Praise for *F*

"A truly remarkable achievement! Kreiman and Sidtis cover virtually every topic ever examined in voice science and blend in their own considerable experience and insight to produce a volume that is both readable and engaging."

Michael J. Owren, Georgia State University

"*Foundations of Voice Studies* is a remarkable book, forging top-quality scholarship with crystal-clear writing to produce an unparalleled treatment of voice production and perception. Anyone interested in voice must have this text."

Gary Weismer, University of Wisconsin – Madison

"A comprehensive, exceptionally-useful treatment of voice-related issues by two of the field's top practitioners; includes the basics of voice production, a model of speaker recognition via the voice, and current research in linguistic, forensic and emotional uses of voice information. The inclusion of online sound files is a particularly valuable addition."

Stefanie Shattuck-Hufnagel, Massachusetts Institute of Technology

"Covering everything from anatomy, physiology and neural substrates to processing and even forensic applications– in a highly accessible format–Kreiman and Sidtis have drawn together perspectives on voice from a wide range of disciplines, making this volume an excellent resource for students, clinical professionals, and scholars alike."

Shari R. Baum, McGill University

"The book is truly an amazing work. The authors are not only pioneers themselves in carrying out fundamental research on many of the key topics covered in the book, but they have managed to organize and synthesize an enormous body of literature and put it together in one easily accessible place. A gem … there simply is nothing like this anywhere."

David Pisoni, Indiana University

Jody Kreiman is Professor of Head and Neck Surgery at the University of California, Los Angeles. She is a Fellow of the Acoustical Society of America and has published over 60 scholarly papers in a variety of journals.

Diana Sidtis (formerly Van Lancker) is Professor of Communicative Sciences and Disorders at New York University and performs research at the Nathan Kline Institute for Psychiatric Research. An experienced clinician, her research has yielded over 90 articles in scholarly journals and edited books.

Foundations of Voice Studies

*An Interdisciplinary Approach
to Voice Production and Perception*

Jody Kreiman and Diana Sidtis

WILEY-BLACKWELL

A John Wiley & Sons, Ltd., Publication

This paperback edition first published 2013
© 2013 Jody Kreiman and Diana Sidtis

Edition History: Blackwell Publishing, Ltd (hardback, 2011)

Blackwell Publishing was acquired by John Wiley & Sons in February 2007. Blackwell's publishing program
has been merged with Wiley's global Scientific, Technical, and Medical business to form Wiley-Blackwell.

Registered Office
John Wiley & Sons Ltd, The Atrium, Southern Gate, Chichester, West Sussex, PO19 8SQ, UK

Editorial Offices
350 Main Street, Malden, MA 02148-5020, USA
9600 Garsington Road, Oxford, OX4 2DQ, UK
The Atrium, Southern Gate, Chichester, West Sussex, PO19 8SQ, UK

For details of our global editorial offices, for customer services, and for information about
how to apply for permission to reuse the copyright material in this book please see our website at
www.wiley.com/wiley-blackwell.

The right of Jody Kreiman and Diana Sidtis to be identified as the authors of this work has been asserted in
accordance with the UK Copyright, Designs and Patents Act 1988.

Library of Congress Cataloging-in-Publication Data

Kreiman, Jody.
  Foundations of voice studies : an interdisciplinary approach to voice production and perception /
Jody Kreiman, Diana Sidtis.
    p. cm.
  Includes bibliographical references and index.
  ISBN 978-0-631-22297-2 (hardback) ISBN 978-1-118-54670-3 (paperback)
  1. Grammar, Comparative and general–Phonology.   2. Voice–Social aspects.   3. Sociolinguistics.
I. Sidtis, Diana.
  P217.3.K66 2011
  414–dc22

                                        2010049389

A catalogue record for this book is available from the British Library.

Cover image: © Ekely/iStockphoto.com
Cover design by Edge Creative

Set in 10/12.5pt ITC Galliard by SPi Publisher Services, Pondicherry, India
Printed in Malaysia by Ho Printing (M) Sdn Bhd

1   2013

To the memory of Peter Ladefoged,
who always encouraged us

Contents

1

Introduction

1.1 Why Should We Care About Voice Quality?

Whenever we speak, our voices convey information about us as individuals. Speakers may sound young, or tired, or elated, or distracted. They may sound as if they are drunk, or lying, or ill, or bearing secret, exciting news. By their voices, adult speakers usually reveal whether they are male or female, and in addition, they may signal that they come from Texas, or Wisconsin, or France. Over the telephone or radio we may recognize the speaker as someone we know, or we may form a distinct impression of the physical appearance of someone we have never seen. The impressions listeners gain from voices are not necessarily accurate; for example, everyone has known the surprise of meeting a telephone acquaintance who does not match the mental picture we have previously formed of them. Despite such occasional mismatches, voice quality is one of the primary means by which speakers project their identity – their "physical, psychological, and social characteristics" (Laver, 1980, p. 2) or their "auditory face" (Belin, Fecteau, and Bedard, 2004) – to the world.

Table 1.1 non-exhaustively summarizes some of the kinds of judgments that listeners make when listening to voices. These human abilities arise from a long evolutionary process, and many animal species, including primates (Cheney and Seyfarth, 1980), wolves (Goldman, Phillips, and Fentress, 1995), penguins (Jouventin and Aubin, 2002), frogs (Bee, 2004), and bats (Balcombe and McCracken, 1992) use vocal quality to signal or perceive size, threat, and kin relationships. Human infants' ability to recognize their mothers' voices is in place at birth (DeCasper and Fifer, 1980), and responses to maternal voices can be measured *in utero*, suggesting such abilities develop even before birth (Hepper, Scott, and Shahidullah, 1993; Kisilevsky *et al.*, 2003). Voice conveys much of the emotion and attitude communicated by speech (Williams and Stevens, 1972; Banse and Scherer, 1996; Ellgring and Scherer, 1996; Van Lancker and Pachana, 1998; Breitenstein, Van Lancker, and Daum, 2001). Alterations in voice quality relative to the speaker's normal vocal delivery may signal

Foundations of Voice Studies: An Interdisciplinary Approach to Voice Production and Perception, First Edition. Jody Kreiman and Diana Sidtis.

Table 1.1   Some kinds of judgments listeners make from voice.

Spoken message

Physical characteristics of the speaker
  Age
  Appearance (height, weight, attractiveness)
  Dental/oral/nasal status
  Health status, fatigue
  Identity
  Intoxication
  Race, ethnicity
  Sex
  Sexual orientation
  Smoker/non-smoker
Psychological characteristics of the speaker
  Arousal (relaxed, hurried)
  Competence
  Emotional status/mood
  Intelligence
  Personality
  Psychiatric status
  Stress
  Truthfulness
Social characteristics of the speaker
  Education
  Occupation
  Regional origin
  Role in conversational setting
  Social status

irony or sarcasm (Van Lancker, Canter, and Terbeek, 1981). Changes in rate and fundamental frequency affect the perceived "competence" (Brown, Strong, and Rencher, 1974) or credibility (Geiselman and Bellezza, 1977) of a speaker. Voice quality provides cues that indicate order of turn-taking in conversation (Schegloff, 1998; Wells and Macfarlane, 1998) and helps resolve sentential ambiguities (Kjelgaard, Titone, and Wingfield, 1999; Schafer, Speer, Warren, and White, 2000). Listeners may also judge the speaker's sexual preference (Linville, 1998; Munson and Babel, 2007), status as native or nonnative speaker (Piske, MacKay, and Flege, 2001), and a myriad of personality factors (Scherer, 1979) based on voice quality cues.

This book describes the manner in which these kinds of information are conveyed to listeners, and how listeners draw conclusions – correctly or incorrectly – about speakers from their voices. Many of the points described are illustrated by recorded examples provided on the accompanying web site.

For example, consider the voice in audio sample 1.1. As you listen to this brief speech sample, you will probably automatically gather information about the speaker. Listeners agree that the speaker is female. Although opinions differ, listeners are likely to think that the speaker is adult but not elderly, cheerful, confident, alert, and in good health. She is American, but does not have a pronounced regional, social, or ethnic accent. She sounds average or slightly above average in height and weight. She seems educated and is speaking carefully. She does not sound like a smoker. You probably do not recognize the voice, but it may remind you of someone you know.

Compare this talker to the voice in audio sample 1.2. This speaker is also female, but the voice sounds like a much older person. She has a New England accent, and the rhythm of her speech is unusual, making her sound rather upper-class or snobby (or merely self-conscious) to some listeners. She is not tired, depressed, or angry, but she is not obviously happy, either, and may be bored. Her voice is somewhat hoarse, suggesting that she is or has been a smoker, but she does not seem ill. Listeners disagree somewhat about her height and weight, but generally estimate that she is average or slightly below average in height, and slightly above average in weight.

The voice of a speaker with a vocal pathology is presented in audio sample 1.3. Even this short sample may produce complex impressions of old age, illness, and unattractiveness, along with a sense of the speaker's emotions or mood, intelligence, and competence. Patients who develop a voice disorder often complain that the disordered voice is not really their voice, and does not convey who they are. In some cases, patients dislike the image they portray so much that they avoid speaking, resulting in significant social and work-related difficulties. Severe voice quality problems may also interfere with speech intelligibility, creating a handicap in the communication of verbal information (Kempler and Van Lancker, 2002).

The strong impressions conveyed by voice quality are often manipulated by the media for multiple purposes. For example, in the classic film *Singin' in the Rain* (Freed, Kelly, and Donen, 1952), the shrill, loud voice of the character Lina Lamont (played by actress Jean Hagen) surprises and amuses because it does not fit her appearance (a beautiful, smiling blonde) or the elegant, poised, sophisticated personality she visually projects. This contrast – a prototypically silly voice in an elegant physique – forms a running joke throughout the film, playing off such lines as, "What do you think I am, dumb or something?" spoken in the abrasive voice stereotypically associated with a vulgar, uneducated, shrewish female. More often, voices are selected to fit the intended message. Documentary films enhance credibility through the use of a male narrator whose voice carries the stereotype of an authoritative figure who is solid, mature, calm, highly intelligent, and dignified. In the field of advertising, impressions conveyed by voice quality are integral to establishing a product image. Consider the characteristics projected by the voices typically used in advertisements for luxury automobiles. Low pitch, breathy quality, and a fairly rapid speaking rate produce the image of an intimate message from a mature but energetic male who possesses authority, sex appeal, social status, and "coolness." These vocal attributes are appropriate to the economic niche for the product and imply that its owners are powerful, sexy, and affluent.

Given the wide range of information listeners derive from voices, it is not surprising that scholars from many different disciplines have studied the production and perception of voice. Table 1.2 lists some of these disciplines, along with a sampling of typical research questions. These research questions encompass much of human existence, and indicate how central voice quality is to human life.

4

Table 1.2 Disciplines incorporating the study of voice and voice quality.

Discipline	Some typical research questions
Acoustics	Deriving reliable and meaningful acoustic measures of voices
Animal behavior	Vocal recognition of kin and social information by nonhuman animals
Biology	Biological and evolutionary significance of vocalization
Computer science, signal processing, information	Transmission, measurement, and synthesis of voice
Forensic science, law enforcement	Reliability and verification of "earwitness" testimony; assessment of truthfulness from voice
Linguistics, phonetics	Meanings of vocal quality in speech
Medicine:	
Developmental biology	Infant voice recognition
Gerontology	Voice quality changes in aging
Neurology	Brain function underlying vocal behaviors
Obstetrics	Prenatal voice perception
Otolaryngology	Voice disorders
Pediatrics	Childrens' processing of vocal information
Physiology	Control of phonation
Respiration	Role of breathing in vocalization
Surgery	Effects of surgical interventions in the vocal tract on voice; cosmetic changes for transgendered voices
Music:	
Singing	The singing voice: many questions
Vocal coaching	The effects of training on the voice
Physics	Vibrating laryngeal tissues; relation of vibration to sound; patterns of airflow through the glottis
Psychology:	
Cognitive psychology	Speaker recognition and its causes; interaction between speech recognition and voice quality
Clinical psychology	Detecting depression, psychopathology, and personality in the human voice
Social psychology	Voices as signals of social relationships including conversational turn taking, sarcasm, and successful con-artistry
Neuropsychology	Brain mechanisms underlying the perception and production of voice cuing personal identity as well as mood and motivation
Psychophysics	Relevant acoustic voice features for perception
Psycholinguistics	Voice information in meaning comprehension for grammatical structure and nonliteral meanings
Sociology	Voice types associated with social groups and their development
Speech science	Normal voice and speech production
Speech pathology	Effects of vocal pathologies on voice quality
Theater arts	Voice as artistic instrument

1.2   What is Voice? What is Voice *Quality?* The Definitional Dilemma

The terms "voice" and "voice quality" are variously used, sometimes apparently interchangeably, and deriving consistent definitions has not proven easy. Adding to the confusion, authors also discuss a range of specific voice qualities (a creaky voice, a breathy voice), qualities associated with a speaker's internal or physical state (a sad voice, a tired voice; a sexy voice), and so on, without benefit of a theoretical framework linking all these usages. We attempt to distinguish these meanings usefully by discussing the terms here.

Although a clear definition of *voice* is a prerequisite to its study, the broad range of functions subserved by voice has made it difficult to provide a single, all-purpose definition that is valid and useful across disciplines, scholarly traditions, and research applications. As voice scientist Johann Sundberg has noted (1987), everyone knows what voice is until they try to pin it down, and several senses of the term are in common use. In scientific usage (and throughout this book), the term "voice" has a physical and physiological base that refers to the acoustic signal (as generated by the voice production system), while "voice quality" refers to the perceptual impression that occurs as a result of that signal, analogous to the distinction between "frequency" (a physical property of vibration) and "pitch" (a listener's sensation). Definitions of voice fall into two general classes. In the first, voice can be defined very narrowly in physiological terms as "sound produced by vibration of the vocal folds." Were this definition applied, voice would include only those aspects of the signal that are attributable to the action of the vocal folds, and would exclude the acoustic effects of vocal tract resonances, vocal tract excitation from turbulent noise, or anything else that occurs during speech production other than the action of the vocal folds. (Chapter 2 describes the voice production process in detail.) This definition corresponds approximately to the linguistic voicing feature that phonetically distinguishes voiced from voiceless sounds (for example, /s/ from /z/) in many languages. Authors who use the term "voice" in this sense (for example, Brackett, 1971) typically distinguish voice from speech. Voice in this sense is also synonymous with the term "laryngeal source," which emphasizes the fact that vocal fold vibrations are the acoustic energy source for much of speech.

Anatomical constraints make it difficult to study voice as narrowly defined. The larynx is located fairly low in the neck (see Chapter 2), and vocal fold function is difficult to observe directly for long periods of time. Short sequences of open vowel phonation can be inspected through the use of a laryngeal mirror (see Sidebar in Chapter 2). Direct views of some aspects of laryngeal vibrations are available using endoscopic imaging technology and either stroboscopy[1] (for example, Hertegard and Gauffin, 1995) or high-speed imaging (for example, Koike and Hirano, 1973; Berry, Montequin, and Tayama, 2001; Deliyski *et al.*, 2008). Laryngeal vibrations can also be studied experimentally using excised larynx preparations (for example, van den Berg, 1968; Berry, 2001). Some authors have used the output of devices like the laryngograph

---

[1]   A technique by which rapid vocal fold vibrations are apparently "slowed" through use of a strobe light so that they can be easily viewed.

(for example, Abberton and Fourcin, 1978) or electroglottograph (Kitzing, 1982) to measure the action of the laryngeal source. However, to study voice in its narrow sense, most researchers adopt the more practical expedient of controlling for all non-laryngeal contributions to the sounds a speaker makes by restricting voice samples to steady state vowels (usually /a/). This practice does not fully eliminate the contributions of non-laryngeal factors (such as vocal tract resonances) to the voice signal, but it does hold such factors relatively constant across utterances and talkers. This approach is the most common implementation of narrow definitions of voice.

Voice as a physiological and physical phenomenon can also be defined very broadly as essentially synonymous with speech. Besides details of vocal fold motions, voice in this sense includes the acoustic results of the coordinated action of the respiratory system, tongue, jaw, lips, and soft palate, both with respect to their average values and to the amount and pattern of variability in values over time.

The term *voice quality* belongs properly to the realm of perception, and refers to how the voice sounds to a listener. Both "voice" and "voice quality" can be defined (and approached) narrowly or broadly, and each is best considered as analogous to a two-sided coin, melding the production characteristics of one side to the perceptual characteristics of the other side. Like the term "voice," "voice quality" can be used very narrowly, to specify a single aspect of the phonatory process such as the perceived amount of unmodulated airflow present in the voice signal; less narrowly, to mean the perceived result of the process of phonation; or broadly, to mean a listener's response to the overall sound of speech. Because these terms appear in various contexts, their specific use also depends on purpose and perspective, so that providing a precise definition of either term is difficult. Definitions of voice quality abound, depending on interest and focus in each particular discipline. Listeners collate a very large amount of material when they gather information from the ongoing speech of individual talkers. Articulatory details, laryngeal settings, F0 and amplitude variations, and temporal patterning all contribute to how a speaker sounds (Banse and Scherer, 1996; cf. Sapir's (1927) notion of "speech as a personality trait"). Broad definitions of voice quality aim to reflect this fact, and generally portray quality as the end result of a complex sequence of cognitive, physiological, and acoustic events, the familiar "speech chain" (Figure 1.1; Denes and Pinson, 1993).

According to the speech chain, sound is produced by the actions of the speech production mechanism. The acoustic signal then travels to the ears of the listener and back to the speaker in the form of feedback. The auditory percept (a stretch of speech) is first processed peripherally within the mechanisms of the ear, followed by neurological activation of the 8th cranial nerve and the auditory pathway to the receiving areas in the brain (as described in Chapter 3). As increasingly complex cognitive processes are invoked, the stretch of speech under analysis may be described in terms of a number of complex messages (Table 1.1). As briefly reviewed above, voice patterns convey information (more or less successfully) about affect, attitude, psychological state, pragmatics, grammatical function, sociological status, and many aspects of personal identity, all of which emerges from this complex enfolding of phonatory, phonetic, and temporal detail.

Precisely which stage in this chain of events receives focus depends on the interest of the practitioner or experimenter, or on the task faced by the listener, and individual definitions of voice quality may vary according to intellectual tradition (Table 1.2).

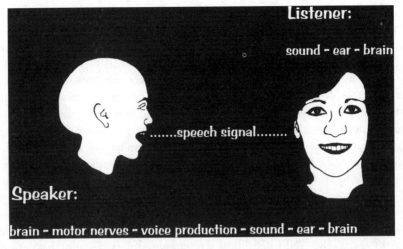

Figure 1.1 The speech chain, showing the transmission of information from a speaker to a listener. Voice production engages systems for respiration, phonation, and articulation.

For example, when surgeons use the term voice quality, they typically think in terms of physiological function, with secondary concern for the exact perceived quality that results from phonation. A typical physiologically-oriented definition characterizes voice quality as "sounds generated by the voice organ ... by means of an air stream from the lungs, modified first by the vibrating vocal folds, and then by the rest of the larynx, and the pharynx, the mouth, and sometimes also the nasal cavities" (Sundberg, 1987: 3). Engineers are often interested in the acoustic waveform that correlates with vocal sound, and therefore define voice quality in terms of acoustic attributes that are (presumptively) perceptually important, without particular regard for the mechanisms that produced the sound. In contrast, psychologists are not especially interested in how the voice is physically produced or in the acoustic features of each utterance, but instead approach voice quality solely in terms of higher-level perceptual attributes.

Given that voice quality is by definition a perceptual response to an acoustic signal, one approach to providing a definition is to specify the nature of the interaction between a sound and a listener that results in quality. This is the approach taken by the American National Standards Institute (ANSI) Standard definition, which defines the quality (or timbre) of a sound as "that attribute of auditory sensation in terms of which a listener can judge that two sounds similarly presented and having the same loudness and pitch are dissimilar" (ANSI Standard S1.1.12.9, p. 45, 1960; cf. Helmholtz, 1885). This definition introduces a number of complications that are not apparent in simpler, narrower, physiologically-based definitions. By the ANSI Standard definition, quality is acoustically multidimensional, including the shape and/or peaks of the spectral envelope,[2] the amplitude of the signal and its fundamental frequency, the extent to which the signal is periodic or aperiodic, and the extent and pattern of changes over time in all these attributes (Plomp, 1976). This large number of degrees

---

[2]   The spectral envelope refers to the way in which acoustic energy is distributed across the different frequencies in the voice.

of freedom makes it difficult to operationalize the concept of quality, particularly across listening tasks. The perceived quality of a single voice sample may also vary from occasion to occasion as listeners focus on different aspects of a sound in different contexts, or as different listeners attend to different aspects of the same sound; and what a given listener attends to when judging voices varies from voice to voice, according to task demands. According to the ANSI Standard definition, quality is a perceptual response in a specific psychophysical task (determining that two sounds are dissimilar), and it is unclear how this definition might generalize to other common, seemingly-related tasks like speaker recognition or evaluation of a single stimulus. Excluding pitch and loudness from what we call "vocal quality" is troublesome, because pitch and loudness are consistently found to be highly important characteristics of voice, on which listeners depend heavily for many kinds of judgments (as described in subsequent chapters). Evidence also suggests that quality may not be independent of frequency and amplitude (Melara and Marks, 1990; Krumhansl and Iverson, 1992), as the ANSI definition seemingly requires. Finally, this definition is essentially negative: It states that quality is not pitch and loudness, but does not indicate what it does include (Plomp, 1976). Such complications have led to frequent criticism of the ANSI definition, which some claim amounts to no definition at all (see, for example, Bregman, 1994, for review).

Dissatisfaction with this situation has led some voice researchers to adopt definitions of quality that simply echo the narrow or broad definitions of voice described above, so that voice quality is characterized in physiological, not perceptual, terms. Consistent with narrow definitions of voice, vocal quality may be defined as the perceptual impression created by the vibration of the vocal folds. More broadly, and parallel to broad definitions of voice, voice quality may be defined as the perceived result of coordinated action of the respiratory system, vocal folds, tongue, jaw, lips, and soft palate. For example, Abercrombie viewed voice quality as "those characteristics which are present more or less all the time that a person is talking: It is a quasi-permanent quality running through all the sound that issues from his mouth" (1967: 91). Similarly, Laver referred to voice quality as "a cumulative abstraction over a period of time of a speaker-characterizing quality, which is gathered from the momentary and spasmodic fluctuations of short-term articulations used by the speaker for linguistic and paralinguistic communication" (1980: 1). Such definitions do very little to specify listeners' contributions to quality, which are essential to defining what is after all a perceptual phenomenon. For example, the perceptual importance of different aspects of a voice depends on context, attention, a listener's background, and other factors (Kreiman, Gerratt, Precoda, and Berke, 1992; Gerratt, Kreiman, Antoñanzas-Barroso, and Berke, 1993; Kreiman, Gerratt, and Khan, 2010), and is affected by the listening task (Gerratt *et al.*, 1993; Gerratt and Kreiman, 2001a; Kreiman, Gerratt, and Antoñanzas-Barroso, 2007). Thus, the measured response to a given voice signal is not necessarily constant across listeners or occasions.

Some of the difficulty that arises when contemplating the nature of quality may be due to the fact that quality is often treated as analogous to pitch and loudness, the two other perceptual attributes of sound specified in the ANSI Standard definition. Authors often discuss *the* pitch or *the* loudness of a signal, presumably because these factors can be scaled unidimensionally, from low to high or faint to strong (Plomp,

1976), and because the anatomy of the auditory system is fairly consistent across individuals, so that responses to fundamental frequency and intensity are reasonably consistent, at least in the auditory periphery (but see Krishnan, Gandour, and Bidelman, 2010, for evidence of listener differences even at this level of processing). In fact, some authors even treat pitch and fundamental frequency, or loudness and intensity, as synonymous in informal writing. This creates the expectation that the acoustic correlates of quality should be fairly consistent from listener to listener, and that the same cues should operate across all voices, as fundamental frequency is the major cue to pitch, but not the only cue (see, for example, Thomas, 1969), and intensity is the primary cue to loudness (Fletcher and Munson, 1933). However, quality is multidimensional. It cannot be successfully scaled unidimensionally; and because more than one possible cue to quality exists, the possibility of listener differences is always present, so that quality can never have fixed acoustic determinants (Kreiman, Gerratt, and Berke, 1994). Given this fact, the perceptual response evoked by a voice signal will always depend on factors like task demands, and listener attention will vary across the multiple facets of the signal, so that some are more important than others from occasion to occasion (although experimental controls can minimize the effects of these factors, as discussed below). For this reason, a single perceived quality may not consistently result from a given signal, relative to the listener. In contrast, pitch and loudness do not ordinarily vary in this way, because of their more-or-less unidimensional nature.

The strength of the ANSI Standard definition is that it incorporates the inherently multivariate nature of voice quality by treating sound quality as the result of a perceptual process rather than as a fixed quantity, and highlights the importance of both listeners and signals in determining quality. Listeners usually listen to voices in order to gather information about the environment, and the information they attend to varies with their purpose and with the information available from a particular utterance. Considered in this light, the ANSI Standard definition has distinct advantages; in fact, its limitations can be reduced by broadening the definition to include different tasks, rather than narrowing its focus to include only a small set of specific acoustic variables. Voice quality may best be thought of as an interaction between a listener and a signal, such that the listener takes advantage of whatever acoustic information is available to achieve a particular perceptual goal. Which aspects of the signal are important will depend on the task, the characteristics of the stimuli, the listener's background, perceptual habits, and so on. Given the many kinds of information listeners extract from voice signals, it is not surprising that these characteristics vary from task to task, voice to voice, and listener to listener.

Studies of familiar voice recognition (van Dommelen, 1990; Remez, Fellowes, and Rubin, 1997) highlight the importance of signal/listener interactions in voice perception. Specific phonatory and articulatory information is key to identifying some individual voices, but not relevant to others (Van Lancker, Kreiman, and Wickens, 1985a), such that three conditions of signal alteration (backwards, rate changed to slower or faster speech) affected the recognizability of individual voices differently. Perceptual processing of voice quality differs qualitatively depending on whether the listener is familiar or unfamiliar with the voice (see Kreiman, 1997, and Chapter 6 for review). Listeners' perceptual strategies can thus be expected to vary depending on the differential familiarity of the voices. Listeners' attention to different cues to voice identity also depends on the total voice pattern in which the cue operates (Van Lancker *et al.*, 1985a; Van Lancker, Kreiman, and Emmorey, 1985b), so that the importance of a single cue varies across voices as well as listeners. Definitions of quality that depend exclusively on aspects of production or on the signal cannot account for such effects. Voice quality is the result of perceptual processes, and must be defined in terms of both signals and listeners.

   Although the great majority of studies of voice maintain a firm distinction between production and perceptual aspects of voice, some recent work in dialogic[3] linguistics abandons this distinction in favor of a view of voice as inextricable from a communicative context, so that production and perception are inseparably linked (Bertau, 2008). In this view, a human voice is a concrete, perceivable event that is inseparable from (and thus indexes) the body that produced it, which in turn shapes the sound of the voice. At the same time, voice manifests the speaker's abstract, unobservable consciousness, thus representing the whole person and "underscoring the physicality of psychological self" (p. 97). Further, the speaking person exists in a communicative context that necessarily includes a listener (somewhat reminiscent of the sound made by a tree falling in the woods), and the voice that is produced cannot be separated from the act of listening that provides the context for production. As Bertau writes,

> So, "voice" is a vocal-auditory event, and it is a concept belonging to a certain socioculturally constructed way of expression. The uttered voice is absolutely individual, coming from a unique body, but this body is located in specific sociocultural contexts and has a history of action, movements, labels, etc. So, the voice, too. As for every human expression, the voice is individual and societal, both aspects being the facets of a wholeness ... (pp. 101–2)

As we will see in subsequent chapters, this viewpoint is helpful when considering the neuropsychology of voice production and perception, both of which suggest that voice reflects the whole physical and social self and is shaped in part by communicative context. This view is also consistent with studies showing how speakers subtly adjust their accents to mutually match elements of the speech of the co-participant. Thus, while the voice pattern is uniquely expressing personal characteristics, it is also capable of adjusting to the voice pattern of the other (Pardo, 2006). Interestingly, this broad view of voice as a perceived manifestation of the total self (or consciousness), cast in another format, is seen in self-help books describing ways to "find and use your natural voice" that "represents us well" (Boone, 1991, p. 6). Such popularized notions are fully consonant with the view that voice expresses who we are, both in isolation and with respect to other individuals.

1.3   Measuring Voice Quality

Given the difficulties inherent in defining voice and voice quality, it is not surprising that considerable confusion also surrounds quality measurement. By its nature, quality is essentially psychoacoustic: It is the psychological impression created by a

---

[3] As the name suggests, this branch of linguistics studies interactional language use, including negotiation, mediation, social identity in partnered communication, identification with and influence of interlocutors, and the like.

physical stimulus, and thus depends on both the listener and the voice, as discussed above. However, the psychoacoustic study of complex multidimensional auditory signals is in its infancy (for example, Melara and Marks, 1990; see Yost *et al.*, 1989, for review), and little research has examined the perceptual processes listeners apply to voice signals. Research has focused instead on deriving and defining static descriptive labels for voices. In this approach, vocal quality is treated as if it can be decomposed into a set of specific features or elements, whose presence or absence characterize a speaker's voice.

The most common approach to the problem of specifying voice quality is simply to create a long list of terms to describe listeners' impressions, essentially decomposing overall "quality" into a set of component "qualities." Listeners then assess quality by rating the extent to which a voice possesses each feature. (Alternatively, listeners may simply mark as present the features they hear in the voice in question.) It can be difficult to determine the basis on which terms in such lists have been selected, and labels like these for quality tend to be rather mixed in their level of description. They may describe voices visually (for example, brilliant, dark), kinesthetically (strained, tight), physically (heavy, thin, pointed), aesthetically (pleasing, faulty), with reference to anatomy (pectoral, nasal), and so on (for example, Orlikoff, 1999).

Such dimensional approaches to measuring voice quality depend on descriptive traditions rather than theory, and have changed only superficially in nearly 2000 years. Table 1.3 includes three lists of descriptive features for voices, one venerable (Julius Pollux, 2nd century AD; cited by Austin, 1806) and two modern (Moore, 1964, cited by Pannbacker, 1984; Gelfer, 1988). A few differences exist among these lists. For example, the oldest list includes terms related to the personality and emotional state of the speaker (confused, doleful), and terms related to articulation and rhetorical ability (articulate, distinct), reflecting the importance of rhetoric in Roman culture (see Gray, 1943, or Laver, 1981, for review). More modern compendia include terms like "breathy" and "nasal" that are commonly used in the study of vocal pathology. However, similarities among the lists are striking. Although alignment of terms across lists is approximate, only eight of forty terms lack at least one close counterpart in the other lists, mostly due to the loss of terms for enunciation, emotion, or rhetorical style in the modern vocabulary for voice, as noted above.

The bomb threat form shown in Figure 1.2 is a modern forensic application of this "list of features" approach to quality assessment and speaker recognition. In completing this form, the listener is asked to judge an eclectic array of vocal descriptors, including the speaker's physical characteristics (age, sex, race), their emotional state (angry, calm), and their identity (familiar, disguised voice), and to describe the dynamics of the utterance (rate, loudness) and the quality of the voice (whispered, nasal, raspy, ragged). As an applied tool, this questionnaire includes commonly known articulatory disorders (lisp, stutter) and nonverbal modes (crying, laughter). This large and heterogeneous set of descriptors has a specific purpose in narrowing down a field of suspects and coordinating voice identity information with other evidence obtained in an investigation. For example, if a listener can correctly judge a caller's sex when completing the form, this alone would eliminate half the population as suspects. However, these descriptors alone would not be useful across the general population in specifying voice quality or uniquely identifying a set of suspects with any degree of confidence.

Table 1.3 Venerable and modern labels for voice quality.

After Julius Pollux, 2nd century AD[a]	Moore, 1964[b]	Gelfer, 1988
High (altam)	–	High
Powerful (excelsam)	Ringing	Strong, intense, loud
Clear (claram)	Clear, light, white	Clear
Extensive (latam)	Rich	Full
Deep (gravam)	Deep	Resonant, low
Brilliant (splendidam)	Bright, brilliant	Bright, vibrant
Pure (mundatam)	–	–
Smooth (suavam)	Cool, smooth, velvety	Smooth
Sweet (dulcem)	–	–
Attractive (illecebrosam)	Pleasing	Pleasant
Melodious, cultivated (exquisitam)	Mellow	Mellow, musical
Persuasive (persuasibilem)	–	–
Engaging, tractable (pellacem, tractabilem)	Open, warm	Easy, relaxed
Flexible (flexilem)	–	Well-modulated
Executive (volubilem)	–	Efficient
Sonorous, harmonious (stridulam)	Chesty, golden, harmonious, orotund, round, pectoral	Balanced, open
Distinct (manifestam)	–	–
Perspicuous, articulate (perspicuam)	–	–
Obscure (nigram)	Dark, guttural, throaty	Husky, guttural, throaty
Dull (fuscam)	Dead, dull, heavy	Dull, heavy, thick
Unpleasing (injucundam)	–	Unpleasant
Small, feeble (exilem, pusillam)	Breathy	Breathy, soft, babyish
Thin (angustam)	Constricted, heady, pinched, reedy, shallow, thin	Thin
Faint (difficilem auditu, molestam)	Whispery	Weak
Hollow, indistinct (subsurdam, obscuram)	Covered, hollow	Muffled
Confused (confusam)	–	–
Discordant (absonam)	Blatany, whiney	Strident, whining
Unharmonious, uncultivated (inconcinnam, neglectam)	Coarse, crude	Coarse, gruff
Unattractive, unmanageable (intractabilem)	–	Shaky
Uninteresting (inpersuasibilem)	Blanched, flat	–
Rigid (rigidam)	Hard, tight	Monotonous, constricted, flat
Harsh (asperam)	Harsh, strident, twangy	Harsh, gravelly
Cracked (distractam)	Pingy, raspy	Strained, raspy, grating, creaky

Table 1.3 (*Cont'd*).

After Julius Pollux, *2nd century AD*[a]	*Moore, 1964*[b]	*Gelfer, 1988*
Doleful (tristem)	–	–
Unsound, hoarse (infirmam, raucam)	Faulty, hoarse, poor, raucous, rough	Hoarse, rough, labored, noisy
Brassy (aeneam)	Buzzy, clangy, metallic	Metallic
Shrill, sharp (acutam)	Cutting, hooty, piercing, pointed, sharp, shrill	Shrill, sharp
–	Nasal	Nasal
–	Denasal	Denasal
–	Toothy	–

Notes:
[a] Cited in Austin (1806).
[b] Cited in Pannbacker (1984).

Redundancies and ambiguities are common in lists of terms, which tend to be exhaustive rather than efficient. To address the problem of which terms to include in a voice quality assessment protocol, some researchers have applied factor analysis, a statistical procedure that reduces large lists of overlapping features to small non-redundant sets. In such studies, listeners evaluate each of a set of voices on a large number of rating scales like those in Table 1.3. Two general approaches have been used in voice quality research. In the first (Holmgren, 1967), voice samples (spoken passages of text) are rated on a relatively small set of scales that have been selected to represent an a priori underlying set of factors. Because no standard factors or dimensions have been established for voice quality, such studies have adopted previously-proposed dimensions (for example, potency, evaluation, activity) and scales (for example, sweet/sour, strong/weak, hot/cold; Osgood, Suci, and Tannenbaum, 1957) that are not necessarily applicable to voice quality. Alternatively, investigators have asked listeners to rate voice samples (again, spoken sentences or passages of text) on large sets of voice quality scales that do not derive from an a priori factor structure (Voiers, 1964; Fagel, van Herpt, and Boves, 1983). Such exploratory studies attempt to ensure that all possible perceptual factors are represented in the derived factors by oversampling the semantic space for voice quality.

In either case, statistical analysis of listeners' ratings produces a small number of orthogonal factors that capture as much of the variance in the underlying ratings as possible. Each original scale is given a weight on each factor, so that scales that are strongly related to the factor receive large weights, and scales that are weakly related to the factor receive low weights. Factors are then given summary labels based on the scales that they comprise. For example, a factor with large weights on scales like "fast," "agitated," "tense," "busy," and "exciting" might be labeled "animation" (Voiers, 1964), while one with large weights on scales like "vivacious," "expressive," "melodious," "cheerful," "beautiful," "rich," and "active" might be labeled "melodiousness" (Fagel, van Herpt, and Boves, 1983).

Department of the Treasury
Bureau of Alcohol, Tobacco & Firearms
BOMB THREAT CHECKLIST

1. When is the bomb going to explode?

2. Where is the bomb right now?

3. What does the bomb look like?

4. What kind of bomb is it?

5. What will cause the bomb to explode?

6. Did you place the bomb?

7. Why?

8. What is address?

9. What is your name?

EXACT WORDING OF BOMB THREAT:

Sex of caller: _____   Race: _____

Age: _____   Length of call: _____

Telephone number at which call is received: _____

Time call received: _____

Date call received: _____

CALLER'S VOICE

☐ Calm   ☐ Nasal

☐ Soft   ☐ Angry

☐ Stutter   ☐ Loud

☐ Excited   ☐ Lisp

☐ Laughter   ☐ Slow

☐ Rasp   ☐ Crying

☐ Rapid   ☐ Deep

☐ Normal   ☐ Distinct

ATF F 1613.1(Formerly ATF F 1730.1, which still may be used)(6.97)

☐ Slurred   ☐ Whispered

☐ Ragged   ☐ Clearing Throat

☐ Deep Breathing   ☐ Cracking Voice

☐ Disguised   ☐ Accent

☐ Familiar *(If voice is familiar, who did it sound like?)* _____

BACKGROUND SOUNDS:

☐ Street noises   ☐ Factory machinery

☐ Voices   ☐ Crockery

☐ Animal noises   ☐ Clear

☐ PA System   ☐ Static

☐ Music   ☐ House noises

☐ Long distance   ☐ Local

☐ Motor   ☐ Office machinery

☐ Booth   ☐ Other *(Please specify)*

BOMB THREAT LANGUAGE:

☐ Well spoken (education)   ☐ Incoherent

☐ Foul   ☐ Message read by threat maker

☐ Taped   ☐ Irrational

REMARKS:

Your name:

Your position:

Your telephone number:

Date checklist completed: _____

ATF F 1613.1(Formerly ATF F 1730.1)(6.97)

Figure 1.2 A typical form for reporting a bomb threat. Listeners completing this form must judge the speaker's personal characteristics (sex, age, ethnicity), and rate the voice on an eclectic selection of characteristics, including terms related to emotional state, articulation, message content, and voice quality.

Voice feature schemes derived from factor analysis do have obvious advantages over large lists of terms. Such protocols typically include between three and six factors (Table 1.4), and thus are manageable for listeners and investigators alike. In theory, factors are independent of one another, reducing concerns about redundancies or

Table 1.4 Factor analytic studies of normal voice quality.

Speakers	Stimuli	Listeners	Input scales	Derived factors	Reference
5 male, 5 female	spoken passage	235	35 7-point bipolar	5 factors: Melodiousness Articulation quality Voice quality Pitch Tempo	Fagel *et al.* (1983)
16 male	sentences	32	49 7-point bipolar	4 factors: Clarity Roughness Magnitude Animation	Voiers (1964)
10 male	spoken passage	20	12 scales representing 4 underlying factors	2 factors: (1) Slow/fast, resting/busy, intense/mild, simple/ complex; (2) Clean/dirty, beautiful/ugly	Holmgren (1967)

overlap across scales, while at the same time they capture much of the information in the scalar ratings, so economy is achieved with minimal loss of information. Finally, this approach preserves the descriptive tradition of quality assessment, because factors are defined in terms of the underlying scales. Thus, factor analytic approaches bring the impression of scientific rigor to the familiar descriptive approach to quality assessment.

Certain limitations to such approaches are also apparent. First, results of factor analytic studies depend on the input scales and stimuli. That is, a factor will not emerge unless that factor is represented in the set of rating scales and is also perceptually relevant for the specific voices and utterances studied. Studies often employ restricted populations of speakers, small sets of voices, and short stimuli. For example, the well-known GRBAS[4] protocol was developed from the results of factor analyses that used five steady-state vowels produced by only 16 speakers (Isshiki, Okamura, Tanabe, and Morimoto, 1969; see Hirano, 1981, for review). Such restrictions significantly limit the extent to which results can legitimately be generalized to the full spectrum of vocal qualities. Further, as can be seen in Table 1.4, results of factor analyses have varied substantially from study to study. The validity of the factors as perceptual features also depends on the validity of the underlying scales, which has never been established. Thus, even a large-scale factor analysis (or multiple analyses) will not necessarily result in a valid or reliable rating instrument for voice quality. Idiosyncrasies in labeling the factors may also obscure differences among studies. For example, in studies of pathological voice quality Isshiki *et al.* (1969) found a "breathiness" factor that loaded highly on the scales dry, hard, excited, pointed, cold, choked, rough, cloudy, sharp, poor, and bad, while a "breathiness" factor reported by Hammarberg,

---

[4] **G**rade (i.e., severity of deviation), **R**oughness, **B**reathiness, **A**sthenicity (or weakness), and **S**train.

Fritzell, Gauffin, Sundberg, and Wedin (1980) corresponded to the scales breathy, wheezing, lack of timbre, moments of aphonia, husky, and not creaky. Finally, Voiers (1964) reported perceptual factors related to statistically reliable constant listener biases and interactions between specific voices and listeners, in addition to factors related only to the target voices. Emergence of such factors suggests that an adequate perceptual model cannot be framed solely in terms of the stimuli, but must also account separately for differences among listeners. Overall, it thus appears that factor analysis has not convincingly identified scales for vocal quality that are independent and valid.

Dependence on underlying descriptive terminology can be avoided by deriving perceptual features for voices through multidimensional scaling (MDS), rather than factor analysis. In MDS listeners assess the similarity of the experimental voice stimuli directly (usually by listening to pairs of voices and rating their similarity), without reference to scales for specific qualities. The analysis produces a perceptual space from these similarity ratings, such that distances between voices in the space are proportional to the rated similarities (more similar = closer together). Dimensions in this space are then interpreted, usually by examining correlations between rated and/or measured characteristics of the input stimuli and stimulus coordinates or clustering of stimuli in the space. Through this process, exploratory MDS can reveal how overall vocal quality (as it determines similarities between voices) relates to scales for particular qualities. Discovery of a dimension that is highly associated with some specific quality provides evidence for the "psychological reality" of that particular quality as an important vocal feature.

Studies applying MDS to normal vocal qualities are listed in Table 1.5. As with factor analysis, results have varied substantially from study to study, with the exception that dimensions related to pitch (F0) emerge consistently across tasks and stimulus types. Some of these differences can be attributed to differences in study design. Note that three of these 11 studies used vowels as stimuli, while the rest used longer, more complex speech samples, which yield additional information and address questions about the broader definition of voice quality. For example, dimensions associated with stimulus duration or F0 variability typically emerge when sentence stimuli are employed, rather than steady-state vowels. Differences have also been reported in the perceptual features derived for male and female voices (Singh and Murry, 1978; Murry and Singh, 1980). However, variability in solutions has emerged due to factors other than stimulus characteristics. In particular, variability in the perceptual dimensions that emerge from studies of fixed sets of stimuli indicates that listeners differ both as individuals and as groups in the perceptual strategies they apply to voices (Gelfer, 1993; cf. Kreiman, Gerratt, and Precoda, 1990, or Kreiman *et al.*, 1992, who studied pathological voice quality). Thus, it does not appear that any specific features, other than F0, are always important for characterizing the quality of all voices under all circumstances.

Multidimensional scaling solutions may also leave large amounts of variance unaccounted for, and published reports may explain less than half of the variance in the underlying similarity judgments, even for simple vowel stimuli (Murry, Singh, and Sargent, 1977; Murry and Singh, 1980). This may occur because of the limited resolution of MDS: The number of extractable dimensions depends on the number of

Table 1.5 Multidimensional scaling studies of normal voice quality.

Speakers	Stimuli	Listeners	Derived dimensions	Reference
8 male	vowels	6	4 dimensions: F0 Glottal source spectrum Jitter Formant frequencies	Matsumoto *et al.* (1973)
9 male	phrase	15	3 dimensions: F0 Intensity Intonation pattern	Carterette and Barnebey (1975)
20 male	word	11	4 dimensions: F0 Utterance duration Speaker's age "Superior" vs. "inferior" voice quality	Walden *et al.* (1978)
10 male, 10 female	sentence	10	3 dimensions: Speaker sex Pitch (male voices only) Utterance duration (female voices only)	Singh and Murry (1978)
20 male	vowel	10	4 dimensions: Pitch Formant frequencies (2 dimensions) Perceived nasality	Murry and Singh (1980)
20 female	vowel	10	4 dimensions: Pitch Perceived breathiness Formant frequencies Perceived effort	Murry and Singh (1980)
20 male	passage	10	4 dimensions: Pitch and effort Perceived hoarseness Formant frequencies 1 uninterpreted dimension	Murry and Singh, 1980
20 female	passage	10	4 dimensions: Perceived effort and nasality Pitch Utterance duration 1 uninterpreted dimension	Murry and Singh (1980)
10 male	sentence	24	4 dimensions: Perceived masculinity Perceived creakiness Perceived variability Perceived mood	Kreiman and Papcun (1991)

Table 1.5 (*Cont'd*).

Speakers	Stimuli	Listeners	Derived dimensions	Reference
20 female	sentence	20 speech-language pathologists	5 dimensions: Pitch Loudness Perceived age Perceived variability Voice quality	Gelfer (1993)
20 female	sentence	20 untrained	2 dimensions: Pitch and resonant quality Variability, age, and rate	Gelfer (1993)

stimuli studied, which has been limited to twenty or less (although additional perceptual features may also be derived from clustering of stimuli in the space). It is possible that more dimensions (providing more explanatory power) exist in the data than can be extracted due to the small numbers of voices involved. Alternatively, large amounts of variance may remain unexplained because the dimensional model of quality implied by MDS and factor analytic studies does not provide a good description of how quality is perceived.

A study of pathological voice quality (Kreiman and Gerratt, 1996) supports the latter explanation. In that study, listeners judged the similarity of all possible pairs of vowel productions obtained from very large sets of speakers (80 males and 80 females) representing a variety of diagnoses and ranging in quality from nearly normal to severely disordered. In this study, use of vowel stimuli limited the information available to listeners, consistent with the narrow definition of voice, so that the perceptual task was somewhat simpler than with connected speech stimuli. Despite this simplification, multidimensional scaling solutions for male and female voices each accounted for less than half of the variance in the underlying data, and revealed two-dimensional solutions in which the most severely pathological voices were separated from voices with milder pathology. Separate analyses of the data from individual listeners accounted for more variance (56–83%). However, stimuli did not disperse in these perceptual spaces along continuous scale-like linear dimensions, but instead clustered together in groups that lacked subjective unifying percepts. Different voices clustered together for each listener; in fact, no two voices ever occurred in the same cluster for all listeners, suggesting that listeners lacked a common notion of what constitutes similarity with respect to voice quality, even when quality is narrowly defined. If listeners lack a common perceptual space for voice quality in its most restricted sense, then a single set of perceptual features for voice quality more broadly defined is not likely to be discoverable.

In the absence of empirical evidence for the validity of particular descriptors or dimensions, it is unclear why some should be included, and others excluded, in a descriptive framework for vocal quality. Further, each traditional descriptive label is holistic and independent, and labels do not combine to form a permutable set. This makes it difficult to understand precisely how qualities differ from one another, or how seemingly similar qualities are related. Finally, in this tradition it is often unclear how quality relates to other parts of the speech chain. In particular, there is no formal theoretical linkage between a given quality and the physiological configuration that produced it (although terms like "nasal" may imply in some cases that such a linkage exists).

The phonetic/articulatory features for voice quality proposed by Laver (1980, 2000; Ball, Esling, and Dickson, 2000) were designed in response to these limitations. In this approach, voice quality is characterized as "quasi-permanent" and derived cumulatively throughout an individual's vocal sound production (Abercrombie, 1967). It is then described in terms of the global long-term physiological configuration that (hypothetically) underlies the overall sound of a speaker's voice. Laryngeal and supralaryngeal aspects of voice are both specified, and are assumed to be auditorily separable. The specific features are derived from phonetics, and include laryngeal raising and lowering, lip rounding and spreading, jaw position (open, closed), tongue tip and body position (raised, lowered, advanced, retracted), pharyngeal constriction or expansion, velum position, and glottal state (modal voice, falsetto, whisper, creak, breathiness, harshness) (see Laver, 1980, 2000, for more details). This model of voice quality was originally developed to describe normal voices, but has been adapted as a clinical voice evaluation protocol called "vocal profile analysis" that is widely used in the United Kingdom and elsewhere (Laver, Wirz, Mackenzie, and Hiller, 1981; Wirz and Mackenzie Beck, 1995).

Vocal profile analysis is analytic, consistent with phonetic models of speech production, and nearly exhaustive in the physiological domain. Because quasi-independent features (or "settings") can combine in different ways, the system can be used to describe a broad range of voice qualities in a single framework, rather than applying vague terms whose relationships to each other are unclear. Thus, for example, "hoarse" voice might appear in this system as "deep, (loud), harsh/ventricular, whispery voice," or "gruff" voice might become "deep, harsh, whispery, creaky voice" (Laver, 1968). The primary limitation of this system is the fact that it models perception in terms of speech production processes without established or documented reference to a listener. That is, by describing voice quality in detailed terms of the supposed underlying physiological configuration, profile analysis indicates where perceptual information about quality *might* be found. However, it does not indicate which of the many aspects specified are meaningful, or, indeed, perceptible to listeners, how listeners actually use different features to assess quality, whether (or when, or why) some features might be more important than others, or how dimensions interact perceptually. The assumption that listeners are able to separate different features auditorily is also questionable, particularly given recent evidence that listeners have difficulty isolating individual dimensions of complex voice patterns (Kreiman and Gerratt, 2000a; Kreiman *et al.*, 2007; cf. Fry, 1968).

The results reviewed above indicate that the validity of dimensional and featural protocols for assessing overall voice quality remains questionable, although clinical applications of such featural systems are common. Despite the proliferation of rating systems, convergence to a general theory of voice perception remains elusive. These protocols model voice quality solely in terms of the voice signal itself, although couching many of the descriptive labels in perceptual terms. Most of these approaches imply that voice quality can reasonably be represented as a list or grouping of descriptors or dimensions – that there is a list of attributes that listeners can and do attend to, and that the same set adequately describes all voices. Whether quality is broadly or narrowly construed, such frameworks imply a well-defined perceptual space for voice quality, applicable to all voices and true for all listeners, which listeners all exploit in essentially the same way. However, substantial evidence and theoretical considerations, many of which have been touched upon in this chapter, contradict these requirements. A well-defined, theoretically motivated set of features for voice has not emerged, despite many years' research; and listeners apparently exploit vocal signals in unique ways. Data thus suggest that efforts to specify a perceptually valid set of scales for voice quality are unlikely to succeed.

A further difficulty with dimensional protocols is their unreliability as measurement tools. Most studies of listener reliability have focused on pathological voices, due to the importance of scalar ratings in clinical assessments of voice quality (for example, Gerratt, Till, Rosenbek, Wertz, and Boysen, 1991). Across studies, scales, and statistics, average interrater reliability has ranged from extremely low ($r^2 = .04$) to extremely high (100% of ratings within +/− one scale value) (see Kreiman, Gerratt, Kempster, Erman, and Berke, 1993, for review). Analyses of the reliability with which listeners judge individual voices indicate that listeners almost never agree in their ratings of a single voice. Even using the simplest of phonated stimuli, the likelihood that two raters would agree in their ratings of moderately pathological voices on various seven-point scales averaged 0.21 (where chance is 0.14); further, more than 60% (and as much as 78%) of the variance in voice quality ratings was attributable to factors other than differences among voices in the quality being rated (Kreiman and Gerratt, 1998). The voice profile analysis system developed by Laver also falls short of desired levels of reliability. Wirz and Mackenzie Beck (1995) reported that 242 listeners who completed a three-day training course in the system's use rated voices within one scale value (of a possible 6) of a target score for 52%–65% of items in a post-test. Studies of rating reliability for normal voices are less common, but not more encouraging. For example, Gelfer (1988) asked trained and untrained listeners to rate 20 normal female voices (speaking sentences) on 16 different quality scales. Kendall's coefficient of concordance revealed only "modest to slight agreement for both groups" (0.14 to 0.69 across scales, with values averaging 0.33 overall) (Gelfer, 1988, p. 325).

In summary, despite a long history of research, significant difficulties continue to plague traditional approaches to vocal quality measurement. Such approaches suffer from possibly irresolvable issues of rating reliability and validity. It is not clear what if any features characterize quality, or how traditional descriptors or dimensions relate to overall quality (broadly or narrowly construed) or to each other. More modern articulatory distinctive-feature approaches are analytical and motivated by phonetic theory, but while they usefully enumerate articulatory possibilities, they do not predict listeners' behavior. Featural systems in general suffer from this limitation, because they model quality as if it inheres in voices, without also accounting for such listener-dependent factors as attention, experience, and response bias.

Given the difficulties, both theoretical and operational, inherent in measuring voice quality, some authors (particularly those studying pathological voices) have argued that perceptual measures of voice quality should be replaced with instrumental measures (see, for example, Orlikoff, 1999, for review). A variety of measures of voice and

Table 1.6 Measurement techniques for voice and vocal function.

Technique	What it does	Sample references
Acoustic measurements	Quantify F0, amplitude, resonance, and temporal parameters in the speech signal	Buder (2000)
Aerodynamic measures	Specify respiratory driving pressure and airflow through glottis and oronasal cavity	Warren (1996)
Anemometry	Measurement of oral and subglottal air flow velocities	Baken (1987), Tropea (1995)
Electroglottography (EGG)	Reflects vocal fold closure and separation cycles	Childers *et al.* (1990)
Functional MRI or PET	Graphic representation of activity during performance of behavioral tasks, for example, of tongue, brain	J. Sidtis (2007)
High-speed imaging	Provides photographic images of rapid movements in speech: tongue, vocal folds	Luchsinger and Arnold (1965)
Magnetic resonance imaging (MRI)/Computerized tomography (CT scans)	Graphic representation of vocal structures: vocal tract, brain	Kertesz (1994)
Movement transduction techniques	Gauges for tracking movements of velum, tongue, jaw, and lips	Baken (1987)
Palatography	Records tongue contacts with alveolar ridge and hard palate	Palmer (1973)
Ultrasound imaging	Use of high frequency sound signals to delineate boundaries between specific structures at rest or during movement	Kent (1997)
Videostroboscopy	Moving pictures of larynx taken in synchrony with a flashing light to reveal phonatory cycles	Baken (1987)

vocal function are available for use in living subjects (Table 1.6). In particular, a spectacular array of acoustic analysis techniques has been developed over the years, largely by speech scientists, enabling researchers to visualize and quantify the properties of the acoustic signals that are the carriers of voice quality information. Of course, these techniques must eventually interface with knowledge about psychophysical processes.

In contrast to perceptual measures, instrumental measures of aerodynamic, acoustic, or physiological events promise precision, reliability, and replicability. Considerations like these have motivated researchers to create several measurement systems for voice, including the Dysphonia Severity Index (Wuyts *et al.*, 2000) and the Hoarseness Diagram (Frohlich, Michaelis, Strube, and Kruse, 2000), whose purpose is to "establish an objective and quantitative correlate of the perceived vocal quality" (Wuyts *et al.*, 2000: 796). A popular software approach to quantitative assessment of voice quality is the Multi-Dimensional Voice Program (MDVP; Kay Elemetrics Corp.). Using sustained vocalization as input, the program calculates 22 acoustic parameters, displaying these values in colorful snapshot form. However, because vocal quality is the perceptual response to a stimulus, development of instrumental protocols for measuring quality ultimately depends on our ability to define quality in a way that accounts for perceptual factors that introduce variability in listeners' judgments. Although it might be possible to devise objective methods to quantify specific quality dimensions, it is more difficult to set up general rules specifying which dimensions are selected and how they combine to produce a final evaluative judgment (Bodden, 1997). Further, no comprehensive theory exists describing the relationships between physiology, aerodynamics, acoustics, and vocal quality, so it is difficult to establish which instrumental measures ought to correspond to perceptually meaningful differences in vocal quality, or why such associations should exist. Existing research has been limited largely to correlational studies, which have produced highly variable results that are difficult to interpret. (See Kreiman and Gerratt, 2000b, for extended discussion.)

1.4 Alternatives to Dimensional and Featural Measurement Systems for Voice Quality

Finding valid and reliable alternatives to traditional voice quality scaling methods requires knowledge of the sources of listener disagreements. Previous studies of pathological voices (Kreiman, Gerratt, and Ito, 2007; see also Gerratt *et al.*, 1993; Kreiman and Gerratt, 2000a) have shown that traditional methods for rating voice quality can be modeled as a kind of matching task, in which external stimuli (the voices) are compared to stored mental representations that serve as internal standards for the quality of interest. Variability in ratings can be predicted with good accuracy (over 84% variance accounted for) by four factors: Instability of internal standards for different qualities; difficulties isolating individual attributes in complex acoustic voice patterns; measurement scale resolution; and the magnitude of the attribute being measured (Kreiman *et al.*, 2007). A protocol that does not rely on internal standards, and that makes it easier for listeners to focus their attention appropriately and consistently, would eliminate these sources of listener disagreement. One such approach (Gerratt and Kreiman, 2001a; Kreiman and Gerratt, 2005) applies speech synthesis in a method-of-adjustment task. In this task, listeners vary the control parameters of a voice synthesizer by moving sliding cursors, until the synthetic token they control represents an acceptable auditory match to a voice stimulus. When a listener chooses a match to a test stimulus, the synthesizer settings parametrically represent the listener's perception of voice quality. Because listeners directly compare each synthetic token they create to the target voice, they need not refer to internal standards for particular voice qualities, which may be varying and incomplete. Further, listeners can manipulate acoustic parameters and hear the result of their manipulations immediately. Such manipulations bring the particular acoustic dimension to the foreground, helping listeners focus their attention consistently, which is the most important factor governing reliability.

Data indicate that this method improves agreement among listeners (to over 95%) in their assessments of voice quality relative to traditional rating scale techniques (Kreiman *et al.*, 2007).

This method of quality measurement also provides other practical advantages. First, quality is measured in acoustic terms, so that the relationship between acoustic parameters and what a listener hears is established directly, rather than correlationally. Thus, measuring quality with synthesis can experimentally establish the perceptual relevance of different acoustic attributes of voice. Mappings between acoustics and quality also mean that hypotheses can be tested about the perceptual relationships between different signals, because quality is measured parametrically. The perceptual importance of different parameters can also be evaluated in naturally occurring complex multivariate contexts. (See Kreiman and Gerratt, 2005, for an example of this kind of application.)

Finally, note that this approach to quality measurement follows directly from the ANSI Standard definition of sound quality, in that it measures quality psychophysically as those aspects of the signal that allow a listener to determine that two sounds of equal pitch and loudness (the synthetic and natural voice samples) are different. In this method, listeners need not focus on single quality dimensions, eliminating concerns about scale validity; and they create a direct mapping between the acoustic signal and a perceptual response, thus modeling quality psychoacoustically.

In summary, voice quality is psychoacoustic in nature, and can most appropriately be measured by developing methods that can assess interactions between listeners and signals, rather than by treating quality solely as a function of the acoustic voice signals themselves. Reductionistic approaches like those reviewed above have not led to a satisfactory model of voice quality assessment by humans; and the study of voice quality has not received benefit of classic psychophysical research methods. Pitch and loudness can often be treated as if they were functions of the signal, because measures of frequency and intensity are fairly well correlated with listeners' perceptual judgments. However, this simplification is inappropriate in the case of quality, because quality is multidimensional and listeners are flexible and variable. This is the case even when the definition of voice is constrained to refer only to laryngeal aspects of sound production. The complexities multiply with broader definitions of voice and voice quality.

Issues of quality measurement have implications beyond the study of quality itself. Once the relationship between a signal and a percept is understood, it may be possible to determine which physiological parameters create perceptually meaningful changes in phonation. At present, it is not possible to determine which aspects of vocal physiology are perceptually important, in part because the relationship between perception and acoustics (which links production to perception in the "speech chain") is poorly understood. In the absence of theories linking physiology to acoustics to perception, observed correlations between acoustic measures of voice and listeners' judgments of a speaker's characteristics remain hard to interpret (Scherer, 1986). Some progress has been made in understanding the acoustic determinants of perceived affect, voice identity, and perception of physiological characteristics like age and sex, as described in the chapters that follow, but much remains to be discovered. Better methods of quality assessment have important implications for understanding aspects of normal voice perception (age, gender, identity, etc.) that are based in physiology, extending them to the impact of habitual speech patterns on listeners' perceptions. An improved understanding of the issues surrounding measurement of vocal quality is a first step toward these broader goals.

1.5   Organization of the Book

This book comprises ten chapters, with Chapter 2 presenting an overview of vocal physiology and acoustics, and describing the technical details of how listeners produce voice and vary their pitch, loudness, and vocal quality. Chapter 3 reviews elementary facts about the neural substrates for voice production, including consideration of the extent to which the elements of vocalization, frequency, amplitude and timing are independently modulated and how different forms of vocalization in humans are related to those of nonhuman animals. We touch upon this question because scientists disagree on neurological correspondences between nonhuman and human vocalizations, and whether the animal substrates, in evolutionary history, are pertinent to explaining the development of human speech and/or language.[5] Chapter 3 also describes the fundamentals of audition as it pertains to voice perception, including information about the auditory periphery, the basic neurophysiology of the auditory system, and the resolution of elementary acoustic elements into complex patterns.

Chapter 4 describes listeners' abilities to judge a speaker's physical and personal characteristics – age, sex, race, and so on – from voice. In Chapter 5, we review behavioral studies of the perception of familiar and unfamiliar voices, beginning with nonhuman animals and ending with a psychological model of human voice recognition. Chapter 6 reviews neuropsychological approaches to voice perception. Drawing on studies of the neurological substrates and processes relevant to perceiving and recognizing vocal patterns, this chapter develops a model of brain function underlying human voice recognition. Chapter 7 returns to the perception of unfamiliar voices, this time in forensic contexts. Chapter 8 examines linguistic prosody, including phonological, grammatical, semantic, and pragmatic uses of voice quality. Chapter 9 reviews the extent to which listeners can judge a speaker's personality, character, attitude and emotional state from voice, along with the influence of voice characteristics on comprehension of affective and attitudinal meanings. Chapter 10, which we call "Miscellany," describes some remaining manifestations of the voice in singing, voice printing and lie detection, advertising, speech synthesis, and problems encountered in film dubbing. As the title of the book implies, our goal is to provide the most current perspectives on voice perception as gained from many sources and disciplines.

---

[5]   The terms "speech" and "language" are used by linguists to refer to different entities. Speech is performance, the motoric, physical realization of language ability; language is competence or the abstract mental ability.

2

Producing a Voice and Controlling Its Sound

2.1 Introduction

The study of voice perception benefits from an understanding of anatomy and physiology, which explains how speakers can differ from one another and how they can vary their voices, and thus tells us what information is available for listeners to exploit when they make judgments of speakers from voice. This chapter describes the anatomy and physiology of voice production, and explains how speakers manipulate their vocal apparatus to change different aspects of the sounds they produce. In this discussion, we assume a basic knowledge of general acoustics (for tutorial reviews see, for example, Fry, 1979; Ladefoged, 1996; or any introductory speech science book). Building on basic concepts of vibration and resonance, we will describe how humans generate sound, and how differences in anatomy and vocal function are reflected in differences in acoustic signals. Later chapters will build on this information to examine not only what conclusions listeners draw from voice signals, but *why* and *how* they draw the conclusions they do.

Figure 2.1 shows the organs associated with normal voice production. Under normal circumstances, voice is produced when airflow from the lungs is converted to acoustic energy by vibration of the vocal folds, which are located within the larynx. These patterns of vibration are then shaped (or filtered) acoustically when the sound passes through the vocal tract above the larynx. The respiratory system serves as a source of power for phonation, by setting air in motion through the vocal tract. The larynx acts as an oscillator to convert this aerodynamic power to acoustic energy, and thus is often referred to as the acoustic voice source. Finally, the vocal tract above the larynx – the pharynx, mouth and nasal cavities – filters the sound. Changes in the way the vocal folds vibrate, or changes in the configuration of the vocal tract above the larynx via movements of the tongue, jaw, soft palate, and lips, will change the sound produced.

Foundations of Voice Studies: An Interdisciplinary Approach to Voice Production and Perception, First Edition. Jody Kreiman and Diana Sidtis.

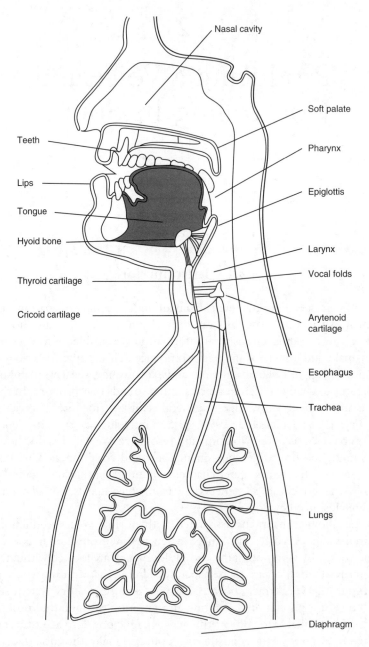

Figure 2.1   Overview of the vocal tract.

Many outstanding reviews of speech physiology exist (for example, Dickson and Maue-Dickson, 1982; Kent, 1997; Zemlin, 1998). Here, we will focus solely on those aspects that are particularly relevant to the production of voice, neglecting many other details that are more relevant to the production of specific speech sounds. The point of this section is to describe how speakers can differ from one another, and to establish what can vary within and across speakers to convey different kinds of information.

2.2   Respiration

2.2.1   Anatomy of breathing

Breathing is an important part of voice production, because the lungs provide the raw power for speech and voice. Obviously, the main function of the respiratory system is breathing – the exchange of gasses – along with smell and temperature regulation. Speech breathing is overlaid on these biologically vital functions, and requires modification of the operations used in quiet breathing. Because of these modifications, human breathing for speech differs significantly from breathing in nonhuman primates, and the evolution of fine control of respiration was essential for the development of modern speech capability in humans (MacLarnon and Hewitt, 1999). This discussion will thus begin by describing the basic function of the respiratory system, followed by the modifications used for speech.

For our purposes, the most important components of the respiratory system are the lungs and the muscles of the chest wall and abdomen. The lungs are a complex branching network of air passages that end in millions of elastic air cells. They have no muscles of their own, but are supported by the diaphragm and contained by 12 pairs of ribs. Between the lungs and the ribs are tissues called the *pleurae*. The *visceral pleura* rests next to the lungs, and the *parietal pleura* lines the chest wall, so the pleurae doubly seal the lungs within the chest cavity. The pleurae are separated by a small amount of fluid, so they can slide against each other, but not pull apart, rather like two sheets of glass with some water between them. The pleurae link the lung tissues to the chest wall, so that when the diaphragm moves or the ribcage elevates or contracts, the lung tissue goes with them. Thus, increasing or decreasing the size of the chest cavity stretches or compresses the lung tissue as well.

The top ten pairs of ribs attach with cartilages to the sternum (or breast bone) to form a closed cage. The two lowest pairs do not attach, and are called *free ribs*. Because these cartilaginous attachments are somewhat flexible, the ribs can move, and the ribcage can expand and contract. The upper ribs can move the least, the lower ribs somewhat more, and the free ribs can move the most. Each rib is connected to the one above and below by the *intercostal muscles* (Figure 2.2). The *external intercostals* run from the bottom of one rib to the top of the next lower rib. When they contract, they elevate the ribs and twist them slightly, with motion that resembles that of a bucket handle swinging up. These actions expand the chest cavity, so that the external intercostals are primarily inspiratory muscles. The *internal intercostals* run from the bottom of each rib to the top of the next higher rib. The internal intercostals are primarily expiratory muscles:[1] Contraction of the outer parts of these muscles lowers the ribs, reducing the size of the chest cavity.

---

[1]   This simplified description of the function of the internal intercostals is adequate for present purposes. In fact, these muscles have a complex function, in that the parts toward the midline elevate the ribs, and are active during inspiration.

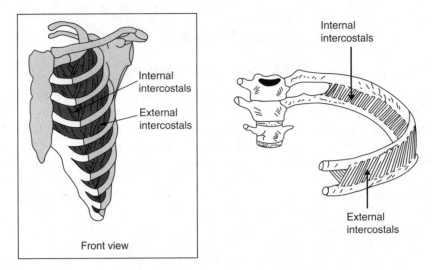

Figure 2.2   The ribs and intercostal muscles.

2.2.2   Mechanics of breathing

Understanding breathing requires knowledge of a few critical physical principles and some properties of air. First, in a container like the lungs, air molecules bounce around at random, hitting each other and the walls of the container. The force of these collisions depends on the number of molecules in the container – the more molecules, the more force exerted on the sides of the container. This collision force is called *pressure*.

Like any gas, air is inherently elastic. Air molecules can be squeezed closely together, or spread farther apart. According to Boyle's Law, pressure and volume are inversely related in a soft walled enclosure (like the lungs) at a constant temperature. Thus, for a given number of air molecules within the lungs, if the lungs expand the pressure within them will decrease, because the same number of molecules now occupy more space, so that fewer collisions occur. Similarly, if the lungs shrink, the pressure within them will increase. Finally, air pressure will always seek to equalize if this is possible. To accomplish this, air will always flow from a region of high pressure to a region of low pressure, until the pressures are equal.

Changes in the pressure within the lungs are created by the actions of the respiratory system. To generate a flow of air into or out of the lungs, the speaker must create a difference between the air pressure inside the lungs and the pressure outside. When the pressure inside the lungs is lower than the atmospheric pressure, air will flow in until the pressures equalize; and when the pressure inside the lungs is higher than atmospheric pressure, air will flow out. In quiet respiration, this means that when the respiratory muscles act to increase the volume of the chest cavity, the air pressure in the lungs decreases relative to the atmospheric pressure. As a result, air will flow into the lungs through the nose and/or mouth provided that the airway is open. When the volume of the chest cavity decreases, the lungs are compressed, so the pressure in the lungs increases relative to the outside pressure, and air is forced out of the lungs. Thus, the action of the respiratory muscles does not directly draw air into or out of the lungs. Rather, these muscles change the size of the chest cavity and the shape of the lungs, causing changes in air pressure that result in the in-and-out flow of air.

Inspiration almost always requires active muscular contractions. Contractions of the external intercostal muscles will expand the chest cavity, as described above. The chest cavity can also be expanded by the primary muscle of inspiration, the diaphragm (shown in Figure 2.1). The diaphragm is a dome-shaped muscle that separates the chest cavity from the abdomen. When it contracts, it moves downward, flattening out the dome and thus increasing the size of the chest cavity.

Both muscular actions and passive forces may play roles in exhalation. The size of the chest cavity can be actively reduced by pulling the ribcage down through contraction of the internal intercostals (along with the muscles of the back), or by allowing the diaphragm to relax and return to its resting state. Because it contracts downward, the diaphragm cannot rise by itself past its rest position, but the abdominal muscles can contract to push the guts upward, pressing up on the diaphragm and further decreasing the size of the chest cavity. Air can also be pushed out of the lungs without the application of muscular forces, because properties of the lung tissues themselves contribute to pressing air out of the lungs. Lung tissues are naturally elastic, and when stretched they will shrink back to their original shape, as a rubber band will. This property is called *elastic recoil*. The ribcage is also somewhat elastic thanks to the ribs' cartilaginous attachments, and it naturally returns to its resting configuration when unopposed by muscular action. Gravity tends to pull the ribs down in the absence of muscular action; and the contents of the abdomen press upward on the diaphragm at end of an inhalation, also acting to shrink the chest cavity. These forces are dependent on the amount of air in the lungs: The more air, the more the lungs are stretched, and the more passive recoil forces are generated.

What this means in terms of airflow into and out of the lungs is that, in the absence of muscular effort, the exact amount of air delivered from the lungs to the vocal tract depends on the amount of air in the lungs. When the lungs are full of air, the recoil pressures are large, the air pressure within the lungs is high, and the lungs deliver a high volume of flow. Similarly, when the lungs are near their resting size, the pressures are lower and flow decreases. To demonstrate the effect of the elastic recoil of the respiratory system for yourself, take a deep breath and then just relax. The air in your lungs will rush out unless active muscular resistance is applied, and the rate of airflow will decrease as more and more air has escaped. To get a sense of how much air pressure can be contributed by elastic recoil, take a deep breath and hold it with your mouth open. Relax the muscles in your ribcage, and feel the pressure develop in your throat. Finally, take a deep breath and use only the respiratory muscles to keep air from rushing out, noting the muscular effort required to oppose the elastic recoil of the lungs and ribcage.

Because we do not usually breathe in too deeply during quiet respiration, elastic recoil, torque from the ribs (which rotate slightly on inspiration), and gravity often provide enough pressure to generate an outward flow of air, and it may not be necessary to use the expiratory muscles at all to breathe out. However, muscular effort is needed to expand the thorax for breathing in, or to contract it beyond its resting position when breathing out. To demonstrate this, take a very deep breath. You should feel the muscles involved in expanding the chest cavity. Now, breathe out as much air as possible. You should again feel the muscular effort involved, including the contributions of abdominal and back muscles when you approach the limit of exhalation.

2.2.3   Modifications of breathing for speech

Breathing for speech differs from quiet respiration in several ways. First, we usually breathe in more air when planning to speak than we do during quiet respiration. The relative durations of inhalation and exhalation are also different during speech. During quiet respiration, about 40% of a breath cycle is devoted to inspiration, and expiration takes up about 60% of the cycle. During speech, inspiration takes up only about 10% of a breath cycle. Exhalation is greatly prolonged (so we can produce long utterances with minimal pausing), and often extends beyond the normal resting capacity of the lungs (Estenne, Zocchi, Ward, and Macklem, 1990). Action of the expiratory muscles is often needed in speech breathing to produce enough airflow to finish an utterance; elastic recoil alone is not enough to produce a very long uninterrupted monologue. Also, speech requires that the relative pressures above and below the vocal folds remain fairly constant (for example, Cavagna and Margaria, 1965). In contrast, airflow and pressure in quiet respiration vary significantly from the beginning of a quiet exhalation to its end, as we saw in the breathing exercises above. Finally, movements of the tongue, lips, jaw, and soft palate mean that the resistance to flow above the vocal folds changes continuously during speech. When the airway narrows or is blocked (for example, during the sounds /t/ or /s/), pressure will increase throughout the system; and when the vocal tract is open (for a sound like /a/, for example), pressure will decrease. These factors make maintaining a consistent pressure below the vocal folds quite a trick. Thus, speech breathing is much more complicated than the simple "breathe in and then relax" of quiet respiration.

Maintaining a relatively constant pressure below the vocal folds requires a dynamic balance between active muscle control and the varying passive elastic recoil forces of the respiratory system (Draper, Ladefoged, and Whitteridge, 1960; Mead, Bouhuys, and Proctor, 1968; Hixon and Weismer, 1995). Unfortunately, surprisingly little is known about the patterns of muscular activity used to regulate air pressure. On average, inspiratory effort may be needed during exhalation when lung volumes are high, to "brake" the excessive expiratory pressure contributed by high levels of recoil, while expiratory effort may be needed when lung volumes are low and there is little or no energy contributed by recoil. However, studies of the movements of the rib cage and abdomen (Hixon, Goldman, and Mead, 1973; Hixon, Mead, and Goldman, 1976; see Hixon and Weismer, 1995, for review) suggest that moment-to-moment balancing of recoil forces and muscular effort requires use of both the inspiratory and expiratory muscles throughout a respiratory cycle. These continuous small muscular adjustments provide fast corrections to subglottal[2] pressure, like those required in response to varying resistance

---

[2]   Subglottal pressure is the air pressure measured below the vocal folds. The glottis is the space between the vocal folds.

above the glottis during speech. In particular, the abdominal muscles are active through-out the expiratory phase of speech breathing, and help regulate subglottal pressure (Hixon *et al.*, 1973, 1976). As noted above, the details of the precise timing of these muscular actions are unknown, and they probably vary from person to person.

Breathing in speech is even more complicated than this brief description might imply. For example, individual speakers differ significantly in the particular patterns of muscular activity they prefer, with greater variability in speaking measures seen in older persons (Morris and Brown, 1994a, b). Speakers also differ in how they organize breathing patterns for speech. For most people, the length of the planned utterance has an effect on the amount of air inspired (Winkworth, Davis, Adams, and Ellis, 1995; Whalen and Kinsella-Shaw, 1997). In reading tasks, speakers differ in how they vary lung volumes to accommodate louder utterances, inspirations at sentence and para-graph boundaries, and length of utterance (Winkworth, Davis, Ellis, and Adams, 1994). Some speakers habitually rely on their abdominal muscles for breathing, while others depend primarily on motions of the ribcage to change the volume of the chest cavity. These differences begin in infancy (Boliek, Hixon, Watson, and Morgan, 1996) and apparently persist throughout life. The particular pattern of muscle activity and chest wall movement also depends on the speaker's age, body type and shape, and posture. For example, gravity will act on the diaphragm and ribs when speakers are upright, but not when they are lying down. Changes in respiratory activity are also associated with changes in loudness, and with the demands of particular segments (for example, more airflow is required to produce /h/ than to produce /t/). Linguistic factors, such as structural (clausal) boundaries, influence lung volume variation (Winkworth *et al.*, 1995; Davis, Zhang, Winkworth, and Bandler, 1996). Speaking appears to co-opt the breathing pattern in a number of ways; for example, in conversa-tional interaction, inspiratory durations during listening were seen to approximate those observed during speaking, and the breathing cycles of conversation partners became synchronous (McFarland, 2001). Much research remains to be done in this area. In particular, existing studies of the movements of the chest wall and abdomen could usefully be supplemented with studies of the action potentials of different mus-cles of respiration (see, for example, Ladefoged and Loeb, 2002). More detailed dis-cussions of these issues are given by Hixon (1987), or by Hixon and Weismer (1995).

2.2.4　Summary

Air flows in and out of the lungs because changes in the volume of the chest cavity cause changes in the air pressure within the lungs relative to the outside atmospheric air pres-sure. Air flows into the lungs when the internal pressure is less than the outside pressure, and it flows out when the internal pressure is greater than pressure outside the lungs. The inspiratory muscles (for example, the diaphragm and the external intercostals) expand the chest cavity during inspiration. Elastic recoil, gravity, and muscle activity (internal intercostals, abdominal and back muscles) may all be involved in exhalation, depending on how much air is in the lungs and how the internal pressure compares to the external pressure. Although speech is normally produced with air flowing out from the lungs, both inspiratory and expiratory muscles may be used to control the amount of air that is delivered during speech. Linguistic and pragmatic factors, such as the length of the planned utterance, placement of structural boundaries, and synchrony with a conversation partner, influence lung volume variation and inspiratory/expiratory cycles.

2.3   The Larynx and Phonation

Once air is flowing in a controlled way from the lungs, it can be converted to sound by the action of the vocal folds, which are located within the larynx (sometimes called the voice box). The vocal folds are also called the vocal cords. The term "folds" is preferred, however, because it provides a better description of the structures, which are small folds of tissue, not strings. These folds oscillate, alternately obstructing and opening the airway as they move back and forth. This oscillation repeatedly interrupts the flow of air from the lungs, creating changes in air pressure that we hear as sound.

The process by which the vocal folds modulate the outgoing air to produce sound is called *phonation*, and sounds whose production includes action of the vocal folds are said to be *voiced*. Understanding the complex process by which voicing is produced requires a grasp of the anatomy of the vocal tract and the biomechanics of vocal fold vibration. These topics will be addressed in the following sections.

Not all the sounds used in speech are voiced. Sounds like /a/, /z/, and /m/ are all produced with vocal fold vibration, but other sounds (for example, /h/ and /s/) are produced without vocal fold vibration, and are called *voiceless*. Try saying "ha ha ha" quite slowly, with your fingers on your throat. You should feel vibrations turning on and off. The pattern you feel is due to the vocal folds, which are vibrating during /a/, but not during /h/. Despite the use of the terms "voiced" and "voiceless," all the sounds of speech, voiced or voiceless, are part of the human voice broadly construed, as discussed in the first chapter.

2.3.1   The larynx

The vocal folds are contained within the larynx,[3] which is suspended by muscles, ligaments, and membranes from the hyoid bone in the neck. It sits in front of the esophagus, as shown in Figure 2.1. Although the larynx has evolved to produce sound, its most important function is sealing the airway to the lungs completely, thus protecting both the airway and lungs from foreign objects or fluids, particularly during swallowing. (Coughing offers further protection to the airway.[4]) The tissue within the larynx is very sensitive, and any foreign particles in the air stream that happen to enter the larynx produce a cough reflex. Sealing the airway also fixes the ribcage, and provides a rigid frame for heavy lifting or pushing. Finally, the larynx serves as a valve to control the amount of airflow through the system. For example, trying to talk while running fast may result in a very breathy voice, because of the primary need to increase the rate of exchange of gasses during physical activity. However, during a consistent, conditioned pace, normal phonation is usual. As with respiration,

---

[3]   Pronounced LAIR-inks.

[4]   A cough usually begins with an initial breath of air. At the beginning of expiration, the vocal folds close the glottis for just a moment, thus increasing the pressure in the lungs even more, so that when the glottis opens the air is expelled with greater force, ideally taking the offending matter with it.

(a)   (b)

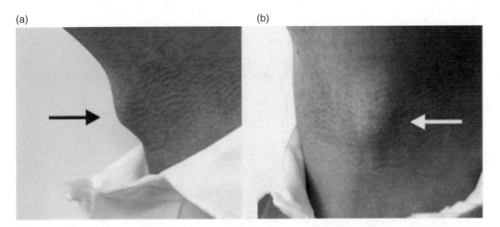

Figure 2.3   Location of the larynx in the neck of a male. The arrow indicates location of the thyroid prominence. (a) side view. (b) front view.

the vocal functions of the larynx are overlaid on these older, more basic, biologically essential functions, which has limited the extent to which sound-producing elaborations to laryngeal structures can evolve (because any changes must preserve the basic ability to protect the airway). As a result, when viewed from an evolutionary perspective, the larynx is a rather conservative structure, and laryngeal anatomy is rather similar across all mammalian species (see Fitch and Hauser, 2003, for review). In contrast, birds have both a larynx and a separate organ (the syrinx) that serves only to produce sound. Because syringes are free of "multiuse constraints," they can evolve in many ways, so that structures vary considerably across birds (see Fitch and Hauser, 2003, or Seddon, 2005, for more details; vocal production in birds is also discussed in Chapter 5).

The larynx comprises a set of interconnected cartilages found in the airway below the pharynx and above the trachea (windpipe). Figure 2.3 shows the approximate location of the larynx in a man's neck. To locate your larynx, place your fingers on your neck and say "ah." You should feel the vibrations getting stronger or weaker as your fingers move toward or away from your larynx. (You can also feel it move upward and then downward during swallowing.) The larynx is suspended in the neck from the hyoid bone (Figures 2.1 and 2.4), which is located just under and roughly parallel to the jaw. (It can be felt above the top of the larynx.) This bone is unique in that it does not connect or form a joint directly with any other bone or cartilage in the body. It serves as a point of attachment for more than twenty different muscles, and may also help protect the airway from injury.

The largest laryngeal cartilage is called the thyroid cartilage (Figure 2.4). It is shaped something like a shield, with an opening towards the back. The rear of the thyroid cartilage has two sets of horns, or *cornua*, one on top (*superior*) and one on the bottom (*inferior*). Ligaments attach the superior cornua to the hyoid bone; the inferior cornua attach the thyroid cartilage to the cricoid cartilage, as described below. The two sides (*laminae*) of the shield meet in the front to form a notch called the *thyroid prominence*, which is easily visible as the "Adam's apple" in many men. It is visually less obvious in women and children, but can still be located easily by touch.

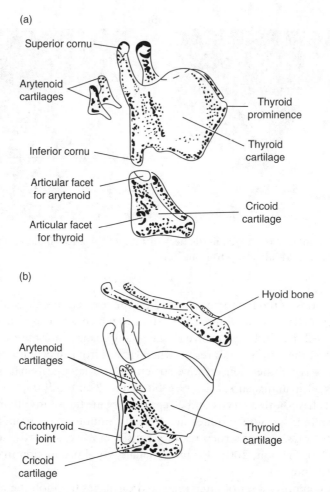

Figure 2.4 Disassembled (a) and reassembled (b) laryngeal cartilages, including the hyoid bone.

Once you have located your thyroid prominence, you should be able to find the general outline of this cartilage for yourself. Feel your neck to locate the laminae. The angle between the laminae ranges from about 90° in men to about 120° in women. (Further differences between men and women in laryngeal anatomy are discussed in Chapter 4, as are changes that occur with aging.) Although this is the largest of the laryngeal cartilages, it is still quite small. Size varies considerably across individuals, but differences in size between men and women are especially notable. In males, the distance from the tips of the inferior cornua to the tips of the superior cornua averages about 44 mm; in females the distance averages about 38 mm. The anterior-posterior dimension averages about 37 mm in males, and about 29 mm in females (Dickson and Maue-Dickson, 1982).

The second major laryngeal cartilage is called the *cricoid cartilage* (from the Greek "krikos," meaning "ring"). This cartilage is shaped like a signet ring, with the large part toward the rear. The cricoid cartilage averages about 25 mm in height in the back, and about 8 mm in the front, although very large differences exist between individuals (Randestad, Lindholm, and Fabian, 2000). The inferior cornua of the thyroid cartilage attach to the cricoid cartilage at the *cricothyroid joint*, so that the larger posterior part of the cricoid cartilage fits within the open part of the thyroid cartilage and the front part of the cricoid cartilage fits just below the bottom of the thyroid cartilage. The thyroid and cricoid cartilages can rock about the cricothyroid joint. This will be discussed further below.

The two *arytenoid cartilages*[5] are the final major component of the laryngeal framework. These paired cartilages are shaped like three-sided pyramids. In men the arytenoids average about 18 mm in height, and in women they average about 13 mm in height (Dickson and Maue-Dickson, 1982). The arytenoid cartilages sit on top of the rear portion of the cricoid cartilage. The joints formed between each arytenoid and the cricoid cartilage are called the *cricoarytenoid joints*. These joints are extremely flexible, and the arytenoids can move in several directions in a motion usually described as "rocking and gliding." Two small bumps (*processes*) project from the base of each arytenoid. The *muscular processes* are located in the rear of each cartilage, while the *vocal processes* project forward from the front of each cartilage, pointing toward the front of the thyroid cartilage.[6]

The vocal folds run across the airway from just below the thyroid notch to the arytenoid cartilages, where they attach to the vocal processes (Figure 2.5). The folds are tiny: In men, they range in length from about 17 mm to about 24 mm, and in women, they are about 13–17 mm long (for example, Zemlin, 1998, but estimates vary; compare Schuster, Lohscheller, Kummer, Eysholdt, and Hoppe, 2005). However, they are quite flexible, and can stretch about 3–4 mm (as described below). The space between the vocal folds is called the *glottis*; thus, the space above them is *supraglottal* and the space below them is *subglottal*. About two-thirds of the glottal opening lies between the vocal folds proper; this part is referred to as the *membranous glottis*. The remaining one-third of the glottis lies between the two arytenoid cartilages, which project into the airway. This part of the glottis is called the *cartilaginous glottis*. The space just above folds is called the *laryngeal ventricle*, or the *ventricle of Morgagni*, and above the ventricle lie the *ventricular folds* (also called the *false vocal folds*). The space below the vocal folds is called the *conus elasticus*.

The vocal folds have a complex, layered structure (Figure 2.6), which is described by the *body-cover model* (Hirano, 1974; see Titze, 1994, for extensive review). The top layer of the folds (the cover) comprises two parts, the *epithelium* and the *lamina propria*. The epithelium is a thin, stiff layer (only about 0.05 mm thick) that protects the folds from impact stresses and friction. The second part of the cover, the lamina propria, is about 1.5–2 mm thick. It has its own layered structure, each layer having a slightly different composition and different vibratory characteristics. The topmost layer of the lamina propria (the *mucosa*) is very squishy and stretchable in all directions; the middle layer can be stretched along the anterior-posterior axis, and the deepest layer resists stretching altogether. Below the cover lies the body of the vocal

---

[5] Pronounced a-RIT-ten-oid.

[6] Three other cartilages are also considered part of the larynx, but these have little apparent function in phonation. The epiglottis is a leaf- or tongue-shaped cartilage that folds over the opening of the larynx to seal it completely (for example, during swallowing). One corniculate cartilage sits on top of each arytenoid, and the cuneiform cartilages are located in the tissue on each side of the entrance to the larynx.

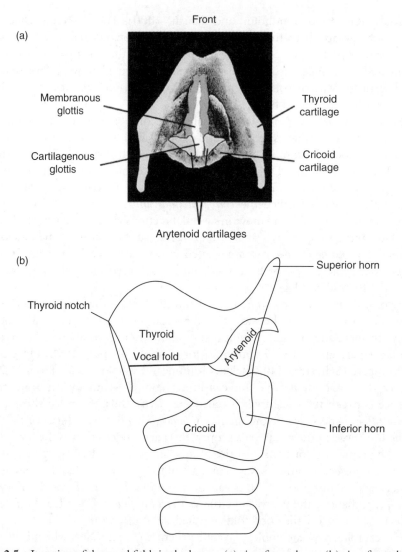

Figure 2.5   Location of the vocal folds in the larynx. (a) view from above. (b) view from the side.

folds, which consists of the *thyroarytenoid muscle* (also called the *vocalis* muscle[7]). This muscle forms the bulk of the vocal folds, and is described in more detail below. The different properties of these layers of tissue mean that the bodies of the vocal folds can be stiffened while the cover remains loose and can move freely around the body. This property is essential for phonation, and will be discussed shortly.

The muscles of the larynx are usually divided into two groups: the *intrinsic laryngeal muscles*, and the *extrinsic laryngeal muscles* (Table 2.1). The extrinsic muscles connect the larynx to other parts of the body, stabilize its position, or move it up and down.

---

[7]   Technically, the term "vocalis" refers to the medial part of the thyroarytenoid muscle, but the terms are often used interchangeably. See, for example, Sanders, Rai, Han, and Biller (1998), for discussion of the complex anatomy of this muscle.

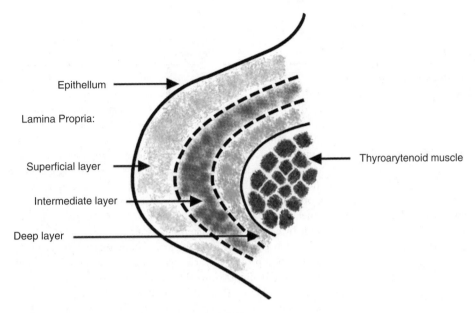

Epithellum

Lamina Propria:

Superficial layer

Intermediate layer

Deep layer

Thyroarytenoid muscle

Figure 2.6 Layered structure of the vocal folds.

The intrinsic muscles connect the different cartilages and change their positions relative to each other. The intrinsic laryngeal muscles are among the smallest and fastest in the body, and provide very quick, precise control of the position of the laryngeal cartilages. By their actions, these muscles can produce complete glottal opening for breathing, or complete glottal closure to protect the airway or support lifting; they can position the vocal folds for vibration to produce sound, or can narrow the glottal opening to produce whisper. These actions will be described in some detail in what follows.

Figure 2.7 shows the vocal folds separated as if for breathing. For phonation to occur, the folds must be brought to midline (as described below), and then they must move apart again for the next breath. The intrinsic muscles are usually subdivided into two groups, reflecting these two different functions. The laryngeal *adductors* bring the folds together, and the *abductor* pulls them apart.[8] These muscles are listed in Table 2.1, and their positions are illustrated in Figures 2.8 to 2.11 (see also, for example, Zemlin, 1998, for detailed discussion).

The two primary laryngeal adductors are the interarytenoid muscle and the lateral cricoarytenoid muscle. Muscles in the larynx are named after the structures they connect. Thus, the lateral cricoarytenoid muscle runs between the muscular process of each arytenoid and the side of the cricoid cartilage; and the interarytenoid muscle runs between the muscular processes of the two arytenoid cartilages (Figure 2.8). The actions of these muscles are shown in an animal model in video examples 1 to 4 on the website. These images were filmed from above (looking down the throat

---

[8] "Adductor" and "abductor" sound very much alike. For clarity, it is common practice in verbal discussion to spell out the letters of the prefixes, as in "A-B-ductors" and "A-D-ductors."

Table 2.1   The intrinsic and extrinsic laryngeal muscles and their actions.

Muscle	Movement produced
The intrinsic laryngeal muscles	
Posterior cricoarytenoid	A paired muscle. Runs between the back of each arytenoid cartilage and the cricoid cartilage. Contraction abducts the vocal folds; opposes cricothyroid muscle to anchor arytenoids during phonation.
Lateral cricoarytenoid	A paired muscle. Runs between the muscular process of each arytenoid cartilage and the side of the cricoid cartilage. Adducts the vocal folds by closing the front part of the cartilaginous glottis and the rear part of the membranous glottis.
Interarytenoid	Connects the backs of the arytenoid cartilages. Adducts the vocal folds by closing the cartilaginous glottis.
Thyroarytenoid	A paired muscle. Runs from the front of the thyroid cartilage to the vocal process of each arytenoid. Contraction tenses and bulges the body of vocal folds, and helps close the middle of the membranous part of the glottis.
Cricothyroid	A paired muscle connecting the thyroid and cricoid cartilages. Tilts the cricoid and thyroid cartilages together, stretching the vocal folds.
The most important extrinsic laryngeal muscles	
Thyrohyoid	Connects the thyroid cartilage and the hyoid bone. When the hyoid bone is fixed in position by the actions of other muscles, contraction raises the thyroid cartilage; when the hyoid is free to move, contraction lowers the hyoid bone and the larynx.
Sternothyroid	Connects the thyroid cartilage to the sternum. Contraction lowers the larynx.
Digastricus	Runs from the jaw to the hyoid bone and on to the mastoid process. Contraction raises the hyoid bone and larynx.
Geniohyoid	Runs from the chin to the hyoid bone. Raises the hyoid bone and larynx when jaw is fixed in position.
Stylohyoid	Runs from the styloid process on the temporal bone to the hyoid bone. Contraction moves the larynx upward and posteriorly.
Sternohyoid	Runs from the sternum to the hyoid bone. Contraction lowers the larynx.

onto the larynx), with the front of the neck at the top of the image and the back of the neck toward the bottom (Figure 2.7). The glottis appears as a dark, wedge-shaped area in the center of the image; in some examples, it is possible to see the rings of the trachea below the open glottis. The vocal folds appear as shiny white bands in the center of the images. They attach to the thyroid cartilage at the front of the neck (top of the image), and to the two arytenoid cartilages at the back of the glottis. The arytenoids appear as the large, bumpy objects at the bottom center of each frame. (The cartilages are covered with mucosa, so it is difficult to see their precise shapes.) The action of each muscle was demonstrated by selectively stimulat-

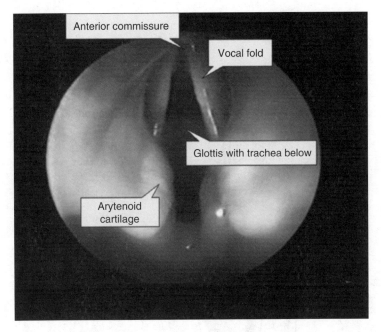

Figure 2.7 The vocal folds and arytenoid cartilages, as shown in video examples 1 to 4.

ing the specific branch of the recurrent laryngeal nerve that innervates that muscle. Stimulation was applied bilaterally, to demonstrate the movement that would be produced by that muscle if it contracted in isolation during normal phonation. For the lateral cricoarytenoid muscle, stimulation was also applied unilaterally, because the motion of the arytenoid is somewhat easier to see when only one side moves at a time. Contraction of the lateral cricoarytenoid (video examples 1, 2, and 3) moves the muscular process of the arytenoid sideways and down, pivoting the vocal processes of each arytenoid toward the midline of the glottis, thus bringing the medial edges of the vocal folds together (cf. Figure 2.8a). Video example 1 shows the movement of the right arytenoid in response to contraction of the right lateral cricoarytenoid muscle; video example 2 shows the result of contracting the left lateral cricoarytenoid muscle. If this muscle contracts alone, the glottis is configured for whispering. (This is easiest to see in video example 3, where bilateral stimulation is applied.) Notice that the lateral cricoarytenoid muscle does not effectively close the cartilaginous part of the glottis, so that a gap remains between the arytenoid cartilages when this muscle acts in isolation.

Video example 4 shows the action of the interarytenoid muscle. Contraction of the interarytenoid muscle slides the backs of the arytenoids together, leaving a gap in the membranous glottis and in the front part of the cartilaginous glottis. (Notice how little the position of the membranous vocal folds changes in this video as the interarytenoid muscle contracts.) When the interarytenoid and lateral cricoarytenoid contract together, their joint action closes the posterior part of the glottis, but may leave a medial gap between the vocal folds.

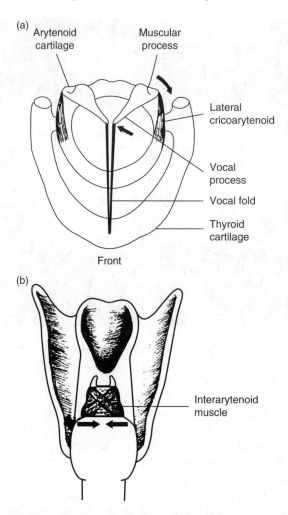

Figure 2.8   The lateral cricoarytenoid muscle (a) and interarytenoid (b) muscles and how they produce the "rocking and gliding" motion of the arytenoid cartilages.

   The thyroarytenoid muscle runs from the vocal process of each arytenoid to the front of the thyroid cartilage (Figure 2.9). It forms the deepest layer and main body of the vocal folds (Figure 2.6). Some authors distinguish separate functional units (the thyrovocalis and thyromuscularis muscles) within this muscle, whose complex structure and function are not completely understood (see, for example, Sanders *et al.*, 1998; Zemlin, 1998, for review). When this muscle contracts, it tenses the body of the vocal folds and bunches them up slightly. This action is demonstrated for each fold separately in video examples 5 and 6, and for both sides together in video example 7. As these videos show, the vocal fold bulging that occurs with contraction of the thyroarytenoid muscle also closes the middle portion of the glottis, so the thyroarytenoid is sometimes grouped with the laryngeal adductors. Contraction also has the secondary effect of reducing the stiffness of the cover of the folds relative to

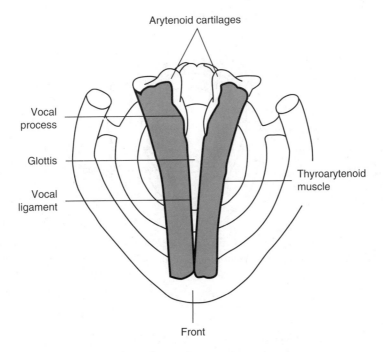

Figure 2.9   The thyroarytenoid muscle.

the body. The ability to control the relative stiffnesses of the different layers of the vocal folds is critical for phonation, as will become apparent in the next section.

Complete closure of the glottis usually requires the joint actions of the cricoarytenoid, interarytenoid, and thyroarytenoid muscles. This is shown in video example 8, which was created by stimulating the branch of the recurrent laryngeal nerve that innervates all three muscles, before the branchings to the individual muscles.

The only laryngeal abductor is the posterior cricoarytenoid muscle (Figure 2.10), which runs between the muscular process of each arytenoid and the back of the cricoid cartilage. Its action is shown in video example 9. At the beginning of this video, the vocal folds are positioned somewhat apart, as if for quiet breathing. When the posterior cricoarytenoid muscle contracts, it pulls the back of the arytenoid cartilages somewhat medially and down, so that the vocal process swings upward and away from the midline. This action opens the glottis widely, as if for a deep or sudden breath. The posterior cricoarytenoid muscle may also act in opposition to the cricoarytenoid muscle to anchor the arytenoids during phonation.

The remaining intrinsic laryngeal muscle, the cricothyroid, is neither an abductor nor an adductor. It connects the thyroid and cricoid cartilages (Figure 2.11). When it contracts, it tilts the fronts of the two cartilages toward each other. This action increases the distance between the front of the thyroid cartilage and the arytenoids, stretching the vocal folds. The *superior laryngeal nerve* innervates the cricothyroid muscle, and is responsible for controlling F0, as described shortly. All the other intrinsic laryngeal muscles are innervated by the *recurrent laryngeal nerve*. Note, however, that both the recurrent and superior laryngeal nerves stem from the vagus

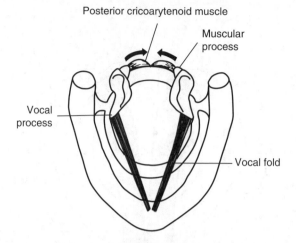

Figure 2.10   The posterior cricoarytenoid muscle and its actions (top view).

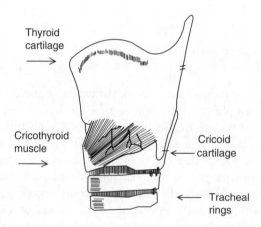

Figure 2.11   The cricothyroid muscle.

nerve (cranial nerve X), which ultimately controls all the intrinsic laryngeal muscles (see, for example, Broniatowski *et al.*, 2002, for review, and Chapter 3 for complete details on the cranial nerves regulating speech).

In summary, the larynx is made up of connected cartilages (the thyroid, cricoid, and arytenoid cartilages). It is suspended from the hyoid bone and sits on top of the trachea and in front of the esophagus. The intrinsic laryngeal muscles control the position of these cartilages relative to each other: The adductors close the vocal folds for phonation or to protect the airway, and the abductor opens them for breathing. The most important intrinsic laryngeal muscle is the thyroarytenoid muscle, which is used for controlling loudness and for changing vocal quality (in the narrow sense), as discussed in Section 2.6. The main adductory muscles are the lateral cricoarytenoid and the interarytenoid. The lateral cricoarytenoid muscle brings the body of the vocal folds together by pulling the back of the arytenoid sideways and down, so that the front edges of the arytenoids (where the vocal folds are attached) are brought together. The interarytenoid muscle closes the gap between the backs of the arytenoid cartilages. The cricothyroid muscle stretches the vocal folds by tilting the thyroid and cricoid cartilages. The only abductory muscle is the posterior cricoarytenoid. This muscle opens the airway by pulling the back of the arytenoid cartilages down and toward the midline, so that the front edges separate.

Sidebar: The Laryngeal Mirror

The invention of the laryngeal mirror revolutionized the study of the voice by making the structures of the larynx visible in a living human for the first time. The history of this critical invention is a fascinating case of serendipity and synchrony. It is also an interesting study in the politics of scholarly credit-taking.

The laryngeal mirror (or laryngoscope) consists of a small round or ovoid mirror at the end of a long handle, which, when placed at the back of the throat and given sufficient lighting, allows users to view the glottis from above. The device with the name "glottiscope" was invented early in the nineteenth century by Benjamin Gay Babington (1794–1866), London physician and polymath, but this and comparable attempts by his contemporaries were considered bulky, difficult to use, and uncomfortable for the patient (Goldman and Roffman, 1975). The laryngoscope was then (re-)introduced to the public simultaneously in England by Manual Garcia II (1805–1906) and by two physicians practicing in Vienna, Austria (Majer, 1980). Garcia, an internationally-known singing teacher, had a large clientele, including the most prominent singers of the time. Garcia reported that his desire to visualize the vocal folds grew so strong that it erupted quite suddenly as the idea to adapt a dentistry mirror for this purpose (Habermann, 1969). In his 1855 publication, he explained the simplicity of the method: Fix a small mirror onto a long, bent handle, turn the client toward the sunlight, and place the apparatus in the throat against the soft palate and uvula. In summer, 1857, Ludwig Türck in Vienna used a small mirror with benefit of sunlight to visualize a patient's larynx. Accounts diverge regarding whether Türck had previously heard of Garcia's achievements. Some reports state that Türck was aware of Garcia's work, and, in fact, was helpful in bringing the procedure into public acceptance (Goldman and Roffman, 1975). However, according to Habermann (1969, citing earlier sources), only after several attempts on his own was Türck first made aware of Garcia's work. In that same year, a visiting physician from Budapest, Johann Czermak, borrowed the apparatus and fitted it with artificial light. Czermak reported his success in visualizing the larynx in 1858 at the Austrian Academy of Science, further promoting its general acceptance in the medical community. For some time, both physicians claimed priority in inventing the laryngeal mirror, but eventually Garcia has received this distinction, with Türck receiving secondary honors.

2.3.2   How the vocal folds vibrate

The intrinsic laryngeal muscles can bring the vocal folds together at the midline of the glottis and stiffen them, but these actions alone do not produce vibration or sound. Instead, a combination of tissue elasticity and aerodynamic forces is responsible for the sustained tissue oscillations that produce voice. As the vocal folds oscillate, they periodically interrupt the flow of air from the lungs, creating changes in air pressure by opening and closing rather than by pressing on air particles as vibrating strings do. (This is one reason why the term "vocal cords" is dispreferred, as it incorrectly implies this type of vibration.) These biomechanical and aerodynamic forces are described in the *myoelastic aerodynamic theory of vocal fold vibration* (van den Berg, 1958).

To begin vibration, the adductory muscles must first bring the vocal folds together. The folds must be closed (or nearly so), but not held together too tightly. Next, the action of the respiratory system generates air pressure below the closed vocal folds. Normally, subglottal pressures of about 3–5 cm H_2O are needed to begin vibration, but once vibration has started it will continue at lower pressures (Titze, 1992; Plant, Freed, and Plant, 2004). When the pressure is sufficient to overcome the stiffness of the folds and the inertia of the air column above the folds, the vocal folds are blown open from below. If the folds are too stiff (held together too tightly), or if there is not enough pressure below the folds, they will not open; but if they are not stiff enough, they will blow open and remain open. Thus, the balance between stiffness and subglottal air pressure must be just right.

As air flows through the opening vocal folds, two factors act to close the glottis again. The first is tissue elasticity. The vocal folds are blown apart laterally by the air pressure from below and, due to their elasticity, naturally regain their original configuration near the midline as air pressure drops with the free flow of air through the glottis. In addition, aerodynamic forces contribute to the closing of the vocal folds. One such force is described by the Bernoulli principle (named after Swiss scientist Daniel Bernoulli, 1700–1782), which states that pressure must go down when air particle velocity goes up, as long as total energy remains equal. Because the glottis is not a smooth tube, air that passes near the edges of the vocal folds has to travel farther than does air at the midline of the glottis. Given a relatively uniform subglottal pressure, air moves faster around the vocal folds than it does at the midline. By Bernoulli's principle, this causes a reduction in pressure away from the midline, which sucks the folds back toward the midline, helping them close. (This same principle explains how airplanes can fly: Wings are constructed such that air flows more quickly over them than under them, creating a lower pressure above the wing that pulls the plane upward.) A second aeroacoustic contribution to glottal closure occurs when vortices form in the airflow as it exits the glottis. Vortices along the superior-medial surface of the folds create an additional negative pressure between the vocal folds, which further contributes to rapid closing and leads to increases in the high-frequency energy in the voice source (McGowan, 1988; Zhang, 2008; Khosla, Murugappan, Paniello, Ying, and Gutmark, 2009). Once the vocal folds are closed, pressure builds up below them again, the folds are blown open, and the entire process repeats for another cycle of phonation. The result of these steps is *self-sustaining oscillation* of the vocal folds.

Vocal fold vibration is rather complex. The folds do not vibrate as single block-like units moving rigidly back and forth across the glottis. Rather, pressure from below opens the folds from bottom to top, and the bottom edges also close before the top edges. Figure 2.12 shows a single cycle of vocal fold vibration, viewed from the front of the neck. At the top of the figure, the vocal folds are closed, and air pressure is building up below them (as indicated by the arrows). As pressure builds, it gradually begins opening the folds from below, so that the bottom edges of the folds separate before the top edges (as shown in the second and third panels of the figure). The top edges of the folds separate in the fourth panel, and air begins flowing through the glottis. At this time, recoil, Bernoulli forces, and forces related to vortices in the airflow immediately begin acting on the bottom edges of the folds, drawing them back together. In panel 7, the upper margins of the vocal folds are still moving laterally, but the bottom edges have returned nearly to midline. In the eighth panel, the lower edges have returned to midline and the glottis is closed. Airflow through the glottis ceases at this point, and pressure buildup begins again below the folds, although the upper edges of the folds are still moving laterally, or may have only begun to return to midline. Finally, in the tenth panel, lateral motion in the upper margins of the vocal folds has nearly dissipated, and the lower edges are beginning to separate, starting the entire process again. (See Berry, 2001, for a detailed but accessible description of current formal models of vocal fold vibration.)

The folds vibrate in this complex fashion because of their complex layered structure. Vibratory movement of the vocal folds takes place primarily in the cover, which rides over the stiffer body. In fact, vibration depends on the difference in stiffness between the body and cover: When the difference in stiffness is absent (because of slackness in the thyroarytenoid due to paralysis, or because of stiffening of the mucosa due to a respiratory infection), the vocal folds cannot vibrate well. Adjusting the laryngeal muscles can change the relative stiffness of the cover and body of the vocal folds, changing the rate and pattern of vibration. Movement of the cover layer of the vocal folds over the body layers – usually called the *mucosal wave* – is easy to see in strobo-scopic images or in high-speed films of the vibrating larynx like those in video example 10 on the website, which shows the vibration of normal human vocal folds. These pictures were taken with a high-speed video system at a rate of 3,000 frames/sec, and are played back here at a rate of 10 frames/sec to show details of the vibratory motion. The speaker is a female, phonating at a fundamental frequency of about 220 Hz. In this video, the rear of the glottis (the arytenoid cartilages) is toward the top of the image, and the front (the thyroid cartilage) is toward the bottom. Note especially the zipping and unzipping motion of the vocal folds, and the mucosal wave traveling across the surface of each fold during phonation. Note also that the rear of the glottis does not close completely. This is a common configuration in normal voices, especially for females.

Descriptions of the mucosal wave usually focus on its propagation along the superior surface of the vocal folds, which is the aspect that is visible when looking from above (as in the video examples). This segment of the wave attenuates quickly as it travels outward away from the glottis. However, the most important part of the wave is its transit along the medial surface of the vocal folds, where glottal opening and

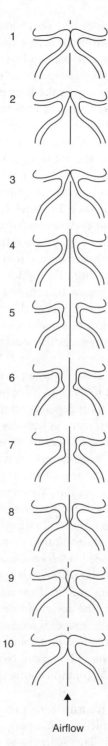

1

2

3

4

5

6

7

8

9

10

Airflow

Figure 2.12   The movements of the vocal folds across the airway for a single cycle of phonation.

closing actually occur. As Figure 2.12 suggests, the wave initiates there, and travels a significant distance along this medial surface before "breaking" across the top of the folds. The wave also has its greatest amplitude along the medial surface of the folds, where it interacts with the opposite vocal fold when the folds collide as the glottis closes. Video example 11 is a computer animation showing these motions. In this animation, the top image shows the vocal fold motion as viewed from above, and the bottom image shows a cutaway view of the same motion.[9] The blue layer represents the vocal fold mucosa (the cover layers); the white area is the vocal ligament, and the pink areas represent the thyroarytenoid muscle. The vocal folds are not adducted especially tightly in this example, so that they do not touch tightly along the entire medial surface. Notice how most of the motion is in the mucosa; the thyroarytenoid moves very little as the folds vibrate. These motions along the medial surface of the folds are what modulates the airflow and produces the acoustic wave that is perceived as voice (Berry, 2001).

Laryngeal vibrations produce sound as follows. As the vocal folds open, air rushes through the glottis and encounters the column of air in the vocal tract above the folds. As the flowing air presses upward against this column of air, it creates an increase in the supraglottal air pressure (a compression) and sets those air molecules in motion. The molecules begin to move, spreading out and moving up the vocal tract. Due to their momentum, air molecules in motion above the glottis continue to move as the glottis closes, even though for the moment no further air is flowing through the glottis. This ongoing motion produces a rarefaction – a decrease in pressure above the vocal folds as molecules in motion continue up the vocal tract, but no further molecules pass the closed vocal folds to take their places. As the vocal folds open, air flowing through the glottis creates another compression; and as the folds close again, momentum in the moving particles creates another rarefaction. Thus, vocal fold vibration modulates the airflow from the lungs, creating a pattern of alternating compressions and rarefactions in the air flowing through the glottis. In this way, vocal fold vibration results in sound. Vortices in the airflow may serve as an additional sound source (McGowan, 1988), but this mechanism of sound generation and its relative importance are not yet well understood, although attention to these matters is increasing (see, for example, Zhao, Zhang, Frankel, and Mongeau, 2002; Krane, 2005; Khosla, Murugappan, Gutmark, and Scherer, 2007).

The complex manner in which the vocal folds oscillate is responsible in part for the acoustic complexity of voice signals. Because the period of a sound is the reciprocal of its frequency, events that happen quickly (with a short period) are associated with high frequencies. Thus, the more quickly the vocal folds close, the more high-frequency energy is generated due to the abrupt change in air pressure that results. As the video examples and Figure 2.12 show, closure of the glottis normally occurs rather abruptly. Although the folds may continue to move together after flow is shut off, this does not cause any further reduction in airflow beyond what happens at closure. However, the folds normally open somewhat more gradually, from bottom to top, as the figure and videos also show. This

---

[9] These images were generously provided by David Berry, PhD, of the UCLA School of Medicine.

slower action is associated with lower frequency energy. These differences imply that *most of the acoustic energy in a normal voice is generated when the glottis closes, not when it opens.*

Figure 2.13 shows how the airflow through the glottis changes as the vocal folds open and close over time, for a male voice with a quick glottal closure (at the top of the figure) and for a female voice with a slower closure (at the bottom of the figure). Notice that the first waveform is asymmetrical: Airflow increases relatively gradually as the folds zip open, but then decreases suddenly as the folds snap shut. The folds also remain closed for a portion of the cycle, as indicated by the lines near 0 between the individual pulses. In contrast, the second waveform is nearly symmetrical, with airflow increasing and decreasing at about the same rate. The folds do not remain fully closed in this waveform, or may not fully close in every cycle.

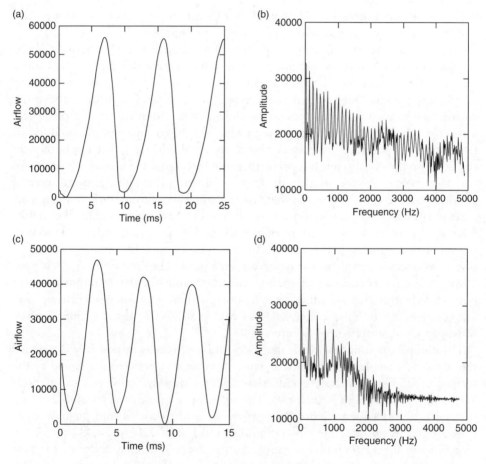

Figure 2.13 Increases and decreases in the flow of air through the glottis as the vocal folds open and close, for two typical normal voices. (a) Changes in airflow over time for a normal male voice. (b) Spectrum of the waveform in panel a. (c) Changes in airflow over time for a normal female voice. (d) Spectrum of the voice in panel c. Units on the y axes are arbitrary.

The panels to the right of the figure show the harmonic energy generated by each of these voice sources (the *source spectra*). The differences in harmonic spacing in the two spectra are due to differences in F0 for the male voice (about 115 Hz) and the female voice (about 220 Hz). Because vocal fold vibration is approximately periodic for both these voices, the frequency of each harmonic in the voice source is a whole-number multiple of the fundamental frequency; hence, harmonics are spaced evenly up the spectrum. Note also that each harmonic has slightly less energy than the one before it. Energy in a normal source spectrum drops off in approximately a straight line, at a rate of about 6 dB/octave.[10] Energy drops off much more quickly in the female voice in the lower part of the figure. Voices characterized by strong, quick vocal fold closure have many high-frequency harmonics in addition to the energy at the fundamental frequency, and are often described as "bright-sounding." Voices generated by gradual or incomplete closure of the vocal folds have most of their energy at or near the fundamental frequency, and sound "dull" or "weak."

Sidebar: Inspiratory Phonation

Voice is usually produced on exhalation. Sound produced on inhalation is called *inspiratory phonation*. An example of this kind of phonation is provided in audio sample 2.1. Although the direction of airflow differs, sound is produced in essentially the same way whichever direction air is flowing. In inspiratory phonation, the vocal folds are adducted as the chest cavity is expanded. Pressure below the vocal folds is lower than pressure above the vocal folds, so air flows from outside the mouth into the lungs. The closed vocal folds are "blown" open from above by this higher pressure. Air flowing inward through the opening glottis combines with recoil forces to close the glottis, as occurs for expiratory phonation. In this case, however, the glottis opens and closes from top to bottom, rather than from bottom to top. Inspiratory phonation is usually produced with a higher F0 than expiratory phonation (about five semitones above the comfortable expiratory voice), and generally requires nearly 50% greater airflow. Such phonation may also be more unstable in frequency than expiratory phonation. (See, for example, Orlikoff, Baken, and Kraus, 1997, for more information.) Inspired utterances occur in natural language, and are usually brief. For example, inspired "ja" occurs in German, Swedish, and Finnish, as an exclamation of assent during conversation. Finnish speakers report that utterances of sentential length may also occur on the inspiration.

[10]   The decibel (abbreviated dB; the B is capitalized because it commemorates Alexander Graham Bell) is a measure of relative sound intensity. It equals $10 \log_{10} (\text{Intensity}_2/\text{Intensity}_1)$. An octave is a doubling of frequency. Two tones with frequencies of 100 Hz and 200 Hz are one octave apart; so are two tones with frequencies of 237 Hz and 574 Hz.

2.4   The Supraglottal Vocal Tract and Resonance

Figure 2.14 shows the supraglottal vocal tract. These structures, like the rest of the anatomy of speech and voice, are primarily designed for purposes other than communication. The lips, tongue, teeth, and jaw are useful for chewing and swallowing food, and the nasal cavities are mostly used for smelling and for heating, humidifying, and filtering air as it is breathed in. The tongue, lips, and jaw are highly mobile, and the shape of the oral cavity can be altered by their movements. For example, protruding the lips makes the vocal tract longer, and pulling their corners back shortens it somewhat. Lowering the soft palate lets air from the lungs (and sound energy) pass through the nasal cavity, and raising it shuts that cavity off. Lowering the jaw enlarges the oral cavity, and moving the tongue changes the shape of the cavity. Changing the shape of the vocal tract by moving these articulators can change the sound that emerges from a speaker, as described below.

Sidebar: I've Lost my Voice!

Most people have had the experience of "losing their voice" during a severe cold. During a respiratory infection, the mucosa of the vocal folds often becomes inflamed. When this happens, the vocal folds swell so that they cannot approximate well during vibration. As a result, glottal closure may be incomplete. The stiffness of the cover of the folds also increases with swelling. Recall that vocal fold vibration depends on the difference in stiffness between the cover and body of the folds. Increasing the stiffness of the cover reduces the ability of the folds to vibrate normally, or to vibrate at all in extreme cases. (See, for example, Colton, Casper, and Leonard, 2005, for more information about a wide variety of voice disorders.)

The sound produced by the vibration of the vocal folds, if it were heard independent of the influence of the rest of the vocal tract, resembles a buzz more than it does what we think of as a human voice, as audio sample 2.2 demonstrates. (The complete, filtered voice can be heard in audio sample 2.3.) In the voices we normally hear, this buzzing sound has been shaped by the acoustic effect of the vocal tract above the vocal folds. The process by which the vocal tract interacts with the vocal source to produce the final sound of a voice is called *resonance*.

More generally, resonance is the process whereby acoustic energy is transferred from a source of vibration to another body. Objects, tubes, and containers (like the vocal tract) have natural resonant frequencies at which they will vibrate best if set in vibration. When set in vibration (for example, by striking a glass with a spoon), an object will vibrate at its natural frequency. The frequency (or frequencies) at which an object vibrates best depends in part on the size and shape of the object. For example, changing the volume of air in the glass by adding or removing water will change the frequency at which it vibrates; and blowing across the top of a large bottle will produce a lower tone than blowing across the top of a smaller bottle.

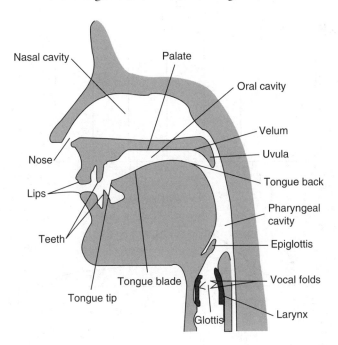

Figure 2.14 The supraglottal vocal tract.

A resonator can be set in vibration by striking it, but it can also be set vibrating by its interactions with something that is already vibrating. How well it vibrates in this case depends on the match between the rate of vibration being applied and the natural resonances of the system. When an object contacts something vibrating at a frequency near its natural frequency, it will vibrate well; when it contacts something vibrating at a rate far from its natural frequency, the resulting vibrations have much less amplitude. Consider this simple example. Imagine a tuning fork and a glass partly filled with water. If the tuning fork is struck, it will vibrate at its natural frequency, and if the glass is tapped, it too will vibrate. If the tuning fork is placed against the glass, the result will depend on how similar the vibratory rates of the glass and the tuning fork are. If they vibrate at rather different frequencies, the glass will begin to vibrate, also, but not very loudly. In contrast, if the frequencies of the glass and the tuning fork are rather similar, the glass will vibrate loudly, or may even break if the fork has been struck hard. In this way, a resonator can also be a filter. It will pass (i.e., vibrate well at) frequencies that are close to its natural frequency, but it will damp out (not vibrate very well at) frequencies that are not close to its natural frequency. Filtering describes the parts of the signal that do not get through; resonance describes the parts that do.

Figure 2.15 shows how a resonator interacts with a vibrating source. The source is shown at the top of the figure, and has a number of harmonics. The resonator is shown in the middle panel, and the output (with harmonic spacing from the source but relative harmonic amplitudes from the filter) is at the bottom. Resonators differ in how close "close" has to be for transfer of energy to occur. A resonator that will respond to or pass a wide range of frequencies (an inefficient filter) has a *broad band-*

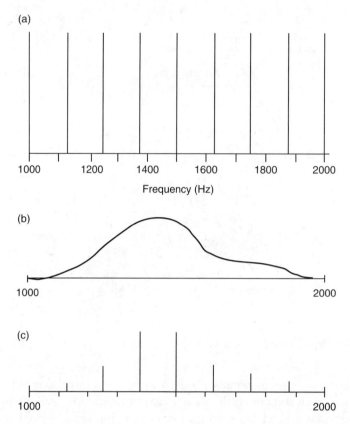

Figure 2.15 The interaction of a vibrating source of acoustic energy with a resonator. (a) harmonics of the voicing source. (b) the resonator's frequency response. (c) result of exciting the resonator with the voicing source.

width; one that only responds to a narrow range of frequencies (efficiently filtering out the rest) has a *narrow bandwidth*.

The *linear source-filter theory of speech production* (Fant, 1960) describes how these principles account for the acoustic characteristics of voice signals. Figure 2.16 shows how the process works. In voice, the source of vibration is the vocal folds. The first panel of the figure shows an average voice source composed of many harmonics, each with slightly less energy than the one before. The second panel shows the resonance characteristics of the supraglottal vocal tract. Because the vocal tract is shaped approximately like a uniform tube, its resonances depend on its length: A longer vocal tract has resonances at lower frequencies than a shorter vocal tract. Resonances of the vocal tract are called *formants*, and their center frequencies are called *formant frequencies*. The formant frequencies shown here are at 500 Hz, 1500 Hz, and 2500 Hz, corresponding roughly to the vowel /ʌ/[11] spoken by a male. (An actual vocal tract has far more than 3 resonances, but usually no more than 6 or 7 are specified.) The set of formants taken together are sometimes called the *vocal tract transfer function*, because

---

[11]   Pronounced "uh."

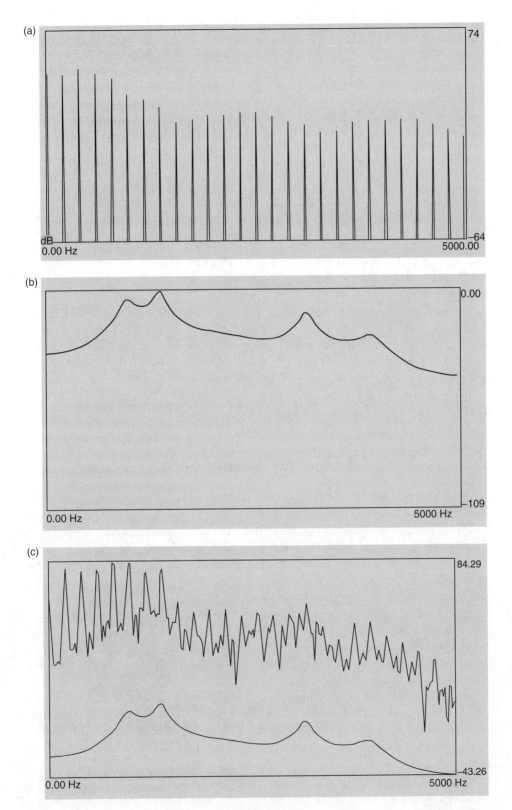

Figure 2.16 Source-filter theory of voice production. (a) The spectrum of voice source. (b) The vocal tract transfer function. (c) The output voice spectrum with the transfer function shown at the bottom of the frame.

they describe how the vocal tract transfers source energy to the air – that is, they describe the relationship between acoustic input and output for the supralaryngeal vocal tract.[12]

When vocal fold vibration sets the air in the supraglottal vocal tract (pharynx, mouth, nasal cavity) vibrating (in the way described above), the vocal tract resonances are acoustically excited, passing the frequencies in the source waveform that are near a resonance, and damping out source energy that is not near a resonance. We can change the tuning of this resonator – the formant frequencies – by moving the jaw, tongue, and/or soft palate, by tensing the pharyngeal muscles, and/or by shaping the lips. Within a speaker, the frequencies of the first three formants (abbreviated as F1, F2, and F3) are usually associated with differences in vowels – with the difference between "beet" and "bat," for example. Across speakers, there are also consistent differences in formant frequencies and bandwidths that are associated with differences in personal voice quality, as discussed in the next chapters.

The final component of source-filter theory is called the *radiation characteristic*. When the voice signal leaves the mouth and radiates into space, it disperses in all directions. This has the acoustic effect of increasing the level of the higher-frequency part of the spectrum by about 6 dB/octave, effectively reducing the relative level of low-frequency energy in the voice. When the three components of the production system – the source, the transfer function, and the radiation characteristic – are combined, the result is the spectrum shown at the bottom of Figure 2.16.

2.5 Kinds of Acoustic Analyses

Many studies of voice use measures of the acoustic signal to characterize a particular sound. Such measures fall into two broad categories: They may assess something about the voice pattern as a function of time (*time domain* measures), or as a function of frequency (*frequency* or *spectral domain* measures). As the name implies, time domain measures generally quantify the duration of speech events or the rate at which they occur. Measures related to the rate of vocal fold vibration (the fundamental frequency, or F0) are particularly important time domain measures of voice, because of the great importance that pitch (the perceptual correlate of F0) has for many aspects of voice perception. A speaker's average F0 is one such measure; in addition, investigators often assess the extent and manner to which F0 varies over a word, phrase, or utterance, for example by calculating the standard deviation of the F0 values or the range from minimum to maximum F0.

Two additional historically-important time domain measures of variation in phonation – *jitter* and *shimmer* – assess short-term changes in the rate and amplitude of vocal fold vibration. Small differences in period length occur from cycle to cycle in the human voice, and jitter is a measure of this kind of variability. Similarly,

---

[12]   This is another simplification. The complete transfer function describes the transfer of energy at all frequencies, not just at resonance peaks (formants). However, many perceptually important details can be usefully summarized in terms of formants and bandwidths, and we will follow that practice here.

shimmer measures small cycle-to-cycle differences in the amplitude of the sound wave. Jitter and shimmer have many physiological causes, including (among other things) small variations or asymmetries in muscle tension, fluctuations in subglottal pressure or randomness in airflow through the glottis, perturbations in muscular innervation, bits of mucous on the vocal folds, changes in the amount of regional blood flow across the heart cycle, and/or interactions of the laryngeal muscles with movements of the tongue (for example, Higgins and Saxman, 1989; Orlikoff and Baken, 1989). Thus, such perturbations in the frequency and amplitude of phonation are necessarily a feature of normal human phonation; in fact, voices synthesized without perturbation sound mechanical or artificial. Many different techniques and algorithms exist for measuring jitter and shimmer, including some that assess the spectral effects of this time-domain variability (Murphy, 2000). These are reviewed in great detail by Buder (2000). Although measurements of jitter and shimmer are sometimes used to quantify the quality of disordered voices (see, for example, Maryn, Roy, de Bodt, van Cauwenberge, and Corthals, 2009, for review), perceptual studies suggest that jitter and shimmer variations are not perceptible in normal voices, or even in many pathological voices (Kreiman and Gerratt, 2005).

Other acoustic measures of voice may be made in the frequency domain. For example, many measures have been proposed to describe the relative amounts of energy in different parts of the spectrum. Such measures may assess the difference in the amplitude of the first harmonic (H1) and the second harmonic (H2), yielding a measure usually called H1-H2. Generally, increasing weakness or breathiness will correspond to an increase in H1-H2 (for example, less high-frequency energy in the voice). Similarly, the amplitude of the first formant (A1) or the third formant (A3) can be measured relative to H1, producing the measures H1-A1 and H1-A3. (See, for example, Hanson, 1997, or Iseli and Alwan, 2004, for discussion of issues surrounding the calculation of these measures.) Other measures describe the overall slope of the spectrum of the voice; or they may assess the extent to which the spectrum deviates from some theoretically ideal configuration (see Kreiman, Gerratt, and Antoñanzas-Barroso, 2007, for review of these and other measures.) Measures of formant frequencies are also usually made in the frequency domain.

A trading relationship often exists between measurement resolution in the time and frequency domains. Time domain measures provide detailed information about durations or rates of speech events over time, but typically smear across the different frequency components of a signal. Similarly, spectral measures can inform us about the precise details of spectral shape or harmonic amplitudes of the voice, but this is achieved at the expense of poor time resolution. These kinds of measures may be thought of as two dimensional: They show how the energy in a signal varies as a function of time or of frequency, but not usually both (although newer signal processing techniques suffer less from this problem than older approaches do). One historically important kind of analysis – sound spectrography – combines intensity, time, and frequency domain information in a single three dimensional display. An example of a spectrogram (also sometimes called a "voiceprint") is given in Figure 2.17 (corresponding to audio sample 2.4). In this figure, the top panel represents the time-domain waveform of the voice (so that time is represented on

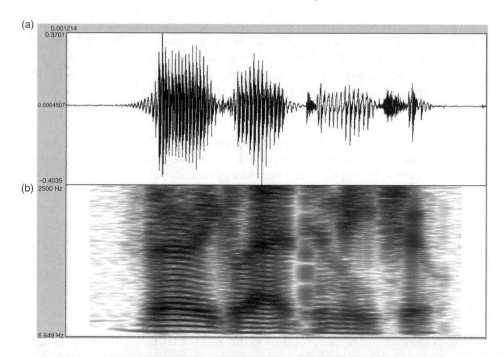

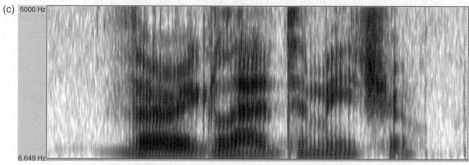

Figure 2.17   A spectrographic display of a male voice (average F0 = approximately 84 Hz) saying the phrase "Very glad to meet you" (pronounced "mee-choo"; audio sample 2.4). Time is on the x axis; frequency is on the y axis; and the intensity of the sound at each frequency is shown by variations in the darkness of the print. (a) the original time-domain waveform. (b) a narrow-band display showing the spectrum from 0–2.5 kHz. (c) a wide-band display showing harmonics from 0–5 kHz.

the x axis, and amplitude on the y axis). In the second and third panels, time is represented on the x axis; frequency is given on the y axis; and the intensity of the sound is shown by variations in the darkness of the marks (darker equaling greater intensity). The display in the second panel was created using settings that provide good frequency resolution, but relatively poor time resolution (a "narrow band" spectrogram). As a result, smaller black lines are visible, representing the harmonics of the voice. This kind of display is useful for measuring F0 contours, because movement of the harmonics corresponds to increases and decreases in F0. However, formants are hard to measure accurately and time information is blurred. The third panel, a so-called "wide band" spectrogram, was created with settings that give good time domain resolution, but relatively poor frequency resolution. This "poor" resolution has the advantage of allowing good visualization of the formant frequencies of the voice, which are visible as wide black stripes. The vertical striations represent the opening and closing of the vocal folds (which can be seen due to the good temporal resolution in this kind of display). (See, for example, Potter, Kopp and Kopp, 1966, or Hollien, 1990, for more information about how spectrograms are made and how to interpret them. Forensic applications of spectrography are discussed in Chapter 10, and an example of F0 measurement using narrow band spectrograms is given in Chapter 8.)

As mentioned above, vocal fold vibration is not perfectly periodic. Irregularities in the rate or extent of vibration add inharmonic components – noise – to the acoustic signal. Noise is also added to the signal by air that leaks through the glottis when the vocal folds do not close completely. In time domain analyses, aperiodicities and noise are visible as jitter, shimmer, and variability in the shape of the acoustic waveform. In a spectrum, noise can be estimated by the "fatness" of the harmonics of the voice, or by the presence of energy between the harmonics of the fundamental, or by both of these things. One common measure of noise is the *harmonics to noise ratio* (HNR; also called the *signal to noise ratio*, or SNR),[13] which measures how much of the voice energy is periodic, and how much is aperiodic. Normal voices usually have a very high harmonics to noise ratio, because most of the energy in the voice is periodic. Pathological as well as "whispery" normal voices may have lower harmonics to noise ratios. Although harmonics to noise ratios are easier to understand as spectral measures, many algorithms exist for calculating them in the time domain as well (see Buder, 2000, for review).

2.6   Controlling the Sound of a Voice

So far in this chapter, we have assembled the components that combine to produce a voice. The respiratory system sets air flowing in a controlled way through the vocal tract; the vibration of the vocal folds converts this aerodynamic energy into acoustic energy; and the resonance properties of the supraglottal vocal tract shape this sound into the final product that we hear. In this section, we will discuss how these different components combine to determine how an individual sounds. Put another way, how can these different aspects of voice production vary within and across speakers?

Steady-state sounds are traditionally described in terms of three main perceptual characteristics: pitch, loudness, and quality. Changes to the mass, length, and tension of the vocal folds alter their vibratory characteristics, and thus change the pitch, loudness, and quality of the voice, as described below. It is important to remember that pitch, loudness, and quality are psychological characteristics, and as such they represent the impact of physical signals on human ears.

---

[13]   Also reported sometimes as the noise-to-harmonics ratio (NHR), with the numerator and denominator reversed.

2.6.1   Frequency and pitch

Under normal circumstances, the fundamental frequency (F0) of an acoustic voice signal is the primary determinant of the perceived pitch of the voice (for example, Gulick, Gescheider, and Frisina, 1989). Listeners are very sensitive to changes in F0, and can reliably detect changes of as little as 2% (2.4 Hz; for example, Smith, Patterson, Turner, Kawahara, and Irino, 2005). F0 in turn corresponds to the rate of vocal fold vibration. Figure 2.18 shows typical F0 ranges for males and females, and for different classes of singing voice on a piano keyboard. (See Chapter 10 for more discussion of the singing voice.) The average F0 for men is about 115 Hz, which means that the vocal folds open and close 115 times per second. For women F0 averages about 220 Hz, and F0 for children averages about 280 Hz (see, for example, Baken and Orlikoff, 1999, for extensive review). A singer's F0 range may exceed four or five octaves. F0 for a bass can be 80 Hz or lower; a soprano can produce an F0 of over 1,000 Hz. Perceived pitch can also be influenced by the resonances of the vocal tract: Voices with higher frequency resonances may sound higher in pitch (or simply "brighter") than voices with lower frequency resonances. Although the relationship between perceived pitch and F0 is not perfectly linear, it is close enough for our present purposes, and we can treat the two as being linearly related.

Sidebar: Pitch of Whispered or Aperiodic Signals

Although under normal circumstances the pitch of a voice is related mostly to the rate of vocal fold vibrations, pitch can also be perceived from whisper, when no vocal fold vibration occurs. In these cases, the perceived pitch of the whispered speech corresponds to the frequency of the second formant (F2), at least for steady-state vowels (Thomas, 1969). To demonstrate this, try changing pitch as much as possible while whispering a prolonged vowel, first with an upward pitch glide, and then with a downward pitch glide. Try several different vowels. Be very careful to keep the vowel sound as constant as possible while changing pitch. Note how the positions of your tongue, jaw, lips, and larynx change as you modify the pitch of the whispered vowels. Constraints imposed by the need to keep the vowel steady will affect the extent to which any one articulator can move, and different articulatory adjustments will be necessary to increase and decrease pitch in a single vowel, or across vowels.

A similar effect is responsible for the perceived high pitch of helium speech. F0 in helium speech is nearly identical to that in speech produced with air, and the small differences that occur cannot account for the large differences in perceived pitch. However, gas density (a constant under all normal conditions) is an important determinant of the speed of sound, which in turn determines the resonance frequencies of the vocal tract. Helium is about 7 times less dense than air, so sound travels much faster through the vocal tract when it is filled with helium than when it is filled with air. This leads to an increase of about 50% in formant frequencies, which accounts for the impression of a higher-pitched voice (Holywell and Harvey, 1964; Bielamowicz *et al.*, 1995). These effects demonstrate that, although perceived pitch is primarily determined by F0, it can be affected by the formant frequencies as well.

The rate of vocal fold vibration (and thus the pitch of the voice) depends on the mass and stiffness of the vocal folds. More precisely, it is proportional to the square root of the ratio of stiffness to mass (Titze, 1994). By analogy, consider a cello's strings: A thicker (more massive) string has a lower frequency of vibration (and produces a lower-pitched tone) than a thinner string; but when either a thick or thin string is stretched and becomes stiffer, its vibratory frequency (and the pitch of the tone produced) increases. Similarly, longer, more massive vocal folds vibrate naturally at a lower frequency than shorter, thinner folds, which is why men usually have lower-pitched voices than women or children do (cf. Hollien, Moore, Wendahl, and Michel, 1966). (This topic will be discussed in much more detail in Chapter 4.) In any speaker, however, the rate of vocal fold vibration will increase when the vocal folds are stretched, and decrease when they are relaxed.

Scientists do not completely understand the manner in which F0 is controlled physiologically. If F0 varies with the ratio of stiffness to mass, F0 should go up as the mass of the vocal folds decreases. In reality, under normal conditions the weight of vocal folds does not change very much within a single individual, except in cases of disease or in the presence of mucous. However, the *effective mass* of the folds may vary with contraction of the thyroarytenoid and cricothyroid muscles. For example, when the thyroarytenoid contracts at a constant level of cricothyroid contraction, the vocal fold is shortened and somewhat bunched up, so the effective mass increases and F0 declines.

However, it is not possible to account for all changes in F0 just in terms of changes in mass. Tension differences appear to have at least as much effect on vibratory rates as changes in vocal fold thickness (Moore and Berke, 1988; see, for example, Titze, 1994, or Zemlin, 1998, for review). The cricothyroid muscle, which stretches the vocal folds, can act independently of the thyroarytenoid to change the stiffness of the vocal folds. When the cricothyroid contracts but the thyroarytenoid does not, the vocal folds lengthen, their effective mass decreases, stiffness increases throughout the folds, and F0 increases. This is the simplest way to increase vocal pitch.

The ability of these muscles to act independently, combined with the complex layered structure and elasticity of the vocal folds, complicates this picture but provides excellent control of F0. For example, when the thyroarytenoid muscle contracts but the cricothyroid muscle does not, the length of the vocal folds decreases, stiffness in the body of the vocal fold increases, but stiffness in the cover decreases due to shortening of the muscle. The net result is a small decrease in F0, but a large increase

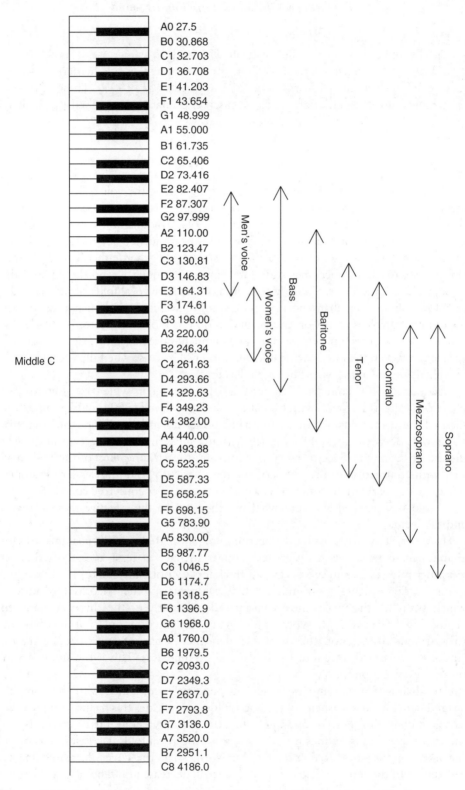

Figure 2.18 Typical F0 ranges for males and females in different voice classifications.

in loudness (Titze, Luschei, and Hirano, 1989). When both the cricothyroid and thyroarytenoid muscles contract, F0 does not change very much due to the opposite action of these muscles. Finally, when all other things are equal, increasing subglottal pressure will produce an increase in F0. To demonstrate this, press gently on your chest while trying to hold pitch constant. Your voice will get louder, but pitch will go up, also. Increasing subglottal pressure without adjusting the tension of the vocal folds produces greater amplitude of vocal fold excursion, stretching the folds by virtue of their greater lateral motion, so frequency goes up. This effect is greatest at low frequencies, when the folds are fairly slack, and explains in part why voice pitch tends to go up during yelling. Controlling these aspects separately is possible, but normally requires vocal training.

2.6.2   Intensity and loudness

Measurement practices for intensity, amplitude, and loudness differ. Intensity is defined as the sound power per unit area. It is measured by assessing sound intensity in the air near a listener's location (usually in units of watts per square millimeter or centimeter). Amplitude is a measure of the amount of energy in a sound wave and is measured as the displacement of air molecules from rest when visualized on a waveform display. Loudness is a psychoacoustic description of the relationship between a sound's intensity and the magnitude of the resulting auditory sensation, or the perceptual correlate of the acoustic intensity of a signal. As with the relationship between pitch and frequency, loudness is not a linear function of intensity; but the association is close enough for our purposes. To assess subjective loudness, as distinct from objective intensity, the sensitivity of the ear must be factored in. Most commonly, this is accomplished by measuring sound intensity relative to a standard threshold of hearing intensity on the decibel scale, which ranges from 0 (threshold of hearing) to 140 (jet aircraft noise at a distance of 120 feet). (See, for example, Roederer, 1995, for extended discussion of the perception of loudness and pitch, and their relationship to physical aspects of sounds.)

Studies of loudness control have focused largely on the association between subglottal pressure and acoustic intensity, and changes in intensity are often attributed primarily to variations in subglottal pressure (for example, Isshiki, 1964; Tanaka and Tanabe, 1986). According to basic laws of aerodynamics, pressure is related to resistance at the glottis and to airflow by the equation:

Pressure = flow × resistance

From this equation, it follows that:

Flow = pressure/resistance
Resistance = pressure/flow

Given these equations, it further follows that loudness (i.e., pressure) can be increased by increasing laryngeal resistance, or flow, or both. How these variables are controlled physiologically remains unknown, however. Changing flow implies adjusting respiratory effort: If glottal adjustment stays constant, more pressure from the lungs should result in more airflow. Changing resistance implies changes in laryngeal adjustment. However, adding laryngeal tension will also tend to increase F0, as described above (see also Hirano, Vennard, and Ohala, 1970).

In practice, these variables appear to interact in complex ways. In particular, although intensity does appear to increase with laryngeal resistance (for example, Holmberg, Hillman, and Perkell, 1988; Stathopoulos and Sapienza, 1993a, b), observational data have revealed no consistent association between increasing intensity and laryngeal muscle activation (which presumably underlies increased resistance; for example, Hirano, Ohala, and Vennard, 1969; Gay, Strome, Hirose, and Sawashima, 1972). Experimental studies have largely been limited to excised larynges, which cannot model the contributions of active contraction of the thyroarytenoid muscle. Experimental data manipulating thyroarytenoid muscle activity directly are generally lacking. Finally, evidence indicates that large differences may occur between speakers in the precise balance between respiratory and laryngeal factors in regulating intensity (Stathopoulos and Sapienza, 1993a). *In vivo* experimental data covarying muscle stimulation, airflow, subglottal pressure, and laryngeal resistance (and controlling for F0 variations) are needed to unravel these complex interactions among variables. Although speakers regulate vocal loudness without much thought or effort, much more research is required to fully explicate the manner in which they accomplish this.

2.6.3   Quality and phonation types

The final perceptual characteristic of a voice is its quality, or timbre. As discussed in Chapter 1, defining and studying quality is not as straightforward as defining pitch and loudness, and no fixed acoustic correlates of quality as a whole can be identified. However, from the point of view of voice production, quality in its narrow sense can be related to changes in the tension and mass of the vocal folds, to the symmetry of their vibration, to the forcefulness with which they are held together (medial compression), and to the amount of subglottal pressure (Zemlin, 1998). Some kinds of changes in the manner of vocal fold vibration do result in reliably perceptible changes in the sound of a voice. This section describes some of these so-called *phonation types*.

The kind of phonation humans usually produce (as described above) is often referred to as *modal phonation* (in the statistical sense of "modal"). Humans can also produce a range of *nonmodal* phonation types. In some cases, the pattern of vocal fold vibration differs discretely from modal phonation. For example, *falsetto* (Figure 2.19a; audio sample 2.5) occurs at the upper frequency limits of a speaker's vocal range, but also reflects a different vibratory mode for the vocal folds. In falsetto, the vocal folds vibrate and come into contact only at the free borders, while the rest of the fold remains relatively still. The folds appear long, stiff, very thin, and may be somewhat bow-shaped. In *period-doubled* or *subharmonic* phonation (audio sample 2.6), cycles alternate in a repeating long-short-long-short or large-small-large-small pattern, as shown in Figure 2.19b. In *vocal fry* (audio sample 2.7; sometimes associated with perceptually creaky voice; see Gerratt and Kreiman, 2001b) the folds open and close

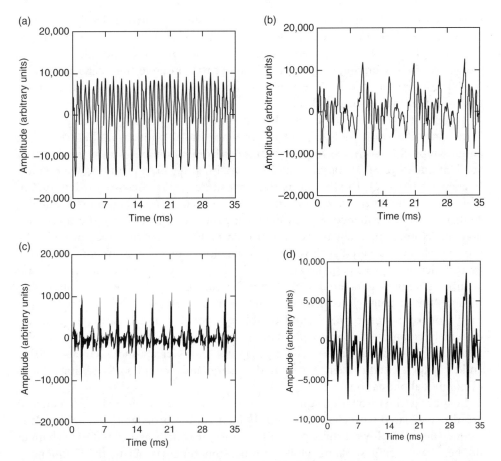

Figure 2.19 Time domain waveforms associated with the nonmodal phonation types in audio samples 2.5 to 2.8. (a) falsetto. (b) period-doubled phonation. (c) vocal fry. (d) breathy voice.

abruptly, and remain closed for most of each cycle (Figure 2.19c). Both period doubling and vocal fry occur very commonly in normal speech, and each has a unique sound that listeners easily identify (audio samples 2.5 to 2.7).[14] (See Chapter 8 for examples of linguistic uses of phonation types.)

Video example 12 shows the vocal folds vibrating in a fry-like pattern in the same normal female speaker presented in video example 10. These images were filmed at a rate of 3,000 frames/sec, and are played back at 10 frames/sec. Although vocal fry is often described as being low in frequency, F0 in this case is about 280 Hz (which is

[14] Terminological inconsistencies unfortunately plague the study of phonation types. The phonation corresponding to the waveform in Figure 2.19b (here called "period doubled" phonation) is also referred to as bicyclic phonation, diplophonia, dycrotic dysphonia, harmonic doubling, and many other names. The term "vocal fry," here applied to phonation resembling the waveform in Figure 2.19c, is also sometimes applied to the kind of phonation depicted in Figure 2.19b. Many other overlapping terms are applied to these and related kinds of phonation. See Gerratt and Kreiman (2001b) for review.

high-pitched for this speaker). Notice that the posterior glottis is tightly closed, in contrast to video example 10. The folds close sharply, and remain closed for much more of each cycle than in modal phonation. In some portions of the video, the folds also appear to be vibrating in a 1–2, 1–2 kind of rhythm, suggesting that some period doubling is present. Finally, note again the mucosal wave traveling across the surface of the folds as they open and close.

In contrast to period doubling and vocal fry, which represent categorical changes in the way the vocal folds vibrate, *breathy* nonmodal phonation (Figure 2.19d; audio sample 2.8) seems to form a continuum from modal phonation (not breathy at all) at one extreme, through "whispery" or "breathy" or "murmured" phonation (somewhat breathy), to whisper at the opposite extreme. Across this continuum from modal phonation to whisper, the vocal folds close more and more gradually, so that less high-frequency acoustic energy is generated. In addition, the vocal folds may not close completely at the end of each cycle, so that the voice may also be mixed with unmodulated airflow through the glottis, producing the sound of noise or turbulence. In whisper, the vocal folds vibrate only slightly or not at all, and acoustic energy is generated entirely by the turbulence that arises as air rushes through the partially-closed glottis. (This is why it takes so much breath to whisper loudly or for a long time.) Period doubling, vocal fry, and breathy voice are all extremely common in normal phonation, and serve a number of communicative functions, as we will see in succeeding chapters. (See Gerratt and Kreiman, 2001b, and the papers cited therein, for more discussion and examples of additional kinds of nonmodal phonation.)

Changes in the resonant frequencies of the vocal tract (the formant frequencies) are also associated with changes in vocal quality in the broader sense. Shifts in the frequencies of the lowest three or four formants are usually associated with changes in the vowel being spoken, while authors sometimes associate the frequencies of the higher formants with "personal quality." Formant frequencies carry significant information about speakers, as we shall see in subsequent chapters. Listeners are quite sensitive to changes in formants, and can reliably perceive shifts of as little as 4–8% in formant frequencies (Ives, Smith, and Patterson, 2005; Smith *et al.*, 2005).

2.7   What Gives Rise to Individual Voice Quality?

The physiology of voice production provides a basis for understanding the manner in which speakers can differ from one another in voice quality, and how individuals can vary their voices from occasion to occasion. Phonatory behavior involves orchestration of respiratory, laryngeal, and vocal tract movements, coordinating over 100 different muscles. To vocalize, we must commandeer an appropriate amount of breath, push a stream of it through the vocal folds (which must be deftly configured and continuously readjusted), and then must work the jaw, tongue, velum, and lips on that moving airstream while simultaneously adjusting the airstream in response to these articulatory movements. This means that speakers can change their voices by altering something about the way air is delivered from the lungs, or by varying something about the way the vocal folds vibrate, and/or by varying the size and shape of the vocal tract above the larynx (including coupling to the nasal tract) – a rather limited number of parameters. However, speakers can vary these things dynamically in an almost infinite number of time-varying patterns. Variations in respiratory driving power can cause changes in loudness; changes in laryngeal parameters lead to variations in the mean frequency of speech, the range of frequencies used, the shape of the F0 contour, the shape and/or timing of glottal pulses, the phonation type, loudness, and so on. Changes in the shape of the vocal tract produce changes in acoustic resonances, resulting in different speech sounds or different accents. Finally, all these things can vary dynamically over time, into a variety of vocalizations including talking, yelling, singing, sighing, laughing, humming, cursing, and reciting memorized material, among others. We can even vary the amount of variability in a voice, producing robotic monotone at one moment and wild fluctuations in pitch, loudness, and/or quality at the next. Thus, an apparently limited number of components in the voice production system yields theoretically a very large number of degrees of freedom in the sounds produced.

Although individual speakers can vary their voices over wide ranges of loudness, pitch, and quality, the precise sound produced is somewhat constrained within each individual by anatomy and physiology (Stevens, 1972; Nolan, 1983). For example, the range of vocal fold vibratory rates is limited by the length and mass of the vocal folds. Speakers can vary F0 over several octaves, but there are definitely higher highs and lower lows that an individual cannot reach. Similarly, speakers can vary the formant frequencies they use by raising or lowering the larynx with the extrinsic laryngeal muscles, by spreading or pursing the lips, by widening the pharynx, by raising or lowering the velum, and so on; but there are limits, and the range of possible variation is determined by an individual's underlying vocal anatomy.

In one traditional model of the sources of differences in vocal quality within and across listeners, a primary distinction is made between organically-based differences between speakers, and differences that are due to learned or habitual behaviors (for example, Garvin and Ladefoged, 1963; Hecker, 1971). In this framework, organically-based differences are derived from relatively unchangeable, physiologically-based characteristics, including mean F0 and formant frequencies. In theory, because they are linked to physiology, in adult speakers such characteristics should be relatively stable over time and thus should be good indices of the speaker's identity, sex, and age. Learned differences between speakers are acquired by experience, and include accent, speaking rate, intonational contours, habitual F0, specifics of voice quality, and so on. Although partially under the control of the speaker, characteristics in this category are often stable because individuals use them to signal group membership and important personal attributes. For example, the central drama and much of the humor in the play *Pygmalion* (Shaw, 1916) occurs because the character Eliza Doolittle changes her group signal by changing her speaking style, without simultaneously changing her social group membership. How much each factor – organic versus learned – contributes to individual quality in humans probably cannot be definitively known.

Both organic and learned characteristics conspire to make family members sound similar to one another. Thanks to heredity, family members often have larynges and vocal tracts that are similar in shape and size. Family members also constitute the environment in which speech is first learned; siblings often grow up in the same linguistic community, and tend to acquire the same pronunciation, intonation, and rhythmic patterns of speech. The combination of physiological, dialectal, and idiolectal[15] similarities can make it relatively easy to identify the voices of family members as "going together" somehow, or can make it very difficult to distinguish among the voices of related individuals, especially if they are close in age (as many parents can testify). An especially interesting example of this phenomenon – the voices of twins – is discussed in Chapter 7.

Finally, this model of differences among voices distinguishes differences between speakers (*interspeaker variations*, like those discussed above) from variations within a single speaker in speaking style (*intraspeaker variability*). Intraspeaker variability occurs in all speakers: We all sound slightly different from day to day, and from time to time within a day. For example, many speakers are hoarse first thing in the morning; and most speakers' voices – in both the narrow and broad senses of "voice" – vary somewhat with changes in emotional state or with fatigue. Many authors assume that such variations in quality over time within a single speaker are small compared to differences between separate individuals. This assumption is convenient when discussing speaker recognition, because it reduces the task of explaining recognition to describing how listeners assess the nature and amount of difference between two voice samples. However, some evidence (for example, Reynolds, 1995; Payri, 2000) suggests that differences within a speaker in quality may sometimes be as great as the differences between speakers. We will return to these issues in Chapters 4 and 7.

A number of other limitations to this framework are apparent (for example, Nolan, 1983). First, individual speakers can vary anything that can be learned (for purposes of disguise, acting, social conformity, or humor), so in practice there is no way to separate learned differences between groups of speakers from learned behaviors within a single speaker. For example, an observed difference in formant frequencies between two speakers might reflect organic differences in vocal tract size, or learned differences between dialect groups in vowel quality, or the habitual smile adopted by one speaker versus the pout adopted by another, or an imitation of the voice of the first talker by the second (Nolan, 1997). Although it is true that a speaker's organic characteristics limit the range of possible vocal productions, a good degree of control remains possible. What individual speakers can vary is constrained by their anatomy, but skilled manipulations of innate anatomical shape can produce extreme or unrecognizable versions of a person's voice. Thus, overlap exists between organic and learned information, and acoustic characteristics like vowel formant frequencies reflect both anatomy and idiolect. Finally, "organic" does not necessarily mean "constant," because many physiological characteristics change (albeit slowly) with growth, aging, and disease (as discussed in Chapter 4).

---

[15]   Idiolect refers to the individualized, unique speech pattern belonging to a single person.

Sidebar: Why Do We Sound Different to Ourselves than We Do in Recordings?

People are often shocked to hear their recorded voice for the first time, and many express a profound and lasting dislike for the sound. Several factors contribute to this effect. First, when we listen to ourselves speaking naturally, our ears receive vibrations from two sources: via the air (the usual channel), and also via the vibration of the tissues and bones of the head ("bone conduction"). Bones vibrate more efficiently at lower than at higher frequencies, so this transmission method effectively boosts the energy in the low frequency part of the voice spectrum. Further, bone-conducted sound does not receive the 6 dB/octave boost that applies to air-conducted sound as it radiates from the mouth. Thus, the sound our ears receive through tissue vibration emphasizes the lower frequencies.

A second factor is the manner in which air-conducted sound reaches our ears. Because of the way sound radiates from the mouth, low frequency sound components (below about 500 Hz) reach the speaker's ears with very little loss of energy, while the higher frequency components are transmitted more efficiently forward than backward toward the ears. This further contributes to the perception of a more resonant, lower-pitched voice.

These two factors combine to make our own voices sound lower in pitch and "richer" in quality than their recorded counterparts. Low-pitched, resonant voices are associated with a variety of socially desirable characteristics (Chapter 9), which may account for the distaste many speakers have for the higher-pitched, less resonant, but true, socially perceived version of their voice they hear in recordings.

2.7.1 The limits of vocal plasticity

Given these articulatory and phonatory possibilities, how much can individuals vary their voices? Consider as an example the great Mel Blanc, who provided voices for Bugs Bunny, Daffy Duck, Elmer Fudd, Foghorn Leghorn, Yosemite Sam, Tweety Bird, Sylvester the Cat, Porky Pig, and all the Looney Tunes characters.[16] Table 2.2 gives details of average fundamental frequency, frequency ranges, speaking rates, and details of articulation for representative characters, and Figure 2.20 shows formant frequencies for the vowel /a/ for each character, along with average values for (non-animated) males, females, and children. As this table shows, Blanc exploited the whole repertoire of possibilities (pitch mean and variability, intonation contours, pharyngealization, articulation, speaking rate, phonation type, loudness, durational features, and so on) to create his memorable gallery of voice characterizations. Apart from the obvious differences in accent (Pepe le Pew's fractured French; Foghorn Leghorn's

---

[16] Voice samples for many of these characters can be found at http://looneytunes.warnerbros.com/ or at www.dailywav.com (along with a multitude of other voice samples).

Table 2.2 Some Looney Tunes characters and their vocal characteristics. Measures are approximate averages.

	Mean F0/ Mode F0	F0 range	Loudness	Speaking rate (syllables/sec)	Voice quality	Pronunciation	Misc.
Bugs Bunny	232 Hz/160 Hz	76–486 Hz	moderate	3.4	Varies widely. Often uses falsetto, vocal fry; occasional breathiness during imitations.	Variable; often with New York accent.	Imitates many voices. Often uses exaggerated pitch contours.
Daffy Duck	223 Hz/220 Hz	75–390 Hz	loud	4.0	Harsh, with vocal fry and turbulent noise.	Lisps. Prolongs syllables, /s/ sounds.	Tends to be agitated.
Porky Pig	238 Hz/220 Hz	70–400 Hz	moderate	5.2	Modal to slightly pressed; no creak or breathiness.	Stutters.	F0 contours never exaggerated.
Taz	undefined	wide	loud	2.8	Rough/harsh, with frequent period doubling and vocal fry.	Snorts, roars, grunts, and other animal noises, with occasional pidgin English.	–
Tweety Bird	323 Hz/220 Hz and 400 Hz (bimodal)	75–575 Hz	moderate	4.7	Very high falsetto.	"Baby talk".	Excursions into ultra-high falsetto on about half of utterances.
Yosemite Sam	Low end of male range	Wide	usually shouting	3.8	Very rough; often period doubled.	Southern accent, extends stressed syllables.	Sometimes uses falsetto.
Pepe le Pew	190 Hz/130 Hz and 235 Hz (bimodal)	50–371 Hz	soft	3.3	Alternately breathy and vocal fry.	French accent.	–

Foghorn Leghorn	192 Hz/110 Hz and 210 Hz (bimodal)	50–250 Hz	loud	4.4	Somewhat pressed; occasional creak.	Southern drawl. Extends final syllables.	Repeats himself. High pitch is unusual. Rate variable.
Sylvester the Cat	210 Hz/190 Hz	37–475 Hz	moderate	3.3	Somewhat pressed. Never breathy.	Forceful releases of stop consonants/ impression of spitting.	–
Elmer Fudd	182 Hz/175 Hz	76–314 Hz	soft	4.4	Somewhat hoarse; period doublings throughout utterances.	Substitutes w for r and l.	Some falsetto.
Marvin the Martian	239 Hz/220 Hz	115–340 Hz	moderate	3.5	Pharyngeal expansion; no creak or vocal fry at all.	Precise pronunciation; extended syllables.	Exaggerated changes in pitch on individual words.

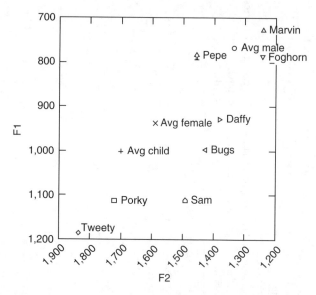

Figure 2.20   Average values of the first and second formant frequencies for a variety of Looney Tunes characters. Smaller-sized or younger characters have higher values of F1 and F2; larger-sized or more mature characters have lower formant values.

Table 2.3   Varying voice quality: A non-professional speaker.

Sample	Modification
2.9	None
2.10	Average pitch increased
2.11	Accent changed
2.12	Speaking rate increased
2.13	Intonation contour more varied
2.14	Accent changed, and mean pitch decreased
2.15	Intonation contour less varied, and rate decreased
2.16	Monotone
2.17	Pharyngealized
2.18	Nasalized

corny Southern drawl; Tweety's baby talk), characters' voices differ in their intonation patterns. For example, Marvin the Martian produces single words with highly exaggerated upward and downward pitch contours, giving his speech a sing-songy sound, while Bugs Bunny will increase F0 to express surprise, but never reduces F0 very far below his typical baseline; and Porky Pig never exaggerates F0 at all, either upwards or downwards. Some characters (Foghorn Leghorn, Pepe le Pew) have rather low-pitched voices overall, while others (notably Tweety Bird) have very high pitched voices on average. Other characters (Elmer Fudd, Taz) produce nearly all their utterances using period doubled phonation or vocal fry, giving their voices an odd, rough quality. The net effect of these and other alterations (as detailed in the table) is a large variety of entirely distinct, instantly recognizable voices, all produced by the same speaker.

A more prosaic set of examples is included in audio samples 2.9 to 2.18. The first audio sample is the speaker's normal voice quality, and the remaining audio samples are attempts to systematically vary pitch, loudness, and pronunciation in different combinations (Table 2.3). Some of these voice samples sound rather similar to the "baseline" sample, while others are difficult to recognize as coming from the same speaker. These examples reinforce the idea that differences within a single speaker can be as great as the differences between different speakers, as discussed previously.

3

Neurological Foundations of Voice Production and Perception

3.1 Introduction

Our goal in this chapter is to assemble fundamental information on cerebral processes underlying various aspects of vocal production and auditory perception that will serve as neurological foundations to voice studies. More detail on these topics is presented in Chapter 6. We begin with essentials of vocal production.

3.1.1 Our personal voice pattern: Producing a voice takes a whole person

Personal characteristics of broad palette are carried in the voice. Any given vocal performance requires a complex orchestration of the vocal apparatus, deriving from expansively represented cerebral influences. Subcortical (including limbic) systems of the brain generate the attitudes, moods, and emotions that find expression in our voices. Temporal and parietal lobes accumulate memories and facts leading to beliefs, assumptions and opinions, which also influence pitch contours and accent, speaking rate, loudness, and other vocal attributes. Intentions, goals and motor programs are managed by frontal lobe systems in circuitry with the subcortical nuclei that contribute to every vocal effort. It is a remarkable fact that this cognitive cornucopia emerging from whole brain interactions is expressed in the human voice. It is not known in detail how the limbic system (seat of emotions), subcortical nuclei (motoric and motivational control) and the cortical lobes (engaged in cognition and planning) operate convergently to formulate the psychological characteristics that are manifest as attitude, mood, and personality, but it has been repeatedly demonstrated that all of these are "heard" along with personal identity in the voice, leading to the oft-repeated statement in medical (Woodson, 1999),

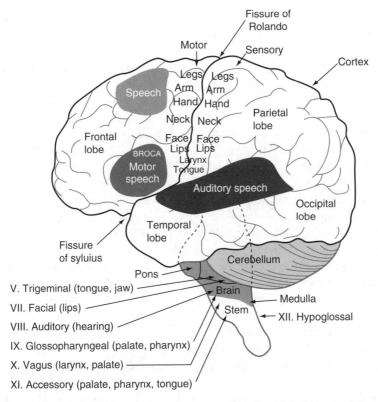

Figure 3.1 Schema of brain structures involved in vocalization. Important structures not seen are the basal ganglia and limbic structures below the cortical mantle, and the periaqueductal grey matter in the midbrain.

religious[1] (Cumming, 1856), and literary writing (Longfellow, 1866) that voice is revelatory of mind or soul. The voice is also a product of our evolutionary past (Locke, 2009). In this chapter we also touch on the controversies surrounding whether human vocal behaviors are significantly related to those of nonhuman animals, and if so, in what ways.

3.1.2 Overview of brain structures and functions in vocal production: It takes a whole brain

As our introductory remarks suggest, producing a vocal pattern requires contributions from nearly the entire brain (see Figure 3.1). Vocalization, which requires "remarkable coordination," draws on functionality across most of this neural resource (Dubner, Sessle, and Storey, 1978, p. 211; Jürgens, 2002). Respiratory,

---

[1] "There is something in the human voice, just as in the human face, that I have often thought is one of the greatest proofs of the infinitude of the resources of God" (Cumming, 1856, p. 80).

laryngeal and vocal tract processes engage cortical, subcortical, limbic, cerebellar, brainstem, and spinal cord structures, which send and receive signals during voice production and control.

The brain and spinal cord constitute the central nervous system (CNS), made up of many kinds of neurons forming many different structures. Major structures are listed in Table 3.1; for a fuller overview, refer to one of the numerous texts on neuroanatomy.[2] Neurons comprise a soma (body), axon (usually the longer portion), and dendrites, and they transmit information through chemical and electrical processes. The axons form tracts that connect parts of the nervous system. They are usually covered with a myelin sheath composed of a lipid substance, giving them a glistening appearance. Thus the somas are referred to as the "grey matter" and the neuronal tracts are called the "white matter." The cortical mantle, a thin (about 1/10 inch) sheath of specialized neurons, covers the four major areas or "lobes" of the brain, or cerebrum: the frontal lobes, responsible for goal setting and planning and execution of voluntary motor acts; the parietal lobes, providing cross-modal associations, visual-spatial processing, and other conceptual operations; the temporal lobes, involved mainly with audition and memory, and the occipital lobes, which process visual input. At the cortical level in humans, the mouth and larynx have ample representation on the motor (frontal lobes) and sensory (parietal lobes) strips on the cerebral cortex – the higher processing and control centers responsible for voluntary action and feedback, respectively. Areas of importance to vocalization on the frontal cortex of the human, but not the nonhuman primate, are the supplementary motor area and the inferior frontal gyrus (Broca's area[3]).

Signals from the cortex carrying out the vocal motor plan travel along the pyramidal (white matter) tract, the neural roadway for voluntary movement, which courses through the subcortex to the brainstem and spinal cord, where the pathways cross ("decussation of the pyramids"), such that the left side of the brain sends and receives signals from the right side of the body, and vice versa. This crossed representation does not hold for the 12 cranial nerves (see below), which innervate the muscles and sensory organs of the head; nerve damage on one side of the brainstem results in weakness or loss of function on that same side of the face, tongue, larynx, or neck. The pyramidal motor pathways originating in the cortical motor strips and descending directly and bilaterally through the internal capsule are equally present in the left and right cerebral hemispheres. In humans, the primary and supplementary motor areas in the cortex, in conjunction with Broca's area, organize a plan and help initiate voice production (Goldberg, 1987; Jonas, 1987).[4]

Immediately beneath the cortex and continuing downward toward the brainstem lies an array of interconnected subcortical nuclei or basal ganglia, the most

[2] For example, Perkins and Kent (1991); Zemlin (1998); Noback, Ruggiero, Demarest, and Strominger (2005); Goldberg (2007); Haines (2007); or Young, Young, and Tolbert (2007).
[3] Broca's area is named after Paul Broca, who in 1861 observed that speech is impaired following damage in the left inferior frontal lobe of the brain.
[4] Cortical stimulation in nonhuman primates of several varieties does not elicit vocalization; instead, nonhuman primate vocalization is elicited from an array of subcortical sites.

Table 3.1   Selected neuroanatomical terms useful for the study of vocalization.

Structure	Definition and location	Function
Amygdala	Structure in the limbic system	Arousal and fear responses
Brainstem	Connects brain to spinal cord; includes pons, midbrain and medulla	Supports cranial nerves; life support systems and arousal
Caudate nucleus	One of the subcortical nuclei	Motor control and psychological set
Cerebellum	Duplicate structures at farthest position inferior (low) and posterior of the brain	Coordination and postural functions
Cerebral hemispheres	The brain is separated into two symmetrical halves	Sensory, perceptual, motoric and cognitive functions
Cingulate gyrus (rhinencephalon)	Part of the limbic system; evolutionarily "old" cortex located along the medial sides of the cerebral hemispheres along the corpus callosum	Attention, arousal, visceral responses, emotional regulation, motivation, monitoring of conditions
Corpus callosum	Large band of white matter fibers connecting the two hemispheres	Provides communication between the two hemispheres
Cortical mantle (cortex)	Thin layer of specialized cells folded into gyri (hills) and sulci (valleys) that covers the entire brain	Higher, voluntary cognitive function, motor and action planning, sensory processing, cross modal associations, thinking, memory
Cranial nerves I–XII	12 pairs of nerves that mostly (from III–VII) exit from the brainstem. Some travel through holes in the skull to reach muscles and sensory organs of face, jaw, and neck	Provide sensory and motor impulses to and from the muscles and sensory organs of the head
Extrapyramidal tract (indirect motor pathway)	Many neuronal pathways with interconnections of the subcortical nuclei: globus pallidus, caudate, putamen, subthalamic nucleus	Movement planning, initiation, control
Frontal lobes	Duplicate divisions of the cerebral hemispheres anterior in the brain	Action planning and motor programs, cross modal associations, memory
Globus pallidus	One of the subcortical nuclei	Movement control
Hippocampus	Located within the temporal lobes	Involved in the transfer from short term to long-term memory
Limbic system	Group of structures lying below the cortical mantle and its white matter; lies within basal ganglia	Emotional and arousal functions
Medulla	Part of brainstem	Life support operations
Occipital lobes	Duplicate divisions of the cerebral hemisphere in posterior portion of brain	Vision

Table 3.1   (*cont'd*).

Structure	Definition and location	Function
Parietal lobes	Duplicate divisions of the cerebral hemispheres posterior to the frontal lobes	Cognition, visual spatial processing and cross-modal associations
Periaqueductal grey matter	Nerve cell bodies within the midbrain	Arousal and initiation of vocalization
Pons	Part of the brainstem	Life support systems
Putamen	One of the subcortical nuclei	Motor control
Pyramidal tract	Neuronal bundle from motor strip on cortex traversing to cranial nerves and spinal cord	Carries cortical motor commands to peripheral nervous system
Spinal cord	Exchanges sensory and motor information with peripheral nervous system	Neural communication with sensory organs for sensation and muscles for movement
Subcortical nuclei	Group of structures lying below the cortical mantle and its white matter	Motor and motivational functions
Substantia nigra	Area in midbrain	Produces l-dopa, neurotransmitter needed for movement
Subthalamic nucleus	One of the subcortical nuclei	The control of movement
Supplementary motor area	Area on anterior frontal lobes	Initiates and facilitates speech
Temporal lobes	Duplicate divisions of the cerebral hemisphere on the lateral portion of brain	Auditory processing
Thalamus	Duplicate structure located above the midbrain within the subcortical structures	Receives and relays sensory information throughout the brain

important of which are the caudate nucleus[5] (crucial for movement control and for maintaining psychological set; Sidtis, Strother, and Rottenberg, 2004), putamen, globus pallidus, the substantia nigra (in the midbrain, where it produces dopamine, which is necessary for movement), and the subthalamic nucleus[6] (Figure 3.2). Cortical impulses travel to these indirect motor pathways, also previously called the extrapyramidal tract, which have numerous interneurons (connecting tracts) projecting to the cerebellum, regulator of coordination and

[5] The caudate forms a large "c" shape with head, body and tail. It partially encircles other subcortical structures as well as several limbic structures.

[6] The importance of the subthalamic nucleus in movement control has emerged recently, when it became the subcortical site of choice for the placement of steadily stimulating electrodes in deep brain stimulation, an effective treatment of movement disorder in Parkinson's disease. The effects of this therapy on speech are variable, although the reasons for this are not well understood (Dromey, Kumar, Lang, and Lozano, 2000).

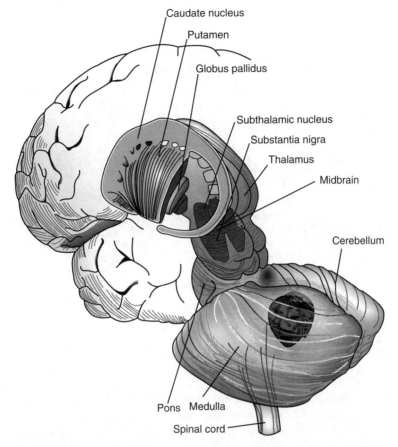

Caudate nucleus

Putamen

Globus pallidus

Subthalamic nucleus

Substantia nigra

Thalamus

Midbrain

Cerebellum

Pons　Medulla

Spinal cord

Figure 3.2　Basal ganglia in situ with limbic structures and most of the cortical layer removed. The cerebellum is present. Substantia nigra produces dopamine, essential for movement. Electrodes for deep brain stimulation as therapy for movement disorders are often placed in the subthalamic nucleus.

posture. The cerebellum is also multiply connected throughout the brain. The basal ganglia orchestrate motor plans and the selection of emotional responses (Marsden, 1982; MacLean, 1987). These structures are involved in initiating and monitoring movement and have complex activating and inhibiting relations in the control of movements, including vocalization.

A loosely related group of structures distributed within and around the basal ganglia make up the limbic system, which modulates mood, emotion, and arousal (Figure 3.3). These structures include the amygdala (emotions), the hippocampus (memory), and the cingulate gyri (numerous roles), spanning the medial portions of the two hemispheres. The first cranial nerve (also called the olfactory bulb; regulates smell) forms part of this system, as does the cingulate gyrus (also called the rhinencephalon) which modulates visceral responses, attention, and set. The amygdala, providing emotional evaluation and response, appears near the tail of the caudate nucleus in both hemispheres. Coordinated activity of the structures of the basal ganglia and limbic system,

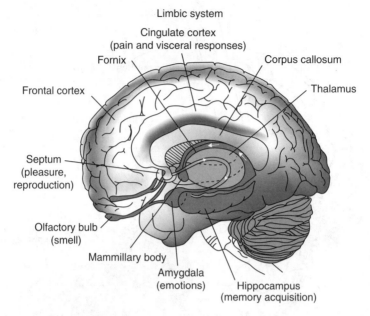

Limbic system

Cingulate cortex
(pain and visceral responses)

Fornix

Corpus callosum

Frontal cortex

Thalamus

Septum
(pleasure,
reproduction)

Olfactory bulb
(smell)

Mammillary body

Amygdala
(emotions)

Hippocampus
(memory acquisition)

Figure 3.3 The limbic system, seat of emotions, has its place within and around the basal ganglia, modulator of motor behaviors.

which are evolutionarily "old," modulates aspects of emotional vocalizations in humans and in nonhuman animals.[7] Recent research highlights how these structures interact with cortical processes (Damasio, 1994; Cabeza and Nyberg, 2000). This is important for our understanding of the voice pattern, as limbic structures are involved in voice production whenever mood and emotion are expressed in the voice. Stimulating these areas routinely produces vocalization in nonhuman primates (see below); and in humans, dysfunction in subcortical-limbic structures is associated with abnormal vocal quality and vocal tics (Van Lancker, and Cummings, 1999).

A left and a right thalamus, coordinators of sensory and motor functions throughout the brain, are seated at the top of the brainstem, in the middle of these structures. Thalamic nuclei integrate sensory feedback with motor control. We do not know exactly how much of a role the thalamus plays in voice production. It sends and receives impulses from most areas of the brain, and likely plays a role in coordinating the diverse functions underlying vocalization.

---

[7] Previous decades emphasized the human cortex as the purveyor of higher cognitive functions, particularly conceptualization and language, unique to humans. Recently, significant responsibilities for human behavior have been identified in basal ganglia/limbic systems (Lieberman, 2000) and entreaties to include affective functions have appeared, as from Panksepp and Burgdorf: "We feel the neuroscience community does need to try to deal more forthrightly with the critically important affective functions of the brain. A proper neuronal conceptualization of affecting processes may be essential for making sense out of many brain functions" (2003, p. 536).

The cerebellum, or "little brain," a double structure located behind and beneath the cerebral hemispheres, coordinates moving structures and maintains posture. It has contralateral connections with cortical control areas, in that the right cerebellum interacts with the left motor areas. Its role in maintaining normal voice is better understood, as damage to that area results in abnormal voice quality, including hoarseness, breathiness, excessive nasality, and distortion of resonance (Sidtis, Ahn, Gomez, and Sidtis, 2010). In some cases of agenesis of the cerebellum (a failure of this structure to develop), vocalization is dysarthric and distorted in timing.

Neural centers controlling articulation, laryngeal behavior, and respiration are stationed at locations on the pons and medulla in the brainstem, and in the spinal cord. Within the brainstem, the reticular formation and the periaqueductal grey matter, the cell-dense region surrounding the midbrain aqueduct (a vertical section of the brain's system of ventricles, which circulate cerebrospinal fluid), perform crucial initiating and facilitating roles for speech. Studies in mammals identify the periaqueductal grey matter as a key structure in emotional expression and as a generator of specific respiratory and laryngeal motor patterns in speech and song (Davis, Zhang, Winkworth, and Bandler, 1996). Voluntary vocal control involves various cortical and subcortical inputs projecting to the periaqueductal grey matter (Bandler and Shipley, 1994). When the periaqueductal grey matter is damaged, muteness ensues in humans; electrical stimulation of these areas elicits vocalization in nonhuman primates. A brain imaging study using PET reported "functional connectivity" between the periaqueductal grey area and an array of cortical, subcortical ("visceromotor"), and cerebellar areas during voicing (Schulz, Varga, Jeffires, Ludlow, and Braun, 2005, p. 1845). Certain muscle patterns during vocalization in nonhuman animals resulting from stimulation of the periaqueductal grey are similar to laryngeal and respiratory patterns published for humans (Davis *et al.*, 1996).

Emerging from the brainstem and spinal cord, the peripheral nervous system is made up of the 12 cranial nerves, seven of which are involved in vocalization, and 31 spinal nerves, a third of which have an influence on respiration (Figure 3.4). The cranial nerves transmit motor and sensory signals to the muscles of articulation, phonation and respiration, with further control of respiration managed by spinal nerves. The facial and oral-pharyngeal muscles modulating speech rely on cranial motor nerves V, VII, IX, XI, and XII. These contribute to voice quality, broadly considered, with respect to resonances of the vocal tract and articulation. The tenth cranial nerve, or "vagal" nerve, from which the recurrent laryngeal nerve emerges on the left and right, provides nearly all the requisite sensory, motor, and autonomic innervation to the larynx, with some motor contribution from the Cranial Nerve XI (the spinal accessory nerve).

Breathing is ordinarily autonomically controlled, but is co-opted during speech to form intonational phrases or "breath groups." This level of control of the outbreath is elaborated in humans relative to other animals, and provides a necessary substrate for normal speaking (MacLarnon and Hewitt, 1999). The respiratory control center of the central nervous system is located in the medulla, the upper portion of the brainstem. Inhibitory impulses to the inspiratory center of the medulla oblongata

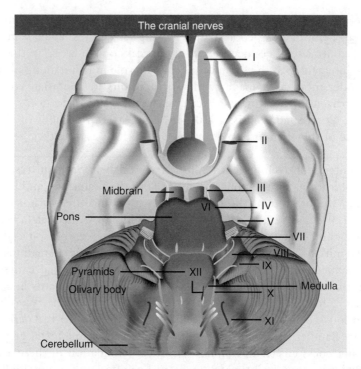

Figure 3.4 Cranial nerves on the inferior aspect (underside) of brain. The facial and oral-pharyngeal muscles modulating speech rely on cranial motor nerves V, VII, IX, XI, and XII, while the larynx is controlled by cranial nerve X (vagal nerve) with some contribution from cranial nerve XI (spinal accessory nerve).

arise from the adjacent portion of the brainstem, the pons. Breathing is mediated by 11 spinal nerves controlling muscles of the neck (cervical nerves) and chest (thoracic nerves), which regulate the diaphragm and intercostal muscles. The vagus nerve also provides sensory information from the thoracic and abdominal viscera, including the lungs, during breathing.

Like other human behaviors, phonation involves both sensory and motor pathways with a range of possibilities for monitoring and modifying the output. Peripheral sensory pathways carry information about acoustic and motor events back to various control centers in the brain, providing auditory and proprioceptive feedback for phonatory control (for example, Yoshida, Tanaka, Saito, Shimazaki, and Hirano, 1992). The proprioceptive senses – providing information about the place and position of parts of the body, especially during movement – allow for monitoring of vocal operations.[8] Temporal lobes allow for auditory monitoring and the nuclei of the basal

[8]   Rush Limbaugh, who recently suffered severe hearing loss, continues to execute credible vocal impersonations of presidents and politicians. When asked how he can mimic without being able to hear himself well, he replied, touching his throat, "I know how the muscles are supposed to feel when I do the voices" (*New York Times*, July 6, 2008, p. 35).

ganglia monitor motor programs involved in vocalizing. Information flowing back from numerous sites and levels of sensory and motor activity is obviously an important aspect of vocalization, but the role and value of self-monitoring during vocal production is not fully understood (see discussion of "The role of auditory feedback" in Chapter 6).

3.1.3 Evidence from functional imaging for neurological structures underlying phonation

Functional imaging techniques using positron emission tomography (PET) or functional magnetic resonance imaging (fMRI) allow "pictures" of the active brain to be made during the performance of behaviors (see Sidebar on "Functional brain imaging using brain scanning"). There are fewer functional imaging studies for vocal production than for perception, primarily because limitations of PET and fMRI present difficulties for studies of phonatory control. To avoid creating movement artifacts in fMRI, some approaches have used "silent" speech and singing to study neurological control of voice production (Ackermann and Reicker, 2004; Callan *et al.*, 2006). Such studies have obvious drawbacks.

Nonetheless, an array of tasks, stimuli, and response conditions has been utilized, leading to a wide range of findings. Some results are consistent with well-accepted brain models, but many are not (Van Lancker Sidtis, 2007). Subcortical and cerebellar responses during rhythmic repetition of syllables were reported (Riecker, Wildgruber, Dogil, Grodd, and Ackermann, 2002). An important unresolved conflict is the finding in imaging studies of bilateral activation during behaviors that are lateralized in lesion and other neurolinguistic studies. Published studies of language processing typically report bilateral hemispheric blood flow responses, for reasons that are not yet well understood (Van Lancker Sidtis, 2007). For example, using the subtraction paradigm (see Sidebar) in PET studies, Murphy *et al.* (1997) found bilateral activation for both articulation and breathing in vocalization tasks while Blank, Scott, Murphy, Warbuton, and Wise (2002) found that bilateral and cerebellar regions were involved in propositional and overlearned articulate speech.[9] Another perplexing result is the failure to observe activations in some of the areas known to be involved in vocalization and speech (Sidtis, Strother, Anderson, and Rottenberg, 1999). These and similar inconsistencies between robust, often-replicated findings from the clinical lesion literature and variable imaging results indicate that imaging results must be interpreted with great caution.

Performance-based analysis of PET data (see Sidebar below) did produce a result consistent with other findings of left hemisphere specialization for timing functions. Subjects produced syllables as quickly as possible during the brain scanning episode. An increase in syllable repetition rate was significantly associated with increased blood flow in the left inferior frontal area and decreased flow in the right caudate nucleus

---

[9] Studies from neurologically compromised subjects suggest that propositional speech is associated with left hemisphere function while overlearned speech is associated with the right hemisphere and subcortical areas; for details see Chapter 6.

measured during the speech production scans (Sidtis, Strother, and Rottenberg, 2003). This finding was replicated in a large clinical sample of subjects with dysarthria (slurred speech) resulting from cerebellar disease (Sidtis, Gomez, Naoum, Strother, and Rottenberg, 2006). Very similar findings for rate relationships between the left hemisphere and caudate activity were reported by Riecker, Kassubek, Gröschel, Grodd, and Ackermann (2006). Some of these approaches have great promise, but given methodological limitations and uncertainty about the meaning of the functional imaging signal, a reliable neural model of vocal production has not yet emerged from functional imaging studies (Sidtis, 2007).

Sidebar: Functional Brain Imaging Using Brain Scanning

Fundamentals:

PET (positron emission tomography) and fMRI (functional magnetic resonance imaging) are techniques for viewing brain activity during behavior. Both methods are based on the assumption that regional blood flow is associated with functional activity. It is also commonly, but not universally, assumed that areas of highest blood flow have the greatest functional significance.

In PET, physiologic images of the brain are acquired through detection of radiation from the emission of positrons, particles released from a radioactive substance injected intravenously. A radioactive isotope is produced in a cyclotron, and is attached to glucose, water, dopamine, or some other compound involved in brain function. Many isotopes used in imaging are short-lived, and as they decay they emit a positron, which in turn annihilates an electron, producing a pair of photons that travel in opposite directions (180 degrees). The PET scanner consists of a series of detector rings containing crystals that emit a signal when struck by a photon. Because the annihilation photons are traveling in a straight line in two opposite directions, it is possible to calculate their origin and hence reconstruct an image of the brain.

The source of signal in fMRI is a local change in the ratio of oxygenated to deoxygenated hemoglobin due to increased need for oxygenated blood. Blood flow is inferred from the ratio of oxygenated to deoxygenated red blood cells. The deoxygenated hemoglobin displays different magnetic resonance properties from oxygenated blood. These different signals can be detected by the MRI scanner, most often using a technique called BOLD (Blood Oxygenation Level Dependent) contrast. The MRI scanner uses a sequence of magnetic pulses (which make the scanner quite noisy) to change the orientation of nuclear particles. As these particles return to their normal orientation (relax), they emit radio signals that are detected by the scanner. The distributions of these signals are used to construct brain images. Assumptions of a correlation between neural activity and BOLD crucially underlie this technique, but controversy remains about their relationship.

Analysis techniques

Both PET and fMRI typically utilize a contrast or subtraction methodology, whereby signals in regions of the brain obtained during one behavioral task or condition are subtracted from the signals obtained during a "rest" condition, or, alternatively, from a task or condition that is believed to differ from the condition of interest in a specific way. The assumption is that when a task state is contrasted with a control state, the difference will reveal brain activity unique to the task state. While some valid outcomes might be obtained, this technique likely also eliminates important areas of signal and/or obscures evidence of important neural systems. Interpretation of activated brain areas often proceeds unconstrained by any external controls (Fellows *et al.*, 2005), and the "meaning" of imaging signals is not yet well understood (Uttal, 2001).

Another approach called "performance-based analysis," in which subjects' verbal performance is predicted from recorded brain activity using multiple linear regression, avoids these pitfalls. This approach uses performance data as a predictive element to identify meaningful signals in the imaging data without resorting to the use of rest states or control tasks (Sidtis *et al.*, 2003, 2006; Sidtis, 2007). This imaging analysis technique has yielded results for speech production that are closer to models derived from traditional studies of lesion data and related observations.

3.1.4 Neural control of vocalization in humans and nonhuman animals

Animal vocalization has a leading part to play in the current debates about the origin of speech and language. There is no convincing cognitive counterpart to human language (the abstract system of grammar) in the nonhuman animal world, but there is little doubt in most people's minds about the continuity of at least some kinds of vocalization across relatively recently evolved species (Burling, 1993; see, for example, Hurford, Studdert-Kennedy, and Knight, 1998, or Wray, 2000, for review). Much understanding has been gained about innate and learned components of vocal calls from birds, but the anatomical and neuroanatomical structures for vocal production in birds differ essentially from those in mammals and primates (See Sidebar "How do mynah birds talk?"). The essential neurological structures supporting elemental vocalization are common across various mammals, although differences in vocal tract shape and larynx placement have generated intense discussion since the 1970s (for example, Lieberman, 1975; see Sidebar on "Evolution of the vocal tract and the capacity for vocal sound"). While the popular notion of the triune brain[10] (MacLean,

[10] MacLean's highly popularized brain model featured three "basic brain types" in evolution, which are "heritages" of man. These were called the "reptilian" brain, which included the midbrain, reticular formation and some portions of the basal ganglia, the "paleomammalian" brain, which corresponds to the "primitive cortex" or limbic system, and the "neomammalian," or neocortex (1990, pp. 338–9).

1990) does not provide a clear model for the evolution of vocalization (Newman, 2003), animal studies are consistent with the notion of an older, elaborated limbic component in common across vocalizing species in audiovocal development, called the "thalamocingulate" division of the limbic system, which is also present in humans (see also Ludlow, 2005). According to MacLean (1987), advent of these structures in mammals enabled the maternal and familial patterns that made critical use of audiovocal behaviors. Correspondences between animal calls and human nonverbal vocalizations are being increasingly described. For example, recent reports describe "laughter" in several nonhuman species (see Sidebar on "A cross-species view of laughter"). Yet the relationship of vocalization as observed in other species or in the human infant to fully-formed adult human speech and language has not been settled.

Sidebar: How Do Mynah Birds Talk?

According to Klatt and Stefanski (1974), the "speech" produced by mynah birds is acoustically very similar to the target human phonation. Mynahs emit periodic phonation whose pitch contours closely match the target human utterance. Formant frequencies also match the overall target pattern remarkably well. Thus, it is not just the perceptual expectations of the human listener that make mynah phonation sound speech-like – it *is* speech-like.

However, the sound-producing organs of mynah birds are very different from the human larynx. The vibratory source is the syrinx, not the larynx. The syrinx is located deep in the bird's chest, where the trachea divides into two bronchi. Parts of the syrinx reside in each bronchus; each half is capable of making sound so that a bird can produce a duet (see discussion of penguin phonation in Chapter 5). The syrinx has muscular folds called the *external labia* that can be adducted somewhat to vibrate and produce a constriction in the soft-walled tube. The frequency of vibration depends on the same factors as in human phonation – the air pressure from below, and the mass and tension of the folds. Mynah birds probably control F0 mostly with lung pressure.

If the syrinx is the source, then the trachea and supratracheal vocal tract are the filter. Mynahs can shorten or lengthen their vocal tracts slightly with extrinsic syringeal muscles, but probably not enough to account for the variability in resonances observed in their speech. Further, the bird's very short vocal tract should produce very high formant frequencies, rather than the good matches to human values that have been reported. Thus, the observed acoustic resonances cannot be the product of the shape of the suprasyringeal vocal tract. According to Klatt and Stefanski, the resonances of the *internal tympanoform membrane* are responsible for producing formant-like resonances. This membrane, which is located in the syrinx near the external labia, produces complex vibrations when air is blown across it. When the external labia vibrate, they set the membrane vibrating. Thus, although mynah speech resembles human phonation acoustically, it is the result of a very different production mechanism than the one that generates human speech.

To probe the question of neural control of vocalization, scientists have used stimulating electrodes, applied to areas of the exposed brain or implanted in brain tissue. Because of the obvious constraints on human studies of these kinds, most of our understanding of the neural control of vocalization is derived from electrical brain stimulation of animals. However, such studies are sometimes performed in humans when purposeful in clinical protocols. For example, in humans, findings have arisen from intraoperative cortical stimulation assaying cortical representation of language.[11] When removing damaged cortical tissue, neurosurgeons explore adjacent cortical areas in the awake surgical patient, as exemplified first in the classic studies of Penfield and Roberts (1959) and continued in later years by Ojemann and colleagues (Ojemann and Mateer, 1979; Ojemann, 1983). These studies focus on the cortical extent of language or speech representation (but see observations from human subcortical surgery in Section 6.2.4). The more extensive cerebral participation in vocalization has been slowly elaborated through studies in animals, primarily in nonhuman primates.

Even with this restricted range of information in humans, important differences from the neurology of animal vocalization have been seen. In animals, vocalization occurs following brain stimulation primarily in subcortical sites, such as the anterior cingulate gyrus (a portion of the limbic system) (Ploog, 1979). Extensive studies of vocalization in the squirrel monkey, macaque, and related nonhuman primates indicate that brain sites for initiating vocal calls extend from the midbrain through the diencephalon (thalamus) to the forebrain. Many of these sites are strongly interconnected to the limbic system (Jürgens and Ploog, 1970; Jürgens, 2002). This implies a major role in vocalization of limbic structures, which mediate emotional responses, rather than cortical structures, which, in humans, are associated with what neurologists sometimes refer to as higher integrative functions. While the details are largely unknown, subcortical control systems are also important in human vocalization (Ludlow, 2005). (See below for discussion of subcortical involvement in formulaic speech.)

As alluded to above, in the brainstem, the periaqueductal grey matter is important for initiation of vocalization in several species of animals and also in humans (Kelly, Beaton, and Magoun, 1946; Jürgens, 2002). Stimulation of this midbrain area has resulted in elicited vocalizations in several species of animals (rats, guinea pig, bat, cat, squirrel monkey, rhesus monkey, gibbon, chimpanzee). Destruction of this brain area in animals results in a complete loss of vocal reactions. Mutism in humans following damage to the midbrain has also been reported (Esposito, Demeurisse, Alberti, and Fabbro, 1999). Studies of rhesus monkeys reveal connections from cortical sites for vocal production to numerous subcortical and brainstem sites, but connections from motor cortex to the larynx were not identified. This is likely a later development in humans (Simonyan and Jürgens, 2003). Stimulation of cortical sites, such as the supplementary motor area, elicits vocalization in humans but not in non-human mammals (Penfield and Roberts, 1959).

---

[11] In intraoperative cortical stimulation studies, after the cortex has been exposed, a surgical patient is awakened and engaged in language tasks, while a stimulating electrode is placed at selected sites on the cortex. Disruption of speech at stimulated sites identifies language areas, or "eloquent cortex" as it is often called, preceding excision of brain tissue for treatment of epilepsy.

Sidebar: A Cross-species View of Laughter

Like love, music, sleep, and many other aspects of human life, laughter is both a vital aspect of our existence and a difficult one to explain. Laughter (discussed in more detail in Chapter 9) is an odd type of vocalization, and one that humans have in common with nonhuman animals – some say. Even a glance highlights the heterogeneity of this putative use of voice in function and form, in animal and man. Panksepp and Burgdorf (2003) provide an entrancing description of ultrasonic squeaks emitted from rats in response to play-tickling that have "more than a passing resemblance to primitive human laughter" (p. 533). Animal behaviorists have identified a breathy, forced exhalation as dog "laughter" (Simonet, Versteeg, and Storie, 2005). Chimpanzees make a laughter-like breathy, panting sound while playing and being tickled (Provine, 2000). Investigation of these behaviors can cast light on affective capacities in nonhuman animals arising out of shared subcortical circuits (Panksepp, 2005). These same circuits evince a "reward" response when experiencing humor (Mobbs, 2003). Laughter has been evoked during stereotaxic neurosurgery in humans, when electrical stimulation is applied to subcortical nuclei (Schaltenbrand, 1965).

Human laughter, which appears early in infant development (Sroufe and Wunsch, 1972), is also acoustically diverse (see Sidebar in Chapter 9; Bachorowski, Smoski, and Owren, 2001). It bears a superficial similarity to the Gibbon vocalization repertoire, which is highly varied and described as musical (Geissmann, 2002). Laughter has been featured in parents' reports of the effects of dolphin therapy on their severely mentally handicapped children (Kuhnert, 2005). For a few of these children, who had not ever phonated, initiated speech, or shown any communicative signs, swimming with the dolphins brought about vocal laughter as a first personal expressive act.

3.1.5 Vocalization from the point of view of evolution

Questions about the cerebral similarities and differences relating animal and human vocalization bring us naturally to a recently revived and currently popular topic–the evolution of human speech and language (Locke and Bogin, 2006; Fitch, 2010). Some researchers have seen evidence of evolutionary development of vocalization in the comparative biology of selected species. Theories of the evolutionary relationship between animal vocalization and human speech take several forms. Some of the debate has revolved around the position of the larynx in evolutionary development, and whether vocal tracts of this or that early human ancestor could shape distinct sounds (see Sidebar on "Evolution of the vocal tract and the capacity for vocal sound"). One conservative view is that animal and human vocal communicative systems evolved independently and separately. In this view, the major focus is on development of grammar as an entity that is wholly different from animal language (Pinker, 1994). Animal and human vocalizations are not seen to correspond in any meaningful way. However, for some, the notion that human language is completely unique and innate only to humans would appear to be at odds with Darwinian theory. A second perspective allows for an intermediate step, with minor, residual connections with animal vocalization as seen in sobbing, laughter, and emotional expression in humans. This view emphasizes the cerebral cortex, noting that human language is localized in cortical areas (although subcortical nuclei have been implicated in grammatical processing; Lieberman, 2002), while animal vocalization is identified with subcortical (including limbic) nuclei. In this intermediate view, human language developed disparately but in parallel with nonlinguistic communication, which originated in animal vocalization (Burling, 1993; Deacon, 1997), and these systems now coexist in modern man.

A third perspective depicts modern human speech as a direct development of early primate vocal behaviors. Lieberman (2002) proposed an intimate network of cortical and subcortical structures in human speech, with the concomitant involvement in human speech of emotional communication expected from subcortical-limbic structures. He argues that the neural substrate that regulates human speech began evolving long before the appearance of modern human beings. Models for human vocalization are derived in large part from experimental studies in nonhuman animals combined with clinical observations in human neurological disease. From clinical observations, it can be concluded that the motor cortex in humans forms part of a complex circuitry required for initiating voluntary, novel speech. From these and observations in comparative animal studies, Ploog (1979) proposed a hierarchical system of neuronal organization in the central nervous system, corresponding with evolutionary development, with brainstem control of vocal gestures, in tandem with higher-level control in anterior limbic cortex in primates, but with cortical representation occurring only in humans. This resembles the notion of two levels of nervous system control for vocalization in humans: an older system, which terminates in the cingulate gyrus (part of the limbic, or emotional, circuit) at the bilateral, rostral (rear) end of the limbic system, and which is capable of emotive and automatic speech behavior; and a newer system that is cortical, unilateral, and involved in voluntary, novel and planned speech (Robinson, 1972, 1976; Ploog, 1975; Myers, 1976). These correspond to disparate neurological circuits for control of "innate" vocal reactions (such as cries in response to pain) and "voluntary" vocalization, which appear to be differentially distributed in human and nonhuman brain organization (Jürgens, 2002). The extent to which human language "grew out" of subcortically represented animal vocalizations, transforming, for example, into primitive singing and/or holistic formulaic expressions in early human communication, or developed as an unrelated, independent behavior, is still debated (Wray, 2002b). In any case, the empirical arguments available from comparative biology hold the possibility of elucidating these questions (Fitch, 2004a, 2010; Locke, 2008) (These topics are discussed in detail in Chapters 5 and 6.)

Sidebar: Evolution of the Vocal Tract and the Capacity for Vocal Sound

The physiology of the vocal tract, presented in Chapter 2, is interesting to consider in an evolutionary context, because many characteristics have evolved to convey biologically important information from one animal to another. However, it is very difficult to obtain reliable information about how the vocal tract has evolved, in large part because the larynx is made up of cartilage and soft tissue, and, except for the hyoid bone, little remains in the fossil record. An influential early proposal by Lieberman and his colleagues (Lieberman, Crelin, and Klatt, 1972; Lieberman, 1975) implicated crucial changes in the position of the larynx in the evolution of human language. Anatomical drawings comparing vocal tracts of nonhuman primates with adult human vocal tracts revealed significant differences. The larynges of nonhuman primates lie higher in the vocal tract; the human vocal tract has a lowered larynx, and this lowering occurs during early infant development with a secondary "descent" occurring at adolescence in males. Further, a reconstruction of the Neanderthal vocal tract suggested that this early species of the Homo genus had a vocal shape closer to that of modern nonhuman primates. The articulatory-acoustic implication, following source-filter analyses of formant capabilities of this type of resonating chamber, was that this extinct hominid, like apes and chimpanzees today, was unable to produce "extreme" vowels such as /i/, /a/, and /u/. However, the descended larynx is not uniquely human (see, for example, Fitch and Hauser, 2003, for review), and more modern research suggests that "the acoustics, musculature, innervation, and peripheral motor control of human and animal vocal tracts are fundamentally similar" (Fitch, 2002, p. 25). Further studies indicated a subtle range of vocal qualities in some nonhuman primates. While these vocal tracts generate a relatively unstable glottal source, they can produce some humanoid phonetic contrasts, and laryngeal air sacs in some species add resonances and have the potential to produce very loud vocalizations (Schon Ybarra, 1995).

There is still little understanding of sound output faculties specific to the nonhuman vocal tract, although comparative studies are rapidly increasing in number (for example, Riede and Titze, 2008, for elk; Todd, 2007, for alligators; see Fitch, 2000a, b for a comparative review). These capacities may have been underestimated, and articulatory gestures in nonhuman animals may be more complicated than originally thought. The laryngeal system in primates appears to have more phonatory (F0) range (maybe even into ultrasonics), but less phonatory precision, than that in humans. Some studies suggested an optimal communication system based on fundamental frequency contrasts, rather than on formant patterning. Nonetheless, Andrew (1976) and others have reported that baboons produce sounds with vocal tract resonances, and evidence reviewed in Chapters 4 and 5 suggests that resonance information carries significant information about speaker identity, physical size, and reproductive fitness across a wide range of species. Further, differences in animal formants or bandwidths were seen to comprise "vocal signatures" allowing for recognizing different individuals (Fitch, 2002, p. 30).

3.1.6   Summary and conclusions for cerebral control of voice production

It takes most of a functioning brain to produce a human vocal pattern. All vocalization is performed by cortical structures in association with basal ganglia and limbic systems, and also involves cerebellar and brainstem activity. Whatever the evolutionary history and relationship of various kinds of animal vocalizations and speech, and whether emotional and overlearned utterances did or did not foreshadow either or human vocalization, remain objects of speculation and future research.

3.2   Essentials of Hearing and Auditory Perception in Animals and Humans

3.2.1   Introduction

We proceed to a survey of animal and human hearing as this information relates to voice perception. The world of audition can be called "wondrous," because so much remains unexplained. Experts lament the relatively slower progress in understanding how the ear functions, compared to vision; Darwin (1872b), for example, described in detail the evolutionary specialization of the eye, but "is silent about the ear" (Ashmore, 2000, p. 65). Most of our knowledge has come from research in the past few decades (Moore, 1982). A great deal is known about the physics of sound and how the vocal system produces sound waves; and the manner in which the peripheral auditory system – the outer, middle, and inner ear – transduces the mechanical vibrations at the eardrum is somewhat understood, although many questions remain, particularly regarding the function of the inner ear (cochlea). At the other end of the auditory roadway, the psychology of auditory perception for speech, music, and other sound objects has been studied extensively. However, for hearing, the manner in which neurophysiology translates into functional capacities for sound processing remains poorly understood. This state of affairs recalls the well-known cartoon by Sidney Harris showing two mathematicians discussing a proof on a chalk blackboard (Figure 3.5). At the beginning and end of the proof, numbers and symbols are orderly and directional, but the middle portion of the derivation states only that "a miracle occurs."

Vision has been much more fully characterized and described in every discipline than has audition, and we compare these two sensory modalities extensively in Chapter 6, because faces and voices constitute striking parallels in our social lives. To preview a few compelling similarities, we note that both faces and voices are complex, unique patterns, laden with affect, semantic and episodic detail, and forming big, personally familiar sets. These phenomena are nearly matched except that voices exist in time and faces in space. From two other important perspectives, however, vision and sound are worlds apart. The first perspective is historical. The objective, externalized rendering of sounds – whether spoken or sung – is about 32,000 years behind the intentional representation of visual images. It is sobering to consider that visual reproductions in

**"I think you should be more
explicit here in step two."**

Figure 3.5 "And then a miracle occurs ..." is on the blackboard, representing complex processes where beginnings and endings are known, but not the relationship between them.

the form of cave paintings were created as long ago as the Upper Paleolithic Period (40,000 to 10,000 BCE), with 30,000 BCE confidently identified, for example, as the date for animal drawings found in the Cave of Chauvet-Pont-d'Arc in Southern France (Richter, Waiblinger, Rink, and Wagner, 2000). During the ensuing millennia, human preoccupation with the visual image through drawings, painting, sculpture, and, later, photography,[12] can scarcely be exaggerated (Gombrich, 1995). In contrast, while early civilizations learned to deliberately produce musical sound quite early – 30,000- and 9,000-year-old bone flutes, for example, were found in Germany[13] (Hahn, 1988) and China – an actual first primitive reproduction of sound occurred

[12] If one wishes to consider the strict analog to sound recording, photography, then the fifteenth century comes to mind with early records of the camera obscura, whereby an inverted image was projected on the opposite wall of a closed box. Precursors to photography appeared in the early 1800s. Nonetheless, even before exact visual replicas were possible, much of visual imagery, including perspective and color, had been explored and analyzed through artistic media.

[13] Bone flutes and other prehistoric artifacts were first discovered in 1973 at Geißenklösterle, a portion of a large cavern, near the present town of Ulm in southern Germany (Hahn, 1988).

at the relatively recent date, in human evolutionary terms, of 1857. The invention was called the phonoautograph, but because the trace was on paper, it had limited playback abilities, such that the captured sound could be seen but not yet heard. Thomas Edison developed the ideas further by inventing the phonographic cylinder, after which the phonograph was patented by Emile Berliner in 1887. Thanks to rapid technological and engineering developments, sound recording is now as pervasive culturally as visual representation, but the huge disparity in cultural provenance and tradition remains a fact.

The second discrepancy between facial and vocal processing is neurophysiological. The two perceptual systems achieve the construction of complex neuropsychological behaviors in interestingly different ways. Vision originates from veridical representations of light energy absorbed by photoreceptors in the retina in a photochemical process that generates a nerve impulse (Peters, Applebury, and Rehtzepis, 1977). Information travels from the retina to cortical visual centers in four bundles of fibers, two of which cross to the contralateral side of the nervous system at the optic chiasm. The optic nerves (Cranial Nerve II; see Figure 3.4) synapse at the lateral geniculate nucleus of the thalamus, a visual way station (a point of synapse onto other nerve fibers or tracts), and from there the visual radiations proceed directly to visual receiving areas of the occipital lobes. Other relay stations serve to process ocular motor activity; visual scenes are built up in large part through elaborate control of movements of the eyes. In contrast to this photochemical process with relatively direct connections to cortical processing centers, input for sound is biomechanical and traverses a less direct and more highly staged path.

3.2.2   Studies of audition in nonhuman animals

The auditory system consists of peripheral and central components, which have interesting similarities and differences across biological species. Much of what we know about auditory function has arisen from nonhuman animal studies, which often assume that nonhuman animal physiology for hearing is sufficiently similar to human hearing to provide an adequate model for deciphering the human system. In many ways, the commonalities in structure and process are striking: For example, the size of the cochlea, the major organ of hearing embedded in bony structures behind the external ear, does not vary greatly relative to overall physical size differences in mammalian species. When uncoiled from its typical snail-shell[14] shape, the cochlea is 10 mm long in the mouse, 34 mm long in humans, and only 50% larger in elephants (Ashmore, 2000). Further evidence for the essential similarity between human and nonhuman animal hearing systems arose when it was shown that phonetic elements crucial to human speech perception, such as 2nd and 3rd formants (see Chapter 2) and voice onset time, could be distinguished by rhesus monkeys (Morse and Snowdon, 1975) and chinchillas (Kuhl and Miller, 1978), respectively. Animal models have been used to establish levels and systems in a general auditory system for the elemental

---

[14]   *Cochlea* comes from the Latin word for "snail-shell," borrowed from Greek *kokhlis*, snail, or *kokhlos*, land snail.

parameters of interest to us: frequency, intensity, and timing, be it in the cat, the rat, or the monkey. In physiology of hearing research, if it has hearing (some species do not have external ears), it could be utilized to learn more about the auditory pathway in general.

Yet hearing competence and hearing practice also differ across species, also in interesting ways. In some cases, a given animal's auditory characteristics are related to the kinds of vocal signals most utilized. (Accordingly, in early studies, the cat's voice was used in studies of the cat's hearing; Watanabe and Katsuki, 1974). For example, bats[15] hear very high frequencies, corresponding to their vocal calls and to their echolocation behavior. The area in the cochlea dedicated to high-frequency reception is large in bats, and vocal structures are engineered for producing ultrasonic pulses. Dolphins have highly developed auditory systems that respond to tones within a frequency range of 1–150 kHz (compared to 0.02–17 kHz in humans), correspond-ing to the frequency range of their vocalizations. Spinner dolphins produce whistles lasting up to 1½ seconds with fundamental frequencies between 2 and 22 kHz and burst clicks ranging upwards of 65 kHz (Bazúa-Durán and Au, 2002, 2004). Dolphin clicks ranging from 120 to 140 kHz have been correlated with sonar or echolocation functions (Au, 1993; Lammers, Au, and Herzing, 2003). Elephants send and receive seismic signals, perceiving these low-frequency sounds through bone conduction and their padded feet (O'Connell-Rodwell, 2005). In these cases, hearing characteristics often correspond to sound production behaviors coordinating with voice recogni-tion. A clear example of extraordinary hearing *not* related to vocal production appears in the desert golden mole, whose middle ear structures are adapted to sense low-frequency vibrations generated by dune grass (Mason and Narins, 2002).

3.2.3   The peripheral and central auditory pathways in humans

As noted above, hearing is remarkably complicated, and the functions of the ear and its connections to the brain are far from understood. In a schematic view (Figure 3.6), hearing a voice begins with the impinging of vibrating air molecules (pressure distur-bances) on the tympanic membrane (the eardrum) at the end of the ear canal. When vibrations of the eardrum are transferred to the middle ear ossicles, they amplify the sound and transduce its acoustic energy into mechanical energy. This mechani-cal energy is then transmitted to the inner ear, where it is again transduced, first into hydrodynamic energy as the motion of the bones sets the fluid in the inner ear into vibration, and then into electrochemical signals as the vibrating fluid sets the basilar membrane in motion, which in turn impinges on the tiny hair cells in the cochlea, stimulating nerve fibers at their bases (Gulick *et al.*, 1989). In the same way that receptors in the retina respond to light energy, the hair cells in the cochlea respond to mechanical disturbance by producing nerve impulses that travel, heavily processed, across multiple and circuitous neuronal tracts to auditory cortex. A spec-tral analysis occurs at this stage of processing as well, because different hair cells are

---

[15]   Bregman (2001) noted that humans, unlike bats, utilize sound-emitting rather than sound-reflecting properties of things in the world (p. 36).

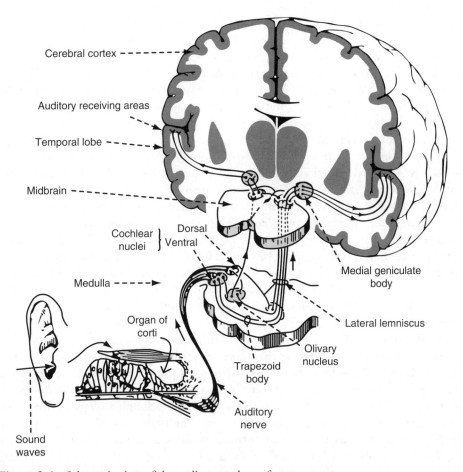

Figure 3.6　Schematic view of the auditory pathway from ear to cortex.

stimulated depending on the spectral characteristics of the sound. The inner hair cells form afferent connections with the approximately 30,000 to 50,000 (estimates vary) neurons that serve each human cochlea. These afferent neurons gather and twist to form the cochlear nerve, a branch of the 8th cranial nerve, seen at the medulla of the brainstem (Figures 3.4 and 3.6). In this way, the vibratory properties of air molecules are closely connected with the performance of the whole auditory system (Ashmore, 2000) as the energy in these vibrations is serially transduced and re-transduced as sound passes through the auditory system.

The auditory pathway next courses from each cochlea through several way stations to the auditory cortex in each hemisphere in an ascending pathway[16] made up of a number of brainstem and subcortical nuclei, many of which perform higher level processing, or coding, of the original signal (Kent, 1997). The trip from ear to

---

[16]　As mentioned above, a descending, efferent (motor) division also exists to transmit cortical information downward.

brain – lengthier and more staged than the ride from the eye – includes four or five way stations, utilizing neural pathways that increase greatly in number at each synapse. Cortical neurons synapse (terminate but communicate with the next fiber tract) at these way stations, sometimes ipsilaterally, sometimes contralaterally, and sometimes both. Most ascending neurons converge at the last way station, the inferior colliculi at the brainstem, and from there traverse ipsilaterally to the medial geniculate body (also at the brainstem) and then to auditory association cortex. Electrical activity along these brainstem way stations can be identified in the auditory brain response (ABR), in which evoked potentials, categorized as ABR waves I–VII, are generated along the auditory nerve, at the cochlear nucleus, and probably at the inferior colliculus and medial geniculate body (sites of later waves are less clearly established). Clues reflecting temporal, spectral and amplitude information are compared and analyzed at numerous points along the auditory pathway, and each neuron sends its signals out to many thousands of other neurons, making synaptic activity enormously complicated (Penrose, 1994). This elaborate, multistage process of transduction and transmission has been the focus of decades of research (see, for example, Gulick, 1971; Keidel, Kallert, and Korth, 1983; Gulick, Gescheider, and Frisina, 1989; Seikel, King, and Drumright, 2000). The task of unraveling and interpreting connectivity in audition remains extremely daunting.

In this system, each ear is represented on both sides of the ascending pathways, but the contralateral side is favored, in that more and stronger connections occur between one cochlea and the auditory cortex on the opposite side. (There is no corresponding asymmetry in neural pathways for vision.) Animal studies have placed the difference at about 60–70%[17] (Schiffman, 1976), although the precise physiology of these connections remains the subject of debate. This asymmetry was first observed in records of gross evoked responses to click stimulation recorded from the auditory areas of the right and left hemispheres of cats (Thompson, 1967). Tunturi (1946) and Rosenzweig (1951, 1954, 1961) further demonstrated that the amplitude of the evoked response is greater at the cortical area contralateral to the ear stimulated by the click in animals, from which it was concluded that the majority of nerve pathways starting in one cochlear nucleus cross to the opposite side of the brain. Anatomical and clinical studies in humans support these observations in animals. In patients with damage to one cerebral hemisphere, under certain testing conditions the auditory information presented to the ear contralateral to the side of lesion shows greater performance decrements than the ear on the side of the lesion (Milner, 1962), again suggesting that the auditory pathway normally carries more information to the contralateral side of the brain. However, as mentioned above, there is considerable interaction between left and right ascending auditory pathways, which is why we can successfully talk on the telephone with the receiver placed at either ear, and why we cannot reliably test cerebral lateralization of sound by merely presenting a sound at a single ear. It is also the reason that damage to auditory areas in one cerebral hemisphere does not produce unilateral deafness.

---

[17]   These numbers are often cited, but definitive neurophysiological evidence underpinning these estimates has not been located.

3.2.4 Representation of timing, intensity, frequency, and quality from the periphery upwards

Everything in sound exists in time. All acoustic signals have a duration, and diverse granularities of temporal detail pervade the auditory process. Portions of acoustic information are successive or simultaneous, and certain timing phenomena are represented by the duration of the nervous system's stimulation. The timing, or phase, of the arrival of the signals at various hearing processing way stations and centers provides data for analysis. Localization of a sound depends on differences at the two ears in time of arrival, especially for low frequency sounds, and on differences in intensity (Thompson, 1967). Frequency and intensity themselves arise from different types of temporal modulations within sound waves.

Among vocal attributes, the processing of frequency information has received the most attention. Here, again, timing is key: Temporal regularity and average repetition rate are determinants of perceived pitch. For the hearing process, frequencies are organized spatially (especially for lower frequencies) – a gradation from high to low – beginning in the hair cells residing along the basilar membrane of the cochlea. This organization is maintained by the 8th cranial nerve bundle fibers, and continues through the auditory pathway to Heschl's gyrus, the auditory receiving area on the temporal lobe of the brain (Thompson, 1967). There, high-to-low frequency-receptive neurons form an orderly band along the cortical gyrus. The spatial representation of frequency, preserved from cochlea to cortex, is called "tonotopicity," discovered and confirmed through studies of single cortical cell recordings in response to tones of known frequencies presented at the ear of nonhuman animals. Representation for frequency also exists at subcortical levels; for example, cats were able to discriminate tones following extensive lesions of auditory cortex (Butler, Diamond, and Neff, 1957). Consistent with this finding, tone frequency discriminations were made by human patients with unilateral temporal lobe damage on either side (Milner, 1962). This does not hold for complex pitch judgments in humans, as we will see in what follows.

Studies in monkeys indicate that the cortical area for extracting fundamental frequency differs from that for processing pitch, which groups harmonics into a single percept (Tian, Reser, Durham, Kustov, and Rauschecker, 2001). These pitch maps, as also revealed by fMRI and MEG studies, are located next to and perpendicular to the tonotopic maps (Bendor and Wang, 2006). Other studies, using high-resolution fMRI, reported numerous cortical fields responding to tonal and band-passed noise sounds in monkey auditory cortex (Petkov, Kayser, Augath, and Logothetis, 2006). It is still unknown exactly how pitch is processed by these cortical areas (Bendor and Wang, 2005).

Intensity is registered by the ear primarily in terms of incrementally greater hair cell recruitment in the cochlea. Early findings that intensity discriminations could be made by animals that lack auditory cortex support the notion that intensity is processed "early" along the auditory pathway (Dewson, 1964). Like frequency, intensity is also coded subcortically and bilaterally through all stages in the brain, but this process is less well understood than that associated with frequency information.

Timbre, or voice quality, in this context generally associated with the spectral shape of the sound wave, is embedded in complex auditory stimuli as they traverse the peripheral hearing system. Because it is derived from processing through the auditory pathway, voice quality, narrowly considered, is a special case of frequency, and is usually understood as a correlate of the amount of energy at each frequency in a sound. Thus, when the auditory system resolves complex waves, information about quality (or timbre) is also derived.

3.2.5   Auditory percepts and the role of cerebral associations

Using the elemental signals of frequency and intensity in various time domains, the auditory system extracts behaviorally relevant information (Wang, 2007). Neurophysical analyses of cortical processing of sound endeavor to explicate how brain cells work together to organize auditory percepts, attempting to discover the neural code underlying perceptual distinctions (Eggermont, 2001). Another approach, called auditory scene analysis, observes performance responses to auditory stimuli to determine how sound is formed into interpretable patterns (Bregman, 1994) (see Sidebar). This approach for speech perception has had detractors, who point to evidence from sine wave speech (Remez, 2005). Remez and colleagues argue that listeners' responses to sine wave speech confound two key tenets of auditory scene analysis: the grouping function and the result of top-down knowledge (Remez, Rubin, Berns, Pardo, and Lang, 1994). Nonetheless, these notions may have interest for the study of voice patterns.

A traditional view of auditory processing from ear to cortex featured discrete auditory receiving areas on the temporal lobe. More recently, studies emphasizing the neural code that underlies auditory perception have shown that initial stages of sound processing in the auditory cortex occur in various cortical fields. While some functions are well documented, such as the processing of frequency in the tonotopic band, many auditory fields remain poorly understood (Petkov *et al.*, 2006). It is now better understood that there are many connections between these areas and other cortical areas, including subcortical nuclei and cross-model association areas of the frontal and parietal lobes (Fair, 1992; Haramati, Soroker, Dudai, and Levy, 2008). Recent studies have indicated that visual, somatosensory and auditory signals converge at early stages of auditory cortical processing. This occurs also in low-level cortical structures that were formerly believed to be unisensory in function. The process of audition, proceeding in a hierarchical progression of simple to more complex aspects of unimodal stimuli, is augmented by convergence of multisensory input, which becomes available at the earliest cortical processing stages (Schroeder *et al.*, 2003). In their discussion of the "distributed auditory cortex," Winer and Lee (2007) describe a confluence of auditory and multisensory streams, which precedes cognitive processing of sound. Reciprocal influences suggest a web of relations among multisensory areas and nuclei in addition to extensive limbic connections. These perspectives are important to our depiction of familiar voice acquisition and recognition as participating in a broad range of cognitive functions, including aspects of memory, affect, thought, motivation and attention. It is also helpful to our understanding of the perception of much communicative information in the voice, including emotions, attitudes, and various types of linguistic-prosodic functions.

Sidebar: Auditory Scene Analysis

A contrasting approach to describing audition, called auditory scene analysis, has arisen from vision studies and from a branch of cognitive studies called ecological psychology (Bregman, 1994). Auditory scene analysis assumes that the perceptual system is tuned to environmental aspects that have biological significance, which may be innate or acquired, and asks the question: What are the steps and processes by which we perceive sounding objects in the world (Bregman, 1994; McAdams, 2001)? Thus, scene analysis focuses on function, not physiological mechanism, examining how basic auditory elements are grouped to make a sound, utilizing the notions of "auditory stream" and auditory groupings, or perceived relations between sound events that affect later perception (McAdams and Bigand, 2001). In this view, both simplicity and complexity co-exist in the auditory cortex, whose role is to arrange input into auditory objects (Nelken, 2004). Bregman (1994, 2001) and others have pursued activation of auditory schemas in listening studies in relation to environmental regularities in sound emission. This approach boldly embraces the "and then a miracle occurred" step in Figure 3.4, because a direct mapping from mechanism to function is neither sought nor expected (Bregman, 1994). For sound, Bregman (1994) states "I have assumed that the auditory system has a set of methods by which it untangles the mass of input and interprets it into a description of distinct sources of sound with their own separate properties" (p. 697), without expecting a direct reverse mapping from function to mechanism. Subjective, perceptual studies of hearing function (not the underlying mechanisms) also provide a context for productive discussion of the evolution, development, and adult abilities in voice identity perception. These perspectives draw heavily on assumptions about grouping within the field of Gestalt perception as developed for vision (Wertheimer, 1944; Neisser, 1976) (see Sidebar on Principles of Gestalt Perception in Chapter 5). These say that to be "grouped" into a coherent auditory object, sound elements have, among others, the properties of proximity, similarity, continuation, organization, belongingness in a context, and innateness. One major effect of these principles, all of which are proposed to be natural processes in hearing, is exclusive allocation of the selected sound elements to a sound object (or event). These principles find full realization in the personal voice pattern, perhaps like no other auditory signal.

3.2.6 Cerebral plasticity in audition

Brain plasticity refers to physical and functional neurophysiological changes in response to behavioral challenges. This is currently a popular topic and the term "plasticity" has many different meanings. Here are a few: laying down of additional neuronal connections or changing neuronal projections (axonal growth) to effect new functions; altering (such as enlarging) the area of cortical representation for a behavior;

growth in neuronal ultrastructure, such as synapse or dendrite count or location; compensatory neural regeneration; and long- or short-term changes in neuronal response properties during behavior. Numerous studies have demonstrated various kinds of cortical plasticity in the auditory receiving area as a response to stimulus input or behavioral manipulations (Recanzone, Schreinerk, and Merzenich, 1993; Nudo, 2003). Long-term neural changes, depending importantly on attention, reward, and task relevance, have been demonstrated in the adult brainstem and auditory cortex of animals and humans (Wang, 2007; Krishnan, Gandour, and Bidelman, 2010). These dynamic cortical changes lead to a view of the central auditory pathway as a flexible processing structure (de Boer and Thornton, 2008). However, very short-term changes arising from behavioral stimulation are also observable, as proposed for imprinting phenomena (see Rauschecker and Marler, 1993).

Earlier, the auditory pathway was thought of as a hard-wired transmission system, but more recently it has been shown that characteristics of neuronal activity can be dynamically altered by exposure and learning (Syka, 2002), lending crucially important plasticity to the system. Additional plasticity is contributed by descending or "corticofugal" systems consisting of multiple feedback loops that affect cortical as well as subcortical processing of sound (Suga, Ma, Gao, Sakai, and Chowdhury, 2003; Suga, 2008). Corticofugal influences are believed to reach as far as the inner ear (de Boer and Thornton, 2008), and provide a mechanism for animals to acquire responses to behaviorally-relevant sounds and for enhancing responses to such sounds (see Suga *et al.*, 2003, for review). Early on, inhibitory interactions in auditory brainstem centers were seen (Watanabe and Katsuki, 1974), and evidence for inhibition of transmitted sound information has been reported for the upper brainstem (Papanicolaou, Raz, Loring, and Eisenberg, 1986), indicating that efferent (coursing downwards from cortex) nerve impulses affect afferent (sensory, upward impulses) transmission.

Thus, recent evidence suggests that the cortical auditory receiving areas (and other cortical representation areas) are more plastic than previously believed, so that several types of nervous system changes may occur as a result of experience (Ehret, 1997). This opens the door to the possibility of individual differences in brain organization, potentially complicating the already complex basic picture. The auditory cortex utilizes temporal and spectral context at several time scales to organize componential features processed by the brain auditory pathway into auditory objects (Nelken, 2004) that are stimulated by the environment. Numerous studies show how controlling sound input affects the area and functionality (response characteristics of neurons) of auditory cortex throughout an animal's life. For example, the auditory pathways and cortices of rat pups were shaped by perceived stimuli – oft-heard frequencies created a larger cortical receiving area for those frequencies in development (Dahmen and King, 2007).

The phenomenon of plasticity is not restricted to cortex. Research reveals variability in representation at different levels of the auditory pathway, emphasizing the plasticity of the developing and adult system as it interacts with environmental input. This results from the aforementioned extensive corticofugal system, which flows downward toward subcortical nuclei along the auditory pathway (for example, Suga *et al.*, 2003; de Boer and Thornton, 2008). It is easy to see how such a set-up would enable rapid acquisition and processing of unique auditory patterns. Processing at lower levels in the brain is also influenced by cognitive-auditory function. This has been shown in studies of brainstem responses. Auditory nerve fibers in the human brainstem normally respond to frequency in a "phase-locked" manner, such that the periodicity of the signal is reflected by the periodicity and interspike intervals of activity in the auditory nerve fibers (the FFR or "frequency following response"). In a study comparing native speakers of Mandarin (a tone language) and English, Krishnan, Xu, Gandour, and Cariani (2005) found that the frequency following response varied with native language: Although a frequency following response was observed in both listener groups, the response was stronger and followed frequencies more accurately for the Mandarin-speaking group than for English speakers. Similarly, the frequency following response was altered after learning foreign pitch patterns (Song, Skoe, Wong, and Kraus, 2008). These effects are not language- or stimulus-specific: Speakers of one tone language still showed the enhanced FFR when listening to words from a second, unfamiliar tonal language, even if the tones were dissimilar in contour shape (Krishnan *et al.*, 2005). Effects also occurred in both speech and non-speech contexts, suggesting that pitch extraction in the brainstem follows the acoustic features of the auditory stream, and not the features of the linguistic tonal system (Swaminathan, Krishnan, and Gandour, 2008). It thus appears that experience tunes the brainstem neurons to optimally (and pre-attentively) extract F0 features that are relevant to speech perception. Kraus and Nicol (2005) reported observing different brainstem response patterns for acoustic material reflecting source characteristics (laryngeal) and filter (vocal tract) characteristics. These results suggest that even at the earliest stages of auditory processing, encoding of frequency depends not only on signal properties, but on their functions as well.

Learning-induced plasticity in audition, although most sensitive in the developing animal, is present also in the adult, although the mechanisms are not well understood. These recent findings, which pertain to plasticity due to learning in the auditory system, promise to open new vistas of understanding hearing behaviors. Insights about plasticity in auditory neurophysiology may lead to clearer descriptions of how voice patterns are acquired and processed, a topic to be treated in detail below and again in Chapter 6.

3.2.7   Cerebral lateralization

3.2.7.1   *Basic concepts*
It is well accepted that speech and language are represented in the left hemisphere (Kinsbourne, 1970, 1974; Geschwind, 1970; Gazzaniga, Irvy, and Mangun, 2002; Pulvermüller, 2002). This fact is as firmly established as it is essentially unexplained. A related, equally familiar view holds that each cerebral hemisphere is specialized for different kinds of cognitive processing. For well over a century, studies using numerous experimental approaches in normal persons and in subjects who have sustained brain damage have confirmed these facts beyond any reasonable doubt. While cerebral laterality is not absolute for most cognitive functions (speech production is the strongest example of laterality), a superiority of processing or a preference in one or the other cerebral hemisphere for many cognitive tasks can be demonstrated from

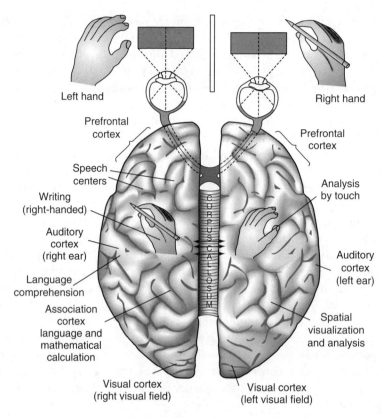

Figure 3.7 Lateralization of functional cerebral processing.

many perspectives (Figure 3.7). Much research and discussion over the past several decades on this topic has led to generalities about "modes" of processing in the two hemispheres. For example, because the left hemisphere excels at language and math-ematical operations, its underlying mode has been called sequential, computational, and/or analytic. The right hemisphere, in contrast, is superior at processing visuospa-tial and auditory patterns and geographical spaces, such that its mode has been called configurational, holistic or Gestalt (Bever, 1975; Young, 1983; Liederman, 1988; Bradshaw and Mattingly, 1995). Although none of these dichotomies fully captures the complex differences that have been demonstrated for cognitive functions in the two hemispheres (Peretz, 2001), they do serve as useful cover terms for possible tendencies.

The distribution of communicative functions between the left and right hemispheres is shown in Figure 3.8. The sounds, words and grammar of language are indeed located in the left hemisphere; familiar voice recognition, as part of communicative-pragmatic competence, is associated with right hemisphere function. Recently a broader interest in communicative function has led to discussion of inference, social context, nonliteral and emotional meanings, and other aspects of language use, commonly referred to as the pragmatics of communication (Brownell, Gardner, Prather, and Martino, 1995).

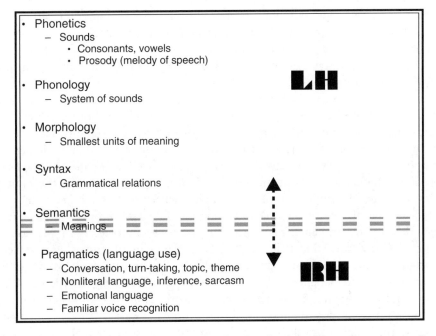

- Phonetics
  - Sounds
    - Consonants, vowels
    - Prosody (melody of speech)
- Phonology
  - System of sounds
- Morphology
  - Smallest units of meaning
- Syntax
  - Grammatical relations
- Semantics
  - Meanings
- Pragmatics (language use)
  - Conversation, turn-taking, topic, theme
  - Nonliteral language, inference, sarcasm
  - Emotional language
  - Familiar voice recognition

Figure 3.8 Schema of hemispheric specialization for "levels" of language structure. Dotted line indicates participation of both hemispheres. LH: left hemisphere specialization. RH: right hemisphere specialization.

(See Chapter 8 for fuller discussion of pragmatics). From work with brain-damaged persons, we know that much of this kind of competence is associated with right hemisphere specialization. Participation in the social principles of communication provides a compatible neural substrate for familiar voice recognition.

3.2.7.2 *Cortical processing of sound: Nature of sound versus function of sound*
Processing of acoustic elements occurs continuously throughout the ascending and descending auditory pathway. As modeled and processed components of the signal move toward cortical areas, a question arises about cerebral specialization for these components. As described above, sound waves impinging at the eardrum traverse to the auditory receiving area in the temporal cortex of the brain, using projections which travel along ipsilateral and contralateral pathways. This fact becomes especially interesting in considering the "typical functional asymmetry" of the cerebral hemispheres (Liederman, 1988, p. 375). What cerebral asymmetries occur for the elements of sound as they emerge from the vocal signal? Complex interactions between the structure of the signal, its function, and inherent hemispheric specialization with respect to cognitive "mode" determine the ultimate manner in which the brain handles an auditory stimulus. We consider two levels of auditory laterality: formal (elemental components of the signal) and functional (use in cognitive behavior).

At the elemental level, investigators have considered the extent to which perception of different vocal attributes depends on each hemisphere. Intensity does not seem to show lateralized representation. There is little evidence from animal or clinical studies that loudness perception or loudness judgments are lateralized to the left or right hemisphere.[18] Along the auditory pathway, comparative processing of intensities emanating from each way station aids in sound localization and in building the code toward the auditory percept.

In contrast to loudness, hemispheric specialization for pitch and timing is clearly established. While sine waves can be processed successfully in both cerebral hemispheres, numerous studies in normal and clinical subjects converge to indicate that complex pitch (or timbre) judgments are most successfully achieved by the intact right hemisphere (Sidtis, 1980). Dichotic listening studies (see Sidebar on dichotic listening) showed higher accuracy at the left ear (right hemisphere) than at the right ear in tasks requiring discrimination of complex pitch patterns. This asymmetry increases with the complexity of the sound. This finding for pitch has been amply verified using several different experimental paradigms (for review see Zatorre, 1988; Samson and Zatorre, 1994; Zatorre and Belin, 2001). Data from clinical studies using epileptic subjects in whom the left or right temporal lobe has been excised (Milner, 1962; Zatorre, 1988) and patients with left- or right-sided focal lesions (Alcock, Wade, Anslow, and Passingham, 2000; Peretz and Zatorre, 2005) are consistent with this view. A similar result was obtained for musical chords, a special category of complex pitch pattern: Brain electrical activity in an evoked response potential study reflected right hemisphere activity (Koelsch, Gunter, Schröger, and Friederici, 2003), consistent with results from dichotic listening studies of chordal stimuli, where a left ear advantage (right hemisphere specialization) was observed (Gordon, 1970). Functional imaging studies of the brain lend support to this idea by reporting that, despite bilateral activation (usually found for cognitive tasks in imaging studies), spectral features were "weighted" to right auditory cortices (Zatorre and Belin, 2001).

The case for timing is different again. Studies in normal (Liégeois-Chauvel, De Graaf, Laguitton, and Chauvel, 1999; Schirmer, 2004) and brain-damaged subjects (Alcock *et al.*, 2000) point to the conclusion that temporal processing is preferentially lateralized to the left cerebral hemisphere in humans. Temporal judgments of various kinds have repeatedly been associated with left hemisphere specialization (Marin and Perry, 1999; Schirmer, Alter, Kotz, and Friederici, 2001), especially fine temporal distinctions. In fMRI studies, signals from the left hemisphere increased with increasing temporal variations in alternating pure tones, while increased spectral variations were associated with lateralized activity in the right temporal lobe (Belin *et al.*, 2000; Zatorre and Belin, 2001; Jamison, Watkins, Bishop, and Matthews, 2006). Rhythmic material, involving complex levels of multiple timing relations, may engage more of the brain (Peretz and Zatorre, 2005).

A prime example of a functional influence on cerebral lateralization arises in the case of F0 contrasts in tone languages such as Thai or Mandarin. In tone languages, changes in pitch height and contour shape signal different meanings in words in the same way that contrasts between consonants and vowels do in nontonal languages.

---

[18] A slight tendency for greater impairments in loudness perception was associated with right temporal lobe surgery as treatment for epilepsy (Milner, 1962).

Table 3.2 Thai language stimuli used in a dichotic listening task comparing tone and consonant contrasts in words with simulated tones in nonsense hums.

Stimulus	Tone	Length (msec)	English gloss
Tone-words			
naa	mid tone	625	field
naa	low tone	650	(a nickname)
naa	falling	575	face
naa	high tone	625	aunt
naa	rising	650	thick
Consonant-words			
daa	mid tone	700	(a nickname)
naa	mid tone	650	field
saa	mid tone	700	diminish
caa	mid tone	650	tea
laa	mid tone	600	goodbye
Hums			
hmm	mid tone	650	(nonsense)
hmm	low tone	550	(nonsense)
hmm	falling	550	(nonsense)
hmm	high tone	575	(nonsense)
hmm	rising	525	(nonsense)

For example, in Thai the syllable "naa" has five meanings, depending on the level and directional movements of pitch (Table 3.2). As mentioned above, complex pitch perception is mediated largely by right cerebral mechanisms, while speech perception is typically associated with the left hemisphere (Sidtis, 1980). When pitch functions "tonemically," where in the brain will this be processed?

To answer this question, Van Lancker and Fromkin (1973) used dichotic listening (see Sidebar) to compare the performance of native speakers of Thai and American English on the five Thai tonal contrasts, five Thai consonant-vowel contrasts, and on five nonsense "hums" modeled after the Thai tones. Wearing stereo headphones, subjects heard two words at once – first a series of Thai tone-words, then a block of Thai words contrasting not in tone but in initial consonant, followed by a block of five "hums," which were nonverbal imitations of the tone-words. Only the native speakers of Thai showed a right ear advantage (more errors at the left ear, corresponding to a left hemisphere specialization) for the Thai tones. Both groups showed the expected right ear advantage for the consonant contrasts and no ear advantage for the nonsense hums. Musical training did not affect this finding (Van Lancker and Fromkin, 1978) (Figure 3.9). These data suggested that, although complex pitch patterns are generally processed at the right temporal lobe, such patterns can be functionally "allocated" for use in the linguistic system, which is lateralized to the left hemisphere (hence the right ear advantage). A similar design demonstrated that native speakers of a click language, Zulu, heard click consonants more accurately in their right ears, unlike English listeners, who showed no such ear advantage (Best and

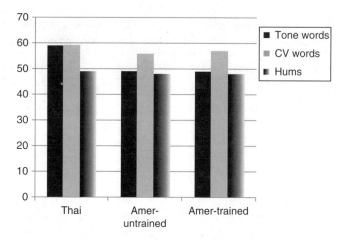

Figure 3.9 Right ear advantages for three sets of stimuli, for musically trained and untrained listeners who heard Thai tones. Native Thai speakers showed a significant right ear advantage to tonal and consonantal contrasts (CV words) in their language, but not to the same tonal contrasts on nonsense syllables (hums). American speakers showed a REA for consonant contrasts only.

Avery, 1999). The finding for tone language speakers has been corroborated by numerous subsequent studies showing impaired perception of tone in patients with left hemisphere brain lesions for Thai (Gandour and Dardarananda, 1983), Chinese (Naeser and Chan, 1980; Liang and van Heuven, 2004; Liang, 2006; Luo *et al.*, 2006), and Norwegian (Ryalls and Reinvang, 1986; Moen, 1991), and in English contrasts such as "green house" versus "green house" (Blumstein and Goodglass, 1972). Data from functional brain imaging studies of normal subjects are also consistent with this conclusion (Gandour *et al.*, 2000; Klein, Zatorre, Milner, and Zhao, 2001). There is some evidence also for left hemisphere preference for linguistic-prosodic contrasts signaling grammatical meanings, such as those found for questions, statements, conditional clauses, and imperatives (Blumstein and Cooper, 1974). These findings are less consistent, possibly because of the competing characteristic, length, which also appears to influence hemispheric side of processing (see below and Figure 3.11). Thus, formal and functional factors interact in determining hemisphere specialization.

Sidebar: Dichotic Listening

In dichotic listening, listeners are challenged by hearing two different sounds at precisely the same time, one stimulus at each ear, over stereophonic headphones. They may be asked to attend selectively to one ear, or to report what they hear at each ear, or respond to a probe that follows the dichotic pair. For example, listeners may hear two different familiar voices (one at each ear) saying two different words, and may be asked to verbally identify both the speaker and the word at one ear (or both) (or multiple choice answer sheets may be provided). The procedure works best when the competing sounds are exactly aligned at point of onset and are acoustically similar. The task is designed to be difficult enough that subjects make errors in reporting what they hear. To interpret the results, two facts are pertinent: The projections of the auditory pathway are stronger on the contralateral side (for example, from the left ear to the right hemisphere), and many cognitive functions are relatively specialized in the left or right cerebral hemisphere (Sidtis, 1982). Thus, better performance at one ear implicates the opposite cerebral hemisphere in processing that kind of stimulus.

Using this paradigm, various questions can be asked about verbal and nonverbal stimuli, and about various elements contributing to higher-order auditory processing (Kimura, 1967; Hugdahl, 1988). In most dichotic listening studies, more errors are made on linguistic stimuli that are heard at the left ear (a "right ear advantage"), and more errors are made on nonverbal auditory stimuli heard at the right ear (a "left ear advantage") (Milner, 1962). Left ear advantages have been reported for complex tones (Sidtis, 1980), chords (Gordon, 1970), and familiar voices (Kreiman and Van Lancker, 1988).

Another study (Francis and Driscoll, 2006) showed that functional use of what are normally phonemic contrasts in English can also affect cerebral lateralization. In this study, one group of listeners was trained to use small differences in voice onset time[19] as a cue to speaker identity, while a control group was trained to treat the same difference as signaling a change from a voiceless to a voiced consonant (for example, from /p/ to /b/) in a single speaker. At test, listeners who were trained to identify talkers showed significantly faster reaction times to stimuli at the left ear than at the right ear, while the control group showed no significant differences between ears. Thus, processing of the stimuli shifted towards the right hemisphere based solely on function, consistent with other results in this area (cf. Kreiman and Van Lancker, 1988).

3.2.7.3 *Hemispheric processing of elements of the sound wave*

In the same way that the lateralization of an acoustic signal can depend on its function, so also can the lateralization of a function arise from the attributes listeners attend to when making their judgments. For example, consider the perception of emotional meanings from prosodic cues in speech. In a task commonly used to test listeners' abilities to perceive emotional-prosodic meanings, sentences with neutral meaning

---

[19] Voice onset time is the elapsed time between release of the closure for a stop consonant and the onset of vocal fold vibration for voicing of the following vowel. Sounds like /p/, /t/, and /k/ in English have relatively long voice onset times (on the order of 50–60 msec); sounds like /b/, /d/, and /g/ have voice onset times close to 0 (e.g., Lisker and Abramson, 1971; Abramson, 1977).

(such as "Johnnie is walking his dog") are recorded with intonations signaling various emotions and played to subjects who identify the emotional intonations. Some studies reported difficulty recognizing prosodic cues for emotional meanings in persons with right hemisphere damage (Heilman, Scholes, and Watson, 1975; Borod, 1993), but similar deficits have also been reported in left-hemisphere-damaged subjects (Schlanger, Schlanger, and Gerstman, 1976; Cancelliere and Kertesz, 1990; Van Lancker and Sidtis, 1992; Baum and Pell, 1997, 1999; Sidtis and Van Lancker Sidtis, 2003) suggesting that this ability is not as strongly lateralized as language is. This discrepancy can be partly resolved by examining the prosodic elements that make up emotional-prosodic stimuli. Pitch mean and variation (processed in the right hemisphere) are primary cues to emotional intonation (for example, angry people often raise their pitch; see Chapter 9 for more discussion). However, temporal cues (processed in the left hemisphere) contribute secondarily to some emotional contrasts (for example, sad people may speak more slowly than usual, leading to changes in the durations of individual segments). Thus, damage in either hemisphere may interfere with successful processing of specific acoustic cues for emotional speech, depending on the task and the stimuli. Untangling formal (or elemental – pitch and timing) from functional attributes (emotional and linguistic content) is crucial to our understanding of how domains in the communication system are lateralized. For familiar voice perception, many dimensions of the signal contribute to right hemisphere specialization of that function. When subjects with left-hemisphere damage perform better in voice recognition tasks than do right-hemisphere-damaged subjects, an array of "natural" right hemisphere abilities – including pattern recognition, emotional experiencing, complex-pitch processing, and personal relevance and familiarity apprehension – are all accountable (for review see Van Lancker, 1997) (Figures 3.10 and 3.11).

3.2.7.4 *Summary of formal and functional influences on cerebral lateralization of sound*

The elemental constituents of sound – intensity, frequency, and timing – can be isolated from perceptual experience, and when they are, tendencies toward hemispheric specialization can be examined. Intensity appears not to have a cerebral side of preference; the pitch of complex signals is better processed in the right cerebral side, and various instantiations of timing are better processed in the left. In many cases these formal attributes of sound and the behaviors that utilize them are in harmony: Timing is a left hemisphere specialty, and timing and sequencing information are key in speech, so that both the crucial auditory element and the behavior associated with it are lateralized to the left hemisphere. Similarly with pitch patterns: Intonation in speech is a primary cue to emotional information, and the right hemisphere processes emotional experience more readily than the left hemisphere. Exceptions come from tone languages, where pitch is a major cue, but the cue is organized into linguistic structure, as described above. Such examples indicate that the hemispheric specialization story is a complex one.

Figure 3.10 schematizes the factors governing the lateralization of auditory behaviors utilizing pitch and temporal information. The symbols in the square depict computational potential reflecting those found in language, novel musical melody, and mathematics. To the extent that stimuli are composed of discrete, permutable,

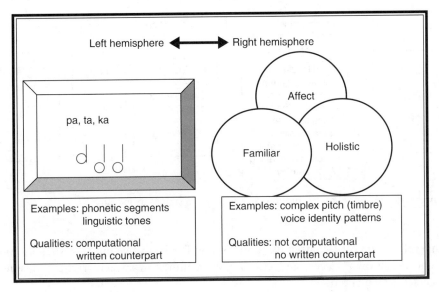

Figure 3.10 Factors and qualities associated with elemental sounds attracted to the left or right hemisphere.

rule-governed features or units, left hemisphere processing is favored. In contrast, the circles on the right side of the figure suggest that familiar, affective, and/or holistic patterns, which are by nature not analyzable into component parts, are lateralized to the right hemisphere. Note that familiar melodies, which usually have no relations with musical notation, fall into the second grouping, whereas novel melodies may more readily engage the left hemisphere. Familiar and affective phenomena overlap in cognitive space. Persons, places, things, voices, faces, phrases, situations, contexts, and so on can be personally familiar; when they are personally familiar, they may assume affective (and other) associations. Personally familiar, affective phenomena tend to be stored and processed in separate "packages," which are rendered in the figure as "holistic"[20] (see Williams and Hollan, 1981). These three cognitive properties co-occur, and provide a supportive substrate for processing auditory events, most especially familiar voices, in the right hemisphere mode.

Vocal parameters may serve many different functions simultaneously. These are schematically listed in Figure 3.11. When pitch is utilized phonemically in a linguistic system (tonemes in languages like Thai), with the same properties of permutability and compositionality as any other phonological units, these qualities determine lateralization to the left hemisphere. Attention to details of sequencing and timing – crucial for speech – favors the left hemisphere. Probably because of a right hemisphere preference for holistic or configurational entities, preference shifts from left to right as stimulus duration increases. A requirement in the stimulus to utilize pitch favors the right hemisphere. Further, when pitch is used to

[20] The terms "holistic," "configurational," and Gestalt-pattern all refer, in slightly different ways, to a complex, fully integrated unity in perception.

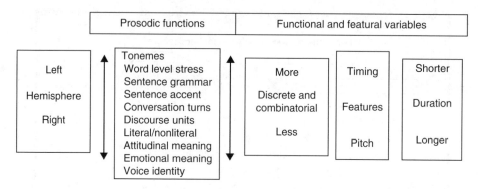

Figure 3.11   A model of cerebral processing of vocal signals in speech.

signal relatively holistic, affective, and/or familiar cognitive entities, such as musical chords, known voices, and emotional meanings in speech, right hemisphere processes are engaged.

At one end of this hierarchy (shown at the top of Figure 3.11), perception of linguistic tone, given that tonemes constitute discrete and combinatorial elements, is lateralized to the left hemisphere. Familiar voice patterns, in contrast, cannot be combined or permutated in the way that speech sounds can, and thus they fall at the other extreme of the functional hierarchy. Between these two extremes, other factors such as duration and linguistic-semantic content contribute to determining hemispheric specialization. Grammatical contrasts[21] such as question versus statement ("He chose the door on the left." "He chose the door on the left?") form a system of discrete elements, but they constitute a smaller set, are longer, and vary more in configurational shape than tones. Even though part of the structured language system, these properties may weaken their status as left-lateralized. Paralinguistic[22] uses of pitch and timing in conveyance of attitude and emotion are graded and continuous in that the higher and louder intonation corresponds iconically to level of emotion and/or attitude ("You saw the teacher?" "You SAW the *TEACH*ER??!!"), likely drawing on right hemisphere specialization. Conventional uses of prosodic elements in cueing literal versus nonliteral meanings ("I hit the sack" can have a literal or an idiomatic meaning), and pragmatic aspects such as conversational turns (vocal signals in speech through timing, intensity and pitch that the speaker is yielding the floor to another speaker) and sentence accent ("She gave John the book"; "She gave John the book") have an ambiguous status between structured and graded. In these cases, hemispheric contributions cannot be strictly predicted and are not known. Voice is the most patterned and unitary, and the most predictably taken up by right hemisphere preferences. These functional allocations of voice quality to linguistic and paralinguistic purposes are further discussed in Chapters 8 and 9.

---

[21]   Linguistic use of vocal contrasts is discussed in detail in Chapter 8.
[22]   Paralanguage refers to meanings in language not restricted to the words and grammar, including attitudes, emotions, and connotations.

3.3 Summary and Conclusion for Audition

Audition is accomplished by biological structures and processes that are similar across many species, all dedicated to transforming acoustic components into psychological entities of meaning in the animal's life. This meaningfulness is dependent on how a given species has evolved to utilize sound in its social setting. All material, heard as a sound, is informed and generated by interwoven streams of intensity and fundamental frequency, coded as temporal signals. These heavily transformed original building blocks are further worked over by cortical sensory and cognitive associations, which in turn may undergo different operations imposed by hemispheric modes of processing. In humans, with respect to vocal communication, this coded auditory material appears as contrasts at various functional levels of language, which signal phonological, grammatical, semantic, and pragmatic aspects, as well as conveying the very large array of personal information carried in each voice.

4

Physical Characteristics and the Voice: Can We Hear What a Speaker Looks Like?

4.1 Introduction

The sound a particular speaker produces ultimately depends on the physical characteristics of that speaker's sound-producing anatomy. It follows that as our physical characteristics change with maturation and aging, how we sound also changes, and physical differences between speakers may be reflected in consistent differences in how they sound. Because of the linkage through the speech chain between physical characteristics and perceived voice quality, listeners often treat voice quality as a cue to a speaker's physical characteristics, and make judgments about physical size, sex, age, health, appearance, racial group, or ethnic background, based on the sound of a voice. Such judgments are common on the telephone, and are actively exploited in animation and radio advertising, where voices are the only cue available to the speaker's physical attributes.

Studies of the extent to which listeners can judge a speaker's physical characteristics are common in the voice literature, in part because of the inherent interest of the topic. Physical characteristics like size, sex, and age are biologically important, and the manner in which such information is transmitted (or manipulated) has important biological and evolutionary implications. Understanding what physical changes are perceptually important, and which do not produce noticeable changes in a person's voice, could provide insight into social relations of many kinds. Finally, such studies also have substantial applied interest. Such knowledge could guide the development of clinical treatments for voice disorders. Understanding the acoustic markers of age, physical size, and gender could improve the flexibility and quality of voice synthesis; and understanding the accuracy with which listeners judge a speaker's physical characteristics could aid in profiling criminals known only from voice recordings, or enhance the accuracy and relevance of court testimony (see Chapter 7 for forensic perspectives).

Foundations of Voice Studies: An Interdisciplinary Approach to Voice Production and Perception,
First Edition. Jody Kreiman and Diana Sidtis.
© 2013 Jody Kreiman and Diana Sidtis. Published 2013 by Blackwell Publishing Ltd.

An additional attractive feature of studies linking speakers' physical characteristics to their voices is that it is relatively straightforward to design and interpret such studies. A speaker's physical characteristics can be measured easily and accurately. Although the problem of measuring voice quality remains, at least one side of the equation relating voice to a speaker's characteristics is knowable, making it easier to interpret a listener's perceptual responses. For example, it makes more sense to ask "Can listeners hear differences in age?" if we know the ages of the speakers in question. This situation contrasts with the perception of personality and emotional state from voice. In these cases, we do not know if difficulties in specifying vocal cues to emotional states have arisen because listeners cannot perceive a speaker's emotions accurately, or because emotions are difficult to define and measure precisely. This issue will be discussed in more detail in Chapter 9.

The present chapter describes the perception of a speaker's age, sexual characteristics, racial or ethnic background, and appearance (height, weight, and facial characteristics) from voice. Each section begins by reviewing the physical differences that underlie any perceived differences, and then proceeds to examine the kinds of judgments listeners can make, and the manner in which they extract personal information about speakers from voices. In this way, we will investigate the acoustic elements that make speakers sound young or old, male or female, fat or thin, and the manner in which those cues relate to the physical characteristics that accompany these biological divisions and changes.

Two important distinctions should be borne in mind throughout the following discussion. First, as described in Chapter 1, authors often distinguish *learned* from *organic* markers of a speaker's characteristics. This distinction separates the things a speaker can manipulate (whether consciously or unconsciously) from the things that follow necessarily from anatomy and physiology. Organic markers have the potential to provide listeners with "honest" cues to the attribute in question, and thus are of particular interest in studies that focus on animal behavior, as we will see in what follows. Secondly, we distinguish *markers* of a characteristic from *stereotypes* of that characteristic. Markers of a characteristic are reliable cues to that characteristic; stereotypes are attributes or combinations of vocal attributes that listeners *expect* to hear from a speaker who possesses certain physical attributes (although speakers do not necessarily produce sounds with these characteristics). As we shall see below, social expectation influences listeners' judgments, and may determine in part what vocal behaviors children learn as they grow.

4.2 Age and the Voice

The sixth age shifts
Into the lean and slipper'd pantaloon,
With spectacles on nose and pouch on side,
His youthful how, well sav'd, a world too wide
For his shrunk shank; and his big manly voice,
Turning again toward childish treble, pipes
And whistles in his sound.

William Shakespeare, *As You Like It*, II.7. 157–163.

From birth to death, humans undergo a number of radical biological changes, many of which leave traces in their voices. These traces can often be detected by listeners, who use this information to assess the speaker's age. As a demonstration, listen to audio samples 4.1 to 4.8, and estimate each speaker's exact age. Correct responses are given in Table 4.4 at the end of this section, and the guesses of a group of 35 listeners are plotted as a function of the speaker's true age in Figure 4.2.

4.2.1   Changes in vocal physiology from birth to childhood

A number of outstanding reviews of the development of the respiratory system, larynx, and vocal tract have been published. In particular, Kent and Vorperian (1995) and Zemlin (1998) provide many details omitted from the following brief summary.

At birth the respiratory system is poorly developed. The lungs are very small (although they almost completely fill the thorax), but they grow rapidly during the first year of life, increasing up to six times in volume. The density of elastic fibers in the lungs also increases during the first years of life, and the elastic recoil of the lungs increases correspondingly. The angle of the ribs is more horizontal in infants and small children than in adults, so children are unable to pivot their ribs very much to increase the volume of the chest cavity. Because of these combined factors, small children generally rely primarily on the diaphragm and on elastic recoil forces, rather than on intercostal activity, for respiration (see Boliek, Hixon, Watson, and Morgan, 1996, or Hoit, Hixon, Watson, and Morgan, 1990, for review).

The larynx is also poorly developed at birth, and consequently control of phonation is poor. A newborn's larynx is high in its neck, at about the level of the 3rd or 4th cervical vertebrae (Tucker and Tucker, 1979). (Adult larynges lie at the level of the 5th cervical vertebra; see section 4.2.2.) The thyroid cartilage and hyoid bone are attached to each other, but separate after birth. The angle of the thyroid cartilage is similar in male and female infants (about 110 degrees in males, and 120 degrees in females), and stays the same until puberty. A newborn infant's vocal folds are tiny, usually about 2.5–5 mm long (although reported lengths are in the range 2.5–8 mm; see Kent and Vorperian, 1995, for review), and the folds are very immature at birth. Fibers are poorly developed, tissue layers are not differentiated, and there is no vocal ligament (Ishii, Yamashita, Akita, and Hirose, 2000).

Because infants' larynges are high in their necks, the supralaryngeal vocal tract does not provide a very good resonating cavity. This limits the extent to which infants could produce the sounds of adult speech, even if they were cognitively up to the task. The tongue is broad and flat, and nearly fills the oral cavity. Infants can move their tongues, jaws, and soft palates, but motions are specialized for suckling rather than for speech, and other motions cannot be well controlled, again limiting their ability to produce the sounds of language (see Kent and Vorperian, 1995, for extensive review). Infants' lack of teeth provides a final limit to their overall range of possible articulations.

From birth to puberty, the vocal tract and respiratory system grow and mature at approximately the same rate as the rest of the body. Patterns of development for males and females are very similar until puberty begins, but acoustic evidence (in particular, consistent sex-related differences in formant frequencies) points to the emergence of sexual dimorphism in the vocal tract in children as young as four years of age (Vorperian and Kent, 2007), and by age seven or eight, boys have consistently lower formant frequencies than girls. (Differences in F0 do not appear until about age 12.) Existing physiological data do not completely explain this difference in formant frequencies, because sex-dependent differences in overall vocal tract length do not exist for these young children (Vorperian *et al.*, 2005). However, recent results from studies using modern vocal tract imaging techniques have shown that significant differences in the *width* of the vocal tract emerge by age two (Vorperian *et al.*, 2009). While these results are preliminary, they suggest that more detailed measurements of the development of the vocal tract may account more fully for the observed acoustic differences between boys' and girls' voices.

By age seven or eight the respiratory system has reached its adult configuration, which changes very little until old age. In the larynx, the hyoid bone (which is cartilaginous at birth) starts to ossify by two years of age. The vocal ligament begins to develop by age four, although initially it is thin and its fibers are arranged loosely. The mucosa is thick in infants, and the superficial layer of the vocal folds does not differentiate until about the age of between three and five years (Hirano, Kurita, and Nakashima, 1983). This explains in part the hoarse vocal quality exhibited by many young children (including the speaker in audio sample 4.2): Normal (adult) vocal fold vibration cannot occur in the absence of the layered structure of the folds, which allows the cover of the folds to ride over the stiffer body. The intermediate and deep layers of the lamina propria do not begin to differentiate until between six and 15 years of age, and are not fully differentiated until age 16 or later. Full maturation of the larynx does not occur until about age 20.

An infant's fundamental frequency at birth is around 500 Hz. Average F0 drops as the larynx grows with age, and decreases to about 275 Hz by age eight. By age six, the vocal folds have grown to about 8 mm in length (Verhulst, 1987; cited by Kent and Vorperian, 1995). F0 range stays the same throughout childhood – about 2.5 octaves – but control improves as the larynx matures physiologically and neurological control develops. (See Vorperian and Kent, 2007, for review.)

4.2.2   Changes in voice with puberty

Prior to puberty, males and females do not differ in the size of their larynges or the overall length of their vocal tracts (Kahane, 1978, 1982; Fitch and Giedd, 1999; Eckel *et al.*, 1999), although the ratio of oral cavity size to pharyngeal cavity size may differ even in young children (Vorperian and Kent, 2007). When puberty begins, both sexes undergo major growth spurts, but the patterns of growth diverge for males and females.

In girls, the vocal tract and larynx continue to grow in proportion to the rest of the body. The vocal folds grow up to 34% in length, reaching an adult size of 12–21 mm. The vocal tract of an average adult female measures about 144 mm in length (Fitch and Giedd, 1999). In males, the vocal organs change in proportions as well as in absolute size. The pharyngeal cavity in males increases in size relative to the oral cavity, and the entire vocal tract grows to an average length of about 156 mm. The larynx also increases dramatically in size. The vocal folds in males grow up to 60%, to an

Table 4.1 Acoustic changes in voice with aging.

Infants/Children	Adults < 60	Adults > 60
F0 is high; male/female differences emerge	F0 decreases with age	F0 decreases with age for females, but increases for males
Pitch range is wide; remains constant after infancy	Pitch range fairly constant	Pitch range fairly constant, but center frequency may shift downward
Formant frequencies are high; male/female differences begin to emerge by age 4	Formants frequencies lower; large male/female differences in formants	Formant frequencies continue to lower
Control of phonation is poor; hoarseness	Phonation is stable	Phonation becomes somewhat less stable; hoarseness/breathiness
Control of loudness is poor	Good control of loudness	Loudness may increase or decrease
Speaking rate is slow initially, but increases with age	Fast speaking rate	Speaking rate declines (due to more frequent breaths)

adult length of 17–29 mm.[1] Most of the difference in growth between males and females is in the membranous part of vocal folds; the arytenoid cartilages (and thus the cartilaginous part of the glottis) grow at very similar rates.

These physical changes are accompanied by large changes in the acoustic characteristics of the voice (Table 4.1). Fundamental frequency decreases with growth in both sexes, largely due to increases in vocal fold length. Development of the vocal ligament also increases the stiffness of the vocal fold somewhat; however, changes in vocal fold length are much larger and generally offset the effects of changing stiffness on F0. The average fundamental frequency in females drops to about 220 Hz by adulthood. Male voices drop about 1 octave in fundamental frequency, to an average of about 130 Hz by age 18 (Titze, 1994).

Males also undergo voice mutation ("change in voice") as a result of laryngeal growth. Although mutation is highly variable and can last up to three years (Hollien, Green, and Massey, 1994), the process usually begins between ages 11 and 14, and lasts between eight and 26 months (with an average duration of about 18 months). During this time, the angle of the male thyroid cartilage decreases to about 70–85 degrees. (The angle remains fairly constant in females throughout life; see Zemlin, 1998, for review.) This narrowing, combined with the disproportionate growth in the membranous part of the vocal folds, results in the protrusion of the apex of the cartilage, called the thyroid notch or "Adam's apple." The bulk of the thyroarytenoid muscle also increases, and the vocal folds thicken and change shape as a result (for

---

[1] The wide range of reported vocal fold lengths may be due in part to racial differences. Reported values for Japanese males range from 17 to 21 mm, compared with 23–25 mm for Caucasian males; values for Japanese females range from 11 to 15 mm, compared with 17 mm for Caucasian females. See Kent and Vorperian (1995) for review and discussion.

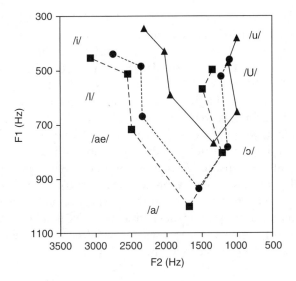

Figure 4.1 Average formant frequencies for vowels produced by children (filled squares), women (filled circles), and men (triangles) (data from Peterson and Barney, 1952, and Hillenbrand *et al.*, 1995). Values of F1 increase from top to bottom on the y axis; values of F2 increase from right to left on the x axis. Thus, data from children (with the smallest vocal tracts and consequently the highest formant frequencies) are below and to the right of adult data.

example, Harries, Walker, Williams, Hawkins, and Hughes, 1997; Harries, Hawkins, Hacking, and Hughes, 1998). This causes important changes in *how* the vocal folds vibrate, in addition to the changes in F0 that occur as the folds increase in length and mass. As the vocal folds thicken, the glottis becomes more rectangular in shape. Because of this change in glottal shape, glottal closure during phonation can be achieved over a greater portion of the vocal fold, and thus over a greater portion of a vibratory cycle. When more of the vocal fold tissue is set into vibration, with greater overall amplitude, a richer harmonic structure results. This change in the spectrum of the voice corresponds to the change in vocal quality we hear as voice change (Titze, 1994). Rapid change in the size and configuration of the vocal folds also causes pitch breaks (sudden, unwanted shifts between modal and falsetto phonation) in male voices as males learn new muscular patterns to control the new shape of the vocal folds. This process is analogous to a person who becomes clumsy for a while after a period of rapid growth. Male singers may also develop frequency "gaps" – ranges of F0 that they cannot produce – although overall F0 range may remain fairly constant (Willis and Kenny, 2008).

The larynx moves lower in the neck throughout life, both in males and in females. By age five it is at about the level of the 4th cervical vertebra; by age 18 it is at the level of the 5th cervical vertebra (Verhulst, 1987; cited by Kent and Vorperian, 1995). As the larynx moves lower, the shape and size of the cavities above the larynx change, and formant frequencies change accordingly. Figure 4.1 shows average formant frequencies for children, women, and men. Across vowels and sexes, formant frequencies average about 16% higher in children than in adults (Peterson and Barney, 1952; Hillenbrand, Getty, Clark, and Wheeler, 1995; see also Vorperian and Kent, 2007). Vowel durations also decline for both sexes until about age 12 as children start to speak faster and faster (Lee, Potamianos, and Narayanan, 1999).

Finally, vocal intensity in children is very similar to that of adults. Physiologically, this is somewhat surprising: Given that children's vocal folds are significantly smaller that those of adults, we might expect them to have quieter voices (although any parent can tell you this is not true). Children generate loud voices by using very high lung pressures – 50–60% greater than those of adults (Stathopoulos and Sapienza, 1993b). Thus, they must work much harder than adults to achieve the same loudness, and require more frequent breaths to sustain their efforts. This is one reason why children's speech is characterized by short phrases relative to adult speech. Because F0 tends to increase with increased lung pressure, children also have difficulty making pitch and loudness changes independently.

4.2.3   The aging voice

Under normal conditions, the larynx, respiratory system, and articulatory system remain fairly stable throughout adulthood. After about age 60, however, changes begin to accumulate throughout the vocal system. (See Linville, 2001, or Kent and Vorperian, 1995, for extended reviews of age-related changes in voice.) Scholars have argued about the reasons for studying such changes. Many claim that it is important to understand how voices age normally, so that common, expected changes can be distinguished from changes due to disease processes. In contrast, Woo, Casper, Colton, and Brewer (1992) argued that changes in voice quality due solely to aging are minimal, and that most voice disorders in older people occur subsequent to disease, not to normal aging. Among the 151 elderly voice patients studied, only six had laryngeal findings consistent with age alone; in the majority of cases a significant medical condition caused the voice problem. Similarly, Hagen, Lyons, and Nuss (1996) found that 30% of voice complaints in their clinical practice were related solely to aging, with the rest deriving from an underlying medical condition. More recent studies have linked vocal aging to general aging processes throughout the body, in an attempt to separate genetic and environmental factors in aging. From this perspective, voice provides a unique window on the aging process, because normal voice production depends on the intactness of both neuromuscular and connective tissues, which may be differentially sensitive to genetic versus environmental factors (see, for example, Ramig *et al.*, 2001, for review).

With increasing age, respiratory support for phonation alters as the cartilages between the ribs ossify and the ribcage becomes more rigid, making respiration less efficient. Collagen fibers in the lungs become cross-linked, and the lungs become progressively less flexible. These changes combine after age 60 to produce a decrease in the vital capacity of the lungs to 2.4–2.7 liters compared with 3.5–5.9 liters in young adults (see Zemlin, 1998, or Linville, 2001, for review). Finally, muscles degenerate and neuromuscular control decreases with increasing age, affecting fine control throughout the respiratory and phonatory systems.

The larynx continues to lower in the neck throughout life. This continued lowering may be due to ongoing growth, or to atrophy of strap muscles and/or stretching of the ligaments that support the larynx in the neck. The thyroid and cricoid cartilages usually begin to ossify in the 20s, and the arytenoids ossify in the late 30s; the entire larynx is usually ossified by age 65. The timing and extent of ossification varies widely across individuals, and it is not clear how it affects voice quality.

With advancing age, changes occur in the vocal folds as well. In some women after menopause, edema may thicken the vocal folds somewhat (Hirano *et al.*, 1983). Because of edema in the mucosal cover of the vocal folds, the cover becomes more loosely coupled to the body of the folds. This results in complicated patterns of vibration, and may lead to hoarseness. Degenerative changes also occur in the folds in both sexes. The number of elastic fibers decreases, while collagen fibers in the deeper layers of the folds increase in number and become cross-linked (Hirano, Kurita, Yukizane, and Hibi, 1989). These changes further alter the mechanical properties of the vocal folds, and are often more marked in men than in women.

Atrophy can occur in all the intrinsic laryngeal muscles (including the thyroarytenoid) with increasing age, reducing their mass and contractile strength. These changes again occur much more commonly in males than in females (see Ramig *et al.*, 2001, for review). Atrophy in the thyroarytenoid muscle can cause bowing by pulling the medial surface of the vocal folds laterally. Bowing produces a weaker, breathier-sounding voice, and is the most common vocal problem in older speakers, particularly in males. Studies have also documented decreases in the speed and force of contraction of the thyroarytenoid with age, along with reduced endurance (see Thomas, Harrison, and Stemple, 2008, for extended review of the effects of aging on the thyroarytenoid muscle). The incidence of glottal gaps increases with age in men, but not in women. Along with bowing, connective tissue atrophy may also contribute to incomplete glottal closure. As the vocal muscles atrophy, the folds become thinner, which may contribute to increasing fundamental frequency, particularly in men, and to increasing levels of jitter and shimmer. Loss of teeth or bone can alter the shape and function of the supraglottal vocal tract, reducing articulatory precision and altering vocal resonances.

Finally, an array of neurological conditions, including those associated with normal aging, may produce a decrease in a speaker's ability to control phonation precisely. Adults over 60 have significantly fewer myelinated fibers in the recurrent laryngeal nerve than do adults under 60, as well as fewer nerve fibers overall in the superior laryngeal nerve and recurrent laryngeal nerve (although large interindividual differences exist; Tiago, Pontes, and do Brasil, 2007). Decreases in the number and size of superior laryngeal nerve fibers with age may result in decreased control of F0 and loudness due to loss of fine control of the stiffness and length of the vocal folds (Thomas *et al.*, 2008), and neurological conditions may cause increasing vocal tremors. Some disease processes, especially those affecting the basal ganglia of the brain, lead to motor speech disorders which may also affect laryngeal control (see Weismer, 1997, for review). Adding insult to injury, efforts to compensate for age-related vocal changes may produce other vocal problems. For example, attempts to lower pitch may produce a gravelly or strained vocal quality.

4.2.4   Aerodynamic and acoustic changes with aging

The many physical changes that accompany aging have aerodynamic and acoustic consequences that affect voice quality. In general, male speakers over 70 years of age expend
a greater percentage of their lung volume on each syllable spoken, and produce fewer
syllables per breath, than do speakers under 25 (Hoit and Hixon, 1987). This may
occur as a secondary effect of age-related changes at the glottis: The presence of a glottal gap may result in inefficient laryngeal valving, which in turn may increase air use
during phonation (Linville, 2001). Older women do not differ significantly from
younger women in patterns of airflow through the glottis. This may occur because
female speakers somehow compensate for age-related changes in laryngeal function,
or because such changes have no significant impact on phonation in healthy older
women (Sapienza and Dutka, 1996). However, older female speakers do differ more
from one another in their patterns of airflow than younger speakers, who are relatively
consistent as a group (for example, Goozee, Murdoch, Theodoros, and Thompson,
1998; Sapienza and Dutka, 1996). In fact, increased variability in most acoustic, aerodynamic, and physiological measures of speech is the hallmark of the aging voice, and
increased between-speaker variability may account in part for the general failure to find
consistent differences between older and younger female speakers in measures of subglottal pressure, glottal resistance, vocal efficiency, or other measures of vocal function.

Acoustic changes in voice with aging are summarized in Table 4.1. Most studies
have examined changes associated with old age, using measures associated with F0.
Note that data about such changes with age are almost always derived from cross-
sectional studies, rather than from longitudinal studies (see Russell, Penny, and
Pemberton, 1995, for an exception), so that differences between individuals are
confounded with differences due to aging. This reduces the likelihood of losing all
one's subjects before the end of the study and makes it possible for an investigator to
complete a study in a single lifetime. However, such a strategy necessarily introduces
the possibility that speaker groups differ in some way other than age. In particular,
cultural trends may contaminate efforts to estimate aging effects in cross-sectional
studies. For example, mean F0 for all women as a group has decreased since 1945
(Pemberton, McCormack, and Russell, 1998), so differences between younger and
older women in F0 may be related to the generation they come from, rather than to
aging. Careful matching of subjects and use of large groups of speakers can minimize
such possibilities. Of course, it is impossible to keep everything except time constant
in a longitudinal study, and differences within a single individual over time may be due
to changes in health, alterations in regional accent due to moves, variability in
emotional state, or a thousand factors other than aging. Thus, neither kind of study
in isolation can fully answer the question of which vocal changes are due solely to
normal aging (see Hollien, Hollien, and de Jong, 1997, for review).

With these caveats in mind, some estimated F0 values for speakers of different ages
are given in Table 4.2. (Estimates are approximate because the effects of aging are
confounded by the effects of smoking and alcohol – both associated with lowered
F0 – on speakers' voices in many older studies; see Hollien *et al.*, 1997, for review).
Longitudinal data using archival recordings showed average decreases in mean F0 for
female speakers of about 13 Hz in 30 years (Decoster and Debruyne, 2000). In a

Table 4.2 Approximate mean F0 values for speakers of different ages. Values in boldface are for nonsmokers; values in parentheses are from studies that combined smokers and nonsmokers. Data from Saxman and Burk, 1967; Stoicheff, 1981; Hollien, 1995; Linville, 1996.

Age	20	40	50	60	70	80	90
Males	(120)	(110)	(105)	(110)	(120)	(130)	(140)
Females	**220** (195)	**210** (190)	**200** (180)	**200** (175)	**200** (175)	**200** (175)	(175)

second longitudinal study of female speakers (Russell *et al.*, 1995) F0 decreased about 45 Hz over 50 years (from a mean of 229 Hz to a mean of 184 Hz). Cross-sectional data also suggest that F0 in adult females decreases slowly but continuously with age. In males, F0 also decreases with age until about age 50, after which F0 apparently increases on average (Hollien and Shipp, 1972). In females, decreases in F0 are probably related to increased vocal fold mass due to edema, loss of muscle tone, ossification, and/or hormonal changes. It is less clear why F0 increases for elderly males. Increases in pitch after age 60 may be an artifact of the cross-sectional experimental design usually employed, as discussed above; or F0 may increase due to increased stiffness of the vocal folds or vocal fold atrophy. One might also expect pitch range to decrease with increasing age, due to declining phonatory efficiency and flexibility, but it is not clear that this happens. For women, range remains fairly constant but shifts downward. Results for males have varied, with some authors reporting declining pitch ranges with age, and others finding no age effects on range (see Linville, 2001, for review).

Older speakers as a group differ significantly from young and middle-aged speakers in overall amounts of F0 variability. One might also expect increasing levels of jitter and shimmer with increasing age, due to decreased motor control, impaired respiratory function, and/or degeneration in laryngeal tissues. These have not emerged for women. Older women's phonation may be less consistently stable than that of younger women, but no significant overall differences have been observed (Linville and Fisher, 1992). Phonatory stability does seem to decrease with increasing age for males, but differences between speakers may relate in part to the speaker's physical condition. Ramig and Ringel (1983) measured F0, jitter, shimmer, and F0 range for 48 male speakers in three age groups (25–35, 45–55, 65–75), in good or poor physical condition. Phonatory stability in these speakers was related as much to physical condition as it was to age. Voices of subjects who were more physically fit showed less jitter, less shimmer, had a better frequency range, and consistently sounded younger than subjects in poor condition. Differences were most pronounced for the oldest subjects.

As the larynx continues to move lower in the neck throughout life, formant frequencies decrease as the supraglottal vocal tract increases in length. Such effects may be sex-specific, although results have varied from study to study. For example, Rastatter, McGuire, Kalinowski, and Stuart (1997) reported significant differences in formant frequencies during continuous speech for old versus young males, but not for females. In contrast, Linville and Rens (2001) found greater lowering of spectral peaks in connected speech for females than for males, although differences occurred for both sexes. The authors suggested that women may undergo more vocal tract lengthening with aging than males do; alternatively, elderly men may compensate for laryngeal lowering by altering their tongue position during vowels more than women do. Results may also interact with the tendency of women of all ages to produce "neat" articulation, as discussed in the next section. Thus, effects of aging on vocal tract resonances probably represent an interaction between the speaker's sex, the physiological effects of laryngeal lowering, and articulation.

Few data are available regarding changes in vocal loudness with advancing age. Effects again appear to depend on the sex of the speaker. Average vocal intensity apparently increases with age for males over 60 (Ryan, 1972), but not for women (Morris and Brown, 1994b). The maximum intensity a speaker can achieve does decline with age for both sexes (Ptacek, Sander, Maloney, and Jackson, 1966). Hearing loss complicates the issue of intensity regulation in old age: Speakers with hearing losses may have difficulty monitoring their vocal loudness, independent of any changes in laryngeal or respiratory function.

Speaking rates (see Sidebar) do decrease with advanced age, although some studies have reported effects of speaker sex, regional accent, and style of speech (reading versus spontaneous speech) on results (for example, Mysak and Hanley, 1958; Ryan, 1972; Shipp, Qi, Huntley, and Hollien, 1992; Quené, 2008; see Jacewicz, Fox, and O'Neill, 2009, for review). Linville (2001) posits several explanations for the decline in speaking rates for males, including aging of the neuromuscular system (which could disrupt articulatory patterns; for example, Weismer and Liss, 1991), respiratory decline (resulting in the need to take more frequent breaths; Shipp *et al.*, 1992), and a general decline in cognitive processes (resulting in difficulties with word retrieval, information processing, and formulation of utterances). Limited experimental data indicate that older speakers (aged 75–85 years) do in fact produce fewer syllables per second than younger speakers (aged under 60), but also take more breaths per utterance resulting in more total pause time within a single utterance (Shipp *et al.*, 1992). When pauses are eliminated from consideration, articulation rates are about 11% faster for adults aged 20–34 than for adults aged 51 to 65 (Jacewicz *et al.*, 2009). Few data are available on speaking rates in elderly women. Published results have varied, with some studies reporting decreases in rate with age (Oyer and Deal, 1985) and some indicating that elderly women's speech rates remain steady (Hoit, Hixon, Altman, and Morgan, 1989).

Sidebar:　Speaking Rates

Speaking rates, usually expressed in words per minute (WPM), are influenced by many factors, including speech task (reading versus monologue), the speaker's age, whether the speaking partner is foreign or native, friend or stranger, young or old. Mean values derived from measurements of 180 subjects were 172.6WPM for conversation and 188.4WPM for reading the Rainbow Passage (Walker, 1988; cited in Kent, 1994). Rates vary considerably with regional and sociological dialect; for example, US Midwestern rates are slower than the speech of New Yorkers. Values for ordinary conversation have been placed between 130–200WPM. Recommendations for reading books aloud for recording are 150–160WPM (Williams, 1998).

Table 4.3 Perceptual characteristics of speakers in different age groups (adapted from Hartman and Danhauer, 1976).

Speaker's perceived age	Pitch	Articulation	Rate	Quality
20–30 years	High	Precise	Fast	Clear
30–40 years	Low	Precise	Slow	Clear
40–50 years	High or low	Imprecise	Slow	Hoarse
50–60 years	Low	Imprecise	Slow; long pauses	Breathy, hoarse

Finally, some authors (for example, Ramig, 1986) have suggested that older speakers systematically alter their articulatory and resonance patterns – in essence, that some changes in vocal characteristics with aging are learned, rather than deriving solely from physiological changes. Given the importance of age in Western culture, it is not impossible that speakers do learn unconsciously to signal (or conceal) their ages with their voices. While studies on this topic have been limited (see Linville, 2001, for review), the suggestion is an interesting one deserving further study. We will return to the issue of vocal signals of group membership shortly.

4.2.5   Perception of age from voice

Authors studying the perception of age from voice have addressed a wide range of rather different questions. The first category of study concerns the characteristics of voices that are perceived as coming from speakers of different ages. Such studies examine the features that characterize a voice that sounds old, versus one that sounds young, regardless of the speaker's true chronological age. For example, Hartman and Danhauer (1976; Hartman, 1979) asked 40 naive listeners to estimate the chronological ages of 46 speakers, aged 25–70. They then informed 24 expert listeners of the mean perceived age for each voice, and asked the experts to write down descriptions of the voices in each perceived age decade. Perceptual features for voices in each decade are summarized in Table 4.3. Speakers with slower speaking rates were perceived as older (cf. Harnsberger, Shrivastav, Brown, Rothman, and Hollien, 2008). Hoarseness, roughness, increased breathiness, and decreases in the precision of articulation also corresponded to increases in perceived age (cf. Honjo and Isshiki, 1980). Voices that were perceived as old were also described as harsh, strained, tremulous, reduced in loudness, and hesitant. Listeners also consistently associate low pitch with old age, despite reported increases in F0 with age in men, suggesting the presence of vocal stereotyping. Further, note that changes in voice are perceived as occurring at much younger ages than they in fact do. This suggests that listeners may tend to underestimate the exact ages for older speakers, again due to vocal stereotyping. We return to this possibility below.

Although many listeners may agree rather well about what a young or old speaker *should* sound like, a second question we might ask about listeners' judgments of age from voice is whether such judgments are accurate. How well can a listener estimate a speaker's age, just from listening to a voice sample? Three different experimental

Table 4.4   Correct ages for speakers 4.1 to 4.8.

Audio sample	Speaker's correct age	Mean guessed age
4.1	25	26.4 years
4.2	3	8.7 years
4.3	70	56.0 years
4.4	46	29.0 years
4.5	41	38.1 years
4.6	7	6.5 years
4.7	11	11.4 years
4.8	85	62.1 years

tasks have been used to address this question. Listeners have sorted speakers into two categories (young vs. old); they have been asked to guess, to the nearest decade, the ages of the speakers (20s, 50s, etc.); and they have been asked to guess the speaker's precise age. Categorization, the simplest task, is not as easy as one might expect. For example, Ptacek and Sander (1966) recorded prolonged vowel samples from young (mean age = 21) and old (mean age = 75) speakers, but listeners were able to identify a speaker's age group with only 78% accuracy (where chance = 50% correct). Accuracy was only 51% (where chance = 33% correct) when young listeners were asked to sort vowels produced by young, middle-aged, and old speakers into the appropriate category (Linville and Fisher, 1985). When listeners are asked to guess the decade of a speaker's age or to guess exact ages, they consistently underestimate the ages of older speakers and overestimate the ages of younger speakers (for example, Shipp and Hollien, 1969; Ryan and Capadano, 1978; Cerrato, Falcone, and Paoloni, 2000). Accuracy of precise age guesses varies considerably from study to study. Shipp and Hollien (1969) reported that age guesses from a spoken sentence were often, but not always, accurate within five years. Ryan and Capadano (1978) reported correlations between true and guessed ages of 0.93 for female speakers and 0.88 for males when listeners heard two sentences of speech. In contrast, Neiman and Applegate (1990) reported that age guesses from sentence stimuli ranged from 14 to 31 years for speakers whose true chronological ages were between 20 and 25, and from 50 to 95 for male speakers whose true chronological ages were between 70 and 75 years. Based on these data, they argued that correlational analyses may overstate listeners' true abilities. Like decade assignments, exact age estimates are always characterized by regression toward the mean, with younger ages consistently overestimated and older ages underestimated. Some evidence suggests this is partly an interaction with the age of the listener. For example, younger listeners tend to underestimate speakers' ages, whereas older listeners tend to overestimate ages somewhat (Braun, 1996).

   Table 4.4 lists the correct ages of the speakers in audio samples 4.1 to 4.8, along with average guesses of 35 UCLA undergraduates who also judged the ages of these speakers. Like the data above, these listeners underestimated the ages of the older speakers, and overestimated the ages of the youngest speakers. The range of age guesses is also very large for most of these speakers (Figure 4.2). In particular, several listeners thought that the youngest speaker (audio sample 4.2) was among the oldest,

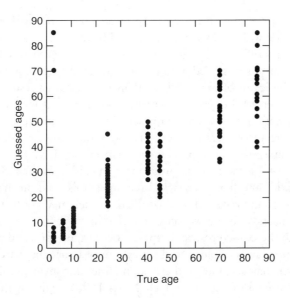

Figure 4.2　Age guesses for speakers 4.1 to 4.8.

presumably due to the speaker's hoarseness and imprecise articulation, which can characterize speech for both children and elderly adults. Data are less variable for the other child than for the older speakers, at least in part because floor effects limit the range of possible guesses below the true age. This is not the case for older speakers, for whom age guesses can range above or below the true value (because these are possible ages for humans), resulting in much more response variability from listeners.

The discussion in this section and the audio examples have highlighted many possible cues to a speaker's perceived age, including speaking rate, F0, breathiness or hoarseness, vocal tremors, vocal tract resonances, and articulatory precision. The question that remains is which of these many possible cues listeners actually use when making their judgments of age, and how these cues explain the variable accuracy of the guesses. Studies of this topic have used categorical rather than continuous estimates of age. For example, Shipp *et al.* (1992) recorded samples of continuous speech from males from three perceived age groups (27–35, 53–57, and 75–85), and then determined which acoustic characteristics predicted group membership for each voice. Both fundamental frequency and speech rate data were good predictors. Mean F0 separated each group of speakers from the others, because listeners consistently associate low pitch with old age, as discussed above. Speakers perceived to be old also differed from perceptually young and middle-aged speakers in total speaking rate and in breath pause time; vocally young speakers differed significantly from perceptually old and middle-aged speakers in the number of syllables produced per second. The decline in overall speaking rate may be the most important indicator of perceived aging in a voice (cf. Helfrich, 1979).

In a study of the cues to perceived age in female voices, Linville and Fisher (1985) asked listeners to judge age from whispered and normal vowels produced by 75 women aged 25–35, 45–55, and 70–80, and then examined which acoustic characteristics were related to these judgments. Perceived age increased as variability in F0 increased, but age estimates increased with decreasing mean F0 (so that voices with lower F0 sounded older). For whispered samples, where F0 was absent, speakers perceived as old had lower values of F1 (suggesting a longer vocal tract) than did other speakers. No such correlation was observed in normally phonated speech, indicating that F0 is a much stronger indicator of perceived age than are vocal tract resonance frequencies. Presence of vocal tremor also leads to perception of increased age, although increased jitter and shimmer are not associated with perceived age (Linville and Fisher, 1992).

Consider the wrong answers listeners gave to audio samples 4.1 to 4.8. As mentioned above, hoarseness and imprecise articulation may have led some listeners to judge that speaker 4.2 (who is three) was in fact an elderly woman. Speaker 4.3 (who is 70) speaks rapidly, and her voice lacks breathiness or creak; but her pronunciation of /s/ is somewhat imprecise. These conflicting cues may contribute to the wide range of age estimates, as listeners focus on different attributes.

Consistent with these discrepancies between social expectation and actual voice characteristics, vocal portrayals of older adults by younger actors and actresses are typically stereotyped, rather than accurate, and are often rather unconvincing. For example, the film *Edward Scissorhands* (Burton and Di Novi, 1990) begins with actress Winona Ryder as a grandmother telling a bedtime story about her youth to her grandchild. In contrast to the voice she uses as a teenager, her grandmotherly voice is extremely hoarse and very quiet, almost whispered. She uses a very slow speaking rate combined with very short phrases and audible inhalations, but there is relatively little change in F0 relative to her youthful voice. The exaggerated hoarseness and slowness, combined with the unchanged F0, give the impression of a woman who is not particularly old, but who is quite ill or seriously depressed. The film *Citizen Kane* (Welles, 1941) features a number of male characters who age as the story progresses, but again depiction of changes in voice with aging is rather simplistic. These imitations of the aging voice sound somewhat like young men caricaturing older ones, although the visual images ameliorate the effect. For example, when actor Orson Welles first appears as a young Charles Foster Kane, his voice is characterized by an extremely fast speaking rate, clear articulation, and large, frequent variations in loudness. As his character ages, the most significant changes in voice are substantial reductions in speaking rate and in loudness, and a decrease in variability. Depiction of age and emotion are difficult to disentangle in this film; in some scenes, Welles's older voice seems a bit breathier or more hoarse than his younger one; F0 is also slightly lower, and his voice sounds more monotone, but these effects are attributable to the emotional content of the scenes as much as to aging (Chapter 9).

4.3   Sex and the Voice

Sexual dimorphism (physical differences between the males and females of a species) is a basic organizing principle of mammalian biology. An individual's sex is one of the most important aspects of that person's identity, and voice is an important way in which males and females identify each other. Many animal species, including big brown bats (Kazial, Masters, and Mitchell, 2004), baboons (Rendall, Owren, Weerts, and Hienz, 2004), and harp seals (Van Opzeeland and Van Parijs, 2004), use voice in this way. Among humans, misidentifications of a speaker's sex are embarrassing and upsetting for all parties, in some cases so much so that older men may seek a physician's help in lowering their vocal pitch to prevent such misidentifications. Similarly, male patients with some kinds of severe voice disorders can speak fluently if they use falsetto, but in general this strategy is avoided because of the misleading or ambiguous information it provides about the speaker's sex.

This section explores the vocal characteristics that mark a speaker as male or female, and the uses listeners make of this information when they distinguish male voices from female voices. As an introduction, listen to the voices in audio samples 4.9 to 4.20, and label each as male or female. Correct answers are given in Table 4.5 at the end of this section.

4.3.1   Physiological, aerodynamic, and acoustic differences between male and female voices

Sex-based differences in laryngeal and vocal tract physiology were introduced in Chapter 2. To review quickly, the vocal tract of an adult female is on average about 15% shorter than a man's (Fitch and Giedd, 1999). Most of this difference is due to differences in the size of the pharynx, which is disproportionally longer in males than in females (Nolan, 1997; Vorperian and Kent, 2007). A man's larynx is about 20% larger than a woman's; the length of the membranous part of the vocal folds differs in men and women by about 60% (Kahane, 1978; Hirano *et al.*, 1983; see Titze, 1989, Rendall *et al.*, 2004, or Fitch and Giedd, 1999, for review). The layered structure of the vocal folds is quite similar in men and women, although hormonal changes in older women may produce edema that changes tissue viscoelasticity (Titze, 1989).

As a result of these physiological differences, male and female voices differ obviously and saliently in fundamental frequency (and correspondingly in perceived pitch). Mean F0 for men and women differs by about an octave. Although considerable variability occurs (and reported means vary as well), male voices have an average F0 of about 130 Hz, and female voices have an average F0 of about 220 Hz (for example, Peterson and Barney, 1952; Hollien and Paul, 1969; Horii, 1975; Hillenbrand and Clark, 2009). For example, F0 for the low-pitched female voice in audio sample 4.2 is 202 Hz; and F0 for the male voice in audio sample 4.3 is 130 Hz. These differences are sufficient to distinguish males from females statistically with about 96% accuracy (Hillenbrand and Clark, 2009). Differences in vocal fold length account for most of the difference between men and women in F0. Rendall *et al.* (2004) note that differences in F0 between sexes greatly exceed their difference in overall body size, suggesting that vocal fold length in male humans has evolved as a dramatic exaggeration that serves as a secondary sexual dimorphic characteristic distinguishing adult males from prepubescent males and females (see also Fitch and Giedd, 1999).

Sidebar: Hormones and the Voice

The mammalian larynx is a hormonal target organ, and fluctuations in sex hormone levels affect laryngeal function throughout life. Growth of the larynx and the emergence of sexual dimorphism at puberty are hormonally triggered: In adult humans, F0 ultimately depends on the amount of testosterone present in late puberty, which determines laryngeal size and vocal fold length (Harries *et al.*, 1997, 1998). The absence of androgens at puberty leads to development of a female voice, while the presence of androgens (at any time, in either sex) leads to the emergence of male vocal characteristics. Virilizing agents can cause permanent lowering of women's vocal pitch, presumably due to increases in the mass of the vocal folds that occur with such treatment (Baker, 1999). In college-aged males, higher levels of testosterone are weakly but significantly associated with lower-pitched voices (Dabbs and Malinger, 1999; Evans, Neave, Wakelin, and Hamilton, 2008).

In females at menopause, decreased levels of estrogen can lead to thinning of the mucosa of the vocal folds, consistent with changes in other estrogen-receptive organs. However, the vocal significance of these changes appears to depend on the demands a particular user places on her voice. Although F0 declines with aging, as described above, serious vocal complaints are common only among professional voice users (see Abitbol, Abitbol, and Abitbol, 1999, for review).

The effects of hormone fluctuations across the menstrual cycle are less evident. In some women, fluctuations may lead to changes in the structure of the mucosa just prior to ovulation; increases in mucous secretions may add jitter and shimmer to the voice (Higgins and Saxman, 1989); or changes in progesterone levels may lead to tissue dryness prior to menstruation. Some professional voice users have reported vocal fatigue and reduced loudness at these times (Abitbol *et al.*, 1999); however, acoustic studies suggest that differences in vocal function across the menstrual cycle, if they exist, are probably below the level that is perceptually significant (Silverman and Zimmer, 1978; Wicklund *et al.*, 1998; Chae, Choi, Kang, Choi, and Jin, 2001; Ryan and Kenny, 2009; cf. Chernobelsky, 2002, who reported that changes in phonation across the menstrual cycle were much more noticeable in professional voice users who used vocally-abusive techniques).

A number of studies have examined the effect of oral contraceptive use on voice. Because oral contraceptives create a stable hormonal balance across the menstrual cycle, one might expect a positive or neutral effect on voice quality to occur with pill use (Van Lierde, Claeys, de Bodt, and van Cauwenberge, 2006). Studies using current-generation oral contraceptives have shown no effects of pill use on voice acoustics or perceived vocal quality (Amir, Biron-Shental, and Shabtai, 2006), even among professional voice users (Amir and Kishon-Rabin, 2004; Amir, Biron-Shental, Tzenker, and Barer, 2005; Van Lierde *et al.*, 2006). The only observed effect of pregnancy on voice (measured shortly prior to delivery) was a decrease in the maximum duration of sustained phonation, presumably because growth of the fetus limits diaphragm motion (Hamdan, Mahfoud, Sibai, and Seoud, 2009). For a comprehensive review of the effects of hormones on voice, see Amir and Biron-Shental (2004).

Although the layered structure of the vocal folds is similar for both sexes (Titze, 1989), differences between males and females occur in the pattern of vocal fold vibration as well as in the rate of vibration. Many (but not all) women's vocal folds open and close smoothly, in a quasi-sinusoidal fashion, while men's folds tend to close more quickly than they open, producing an asymmetrically shaped source pulse in the time domain (Titze, 1989). This can be seen by comparing the glottal pulse in Figure 4.3a (a normal male voice source) with those in Figure 4.3b and c (two pulses from the

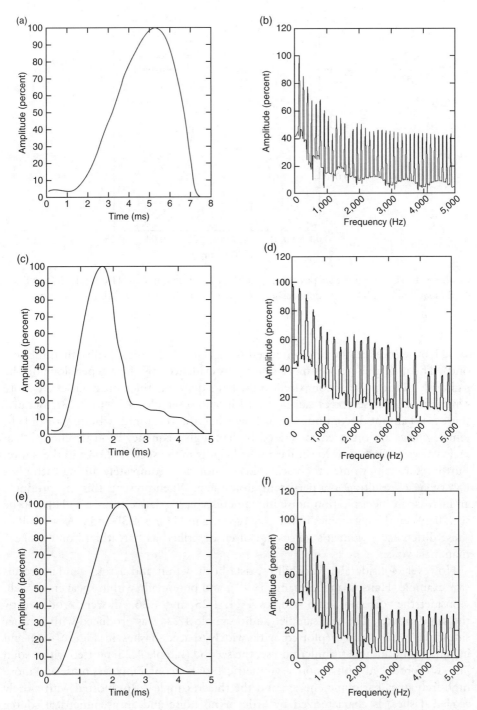

Figure 4.3 Source pulses and source spectra for normal speakers. (a) A single source pulse from a normal male speaker. (b) Spectrum of the source pulse in A. (c) A single source pulse from a female speaker with an efficient vocal source. (d) Spectrum of the source pulse in C. (e) A single source pulse from breathy voice produced by the same female speaker. (f) Spectrum of the source pulse in e.

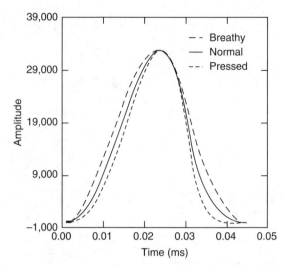

Figure 4.4. Glottal pulse shapes corresponding to audio samples 4.24 (closely dashed line), 4.25 (solid line), and 4.26 (widely dashed line). Units on the y axis are arbitrary.

same female speaker, the first produced with a breathier voice quality than the second). The male pulse closes more sharply, as evidenced by the steeper slope on the right side of the pulse as compared to the left side, while the female pulses are more symmetrical. (These voices can be heard in audio samples 4.21 to 4.23.) Because there is no abrupt discontinuity in airflow when the vocal folds vibrate sinusoidally, female voices are often characterized by less high frequency acoustic energy than male voices, indicated by lower harmonic heights in the spectra shown in the figure. Further, for many women the vocal folds do not close completely during each phonatory cycle, resulting in a persistent glottal gap. When present, this gap produces an increase in the aspiration noise in women's voices relative to men's. This can be seen between the harmonics in the voice spectra in Figures 4.3b and f. As a result of these differences, women's voices are often described as "breathier" or "weaker" than male voices.

However, considerable variability exists both within and across gender groups (for example, Hanson and Chuang, 1999), and potentially within speakers as well. Consider the voices in audio samples 4.24, 4.25, and 4.26. All were produced by the same speaker. The first sample (audio sample 4.24) was produced with a rather sinusoidal voice source (plotted with widely spaced dashes in Figure 4.4) and includes quite audible turbulent noise; the second (sample 4.25; plotted with a solid line) was produced with a more asymmetrical source containing less noise and more high-frequency harmonic energy; and the third (sample 4.26; plotted with closely spaced dashes) is characterized by little or no noise and an asymmetrical source with a relatively long closed phase. The sources of this kind of variability in the female voice source (which are not physiologically necessary) will be discussed in section 4.3.5 below.

Men and women also differ in patterns of frequency variation. Women's intonation is often described as "more dynamic" than men's: A number of authors have reported that women use a wider pitch range and change pitch more sharply, while men's voices are typically more monotone (for example, Fitch and Holbrook, 1970; Stoicheff, 1981; Hudson and Holbrook, 1981; Graddol and Swann, 1983). Received wisdom states that women (particularly younger women) also use rising, question-like intonation on statements ("uptalk") more often than men do, and rising pitch contours have been associated with more effeminate speech in males (Terango, 1966). (Note, however, that recent personal observations suggest that use of rising intonation on statements is spreading throughout the population, at least in Southern California where such contours are frequently used by males and by older adults of both sexes. Uptalk is discussed further in Chapter 8.) Descriptions of female voices as "high pitched, shrill, over-emotional, and swoopy" have been disputed by Henton (1989), who argues that F0 ranges for male and female speakers are in fact the same when frequency range is expressed in logarithmic semitone units (which corrects for differences in F0, and may correspond to how the ear processes frequency), rather than in Hertz.[2] When published data were reanalyzed using the semitone scale, Henton found no differences between male and female speakers in pitch variability. However, a further reanalysis of these same data using the ERB scale[3] (which more precisely models the way the ear processes frequency) indicated that female voices in fact *are* characterized by more variability in pitch than are male voices (Daly and Warren, 2001). Daly and Warren further reported differences between males and females in "pitch dynamism" for a storytelling task versus a sentence-reading task (which was used in most of the studies reviewed by Henton, 1989), no matter which scale was used to measure frequency. They suggest that this more natural task elicited more usual behavior, and more pitch variability, from their female speakers.

Differences between men and women in vocal tract length and configuration produce differences in the resonances of the vocal tract. Formant frequencies are about 20% higher in females than in males (Figure 4.1; Peterson and Barney, 1952; Hillenbrand *et al.*, 1995), and resonances cluster closer together in male voices than in female voices (Nolan, 1997; Ey, Pfefferle, and Fischer, 2007). These differences statistically distinguish males from females, but with slightly less accuracy than does F0 (92% versus 96% correct classification; Hillenbrand and Clark, 2009). The spectra of fricative sounds like /s/ and /ʃ/ also have lower center frequencies for male speakers than for female speakers, again presumably due to the differences in vocal tract length (Schwartz, 1968; Stevens, 1998). Unlike F0, these differences are proportional to overall differences in body size between the sexes (Rendall *et al.*, 2004). Consistent formant frequency differences between boys and girls may also occur, suggesting that learning, differences in patterns of growth in specific regions of the vocal

---

[2] Frequency range in semitones is equal to $39.86 \log (\text{F0 max}/\text{F0 min})$.

[3] ERB stands for 'equivalent rectangular bandwidth'; $\text{ERB} = 1.67 \log (1 + f/165.4)$, where f = frequency in Hz.

tract (but not in overall length; Vorperian *et al.*, 2009), or a combination of these factors play an important role in this vocal attribute. For example, Bennett and Weinberg (1979) reported sex-related differences (in the direction of adult values) of about 16% in F1, and of about 10% in F2, for six and seven year olds.

Women's pronunciation is often described as more "precise" than that of men. Women tend to produce the rhetorically correct forms of words more often than men do; for example, women pronounce individual sounds more accurately ("thin" vs. "tin") and omit sounds less often ("ing" vs. "in"). In contrast, men often reduce or omit vowels and simplify consonant clusters by omitting some segments (Whiteside, 1999). Similar findings have been reported for a variety of languages in different cultures. For example, female speakers of Canadian French typically produce the /l/ in the words "il," "elle," "la," and "les" much more often than men do (Sankoff and Cedegren, 1971; cited by Smith, 1979). Many studies report that women are more intelligible than men (for example, Bradlow, Torretta, and Pisoni, 1996; Ferguson, 2004; Hazan and Markham, 2005). Differences between men and women in grammar, speech style, and vocabulary also have been reported (see Smith, 1979, for extended review). Finally, although women are widely assumed to be more talkative than men, men and women in fact speak about the same number of words (approximately 16,000) in a day (Mehl, Vazire, Ramirez-Esparza, Slatcher, and Pennebaker, 2007), and men and women speak equally fast, at least in informal conversation (Jacewicz *et al.*, 2009).

In summary, information about a speaker's sex is redundantly represented in speech signals. Cues may be found in both static aspects of steady-state phonation (like mean F0, overall spectral shape, and formant frequencies) and in dynamic features of connected utterances (pitch contours, speaking rate, and details of pronunciation). Of these cues, F0 and formant frequencies are the most closely related to physiological differences between men and women, and combinations of these two acoustic features are statistically sufficient to classify voices as female or male with near-perfect accuracy (Bachorowski and Owren, 1999). Differences in F0 and formant frequencies are attributable to the disproportionate growth of the larynx and pharynx that occurs in males at puberty. The increase in vocal tract length in males may be an adaptation designed to give males more imposing, resonant voices – to exaggerate size, in other words – and differences in F0 may also have evolved to distinguish sexually mature males from younger males and females. Such adaptations are common among male mammals (Fitch and Giedd, 1999). The extent to which listeners actually rely on different cues to assign a sex to a speaker is the topic of the next section.

4.3.2   Recognizing an adult speaker's sex from voice

Table 4.5 gives the correct sexes for the speakers of audio samples 4.9 to 4.20. This exercise confirms the commonsense view that recognizing a speaker's sex from a brief voice sample – even from a single vowel – is usually, but not invariably, easy, and accuracy is always imperfect, especially when there is intent to deceive. Several of these voice samples were in fact intended to deceive. Sample 4.13 was produced by a male phonating in falsetto with the corners of his mouth retracted, which increased both

Table 4.5 Speaker sex for the voices in audio samples 4.9 to 4.20.

Audio samples	Speaker's true sex
4.9	Male
4.10	Female
4.11	Female
4.12	Female
4.13	Male
4.14	Male
4.15	Female
4.16	Female
4.17	Male
4.18	Male
4.19	Male
4.20	Female

F0 and formant frequencies, and sample 4.15 was produced by a female phonating at a very low F0, with pharyngeal expansion and a drastically lowered larynx, both of which shifted resonances into the male range. Such effects should not be surprising, given the plasticity of the human voice production mechanism, the multiplicity of ways in which sex is represented in voice, and the fact that values for F0 and formant frequencies overlap somewhat for males and females.

The ability to discriminate male from female voices emerges early in infancy. Infants as young as six months old are able to consistently distinguish male from female voices (Miller, Younger, and Morse, 1982). Children aged between six and nine can identify the gender of an adult's voice from a spoken (> 98% correct) or whispered vowel (about 79% correct) as accurately as an adult can (Bennett and Montero-Diaz, 1982). Published data confirm that recognizing an adult speaker's sex from a brief voice sample is usually (but not always) accurate. In fact, information about a speaker's sex seems to be highly robust in the presence of acoustic distortion, consistent with the multiplicity of cues available to listeners. Table 4.6 presents data from a number of studies in which panels of adult listeners judged the sex of adult speakers under a variety of experimental conditions. Accuracy of sex recognition from voice remains good even when the speaker produced a single /s/ or /ʃ/ or a whispered vowel, when stimuli were filtered to remove much of the acoustic signal, or when stimuli are less than two phonatory cycles in duration. As stimuli increase in length and complexity, they contain more (and more kinds of) acoustic information, including pitch contours and more details about pronunciation; and (not surprisingly) sex recognition scores increase accordingly. When stimuli are as long as a syllable, judgments are consistently near 100% accurate.

A number of studies have reported that male voices are "easier to recognize" than female voices, in that listeners typically assign male voices to the correct category more often than they do female voices (for example, Coleman, 1971; Lass, Hughes, Bowyer, Waters, and Bourne, 1976; Bennet and Montero-Diaz, 1982; Perry, Ohde, and

Table 4.6   Accuracy of sex recognition for adult speakers and listeners hearing different kinds of stimuli.

Stimuli	Recognition accuracy	References
Voiceless front fricative (f, th)	55%–71.5%	Ingemann (1968); Schwartz (1968)
Voiceless central fricative (s, sh)	72.5%–91.5%	Ingemann (1968); Schwartz (1968)
Whispered vowel	75%–97.5%	Ingemann (1968); Lass *et al.* (1976); Schwartz and Rine (1968)
2 cycles of phonation	appx. 80%–90%	Owren *et al.* (2007)
Low-pass filtered vowel	91%	Lass *et al.* (1976)
Vowel	96%–100%	Lass *et al.* (1976, 1979)
Monosyllabic word	99%	Lass *et al.* (1979)
Bisyllabic word	95%	Lass *et al.* (1979)
Low-pass filtered sentence	97%	Lass *et al.* (1980)
Backward sentence	99%	Lass *et al.* (1978)
Sine wave replica of a sentence	≈ 83%	Fellowes, Remez, and Rubin (1997)
Sentence	98%–100%	Lass *et al.* (1979, 1980)

Ashmead, 2001). An alternative explanation for such findings is that they represent response biases. Consider the following exaggerated example. Listener A hears a series of voice samples, and is asked to judge whether the speakers are male or female. He cannot hear any differences among the voice samples, but because he is forced to make a selection, he responds "male" to every sample. Because of this strategy, he achieves a score of 100% on the trials where the voice is in fact that of a male speaker, and a score of 0% when the voice is that of a female speaker. The experimenters conclude that for the class of voices under study, maleness is easy to perceive and femaleness is impossible to perceive. However, it should be obvious that this listener is performing at chance, achieving a correct response on only 50% of the total trials. This listener's apparently perfect performance on male voices is merely the result of a bias in favor of responding "male."

The *theory of signal detection* (for example, Green and Swets, 1966; Macmillan and Creelman, 2005) provides statistical methods for estimating listeners' perceptual acuity independent of the influence of response biases in favor of one category or the other. In this framework, listeners' responses can fall into one of four categories. If a signal is present (a "signal" trial), and listeners respond "signal present," they score a *hit*. If a signal is present but listeners do not detect the signal, they score a *miss*. If a signal is absent (a "noise" trial) and they respond "present," they score a *false alarm*; and if no signal is present and they respond "signal absent," they score a *correct rejection*. (In studies of voice, which of the two response choices – male or female; old or young – is designated "signal" and which is designated "noise" is an arbitrary decision.) Hit rates and false alarm rates can vary independently of one another, because they reflect scores on different classes of trials: Hit rates reflect the number of correct responses on "signal" trials, and false alarm rates reflect the number of incorrect responses on "noise" trials. As above, a hit rate of 100% can be achieved by the simple strategy of responding "signal present" on every trial. However, this strategy also

Table 4.7   Cues to a speaker's sex.

Cue	Female Speech	Male Speech
Mean F0	Averages about 220 Hz	Averages about 110 Hz
F0 dynamics	More variable; more rising pitch contours	More monotone; more falling pitch contours
Vocal tract resonances	Higher in frequency	Lower in frequency
Speaking rate	May be slower	May be faster
Articulation	More precise	Less precise

provides a false alarm rate of 100%. A 0% false alarm rate can be achieved by responding "signal absent" to every trial; but this strategy will also result in a hit rate of 0%. Thus, examining either parameter alone gives an incomplete picture of listeners' actual ability to distinguish the response categories. However, the ratio of hits to false alarms provides a more reasonable measure of performance. (Many other, more sensitive measures of performance are available; see, for example, Swets and Pickett, 1982, or Macmillan and Creelman, 2005, for discussion.)

When published data on the perception of sex from voice are re-evaluated in a signal detection framework, it seems possible that the consistent finding that maleness is "easier" to perceive accurately than femaleness reflects a social bias in favor of responding "male" when a signal is ambiguous with respect to sex. However, because response bias and accuracy can be separated in the signal detection model, it also remains possible that an accuracy advantage could exist simultaneously with a response bias in favor of male voices. For example, it is possible that male quality is somehow "marked" biologically because it only emerges if testosterone is present at sufficient levels during puberty, so that a male voice represents a deviation from the straight line of vocal development. This markedness might make it easier for listeners to identify male voices than female voices, because presence of low F0 and formant frequencies in the male range unambiguously signals a male voice, while higher F0 and formant frequencies could represent a female speaker, a prepubescent male, or a male whose voice has not changed completely (Owren, Berkowitz, and Bachorowski, 2007). Although most experimental designs employed to date in studies of sex perception from voice have not adequately separated response biases from response accuracy, Owren *et al.* (2007) reported that listeners are in fact more accurate in "male" judgments even when response biases are taken into account. These results follow from the asymmetries that occur in development of the voice production mechanism, and underscore the usefulness of biological explanations in the study of voice perception (without which the prediction that maleness is easier to hear is somewhat counterintuitive).

The primary cues to an adult speaker's sex are summarized in Table 4.7. When asked to describe stereotypically male and female voices, listeners responded that they expect male voices to be deep, demanding, and loud, and female speakers to have good enunciation, high pitch with substantial dynamic variation, and a fast and variable speaking rate (Kramer, 1977). These results suggest that listeners potentially exploit the full range of information available to them when they judge a speaker's sex from a voice sample. However, studies of the cues listeners use when judging a speaker's sex have utilized a rather simple set of cues, focusing mostly on the relative contributions of F0 and formant frequencies to perceived maleness or femaleness, possibly because these acoustic attributes are linked closely to physiological differences in body size and vocal fold length, as discussed above. Early studies separated the contributions of F0 and formant frequencies by having male and female speakers produce vowels using an electrolarynx as the vibrating source instead of the larynx. This device (which is sometimes used by laryngectomized individuals) produces a buzzing sound at a constant frequency. When held against the neck, it provides an acoustic source that excites the vocal tract in place of laryngeal vibrations. Examples of voices generated with an artificial larynx are given in audio samples 4.27 and 4.28. The speaker of the first sample is a female; the second is a male. F0 in both cases is 70 Hz (which is low even for a male voice). Despite the constant low F0, it is easy to distinguish the speakers by sex, although it is harder to determine sex from each sample heard out of the context of the other (particularly for sample 4.27). Note also that (due to the female speaker's higher frequency vocal tract resonances) the voice in audio sample 4.27 sounds higher pitched than that in audio sample 4.28, despite the fact that F0 is constant for both speakers.

Experimentally, this alternative sound source makes it possible to combine the fundamental frequency of one sex with the vocal tract of the other, although the resulting stimuli are monotone and sound highly unnatural (as audio samples 4.27 and 4.28 demonstrate). In one such study, Coleman (1971) asked male and female speakers to read a short passage using an electrolarynx with a steady F0 of 85 Hz. Given the unambiguous combination of a very low F0 and male formants, listeners easily identified male speakers as male; but the low F0 apparently influenced listeners somewhat in favor of "male" responses, so that female voices were identified correctly only 79% of the time. Thus, formant frequencies (even combined with uncontrolled cues like articulatory precision and speaking rate) did not predict listeners' responses, confirming the importance of F0 in perception of a speaker's sex. A subsequent study (Coleman, 1976) suggested that F0 alone is also inadequate to unambiguously specify a speaker's sex. In this study, males and females whose vocal tract resonances were extreme for their sex again produced speech, this time with an electrolaryngeal source of 120 Hz or 240 Hz. Although the speakers' natural fundamental frequencies were good predictors of perceived sex, combining either artificial source with the opposite vocal tract resulted in a voice that sounded male. (Response biases or the unusual nature of the stimuli may also have contributed to this result.) Thus, although F0 may be the main cue to a speaker's sex, it is neither the only cue nor a sufficient cue when other conflicting information is present. Additional details (for example, pitch contours) are apparently required to disambiguate stimuli created by mixing F0 and resonance cues.

More recent studies have applied speech synthesis rather than electrolarynges, but continued the strategy of mixing and matching male and female vocal tracts and fundamental frequencies. For example, Whiteside (1998) synthesized 10 short vowels (50–100 msec long), mixing and matching the voice sources and vocal tracts of three male and three female speakers. She found that in general mean F0 was the best predictor of the perceived sex of the hybrid stimuli, usually overriding the vocal tract resonance information. However, in some cases the presence of a marked drop in F0 at the end of a stimulus could produce a vowel that sounded male even when mean F0 was more typical of a female, suggesting dynamic information about patterns of pitch also plays an important role in the perception of a speaker's sex. Similarly, Hillenbrand and Clark (2009) found that perception of most (but not all) male and female voices could be shifted in sex by scaling both F0 and formant frequencies up and down, respectively. Modifying either F0 or formants alone had a much smaller effect; and effects were smaller for sentence stimuli than for syllables, pointing to the importance of prosodic and/or articulatory cues in sex recognition.

Similar (but much longer) synthetic stimuli are included in audio samples 4.29 to 4.36. Audio samples 4.29 and 4.30 are synthetic copies of natural male and female voices saying the vowel /a/. Audio sample 4.31 is a synthetic voice created with the male source from audio sample 4.29, and the female vocal tract from audio sample 4.30; and in audio sample 4.32 the female source from audio sample 4.30 has been combined with the male vocal tract from audio sample 4.29. In all of these first four stimuli, the pitch contour is level. Finally, the voices in audio samples 4.29 and 4.30 have been resynthesized with falling intonation contours (often associated with perceived male voice quality) in audio samples 4.33 and 4.34, and with rising pitch contours (associated with female voice quality) in audio samples 4.35 and 4.36. All stimuli created with a male source (samples 4.29, 4.31, 4.33, and 4.35) sound unambiguously male regardless of the vocal tract employed, although those that have a female vocal tract sound as if they might have come from a smaller or younger male than the original male sample. Stimuli created with a female voice source but a male vocal tract are ambiguous with respect to the "speaker's" sex, and sound neither particularly male nor convincingly female. Although the falling F0 contour in stimulus 4.34 does perhaps increase the masculinity of the voice, overall these stimuli are consistent with Whiteside's finding that when both resonance and F0 information are present, F0 is usually a stronger cue to sex than resonances are.

In summary, recognizing an adult speaker's sex from continuous speech is usually easy, presumably because of the large variety of pitch, resonance, articulatory, and intonational cues present in longer stretches of speech. Studies of sex recognition from vowels suggest that mean F0 is a necessary, but not necessarily sufficient, cue to an adult speaker's sex. Formant frequencies and patterns of F0 variation interact with mean F0, resulting in ambiguous stimuli or even overriding the F0 information (as audio samples 4.34 and 4.35 particularly demonstrate).

4.3.3   Recognizing the sex of children's voices

The problem of sex recognition is even less simple for the voices of children. As described in Section 4.2.1, only limited differences in vocal anatomy or physiology between boys and girls have been demonstrated prior to the onset of puberty, although acoustic data predict that such differences should exist (Vorperian and Kent, 2007). In fact, listeners are often able to determine the sex of very young children from rather short voice samples, indicating that sex is robustly represented in children's speech (although the sex of an infant cannot be accurately determined from its cries, even when the cry samples are as long as 15 seconds; Murry, Hollien, and Muller, 1975). Typical results are given in

Table 4.8   Accuracy of sex judgments from children's voices by adult listeners.

Speaker's age	Stimulus	Correct sex recognition	Study
3–5 years	2 minute sample	79%	Meditch (1975)
4 years	vowel	64.5%	Perry *et al.* (2001)
5–6 years	30 sec sample	74%	Weinberg and Bennett (1971)
6–8 years	whispered vowel, vowel, sentence	66%, 65%, 70% respectively	Bennett and Weinberg (1979)
7–9 years	vowel, sentence	55–65%; 74% respectively	Perry *et al.* (2001); Gunzburger *et al.* (1987)
12 years	vowel	69%	Perry *et al.* (2001)
16 years	vowel	97%	Perry *et al.* (2001)

Table 4.8. As this table shows (and as audio samples 4.2 and 4.6 confirm), listeners recognize the sex of a child at above chance levels, but not perfectly. Accuracy remains fairly constant until puberty, when it increases sharply; and accuracy also increases somewhat when listeners hear a sentence as compared to a vowel.

Attempts to identify the cues listeners use in making these judgments suggest that children learn to speak like girls or boys, but that the characteristics that mark them as male or female vary. The fact that sex can apparently be identified as accurately from a whispered vowel as from a voiced vowel (Bennett and Weinberg, 1979) suggests that formant frequencies are a sufficient cue to a child's sex; and formant frequencies may differentiate the voices of boys and girls as young as four (Sachs, Lieberman, and Erickson, 1973; Busby and Plant, 1995; Perry *et al.*, 2001; Vorperian and Kent, 2007). Differences between boys and girls in formant frequencies remain significant even when children are matched for physical size and weight, and thus may be attributed in part to learning, rather than solely to anatomy. Significant sex differences in F0 have been reported by age seven despite the lack of a physiological basis for such differences (Hasek, Singh, and Murry, 1980); however, other studies have reported that F0 differences do not emerge until age 12 or later (Busby and Plant, 1995; Perry *et al.*, 2001; cf. Sachs *et al.*, 1973, who reported that boys had significantly *higher* fundamental frequencies than age, height, and weight matched girls). In studies using longer stimuli (phrases or sentences), both articulatory and pitch cues have served to identify children as male or female, with males speaking more monotonously and females using more precise articulation, as adult males and females do (Bennett and Weinberg, 1979; Gunzburger, Bresser, and ter Keurs, 1987).

In conclusion, it appears that sexual dimorphism does not entirely explain listeners' ability to distinguish boys' voices from girls' voices. Although static cues like formant frequencies and F0 depend broadly on physiology in adults, sex-based differences in laryngeal physiology are minimal in children, and do not completely explain differences in F0 or in quality that are exhibited by girls and boys (although better measurement approaches and modern vocal tract imaging protocols may revise this picture in the future; Vorperian *et al.*, 2009). The lack of consistent differences between boys and girls in mean F0 is not surprising, given that children's control of F0 is relatively poor. In contrast, relatively simple articulatory techniques (spreading or pursing lips, for example) are available to manipulate vocal tract resonances. Because these articulatory adjustments are not difficult for children to implement, the more consistent finding that formant frequencies reliably distinguish the speech of boys and girls is also not particularly surprising. Differences between young boys and girls in dynamic, learned aspects of speech like patterns of frequency variability and details of pronunciation have also been observed. Thus, learning affects nearly every aspect of sex presentation from voice, and from a very early age.

4.3.5   Attractive voices, sexy voices, and reproductive fitness

Her voice was ever soft,
Gentle, and low, an excellent thing in woman.
> William Shakespeare, *King Lear*, V.3, lines 275–276

The large and perceptually salient differences that exist between male and female voices suggest that evolutionary pressures may have contributed to the development of vocal sexual dimorphism. Two possible mechanisms for the evolution of sexual dimorphism in the vocal tract have been proposed. First, females may perceptually use vocal signals during mate selection to assess the quality of a male (for example, Collins, 2000). Consistent with this view, a variety of animals use voice quality to signal reproductive fitness as part of the process of attracting mates. For example, the minimum formant frequencies produced by male red deer while roaring are good indices of fitness, because they provide accurate information about size to potential mates (Reby and McComb, 2003), and female red deer are able to hear changes in formant frequencies corresponding to the difference between a large and small animal (Charlton, Reby, and McComb, 2007, 2008). Similarly, in gray tree frogs the duration of an advertisement call has been shown to be a good index of genetic quality, and females greatly prefer calls of long duration (Welch, Semlitsch, and Gerhardt, 1998; cf. Burke and Murphy, 2007, who report that female barking tree frogs assess both call duration and call rates when selecting a mate).

A similar situation may have emerged during human evolution, although virtually all arguments are necessarily based on speculation and correlational data. In humans, bilateral physical symmetry (the extent to which one side of the body is identical to the other, for example with respect to the length of the fingers or the diameter of the wrist) is an inheritable marker of sexual and reproductive fitness, and ratings of vocal attractiveness are significantly correlated with measures of physical symmetry (Hughes, Harrison, and Gallup, 2002). This suggests that voice in turn is a good marker of speakers' genetic quality and thus of their potential fitness as a mate. Emerging evidence points to the ongoing importance of vocal quality in signaling reproductive fitness in modern humans (Locke and Bogin, 2006; Locke, 2008). The shoulder-to-hip ratio in men and the waist-to-hip ratio in women (both measures of reproductive fitness) are correlated with ratings of vocal attractiveness by the opposite sex, and listeners' ratings of vocal attractiveness are correlated with the speaker's level of sexual activity (Hughes, Dispenza, and Gallup, 2004). Further, female listeners are more sensitive than male listeners to the presence of frequencies below 220 Hz in male voices (Hunter, Phang,

Lee, and Woodruff, 2005), and are more sensitive to low frequencies in general around the time of ovulation (Haggard and Gaston, 1978). Because lower F0 is associated with higher levels of testosterone (for example, Evans *et al.*, 2008), these sensitivities could have evolved to help distinguish male from female voices, and adult from juvenile males (Hunter *et al.*, 2005; Feinberg *et al.*, 2006). Females prefer voices with lower F0, and voices for which F0 is concordant with vocal tract length, while dispreferring voices with low F0 but higher resonances (resembling an adolescent male voice; Feinberg, Jones, Little, Burt, and Perrett, 2005). Preferences for voices with low F0 vary across mating contexts as well as across the menstrual cycle: Low-pitched voices are judged more attractive in contexts that emphasize short-term liaisons, but F0 has little influence on attractiveness in the context of long-term, committed relationships. (This may occur because women sometimes associate low F0 with physical dominance and untrustworthiness in males, either of which can be costly in a long-term relationship; Vukovic *et al.*, 2010.) This difference is largest when women are fertile; and male F0 was significantly correlated with self-reports of mating success (Puts, 2005). These findings must be interpreted carefully—differences are often small, correlations relatively weak, and conclusions often depend on rather long chains of somewhat indirect reasoning, but cumulatively they are at least consistent with the notion that mate selections can be influenced to some extent by voice quality, so that female choice is a possible mechanism for the evolution of sexual dimorphism.

Sidebar: Why is F0 so Important?

F0 is the one vocal feature that can be counted on to emerge as an important cue in almost any study of voice, whether its focus is perception of age and sex, speaker recognition (Chapters 5 and 7), recognition of emotion and personality from voice (Chapter 9), or any other kind of judgment based on voice. It forms a valuable vocal cue for a number of reasons. First, human ears are very sensitive to changes in frequency. Young listeners can hear frequencies from 20 Hz to 20,000 Hz or more, and most people are able to distinguish differences in frequency of less than 2 Hz in the typical F0 range (100–500 Hz; see, for example, Gescheider, 1997, for review). Frequency information is also redundantly represented in acoustic signals. That is, listeners can determine F0 either from the fundamental frequency or through the spacing of the harmonics of the fundamental (whose frequencies equal whole number multiples of the fundamental). Thus, F0 information is robust against environmental noise (which may mask part of the voice signal) and hearing loss.

We are also able to control F0 very finely. The cricothyroid muscle (which tilts the thyroid and cricoid cartilages towards each other, stretching the vocal folds and altering F0) is innervated by its own nerve (the superior laryngeal nerve), allowing specific and precise adjustments to F0. Synergistic contractions of the thyroarytenoid muscle (which shorten the vocal folds and bulge them towards midline) also contribute to precise tuning of F0 (for example, Titze, 1994).

In addition to its virtues of robustness and flexibility, F0 provides a variety of at least somewhat honest cues to an individual's characteristics. Because it varies with physiology, it provides some information about an individual's overall physical size and physiological state. It also varies consistently with changes in respiratory status, neural activity/arousal, and articulation. Thus, F0 displays correlations with an individual's physical characteristics and internal state, but is also finely controllable and highly salient to listeners. These combined factors make it an ideal conveyor of information.

Finally, in that half of the world's languages that do not use lexical tone, F0 does not interact too much with referential meaning in the spoken message. However, even in nontonal languages, changes in F0 affect the connotation of the word or sentence – for example, emphatic versus neutral, happy versus sad, given versus new information, objective versus sarcastic, or ironic versus neutral (as discussed in Chapters 8 and 9).

A significant limitation of studies showing the overwhelming importance of F0 as a cue to a speaker's characteristics and internal state is the fact that almost all such studies have been conducted using speakers of English. Many of the world's languages do use F0 in the form of lexical tones (changes of F0 over the duration of the word, superimposed on the intonation contour of the sentence) to carry word-level meaning. These functions are described in Chapter 8. Little information is available regarding how lexical tone interacts with the speaker-indexical aspects of F0, if it does.

One interesting study investigated the development of women's preferences for different voices from childhood to adulthood. Saxton *et al.* (2006) argued that if vocal attraction is related primarily to mating behavior, then childrens' preferences should differ from those of adults; but if vocal attractiveness has some other primary function (social coordination, identifying allies ...), then preferences for specific voice types should remain fairly stable across age groups. Female listeners in three age groups (7–10, 12–15, 20–54) heard the voices of 12 males in pairs, and selected their preferred voice from each pair. Adolescent and adult listeners shared similar preferences (r = 0.87). Both liked voices with low F0, although the association was stronger for adults. In contrast, children preferred different voices altogether (r = 0.23), and their preferences were unrelated to F0. These findings suggest that young females are not very attuned to cues that reflect mate value. This kind of awareness apparently begins at puberty, but requires some time and experience to develop fully.

An alternative explanation for the emergence of sexual dimorphism in the vocal tract argues that vocal signals play a role in male dominance competition, with the mate going to the winner (for instance, Puts, Hodges, Cardenas, and Gaulin, 2007). In other words, it is possible that sexual selection pressures for vocal evolution are a large but secondary effect of the more general manner in which voice signals an individual's size and general fitness. For example, the rate and duration of "contest wahoo" calls made by male baboons reflect the male's competitive ability, with younger, more fit, higher-ranking males producing longer-lasting calls with higher F0. As a male falls in rank, F0 decreases and calls shorten, and formant dispersion decreased as animals decrease the mouth opening used to produce the calls (Kitchen, Fischer, Cheney, and Seyfarth, 2003; Fischer, Kitchen, Seyfarth, and Cheney, 2004).

This hypothesis of an indirect mechanism related to dominance displays for the development of dimorphism suggests three predictions about human behavior: (1) Males whose voices are low in F0 should be perceived as more dominant by other males; (2) male speakers should modulate their F0 depending on the relative dominance of their conversational partner when competing for "resources" (like a date with a female in the next room); and (3) males with lower F0 should report more mating success. Some evidence for these predictions has been reported (Puts, Gaulin, and Verdolini, 2006; Puts *et al.*, 2007). Changes in F0 and in formant dispersion affect perceived dominance, and a man with a low-pitched voice or closely-spaced formants is perceived as physically and socially dominant, although effects of formant dispersion on perceived dominance are greater than those of F0 (Puts *et al.*, 2007). When males converse with other males, the vocal pitch they use also depends in part on how the speakers view their relative status: Men who believe they are physically dominant to their competitor lower their pitch when talking to him, but men who think they are less dominant raise F0. (Changes are small – only about 4 Hz on average – but are perceptible.) Finally, men with lower F0 also reported higher rates of "mating success" than men with higher F0 (Puts *et al.*, 2007).

In conclusion, data support both the "female choice" and "male competition" explanations for the development of sexual dimorphism in voice. Because the effects of formant dispersion and F0 on men's dominance judgments are much larger than the effects on females' attractiveness judgments, it seems more likely that men's voices evolved to signal dominance to other men, and that women secondarily learned to prefer aspects of voice that convey information about mate quality. Although we can only speculate, one scenario consistent with modern behavioral data is that low voice pitch evolved because it increases mating success by increasing the aura of physical dominance (thus helping some men increase mating success by excluding others from "resources"), and because it influences female mate selection through association with heritable markers of reproductive fitness.

Although the evolutionarily based vocal cues to reproductive fitness are fairly subtle, media representations of sexy voices are another matter altogether. Among speakers of American English, attractive voices are usually described as resonant, low to moderate in average pitch, having good articulation, and without shrillness, nasality, or extreme pitch modulations (Zuckerman and Miyake, 1993). Perceptual data are not entirely consistent with these descriptions. For example, males generally prefer female voices with higher F0 to those with lower F0 (Feinberg, deBruine, Jones, and Perrett, 2008); and female French speakers found male voices significantly more pleasant when the speakers used rising pitch contours and lower overall F0, compared to monotone or falling contours (Bruckert, Lienard, Lacroix, Kreutzer, and Leboucher, 2006). When asked to speak in a sexy manner, most speakers (male and female) will reduce F0 (about 20 Hz on average), increase breathiness, and speak much more slowly than usual (Tuomi and Fisher, 1979). Most listeners have no difficulty associating these slow talking, low-pitched, soft, hoarse or breathy utterances with a message of sex appeal; and listeners agree reasonably well about which voices are attractive (Zuckerman and Driver, 1989).

Scholarly studies of sexy voice have focused on female speakers. Henton and Bladon (1985) noted that female speakers often phonate with a persistent glottal gap. Such a configuration may arise from anatomy, or could be caused by "intentional" incomplete adduction of the vocal folds. They speculate that this kind of phonation (which is not aerodynamically efficient and does not increase the intelligibility of the spoken message) may be used to communicate intimacy by imitating the sound of sexual arousal. Thus, they claim, stereotypically sexy female phonation may be part of a ritualized courtship display. Similar mechanisms may also operate in non-human animals. For example, in Barbary macaques female copulation calls are longer, slower, and higher in F0 when the female is most fertile, and playback experiments show that males can perceive and use this acoustic information to increase their reproductive success (Semple and McComb, 2000). F0 may also increase slightly in some human females during the most fertile portion of the menstrual cycle (Bryant and Haselton, 2009).

A more moderate view is that a sexy female voice is simply a voice that displays extreme amounts of female voice characteristics. Thus, stereotypically sexy voices like that of actress Marilyn Monroe are marked by extreme intonation contours, extra high pitch, extra breathiness, and an extra slow speaking rate. These characteristics represent Western cultural standards for a female voice, but are exaggerated. Of course, some sexy voices differ from this stereotype. For example, actresses Marlene Dietrich and Lauren Bacall were noted for their sexy voices, which differ from the stereotype above primarily in F0 (which is lower than average). This suggests that a distinction can be drawn (based mostly on F0) between the "childish" sexy voices belonging to speakers like Marilyn Monroe, and "mature" sexy voices.

Sexiness in male voices has not been studied in similar detail, although informal examination of stereotypically sexy male voices in the media suggests that similar cues (low pitch, slow speaking rate, breathiness) are in operation for both male and female voices. As mentioned above, lower F0 in males is associated with higher testosterone levels (Dabbs and Malinger, 1999; Evans *et al.*, 2008), and female listeners agreed very well that males with lower F0s were likely to be more attractive, more muscular, and have chest hair (Collins, 2000). Because pitch acts as a cue to sexual maturity and reproductive capability, female preferences for male voices with low fundamental frequencies are potentially adaptive. Using speech synthesis to manipulate F0 in natural voices, Feinberg *et al.* (2005; 2006; Vukovic *et al.*, 2010) found that male voices with a lower F0 are more attractive to females than the same voice with a higher F0, and that females prefer such "masculinized" voices more when they are fertile than during non-fertile phases of the menstrual cycle. Male voices whose F0 and formant frequencies were raised to mimic pre-pubescent male voices were perceived as less attractive than older-sounding male voices. Similarly, Riding, Lonsdale, and Brown (2006) reported that voices resynthesized with F0 equal to 1.3 times the original value were significantly less attractive to female listeners than the same voices with their original F0 or F0 equal to 0.7 times the original value. These results suggest that voice in fact does serve as a secondary sexual characteristic, and that attractive male voices are those that reflect full sexual maturity. Interestingly, prepubescent females do not consistently prefer voices with low F0, as noted above. Reliable associations between F0 and perceived vocal attractiveness emerge at adolescence, and strengthen into adulthood as women develop and learn to assess mate fitness, consistent with this interpretation (Saxton *et al.*, 2006).

Patterns of voice use also predict males' success at seduction (defined rather charmingly as succeeding in arranging a second meeting with a female; Anolli and Ciceri, 2002). Seduction in this sense begins with a display phase to attract the female's attention. Voice in this phase is characterized by higher pitch, increased intensity, and faster speech rates relative to the speaker's baseline phonation. This "exhibition voice" is gradually modified by lowering pitch, decreasing volume, and decreasing pitch variability as the interaction proceeds to a "self-disclosure phase." Speech rate remains high or even increases as the seductive interaction proceeds, but pitch variability decreases consistently with time. Males who modulated their voices in this manner were successful in arranging subsequent meetings with their female conversational partners, while males who did not vary their voice across the interaction were not successful.

In a different approach to male voice quality, Avery and Liss (1996) examined the acoustic characteristics of voices that were perceived as sounding either more or less masculine. In this study, 35 female listeners rank-ordered the voices of 37 men in terms of the masculinity of voice. A high fundamental frequency alone was not enough to make speech sound less masculine. Instead, dynamic aspects of the voice proved better predictors of perceived masculinity. Voices judged less masculine were characterized by more extreme and faster pitch variations, more rising intonation contours, and more accurate articulation (all of which have been associated with female speech, as noted above). Less-masculine sounding voices also had higher formant frequencies and higher-frequency fricative spectra than did more-masculine sounding voices, consistent with shorter vocal tracts. These last differences might have resulted from lip retraction, the authors speculate: In essence, the less-masculine sounding speakers may have spoken with a smile.

4.3.6   Sexual orientation and vocal quality

The study of how (or if) listeners perceive a speaker's sexual orientation from voice provides another example of competing hypotheses regarding the social and/or physiological origins of differences in perceived voice quality. Pierrehumbert, Bent, Munson, Bradlow, and Bailey (2004) described three hypothetical sources of differences between the voices of gay and lesbian speakers and straight (heterosexual) speakers. Differences may derive from biologically determined differences in anatomy; they may occur due to differential attention to male or female models as the child acquires language; or they may arise as a socially learned means of signaling group membership. As with other topics in this chapter, studies have fallen into two general categories: Studies of the accuracy with which listeners can determine a speaker's underlying sexual orientation, or studies that ask listeners to assess the extent to which a speaker sounds gay or lesbian or straight (without regard to the speaker's true orientation) and then examine the cues listeners use to make their judgments and the consistency among listeners.

To date, studies of relationships between sexual orientation and vocal quality have focused almost entirely on the voices of openly gay male speakers of American English. Results from these studies suggest that listeners can assess sexual orientation, at least to some extent. For example, Linville (1998) played recordings of five openly gay and four straight men to listeners, who were able to distinguished them correctly about 80% of the time. More recently, Smyth, Jacobs, and Rogers (2003) used a set of 25 speakers (17 gay and eight straight) to examine listener accuracy as a function of speaking style. With this larger set of speakers, sexual orientation was correctly judged only 68% of the time overall. 45% of gay speakers did not sound gay, while 28% of straight speakers were perceived as gay. This percentage increased to 35% when the speaking task involved reading a scientific passage, which may have elicited a more formal speaking style. These results underscore the heterogeneity of the population with respect to speaking style: Many gay men do not sound particularly gay, and many straight men employ features of stereotypically gay speech at least occasionally.

Little agreement has been achieved about the cues listeners use to classify a speaker as gay or straight (see Munson, McDonald, DeBoe, and White, 2006, or Munson and Babel, 2007, for extensive review). Early studies focused on voice fundamental frequency, possibly on the assumption that gay males "imitated" female voice quality, and thus should display higher pitch, greater breathiness, and more pitch modulation than straight males (Gaudio, 1994). Data have not supported this hypothesis. Lerman and Damste (1969) found no consistent differences in mean pitch for 13 openly gay men compared to 13 straight men, each of whom performed six speaking tasks. More recently, Gaudio (1994) found no differences in mean pitch or in pitch variability between groups of gay and straight men who recorded a neutral passage and an emotional monologue, although listeners were able to classify the speakers as gay or straight with good accuracy (cf. Smyth *et al.*, 2003; Rendall, Vasey, and McKenzie, 2008). The parallel assumption – that lesbians imitate male voice quality and thus should speak with a lower F0 and more monotone pitch contours – also seems to be untrue. Lesbian and straight females did not differ in mean pitch or in pitch variability in the two studies that examined such differences (Waksler, 2001; Rendall *et al.*, 2008). Finally, Munson *et al.* (2006) found no differences between gay and lesbian and straight males and females in breathiness (measured as the difference in amplitude between the first and second harmonics).

Although perceived masculinity and femininity are related to perception of sexual orientation from voice, the concepts are different, so that a male who sounds relatively feminine does not necessarily sound gay. F0 is more strongly related to masculinity and femininity than it is to perceived sexual orientation (Munson, 2007). Smyth *et al.* (2003) reported that listeners perceived some low-pitched voices as sounding gay, but were less willing to rate these same voices as "feminine sounding" because the low pitch was inconsistent with femininity.

Articulatory differences seem to provide better cues than F0 to speakers' perceived sexual orientation. Linville (1998) reported that spectral peaks for the sound /s/ were higher in frequency, and /s/ durations were longer for the gay than for the straight men. More recently, Pierrehumbert *et al.* (2004) reported that in sentences gay and lesbian speakers all produced vowels with more widely dispersed formants relative to those produced by straight speakers, consistent with more precise articulation. They argued that this pattern of more precise articulation represents an expansion of the vowel space as a way of identifying the speaker with a specific group (cf. Linville, 1998, who similarly argued that changes in /s/ articulation represent a learned articulatory characteristic that serves as a perceptual index of group identity). These articulatory data are not consistent with the hypothesis that anatomical differences are responsible for differences in voice quality (because when vowel spaces are expanded, vowels are not uniformly affected, as they would be if changes were structurally based) or with the alternative hypothesis that perceived differences in vocal quality represent a shift to vocal patterns used by the opposite sex, because the direction of change in vowel formants was the same for both gay and lesbian speakers, and not opposite as this hypothesis predicts (see Munson and Babel, 2007, or Rendall *et al.*, 2008, for review and more discussion).

4.3.7   Perception of sex in the voices of transgendered individuals

The study of the voices of transgendered individuals presents an interesting test case for arguments about the relative importance of organic versus learned cues to a speaker's sex, and also provides a test of the limits of vocal plasticity. Individuals who have undergone transgendering surgery are faced with the challenge of producing a female (or male) sound with what remains a male (or female) vocal tract and larynx. This is especially difficult when speaking over the telephone, when visual information is not available (Van Borsel, De Cuypere, and Van den Berghe, 2001), or when talking to strangers or in formal situations (Pasricha, Dacakis, and Oates, 2008).

Consistently and convincingly generating one kind of voice with another kind of vocal apparatus is not a trivial problem. Because a speaker's sex is redundantly represented in voice, a speaker wishing to alter his or her sexual presentation must successfully alter many different dimensions of voice, including pitch, intonational patterns, and pronunciation. Most research on voice conversion by transsexuals has focused on male-to-female conversion, which presents a more difficult vocal problem than female-to-male conversion (for which pitch-lowering steroid treatments are often effective; de Bruin, Coerts, and Greven, 2000; Van Borsel, De Cuypere, Rubens, and Destaerke, 2000). Even if an individual learns to use a high F0 during speech, F0 alone does not predict the patient's satisfaction with her new voice (McNeill, Wilson, Clark, and Deakin, 2008); yawns, coughs, and laughs still tend to sound male; and any vocal characteristics that are not successfully altered will work against the attempted change, contributing to produce a profoundly ambiguous and sometimes disturbing stimulus. Response biases also work against successful male-to-female voice conversion, in that even one or two remaining male vocal characteristics can be sufficient to produce the impression of a male voice, whereas a speaker must in general be almost perfectly female to produce a consistent female impression. Thus, the study of voice quality in transgendered individuals can shed light on how far vocal plasticity can be pushed to overcome the limitations inherent in vocal anatomy.

Various methods have been tried, but voice quality is very resistant to convincing male-to-female change after gender reassignment surgery. Generally, a fundamental frequency of at least 155 Hz is needed to achieve a female impression (Wolfe, Ratusnik, Smith, and Northrop, 1990). Hormone therapy does not change voice pitch in males

(Mount and Salmon, 1988), so a number of surgical interventions have been devised. Surgeons have increased the tension in the vocal folds by surgically approximating the cricoid and thyroid cartilages; by removing part of the thyroid cartilage and the vocal folds (so that the folds are reduced in length and tension is increased); or by making a window in the thyroid cartilage and stretching the vocal folds forward, effectively moving the anterior commissure (but also accentuating the thyroid prominence). Attempts have also been made to alter the consistency of the folds by creating scar tissue, or to decrease the mass of the folds by stripping tissue. Finally, the front edges of the vocal folds may be sutured together, decreasing their length and effective vibrating mass. Because F0 is a primary cue to a speaker's sex, such surgical interventions may increase the perceived femininity of a voice. However, they are invasive and long-term success rates are variable (see, for example, Gross, 1999; Kunachak, Prakunhungsit, and Sujjalak, 2000; or McNeill, 2006, for review); and simply increasing F0 generally produces a voice that is more feminine, but not necessarily female (Van Borsel, Van Eynde, De Cuypere, and Bonte, 2008). In fact, voices with very high F0s may remain unambiguously male as long as other cues to the speaker's sex retain their male values (Gelfer and Schofield, 2000).

Research has confirmed that many characteristics other than mean F0 are important to producing a convincingly female sound (for example, Gunzburger, 1993; Gelfer and Schofield, 2000; de Bruin *et al.*, 2000), and the success of male-to-female voice conversion depends on the extent to which these additional characteristics assume female values. For example, greater perceived vocal femininity is associated with increased breathiness, more upward shifts in F0, less downward shifts in F0, more variable intonation contours, longer word durations, less loudness (and less variation in loudness), and higher formant frequencies. One interesting study (Gunzburger, 1993) compared the male and female versions of the voices of six transgendered speakers. Most speakers increased mean F0, F0 ranges, and durations when speaking in their female voice; most also raised formant frequencies by retracting the corners of their lips and/or raising their larynges to shorten their vocal tracts. Perceptual tests showed that the utterances of the speaker who produced the greatest contrasts in F0 and loudness between male and female vocal productions were correctly classified as male or female 99% of the time. However, utterances from a second speaker whose male and female utterances showed no difference in F0 (and whose patterns of vocal intensity were not typically male or female) were still classified correctly 74% of the time. This second speaker used "neat" articulation and resonance cues to compensate for the lack of F0 cues and misleading intensity cues. These patterns confirm that a male or female voice quality depends on a constellation of static and dynamic cues, and not simply on mean F0. As some have argued (Whiteside, 1999; Hillenbrand and Clark, 2009), a female voice cannot be created by simply scaling up male vocal parameters, because culture-, accent-, and dialect-dependent cues to a speaker's sex can be essential to a successful transformation.

The difficulties of creating a convincingly transgendered voice are reflected in a number of film performances. Because of the difficulty of creating a convincing transformation, most portrayals of men passing successfully as women are comedies. In films like *Some Like It Hot* (Wilder, 1959), *Mrs. Doubtfire* (Radcliffe, Williams, Williams, and Columbus, 1993), and *Tootsie* (Pollack and Richards, 1982), male actors pose as females, fooling everyone. These films vary a good deal in terms of how

Table 4.9   Characteristics of transgendered voices in the movies.

	Jack Lemmon, *Some Like It Hot* Female voice is:	Robin Williams, *Mrs. Doubtfire* Female voice is:	Hillary Swank, *Boys Don't Cry* Male voice is:
Mean F0	Slightly higher overall, but inconsistent	Higher	Higher
Intonation	Little change	Wide contours	More monotone
Speaking Rate	Little change	Slower	Faster speaking rate
Articulation	No change in precision. Formants raised due to constant smiling.	Much more precise (British accent)	Less precise
Voice Quality	Some falsetto and falsetto giggles; creakiness at ends of utterances. No breathiness	Some falsetto; sounds male due to pitch drops/vocal fry at ends of phrases	Breathier

convincing (or unconvincing) the male-to-female transformations actually are. In *Some Like It Hot*, actors Tony Curtis and Jack Lemmon impersonate women and join an all-female band after witnessing a gang killing in 1920s Chicago. Jack Lemmon makes minimal and inconsistent adjustments to his vocal quality in imitating a woman, and the male-to-female vocal transformation is not at all convincing on examination (Table 4.9).[4] The male character he plays is somewhat hysterical and uses wide pitch variations to express this, so the female version of his voice is not marked by increased pitch variability but merely retains the male pattern. He does increase F0 slightly and uses a falsetto quality during some utterances, but phonation is largely modal, and frequency falls mostly into the higher end of the normal male range with substantial creakiness, particularly at the ends of utterances. His rate of articulation is high in both male and female guises, reflecting his character's underlying excitability. The humor of the portrayal (which is very funny indeed) arises in part from the inconsistency between the limited vocal cues and the exaggerated visual image, from the enthusiasm with which the character embraces his female role, and from the gullibility of those with whom he interacts.

Several strategic choices make Robin Williams's performance as Mrs. Doubtfire (Radcliffe *et al.*, 1993) more convincing than Jack Lemmon's. First, Mrs. Doubtfire is an older woman, so that viewers can tolerate a lower F0 overall (although Williams does use some falsetto). Secondly, Mrs. Doubtfire has a British accent and pronounces words carefully, as a woman would. Williams also uses a slower speaking rate and a wider F0 contour when speaking as Mrs. Doubtfire than he does as a male. Residual cues to his true sex do appear: in particular, F0 drops very low at the ends of utterances, making the voice sound unambiguously male at those points.

[4] Tony Curtis apparently had difficulty maintaining a high F0 for long periods of time, and his female voice was partially dubbed by actor Paul Frees (Internet Movie Database; http://www.imdb.com/title/tt0053291/trivia; accessed July 30, 2005).

Female-to-male transformations in film vary a good deal in detail and quality. In many cases (for example, in *Swiss Family Robinson* (Anderson and Annakin, 1960) or in any adaptation of Shakespeare's *Twelfth Night*), a woman impersonates a boy or a young man, which requires changes in vocabulary and speaking style, but little or no change in vocal quality. These performances can be convincing. For example, actress Hillary Swank plays a young woman posing as a young man in the film *Boys Don't Cry* (Peirce, 1999). The male voice she uses is actually significantly higher in F0 and somewhat breathier than her normal female voice (as heard in interviews), reflecting the sensitivity and youth of the character. However, she speaks significantly faster as a male, and uses much less precise pronunciation than she does in her normal speech, resulting in an overall impression of a young man. In contrast, in the musical comedy *Victor/Victoria* (Edwards, 1982), actress Julie Andrews impersonates a female impersonator primarily by lowering her F0 and hiding her lack of a thyroid prominence with a scarf. The discrepancy between her appearance and voice and her claim to be male is appropriate for a comedy, and is a joke even to the characters in the film.

4.4   Race and Voice

Studies of the perception of race from voice have been largely limited to comparisons of the voices of Americans of African and European descent. The theoretical status of these studies is somewhat problematic. The simple hypothesis that listeners can distinguish a speaker's race from samples of connected speech is (from our perspective) not particularly interesting, because well-documented dialectal features of African-American English readily signal the race of some African-American speakers (for example, Mufwene, Rickford, Bailey, and Baugh, 1998). The hypothesis that African-American and Caucasian speakers have reliable differences in voice quality apart from such dialectal differences implies that there are consistent differences in vocal anatomy and physiology between the two groups. A finding of consistent physiological differences between groups of speakers would imply that it is at least possible that group membership is consistently coded in the speech signal; but if differences are entirely due to learned factors like dialect, then racial identity is something speakers may or may not project. This issue has not been adequately addressed in the voice literature. Relevant physiological data are almost completely lacking, and experimental designs have not consistently separated the effects of learned versus organic factors, or the effects of listener sensitivity from response biases, as we will see below.

4.4.1   Physiological data

Few data are available about race-dependent variations in vocal anatomy. One early dissection study undertaken in South Africa (Boshoff, 1945) compared larynges from 102 Black Africans (88 male, 14 female) with those from 23 Caucasian Africans. This study reported minor differences between speaker groups; for example, Black Africans had more flexible thyroid cartilages, a somewhat larger cricoid height, larger vocal folds, and occasionally "aberrant muscles." Unfortunately, no data are provided about the age or physical size of the subjects, so it is not possible to determine if findings reflect actual racial differences or simply sampling error. More recently, Ajmani (1990) measured laryngeal cartilages from adult Nigerians, and reported no significant differences in size between subjects of European or African descent. Given that substantial variability in laryngeal anatomy exists within racial groups, both reports must be interpreted with caution. Some additional data comparing vocal tract size and volume for carefully matched male and female Caucasian, African-American, and Chinese speakers (20 males and 20 females in each racial group) have been generated using acoustic reflection imaging technology (Xue and Hao, 2006; Xue, Hao, and Mayo, 2006). Differences between racial groups depended on the sex of the speaker. For males, Chinese speakers had oral volumes that were 20–25% greater on average than those of Caucasians or African Americans, and total vocal tract volumes that were 13–17% greater. For female speakers, Caucasians had pharyngeal volumes that exceeded those of African American and Chinese speakers by 19–21%. No other significant differences in vocal tract dimensions or volumes across races were observed, and these results are hard to interpret.

4.4.2   Acoustic differences

It is difficult to formulate hypotheses about what the acoustic cues to a speaker's race should be, given the limited evidence available regarding physical differences in vocal anatomy. Some authors have reported that African-American speakers have lower F0 overall than Caucasian speakers (Hollien and Malcik, 1967; Hudson and Holbrook, 1982) or that the amplitudes of the second and third harmonics were higher for speakers of African origin than for Europeans (Kovacic and Hedever, 2000). However, other authors (including Morris, 1997; Xue and Fucci, 2000) found no differences between African-American and Caucasian speakers in measures of mean F0 or F0 perturbation (jitter, shimmer, and spectral noise). Formant frequencies do not vary systematically by race (Walton and Orlikoff, 1994; Andrianopoulos, Darrow, and Chen, 2001), nor do patterns of airflow through the glottis (Sapienza, 1997). Thus, acoustic evidence, like physiological evidence, provides little motivation for studies of the perception of race from voice.

4.4.3   Perceptual differences

Early studies of listeners' abilities to identify a speaker's race from a voice sample did not control for learned differences in dialect and articulation (see Thomas and Reaser, 2004, for extensive review). A study by Dickens and Sawyer (1962) is typical, and demonstrates the limitations of many studies in the literature. In this study, voice samples (sentences) were recorded from ten Caucasian and ten African-American speakers. Groups of African-American and Caucasian listeners were asked to listen to each sentence and to determine the race of the speaker. Results are summarized in Table 4.10. Listeners were able to discriminate the two races at above chance levels, but it is not clear what the basis for their judgments was. Dickens and Sawyer claim in their discussion that each listener group is more accurate at recognizing their own

Table 4.10   Accuracy of race judgments. Data from Dickens and Sawyer (1962).

	African-American speakers	Caucasian speakers
African-American listeners	77.4 %	58.8%
Caucasian listeners	53%	93%

Table 4.11   Response biases in judgments of race. Data from Dickens and Sawyer (1962).

	African-American listeners	Caucasian listeners
% "African-American" responses	59.4%	30.2%
% "Caucasian" responses	40.6%	69.8%

race; but upon examination it appears that each listener group had a substantial response bias toward their own race, with Caucasians responding "white" more often and African-Americans responding "black" more often (Table 4.11).

Similar results were obtained in a series of studies by Lass and colleagues (for example, Lass, Tecca, Mancuso, and Black, 1979; Lass, Almerino, Jordan, and Walsh, 1980). Race was recognized with reasonable accuracy (about 80% correct) when stimuli were sentence length, and thus included substantial information from pronunciation and intonation. Accuracy decreased with stimulus length, reaching chance levels when stimuli were vowels. This consistent decrease in accuracy with decreasing articulatory information suggests that cues to a speaker's race are articulatory and learned, rather than anatomical and innate. More recently, Walton and Orlikoff (1994) studied a population of newly admitted African-American and Caucasian prison inmates who were not formally matched for dialect. Listeners heard vowels in pairs, and specified which of the two speakers was African-American. They achieved 60% correct recognition overall, although accuracy ranged from 52–70% across listeners; analyses did not control for response biases. Thomas and Reaser (2004) reported that both African-American and Caucasian listeners had difficulty recognizing the race of African-American speakers when dialect was controlled (correct recognition = about 56%), but were nearly perfect at recognizing the race of Caucasian speakers of standard American English (about 94% correct) and control speakers of standard African-American English (about 92% correct). Unfortunately, no significance tests were undertaken to determine if recognition remained above chance when dialect was controlled. Finally, Perrachione, Chiao, and Wong (2010) found that both African-American and Caucasian listeners misclassified a consistent subset of African-American voices as Caucasian (based on sentence-length stimuli), but not vice versa. When new listeners were trained to recognize these misclassified speakers, Caucasian listeners (but not African-American listeners) showed an own-race advantage, based on speech characteristics. These results again point to dialect, and not anatomy, as the source of "sounding Black."

In conclusion, accuracy of classification by race appears to decline with declining articulatory information, suggesting that significant information is contained primarily in articulatory patterns. This points to learned, rather than organic, differences between speakers, but the definitive answer to this question awaits better science.

4.5   Inferring a Speaker's Physical Size and Overall Appearance from Voice

The final topic in this chapter is the issue of whether listeners can estimate a speaker's physical size or overall appearance from voice. As listeners, we all sometimes form strong opinions about what a speaker should look like from hearing a voice. This impression may include only a speaker's height and weight, but sometimes we also form opinions about the speaker's particular facial characteristics. Despite the strength that such opinions tend to have, most of us also know from experience that we are doomed to disappointment, or at least to surprise, when we finally see the owner of a voice for the first time. Apart from its social interest, this kind of study has some practical implications as well. For example, law enforcement officials are interested in the extent to which voices can give reliable information about the appearance of a suspect who has been heard, but not seen.

4.5.1   Matching voices to faces

Because moving the articulators during speech necessarily causes changes in the face, information carried in the voice allows subjects to match voices to images of moving faces, and vice versa. Numerous experiments (for example, Kamachi, Hill, Lander, and Vatikiotis-Bateson, 2003; Lachs and Pisoni, 2004; Rosenblum, Smith, Nichols, Hale, and Lee, 2006) have shown that listeners can match a moving face to audible speech, or recorded speech to a moving face, with better than chance accuracy (generally about 60% correct; Lander, Hill, Kamachi, and Vatikiotis-Bateson, 2007). Performance on these tasks is impaired if the tokens differ in the manner in which they were produced (statement/question, conversational/clear speech), but does not depend on the subject's knowledge of the language being spoken (Lander *et al.*, 2007). These findings suggest that such cross-modal matches depend on phonetic information that is represented in both the face and the speech signal.

In contrast, matching a voice to a static image of a speaker's face is an almost impossible task. In a study by Lass and Harvey (1976), listeners heard a voice reading a paragraph-long passage, and then attempted to determine which of two photos represented the speaker. In one condition, listeners saw photos of heads and shoulders; in a second condition, they were shown the speakers' full bodies. Recognition rates ranged from 47% to 65% correct, and were not above chance levels overall.[5] In a similar experiment, McGlone and Hicks (1979) asked listeners to match a two-sentence stimulus to one of two photos showing the speakers from the waist up. Identification

---

[5]   Lass and Harvey report their results as exceeding chance, but reanalysis of their data using more sensitive statistical tests suggests that listeners' performance did not exceed levels expected from guessing.

rates were again at chance. Accuracy does improve to above-chance levels (about 77% correct) when foils used in the identification task are not matched to the speakers in age or in race (Krauss, Freyberg, and Morsella, 2002). It should not be surprising that listeners have difficulty matching a voice to a face, because the anatomy related to voice quality does not have much to do with external appearance. As described in Chapter 2, the primary determinants of vocal quality include the layered structure of the vocal cords, the size and shape of the vocal tract, and the particular manner in which speakers utilize their anatomy to produce speech. These factors have no connection to such important determinants of facial appearance as hair, figure, eyes, and complexion.

4.5.2   Physical size and vocal quality

Even though listeners cannot match a voice to a photograph of the speaker, they might be able to estimate a few specific aspects of appearance from voice quality. In particular, body size is a critical biological parameter: How large you are has important implications for such basic functions as obtaining food and mates, and communicating your superior size to other animals could help obtain resources while possibly avoiding conflicts. Information about size can also indicate an individual's sex in dimorphic species, and can give a rough estimate of an individual's age, or at least child vs. adult status. An association between voice and size could thus provide an evolutionary advantage to larger animals.

Because vocal fold size and vocal tract length are related to overall body size in many animals – both are larger in human males than in females or children, for example – logically it follows that the acoustic correlates of these anatomical features (F0 and formant frequencies) should covary at least somewhat with the overall size of the animal, at least in sexually dimorphic species (see Taylor and Reby, 2010, for extensive review). The extent to which this is true across species has been the object of intense study, and animals in fact differ widely in the manner and extent to which they display this expected relationships between overall size, vocal tract configurations, and acoustic vocal attributes. In general, larger animals produce longer calls (possibly because of greater lung capacity), with lower F0, and with formants lower in frequency and/or closer together (Ey *et al.*, 2007; see also Rendall, Vokey, and Nemeth, 2007); but many variations occur. For example, vocal fold size and F0 are uncorrelated in reptiles (Asquith and Altig, 1990), and body size is uncorrelated with F0 in Japanese macaques (Masataka, 1994); the size of hamadryas baboons is better predicted by F0 than by formant dispersion (Pfefferle and Fischer, 2006); but formant dispersion predicts body size in red deer (Reby and McComb, 2003) and body size (Riede and Fitch, 1999) and weight in dogs (as subjectively judged by humans; Taylor, Reby, and McComb, 2008); and F0 is associated both physically and perceptually with weight in male scops owls (Hardouin, Reby, Bavous, Byrneleau, and Bretagnolle, 2007).

In some species, the vocal tract has evolved to produce calls that exaggerate the size of the animal. For example, in human males the larynx descends a full vertebra lower than it does in females, suggesting that the original function of the descent of the larynx in the neck may have been to exaggerate cues to body size (Fitch and Giedd, 1999). Saiga (small Eurasian antelope) tense and extend their noses prior to roaring by pulling back their flexible nasal vestibulum, which elongates the nasal vocal tract by 20% and lowers resonances by a similar amount (Frey, Volodin, and Volodina, 2007). Elephant seals also have evolved long noses that similarly serve to elongate the vocal tract and exaggerate their sizes (Sanvito, Galimberti, and Miller, 2007). Red deer achieve a similar goal by lowering their larynges to the level of the sternum during roaring, resulting in resonances that are much lower in frequency than would be predicted by the resting length of the vocal tract (Reby and McComb, 2003). Because larger red deer (with longer necks) have lower resonances than do smaller animals, these calls still provide information about the animal's relative size. Similarly, black and white colobus monkeys have evolved air sacs that serve as additional resonators, producing resonances consistent with a vocal tract that is 29 cm long versus the actual 7–8 cm vocal tract of the animals. As with red deer, the acoustic features of the call do correlate with the animal's size, so information about relative size is preserved (Harris, Fitch, Goldstein, and Fashing, 2006). Thus, calls may simultaneously serve as both honest (within species) and deceptive (across species) indices of an animal's size (see Ey *et al.*, 2007, for extended review).

In humans, F0 decreases as children grow, and is lower overall for adult males than for females, as discussed previously, so that a rough correspondence between size and voice pitch does exist. However, *within* groups of males, females, and children, fundamental frequency seems to be largely independent of an individual's body size, despite the common view that a low-pitched voice goes with a large person (for example, Graddol and Swann, 1983; Kunzel, 1989; van Dommelen, 1993; see Rendall, Kollias, Ney, and Lloyd, 2005; Rendall *et al.*, 2007; Ey *et al.*, 2007; or Smith, Walters, and Patterson, 2007, for review). Several explanations for the failure to find reliable correlations between F0 and size within age- or sex-specific groups have been suggested. Smith *et al.* (2007) argued that the association is reduced because speakers routinely vary F0 during speech by an octave or more, and in so doing distort potential cues to size in order to convey other kinds of information (emotional state, attitude, question versus statement, and so on, as described in later chapters). Other authors have argued that F0 is a poor index of body size because the human larynx differs in critical ways from that of most other animals. Recall that in humans the larynx is suspended from the hyoid bone (which in turn does not articulate with any other bones in the body), and that it can move up and down in the neck rather freely. Because the size of the larynx is not constrained by any other nearby bony structures, it can grow somewhat independently of the rest of the head or body. Such independent growth occurs in males at puberty, and is even more extreme in certain other animals (Fitch, 1997). For example, in male hammerhead bats the larynx fills almost the entire chest cavity (Fitch and Hauser, 2003). Because growth of the larynx is not constrained by the growth of the overall body, there is no particular reason why F0 should be correlated with body size within age- and sex-matched groups of speakers (although F0 discriminates well between men, women, and children, as noted above).

In contrast, the vocal tract in humans (and in most other animals) is much less free to grow independently of the rest of the body, because it is largely contained within the skull. Because the vocal tract cannot be extended limitlessly without compromising swallowing ability, resonances of the vocal tract might provide at least somewhat honest cues to an animal's true size, with lower frequencies corresponding to larger animals

(Fitch, 1997; Fitch and Hauser, 2003). This suggests that formant frequencies should provide much more robust cues to body size than F0 (Fitch, 1997). MRI data confirmed that vocal tract length is highly correlated with total body length in a sample that included males, females, and children, aged two to 25 (r = 0.93; Fitch and Giedd, 1999), and in fact formant frequencies are highly correlated with size and weight in some non-human animals as well (for example, Schon Ybarra, 1995; Fitch, 1997; Pfefferle, West, Grinnell, Packer, and Fischer, 2007).

Many species use vocal tract length as a cue to size; for example, rhesus monkeys reliably associate lower formant frequencies with the face of a larger versus smaller animal (Ghazanfar *et al.*, 2007); female red deer can discriminate the calls of large animals from those of smaller animals based on changes in formant frequencies (Charlton *et al.*, 2007, 2008); and playback experiments demonstrate that male red deer respond more (and extend their own vocal tracts) when they hear stimuli whose formants are manipulated to represent larger-sized callers (Reby *et al.*, 2005). As with F0, the relationship is much stronger between age- and/or sex-matched groups than it is within these groups, possibly because of the many other factors that affect call characteristics (see Ey *et al.*, 2007, for review). These principals may apply to humans as well, although the particular biological mechanisms involved remain unknown. However, humans differ somewhat from the typical case, in that the human larynx sits much lower in the neck than primate larynges do, making vocal tract length at least potentially somewhat independent of skull size. Further, humans can significantly modify the shape of the vocal tract through movements of the tongue, jaw, and lips, as discussed in Chapter 2. Thus, the facts of vocal anatomy and acoustics do not make clear predictions about the extent to which formant frequencies should reflect physical size in humans, and studies have reported weak, moderate, and zero correlations between formants and heights in men and women (for example, Kunzel, 1989; van Dommelen and Moxness, 1995; Collins and Missing, 2003; Gonzalez, 2004; Rendall, Vokey, Nemeth, and Ney, 2005; Evans, Neave, and Wakelin, 2006; see Rendall *et al.*, 2007, for review).

4.5.3 Perception of size from voice

Studies of human listeners' abilities to judge a speaker's true physical size (height and weight) from voice samples have had variable results, consistent with the weak relationship between F0, resonances, and size in adult humans. Early studies by Lass and colleagues (for example, Lass and Davis, 1976; Lass and Brown, 1978; Lass, Mertz, and Kimmel, 1978) claimed that listeners could make these judgments, and then examined the "cues" underlying listeners' behavior (for instance, Lass *et al.*, 1979, 1980; Lass, Scherbick, Davies, and Czarnecki, 1982). Unfortunately, these studies were fraught with methodological problems (Cohen, Crystal, House, and Neuberg, 1980; see also Lass, 1981), particularly with the statistical approach applied. When evaluating their data, Lass and colleagues calculated the average difference between each guess and the correct height and weight. Because listeners both over- and under-estimated speakers' heights and weights, positive and negative deviations from the true values cancelled each other out, producing very small average differences despite significant absolute variability in listeners' responses. This procedure reduced the variance in the data, so that listeners' accuracy was overstated. When data were reanalyzed to examine correlations between estimates and true values (van Dommelen, 1993; Gonzalez, 2003), accuracy was not impressive: The correlation between the speakers' actual and estimated heights and weights ranged from –0.02 to 0.35, and did not reach statistical significance.

Subsequent studies trying to provide less ambiguous evidence regarding the perception of height and weight from voice have had generally negative results. Gunter and Manning (1982) found that listeners were rather inaccurate in their judgments of height and weight. Height estimates differed from the speakers' true heights by 2.5–3.2 inches (above and below the correct value), and weight estimates were off by 16–19 pounds. Good performance was obtained only by listeners who consistently guessed values near the population mean. Statistically, this response strategy will produce the lowest overall error, because the mean is the best estimate of the central value of a normally-distributed population. van Dommelen and Moxness (1995) similarly found correlations between true and estimated height in the 0.5 range, indicating a reliable but weak association between a male speaker's true and perceived size; but no significant associations were found for female speakers. Bruckert *et al.* (2006) found no significant correlation between perceived and true height for male French speakers, and only a small correlation (r = 0.4) between estimated and true weight.

Interestingly, estimates of height and weight from different experimental conditions are often well correlated (r = 0.64 – 0.94), indicating listeners are very consistent in their impressions, even though they are inaccurate (for example, van Dommelen, 1993; van Dommelen and Moxness, 1995). Rendall *et al.* (2007) hypothesized that this discrepancy between accuracy and agreement arises at least in part because listeners are typically asked to estimate speakers' sizes directly. Listeners require a difference in vocal tract length of about 4.8% (corresponding to a difference in height of 10 cm, or about 4 inches) before they perceive a difference in voice quality. Tasks that ask for direct height estimations (usually within an inch) may underestimate listeners' abilities to detect differences in size by asking for judgments that are below the limits of perception. In fact, Rendall *et al.* found that listeners were able to determine which of a pair of speakers was the larger about 80% of the time as long as speakers differed in size by more than 10 cm (cf. Smith, Patterson, Turner, Kawahara, and Irino, 2005, who also reported that listeners can make accurate judgments of the relative sizes of two speakers, even when size is scaled to include much smaller and much larger individuals than those encountered in everyday experience). However, if the voice samples were modified by altering either F0 or formant frequencies, performance dropped to chance levels or below. Rendall *et al.* concluded that listeners are sensitive to formant cues to size, but that their ability to make correct judgments is impaired when F0 cues conflict with the more reliable formant cues. (See also Bruckert *et al.*, 2006, who report similar results for speakers of French.) They suggest several explanations for listeners' apparently misguided reliance on F0: Listeners may overgeneralize the fact that F0 does distinguish males from females from children; their reliance on F0 cues may derive from the general environmental association of low pitch with large size (for example, in the sounds made by trucks vs. compact cars, or large dogs vs. mice); or their performance may reflect a chain of association that links size to F0 indirectly (maleness → large size → aggressiveness → low F0). These diverse speculations highlight the difficulty of interpreting listener behavior in the face of the extremely plastic human vocal system.

The association between body size and formant frequencies also predicts that low-pitched, noisy cries should provide the best information about an animal's true size, because in such calls the harmonics are close together and formant information is most clearly represented in the speech signal. If such calls provide good information about an animal's size, they should be favored as signs of aggression, which may explain why growls are generally low-pitched and noisy. Further, if listeners associate long vocal tracts with larger bodies, animals should elongate their vocal tracts during phonation (or over evolutionary time) to maximize their perceived size, by protruding their lips, lowering the larynx, or elongating the nose. Thus, aggressive calls should be made with protruded lips and nearly closed mouths; and cries of submission should be made with retracted lips, because retracting the lips shortens the vocal tract, making the animal sound less threatening. Both these kinds of behavior are widespread among mammals, including nonhuman primates, dogs, goats, pigs, and deer. For example, red deer (and possibly lions) lower their larynges prior to roaring to enhance their perceived size (Fitch, 2000b; see Fitch and Hauser, 2003 for review). (Red deer also appear to use formant information to assess the size of the caller, and lower their own larynges when they hear the call of a "larger" animal; Reby *et al.*, 2005). The extent to which these observations apply to humans is not known, although the human smile may have its origins in this kind of behavior (for example, Ohala, 1980; smiling will be described further in Chapter 9).

4.6   Summary and Conclusions

In conclusion, we would like to highlight two themes that unite the topics discussed in this chapter. The first is the importance of distinguishing vocal attributes that are the result of physiological characteristics ("organic") from those that are learned behaviors. Studies that examine the balance between organic and learned factors (in the context of vocal plasticity) often provide the most satisfying explanations of the behavior in question, because they tell us not just "what" and "how," but also *why* speakers sound the ways that they do, which in turn helps us understand why listeners reach the conclusions that they do.

The second theme is the usefulness of a biological perspective when studying vocal quality. A number of the topics in this chapter (for example, the perception of a speaker's size and the perception of sex from voice) have been studied independently by voice scientists. However, recent studies of the behavior of nonhuman animals make it clear that age, size, sex, and reproductive fitness are inseparably linked in the vocalizations of many animal species. For example, the perception of size plays an important role in attracting or selecting mates; and the ability to convey size through vocalization helps establish and maintain dominance, and thus access to mates. The message here is that we share many vocal behaviors with other animals, and that broader perspectives on how voice functions across species can lead to a deeper understanding of why our human voices function as they do, and how it came to be that way. We will expand on this theme in the next chapter.

5

Recognizing Speaker Identity From Voice: Theoretical and Ethological Perspectives and a Psychological Model

5.1 Introduction

Recognizing significant voices in our midst is an ability shared by many animal species. It pervades much of biological experience, appearing first when an infant recognizes the voice of its mother, and expanding to the repertory of personally familiar voices known to many kinds of mature animals. Given that both the larynx and the peripheral auditory system are evolutionarily relatively conservative, it is not surprising that some vocal functions show behavioral similarities across species; and it is useful to look to simpler systems in other animals for clues to how humans have arrived at certain behaviors. However, familiar voice recognition has its greatest flowering in humans, in whom no upper limit to the number of personally known voices has yet been established, and in whom the skill, in tandem with the colossus speech perception, plays a huge role.

This chapter surveys the field of familiar voice recognition, first by defining "familiar" and "unfamiliar" tasks in voice studies, then by reviewing studies of recognition abilities and strategies in nonhuman animals. We proceed to an overview of studies of human voice perception. Arising from these perspectives, we introduce a psychological model to account for perception and recognition of familiar and unfamiliar voices.

5.2 Kinds of Tasks and Theoretical Preliminaries

The topic of speaker recognition encompasses a number of rather different kinds of judgments and responses, so we begin this chapter with a few illustrations. Listen carefully to audio sample 5.1 and try to remember it. Now listen to sample 5.2. Does this voice sound familiar? If so, can you name the talker? (Answers to these exercises are given in Table 5.1 at the end of this section.) Next, listen to audio

Foundations of Voice Studies: An Interdisciplinary Approach to Voice Production and Perception, First Edition. Jody Kreiman and Diana Sidtis.

Table 5.1 Descriptions of audio samples 5.1–5.7.

Audio samples 5.1, 5.5, and 5.7 were are all produced by the same talker.
Audio sample 5.2 is the voice of actor Peter Lorre (known for the films *M*,
  Casablanca, and *The Maltese Falcon*, among many others).
Audio samples 5.3 and 5.4 are from different talkers.
Audio samples 5.5 and 5.6 are from different talkers

samples 5.3 and 5.4. Were these two samples produced by the same talker, or by two different talkers? What about the voices in samples 5.5 and 5.6? Are these the same talker or two different talkers? Now listen to audio sample 5.7, and try to remember the voice sample you heard at the beginning of this exercise (sample 5.1). Is the speaker of sample 5.7 the same person, or is it someone different?

These exercises used voices that were familiar and unfamiliar, disguised and undisguised, and required you to remember, recognize, compare, name, and discriminate among stimuli. *Discrimination* tasks require listeners to compare two voice samples to one another in short-term memory. *Identification* tasks involve comparing a voice the listener has just heard to an exemplar or representation stored in long-term memory. The stored exemplar may be created through listening exposure in the media (recognizing a familiar/famous voice) or through personal interactions with the speaker (recognizing a friend or family member – a familiar/intimate voice). *Recognition* occurs once listeners determine that the voice they have heard is familiar, whether or not they are able to name the speaker. Voice *identification* implies naming, and thus requires the additional (and sometimes problematic) step of associating a name (or a list of identifying characteristics, if naming fails) with the voice. *Speaker verification* tasks are a special case of identification tasks where the "listener" is a computational algorithm rather than a human. In speaker verification, using a machine, a voice sample is compared to a stored template (constructed from many individual exemplars) for the voice of the person the speaker claims to be, and the claim is accepted or rejected depending on the extent of a match between the sample and the template.

Other kinds of tasks (*identification after training* or *recognition after training*) occur mostly in experimental studies, in which listeners are exposed in a controlled manner to a voice or a set of voices with which they were not previously familiar. This kind of task is quite artificial, and does not correspond particularly well to recognition tasks that occur in everyday life. However, experimenters who wish to study recognition of personally familiar voices may find it very difficult to create a set of stimuli that are uniformly familiar to a large group of listeners, and listener training solves this dilemma, in addition to allowing experimental control over the extent of exposure and the kind of stimuli listeners have heard. (Trained-to-recognize and verification tasks are discussed in more detail in Chapters 6, 7, and 10.)

In Chapter 2 we discussed the great extent to which an individual can intentionally vary vocal quality. In fact, even without conscious manipulation, no speaker ever produces an utterance in exactly the same way twice. Differences within a single speaker in vocal quality (whether intentionally or incidentally produced) across occasions and utterances are called *intraspeaker variability*; differences between speakers are called *interspeaker variability.* Speaker recognition, identification, discrimination, and verification tasks all require listeners (or machines) to determine whether the nature and extent of differences between target and test voice samples can be better explained by intraspeaker variability (in which case voices are judged to be the same) or interspeaker variability (in which case they are considered different).

In constructing experiments, investigators can create trials where listeners know a match to the test voice exists and are forced to select a single response from a set of possible choices. Such *closed-set* trials have no true analogs in everyday experience, where the possibility of no match always exists. In *open-set* trials, a match to the target may or may not exist. This type of experimental design provides a more valid model of the task listeners usually perform, but makes it difficult to quantify listeners' performance accuracy, because chance levels of performance are undefined when the number of possible response options is unknown, and because the probability of a correct identification must be 0 when the target voice is not a response option.

With respect to theory, our discussion in this chapter takes place in a general framework that describes voice perception as an interplay between "featural" processing and "Gestalt" pattern recognition. As discussed in Chapter 1, featural processing presupposes decomposition or deconstruction of the stimulus into useful, additive elements. In this atomistic approach, the perceptual process involves perceiving and classifying the presence and absence of a previously established and known set of features. Gestalt recognition, on the other hand, implies apperception as a whole. Certain characteristics of the stimulus lead to the correct interpretation using an interactional part-whole process, determined by the intrinsic nature of the entire stimulus, that relies on context, familiarity, and memory (Wertheimer, 1944). In the act of recognition, specific, selected elements arise and cohere to effect recognition of the Gestalt (see Sidebar). The best examples of this process occur in facial and vocal caricatures: The artist selects only a few elements to copy, but the target is immediately identifiable, despite the fact that the selected features vary from target to target.

Sidebar: Gestalt Principles

Principles of Gestalt pattern perception were derived from studies of the organizing principles in visual patterns (Wertheimer, 1944; Hochberg, 1971; King and Wertheimer, 2007;). The approach states that "seeing, hearing, and remembering are all acts of construction" (Neisser, 1967, p. 10). Practitioners of this approach worked for many years to discover rules to predict how wholes are perceived out of incomplete elements. While many explanatory principles have been established for perception of visual patterns, (Hochberg, 1971), acceptable methods of quantification have not emerged (Kubovy and Wagemans, 1995), and extension of these principles to auditory patterns, for the most part, has not been adequately developed. An exception lies in auditory scene analysis, where some Gestalt principles have been adapted (McAdams and Bigand, 1993; Bregman, 1994, pp. 196ff.). In this framework, properties are experienced in relation to organization of the whole, and certain principles of organization are automatic and innate. Primitive processes partition the sensory evidence and then schema-based attentional processes select from the evidence to construct the auditory object. The schema-based process is affected by familiarity (Bregman, 1994, pp. 669–670). Some of these principles could be usefully considered to underlie voice perception.

Figure 5.1 illustrates this distinction schematically (and whimsically). In this figure, familiar voices are represented as distinctive, unique, and salient objects, while unfamiliar voices are represented as features more or less evenly distributed. It is well known in psychological research that recognizing complex unitary patterns engages different perceptual mechanisms than does attention to percepts composed of constituent features. We will provide evidence below that the role of individual voice parameters in the perception of a given voice depends on the extent to which the listener's task requires recognition of the whole pattern (when the voice is a familiar one) or attention to featural details (in discrimination tasks, for example), and we will argue that as a result perception proceeds differently in the listener for these two different kinds of competence. We will explain how prototypical vocal templates underlie perception of unfamiliar voices, while unique Gestalt patterns are utilized for familiar voice recognition. Auditory-acoustic features operate differently in these two kinds of perception.

5.3 Recognizing Familiar Voices

On first consideration, it may seem that recognizing a familiar voice somehow depends on the ability to discriminate among unfamiliar voices (for example, Fischer, 2004). After all, voices are all unfamiliar when we first encounter them, and it seems intuitively that learning means incrementally establishing how a specific voice can be reliably recognized. Despite this common intuition, we will propose that familiar voices are rapidly acquired into memory, not learned incrementally in the traditional sense (this is further elaborated in Section 6.5). Further, many years of research guided by the assumption

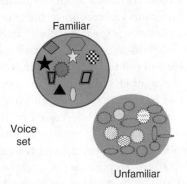

Figure 5.1 Caricatured perceptual spaces for familiar and unfamiliar voices.

of incremental learning of voice patterns have not yielded a satisfactory explanation – or even a very good description – of human abilities to recognize or discriminate among voices, and a growing body of data contradicts this intuitive view.

In this section, we will see that ethological and evolutionary data about familiar voice recognition shed significant light on human abilities to recognize voices. These data indicate that familiar voice recognition is the more widespread ability, on which the ability to discriminate among voices may depend (rather than vice versa). For this reason, we will begin our discussion with familiar voice perception, and then account for discrimination in that context, rather than vice versa.

5.3.1   Voice recognition by infants and children

The ability to recognize the voice of one's mother is present at birth in normally hearing humans. In fact, recognition begins even before birth. Fetuses *in utero* are exposed to sounds generated by the mother's body (her heartbeat, vascular, respiratory, and digestive sounds, and of course the sound of her voice), and they begin responding to sounds at about 20 to 30 weeks gestational age (Shahidullah and Hepper, 1994). Fetuses also hear sounds originating outside the mother, but these sounds are low-pass filtered as they pass through the mother's body and the fluid that surrounds the fetus. As a result of this filtering, sounds from 500–4,000 Hz decrease in intensity by about 20 dB, and higher frequency components are attenuated by as much as 40–50 dB before they reach the fetus. Thus, high-frequency acoustic energy probably has little or no perceptual importance prior to birth. Additional filtering occurs when sound reaches the fetus through the vibration of its bones, further enhancing the lower frequencies in the sound (see Gerhardt and Abrams, 2000, for review). Despite this filtering, the mother's voice heard *in utero* is as loud or louder than it is *ex utero* (Richards, Frentzen, Gerhardt, McCann, and Abrams, 1992; DeCasper, Lecanuet, Maugais, Granier-Deferre, and Busnel, 1994). Mean F0, F0 variability in phrases, and speech rhythm can be perceived *in utero*, as can differences between voiced and unvoiced consonants; in fact, about one-third of phonemes can be recognized (see Spence and Freeman, 1996, for review).

This acoustic information is sufficient for fetuses to learn to recognize the voices of their mothers, and a number of studies have demonstrated that both fetuses and newborn infants can recognize their mothers' voices and discriminate them from the voices of unfamiliar speakers. For example, Kisilevsky *et al.* (2003) measured the heart rates of 60 fetuses (38 weeks gestational age) in response to recordings of the mother's voice and the voice of a strange woman, both played through a loudspeaker held above the mother's abdomen, and both reading the same poem. They found that fetal heart rates increased by about five beats per minute in response to the sound of the mother's voice, and decreased by about four beats per minute in response to the stranger's voice. The different behavioral effects of the two voices indicate that fetuses are capable of remembering and recognizing their mothers' voices (see Sidebar). In a related study, Hepper, Scott, and Shahidullah (1993) recorded ultrasound images of ten fetuses (36 weeks gestation) while their mothers spoke normally, or while a recording of her voice was played via a speaker on her abdomen. They found that fetuses moved less[1] when hearing their mothers speak normally (corresponding to what they normally hear *in utero*) than they did when they heard voice recordings, which lacked acoustic characteristics related to vibration of the mother's tissue as sound was transmitted through her body to the fetus. These results further support the hypothesis that fetuses learn to recognize voices prior to birth.

A number of studies using a variety of experimental techniques (see Sidebar) have documented infants' ability to recognize their mothers' voices immediately after birth, even when they have not heard her voice since birth. At two hours of age, 45% of 25 newborn infants oriented to their mother's voice, versus 16% that oriented to the voice of a strange female (Querleu *et al.*, 1984). Slightly older newborns (aged 27–95 hours) moved less when they heard their mother's natural voice than when they heard the voice of a stranger, and they moved less when their mother spoke naturally than when she spoke "motherese" (which they had not heard *in utero*; Hepper *et al.*, 1993). In a classic study (DeCasper and Fifer, 1980), two- or three-day-old infants who listened to voices as they sucked on a non-nutritive nipple changed their patterns of sucking in order to hear the voice of their mother (vs. a stranger) when the voice they heard was contingent on the pattern of sucking. Finally, a similar experiment showed that infants (38–60 hours old) preferred the sound of their mother's voice filtered to mimic the womb (the sound they were used to) versus the sound of her voice in air (Spence and DeCasper, 1987; Spence and Freeman, 1996). These studies provide further evidence that infants learn their mothers' voices prenatally.

Neurophysiological evidence confirms that the mother's voice has special meaning to an infant. Event-related electrical potentials (spikes of brain activity in response to stimuli) recorded from the scalps of four-month-old infants differed in amplitude when the infants heard the voices of their mothers or a strange female, suggesting that infants pay more attention at the neurological level to their own mothers' voices than to the voices of strangers (Purhonen, Kilpelainen-Lees, Valkonen-Korhonen, Karhu, and Lehtonen, 2004). The timing and pattern of neurophysiological responses also differs when infants hear their mothers' voices, suggesting that infants process their mothers' voices faster than they do the voices of strangers (Purhonen, Kilpelainen-Lees, Valkonen-Korhonen, Karhu, and Lehtonen, 2005), and that infants have a demonstrable neural correlate of the mother's voice by at most four months of age.

The impressive voice recognition abilities infants display with respect to their mothers' voices notwithstanding, infants are not able to recognize their fathers' voices reliably, even when they have been exposed to his voice postnatally for up to ten hours (DeCasper and Prescott, 1984). At age four months, infants still do not recognize their fathers' voices reliably, even when the fathers speak "motherese" (Ward and Cooper, 1999). Both newborns and four-month old infants are able to discriminate reliably among male voices. These results suggest that learning maternal and paternal voices follow different developmental courses. Recognizing and responding to the mother's voice appears to be an important ingredient for fostering infant/mother bonding, which in turn is essential for the survival of the infant given its total dependence on its mother. Because the mother's voice is so strongly related to the infant's survival, the ability to identify and bond could have evolutionary survival value

---

[1] In this paradigm, less movement is interpreted as attentive listening.

(Purhonen *et al.*, 2005), and in fact recognition of mothers by infants, infants by mothers, and mutual voice recognition between parents and offspring are all common in animals, as we will discuss in the following section. The ability to focus on the mother's voice also makes it easier for the infant to separate voices when more than one person is speaking at once (a common occurrence in most households), thereby providing infants with the information they need to learn the sounds of speech. Separating the voices of simultaneous talkers in this manner is otherwise a very difficult task, even for older infants (Barker and Newman, 2004), but the importance of the mother's voice apparently motivates infants to pay more attention to this stream in the background of sound. Fathers' voices, on the other hand, play a different, evolutionarily less-central role in the lives of very young children. Thus, the manner in which infants recognize their fathers may differ from that used with mothers. Infants may require different cues – for example, smell, vision, and touch – in addition to voice in order to reliably recognize their fathers (Ward and Cooper, 1999).

It is not known for certain what cues newborns use to recognize their mothers' voices, but it is possible to make educated guesses. F0 mean and variability and speech timing are the most likely early cues, because this information is available to the fetus *in utero*. Evidence suggests that infants rely largely on cues related to intonation, but not timing. For example, one-month-old infants can discriminate their mother's voice from that of another female when the pitch contour is normal, but not if the voices are monotone (Mehler, Bertoncini, Barriere, and Jassik-Gerschenfeld, 1978). Further, newborns do not consistently prefer the sound of their mother whispering (which preserves speech rhythm, vocal tract resonance information, and pronunciation, but not F0) to the sound of an unfamiliar female whispering, although they can successfully discriminate between two unfamiliar whispered female voices (Spence and Freeman, 1996). These data help explain the importance of F0 in voice perception: It is the cue we use earliest in life.

Sidebar: How Do We Know What Infants and Fetuses Can Hear?

Measuring perceptual responses to complex auditory stimuli is not easy, even in adults, as described in Chapter 1. The problem is compounded in infants who cannot understand instructions or produce verbal or written responses; and it is even greater in fetuses. Two techniques are available for evaluating fetal responses to sounds. First, ultrasound can be used to assess the number or kinds of movements the fetus makes as it hears sounds. For example, researchers can measure fetal blink responses to sound, or can count movements of the fetus's head, torso, and limbs (see Hepper *et al.*, 1993, or Gerhardt and Abrams, 2000, for review). Alternatively, researchers can measure changes in the fetus's heart rate in response to different kinds of stimuli, using a standard cardiotocograph (for example, Kisilevsky *et al.*, 2003). Bodily movement or changes in heart rate may indicate a response to a stimulus or task.

A few more possibilities are available to assess the responses of newborn or very young infants. For example, researchers can count and compare the numbers and kinds of movements the infants make in response to different kinds of stimuli (for example, Querleu *et al.*, 1984). The infant may orient toward the sound or gaze at an image; it may move its head, arms, or legs; or it may do nothing. Researchers can also examine rates of sucking on a non-nutritive nipple in newborns (DeCasper and Fifer, 1980). In this paradigm, infants suck on the nipple to establish the baseline interval between bursts of sucking. Next, researchers play a sound to the baby. What happens next depends on the infant's response to the voice. For example, if the infant increases the interval between bursts of sucking (thus slowing its overall sucking rate), it hears its mother's voice, and if it increases the rate of sucking, it hears an unfamiliar voice (or vice versa). Across a set of trials, the number of times the infant "selects" its mother's voice by sucking appropriately is a measure of the infant's recognition of and preference for its mother's voice. Sucking paradigms can also be used to determine whether infants can discriminate between two voices, because infants typically increase their sucking rates when they hear a change (for example, Spence and Freeman, 1996).

It is also possible to study event-related brain potentials in very small infants (for example, Purhonen *et al.*, 2004, 2005). These potentials are small amounts of brain electrical activity that occur in response to stimuli. Event-related responses are time-locked to the stimuli, and reflect sequential steps in cerebral processing. They are recorded using surface electrodes on the infant's scalp. Because infants' brains are immature at birth, their neuronal responses differ significantly from adults', but some useful patterns can still be observed. Typically, researchers using this paradigm look for differences in the amplitude of the electrical response and the timing of different peaks as infants listen to streams of stimuli, and make inferences about the cognitive and neurological processing that is taking place in response to the stimuli.

As infants grow and develop, additional experimental techniques become practical. For example, researchers can play competing stimuli through different speakers, and then measure the direction and duration of the infants' head turns in response to the different stimuli, with the preferred stimulus hypothetically meriting the most visual attention (for example, Barker and Newman, 2004). Once babbling begins, it is also possible to record the amount of time that infants vocalize in response to different kinds of stimuli as a measure of their engagement with the different signals (Brown, 1979).

In all of these cases, the dependent variable (the thing being measured) is a normal infant behavior that occurs regularly outside the context of the experiment. For this reason, the meaning of the behavior *within* the experimental context – and our ability to draw inferences about what infants hear or recognize – derives entirely from the structure of the experiment. For example, if an infant moves its legs or turns its head to gaze at a screen, it is only possible to associate these actions with the sound being played if the infant responds differently (for example, fails to move or stops moving) when it hears a different voice. Without proper experimental controls, babbling and waving limbs are adorable, but difficult to interpret.

Voice recognition abilities in children continue to develop quickly after birth. By age three, children can recognize the voices of familiar cartoon characters about 70% of the time. This recognition improves to about 92% correct by age four, and it approaches 100% by age five (Spence, Rollins, and Jerger, 2002). Four- and five-year-old preschoolers matched a classmate's voice to a picture 62% and 55% of the time respectively, although performance varied widely from child to child (Bartholomeus, 1973). Although familiar voice recognition is present at birth, children do not consistently discriminate unfamiliar voices at adult levels until age ten (Mann, Diamond, and Carey, 1979).

Parents are able to recognize the cries of their infants at well above chance levels. Mothers may begin learning the voices of their babies as early as three days postpartum (Formby, 1967). 80% of mothers recognized their newborns from a set of three 15–second cries after between three and eight days (Morsbach and Bunting, 1979); and by the time infants are one month old, 80% of mothers could identify their own infant's crying at above chance levels from a set of six crying babies (Green and Gustafson, 1983). Hit rates for these mothers averaged 92%, with a false alarm rate of 33%. Mothers of older infants were even more accurate: The cries of infants aged between three and five months were correctly identified 91% of the time from a set of eight, with a low false alarm rate of 8% (Murry, Hollien, and Muller, 1975). Fathers are less accurate as a group than mothers, with only 45% able to identify the crying of their one-month-old infant at above chance levels (Green and Gustafson, 1983). It is unclear whether this difference in performance is due to differential exposure to the infants' cries, or whether women also benefit from additional cues provided by hormonally-mediated physical responses (for example, milk letdown in nursing mothers) to the sound of their child (see, for example, Soltis, 2004, for a review of the role of crying in mother/child interactions).

5.3.2   Familiar voice recognition by nonhuman animals

The evidence for *in utero* voice recognition in humans suggests that there is an evolutionary advantage to recognizing a mother's voice, as described above (Locke, 2008). An adult's ability to recognize its own offspring conveys advantages as well. Voice recognition can facilitate reunions when mobile offspring wander off, or when a foraging parent returns and must locate its offspring in a noisy breeding colony. Such abilities help ensure that the adult's care is invested properly, so that its own offspring (and thus its genes), and not those of another animal, survive.

In this section, we review voice recognition abilities of a variety of species, ranging from penguins to goats, and from bats to primates. Two distinct kinds of recognition ability have been studied and will be reviewed in turn: the ability of parents and offspring to recognize one another, and the (more unusual) ability of an adult to recognize an unrelated animal. This discussion serves two purposes. It provides a broader perspective on human abilities to recognize and remember voices, and it supplies strong evidence for the claim that familiar voices are in fact "basic" in biologically-important ways.

5.3.2.1   *Parent/offspring recognition*

Providing significant amounts of care to needy infants is taxing for parents, and adults of many species refuse to feed or care for any but their own offspring. Some species face the additional problems of locating offspring in a crowd or after an absence. Such difficulties are particularly problematic in herd animals or in animals that breed in colonies. In these cases, voice recognition is one tool parents have to enable them to locate and reunite with their offspring, and to ensure that their care effort is invested properly. For the infant's part, the ability to recognize its parent allows it to solicit food and/or care from the appropriate adult, thus maximizing the likelihood of success while minimizing the chances of a physical rebuff from another adult. For example, six-day-old laughing gull chicks will run towards the sound of their parent's voice, but move away from the sound of a strange bird (Beer, 1969). Put together, these functions provide a potentially large evolutionary benefit, both in terms of maximizing the chances of infant survival and limiting the adult's unnecessary expenditure of resources (which increases its likelihood of reproducing again; Terrazas, Serafin, Hernandez, Nowak, and Poindron, 2003). Voice recognition in most animals is not an ability that extends beyond the identification of parents and/or offspring. Instead, it seems to represent a specific adaptation that enhances infant survival.

Animals have many ways of achieving these broad goals, and different adaptations have evolved depending on the environmental challenges to recognition that confront each species. For some animals, voice recognition is used as an adjunct to visual and olfactory recognition. Visual cues to identity are of limited use when many similar-appearing animals are in the same general location, and an animal's smell can only be assessed from close up. In contrast, vocal cues carry efficiently over long distances, and calls can be simple or elaborate, depending on the amount of information needed to ensure recognition (Searby and Jouventin, 2003). Common domestic sheep, for example, use fairly simple vocal recognition strategies, presumably because identity can be confirmed by smell before nursing takes place. Ewes and their lambs can recognize each other based solely on their calls: Both mothers and offspring responded to each other's calls by calling back significantly more often than they returned the call of another animal (Searby and Jouventin, 2003). Acoustic analyses of the calls suggested that a combination of mean F0 and the spectral shape of the calls (in other words, voice quality, narrowly defined) reliably distinguished animals from each other. To test this hypothesis, the animals also heard calls that had been shifted in frequency by 50 Hz, or that were played backward (to distort temporal cues). Playing the calls backward had no effect on recognition, but the animals failed to respond to calls whose mean F0 had been altered. Note that these experiments do not prove that a Gestalt pattern is NOT used for recognizing familial voices. In initial playback studies, the only strategy available to investigators is cue manipulation, which inherently emphasizes featural aspects of the recognition process (cf. Payne, 1998, p. 98).

Like sheep, mother goats (who also use smell and visual cues to recognize off-spring) can discriminate their own kids from an unfamiliar kid of the same age, based only on the sound of its cries (Terrazas *et al.*, 2003). Goats appear to use a more complex set of cues to recognize their infants, including the duration of the bleat, its fundamental frequency, the peak frequency and number of harmonics, and the numbers of segments in the cry. Although data from playback experiments confirming the importance of these cues are not available, in combination they are sufficient to distinguish animals statistically with almost perfect accuracy, suggesting that, in some combination, they provide a sufficient basis for recognition. The additional complexity of this system allows mother goats to learn the voices of their kids with remarkable efficiency: Recognition occurs reliably by the time the kid is 48 hours old.

Parent/offspring voice recognition is often symmetrical among so-called "following species" like goats and sheep, whose offspring typically follow after their parents in a herd environment. In these species, parents and offspring use contact calls to reunite when separations occur, and recognition of either by the other can advance this goal. In contrast, parent/offspring voice recognition is often asymmetrical in "hiding" species like fallow deer (Torriani, Vannoni, and McElligott, 2006). Newborn hiders conceal themselves to avoid predators, and only emerge from hiding when a parent calls. Because newborn survival depends on concealment, calling to a parent is counterproductive, and parent recognition of offspring cries serves no purpose. Thus, calls of adult female fallow deer are acoustically distinctive, but those of fawns are not significantly so; and fawns can discriminate the calls of their own mothers from those of other females, but hinds are unable to tell the calls of different fawns apart (Torriani *et al.*, 2006). These data show how the survival behaviors of different species (for example, herding and following vs. hiding) have shaped voice recognition behaviors.

Voice recognition in penguins provides another classic example of how voice recognition systems have evolved to meet different environmental demands. Adélie, macaroni, and gentoo penguins build nests, on which only family members are allowed. Thus, some kind of recognition system is essential for these animals. However, penguins apparently all look as much alike (and smell alike) to each other as they do to humans; and it has been shown that they are unable to recognize each other without the use of voice information (Jouventin, 1982). The exact role of voice varies across penguin species, however. For example, some penguins use their nest as a landmark to facilitate reunifications, so calls in these species serve primarily to alert the chick to the return of a foraging parent, as a summons to the nest, or as a confirmation of identity; but nest location is the primary cue to an individual's identity (Jouventin and Aubin, 2002; Searby, Jouventin, and Aubin, 2004). In contrast, king and emperor penguins do not build nests, but instead incubate their eggs on their feet. Because these birds lack nests, they face the difficult task of locating mates and offspring in a crowd of tens of thousands of moving, noisy birds, without the help of geographic cues or use of visual or olfactory information. Voice recognition is therefore critical if adult emperor and king penguins are to recognize their breeding partners when switching duties during incubation or chick rearing, or if chicks and parents are to recognize each other and reunite as the chicks become more independent and mobile. In all penguins, the task of voice recognition is complicated by the sound-masking effects of the bodies of the birds and the arctic wind, which block and/or distort the calls to variable extents. To overcome these difficulties, the birds' calls must be both complex (so that a single individual can be identified out of many thousands of possible candidates) and redundant (so that loss of part of the signal in transmission does not preclude the possibility of recognition based on the parts that remain (Lengagne, Lauga, and Aubin, 2001).

Nesting and non-nesting penguins have evolved very different voices, and very different systems of voice recognition, in response to these different ecological pressures. Nesting penguins apparently rely primarily on a frequency-based recognition system. Playback experiments using acoustically altered calls show that these birds are sensitive to the calls' F0, which must be within 25 Hz of the original call for it to be recognized. The duration and temporal pattern of the calls are unimportant, and playing signals backwards has no effect on recognition. Despite its simplicity, this recognition system is very effective: Chicks can recognize parents even when calls are produced in context of equally loud competing calls from other birds, and because calls appear from playback experiments to be unidimensional; chicks can recognize their parents based on a single syllable of a multi-syllable call (Jouventin and Aubin, 2002).

In contrast, non-nesting penguins have evolved a highly complex vocal system that is unique among penguin species. In birds, sound is produced by the syrinx, which is located in the chest at the junction of the bronchi. Each branch of the syrinx can produce sound independently, but most birds (including Adélie, gentoo, and macaroni penguins) do not use the two sources at the same time.[2] (See Sidebar in Chapter 3 for more information about the syrinx.) King and emperor penguins, the exceptions to this rule, use both voices simultaneously (the "two voice system;" Aubin, Jouventin, and Hildebrand, 2000) to produce complex calls with two separate sources that are close together in frequency. Because these frequencies are close together, they create a pattern of beats that varies between individuals. As a result of this complex system, a huge number of distinct voice patterns can be created, ensuring that each call contains enough distinct cues to ensure reliable recognition. A number of experiments (reviewed by Lengagne *et al.*, 2001) indicate that adult and juvenile king and emperor penguins attend to this beat pattern when identifying their family members. Time, frequency, and beat information are all important for successful recognition in these species: The birds do not recognize signals that are played backward or that have their frequency modulations[3] removed, or that have the pattern of frequency modulation altered; and recognition fails if one of the two voices is suppressed experimentally. Recognition also fails when the pattern of beat amplitudes is altered. These penguin species can tolerate more variability in mean F0 (up to about 100 Hz) than can Adélie or gentoo penguins, and the specific difference in frequency between the two voices appears unimportant for recognition, suggesting that spectral information does not play a role equal to that of time and frequency variations in voice (Lengagne *et al.*, 2001).

These complex calls and elaborate recognition strategies seem to have evolved as an adaptation to the loss of nest location cues in a context in which recognition of mates and offspring retains its high survival value for all concerned. Increased call complexity

---

[2]   As noted in Chapter 2, the syrinx is able to evolve in these various and complicated ways because its only function is to produce sound.

[3]   Slow changes in the mean F0 over time. Vocal tremors and vibrato are both examples of frequency modulations.

helps make calls highly robust in the face of masking noise and sound absorption by the bodies of the birds (Aubin *et al.*, 2000). In fact, emperor chicks can recognize their parents when voice signals are 6 dB *softer* than the ambient noise (Aubin and Jouventin, 1998). The elaborate calls produced by non-nesting birds, compared to the relatively simple calls of nesting penguins, suggest that call complexity has evolved as an adaptation to the different challenges the species face with respect to the general biological problem of partner and offspring identification (Lengagne *et al.*, 2001).

Nesting Macaroni penguins have evolved a voice recognition system that is intermediate in complexity between those of other nesting penguins and the non-nesting species. Macaroni penguins use a "double signature system," in which either the tempo of syllables in a multi-syllable call *or* the harmonic structure of the call is sufficient for recognition (Searby *et al.*, 2004), but neither alone appears to be crucial and recognition is most successful when both are present. This combination of elemental temporal and spectral cues is more redundant than the system used by other nesting penguins, but less so than that of the non-nesting penguins. Playback experiments indicate that Macaroni penguin chicks, studied in the field, respond to only about 39% of recorded calls (compared with about 80% responses from chicks of non-nesting species), whereas calls from parents elicit responses over 99% of the time. These data reinforce the importance of geographic cues in nesting penguins: Voice recognition appears to function as an additional cue to parent identity in these species, but is not in itself a substitute for the sight of a penguin on the appropriate nest. In this situation, a basic set of acoustic cues may be sufficient to the purpose, although non-featural pattern recognition strategies that cannot be examined via cue manipulations may also operate, as noted above.

Similar sets of complex voice patterns and recognition cues exist in other species (avian and non-avian) that also breed in colonies, produce mobile offspring, forage, and thus must rely on voice recognition if offspring are to survive. Sound is a particularly efficient means of recognition in such colonies, because unlike sight and smell it spreads widely in all directions and does not require close contact between parent and child to be effective (for example, Searby *et al.*, 2004). For example, black-headed gull chicks use high-energy "begging" behavior (which is tiring and can attract predators) to solicit food from their parents, and to maximize the return on investment (and to avoid being pecked by a stranger) they need to recognize their parents' voices (Charrier, Mathevon, Jouventin, and Aubin, 2001a). Seals also breed in large colonies that can include 70,000 animals, and because feeding grounds are often far from breeding shores, mothers must leave pups unattended while foraging for food, sometimes for several weeks at a time. Playback experiments (reviewed in Insley, 2001) have shown that mothers recognize pups by voice in seven different species of seal; in four of these (sub Antarctic fur seals, Galapagos fur seals, California sea lions, and northern fur seals), pups also recognize their mothers. Insley (2001) has argued that ensuring reliable reunions in the context of coloniality and offspring mobility may have motivated what was originally a unidirectional recognition system (mothers recognize pups, but not vice versa) to evolve into one of mutual recognition. As evidence, he cites the case of northern fur seals. Both mothers and pups respond selectively to each others' calls. However, northern fur seal mothers bear relatively many pups over their lifetimes, so a missed reunion is more costly to the pup (who will die) than it is to the mother (who will bear another pup next season). For this reason, pups expend far more energy calling and responding to calls, and also make more mistaken identifications, than mothers do. In essence, pups appear to be oversampling the range of possible mothers, ensuring a high hit rate at the expense of a high false alarm rate. Thus, although recognition is mutual, it is also asymmetrical, suggesting that pups' ability to recognize their mothers is a relatively new ability that is still evolving.

There are variations in the extents to which given seal species depend on vocalization, as is also the case for penguins. For example, arctic fur seals use vocalization and rendezvous points to locate each other initially, but final identification depends on olfaction, not voice (Dobson and Jouventin, 2003). In contrast, mother/pup reunions in sub Antarctic fur seals depend mostly on voice recognition, with both mothers and pups continually calling until reunion is accomplished (Charrier, Mathevon, and Jouventin, 2001b). Playback experiments suggest that fur seals use a complex recognition strategy based on both time and spectral domain information to recognize each other (Charrier, Mathevon, and Jouventin, 2002; Mathevon, Charrier, and Aubin, 2004). The temporal pattern of frequency modulation is of primary importance; if this pattern is modified, recognition does not occur. Seals also attend to the shape of the overall voice spectrum, particularly to F0 and the lower part of the spectrum (modifications to which also impair recognition). These parameters vary more between individuals than within individuals, and provide enough information to distinguish one pup from another. As a set, they are also very resistant to degradation by the noisy breeding colony environment.

In foraging, colonial species like seals, mothers cannot forage until they are sure that their pups can recognize their voices, if they are to have any hope of reuniting with their offspring. As a result, learning must take place extremely quickly after birth. In sub Antarctic fur seals, playback experiments have shown that at birth pups respond to the calls of any female. However, by the time that they are between two and five days old they only respond to their own mother, who is then free to leave on a foraging trip (Charrier *et al.*, 2001b). Although pups' voices change as they grow, playback experiments also showed that mother seals retain the ability to identify all the different versions of their pup's voice that they hear. For instance, mothers whose pups were in the age range eight to ten months responded equally to contemporary calls and to calls recorded when their pups were newborn, and they ignored any calls coming from other, unrelated pups (Charrier, Mathevon, and Jouventin, 2003). These data indicate that female sub Antarctic fur seals must retain memories of all the successive versions of their pup's voice. This is somewhat less surprising given the heavy burden played by voice recognition in this species. If mothers (who leave the pups for up to two to three weeks at a time) fail to recognize their infants, the pups will die, so among sub Antarctic fur seals voice recognition is the sine qua non of breeding success.

In contrast, evening bat mothers go out to forage immediately after the birth of their young, leaving the pups in dark crèches that may contain thousands of other bats. Mothers and pups do successfully reunite after these separations, which suggests that either the mothers learn their pups' calls incredibly quickly (within minutes of birth), or else the calls have a genetic component (Scherrer and Wilkinson, 1993). The pattern of frequency modulation in an individual's calls is distinct and remains so throughout that individual's life, and it is possible to sort over 1,800 pups based on their calls without any acoustic overlap. Further, statistical analyses of the calls of wild bats assigned each animal to the correct family with almost 70% accuracy. These observations suggest that calls are in fact inheritable in this species. In comparison, consider the case of long-tailed tits, a bird species that breeds cooperatively. Individuals provide care almost exclusively to their relatives, whom they distinguish from unrelated individuals based on the features of their calls (although they do not distinguish specific individuals among their kin). Cross-fostering experiments indicate that tits learn their calls from the adults that care for them as nestlings, thus ensuring that they share their vocal features with their relatives and with their siblings (Sharp, McGowan, Wood, and Hatchwell, 2005).

Learning to recognize a parent's or infant's voice apparently follows a somewhat more leisurely course in animals whose environment and/or behavior makes voice recognition less difficult or less critically important. For example, Japanese macaques do not recognize their mothers until about 22 days of age (Masataka, 1985), and infant barbary macaques apparently do not recognize their mothers reliably until ten weeks of age (Fischer, 2004). In fact, although pressures of communal living have led many species to develop infant/mother recognition systems, such systems are simpler overall in non-colonial animals. For example, rhesus monkeys are highly mobile, and juveniles are frequently out of visual contact with their mothers, so the ability to recognize each other auditorily is important. Playback experiments have shown that rhesus monkey infants increase cooing rates when they hear their own mothers vocalize, compared to an unfamiliar female (Hansen, 1976). However, it is not clear if mothers recognize the juveniles, or if they remember or adapt to changes in their infants' calls with age. In other primate species, the responsibility for reunification rests on mothers, and infants may not recognize their parent until they are much older (Altmann, 1980). Unidirectional recognition is adequate for these species, because the parents and infants are generally not widely separated, do not separate for extended periods, and can rely on vision and smell as adjuncts to vocal identity cues.

In summary, different species (including many not mentioned here) have evolved a variety of solutions to the problem of vocally recognizing a parent or an infant. The details of the observed variations can often be understood in terms of the varying ecological and evolutionary demands faced by different animal species. In some cases, mothers and infants must be able to recognize each other's vocalizations; in others, one-way recognition is sufficient. The need for signal redundancy varies, as does the need for complex calls (which depends in part on the number of individuals present, from whom the target must be distinguished). Playback experiments suggest that in several species, call repertoires consist of a large number of complex, unique vocal patterns. As this brief review shows, species solve these problems in different ways, depending on the particular environment involved. The variety of solutions that has evolved, along with the widespread presence and sophistication of voice recognition, attest to the fundamental importance this ability has in enabling offspring to survive.

5.3.2.2 Recognizing other animals from voice

A few nonhuman animals have been shown to recognize the voices of others who are not their parent or offspring, or who are not even relatives. For example, many territorial frogs and songbirds discriminate neighbors from strangers using a combination of acoustic and location cues: A familiar call from an expected location will not evoke an aggressive response, but an unfamiliar call (presumably from a frog attempting to take over the breeding territory) will evoke aggressive vocalizations, chases, splashes, or physical attacks (Bee, Kozich, Blackwell, and Gerhardt, 2001). In many animals such responses are location dependent – a familiar call from a new location triggers the same aggressive response as an unfamiliar call – and hence do not constitute true voice recognition (Bee and Gerhardt, 2002). However, in at least one species (*Rana catesbeiana*, the North American bullfrog) males respond significantly less aggressively to a familiar voice in a new location than to an unfamiliar voice independent of location, suggesting that they can discriminate the familiar voices of their neighbors from unfamiliar voices, and can use this information to limit unnecessary aggressive interactions (Bee and Gerhardt, 2002).

Other data on this kind of voice recognition come from studies of primates. Primates tend to live in social groups marked by stable dominance relationships among group members, and many behaviors are influenced by the identities of the animals involved and their kin relationships. For this reason, social primates require the ability to discriminate among and identify other group members. It has long been known from seminal studies performed in the wild by Cheney and Seyfarth (1980) that female vervet monkeys can recognize the voices of their juvenile offspring, and can recognize an unrelated juvenile and associate it with its mother. When a female hears her offspring's voice in a playback experiment, she stops what she is doing, looks up, and/or approaches the speaker, while unrelated females look at the caller's mother, but never approach the speaker. These findings have been replicated more recently in female baboons (Cheney and Seyfarth, 1999), who also recognize the screams and threat grunts of both their own relatives and of unrelated individuals. In contrast, rhesus monkeys respond consistently to the voices of kin who are not immediate family members (by stopping what they are doing, looking around, and/or approaching the speaker), but almost never to those of unrelated animals (Rendall, Rodman, and Edmond, 1996). In addition, a habituation/discrimination experiment indicated that the monkeys can also discriminate among voices of their different relatives: They stopped responding to the voices of the original animals, but responded again when the voice they heard changed to that of a new individual. Although discriminating among and recognizing voices are different abilities, the combined results of these experiments suggest rhesus monkeys can in fact recognize a variety of individuals by voice.

Field studies of African elephants similarly reveal an impressive ability to recognize the voices of family members and non-related associates. Female elephants live in family groups, but associate with other groups (their "bond" group) in the same geographical area. Playback experiments (McComb, Moss, Sayialel, and Baker, 2002) showed that elephants could distinguish the voices of family and bond group members from those of other females: They responded to the first class of voices by calling or by approaching the loudspeaker, but to the second class of voices either by listening or by bunching together and retreating. The extent of the defensive response to the relatively unfamiliar voices could be predicted by how much the elephant groups had been in contact: They simply listened to calls from elephants that were unrelated but encountered relatively often in the bush, but bunched and retreated when they heard calls from elephants that were seldom encountered. From these data and from estimates of the total elephant population in the area, McComb *et al.* concluded that the elephants were familiar with the calls of around 100 adult females, and could correctly classify them into an "us versus them" scheme that was further scaled according to the extent of familiarity.

Analyses of the calls of chimpanzees (Marler and Hobbett, 1975), rhesus monkeys (Rendall, Owren, and Rodman, 1998), and baboons (Rendall, 2003) suggest that vocal tract resonances provide reliable cues to an individual's identity. Rendall and colleagues measured F0, formant frequencies, and noise characteristics from coo, grunt, and scream vocalizations – over 1,000 calls in all – from 21 wild rhesus monkeys. Coos and grunts are both characterized by clear formant structures, but screams are broadband noise, with no measurable resonance peaks. Statistically, coos provided the most information about which animal had produced a given call. Grunts were next, but it was not possible to correctly identify an animal from its scream vocalizations.[4] Formant frequencies were sufficient to identify an animal 78% of the time; a coo's fundamental frequency produced 61% correct classification, but screams were not sufficiently distinctive on any measured acoustic dimension to permit classification at statistically significant levels. Playback experiments confirmed that the monkeys did not recognize voices from screams. Vocal tract resonances are also better predictors of the identity of individual baboons than are such source-related characteristics as F0, jitter, H1–H2, or the intonation pattern of the calls (Rendall, 2003). Measurements confirmed that vocal tract resonances in baboons are relatively unchanging across calls within an individual, and thus may serve as stable indicators of individual identity.

Physiological evidence is consistent with the idea that vocal tract resonances should provide stable indices of personal identity in primates. Primate vocal systems resemble those of humans, and many species use vocal fold action like human vibration to provide vocal tract excitation, with the vocal tract filtering the sound as it does in humans. A number of differences in anatomy also occur across species, however. Some species (including macaques) have a relatively rigid lip on the medial edge of each vocal fold that lets them produce vibratory modes that humans cannot. For example, they can produce very loud noise-based sounds, sounds that are near-sine waves, frequency sweeps that cover many octaves in a fraction of a second, and simultaneous periodic and aperiodic vocal fold vibration. Supralaryngeally, some primates have a "sac" that may act as an extra resonator for sounds that are intended to carry for long distances. In addition, primates have thinner tongues than humans, and their larynges are higher in the neck. This suggests that they are less able to vary the resonances of the vocal tract dynamically than humans are, further supporting the idea that these structures can provide stable acoustic cues to individual identity. Finally, some evidence indicates that primates are less sensitive to frequencies below 500 Hz (i.e., the range of F0) than are humans and are more sensitive in higher frequency ranges nearer the formant frequencies. (See Fitch, 2000a; Fitch and Hauser, 1995, 2003; or Schon Ybarra, 1995, for review.)

---

[4] Although the identity of a screaming individual cannot be ascertained through spectral cues, some information is available through the temporal pattern of the cries. Screams are issued in burst patterns, rather than as one long vocalization. This may occur due to constraints on facial expression during screams, which are always issued with a fear grimace and exaggerated lip retraction. This significantly alters the formants by shortening the vocal tract, thus distorting the spectral cues relative to other cry types (Rendall *et al.*, 1998).

In comparison, analyses of elephant contact calls indicate that both source and filter information are important for recognizing an individual. Calls could be correctly matched to the caller 77.4% of the time based on the combined source and filter attributes, but only about 40–43% of the time based on either alone (McComb, Reby, Baker, Moss, and Sayialel, 2003). Elephants produce "infrasonic" calls, including seismic alarm calls, with very low F0 (typically around 16 Hz), which can be heard and recognized reliably by other elephants over distances of at least 1–2.5 km, and possibly up to 4 km (Payne, 1998; O'Connell-Rodwell, 2005). Recordings of the calls at increasing distances showed that detection and recognition probably depend on harmonics around 115 Hz – well above the infrasonic range – that are amplified by vocal tract resonances and thus stand out above background noise (wind, rustling trees, blowing dust) at long distances. F2 in elephant calls occurs at about 115 Hz, consistent with a very long vocal tract and with the trunk functioning as part of the filter.

In summary, many different animal species share a specialized ability to recognize voices, but evince different voice recognition strategies. In some species, auditory recognition supplements vision, olfaction, and location cues, while other species depend entirely on voice to recognize each other. The observed variability can be understood by examining the needs of the animal and the environmental challenges to recognition. In general, simple recognition strategies have evolved in situations where additional nonvocal cues are available, or where informational demands are light, while complex vocal signals containing a multitude of possible cues to the caller's identity have emerged when other cues are lacking or where signal redundancy is needed because of environmental demands. These conclusions are offered with the caveat that playback studies (from which these findings derive) have only tested hypotheses about the importance of specific acoustic cues in voice recognition. Such studies of necessity presuppose feature-based models of voice recognition, because it is not apparent how to study perception of integral auditory patterns in nonhuman animals. The fact that recognition rates reported in studies using these reductionist paradigms seldom rise above 70% itself suggests that other processes are in play. It might be inferred from these results that utilization of complex patterns, not directly probed in these studies, at least potentially accounts for successful vocal recognition in the wild. The data simply do not exist to address this possibility at present.

5.3.3   Familiar voice recognition in adult humans

We had scarcely sat down when a darkness came that was not like a moonless or cloudy night, but more like the black of closed and unlighted rooms. You could hear women lamenting, children crying, men shouting. Some were calling for parents, others for children or spouses; they could only recognize them by their voices.

Pliny the Younger, letter to Tacitus describing the destruction of Pompeii[5]

For humans, recognizing familiar voices is a ubiquitous experience, achieved by virtually all normal listeners every day of their lives. Most people commonly have the experience of recognizing a familiar voice from the single word "hello" on the telephone.

---

[5]   *The Letters of the Younger Pliny*, translated by Betty Radice (New York: Penguin Classics, 1963), p. 172.

Speakers expect to be recognized from this short voice sample (which in itself provides information about who the caller might be), and it can be embarrassing to fail to recognize a friend or family member. Sociolinguistic analyses have shown that familiar callers expect to be recognized by their voices rather than by giving their names; even brief hesitation by the listener in recognizing the caller by voice will result in an awkward moment, or "trouble," in the progress of the conversation (Schegloff, 1979). An occasional crank caller will even exploit this fact, pretending to be a known speaker and listening to the victim struggle to place the voice. Other kinds of errors can be equally problematic. For example, in *Bonfire of the Vanities* (Wolfe, 1987), Sherman accidentally dials his home number instead of his mistress's, reaches his wife, fails to recognize her voice (although he realizes it is not his mistress, Maria), and embroils himself in difficulties:[6]

> *Three rings, and a woman's voice: "Hello?"*
> *But it was not Maria's voice. He figured it must be her friend Germaine, the one she sublet the apartment from. So he said: "May I speak to Maria please?"*
> *The woman said: "Sherman? Is that you?"*
> *Christ. It's Judy! He's dialed his own apartment. He's aghast – paralyzed!*
> *"Sherman?"*
> *He hangs up. Oh Jesus. What can he do? He'll bluff it out. When she asks him, he'll say he doesn't know what she's talking about. After all, he said only five or six words. How can she be sure? (p. 17)*[7]

The functions and evolutionary (or other) benefits of voice recognition ability for humans are similar in many ways to the advantages gained from these abilities by nonhuman animals, and ability to extract information from voices clearly predates language by many millennia. Voice recognition enables mobile individuals to locate and identify members of a family or group who are out of sight, and allows them to determine whether an approaching individual is or is not an outsider. These abilities facilitate cooperation among individuals and members of a group, thus enhancing the likelihood of survival. Voice recognition ability also helps mothers and infants identify and bond with each other, as described above. Like other animals, humans do not need to learn the voice of every individual they encounter in life. Rather, they recognize the individuals that are personally relevant to them, against a background of irrelevant, unfamiliar, and usually unattended voices.[8] Recognizing familiar voices differs in structure and process from perceiving unfamiliar voices, as we will continue to describe; in fact, studies show that these two cognitive processes are subserved by different brain mechanisms, as described in Chapter 6. Finally, humans rely heavily on visual information when recognizing others, as other animals rely on olfaction, vision, geographical or other cues.

---

[6]   That the process of recognizing voices can be influenced by expectation (also known as psychological set) was shown by Ladefoged (1978). In this fictional example, expectation leads the character Sherman, for a split second, to know only whose voice the "hello" did NOT represent. It required four more words for him to be sufficiently free of psychological set to recognize his wife's voice.

[7]   Sherman misses the point that HE definitively recognized his wife's voice in five words.

[8]   In fact, as an index of how little attention we pay to unfamiliar voices, listeners will not usually notice a change in talker in mid-conversation, even if the speaker's sex changes and even if they are specifically instructed to listen for such a change (Howard Nusbaum, personal communication, 2007).

Human recognition abilities, as far as is known, do differ from those of other animals in several critical ways. While recognition in most other species is limited to a relatively small number of relatives or troop members, the modern human "troop" is huge. For example, the first author's set includes Fred Astaire and Katharine Hepburn, her co-author, her neighbors, her mother, many present and past members of the UCLA Phonetics group, the public address announcer at Dodger Stadium in Los Angeles, Bugs Bunny, all the spouses of her husband's siblings, and her daughter's friends, among many, many others. In fact, there may not be an upper limit to the number of voices a human can learn to recognize. (One estimate places the memory capacity of the human brain at 10^{8432} bits; Wang, Liu, and Wang, 2003). We conclude from this that the human brain's ability to store and access complex patterns, based on perceptual experience, is very large indeed.

Beyond flagging a voice as familiar, humans are often (but not unfailingly, alas) able to associate a name, a face, and a body of personal information with the voice (old friend, laughs at your jokes, fond of tea, plays viola da gamba and piano, likes Wagner and the color maroon), adding an additional dimension of complexity to the recognition task. Familiar voice patterns usually resonate with a packet of associated pieces of information, including biographical, affective, physical, and historical details (Van Lancker, 1991). Finally, human voice recognition is robust relative to recognition in most other animals, by which we mean that more patterns are recognized under more varied conditions; and no one acoustic cue, or small set of cues, is critical to recognition of all voices, so that recognition can occur even under less-than-ideal conditions, as we will discuss shortly. The number of voices humans can recognize, the varied contexts in which recognition can take place, and the diversity of perceptual strategies brought to the recognition task indicate that human voice recognition abilities represent a substantial elaboration on the ability found in other species, appropriating additional cognitive operations of all kinds: linguistic naming, extensive cross-modal perceptual associations, emotional associations, and declarative, semantic, and episodic memory functions (although other species manifest some of these attributes in rudimentary forms).

5.3.3.1 How well do human listeners recognize familiar voices?

As suggested above, when they recognize and possibly name the person who produced a voice sample, humans do a highly complex task extremely well compared to the recognition abilities demonstrated in other animals. Studies of human listeners' abilities to identify a familiar speaker have taken two approaches to the topic. In the first, researchers study speakers and listeners who are familiar with each other through daily contact (familiar/intimate voices). These studies examine recognition of the voices of an individual's friends and family members, and thus necessarily include relatively small numbers of speakers and/or listeners. For example, Ladefoged and Ladefoged (1980) examined the ability of a single über-expert listener to recognize the voices of 53 speakers (29 familiar, 13 somewhat familiar, and 11 unfamiliar). The expert (Peter Ladefoged) correctly named 31% of the speakers after hearing the single word "hello," and he correctly recognized 66% of the speakers when the stimulus was a sentence. The overall false identification rate equaled 11%. Note that this is a very difficult "open-set" task, in which a successful response requires first correctly judging that the voice is familiar, discerning whose voice it is, and then, as an additional step, retrieving the name associated with that voice, all without benefit of context, when the set of possible responses included everyone whose voice the listener was even slightly familiar with. Name retrieval adds an extra dimension of complexity to voice recognition tasks above and beyond merely recognizing that the voice is familiar and knowing whom it belongs to, as we will discuss further below.

Several similar studies examined recognition of the voices of the listeners' friends and relations, but used untrained listeners rather than a prominent phonetician (see Sidebar on "Trained to familiar voices procedure" in Chapter 6). These studies have varied significantly in experimental design, as indicated in Table 5.2. Correct identification rates vary widely with design and also from speaker to speaker within a study, ranging from 20–60% correct for familiar voices saying the word "hello", with corresponding false alarm rates of 30–45%. Some differences in the level of performance can be attributed to response criteria: Studies reporting higher accuracy also generally reported higher rates of incorrect identifications as well. Several other rather unsurprising findings have emerged from these studies. For example, recognition accuracy generally increases when the talker is highly familiar to the listener as compared to less familiar talkers. Accuracy also increases with increasing stimulus durations. Finally, recognizing a familiar voice is easier when speakers talk in a normal tone, and harder when they whisper or use falsetto.

In a second approach, familiar voice recognition can be studied using familiar/famous voices. Thanks to the mass media, this approach is much simpler to implement, because many listeners are familiar with the voices of similar sets of actors, politicians, newscasters, and other celebrities. Listeners do fairly well when asked to identify a famous voice in an open-set task (where the speaker could be anyone, living or dead): Listeners correctly named 27% of the speakers when presented with a two-second voice sample without context (Van Lancker, Kreiman, and Emmorey, 1985a), and 48% from a 20-second sample, even when voices were recorded across five decades (Meudell, Northen, Snowden, and Neary, 1980). Recognition rates increased when speakers were provided with a closed set of choices, with pictures, and/or with a list of speakers' names (Table 5.2). More recently, Schweinberger, Herholz, and Sommer (1997a) played listeners samples of famous voices varying in duration from 250 ms to 2 sec. Listeners heard longer and longer samples until they categorized the voice as "famous" or "unfamiliar." Accuracy was very close to 0 for stimulus durations of 250 ms, but increased rapidly with duration up to 1 sec. For the longest durations, listeners correctly responded "famous" 68% of the time, with a false alarm rate of 33%.

5.3.3.2 Familiar voice recognition: Reliable features or complex patterns?

These data (and everyday experience) confirm that human voice recognition abilities are quite impressive compared to those of other animals. Studies to date report that nonhuman animals appear to use a variety of cues and strategies to recognize the voices of their kin. However, the specific questions about the process depend on the imagination of the investigator, and in many cases animals may ultimately rely on nondecomposable patterns in ways that have not been investigated to date. Is human familiar voice recognition an elaborated version of any of these kinds of processes, or do

Table 5.2 Recognition rates for the voices of personally familiar speakers.

A: familiar-intimate voices

Task	Correct recognition	Study
Naming, "hello"	31%	Ladefoged and Ladefoged (1980)
Sentence	66%	Same as above
Naming, 2.5 minute passage	90–100%; mean = 98%	Hollien *et al.* (1982)
Naming, barely familiar voices 15.3 sec sample	79%	Schmidt-Nielsen and Stern (1985)
Highly familiar voices 5.3 sec sample	92%	Same as above
Naming, "hello"	Hit rate 47–60%; false alarm rate 30%	Rose and Duncan (1995)
Sentence	Hit rate 90–100%	Same as above
Naming, 15 sec sample, normal voice	Hit rate 97%; false alarm rate 29%	Wagner and Koster (1999)
15 sec sample, falsetto	Hit rate 4%; false alarm rate 1%	Same as above
Select name from list, 0.5 sec /a/	Hit rate 12–93%; false alarm rate 1–50%	Lavner *et al.* (2000)
Naming, highly familiar voices, "hello"	Hit rate 20–33%; false alarm rate 5.33%	Yarmey *et al.* (2001)
Low familiarity voices, "hello"	Hit rate 4–13%, false alarm rate 23–46%	Same as above
Naming, highly familiar voices, whispered "hello"	Hit rate 20%, false alarm rate 41%	Same as above
Low familiarity voices, whispered "hello"	Hit rate 5%, false alarm rate 41%	Same as above
Naming, highly familiar voices, 2 min whispered spontaneous speech	Hit rate 77%, false alarm rate 15%	Same as above
Naming, low familiarity voices, 2 min whispered spontaneous speech	Hit rate 22%, false alarm rate 47%	Same as above

B: familiar-famous voices

Task	Correct recognition	Study
Naming; 2 sec sample; open set	27%	Van Lancker *et al.* (1985a)
6 names provided	70%	Same as above
Naming; 20 sec sample; open set	48%	Meudell *et al.* (1980)
4 pictures provided	60%	Same as above
4 pictures + names provided	82%	Same as above
"Familiar" judgment without naming; 0.35 sec stimulus duration	Hit rate 10%; false alarm rate 5%	Schweinberger *et al.* (1997a)
2 sec stimulus duration	Hit rate 68%; false alarm rate 33%	Same as above

different kinds of perceptual and cognitive processes underlie humans' more sophisticated recognition abilities?

Like approaches to animal vocal recognition, most studies examining the way in which humans recognize voices assume that there exists a fixed set of cues on which humans rely, and then seek to identify these cues. Studies typically manipulate a rather limited set of acoustic parameters and examine the effect each manipulation has on recognition scores. For example, many such studies have examined the relative importance of source versus vocal tract information in recognizing a familiar speaker, while the majority of parameters listed in Table 5.3 remain unstudied. Data from primates (reviewed earlier in this chapter) suggest that vocal tract resonances might provide reliable cues to a speaker's identity. On the other hand, in humans, variation in resonances conveys semantic information (the vowel, and hence the word, being spoken), and thus might be less informative about the speaker's identity than is the case for primates. If this is so, voice source information might be relatively more important in humans for determining speaker identity. Patterns of variability in resonances and/or F0 might perform the complex function of signaling both linguistic meaning and personal identity. Further, the large constellation of vocal parameters carried in speech are available singly and in any combination for any unique voice pattern. In the end, it will be seen that recognition of a given voice draws unpredictably on any and all of these parameters as well as from the array listed in Table 5.3 (and possibly others that we have not listed).

A number of problems are apparent in testing familiar voice recognition in non-human and human animals alike. (These issues are explored further in Section 6.3.1). Some are procedural. For example, it can be hard to assess recognition ability in the face of listeners' differential familiarity with famous target speakers, but it can be equally difficult to locate enough participants who are sufficiently mutually familiar when using (for humans) non-famous (familiar-intimate) voices. The "I know who that is but I just can't think of the name" problem also plagues studies of familiar voice recognition, which may overestimate performance when asking listeners to respond "familiar/unfamiliar" but may underestimate actual recognition if they require name retrieval. (See Schweinberger *et al.*, 1997a, for a discussion of response biases in this kind of research.) For animals, establishing previous familiarity and reliably recording the familiarity response is even more challenging. Finally, most studies in this tradition, because they often arise from forensic exigencies, lack a well-developed theoretical motivation, and it can be hard to interpret the conflicting findings that sometimes emerge from seemingly similar research (see Chapter 7). In particular, it is difficult to reconcile the finding that individual cues are variably important across voices with a model of speaker recognition based on linguistic-style "distinctive features" for voices like that implied by studies in this tradition.

In fact, results of early studies using a restricted set of auditory-acoustic parameters did not provide an unambiguous answer to the question of the relative importance of source and vocal tract information as cues to speaker identity. Abberton and Fourcin (1978) asked eight female listeners to identify the voices of five classmates by circling the speaker's initials from a list for each trial (a closed-set task with no naming required). Listeners heard seven versions of the phrase "Hello! How are you?" These

Table 5.3 A partial list of vocal characteristics potentially contributing to voice recognition in humans[a].

Source and filter characteristics
    F0 mean, variability and range
    Intensity mean, variability and range
    Resonances (formants) and anti-resonances
        Frequencies
        Variability
        Bandwidths
        Relative spacing of formants

Mode of vocal fold vibration (voice quality narrowly considered)
    "Modal"
    Murmured
    Glottal attack
    Creaky voice
    Breathy voice
    Harmonics-to-noise ratio

Temporal characteristics
    Rate
    Mean syllable length
    Words per minute
    Pausing
    Phrase length
    Rhythm or meter
    Vowel and consonant lengths
    Stress patterns

Articulatory setting
    Oral
    Pharyngealized
    Lip protrusion

Articulatory characteristics
    Degree of hyperarticulation
    Coarticulation
    Vowel reduction

Degree of nasality
    Hypernasal/hyponasal

Prosodic line
    Predominately falling, rising
    Monotonic, hypermelodic

Syllable structure
    Broad
    Clipped
    Slurred

Other
    Dialect/accent
    Idiolectal variants (of great variety)

---

[a] A comparable table of potential vocal parameters for vocal recognition in various nonhuman animals is not yet possible.

conditions included the natural voice (source + vocal tract information), whisper (vocal tract information, but no source information), the output of a laryngograph (a device that records the estimated position of the vocal folds across the glottis; source information, but no vocal tract information), and several synthetic stimuli in which different aspects of average F0 and F0 contours were manipulated. Listeners correctly identified the speaker 99% of the time from the natural speech tokens. The recognition rate for whisper was 90%, but it was only 65% from the laryngograph signal. In contrast, LaRivicrc (1975) asked 12 listeners to identify eight familiar male speakers from a normal vowel, a whispered vowel, or a vowel that was low-pass filtered to remove vocal tract information. Listeners correctly recognized the speakers 40% of the time from natural vowel stimuli, 22% of the time from whisper, and 21% of the time from filtered vowels, suggesting that listeners can identify a speaker based solely on either source or vocal tract information, with the average contributions of each being equal. However, this average pattern was not true for each individual speaker: The more extreme a speaker was on some parameter, the more listeners appeared to rely on that parameter, and the greater the error rate for that particular voice when that information was eliminated.

More recent studies using speech synthesis suggest that, as with primates, recognizing a familiar human voice may utilize resonance information somewhat more than F0. Kuwabara and Takagi (1991) manipulated formant frequencies, bandwidths, and F0, and found that changes in formant center frequencies of more than 5% destroyed personal quality, but changes in F0 and bandwidths had less effect on speaker recognizability. Consistent with this result, humans are able to identify familiar speakers based on "sine wave replicas" of their voices, in which the resonances are replaced by sine waves with the appropriate frequencies (so that listeners have information about formant frequencies, but not about F0 or formant bandwidths; for example, Fellowes, Remez, and Rubin, 1997).

In an even more elaborate study, Lavner, Gath, and Rosenhouse (2000) raised and lowered formant frequencies individually and by shifting the entire spectral envelope up and down; they modified the shape of the glottal source pulses as well as F0; and they mixed and matched vocal tracts and sources for each of 20 male speakers who had lived together in the same kibbutz for at least five years. When asked to select the correct response from a list of 29 names, listeners were correct 49.6% of the time overall, but performance varied by stimulus condition and by voice, and no acoustic manipulation had the same effect on all of the voices. Changing formant center frequencies had the largest negative effect on recognition. Overall, shifting the higher formants (which are less important for vowel recognition) disrupted recognition more than shifting the lower formants. However, different formants appeared to contribute differentially to identifiability for individual speakers, and some voices remained equally identifiable in all conditions of modification. Modifications to F0 also interfered with recognition, but to a lesser (and voice-dependent) extent. The exact shape of the glottal source pulses had little independent effect on voice recognizability. It thus appears that vocal tract information is somewhat more important overall than source information for identifying known speakers, although the importance of any given parameter may vary considerably from speaker to speaker. As mentioned above, listeners apparently exploit all possible sources of information – pitch, loudness, quality, and their patterns of variation over time, as well as many other parameters not specified here, and in various combinations, when recognizing a voice (see Table 5.3).

Other studies have examined the kind of speech sample and amount of speech needed to recognize a familiar voice. In an early approach to this question, Pollack, Pickett, and Sumby (1954) studied the effects of stimulus duration on the identification of eight personally familiar voices from samples of connected speech. Performance improved rapidly with increasing duration up to about one second, but improvement slowed thereafter.[9] When listeners recognized familiar speakers from isolated vowels, recognition accuracy also increased with stimulus duration until it peaked at 65% correct for durations of 500 to 700 ms (although recognition rates exceeded chance levels for stimuli as short as 25 msec; Compton, 1963). More recently, Schweinberger *et al.* (1997a) played listeners samples of famous voices varying in duration from 250 ms to 2 sec. Recognition accuracy was very close to 0 at 250 ms, but increased rapidly with duration up to 1 sec. These increases in accuracy appear to be related more to the increased variety in speech sounds available in longer stimuli, rather than simply to the increased duration per se: Recognition rates are better predicted by the number of phonemes in the speech sample provided under laboratory conditions than by duration alone (Bricker and Pruzansky, 1966), due to the additional information on rate, syllable shape, articulation, and F0 variation, encompassing a larger array of possible parameters.

What these have in common with the studies of animals reviewed above is their exclusive focus on the role of F0, resonances, and rate in speaker recognition, without considering other vocal characteristics present in the voice signal. In fact, very many different parameters, at various levels of description, can hypothetically play a role in specifying the quality of a known individual's voice. A small subset of these is listed in Table 5.3. Studies examining such small sets of features (whether in animal or human vocalization) miss the point that perceptually important features emerge idiosyncratically in different patterns, and that it is the unique relationship of a constellation of parameters taken from a very large set that signals a given unique pattern.

An alternative view of the voice recognition process abandons the assumption that a relatively small and fixed set of cues underlies familiar voice recognition, and proposes that familiar voices are recognized as Gestalt-like patterns, drawing variously and inconsistently from a very broad set of potential auditory parameters like those listed in Table 5.3 (cf. Kuwabara and Sagisak, 1995, who concluded that no single acoustic parameter alone can account for perception of voice identity). In this view, as mentioned previously, processing a voice sample involves an interplay between a holistic, synthetic Gestalt process and attention to salient details. From this perspective, it is not useful to specify a small set of parameters that universally underlies voice quality judgments, because many cues are available, and the cues to a particular speaker's identity logically depend on their relation to the complete vocal pattern in which the individual cues operate. Recognition also depends on the particular listener,

---

[9] Pollack *et al.* (1954) report their results using a measure of the percentage of information transmitted, in bits. They found about 45% information transmitted when stimuli lasted 0.2 sec (one monosyllable); about 78% at 0.4 sec; over 90% at 1 sec, and 100% by 2 sec in duration.

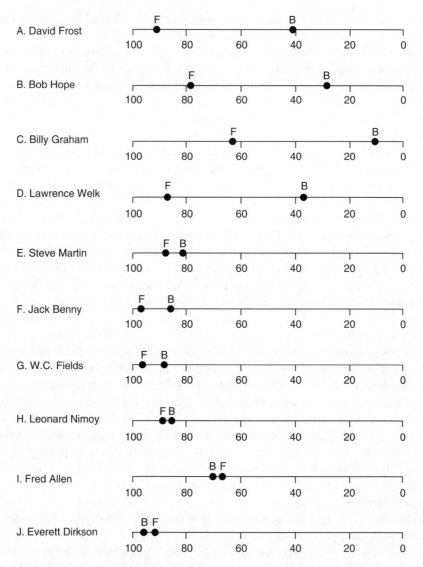

Figure 5.2   Differences in recognizability for famous voices played forwards (F) and back-wards (B).

because familiarity is a function of both the voice and the listener (what is known, how it is known, and the person who knows it).

Support for this view comes from behavioral studies of normal listeners. In one such study, listeners heard samples of 45 famous voices played backwards or with the speaking rate altered. Featural models predict that alterations would affect all voices equally, but this did not occur: Some voices were easily recognized despite the altera-tions, but others could not be identified (Van Lancker *et al.*, 1985a; Van Lancker, Kreiman, and Wickens, 1985b; Figure 5.2); and different voices were affected by dif-ferent alterations (Figure 5.3). Finally, it was not the case that voices of speakers who were notable as fast or slow talkers were most affected by rate alterations, or that

	Backwards	Expanded	Compressed
David Frost	X		
John F. Kennedy		X	
Edgar Bergen			X
Vincent Price			X
Johnny Carson		X	
Bob Hope	X		
Maurice Chevalier			X
Lawrence Welk			X
Tony Randall			X
Martin Mull		X	

Figure 5.3 Differential effects of backwards presentation, slowed rate, and increased rate on recognizability of famous voices. X marks cases with mean scores more than one standard deviation away from the mean difference between the normal score and the score in the altered condition, and thus represents significant interference with recognition.

recognition of the voices of speakers with strong foreign accents was most impaired by backwards presentation. No matter how extreme a voice was on some dimension, the importance of that dimension as a cue was influenced by the other characteristics of the voice, rather than just that cue alone. For example, actor Maurice Chevalier had a strong French accent when speaking English, but also a rather low-pitched, breathy voice, distinctive syllable rates and "different sounding" vowel qualities; his voice was easily recognized backwards. Other actors with similarly salient accents were not recognizable when their voices were played backwards (see Figure 5.3). These data suggest that recognition depends both on the relative salience of a cue or cues, and on the context of the other cues present in a voice. The simple feature-based model of familiar voice recognition assumed by most research cannot accommodate these findings, because the values of individual cues from a fixed set are not adequate to predict whether or not a voice will be recognized.

Data from priming experiments (Schweinberger, Herholz, and Stief, 1997b) also point to this conclusion. In one such studies, listeners heard famous and unfamiliar voices, and were asked to respond "famous" or "not famous" as quickly as possible. Reaction times to famous voices were significantly faster when listeners had previously heard a different exemplar of a famous voice, but no similar advantage was observed for unfamiliar voices. Because the priming effect was produced by a different sample of each voice, it appears that the benefit derives from the complete voice pattern, not from the specific details of a given sample, consistent with the view that familiar voices are processed as patterns, and not as bundles of features.

In summary, studies of animal and human voice recognition have usually assumed that a universal set of features commonly cues familiar voices, and investigators have manipulated a few of these features, usually F0, resonances, and/or temporal elements. In some cases, listeners responded to some manipulations but not others. In many cases, when the results were carefully evaluated in animal and human listeners, it was seen that these reductionistic approaches do not suffice to explain listeners' behavior. Some of these studies support the notion that selections from a large range of auditory-acoustic cues may participate unevenly across vocal patterns in the recognition process in humans, and that processing of unique patterns is in play. Methods for accommodating the multivariate properties of familiar voice patterns will aid in better understanding this ability.

5.3.4   Perceptual processes associated with recognizing or discriminating among unfamiliar voices

A different relationship between pattern and features appears to exist for tasks that require listeners to remember or discriminate among unfamiliar voices. For familiar voices, features operate in idiosyncratic ways that depend on the context of an overall pattern. In contrast, data from behavioral studies of normal subjects, from lesion studies, and from brain imaging (the latter two reviewed in the next chapter) all indicate that remembering a new voice requires both reference to a "standard" or "average" pattern of some kind (for example, an average-sounding young male Californian) and assessment of the manner in which the new voice differs from that standard.

One kind of evidence for this view comes from a study comparing patterns of incorrect responses listeners made in long-term memory and discrimination tasks using unfamiliar voices (Papcun, Kreiman, and Davis, 1989; Kreiman and Papcun, 1991). In this study, two groups of listeners heard the voices of male UCLA students, matched for age and dialect. One group of listeners heard pairs of voices and judged whether they represented the same or two different speakers; the second group heard a single voice that they tried to select from a ten-voice lineup after a delay of one, two, or four weeks. Not surprisingly, overall listener accuracy declined as the time between hearing a voice and recognizing it increased, although discrimination accuracy did not differ from recognition accuracy after one week. The likelihood of correctly identifying the target – the hit rate – did not change with delay. However, the pattern of false alarms changed notably with increasing delay. Over time, listeners were increasingly likely to mistake an "average-sounding" voice for the target, no matter what target voice they originally heard. This pattern of results – loss of details over time, with responses converging on a few "average-sounding" voices – suggests that listeners remember an unfamiliar voice in terms of a "prototype" (Mervis and Rosch, 1981) or an average, basic pattern that captures the central trend for a population of voices, and a set of deviations from that prototype. Over time, listeners forget the deviations, and consequently over time recognition responses converge on the average-sounding voices. Thus, recognizing or discriminating among unfamiliar voices requires both reference to a pattern – the prototype – and featural analysis to determine how the target voice differs from the prototype.

Multidimensional scaling provides further details about the nature of what is remembered and what is forgotten over time about unfamiliar voices (Kreiman and Papcun, 1991). As noted in Chapter 1, this kind of analysis derives a "space" from measures of the similarity of pairs of stimuli, such that stimuli that are similar are closer together than stimuli that differ more widely. By interpreting the dimensions of this space, experimenters gain insight into the attributes that make voices similar or confusable. Analyses of similarity ratings from the voice discrimination task produced four dimensions: masculinity, creakiness, variability, and mood. Confusions and similarity ratings from the long-term memory task produced three dimensions (masculinity, breathiness, and variability), suggesting a simpler cognitive strategy overall. The first dimension, masculinity, was much more important in the memory space than in the discrimination space, suggesting that this attribute plays a bigger role in remembering voices than in simply telling them apart. The other dimensions in the discrimination space were not significantly correlated with the dimensions in the memory space, suggesting loss from memory of details about the voices. These results indicate that over time listeners do not simply remember the same things that they listen for in a discrimination task, only less well; some things are lost, and other things correspondingly gain importance, in memory over time.

In summary, memory tasks using unfamiliar speakers require listeners to associate the target voice with some population of voices, and to identify the features that differentiate that voice from an average-sounding one – a prototype, defined as a central tendency in a distribution of exemplars (Patel, 2008). To do this, listeners appear to kludge together elemental pattern recognition processes with ad hoc featural analysis. We seem to use a hodgepodge of cognitive strategies to perform these tasks, relying on whatever works best under the circumstances. This is not especially surprising given the limited interest and lack of personal relevance unfamiliar voices have to the average listener (be it person or penguin) under normal circumstances. Depending on the content of the voice sample, how "average" the voice sounds, the listener's motivation to learn the voice, the task demands, and the listening situation, the information available to listeners may vary widely, and across cases a given vocal attribute may or may not be helpful, especially if the voice is not particularly distinctive. We review brain processes underlying familiar and unfamiliar voice perception in the following chapter.

5.5   Summary of Animal and Human Studies

Given the diversity and complexity of vocalization behaviors across species, studies of familiar vocal recognition have barely scratched the surface of the phenomenon. Studies of the acoustic features underlying these behaviors in a variety of animals show that voice recognition is highly adaptable to a large array of behavioral and environmental determinants. However, these studies have only indirectly entertained the possibility that holistic pattern recognition strategies may also play a role in voice recognition in nonhuman animals, and thus the results of these studies may misrepresent or underestimate animals' abilities in these tasks. Some pertinent evidence has been published: Statistical analysis of the calls of the aromobatid frog (*Allobates femoralis*) showed that acoustic features were only moderately successful at identifying the calling individual (about 65% correct), indicating that featural models may be inadequate to predict recognition behavior (Gasser, Amézquita, and Hödl, 2009). The authors conclude that these frogs may rely on combinations of features or on whole pattern recognition instead of single properties when distinguishing neighbors from strangers. Given the view that any stimulus can be decomposed and deconstructed (thereby obliterating its holistic integrity), it is questionable whether this approach can yield a veridical picture of vocal recognition competence. A modest set of elementary parameters can be posited as accounting for construction of the perceptual object under investigation, and when the listeners (animal or human) are not responsive or are only partially responsive, it is difficult to say why. Of course, decomposition and analysis techniques represent a reasonable first line approach to understanding voice recognition; admittedly, there is much less available to the researcher to investigate how complex auditory patterns are perceived. Yet several of the animal and human studies reviewed above have yielded the possibility that complex Gestalt pattern recognition better explains the results.

The small number of familiar voices recognized by most animals increases the appeal of a pattern recognition strategy for voice recognition. It is not parsimonious to posit a featural system – even one based on only a few parameters – when most animals recognize only a few other individuals. For example, penguins recognize the voices of parents, offspring, and mates; Vervet monkeys recognize the voices of their immediate cohort. (An exception appears in the allegedly large repertory of voices known by elephants.) Such featural systems also cannot account for the fact that most animals generally ignore unfamiliar vocalizations, suggesting that a familiar pattern has special status. It is both parsimonious and plausible that each vocal identity is acquired and stored as a unique, complex pattern. We look to the visual modality for an analogue: In fowl, presentation of a single image at the right maturational moment locks that image into the chick's long-term memory in a process called imprinting. We submit that a corresponding process may be in place for familiar voices (this proposal is explored in detail in Chapter 6.5). While it is of interest to explore sets of auditory-acoustic parameters that appear to be salient in animal vocalizations, it does not follow that any or all of these parameters viewed separately or additively are satisfactorily representative of the material used in the veridical recognition process. In fact, efforts to reduce the patterns to a set of regularly occurring elements may detract from a more compelling fact, namely, that individual, multivariate patterns are produced and heard. These points lead to our view that auditory-acoustic parameters play an important role, but not the only role, in voice recognition, and that the role they play differs across voices. Unitary patterns are notoriously difficult to study (and may, in principle, be impossible to analyze into fully revealing elements). Nonetheless, we propose that the Gestalt principles of recognition known in other psychological behaviors, especially vision, must be taken into account and thoughtfully adapted to understand familiar voice recognition. Evidence reviewed in these chapters points to a highly sophisticated interplay between parameters and patterns.

In humans, for whom more extensive and sophisticated studies can be performed, analysis of vocal identity recognition by addition or subtraction of auditory-acoustic parameters, such as fundamental frequency, fundamental frequency variability, temporal parameters, and so on, accounts only weakly for our prodigious skill in familiar voice recognition. It is difficult to grasp how so many unique patterns can form a functional array in a human voice recognition arsenal. On the other hand, attempts to show how a small set of auditory-acoustic features combine to reliably

Unfamiliar voice discrimination

    Featural comparison

        (Pattern recognition)

    Processing: "bottom up" > "top down"

    Time to decision: open-ended

Familiar voice recognition

    Pattern recognition

        (Featural comparison)

    Processing: "top down" > "bottom up"

    Time to decision: 2–3 sec

Figure 5.4 Top-down versus bottom-up processing of voice information.

generate the very large repertory of voices we can recognize have been disappointing. It is likely that the capacity of human memory for voices has been seriously underestimated.

5.5.1   A model: The fox (features) and the hedgehog (patterns)

The view of voice perception proposed here makes the basic assumption that all voices constitute complex auditory patterns, which we designate as perceptual objects or events from the perspective of normal perception. The voice is not readily reducible to componential constituents; like many patterns, no list of parameters can reasonably be thought of to exhaustively "add up" to the total voice pattern. In the case of personally familiar voices, very few predictable features may enter into the recognition process. Rather, a few idiosyncratic, salient cues, drawing from a very large constellation of possible cues and occurring within a unique context of other vocal qualities, provide adequate information for identification, and the whole pattern is apperceived. For unfamiliar voices, in matching or evaluation tasks, use of elemental feature analysis and comparison plays a greater role. That is, in addition to perceiving the unfamiliar voice as an overall auditory pattern, the listener "extracts" elementary acoustic features such as pitch, vocal quality, and rate, and possibly more complex attributes like "sharpness" or "masculinity," and uses them for comparison (see Figure 6.8). Normal listeners' performance on unfamiliar voices, in discrimination and long-term memory studies, suggests that both general characteristics and distinct features are utilized to compare and remember unfamiliar voice patterns (Kreiman, 1987).

    This notion is shown schematically in Figure 5.4. Complex, unitary patterns (like familiar voices) that are apprehended as a whole rely more on a "top-down" direction of processing, using only a few signature features, which will differ for different voices. During recognition, the auditory percept is aligned to a unique pattern or long-term memory image of the voice. In contrast, in matching or assessing unfamiliar voices, a

Figure 5.5   A fox and a hedgehog.

larger array of vocal features is available for evaluating the voices, and processing is generally "bottom up" (or stimulus-driven) in nature. The prototypical templates used in a matching or identification process for unfamiliar voices may consist of idealized standards for "average" voices (Papcun et al., 1989; cf. Patel, 2008). In this type of perception, pattern characteristics have a less prominent role, by definition, than do the values of the individual features themselves.

We call this the "Fox and Hedgehog" model of voice perception (Figure 5.5), drawing on the characterization of Greek poet Archilochus (seventh century BCE),[10] who wrote that the fox knows many things, but the hedgehog knows one big thing. For voices, the little things, or features, are utilized more successfully in unfamiliar voice perception, whereas the familiar voice is one big thing, in which "features" appear in idiosyncratic combinations cohering and/or "emergent" to yield a complex, integrated pattern. As the studies reviewed in this chapter show, in any act of voice perception both kinds of knowing pertain, in different degrees. As we will argue in the next chapter (Section 6.6.2), how much fox and how much hedgehog is operative for any single act of voice perception depends on the listener's relationship to the vocal stimulus, and can be accounted for by cerebral hemispheric specialization.

[10]   The Fox and hedgehog viewpoints were elaborated in a 1953 essay by Sir Isaiah Berlin, reprinted in *Russian Thinkers* (Viking, 1978).

6

The Brain Behind the Voice: Cerebral Models of Voice Production and Perception

6.1 Introduction

In this chapter, we review evidence from neuropsychological studies that shed light on the brain mechanisms that underlie voice processing. These studies lead to a model in which features and patterns are utilized in different ways depending on how the listener relates to the voice – whether the voice is familiar or unfamiliar. Every individual voice is produced as a consequence of the full biological and biographical background of the speaker. If the voice is familiar to the listener, it is recognized in association with an array of these associations, so that it takes a whole brain to produce a voice, and it takes a whole brain to recognize a voice. One goal in this chapter is to bring together neurological evidence of cerebral participation in voice perception and production. Further, we propose that familiar voices are quickly acquired, not incrementally learned; they roll into the arsenal of personally familiar voice patterns through a process performed by brain mechanisms subserving arousal, emotion, motivation, and attention, and are stored through temporal-parietal lobe mechanisms of memory and cross-sensory associations. Cerebral side-of-processing for voice perception varies with familiarity, as pattern recognition mechanisms native to the right cerebral hemisphere are more successfully engaged for familiar, distinct patterns, while the feature-analytic processes inherent in discriminating unfamiliar voices are better modulated by left cerebral areas. Drawing on a rich history in several branches of psychology that approach learning and memory in terms of exemplar versus rule-based models of categorization and classification (Juslin and Olsson, 2004; Rouder and Ratcliff, 2006), we have proposed a model in which voice perception, including familiar voice acquisition and recognition, systematically participates in these two modes (see Section 5.5.1). Applications of featural (rule-based) and/or pattern (exemplar) processing vary with numerous factors, all mainly related to listener familiarity with the voice. Material reviewed here expands and elaborates the "Fox and Hedgehog" model of voice perception introduced in the previous chapter.

Foundations of Voice Studies: An Interdisciplinary Approach to Voice Production and Perception,
First Edition. Jody Kreiman and Diana Sidtis.

6.2   Neurological Substrates of Voice Production

Many brain mechanisms underlie voice production, reflecting the many physical, emotional, cognitive, and experiential factors associated with the sound a speaker produces at any given moment. This section provides a brief overview of these mechanisms, and describes the manner in which control of voice production varies depending on the circumstances under which it occurs. See Chapter 3 for more specifics and details of the brain structures and mechanisms associated with voice production.

6.2.1   The role of auditory feedback in voice production

Because of the prime position of auditory feedback in acquiring and producing one's own voice, we begin with a brief review of this complicated process. Voice patterns emerge out of interactive processes of phonation, articulation and audition. For example, babies instinctively vocalize, yet, as mentioned in Chapter 1, personal voice patterns require exposure to self and others in processes of social learning. Prelingually deaf children, when taught oral language, have distorted voice patterns (Monsen, 1979), with deviant pitch, breathiness, and abnormal quality (Arends, Povel, Van Os, and Speth, 1990; Morrison, 2008). Vocal abnormalities were identified even on sustained vowels (Campisi, Low, Papsin, Mount, and Harrison, 2006). Thus one's personal voice quality is both biologically present at birth and sculpted not only by physical maturation but also by external social and neuropsychological influences.

Among important influences in this interplay of articulation and audition is auditory feedback of one's own voice. Auditory feedback and self-monitoring are experienced by all language users, most saliently when self-repair of speech errors occurs. Continuous, semi-conscious decisions we make about the clarity, volume and rate of our speech depend on many factors besides ambient noise level: Whether our interlocutor is a native speaker, hard of hearing, demented, attentive, young or elderly, and so on. Further, to acquire vocal competence, humans, like some birds, must hear the adult language at a certain time in their development (called the sensitive or critical period), and they must hear their own voices producing it (Brainard and Doupe, 2002). However, much about auditory feedback remains mysterious. When adult women sound like young girls, or adult men speak with high or excessively low F0, when someone adopts a vocal style that does not fit their physical persona, we might well wonder about the complex status of personal voice quality in the auditory feedback process.

Artificially induced disruption arising from listening to oneself can be readily demonstrated by electronically delaying auditory feedback presented over headphones carrying a signal from the talker's microphone. When talkers hear themselves at a 0.4 second delay, dysfluencies and abrupt shifts in voice quality occur. False synthetic representation of the pitch of one's own voice elicits compensatory adjustment in fundamental frequency by the vocalizing subject (Hain, Burnett, Larson, and Kiran, 2000). Similarly, artificial changes in the formant pattern of a vowel, when fed back to the speaker, cause changes in pronunciation (Houde, Nagarajan, Sekihara, and Merzenich, 2002). These studies reveal a control system that makes use of feedback.

How prominent, and how determining is auditory feedback during normal language use? When hearing loss affects adults (who have a fully established motor speech ability), slow changes in phonated and articulated speech ensue, suggesting that a degree of ongoing self-monitoring is necessary to maintain normal speech (Goehl and Kaufman, 1983). Details of this process remain unclear. A perplexing clinical contrast appears in jargon aphasia, a condition in which speech consists of fluently produced nonsense words, while hearing is not impaired. A specific failure of self-monitoring has been proposed as a consequent of the lesion (Marshall, Robson, Pring, and Chiat, 1998).

Other evidence suggests that self-monitoring processes for speech are neurologically independent of listening to the speech of others. Brain responses to self-spoken speech differ from passively heard speech. Evoked response (EEG) studies revealed a delay in response in the left temporal lobe during the speaking condition as compared to the listening (alone) condition (Curio, Neuloh, Numminen, Jousmäki, and Hari, 2000). Speech-related inhibition of auditory cortex during phonation has been reported for humans and monkeys, implicating a special circuitry for self-monitoring that temporarily reduces auditory processing. Suppression of auditory cortex neurons was observed in marmoset monkeys during their own vocalization (Eliades and Wang, 2005). That voice, speech, and language are monitored independently is suggested by the statement recorded by Peretz (2001, p. 205) from a patient with auditory agnosia (inability to make sense of meaningful sounds): "I know I am speaking but I can't hear the words right … I can hear the voice."

6.2.2 Individual voice quality: Is the voice pattern localized in the brain?

Specific functional brain sites for the production of personal individual voice quality have not been established. This should not be surprising, given the many factors that contribute to what it means to "sound like" oneself. An array of neurological systems contributes to the production of voice in the broad sense, because each voice pattern results from a confluence of contributed factors. There is a "whole brain" underlay to this effect, which includes physical characteristics and learned habits, personality, and mood states, reflecting the whole person (Boone, 1991). Thus, although specific elements of the voice pattern, such as pitch, loudness, or speech timing in articulation can be selectively affected by brain damage, there is no particular brain site that, when damaged, predictably results in a speaker specifically no longer sounding like himself or herself, in the way that specific foci of brain damage affect phonology or syntax in speech.

Nevertheless, significant alteration to an individual aspect of the signature vocal pattern can affect recognizability. For example, distorted articulation of vowels might make it difficult or impossible to identify the speaker; or identifiability might be compromised when a previously mellifluous vocal pattern is made monotonous by a basal ganglia stroke. Timing errors in speech may follow left hemisphere, subcortical, or cerebellar damage, while changes from hypomelodic (reduced speech melody) or hypermelodic (exaggerated speech melody) pitch patterns may result from left or right hemisphere and subcortical damage (Sidtis and Van Lancker Sidtis, 2003). When one or more features of speech production are distorted following left hemisphere damage, speech may appear to have suddenly acquired a "foreign accent," which may also compromise identifiability (see Sidebar).

Sidebar: Foreign Accent Syndrome

Persons listening to patients with foreign accent syndrome actually have the impression that they are hearing a foreign accent. Descriptions of this syndrome include anecdotes about patients no longer sounding like their former selves. Several examples have been reported, starting with Monrad-Krohn's (1947) account of a native Norwegian patient whose speech, following brain injury, sounded as if her native language were German. This created social difficulties for the woman, who lived in occupied Norway during World War II. In this case, personal recognizability at a social level was compromised, as the subject was mistaken – by strangers – for a foreigner. Whether family and friends failed to recognize her personal voice quality after injury was not reported. Prosodic contrasts in word pairs, phonologically distinctive in Norwegian, were affected; timing and pitch direction constitute the main cues to these contrasts. When these contrasts were lost, the subject appeared to be speaking German. Other cases, mostly involving left hemisphere or subcortical damage, have been reported in which the patient's signature voice quality changed significantly. Affected speech components included articulation, timing, stress, and intonation. In one case of left basal ganglia infarct, sporadic misproductions were not those a native speaker would make, causing the listener to conclude that the speech was that of a foreigner (Gurd, Bessel, Bladon, and Bamford, 1988). Another person spoke with altered voice quality following a subcortical stroke and reported that he was no longer able to imitate dialects (Van Lancker Sidtis, Pachana, Cummings, and Sidtis, 2006). The "foreign" quality of the disordered speech results from a perceptual impression of the listener (Carbary, Patterson, and Snyder, 2000) but the listener may include the patient. In one case report, a person with foreign accent syndrome complained: "It's not me, you know, it's somebody else" (Miller, Lowit, and O'Sullivan, 2006, p. 406).

6.2.3 Cerebral lateralization of elements of voice production

Although we cannot identify a neurological structure responsible for the whole voice pattern, we do know something about how certain elements of voice, such as frequency and timing, are managed in the brain, and information is emerging about how different vocal tasks – speaking spontaneously, reading aloud, repeated speech, singing – are parceled out. To discuss these conditions, it is useful to view the brain on the horizontal dimension – comparing left and right sides – and the vertical dimension, considering the relationships between cortical, subcortical, and brainstem structures.

Even a careful look at a human brain reveals general physical symmetry: Cortical, subcortical, limbic, thalamic, cerebellar and brainstem structures in the left side are mirrored in the right. Minor morphological (shape) variations between the two hemispheres appear to have little discernible functional significance (Geschwind and Galaburda, 1987). Functionally, however, a dramatic asymmetry exists. Few facts are as clear, and simultaneously as puzzling, as the allocation of cognitive functions to one or the other cerebral hemisphere.

While many cognitive abilities are lateralized to the left or right cerebral hemisphere, most striking by far is the case for speech and language. Hundreds of years, if not millennia,[1] of observations of patients with brain lesions have yielded a consistent model of speech and language representation in the brain. Although rare exceptions occur, language abilities are most often impaired following left hemisphere damage in right handed individuals (to the frontal, temporal, and/or parietal lobes), but almost never following right hemisphere damage of any kind (but elements of speech production and perception are reliant on other than left cortical areas, as described below).

In contrast, production of prosodic cues in speech involves both cerebral hemispheres, subcortical systems, and the cerebellum (Kent and Rosenbek, 1982), as can be inferred from the effects of focal brain damage. Control of amplitude in speech is at least partially modulated by subcortical nuclei,[2] but neurological systems modulating respiratory competence also regulate this vocal feature. Timing control in vocal production is performed more efficiently by the left hemisphere. Damage to left cortical structures is associated with timing deficits in production, affecting temporal relations in speech and rhythm in music. In nonfluent aphasia due to left hemisphere damage, for example, odd-sounding production of words and phrases turns out to be abnormal timing in vocal control (Danly and Shapiro, 1982; Baum and Pell, 1997; Schirmer, Alter, Kotz, and Friederici, 2001; Seddoh, 2004; Van Lancker Sidtis, Kempler, Jackson, and Metter, 2010).[3] Conversely, individuals suffering from right hemisphere stroke (with intact left hemispheres) have preserved rhythmic capacity in familiar songs alongside strikingly impaired melodic (F0) production (Alcock, Wade, Anslow, and Passingham, 2000; Murayama, Kashiwagi, Kashiwagi, and Mimura, 2004). Observations using Wada testing[4] yielded failure of melodic production during right-sided injection, while performance on rhythm was preserved, presumably due to intact left hemisphere function (Bogen and Gordon, 1971).

Modulation of fundamental frequency in speech can be impaired separately from the timing functions required for articulation. Subjects with dysprosody (impaired melody of speech) speak on a monotone but retain temporal distinctions (Sidtis and Van Lancker Sidtis, 2003). When subcortical damage is sustained, dysprosodic production may be confined to speech, leaving F0 control for singing intact (Van Lancker Sidtis *et al.*, 2006). In a study of two musically-trained stroke patients with dysprosody, other vocal elements were spared. Both subjects spoke on a striking monotone, and both retained timing parameters in speech and singing. One patient, with right hemisphere damage, lost his former ability to sing; the other patient, whose damage was restricted to subcortical nuclei, retained F0 control in singing. Thus there is evidence that speech

---

[1] A passage from Proverbs 135, "If I forget you, O Jerusalem, May my right hand forget her skill (sometimes translated "wither"), my tongue cling to the roof of my mouth" has been cited as ancient awareness of the effects of left hemisphere damage, which are right sided weakness and speech disturbance.

[2] This is assumed because many patients with Parkinson's disease, who suffer progressive dysfunction of basal ganglia structures due to lack of the neurotransmitter dopamine, have low vocal volume as part of the clinical description of their voice disorder. They also have reduced respiratory function.

[3] In the classic formulation of Goodglass and Kaplan (1972) and Luria (1980), nonfluent aphasia was associated with "impaired melody of speech." Later studies revealed that the deficit was less in pitch control than in details of timing.

[4] A clinical protocol whereby each cerebral hemisphere is briefly anesthetized prior to neurosurgery, and neuropsychological tests are administered to determine competences of the hemispheres.

and singing are distinct vocal modes, and F0 and timing (within both these modes) are separately and independently modulated in the brain. Similar dissociations between F0 and rhythm production have been reported in right hemisphere damage (Alcock *et al.*, 2000; Murayama *et al.*, 2004). This implies that voice production processes vary with vocal task and that they are under control of different neurological structures.

To summarize, as described in Chapter 3, amplitude is centrally and bilaterally controlled, at least partially due to its association with respiratory function. Temporal relations in vocal production rely more on left hemisphere abilities and F0 is modulated by the right hemisphere. However, basal ganglia, limbic, cerebellar and brainstem structures are involved in all of vocal production.

6.2.4　Production models of vocalization: Comparison of vocal modes

A common approach to understanding a complex, dynamic system in behavior is to design a model of the process (Levelt, 1989; Kent, 2000[5]). The earliest-known working model of speech production was developed by Wolfgang von Kempelen (see Sidebar and Figure 6.1), whose apparatus of metal and wood embodied the moving parts of the larynx and oral-nasal tract. In modern approaches, the neurological control of voice quality must be incorporated by designing systems modeling laryngeal tone and vocal tract resonances. Gestures of the tongue, velum, and lips shape the distinct voice pattern arising from the affective and conceptual background of the speaker and utterance.

Sidebar:　The First Speaking-Machine

Wolfgang von Kempelen (1734–1804) was an inventor, artist, and early linguist/phonetician from Austria-Hungary. His book entitled *Mechanismus der menschlichen Sprache nebst der Beschreibung seiner sprechenden Maschine* (Mechanisms of human speech toward a description of a speaking machine), published in Vienna in 1791, describes his construction of a talking machine. The 500-page tome included enlightened discussions of animal communication (said to function mainly to express emotions), the evolution of human speech (occurred in stages), sign language, speech reading, phonetic descriptions of Latin, French, and Italian and numerous drawings of his invention. His discussions of how the conditions of the soul (*Seelenzustände*) affect breathing, and therefore the sound of speech, reflect insights into personal voice quality.

The speaking machine consisted of bellows to represent the lungs, which were manipulated by the operator's right arm. A reed simulated the vocal folds, and reeds and tubes controlled by the left hand produced voiced and voiceless consonants. Levers provided fricatives (/s/, /z/, /ʃ/, /ʒ/). The model described and illustrated in the book allowed for monotonic voice only, but a later upgrade was provided with a handle to allow for varying intonation. This version can be viewed in the division of musical instruments at the Deutsches Museum in Munich, Germany.

---

[5] Appropriately, in Kent's diagram of speech production, affect and communicative intentions initiate and directly feed the preverbal message (2000, p. 393).

(a)

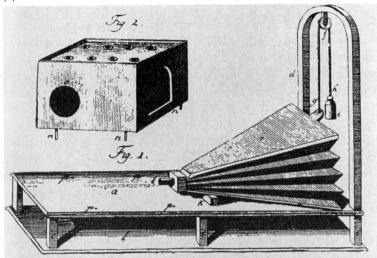

Abb. 5. Die Sprachmaschine von Kempelen. Ein Modell ist im Deutschen Museum zu München zu sehen

(b)

(c)

Figure 6.1 Von Kempelen's speaking machine (Deutsches Museum) showing bellows (above), laryngeal and vocal tract simulation below.

Data derived from lesion, stimulation, single-unit recording and brain imaging studies in humans and nonhuman animals indicate that central control of vocal behavior is hierarchically organized into interleaved networks (Jürgens, 2002). In humans, all vocalization utilizes a cerebral hemisphere, the basal ganglia and limbic system, cerebellum, and brainstem leading to cranial nerve innervation of the larynx and vocal tract structures; but different vocal tasks engage the cerebral networks in unique combinations (see Chapter 3 for detailed review). Production of novel utterances engages left-sided cortical areas of the brain including the inferior frontal gyrus (Broca's area), sensori-motor strip, and supplementary motor area, aroused by the reticular formation and the aqueductal grey matter in the brainstem, exchanging commands via the pyramidal and extrapyramidal tracts to the peripheral nervous system (cranial and spinal nerves) (for overview see Figures 6.2a, b). Ongoing auditory monitoring is carried on by the superior temporal gyrus while complex motor gestures are monitored by nuclei of the basal ganglia. Integration of speech motor gestures is aided by the thalamus and the cerebellum, especially the right cerebellum (contralateral to the left cerebral hemisphere where speech and language are represented). Speech that is read aloud or repeated is also modulated by the left hemisphere, and left hemisphere cortical damage can disrupt spontaneous speaking, reading aloud, and repetition of speech. However, configurations of left hemisphere-subcortical circuits engaged for speech repetition and reading aloud differ from those involved in spontaneous speech. Other modes, previously referred to as recited, "automatic," "formulaic," and emotional speech, as well as singing, are functionally represented in the right hemisphere as well as in the left, and rely heavily on subcortical processing.

At first, it might seem trivially obvious that spontaneous speech differs from the read or repeated versions of the same utterances. After all, when reading aloud or repeating, the speaker is not concentrating on the ideas, but is merely mouthing the words, and the qualitative differences in voice and articulation seemingly can be accounted for by differences in attention and effort. However, in neurological disease, where the underlying control systems are highlighted, it becomes clear that such simple explanations are not adequate. Subcortical dysfunction, causing motor speech disorders, interferes more with spontaneous than read or repeated speech. For example, in Parkinson's disease, the basal ganglia are compromised due to deficient dopamine infusion from the substantia nigra, resulting in dysarthria (slurred, low volume, monotonous and sometimes rapid speech). In Parkinsonian dysarthria, voice quality improves significantly for reading and repetition, when compared to spontaneous speech (Kempler and Van Lancker, 2002; Sidtis, Rogers, Godier, Tagliati, and Sidtis, 2010). Task effects in Parkinson's disease are dramatic because dysarthria was formerly believed to be uniform and consistent across speech contexts.[6] Vocal task differences are important for voice studies, because voice production abilities have been seen to substantially differ with mode of vocal production: speaking spontaneously, reading aloud, repeating, producing automatic (overlearned, formulaic) material, and singing.

Dramatic discrepancies between performance abilities for singing and speech are seen in several speech disorders. For example, stuttering is task-specific, occurring

---

[6]   Comparable effects have been found in other speech disorders (Kent, 2000), and are to be expected in careful testing of normal speakers. For example, the severity of vocal difficulties in spasmodic dysphonia is affected by speech task conditions (Roy, Gouse, Mauszycki, Merrill, and Smith, 2005).

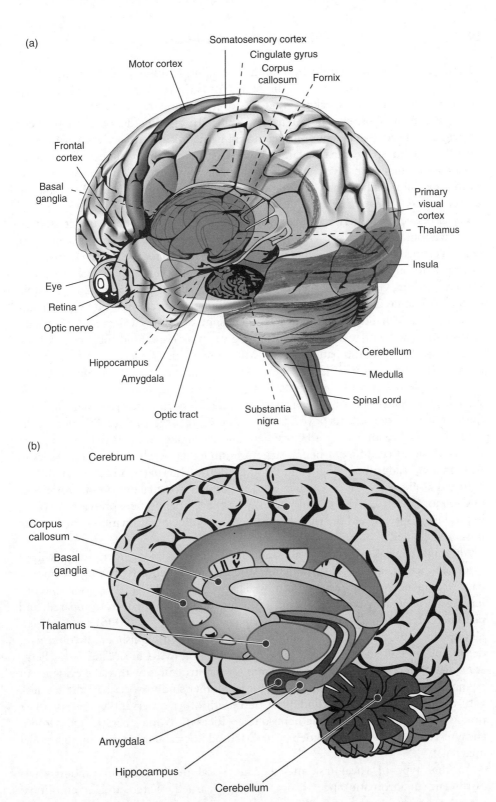

Figure 6.2 (a) Schematic model of brain mechanisms, including the brainstem. (b) Schematic model highlighting subcortical and limbic systems.

during speech but not during humming or singing (Ludlow and Loucks, 2003). Stutterers are able to fluently sing the same words (in the form of lyrics) that they produce dysfluently in a speaking mode (Glover, Kalinowski, Rastatter, and Stuart, 1996; Packman, Onslow, and Menzies, 2000). In another dissociation between singing and speech, some children diagnosed with autism, who are essentially non-verbal and do not speak, can sing familiar songs. And while the etiology of Parkinson's disease also remains unsolved, speech intelligibility improves significantly when the words are sung rather than spontaneously spoken (Kempler and Van Lancker, 2002).

Other dissociations between singing and speech reflect a difference in hemispheric specialization, leading to the view that singing is a capacity of the right hemisphere (RH). Persons with severe speech deficits or aphasia due to focal left brain damage are often able to sing familiar songs fluently and competently (Hughlings Jackson, 1874; Hébert, Racette, Gagnon, and Peretz, 2003; Racette, Bard, and Peretz, 2006). Audio samples 6.1 and 6.2 provide an example. These samples were produced by a normally developing right-handed adult whose left hemisphere was surgically removed in cancer treatment and who was therefore profoundly aphasic (Burklund and Smith, 1977). In audio sample 6.1, the patient sings "My country, 'tis of thee" with consistently correct F0 and normal articulation (Smith, 1966; Van Lancker and Cummings, 1999). Audio sample 6.2 provides a sample of the patient's regular (non-singing) speech, showing that the contrast between the speech disability and the preserved singing is quite dramatic. For students of voice, it is of interest that the voice can be successfully controlled by the isolated right hemisphere during singing. Some fMRI data support the conclusion that different neural structures underlie speech and singing (Riecker, Ackermann, Wildgruber, Dogil, and Grodd, 2000). Ackermann and Riecker (2004) reported a series of vocal production studies pointing to separate roles in voice production for the left and right hemispheres, with the left hemisphere primarily involved in producing speech, and the right hemisphere in producing intonation contours and musical melodies.

Although clinical evidence of all kinds attributes vocal song to right lateralized cerebral function, some voice production studies using functional imaging techniques have yielded inconsistent results. Formby, Thomas, and Halsey (1989) found no differences in brain activity when singing, speaking, and humming were compared, and no differences between singers and nonsingers. Callan *et al.* (2006) reported left hemisphere activation for covert singing, with some right hemisphere involvement, depending on task and on contrasts performed. Using fMRI in singing tasks, Perry *et al.* (1999) reported bilateral activation in several structures, with some evidence of asymmetry focusing on the right frontal area. Another study associated a rhythm task with the right hemisphere, a finding at odds with other observations that associate timing regulation with the left hemisphere (Riecker, Wildgruber, Dogil, Grodd, and Ackermann, 2002; see Sidebar on Methodological limitations of functional imaging).

Another type of vocal task may engage vocal mechanisms in unique ways. Formulaic (or automatic) speech comprises overlearned, recited, and/or emotional utterances of various kinds, including counting, speech formulas (salutations and conversational fillers), swearing, nursery rhymes, familiar lyrics and familiar songs, and other such expressions[7] (Code, 1987; Van Lancker and Cummings, 1999; Wray and Perkins, 2000; Wray, 2002a; Van Lancker and Rallon, 2004) (see Sidebar). These kinds of utterances, now generally grouped under the rubric "formulaic language," also depend on neurological mechanisms that differ from spontaneous speech, but resemble those for singing. For voice scientists, questions of hemispheric control of vocal production varying with mode of vocal production arise. Measures of voice and articulation in dysarthric speakers differ for novel and formulaic vocalization tasks (Sidtis, Cameron, Bonura, and Sidtis, 2011), again suggesting that the underlying articulatory mechanisms for these modes of speech production differ. Neurological data are consistent with this view. Abilities to produce formulaic language are compromised not only by right hemisphere impairment (Van Lancker Sidtis *et al.*, 2006; Van Lancker and Postman, 2006) but also by subcortical damage (Speedie, Wertman, Ta'ir, and Heilman, 1993; Van Lancker Sidtis *et al.*, 2006; Sidtis, Canterucci, and Katsnelson, 2009). On the other side of the coin, hyperfunction of the basal ganglia/limbic system in persons with Tourette's syndrome is associated with semi-compulsive emotive utterances (called coprolalia or "foul speaking;" Van Lancker and Cummings, 1999). In related observations during surgery for treatment of epilepsy, formulaic vocalizations occurred when subcortical sites were electrically stimulated (Schaltenbrand, 1965; Petrovici, 1980).

The notion that a right hemisphere–subcortical circuit plays a role in singing as well as in formulaic verbal behavior in humans (see below) is especially interesting when considering the relationship of human phonatory behaviors to animal vocalization. Some authors argue that these kinds of vocalizations resemble animal calls, and thus may offer clues to the evolution of vocal control mechanisms (Wray, 2000; Code, 2005). Both singing and formulaic expressions have been proposed as antecedent to the evolution of human language (Jespersen, 1950; Wray, 2002b; Code, 2005; Patel, 2008). Animal vocalization is almost exclusively social in nature, with some vocalizations indicating anger and warning and others facilitating social interactions.[8] Similarly, some formulaic language in humans, such as swearing and other interjections, is likely mediated by limbic system structures and, presumably, was originally intended to perform the social functions of repulsing intruders and expressing anger and dissatisfaction. In humans, the older system may also continue to perform in singing and in emotional and routinized vocal behaviors. Considering that this hard-won, hard-wired vocalization substrate was inherited from our forebears after millennia of evolution, Fitch (2004a) proposed a "prosodic protolanguage" in human development as precursor to both modern language and music. Indeed, Fitch (2006) associates animal vocalization not with human language, but with the development of musical behaviors in humans.

[7]   We are grateful to Alison Wray for giving these phenomena a unifying name in her book *Formulaic Language and the Lexicon* (Wray, 2002a). Her Figure 1.2 lists approximately 80 terms that have been used to refer to holistic expressions of various kinds (p. 9).

[8]   A few referential meanings for distinctive calls in primates have been identified (for example, Cheney and Seyfarth, 1980; Hihara, Yamada, Iriki, and Okanoya, 2003).

Sidebar: The "Automatic" versus Voluntary Dichotomy
in Vocalization Lore

The term "automatic speech" has been both useful and troublesome in characterizing vocal behavior. The well-worn polarity between automatic and voluntary has had several applications in matters of voice. One use was introduced by Hughlings Jackson (1874) to characterize preserved vocalizations in severe language deficit following brain damage. "Automatic speech" referred to emotional outbursts, swearing, clichés, greetings, yes, no – a hodgepodge of utterance types which had in common only that they were nonpropositional, or as we might say today, nonnovel – not generated by grammatical rules applied to a repertory of words. The terms "voluntary" and "propositional" speech were used for novel or newly created utterances.

The other important use of the automatic–voluntary duality comes from the comparative biology of vocalization. Only humans are said to have voluntary vocalizations, in contrast to nonhuman animals, whose "automatic" vocalizations are often viewed as springing forth reflexively from autonomic physiology.

The traditional terms, automatic and voluntary, are colorful and provocative, but neither stands up well to careful scrutiny. First, in looking at the nervous system, reliable operational definitions of both terms fail us. Sometimes the dichotomy corresponds to conscious versus nonconscious; sometimes to combinatorial versus holistic. "Low-level" grammatical processes in spontaneous speech, such as subject–verb agreement, proceed, in one sense of the term, automatically. On the other hand, emotional utterances (called "automatic" in animal vocalization) are voluntarily produced and human speech is imbued with affect throughout (Panksepp, 2003). Recurrent stereotyped utterances (such as *bi di bi di*) can be delivered by the severely aphasic person in such a way as to "voluntarily" express a need or wish. Secondly, research in nonhuman animal vocalization has brought serious question to the claim that calls are not "voluntary." Primates produce calls with referential and intentional content in a large range of social situations (Cheney and Seyfarth, 1980, 1990; Marler, 1998). Reflexive and volitional control systems join to produce vocal sound, and volitional control of activity involves both cortical and subcortical systems (Ludlow, 2005).

We take these dichotomous terms to be merely suggestive of important differences, but we use the terms loosely. The pertinent vocal behaviors in both human and nonhuman animals are better described in terms of numerous characteristics that are hierarchical or continuous.

6.3   Neuropsychology of Face Perception: An Analog to Voice Perception

Although voice quality information is carried in the speech signal and commingles inextricably with speech sounds, signaling for voice and speech have very different characteristics. In our perspective, voices and faces are more similar to each other than

DENNIS the MENACE

"HELLO, MR. WILSON... GUESS WHO?"

Figure 6.3   Dennis senses the correspondence between faces and voices at a deep level.

are voices and speech. The human voice can be described as an "auditory face" (Belin, Fecteau, and Bédard, 2004; Figure 6.3), and facial processing in humans provides a powerful and revealing analogue to voices (Table 6.1). A number of factors distinguish speech and voice: Speech is sequential and continuous, and is decomposable into a small, finite set of discrete elements (phonetic units and phonemes; Sawusch, 1986), with describable structure (syllables, consonants and vowels, regularly occurring voiced and voiceless portions, and so on). Crucial contrasts, such as those distinguishing different stop consonants, occur within very small units of time, as little as ten milliseconds. By comparison, any perspective on structural description of the acoustic material serving to cue vocal identity takes a very different stance. The pertinent decomposable elements are not known, and may not be rationally and completely describable. Longer samples of sound (between one and three seconds) usually form the basis for identification. The characteristics "sequential" or "analyzable into component parts" do not pertain[9] (see schema in Figure 5.1).

In contrast to speech, the face, like the voice, constitutes a pattern that is not readily decomposable (Table 6.1). In the process of identifying faces, different and idiosyncratic aspects (relation of eyes to nose, mouth shape, closeness of eyes) emerge in thousands of combinations. Both faces and voices are used to communicate an array of nonverbal personal, affective, and social information. They both surround us in familiar and unfamiliar guises. Voices and faces are similar in forming unique, nondecomposable patterns, but they can also be "sketched" or caricatured in terms of selected idiosyncratic features. They are both "indexical," in that they signal personal information or attributes such as

[9]   Proposals by Port (2007; Port and Leary, 2005) and studies by Pisoni (1993), Goldinger and Azuma (2003) and Palmeri, Goldinger, and Pisoni (1993) dispute the traditional description of speech perception as abstracted sequential and segmental elements, positing instead a role of voice information and dynamic, local emergence of perceptual cues.

Table 6.1 Commonalities between faces and voices as objects of perception.

- Complex patterns (Gestalt-like, holistic)
- Familiar and unfamiliar stimulus conditions
- Familiar-famous (cultural) and familiar-intimate (friends, family) versions
- Posed (given voluntary shape) and spontaneous expression
- Subject to disguise
- Keys to personal identity
- Maintain format through time and effects of aging
- Can be altered cosmetic-surgically (plastic surgery; laryngoplasty)
- Figure importantly in interpersonal relations
- Comprised of analytic (details) features and synthetic wholes (pattern)
- Subject to influence of both nature (innate capacity) and nurture (learned elements)
- Samples represented by distant transmissions: Radio and television
- Ubiquitous
- Important in phylogeny and ontogeny
- Subject to pathologies (voices more than faces)
- Congenital anomalies affect face together with voice
- Forensic interest
- Expression: flat to animated
- Records can be made (visual, acoustic)
- Evoke strong personal response
- Hemispheric specialization studied in normal persons using split-visual field and dichotic listening
- Hemispheric specialization studied in unilateral brain damage
- Brain function studied using functional imaging

age, gender, and mood; further, particular faces and voices are familiar or "personally relevant," and are instantly recognizable under normal circumstances (Bruce and Young, 1986; Bruce, 1990); and for both, familiarity can be cultural or personal. Both, being inalienable features of human existence and keys to communication, figure importantly in nearly every human encounter – we use the term "ubiquitous." Both can be intentionally altered through disguise techniques. Voices and faces play a great role in ontogenetic and phylogenetic survival: Individuals learn to rely on vocal and facial signals for crucial information about friend or foe status, identity of family members, threat or danger level, and the subtler continuous cues of social communication.

A few differences do exist as well (Table 6.2). Obviously, voices exist in time, and faces exist in space.[10] Voices can be heard *in utero*, much earlier in development than the face can be seen. They may become damaged by disease or extirpated in surgery;

---

[10] This is an eminent difference. Sound material representing voice is fleeting. Visual images representing faces are abiding. That the visual modality is more present, salient, and obvious is reflected in the old conundrum: If a tree falls in the forest, and no one is there to hear it, does it make a sound? No companion joke has arisen about the visibility of the falling tree.

Table 6.2   Some differences between voices and faces as objects of perception.

- Temporal vs. spatial domain
- Voices occur at various distances (behind listener, telephone); faces immediate[a]
- Disease interferes more with voice than face
- Voices produce energy; faces less so
- Only voices are accessible to the intrauterine fetus
- Maternal voices are recognized at birth; faces not until three to six months
- Faces can be more readily described using words or graphics than voices

[a] This difference is changing in some ways because of advancing video technology.

although rare accident and burn injuries occur, any such parallel for faces is weak. Vocal expression covers a broad range from spoken monotone, through revelation of emotional, personal and social cues in the speaking voice, to the heights of musical expression. Faces, while indeed expressive of mood and attitude, have less versatility. It has been reported that feelings of familiarity without the ability to identify occur more commonly for voices than for faces (Hanley and Turner, 2000).

Nevertheless, given the extent of the analogy between the two modalities, we can reasonably apply findings about faces to generate hypotheses about voices, and to interpret findings about voices. This is particularly useful because far more is known about the processing of faces than of voices, due to large asymmetries that exist in the amount of study devoted to the two topics[11] (Figure 6.4a). During the 1990s, studies of faces outnumbered voice studies by two to one.[12] Further, thematic questions differed considerably between the two topics (Figure 6.4b). Most studies of face perception focused on neuropsychology and on structure/function correlations in brain processing, with secondary emphasis on perception and cognition in normal individuals, and with about equal numbers of studies of familiar and unfamiliar faces. In contrast, voice studies mostly involved automatic speaker recognition by machine, employing unfamiliar voices. Studies of pathological voices and perceptual and cognitive studies weighed in next, with only a small number of studies addressing questions about brain or mental function underlying voice discrimination and recognition abilities. Interest in the neurology of voice perception has increased recently, mostly due to the advent of functional brain imaging. Nonetheless, the face-to-voice ratio in numbers of scientific studies has remained high.

6.3.1   Familiarity as an independent characteristic

The attribute "familiarity" has been neglected in neuropsychological research. The attribution of familiarity is itself a separable neuropsychological process associated with right hemisphere specialization (Cutting, 1990), affecting recognition of faces,

[11] This discrepancy is not so surprising when one considers the 32,000-year lag in intentional representations of visual (cave paintings) versus auditory (phonographic cylinder) materials; see Chapter 3 for details.
[12] Based on citation counts in Medline (http://www.ncbi.nlm.nih.gov/sites/entrez/) and Psychological Abstracts (http://www.apa.org/psycinfo/).

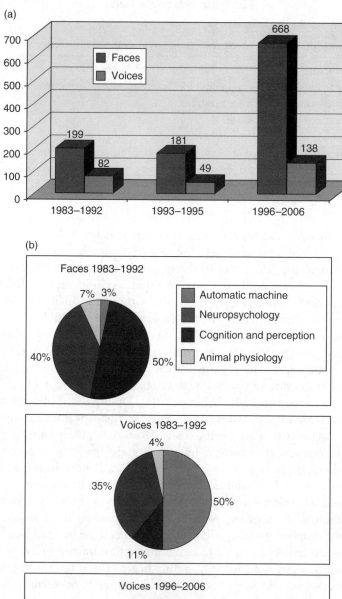

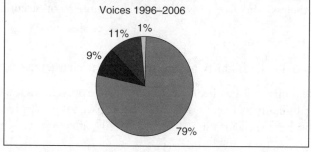

Figure 6.4 (a) Numbers of studies of face and voice perception as measured from Medline database surveys from three different time periods. (b) Comparison of subdisciplines in published studies of face and voice perception. Machine recognition studies have dominated voice studies (at 79%) for the past decade.

voices, and surroundings (including pets and handwriting; Van Lancker, 1991). Most agnosias – failures to recognize faces, objects, locations and the like, despite the preserved ability to visually perceive them – are likely attributable to a failure to invoke the familiarity feeling, and are associated with right hemisphere damage (Bauer and Rubens, 1985). For example, recognizing familiar handwriting involves a special combination of pattern recognition and familiarity evaluation; this function was impaired after right but not left hemisphere damage (Heckmann, Lang, and Neundörfer, 2001). People can lose the feeling of familiarity for their surroundings (apartment, local neighborhood), although they can still navigate through them (Landis, Cummings, Benson, and Palmer, 1986). A "pure" failure of the recognition sense presents in a striking condition called Capgras syndrome (see Sidebar), which confirms that the familiarity sense is an independent neuropsychological attribute.

The earlier dearth of scientific interest in "familiarity" in general (Van Lancker, 1991) arises in part from experimental design challenges inherent in this kind of research. Examination of personally familiar material brings in precisely those features that scientists try to avoid: subjective judgments, personal biases, idiosyncratic processing, stimuli necessarily tailor-made for individual subjects. Validity depends on selecting stimuli that are uniformly familiar to the subjects, but the difficulty of achieving such uniformity is obvious. Further, it is likely that stimuli are familiar in different ways in different contexts: We might expect recognition processes to differ for faces and voices of family and friends (familiar-intimate) compared to faces and voices that are familiar from media exposure (familiar-famous). The comparison of familiar-intimate with familiar-famous materials in an experimental setting presents an additional challenge, because two sets of familiar exemplars must be accumulated, each having uniform levels of familiarity to the subjects. Acquisition and storage details for these two categories of personally familiar phenomena may well take different forms, for example, in establishing the constellation of characteristics associated with the voice. Only hints about the relationship between familiar-famous and familiar-intimate face recognition appear in the literature, and even less is known about familiar voices. In a few classic and rare studies on the topic, Warrington and James (1967) found no correlation between abilities to recognize familiar-intimate and familiar-famous faces, whereas Benton (1980) observed that prosopagnosic patients erred on family faces as well as those of famous television personalities.

Evidence that familiar stimuli are handled differently from unfamiliar stimuli comes from studies showing that recognizing familiar faces and discriminating among unfamiliar faces are dissociated in the brain. For faces, abundant evidence exists that subjects can recognize without the ability to discriminate, and discriminate without the ability to recognize; for example, Malone, Morris, Kay and Levin (1982) reported a double dissociation between discrimination and recognition of faces in two patients who could achieve one but not the other task, and they mention four cases of prosopagnosia in whom unfamiliar face discrimination was preserved (see also, for example, Grafman, Salazar, Weingartner, and Amin, 1986, or Carlesimo and Caltagirone, 1995). Studies of brain electrical activity using surface and depth electrodes also reported different responses to familiar and novel faces (Seeck *et al.*, 1993). Early studies examining brain-injured subjects suggested that discriminating between unfamiliar faces and recognizing familiar faces engage different cerebral mechanisms (Benton and Van Allen, 1972; Young, Newcombe, de Haan, Small, and Hay, 1993; see Benton, 1980, for review). Warrington and James (1967) claimed that a right parieto-occipital lesion corresponded to a recognition deficit, while a right hemisphere temporal lobe lesion was associated with face discrimination deficits.[13] In section 6.4.1 we will review evidence for a dissociation between familiar and unfamiliar voices drawn from studies of unilaterally brain damaged subjects.

It is known that familiarity ratings can be influenced by manipulating context. "Familiarity" can be confused with frequency, and increased frequency can induce an affective response (Zajonc, 1968). The converse pattern also occurs: Stimuli with greater affective loading seem more familiar (Gerard, Green, Hoyt, and Conolley, 1973). Related findings showed higher familiarity ratings for rapidly presented familiar and unfamiliar faces when the faces were smiling (Baudouin, Gilibert, Sansone, and Tiberghien, 2000). Even arousal induced by exercise made objects seem more familiar (Stephens, 1988). It is well known that these factors all influence recognition (Myers, 1915).

6.3.2   Familiar face recognition

The prodigious memory cache of familiar voices available to each of us has been alluded to, but no quantitative data are available. A few such studies have appeared for faces. Bahrick, Bahrick, and Wittlinger (1975) showed that subjects recognized familiar persons (in arrays including unfamiliar faces) at very high rates from high school yearbook pictures going back as far as 50 years, although in many cases subjects could not name the former classmate. This and similar studies found no demonstrable upper limit to the number of faces individuals can accurately recognize as "familiar" throughout their lives (Bruck, Cavanagh, and Ceci, 1991). Aging does not noticeably affect face recognition competence (Baeckman, 1991), although some decrements for more recently-acquired faces may occur in old age (Wahlin *et al.*, 1993). The case for lifelong retention of a repertory of familiar voices is likely similar, but only anecdotal evidence is available[14] due to the difficulty of obtaining a vocal equivalent to yearbook photos for testing.[15] If this study could be performed, we might find that familiar voices stand the test of age more resiliently than familiar faces, both for listeners and as indices of speaker identity. For example, the youthful actor in the "Duel at Sundown" episode of the 1950s television show "Maverick" is hard to identify by face, but once his voice is heard – which has changed less than his face in 50+ years – he instantly recognizable as Clint Eastwood. This demonstration works for most contemporary audiences we have tried.

6.3.3   Hemispheric specialization for face processing

Brain damage can interfere with face recognition, leading to "prosopagnosia," which was first described by Joachim Bodamer (1947) as agnosia for the recognition of faces and expressions, without disturbance of perception of the parts of the face. Later studies

---

[13]   Such differences were also reported using evoked responses in nonhuman primates (Pineda, Sebestyen, and Nava, 1994). See the discussion in Chapter 5 of animal precursors to developmental voice recognition.
[14]   For example, the case of a man who correctly recognized the voice of an army buddy on a crowded New York street, 50 years after their last encounter. Additional anecdotal reports tell of individuals recognizing long-lost acquaintances who were not readily recognized by appearance, but only when heard speaking.
[15]   With internet resources and digital recording facilities, it may soon be possible to assemble large sets of familiar-famous voices for this purpose.

uncovered separate cognitive processes for familiar face recognition, unfamiliar face discrimination, and recognition of facial expression. (Failure to distinguish these different neuropsychological functions has often led to confusion in the scholarly literature.) In real life, the prosopagnosic patient must rely on known items of clothing, on the sound of his wife's voice (anecdotally demonstrating the dissociability of voice and face in the recognition repertory),[16] or mother extraneous props, to recognize her (Damasio, Damasio, and Van Hoesen, 1982). Viewing a photograph of his wife, the victim of prosopagnosia can report that he is seeing a face and he can describe the face in detail, but he cannot "recognize" or identify it (Benton, 1980), and viewing the face evokes no feeling of familiarity.

Sidebar: Capgras Syndrome

Named after Joseph Capgras (1873–1950), a French psychiatrist who, with co-author K. Reboul-Lachaux, first described the disorder in 1923, Capgras syndrome is a deficit of the familiarity sense, involving the belief that a familiar feature in the afflicted person's life has been replaced by a foreign version of that feature (Capgras and Reboul-Lachaux, 1923). The patient perceives the person, place, or thing normally and clearly, but no longer experiences personal familiarity or personal relevance in association with the perception. In one form, the patient insists that a wife or other relative has been replaced by an imposter. This is a very strong belief, because counterevidence is abundant (for example, she looks exactly like the wife; she lives in the house, cooks, cleans and knows the names of the children) and counseling has no dissuading effect. Personal objects, pets, living quarters, geographical surroundings, and even self recognition may also be affected. The patient complains that these elements indeed look like the previously personally-relevant phenomena, but simply are not the same ones. The lack of the familiarity sense leads to a persistent belief that they have been replaced (Young, Reid, Wright, and Hellawell, 1993). This neuropsychological syndrome in its variety of manifestations is often associated with right hemisphere injury (Cutting, 1990; Silva, Leong, and Wine, 1993; Neuner and Schweinberger, 2000; Bourget and Whitehurst, 2004), contributing to the body of evidence that the right hemisphere stores and processes personally familiar phenomena (Van Lancker, 1991). A few voice-specific Capgras delusions have been reported; for example, a blind patient believed that her cat had been replaced, based on its meow (Reid, Young, and Hellawell, 1993). In a sighted person, a Capgras delusion involving voices was characterized by reduced autonomic

---

[16] We have noted such comments several times in the neuropsychological literature on prosopagnosia, anecdotally and indirectly implying a dissociability of voice and face in the recognition repertory, but also indicating a failure to acknowledge that voices have status as a comparable neurocognitive category. Critchley (1953), for example, described a patient with a wound to the occipital lobes who could not recognize faces "but could promptly recognize voice" (p. 294). This neglect has persisted in neuropsychology (cf. Bauer and Rubens, 1985; Duchaine, 2006) and reflects the dominance of the visual modality in neurobehavioral thought.

responses for familiar voices but not for familiar faces (Lewis, Sherwood, Moselhy, and Ellis, 2001). Adventitiously occurring familiarity agnosias (failing to recognize formerly familiar persons, places, and things), also called "jamais vu," and hyperfamiliarity (spurious sense of familiarity for unfamiliar items, such as faces), also called "déjà vu," may be milder versions of this syndrome (Young, Flude, Hay, and Ellis, 1993; Rapcsak, Polster, Comer, and Rubens, 1994).

Prosopagnosia has been associated with lesions in the right hemisphere, often in the parietal-occipital areas (Yin, 1970; Vilkki and Laitinen, 1974; Whitely and Warrington, 1977), based on CT-scan evidence (Landis *et al.*, 1986; De Renzi, 1986). Studies of normal subjects also show that the left visual field/right hemisphere is superior in tasks involving facial discrimination and recognition (Leehey and Cahn, 1979; Bradshaw and Nettleton, 1983; Young and Ratcliff, 1983). Although a few clinical studies of famous face perception (Marzi and Berlucchi, 1977; Umiltà, Brizzolara, Tabossi, and Fairweather, 1978) have reported that bilateral damage is required for prosopagnosia (cf. Meadows, 1974; Hamsher, Levin, and Benton, 1979; Bruyer, 1981; Damasio, Damasio, and Van Hoesen, 1982), such counterclaims likely arise from the facts that for most behaviors, both hemispheres are needed for optimal performance, and the design of the experiment and the task demands can influence results. Models of hemispheric function predict that the hemispheres process some kinds of stimuli equally well, but in different ways. In visual stimuli, exposure time and spatial frequency (roughly corresponding to sharp vs. degraded forms) affect laterality (Glass, Bradshaw, Day, and Umiltà, 1985), with shorter presentation times and more degraded targets associated with right hemisphere superiority. In the same way that hemispheric specialization has been associated with spatial frequencies, the length and acoustic content of synthetic auditory stimuli have been found to affect lateralization (Poeppel, 2003).

In summary, although these issues remain to be resolved, it is reasonable to conclude that both hemispheres are able to perceive and identify faces, but they do so using different processes (Gazzaniga and Smylie, 1983). The right hemisphere excels at establishing and maintaining personally relevant (familiar) phenomena in the life of each person, which include faces and voices. This interacts with a superiority for processing complex patterns, and, in a related function, for storing and managing contextual material (Joanette and Brownell, 1990) and emotional experiencing (Borod, 1993). These elements converge to form a basis for a right hemisphere specialization for face and voice perception and recognition, and combine with the associated sense of familiarity and establishment of affective personal relevance resident in that hemisphere. The right hemisphere recognizes with a more emotional, personally familiar response, and is able to recognize the names as well as the other information associated with the face (Van Lancker and Ohnesorge, 2002), while the left hemisphere identifies (or classifies) and names (Sperry, Zaidel, and Zaidel, 1979; Semenza and Zettin, 1988), and contributes to successful matching and discrimination of facial features.

6.4   The Neuropsychology of Voice Perception

6.4.1   Classical neurobehavioral studies

With these structures and processes in mind, we now turn to the neurological structures and processes that underlie voice perception. The first published neuropsychological studies of voice perception (Assal, Zander, Kremin, and Buttet, 1976) examined perception of unfamiliar voices in patients with brain damage, but the purpose, to probe abilities to discern different voice patterns, foreshadowed the recognition question. Listeners were asked to judge whether speakers were male, female, or child, and to detect foreign accents in a set of unfamiliar female voices. Although the authors found no significant effects of side of lesion, in a strikingly prescient interpretation, they inferred from patients' performance on a same/different voice discrimination task that "the right temporal/parietal region seems to play a key role in vocal recognition" (Assal, Aubert, and Buttet, 1981, p. 256). The studies on unilaterally brain-damaged persons were followed by experiments using dichotic listening (see Sidebar in Section 3.2.7) in normal subjects, showing that listeners were faster at recognizing gender from stimuli presented at the left ear, again suggesting a right hemisphere superiority for perception of voice patterns (Assal *et al.*, 1981).

The first study using personally familiar voices in brain-damaged subjects was published by Van Lancker and Canter in 1982. Voices of famous male entertainers were edited to eliminate background noise and revealing semantic content. A pretest, consisting of written transcriptions of the speech samples, was administered. Any sample for which the transcription led to correct identification of the speaker was edited or eliminated, in order to ensure that genuine identification would be made from voice alone. Seven samples of between nine and 14 seconds in length were played to 30 unilaterally brain-damaged subjects (21 left brain damaged and nine right brain damaged) who had sustained single lesions from stroke. Responses were made by pointing to one of four pictures, for which the written and spoken name were also given, so that selective deficits in face recognition, reading, or speech comprehension would not interfere with the results. Van Lancker and Canter found that right hemisphere damage interfered significantly with recognizing familiar voices (a deficit they termed "phonagnosia"), whereas left-hemisphere-damaged patients recognized voices, in many cases as well as normal listeners. Even severely aphasic patients, some with a diagnosis of global aphasia, who could neither speak nor understand what was being said, recognized who was speaking with ease. From our contemporary perspective, this finding is not surprising, given the obvious parallels between face and voice recognition: Both are complex patterns (one auditory, one visual) and the right hemisphere is superior at pattern recognition; and many studies have identified the right hemisphere as modulator of facial perception. At that time, however, the right hemisphere was viewed as engaged primarily in higher-level visual pattern processing, and the left with language. Voice quality is carried in the speech signal, and speech is exclusive to the left hemisphere, or so it was believed. In that context, the finding that the right hemisphere contributed so significantly to voice recognition was a surprise.

Table 6.3 Performance scores on two tasks: recognition of famous voices and discrimination of unfamiliar voices by three groups (normal-control subjects, persons with left hemisphere damage and those with right hemisphere damage).

		Side of Lesion	
Task	Normal (%)	Left (%)	Right (%)
Recognition	82.1	81.8	62.9
Discrimination	87.2	76.4	69.9

Another protocol was developed to compare the ability of clinical subjects, including those with left, or right cerebral damage, to identify familiar-famous voices and to discriminate among unfamiliar voices (Van Lancker and Kreiman, 1986, 1987). Clinical and normal control subjects identified 25 famous speakers by pointing to the correct picture or written name from among four choices (matched for speaking style and appropriateness, given the import of the utterances; for example, newscasters were grouped with other newscasters, and comics with comics). They also heard 26 pairs of unfamiliar voices and were asked to say whether the speakers were the same or different. All samples were approximately three seconds long. The results replicated the Van Lancker and Canter (1982) study. Healthy (normal-control) subjects performed well on both tasks (Table 6.3). Patients with damage to the right hemisphere performed significantly worse than control subjects on both tasks; patients with damage to the left hemisphere differed significantly from control subjects on the voice discrimination task, but not on the voice recognition task. Although the difference between recognition and discrimination in the left-sided lesion group is small, it invites some speculation. In our formulation, recognition of famous voices is the result of a Gestalt-recognition process in which specific acoustic cues are utilized in a manner idiosyncratic to particular famous speakers and individual listeners. This is largely mediated by the right hemisphere. In contrast, discrimination relies in part on left hemisphere featural analysis that is hampered by a left-sided brain lesion. That both pattern and feature-analytic processes are required for successful discrimination is suggested by the impact of either left or right brain damage on the voice discrimination task.

To classify patients on the two tasks, listeners were considered "deficient" on either task if they scored more than 1.5 standard deviations below the mean of the normal-control group. Lesion sites predicted patterns of task deficiency. All patients with familiar-recognition deficits had right parietal lobe lesions; two had additional right frontal or occipital damage. Patients with unfamiliar-discrimination deficits had lesions involving either the right or left temporal lobe, with the lesions extending beyond the temporal lobe in two-thirds of the cases. Examination of the subset of subjects who performed very well or very poorly on either task (Table 6.4) suggested that performance on the two tasks is independent: Some listeners could discriminate

Table 6.4 Individual case examples of dissociated high and low performance on voice recognition and performance tasks. Low performance is indicated by bold type. Chance is 25% on this protocol (adapted from Van Lancker *et al.*, 1988).

Case	Age	Discrimination score (%)	Recognition score (%)	Lesion site
1	61	**50**	92	R temporal L temporoparietal
2	62	**58**	84	L frontotemporo-parietal
3	59	**69**	92	L temporal
4	74	73	**16**	R parietal, L parietal
5	82	89	**50**	R parietal, L occipital
6	69	**58**	**41**	R temporoparietal

but not recognize, while familiar voices could be correctly and reliably recognized by people who were unable to discriminate between two different speakers (Van Lancker, Kreiman, and Cummings, 1989). We concluded from these studies that voice recognition should not be modeled as a process based in or dependent on discrimination: Although voice recognition and discrimination utilize the same acoustic signal (i.e., the voice), they are not ordered processes, they are not dependent on each other, and they are processed by different cerebral systems (Van Lancker, Cummings, Kreiman, and Dobkin, 1988).

Later studies using a large group of patients with unilateral brain lesions (n = 36, plus 20 control subjects) lend support to these early studies and carry them a step further (Neuner and Schweinberger, 2000). Person recognition deficits were associated with bilateral or right hemisphere damage in nine of the 10 subjects having this difficulty, further supporting the notion of personal relevance as residing in the human right hemisphere (Van Lancker, 1991). Four of these subjects were able to discriminate unfamiliar voices, supporting the view that familiar recognition and unfamiliar voice discrimination are dissociated neuropsychological abilities. Further, impairments in face, voice, and name recognition were dissociable from one another: In four patients, voice recognition was impaired (scores at chance levels), while face, name, and sound recognition were preserved.

In summary, we propose that results from converging studies are consistent with the traditional model of brain function in which the left hemisphere more successfully modulates analytical processing, while the right hemisphere is specialized for recognizing patterns (Bever, 1975), and that these polar cerebral modes correlate with functional voice perception modes. Discriminating among unfamiliar voices requires both featural analysis and a kind of pattern recognition, and thus requires both left and right hemisphere participation. Recognizing a familiar voice involves processing a unique pattern. Familiar recognition is achieved by identifying a few idiosyncratic distinctive cues from a very large constellation of possible auditory cues in relation to the overall pattern, consistent with right hemisphere dominance. It is this complex interplay between pattern and featural processing that is depicted by the "Fox and Hedgehog" model proposed here, metaphorically representing the view that little things (features) and one big thing (the pattern) emerge and interact differently in the perception process, depending on familiarity of the voice. This model recalls studies elaborating exemplar versus rule-based theories of categorization (Rouder and Ratcliff, 2006), and discussions of analog versus structure in linguistic studies (Skousen, 1989; Skousen, Lonsdale, and Parkinson, 2002). Many phenomena in learning and memory are best described by interactions of these two processes.

6.4.2   Results from functional brain imaging studies

The lesion data reviewed in the previous section suggested that brain areas exist that are specifically associated with the neuropsychological ability to discriminate or recognize voices. Using extracellular recordings of neuronal firing rates, regions have been found in the auditory cortex of both cats and marmosets (a highly vocal primate) that are selectively responsive to species-specific vocalizations, but do not respond to other animal calls, calls presented backwards, or environmental noises (for example, Wang and Kadia, 2001; Poremba *et al.*, 2004). With the advent of functional imaging, studies previously applicable only to nonhuman animals can be extended to humans. Recent data from such studies point to the existence of similar brain regions that are selectively sensitive to voice stimuli (see Table 6.5). A variety of imaging methods have been used, including functional magnetic resonance imaging (fMRI, which exploits magnetic field changes to measure increases in oxygenated blood as a marker of changes in blood flow from which inferences about brain activity are made), positron emission tomography (PET, which uses isotopes to measure task-dependent changes in the blood flow to different regions of the brain), electroencephalography (EEG and event related potentials, or ERPs, which measure the electrical brain potentials evoked by different stimuli in different regions of the brain via surface electrodes), and magnetic encephalography (MEG, a technique for measuring time courses in magnetic fields generated by electrical brain activity). Comparing results across these different methodologies is not a straightforward process, and evaluating functional imaging data can be quite difficult (see Sidebar on Methodological limitations of functional imaging). At their best, imaging data can add depth and context to lesion data; at their worst, they present counter-intuitive findings that seemingly contradict results from lesion studies without offering interpretations that explain the contradictions.

Functional neuroimaging studies using PET and fMRI have produced a variety of results, some consistent with lesion studies and some not (see Sidebars in Chapter 3). Most of these studies use contrast or subtraction analysis, which has intrinsic limitations (see Sidebar on Methodological limitations of functional imaging). For example, subtracting data reflecting brain responses for one task from responsivity acquired in a contrast task may result in canceling out network areas common to both tasks. Because reliable, consistent, or convincing interpretation of the myriad results is extremely challenging, we provide Table 6.5, which lists the most important and representative studies at this time. This table notes findings for the posterior and anterior superior temporal gyrus (upper area of temporal lobe) and for the temporal parietal area, as well as for a variety of other brain sites.

Table 6.5 Selected reported results from functional imaging studies using voice stimuli in order of date. Key for abbreviations is footnoted.

Study	Stimulus (task)	Subjects	Contrast	Side	STG post	STG ant	TP	Other areas
Imaizumi et al., 1997	Words; Identify speaker (trained familiar) or emotion	6 R-handed subjects (all male) ages 18–25 years	Identify speaker (trained familiar) minus emotion	L	–	–	+	PF, FO, IPL, VA, BG
				R	–	–	+	MTG, VA
Belin et al., 2000	Vocal and nonvocal sounds (passive listening)	14 subjects (six males, eight females) ages 22–47 years	Nonspeech vocal sounds minus scrambled versions	L	–	–	–	–
				R*	–	–	–	–
Nakamura et al., 2001	Spoken sentences (identify familiar-intimate voices or vowels)	9 subjects (all male) ages 20–34 years	Identify familiar-intimate voices minus identify vowels	L	–	–	–	PF, PC
				R	–	–	+	PF, PC, MTL
Shah et al., 2001	Phrases and faces of familiar-intimate v. unfamiliar type	10 subjects (all male) ages 25–33 years	Voices minus faces	L	+	+	–	PF
				R	+	+	–	PF
Belin et al., 2002	Vocal and nonvocal sounds (passive listening)	8 subjects (four men, four women) ages 22–47 years	Vocal sounds minus non-vocal sounds	L	+	–	–	ANT MTG MTG, PC
				R*	+	+	–	PC
			Vocal sounds minus scrambled voices, AM noise	L	+	–	–	MTG
				R*	+	–	–	
			Frequency-filtered vocal sounds	L	+	–	–	MTG
				R	+	–	–	MTG
Belin and Zatorre, 2003	Spoken syllables by trained familiar voices (passive listening)	14 subjects (five males, nine females) ages 20–40 years	Adaptation to syllable minus adaptation to speaker (trained familiar)	L	–	–	–	–
				R*	–	–	–	
Von Kriegstein et al., 2003	Spoken sentences by trained familiar voices and speech-envelope noises (identify target voice, sentence or noise)	14 R-handed subjects (six men, eight women); ages 20–51 years	Identify target voice (trained familiar) minus speech	L	–	+	–	Mid-ant MTG
			envelope noise	R	–	+	–	Mid-ant MTG, PC, VA

Table 6.5 (*Continued*)

Study	Stimulus (task)	Subjects	Contrast	Side	STG post	STG ant	TP	Other areas
Stevens, 2004	Spoken words, pure tones (2-back memory for voices, words or tones) Trained familiar voice	10 subjects (six men, four women); 9 R-handed, 1 L-handed; ages 23–44 years	Identify target voice (trained familiar) minus identify sentence	L	–	–	–	
				R*	–	–	–	PC
			Memory for target voices (trained familiar) minus memory for words	L	–	–	–	
				R	–	–	–	Post-cingulate, PF, IPL
			Memory for target voices (trained familiar) minus memory for tones	L	+	–	–	IPL
				R	+	–	–	
Rämä et al., 2004	Spoken words in virtual space (memory for trained familiar speaker or location)	14 R-handed subjects (4 men, 10 women) ages 18–27 years	Memory for voices (trained familiar) minus phase-scrambled controls	L	+	+	+	PF, insula, IPL
				R	+	+	+	PF, insula, IPL, SPL, cerebellum
			Memory for voices (trained familiar) minus memory for location	L	–	–	–	IFG, insula
				R	–	–	–	IFG, insula
Fecteau et al., 2004	Linguistic and non-linguistic vocal sounds, animal vocalizations, nonvocal sounds (passive listening)	15 subjects (9 men, 6 women) mean age 22.6 years	Human > animal vocalizations	L	–	–	–	–
				R*	–	–	–	–
			Animal vocalizations > nonvocal sounds	L*	–	–	–	–
Von Kriegstein and Giraud, 2004	Spoken sentences and noise (identify familiar-intimate or unfamiliar voices and content)	9 subjects (5 men, 4 women) ages 27–36	Familiar-intimate > unfamiliar voices	L	–	–	–	Fusiform gyrus
				R	–	–	–	Fusiform, SPL
			Unfamiliar > familiar-intimate voices	R*	–	–	–	IPL, amygdala, bilat PF
Lattner et al., 2005	Spoken sentences with manipulation of pitch and formant structure	16 subjects (8 men, 8 women) ages 20–28 years	High > low voice pitch	R*	–	+	–	Insula
			Female > male vocal spectra	L	+	–	–	
				R	+	–	–	Thalamus IPL
			Altered > natural voices	R*	+	+	–	–

Study	Stimuli (paradigm)	Subjects	Contrast	Hemisphere				Regions
Rämä, Courtney et al., 2005	Spoken words, faces (trained familiar) and scrambled versions (memory for identity)	12 subjects (5 men, 7 women) ages 18–34 years	Voices > control (encoding)	LR*	+	+	–	IFG, insula, IPL, PF; IFG, insula, IPL, MTG
			Voices > control (recognition)	L	+	+	–	IFG, insula, IPL, fusiform gyrus; IFG, insula, IPL, PF, fusiform gyrus
				R*	+	+	–	
Von Kriegstein et al., 2005	Spoken sentences by familiar-intimate (colleagues) and unfamiliar voices	9 subjects (five men, four women); ages 27–36 years	Voice (familiar-intimate; unfamiliar) minus verbal content recognition	L	–	–	–	IFG, OFC, SPL, cerebellum; IFC, OFC, SPL fusiform gyrus, cerebellum
				R	+	–	+	
			Familiar minus unfamiliar speaker	L	–	–	+	Fusiform gyrus TL
				R	–	–	+	Fusiform gyrus medial TL, PC, IFG
Fecteau et al., 2005	Human vocalizations and nonhuman sounds	15 subjects (9 men, 6 women) ages 19.9–25.3 years	Human vocalizations minus nonhuman sounds	L*	–	–	–	IFG
				R	–	–	–	–
Warren et al., 2006	Vocoded spoken monosyllabic words by unfamiliar voices (passive listening)	12 Right-handed (six males, six females) ages 21–41 years	Human vocalizations minus sounds	L	–	–	–	IFG
				R*	–	–	–	–
			Changing minus fixed speaker	L	+	+	–	–
				R*	+	+	–	
			Number of frequency channels	L	+	+	–	MTG
				R	+	+	–	MTG

Legend to Table 6-6: asterisk (*) = significantly greater activation; fMRI in normal font; PET studies are in bold font; PET studies are in bold abbreviations: a-l: antero-lateral; AM: amplitude-modulated; ant: anterior; BG: basal ganglia; fMRI: functional magnetic resonance imaging; FO: frontal operculum; HG: Heschl's gyrus; IFG: inferior frontal gyrus; IPL: inferior parietal lobe; lat: lateral; L: left; MGB: medial geniculate body; MTG: middle temporal gyrus; MTL: mesial temporal lobe; OFC: orbitofrontal cortex; PAC: primary auditory cortex; PC: precuneus; PET: positron emission tomography; PF: prefrontal areas; p-m: postero-medial; post: posterior; PT: planum temporale; R: right; SPL: superior parietal lobe; STG: superior temporal gyrus; STS: superior temporal sulcus; TL: temporal lobe; TP: temporal pole; VA: visual area.

Sidebar: Trained-to-Familiar Voices Procedure

To overcome the difficulties inherent in using naturally acquired, personally familiar voices, several laboratories engage listeners in a training process, which begins with associating a voice to a name or a face repeatedly until some performance criterion is reached. For example, Winters, Levi, and Pisoni (2008), following methodology developed by Nygaard, Sommers, and Pisoni (1998), familiarized listeners to ten talkers in four days of eight training sessions, each of which consisted of seven phases. Over the first familiarization phase, potential subjects attend to voice/name pairings of five words produced by each of ten talkers. In the refamiliarization phase, subjects attend to the same word spoken by all talkers and then, on hearing all five words again, attempt to identify the speaker with feedback provided. These sessions end with an evaluation task followed by a generalization test, which includes words not previously presented. Overall, listeners hear several hundred words produced by each talker over a period of four days. Very little is known about the requisite amount of time or the typical conditions surrounding how people naturally acquire familiar voice patterns; we speculate about this in Section 6.5 below. The laboratory procedure obviously lacks the variegated social and affective contingencies ordinarily surrounding personal familiarity.

As Table 6.5 shows, stimulus type and task vary widely across studies. Of the 16 studies included, seven used unfamiliar voice stimuli, five used familiar-intimate voices of colleagues, and four used laboratory trained-to-familiar voices. None used culturally familiar voices.[17] (See Sidebar on Trained-to-familiar voices). The studies perform analyses on contrasts; for example, Belin, Zatorre, and Ahad (2002) subtracted nonvocal sounds and scrambled voices from vocal sounds; von Kriegstein, Eger, Kleinschmidt, and Giraud (2003) contrasted sentences spoken by trained-to-familiar voices with noises within the speech spectrum; and Shah *et al.* (2001) subtracted areas of signal observed in association with voice stimuli from areas of signal observed in association with face stimuli. This practice forces extremely detailed assumptions about organization and relatedness of brain areas in processing. It is often unclear why these contrasts are used or whether these choices of stimuli have any bearing on brain function. All of the studies report bilateral activation in several regions of interest. All seven studies using unfamiliar voices contrasted with nonvocal sounds or with acoustically manipulated speech reported significantly greater right-sided activation on at least one contrast analysis. Two of the five studies using familiar-intimate voices report significant right hemisphere activity on at least one analysis; one of the four studies using trained-to-familiarity stimuli resulted in significantly greater right sided activation. Reported activation in the temporal-parietal area (a cortical site implicated in earlier familiar-famous voice studies) appeared in two

---

[17] Familiar-famous voices were used in early normal and clinical studies by Van Lancker and Kreiman (1984, 1986, 1987; Kreiman and Van Lancker, 1988) and Neuner and Schweinberger (2000).

familiar-intimate and two trained-to-familiar voice studies, but not in the seven unfamiliar voice studies. Numerous other regions, mostly in the cortex, yielded significance using the subtraction method. Subcortical areas, which we will argue are crucial in familiarity processing, seldom survive the screening process inherent in the subtraction and other comparison procedures typically used; these areas play an important role in establishing set or readiness to perform the task (Sidtis, Strother, and Rottenberg, 2004). Superior parietal and other areas are generally not investigated in these procedures.

fMRI studies contrasting unfamiliar voices with nonvocal sounds have reported voice-selective areas in the auditory cortex along the superior temporal sulci (STS) in both hemispheres (Belin, Zatorre, Lafaille, Ahad, and Pike, 2000; Belin *et al.*, 2002), especially on the right side (Belin and Zatorre, 2003; von Kriegstein and Giraud, 2004). Using near-infrared spectroscopy, a technique similar to fMRI in that it detects hemoglobin changes in the brain, a right-temporal cortical response to vocal (compared to nonvocal) sounds was observed in seven-month-old (but not four-month-old) infants, suggesting early development of a voice-sensitive brain system (Grossmann, Oberecker, Koch, and Friederici, 2010). (Note that infants recognize familiar voices at three days, and that near-infrared spectroscopy is capable only of scanning cortical and not other brain tissue.) The claim is that these areas are not merely sensitive to voices – they are *selective* for voices, and do not respond to other sounds, even when those sounds are matched to the voice stimuli (scrambled voices, amplitude modulated noise). Although voices generate bilateral responses, responses are reported as "stronger" (significantly different) in the right hemisphere, on average. Some of these results are indeed compatible with lesion studies and with general knowledge about auditory receiving areas on the cortex. Other studies have implicated cerebral regions beyond those identified in lesion studies. For example, using trained-to-familiar voices, von Kriegstein and colleagues (von Kriegstein, Kleinschmidt, Sterzer, and Giraud, 2005) claimed to identify a familiar voice recognition network in the right temporal-occipital ("fusiform") areas. Familiar-intimate voice stimuli have also been reported to activate the fusiform face area, a part of the cortex that has been reported to be active during face recognition (Shah *et al.*, 2001). Similar activation did not occur when listeners heard unfamiliar voices (von Kriegstein *et al.*, 2005). Still other reports focus on prefrontal cortex as an area sensitive to human voices (Fecteau, Armony, Joanette, and Belin, 2005).

Another type of functional imaging, electrophysiological records, has been used to identify cortical voice processing areas, with variable results. Several such studies have claimed that the process of separating voice from linguistic information occurs in the first 100 ms (Schweinberger, 2001; Knösche, Lattner, Maess, Schauer, and Friederici, 2002; Kaganovich, Francis, and Melara, 2006). Evoked potential data (Levy, Granot, and Bentin, 2001) first identified an area along the superior temporal sulcus (STS) that is sensitive to voices, but later studies found that manipulation of attention to the stimuli significantly affected the brain responses, so that voices were no longer distinguished from voice-like stimuli (Levy, Granot, and Bentin, 2003). Different patterns of neural firing appeared in response to voices and musical instruments, but the observed pattern of brain potentials did not differ across different classes of musical instrument (so a cello might be different from a soprano, but not from a trumpet). These data suggest that the cerebral specialization found for voice quality is not a byproduct of any linguistic content the voice samples may possess, because neither the sung notes nor the musical instruments had linguistic content. Two additional electrophysiological markers, the Mismatch Negative and P3a waves, were found to successfully reflect responses to familiar versus unfamiliar voices (Titova and Näätänen, 2001; Beauchemin *et al.*, 2006). Brief vowel stimuli were utilized, but the way in which stimuli were familiar – whether familiar-intimate, familiar-famous, or trained-to-familiarity – was not described. Evoked responses to one's own name spoken in a familiar voice showed greater involvement of the parietal lobe, suggesting higher level processing of this deeply familiar stimulus (Holeckova, Fischer, Giard, Delpeuch, and Morlet, 2006).

From a broader perspective, these functional imaging studies land squarely in two camps, both of which detract from a convincing, veridical depiction of familiar voice recognition. The first is the localizationist stance, where a circumscribed area in the brain, usually sought on the cortical mantle, is identified as the effective spot. The second is cortical bias, with little or no effort to discover a functioning network in the brain. Even cortical areas are restricted, such that the superior parietal cortex is seldom included in region of interest analyses. Limbic and subcortical nuclei are not evaluated in these approaches, so the crucial differences in depth and nature of processing between unfamiliar and familiar voices cannot be illuminated. Questions about whether tasks evaluating trained-to-recognize voices bear any resemblance to valid familiar voice recognition are not posed (see Sidebar on Trained-to-recognize Voices). These approaches thus yield an impoverished description. We find it of limited usefulness to search for a unique cortical area for familiar voice recognition, given the broad spectrum of integrated cerebral functions that indispensably and essentially contribute to the process, as we will demonstrate below (see Sidebar on Methodological limitations of functional imaging).

Sidebar: Methodological Limitations of Functional Imaging and a Proposed Solution

Background: Aggregates of voxels (fMRI and PET technologies) constitute the dependent variables (measures) of imaging experiments, yielding areas of signal that are referred to as "brain activation." These areas are interpreted to reflect neuronal responses to a behavioral task. Areas are compared to each other within and across subjects as being "more active" or "less active." There are numerous threats to scientific validity and reliability in techniques of signal acquisition, quantitative analysis, and interpretation.

1.   Functional imaging techniques measure cerebral blood flow or related phenomena. However, the relationship between cognitive or mental function and cerebral blood flow is quite indirect, in that cerebral blood flow is affected by many factors other than neuronal activity, including the biochemical influences of neurotransmitters and neuromodulators (Drake and Iadecola, 2007).

2. The scalar properties of various brain areas are not known, so that it is not meaningful to say that one area is "more active" than another based on differences in signal. The conservative assumption is that different areas have different scalar properties, given that the vascular tree is not evenly distributed throughout the brain and that no evidence to the contrary exists. This can be inferred from the different responses of brain areas to disruptions in bloodflow. For example, the hippocampus and basal ganglia are more susceptible to hypoxic-ischemic damage from interruptions of flow of oxygen. Therefore comparing "activation" sites within and across subjects and subject groups inherently includes a threat to validity.

3. The meaning of increased signal in brain areas is not known. Increased signal could mean that the area is aroused to perform the task because it always performs that task; it could mean that the area is responding because it is performing a task that it usually does not perform; it could mean that the area is working to inhibit processing related to the task (it has been said that at least 50% of the brain is dedicated to inhibitory processes); or increased signal could mean that blood flow is occurring "in tandem" (on homologous areas in the opposite hemisphere) to processing elsewhere.[18] Appropriate isomorphism between the empirical relations and the dependent variable (see Stevens, 1951; Van Lancker Sidtis, 2007) is lacking.

4. Most studies utilize task contrasts as an early stage of analysis. This means that the signal obtained in one task or setting is subtracted from (or otherwise contrasted with) the signal gained in a different task. This is the "pure insertion" assumption, which asserts that complex behaviors are an additive collection of simple behaviors. For example, a study presents meaningless and meaningful words to subjects. Signal obtained in the meaningless word condition is subtracted from signal obtained in the meaningful word condition. Brain areas remaining after this operation are presented as areas for processing meaning. There are no independent data to suggest that complex brain activity is made up additively of simpler stages of processing. In fact, a great deal of evidence outside of the field of imaging suggests that this is rarely the case.

5. Some studies begin with contrasts of the experimental task with resting states obtained from the subjects. However, studies have shown that resting state signals are more highly correlated with the accompanying tasks than with resting states in other tasks (Sidtis, 2007). Therefore, contrasts using resting states inherently contain a threat to validity.

6. Because the meaning of the brain signals obtained in functional imaging is not understood, and a method for confirming the reliability of the measure is not utilized, interpretation of the signals is unconstrained. It is impossible, using contrast techniques, to determine which of the findings are reliable and valid.

---

[18] Ubiquitous bilateral signal in language and other tasks may be attributable to this physical process.

7. Most imaging studies identify "hot spots" of signal, without a reliable ability to recognize dynamic systems of brain function, which undoubtedly constitute the most important aspect of brain–behavior relationships.

8. Interpretations of results derived from functional imaging studies are self-referential and non-concordant with findings drawn from a century of studies of brain-behavior relationships using a variety of paradigms (cf. Fellows *et al.*, 2005). For example, every functional imaging study of language (naming, listening to sentences, any task you wish) reports bilateral "activation" signal. Yet a huge preponderance of converging evidence from numerous experimental paradigms has taught us that language is processed exclusively (miniscule exceptions have been duly noted) in the left hemisphere. The world of imaging has yet to explain this fact, producing, instead, an ad hoc listing of possible, unsubstantiated explanations for right sided signal during language tasks (Van Lancker Sidtis, 2007).

A proposed solution: Performance-based analysis (Sidtis, Strother, and Rottenberg, 2003) is a technique for obtaining functional imaging signals that are quantitatively tied to behavioral measures obtained during scanning, without the need for contrast procedures. Regression procedures are utilized to identify relationships among brain areas that can predict objective measures of performance. By tying brain imaging data to behavioral measures without using task contrasts, decreases as well as increases in brain activity can be highlighted, and networks of signal in the functional image can be identified, which in the case of speech agree with clinical studies.

While we are gratified that brain function underlying voice recognition – especially personally familiar voices – has finally become a topic of serious scientific study, we suspect that the cortical-localizationist approach, especially as utilized in brain activation paradigms, is inadequate (Uttal, 2001). Its shortcomings are compounded by the uncertainties about the meaning of activation signals in functional imaging (Sidtis, 2007; Van Lancker Sidtis, 2007; see Sidebar). Voice recognition abilities have evolved as instinctual behaviors in a wide range of animals and are innate in humans, suggesting a whole-brain participation in the process. Personal voice identity recognition is better described as a brain state involving the brain stem and resonating through limbic and basal ganglia systems to neocortical areas. We refer the reader to Chapter 3, the earlier review of brainstem plasticity, and to the evidence for brainstem, midbrain, and subcortical/limbic arousal and attentional systems described for vocalization, which points to extensive integrated cerebral systems underlying processing for voices.

6.4.3   Familiar voices in a world of unfamiliar ones

As described in Section 5.3.3.2, presentation of altered familiar voices (Van Lancker, Kreiman, and Wickens, 1985; Lattner, Meyer, and Friederici, 2005) and priming studies of voice recognition (Schweinberger, 2001) lead to the conclusion that familiar voices are apperceived as unique Gestalt-like patterns. Attempts to extract a consistent set of decomposable features that emerge across familiar voices have failed to convincingly support the notion that feature analysis underlies familiar voice recognition. Neuropsychological evidence of a right hemispheric participation in this behavior is consistent with this view. Converging evidence from a variety of paradigms, including electrode recording of auditory cortex and lesion studies, indicates the importance of the temporal-parietal junction in the right hemisphere as cortical contributor to processing speaker identity. The existence of a voice-specific region or regions in the cerebral cortex, comparable to cortical language areas in humans, is consistent with the evolutionary and behavioral importance of familiar voices, and with the fact that voice learning begins before birth in humans and is therefore innate by definition.

However, just as featural analysis does not lead to understanding of familiar voice recognition, so also is the cortical localization approach not adequate to accommodate the global cerebral involvement underlying acquisition and the maintenance of familiar vocal patterns. To account fully for familiar voice cognition, Gestalt-configurational processing and its associations in parietal, frontal, subcortical, and brainstem systems must be elaborated and described. Processes for discriminating new voices involve systems different from those for recognizing familiar voices. The remainder of this chapter provides this comprehensive view of brain structures underlying voice perception. To adequately represent cerebral processing for voice perception, we begin by characterizing differences between discrimination of unfamiliar voices and recognition of familiar voices.

How does the highly evolved ability to acquire and maintain a large repertoire of familiar voices, which is present at birth in many species, relate to processing of unfamiliar ones? As mentioned above, data from behavioral and lesion studies indicate that recognizing familiar voices and discriminating among unfamiliar voices are separate, unordered activities: Recognition does not depend on a prior ability to discriminate, nor does discrimination depend on recognition processes. This suggests that the neurophysiological and cognitive processes involved in perceiving unfamiliar voices are different from those used for familiar voice recognition. Memory processes also operate very differently for the two genres of sound, as described in Chapter 5.

Further, the significance of a human's ability to "recognize" (match or identify) a voice heard in the laboratory, or once or twice previously, and/or lacking in personal relevance, is not very clear. Under some circumstances, our attention may be drawn to biological characteristics or intonational nuances of unfamiliar voices; it may be natural to continually evaluate such parameters in the voice as female, younger, fast rate, pleasant. However, for most animals, including humans, unfamiliar voices are not particularly salient stimuli. As an exercise, the next time you walk in a crowd, notice your reactions to the unfamiliar voices that surround you. Although an occasional voice may penetrate consciousness, this usually occurs because of the words being spoken, and not due to the characteristics of the voice itself, although nuances of intonation may be noted. For the most part, unfamiliar voices are simply an unattended part of the background of noise that surrounds us, out of which a familiar voice "pops," for example if a friend passes audibly nearby. The ability to discriminate the voices of different talkers is useful for streaming the voices of people talking simultaneously, but such abilities do not provide a survival advantage comparable to that associated with familiar voice recognition. When it occurs, trafficking with unfamiliar voices happens in contexts and circumstances that differ essentially from those under which we learn a new voice, in which we are interacting with a person who has some kind of relationship to us. This implies that very different kinds of neuropsychological process (and cognitive process; see, for example, McAdams, 2001), developed over evolutionary time, underlie these tasks. We will provide evidence for these different processes in the remainder of this section, reviewing results that implicate most of the brain in voice recognition.

6.4.4   Neuropsychological factors in voice recognition: Attention, cross-modal associations, emotion, familiarity

The scenario above describes the saliency of the personally familiar voice in a background buzz of unfamiliar ones. Voices in the immediate environment may reveal a mélange of dialects, attitudinal nuances, accents, and moods (see Chapters 4, 8, and 9), and sometimes these attract our attention, but these impressions are fleeting. Returning to the city sidewalk filled with sounds, let us now recall typical concomitant mental experiences that arise on hearing a familiar voice: focused attention, affective impressions, associated memories, motivation or desire (to remain, to escape), and, not to be minimized, a feeling of familiarity or personal relevance (see Sidebar on Familiarity in evolutionary development). These responses imply a significant role of attention in voice processing: Familiar voices naturally capture attention in ways that unfamiliar voices do not. Recent neurophysiological studies of audition (Gilbert and Sigman, 2007; de Boer and Thornton, 2008) reveal that attention and related cognitive attributes are indispensable in successful perception and recognition of heard stimuli. These studies use techniques that trace neural pathways and record single cells to examine neural changes in auditory systems following behavioral manipulations, rather than focusing on putative cortical responses to contrasted stimuli, and highlight the extent to which attention, interest, motivation, and emotion must be present in the acquisition process, converging to enable nearly instant acquisition of a voice pattern into the personal pantheon of familiar voices. Results suggested that interested fixation facilitates responses in monkeys, such that when animals are presented with the task, comparable neuron activity is not present without such interested fixation. This is due at least in part to the rich interconnections of parietal areas with limbic and hypothalamic structures, which mediate emotion and motivation. These connections enable the motivational factors typically seen in learning (Hyvärinen, 1982a). The animal's intention is important to neuron firing in the parietal cortex, where multisensory associations in memory formation occur, and attention, motivation, and intention are closely related to sensorimotor processing (Hyvärinen, 1982b). Regions in the superior parietal lobe have been found to perform voluntary orienting to relevant aspects of the environment supporting multiple attentional systems (Ciaramelli, Grady, and Moscovitch, 2008) and establishing memory and enabling recollection (Simons *et al.*, 2008).

The strong interactions between temporal and parietal areas during learning and memory support our position that multiple cognitive operations converge in the process of voice recognition. In this view, familiar voice recognition involves a process that is highly associated with images, properties, emotions, episodes, impressions, and so on (see Figure 6.7). Cerebral cross-modal associations involving auditory processing occur throughout the brain, and many converge in the parietal lobes. Further, microelectrode studies in awake monkeys have revealed structural and functional multisensory convergence in the auditory cortex (Schroeder *et al.*, 2003). Previously we mentioned that multisensory convergence and integration occur early in sensory processing (Kayser and Logothetis, 2007). This is achieved through cortico-cortical connections and numerous connections to subcortical nuclei. The functionality of these anatomic projections is not always known, but these provide clear candidates for cross-modal interactions at early stages of sensory processing leading to sensory integration, including feedback and feed forward processes.

From these studies of audition, we describe the voice recognition process as engaging a range of cerebral systems, including those responsible for long-term and short-term memory (limbic and hippocampal structures), multisensory associations (parietal lobes), processing of linguistic and prosodic auditory information relating to the voice pattern (temporal lobes), attention and management of the talk interaction (frontal lobes), and motor systems governing the exchange of speech (basal ganglia). The voice thus becomes personally relevant through processes involving cognition and emotion throughout the brain, and establishing personal familiarity in the surroundings is a elemental function (described in more detail in the following section; see also Sidebar on Familiarity in evolutionary development).

Sidebar: Familiarity in Evolutionary Development

Much proverbial ink has been spilled on the question of the origins of the exclusively human abilities: language and music. Are they related? What were the precursors? Did one or the other, or both, arise from nonverbal gesture, vocal cries, courtly songs, work, hunting or war chants (Jespersen, 1950), formulaic expressions (Wray, 2000; Code, 2005), or stereotyped utterances in the right hemisphere (Jaynes, 1977)? We submit that personal voice recognition, inherited and continuously elaborated from a long phylogenetic line of masters at the skill, antedated any and all of these abilities. A favored and prominent actor on the stage of evolution must have been personal *familiarity*, crucially allowing individuals to distinguish family and friend from stranger and foe. Familiarity, a neuropsychological function much neglected in modern studies, with its tight bonds to attention, motivation, affect, and intention, was in highest probability continuously and intensely practiced whenever our ancestors gathered into groups. While faces could be identified during daylight nearby, vocalizations allowed recognition to occur at distances and in the dark. Personal voice identification is much, much older than we are – in all likelihood, older than the split from reptiles. In the beginning was the familiar voice pattern.

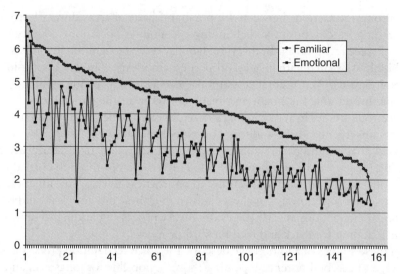

Figure 6.5 Emotionality and familiarity are independent but closely related cognitive attributes. The relatively straight line shows ratings of familiarity for each stimulus; the jagged line indicates ratings of emotionality for the same items. Ratings given to each item are on the y axis; the indvidual rated items are on the x axis.

In addition to attention and motivation, which have been more often studied in auditory learning, we again emphasize the pervasive role of affect in all of cerebral processing, especially in familiarity perception (Panksepp, 2003). Here, process theory as articulated by Brown (1998b, 2002) provides a foundation in maintaining that affect is universally generated through conceptual systems, and that affect arises through cerebral regions other than the limbic system (see Sidebar on Microgenesis). These perspectives, formerly explored by Zajonc (1980), were otherwise seriously neglected in earlier years, but have been recently resumed (Panksepp, 1998, 2008; Shanahan, 2007). Familiarity and affect are intimately intertwined and can be variably influenced by the effects of frequency and arousal. We have presented evidence that familiarity is an independent neuropsychological parameter (see Section 6.3.1 and Sidebar on Capgras syndrome), separable from other parameters such as emotionality and frequency. In a study comparing rated familiarity and emotionality of culturally familiar persons and places (for example, the Eiffel Tower, Elvis Presley, Mother Theresa, Wayne Gretzky, Wonder Woman, Taco Bell; Van Lancker and Ohnesorge, 2002), these two sets of ratings were significantly different but highly correlated. This relationship can be seen graphically in Figure 6.5. In voice recognition performance, from other studies we expect a strong relationship between familiarity and affect, which together form the essence of familiar voices.

6.5   How are Familiar Voices Acquired?

The psychological gulf, as we view it, between recognizing a familiar voice and discriminating among unfamiliar voices raises the question of how listeners learn new voices. Under the recognition circumstance, we process, acquire, and assess a "packet" including many kinds of information about a person other than the voice (face, relationship to us and its history, context of the interaction, content of the exchange, biography, emotional associations, remembered past and projected future scenarios; Damjanovic and Hanley, 2007). Unfortunately, not only are there almost no data about the processes of familiar voice acquisition; the question has hardly been seriously posed. Familiar voice recognition studies in infants and children reviewed in Section 5.3.1 merely demonstrate that children do acquire familiar voice patterns, not how they do so. Studies of voice perception in which voices are learned through exposure in the laboratory setting appear to assume that the training procedure simulates normal familiar voice acquisition, although the multifaceted familiar voice packet schematized in Figure 6.7 can, at best, be only scantily established. The intention, to move unfamiliar voices to the status of personally familiar voices, is done primarily by quantity of exposure to the target voices, not quality of exposure (see Trained-to-familiarity Sidebar above). The role of quantity of exposure in acquiring a new personally familiar voice in normal settings is not known.

Under normal conditions, however, given the widespread cerebral commitment to interaction with a familiar voice (of a person) under normal conditions, it is likely that a lasting representation of the voice can be and usually is rapidly established. Perception of an unfamiliar voice, while often of biological or social interest to the listener, has no personally relevant status in the ecological setting and therefore does not engage a similar range of cerebral systems, so that the familiar voice acquisition process is difficult to simulate in laboratory settings. Whether familiar voice status can be adequately simulated in the laboratory by using unfamiliar voices in a series of training sessions might be an empirical question but is difficult to answer definitively. It is obviously a more pragmatic approach to examining the effects of voice information in various performance tasks than using veridically, personally familiar voices. Our view is that important brain structures, such as limbic system emotional and parietal lobe association areas, are not engaged at all or are not sufficiently engaged in laboratory learning experiments, so the use of learned-to-familiarity voices does not and, without taking extreme measures in the training sessions, cannot fully represent valid personally-familiar voice recognition. We offer some speculations about alternate views of the process of voice learning here.

Acquiring a familiar voice pattern implies, by definition, that the voice becomes personally familiar, which entails enrollment of several additional brain structures to those involved in processing unfamiliar voices. Most importantly, negative or positive emotional and memorial associations naturally ensue when a new voice takes on familiar status. This is the work of the limbic system, the cluster of nuclei encircling the subcortical motor nuclei, including the fornix, amygdala, cingulate gyrus, and hippocampus (see Chapter 3). These limbic structures are involved in emotional experiencing and in memory, which are also represented as informational networks in other areas of the brain. Acquiring a new familiar voice pattern is more like one-trial learning, imprinting, or flashbulb memories than like any kind of repetitive exposure described by a learning curve. In the following paragraphs, we characterize these alternate forms of learning, which differ from incremental learning, as analogic examples of the type of process that must be in play in acquiring familiar voices.

One-trial learning is a special case in classic learning theory. Rather than acquiring a skill or a piece of information over a period of time through repeated exposure or practice, in one-trial learning organisms (for example, rats) "learn" (acquire a conditioned response) immediately or very quickly as the result of "strong contingency" with reinforcement (Lattal, 1995).[19] Unlike a common reinforcement, such as food, this "strong contingency" reinforcement is so effective that the response is acquired after one trial (the pairing of a stimulus and response). A classical example is seen in predatory mammals, who attack and kill their prey routinely and efficiently, until the meat of a target prey (for example, sheep) is contaminated on one single occasion with an emetic, causing the predator (a wolf, for example) to become very ill. Following a single such experience, the wolf not only declines to engage in the usual attack routine, but actually may exhibit play behavior on next encountering a sheep (Palmerino, Rusiniak, and Garcia, 1980; Garcia and Riley, 1998).

Another kind of "learning" that resembles familiar voice acquisition is imprinting. Imprinting was first studied, primarily in birds, by Austrian naturalist Konrad Lorenz (1903–1989), founder of ethology (the study of animal behavior) (Lorenz, 1935). The baby bird at birth immediately "recognizes" its mother, or any moving object (such as a red balloon) encountered at the right time window, and will form an immediate bond.[20] This well-known phenomenon is less elaborated and less intense in mammals, although early maternal voice recognition might well be a candidate for imprinting in many mammals, including humans. Brain biochemistry and brain localization for imprinting have been extensively investigated in avians (Horn, 1985; Knudsen, 1987). In chicks and other fowl, forebrain hemispheres with strong connections to striatal (subcortical) and brainstem structures have been identified through lesion and labeling (tracing paths of neurons) studies as operative in imprinting. The imprinting process in these creatures is based on linking together of various brain regions involved in visceral and endocrine functions as well as emotional expression (Horn, 1985), and the nature of the accompanying cerebral changes is a contemporary topic of active research (Rauschecker and Marler, 1987). Genetic determinants control the basic neuronal circuitry in some species studied, but flexibility allows for experience to shape the auditory system (Knudsen, 1987). Even in songbirds, for whom a critical period for acquiring an auditory pattern is well established, these sensitive periods are labile and flexible (Marler, 1998).

Our perspective on this is that familiar voice acquisition resembles imprinting in the speed and thoroughness with which voices become familiar. We propose that throughout the lifespan, personally familiar voices are acquired in a manner similar to the near instantaneous uptake described for imprinting in water fowl. We speculate that, unlike imprinting, the innate ability to recognize Mom's voice generalizes and thus remains open throughout adulthood as a specialized competence, whereby a necessary and sufficient combination of contextual and auditory cues, engaging the appropriate range of cerebral systems, leads to a rapid lock-in of the sound object.

---

[19] "Contingency" of reinforcement is a relation between environmental events (i.e., stimuli) and responses (Catania, 1998; Lattal, 1995).

[20] Imprinting is depicted as primarily a visual process, but a significant role of vocalization has been described (Hess, 1973; Bolhuis and Van Kampen, 1992).

The third example, flashbulb memory, also involves contextual support (Gold, 1985). This well-described type of instantaneous memory acquisition was originally reported by Brown and Kulik in 1977. People report remembering exactly where they were, what they were wearing, the time of day, the ambient smells and sounds, and other contextual details, on hearing personally affecting news or surprising information. For example, a recent article documented such memories established by people in the United Kingdom on learning of the death of Diana, Princess of Wales (Hornstein, Brown, and Mulligan, 2003). (These reports are not always completely accurate; Neisser and Harsch, 1992.) This type of memory process has engaged considerable interest. Features of the action include arousal, surprise, personal relevance, and consequence to the person, in addition to affect, attention, distinctiveness and poststimulus elaboration (Christianson, 1992), perhaps belonging to a preattentive or automatic mechanism (Neisser, 1967). For our purposes, gaining a flashbulb memory is associated with high levels of arousal that narrow attention (Conway, 1995), leading to a "Now Print" type of command in the nervous system (Livingston, 1967). In all these instances, personal relevance is a key feature leading to encoding of the stimulus. Flashbulb memories constitute an example of the relationship between stress and speed of learning mentioned earlier (Denenberg, 1967; Fair, 1988), and between arousal, emotion, and personal relevance in establishing a record of an experience. They are also unusually well-preserved over a lifetime (Christianson, 1992). Scientists studying flashbulb memories have suggested that this memory mechanism had strong survival value, and thus (along with familiar voice recognition) may have preceded language (Conway, 1995).

These three examples of extraordinary learning and memory functions are offered to provoke new ways of looking at familiar voice pattern acquisition. These examples of near-instantaneous acquisition of information all demonstrate the coordinated roles of emotion, episodic and declarative memory, personal relevance, and attention, rendering a special status to some kinds of knowledge acquisition. We propose that routine and extensive coordination of emotional, memory, sensory, attentional, and motor processes in the brain underlies familiar voice acquisition, and that this all occurs very rapidly. We speculate that some kind of alerting mechanism commands several brain systems to quickly process new information according to an innate perceptual processing ability that is both present at birth and highly elaborated during child development (unlike attention to faces, which initially declines in infancy; Johnson, Dziurawiec, Ellis, and Morton, 1991). This mechanism could be subcortical; for example, the reticular formation forms a system in the core of the brainstem connecting to subcortical and cortical sites, regulating basic life processes, including sleep. It functions as a global monitor of changes in status quo (Fair, 1992), and plays a major role in alertness and motivation. Another obvious candidate is the amygdala, which mediates arousal to stimuli and emotional memories (Adolphs, Cahill, Schul, and Babinsky, 1997). Brain functions of this kind could signal the network to "jolt into action" at the appropriate time and place, engaging the full range of cerebral function required to acquire a personally relevant voice pattern.

As noted above, studies in nonhuman primates reveal rich connections of auditory receiving areas with the posterior parietal lobe,[21] which is strongly affected by

---

[21] Brodmann areas 5, 7, 40, 39.

motivational and attentional inputs from other cerebral areas. Cortical regions are connected to a phylogenetically much older system whose principle relations were (and still are) with the limbic system – especially the amygdala and hippocampus (Fair, 1992), structures directly involved in emotion and memory. Reciprocal connections to the posterior parietal area occur with at least 10 sites across the cortex and limbic and subcortical nuclei (Hyvärinen, 1982a, b). Multimodal visual, somatosensory, auditory and vestibular signals are combined in the posterior parietal cortex (Critchley, 1953; Benson, 1994; Andersen, 1997) supporting establishment of episodic memory (Wagner, Shannon, Kahn, and Buckner, 2005; Haramati, Soroker, Dudai, and Levy, 2008).

Investigative studies of memory processes in the parietal lobes also highlight the importance of personal relevance, attention, and affect (Fair, 1992). Studies of parietal function suggest that the acquisition of personally relevant associations "is more episodic and also more energy intensive than is the formation of memories mediating generic recognition of the same sorts of data" (Fair, 1992, p. 3), mirroring our distinction between the conditions surrounding processing of familiar versus unfamiliar voices. Long-term memory formation involves motivationally or emotionally significant data generating various levels of arousal (Fair, 1992, p. 72), orienting (Sokolov, 1960), or "coactivation" by brain areas involved in arousal. Studies have found a relation between stress – a type of strong arousal – and speed of learning (Denenberg, 1967; Fair, 1988). If the intensity factor, such as affect, motivation, or circulation of stimulating drugs, is sufficient, the time factor in acquiring the learning becomes "negligibly small" (Fair, 1992, p. 107); under proper circumstances, as discussed above, one exposure may be sufficient to bring the input into long-term memory. Studies using electrophysiological measures suggest that naming familiar voices is preceded by activation of awareness of person-specific semantic information, supporting our notion of a complex constellation of properties surrounding and supporting the familiar voice pattern (Schweinberger, Herholz, and Sommer, 1997a).

In summary, we propose that a voice pattern, under specialized circumstances, ascends quickly and precipitously into a listener's familiar-intimate or familiar-famous repertory (we do not know whether these differ) through engagement of brain structures responsible for attention and executive control, emotions, semantic/declarative memory (establishing biographical and contextual facts attached to the voice), and procedural memory (coding the operational details of the conversational interaction or discourse). Vision and audition, touch and smell may also be involved. Thus engaged are the frontal lobes (attention and executive control), temporal structures (audition and pattern recognition), parietal lobes (cross-modal associations and declarative memory), limbic structures (emotional engagement), and subcortical structures (motor execution and procedural memory), working in combination to establish a voice Gestalt-pattern (Figure 6.6).

6.6 A Neuropsychological Model of Voice Perception

Voice perception is best approached as an interaction between the acoustic object and the subjective perceiver (Bertau, 2008). Voices are holistic patterns that occur in time. Recognition occurs as a process of closure, a sudden attainment of a complex entity.

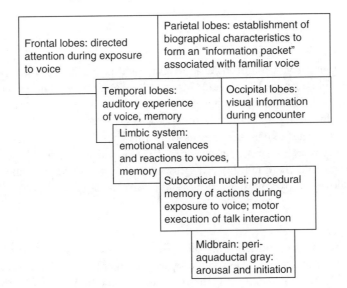

Figure 6.6 Brain areas involved in acquiring a personally familiar voice pattern.

For familiar voices, the effect of individual acoustic parameters is unpredictable and inconsistent across voice patterns. The phenomenological view of voice patterns described in Chapter 1 implies, for voices familiar to the listener, that the individual voice pattern as a whole provides the appropriate cue to itself. The configural properties of the voice are reproduced as part of the interactional process of talking and listening. It follows that differing instantiations of the voice pattern, even affected by background noise, aging, or mood, to mention a few, suffice to represent the voice. Each occurrence of the familiar voice object, in a sense, is novel, as described for mental states in microgenesis. Each entity in thought is novel in view of its temporality and its change across micromoments (Brown, 1998b); yet the brain forms categories, leading to an illusion of stability. This conceptualization of mental processes accommodates the very large number of known voice objects, each of which occurs in changing, "novel," and dynamic form, and yet each belongs to a single, unique category (her voice or his voice). This dynamic process approach to familiar voice perception offers an accounting that is lacking in compositional analysis of a static entity (see Sidebar on Microgenetic theory).

Sidebar: Microgenetic Theory of Brain Function

Microgenetic or process theory provides a counterpart to current paradigms of brain function that utilize assumptions about localization of neuropsychological abilities. Microgenesis refers to psychodynamic processes unfolding in a present-time scale from global to local instantiation of a realized percept or experienced mental event (Werner, 1956; Werner and Kaplan, 1963; Rosenthal, 2004). A key feature is that form, meaning and value are not independent, but unfold simultaneously from resources within the entire brain. Our perspective on familiar voices is resonant with the process model of brain function in which configurations play a major role as original status of the cognitive content (Benowitz, Finkelstein, Levine, and Moya, 1990; Brown, 1998a, b). The mental content is "not constructed like a building," but unfolds from "preliminary configurations [that] are implicit in the final object" (Brown, 2002, p. 8). Affect and familiarity might be better accommodated in these approaches. Accounts of familiar voice recognition that attempt to utilize acoustic building blocks in the explanation are likely to fall short of satisfaction – "would be like trying to illustrate the flow of a river with a set of bricks" (Brown, 2002, p. xxxvi).

As mentioned above, inducting a voice pattern into one's pantheon of personally familiar voices is not accurately described by an incremental learning curve. Acquiring a personally relevant voice pattern is the result of a whole brain response that involves the auditory processing of the temporal lobes, short-to-long-term memory shunting by hippocampi, the emotional valences of the limbic system, executive oversight of the frontal lobes, coordination across parietal lobe association cortices, and accruing packets of associations (Figure 6.7). Processing details for unfamiliar voices are essentially different, selecting features that reflect deviations from stored prototypes (Figure 6.8).

As noted in Chapter 3 and elsewhere in this chapter, all the structures of the brain involved in voice and face discrimination and recognition exist bilaterally. The temporal lobes, which contain the auditory receiving areas, the hippocampi, which are crucial to learning and memory of auditory (and other) events, the amygdala, which, as part of the encircling limbic system, react to emotionally laden stimuli, are all nearly identical in size and shape in each cerebral hemisphere. The small morphological differences identified for a few structures, comprising minor size or shape differences between left and right appearances, have not been shown to have consistent functional implications (Geschwind and Galaburda, 1985). Nevertheless, converging findings from different scientific paradigms lead to the conclusion that the acoustic material of speech is processed preferentially in the left hemisphere[22] (Studdert-Kennedy and Shankweiler, 1970; Bever, 1975), while the acoustic material for voice recognition is preferentially processed in the right hemisphere. The model of voice perception presented here is in harmony with other known attributes of the right hemisphere: processing of social context, emotional meanings, complex patterns, and personal relevance (Van Lancker, 1991, 1997; Bradshaw and Mattingly, 1995; Brownell, Gardner, Prather, and Martino, 1995; Myers, 1998). This model of voice processing in the brain fits well with other discoveries about the role of the right hemisphere in prosodic function (Borod, 1993; Adolphs, Damasio, and Tranel, 2002). Information about the speaker revealed in the speaker's voice

[22] Studies of persons who have undergone left hemispherectomy in early childhood, more than those with right hemispherectomy, reveal subtle syntactic deficits even though language has developed normally (Dennis and Whitaker, 1976; Van Lancker Sidtis, 2004).

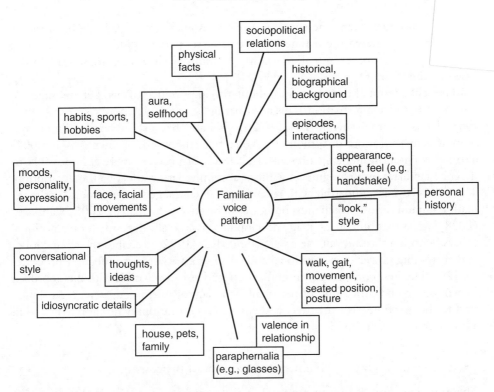

Figure 6.7 A schema of associations to a familiar voice pattern. A rich, subjective, unstructured array of qualities and characteristics accompanies the known voice. The attributes "surround" the voice pattern as personally relevant factors.

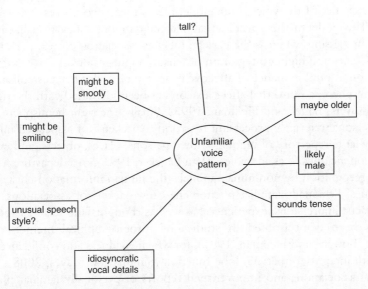

Figure 6.8 A schema of associations to an unfamiliar voice pattern. A sparse, unstructured array of guesses accompanies the unknown voice.

includes emotional state, personality, socioeconomic status, geographic history, mood, attitude toward the listener, and, of course, personal identity. All of this is interwoven in the speech signal, in a complex auditory pattern, automatically processed by the listener.

Judgments about the speaker and about the importance of his/her message are conferred by voice information. This information is, in a way, "more elemental" than the verbal content (Bolinger, 1964, 1972b), probably because subcortical limbic systems are engaged more directly by the voice than the words. Brown (1972, 2002) also views emotion as being present at all levels of processing. It is impossible to describe familiar voice recognition without accommodating affect to the description. This perspective is compatible with recent shifts in language study to social and pragmatic communication, which must be viewed subjectively (Shanahan, 2007). Panskepp (2008) argues that human language development is crucially dependent on emotional processes arising throughout the basal ganglia. Fair (1992) describes the frontal lobes as contributing powerful motivational and affective associations to memory processes (p. 125). This new context of communication studies is compatible with our approach to acquisition and processing of personally familiar voices. In neuroscience, a similar shift to the overriding role of affect and emotion in evolutionary development and in all of cognitive processing is underway.

6.6.1   Hemispheric modes of processing

These findings can also be understood in the context of a model of the brain that describes the right hemisphere as a superior Gestalt pattern recognizer, and the left hemisphere as specialized for detailed, analytic tasks (Bogen, 1969; Bever, 1975). The model proposes that voices are processed by the interplay of Gestalt recognition and feature analysis. This interplay occurs in varying degrees across voices as determined by characteristics of the voice. Our model places these two process types on a continuum. The model further specifies that bilateral temporal lobes specialize in detailed auditory processing, whereas the parietal lobe, as association cortex, performs cross-modal matches and higher integration of sensory input, using affective and memorial information. A predominance of affective processing has also been established for the right hemisphere; a nonverbal affect lexicon has been identified with the right hemisphere (Bowers, Bauer, and Heilman, 1993). Finally, the right hemisphere has a key role in personal relevance processing by storing "packets" of associated information for a very large repertoire of unique, known persons, places, objects, and events; this information includes faces and voices (Van Lancker, 1991). In a departure from familiar voice recognition by nonhuman animals, the human information cluster includes their names. Personally familiar phenomena carry packets of associations – history, images, facts, impressions, experiences, as well as thoughts and feelings about them. This has been demonstrated in studies of autobiographical memory (Cimino, Verfaellie, Bowers, and Heilman, 1991), for which vividness and confidence are associated with integrity of parietal lobe function (Simons and Mayes, 2008). Deficient emotional associations and impoverished reports of personally familiar phenomena are seen following right hemisphere damage. This disability is likely to interact with familiar voice processing and cause this function to be diminished.

We must confess that we are handicapped in our desire to characterize the voice pattern in a truly revealing way. This caveat reflects the fact that linguistically structured tones in a tone language and phonetic elements in speech can be transcribed and written down, but voice patterns cannot. When discussing faces and voices, the notion of a pattern must be primary. Gestalt doctrine – the notion that much of perception involves establishment of schemata or patterns (Corcoran, 1971; Reed, 1972; Neisser, 1976) – is generally accepted. This ability is held to be "wired-in" or innate (Pomerantz, 1986). It remains a problem how to define this process. It may be virtually impossible to characterize right hemisphere pattern recognition processes using left hemisphere verbal-analytic terminology. However, differences between the two kinds of processing can be highlighted. Both featural-analytic and holistic-configurational approaches have been demonstrated in face perception (Farah, Hammond, and Mehta, 1989; Farah, Levinson, and Klein, 1995). These follow different maturational schedules in children, so that equal performance on tasks emphasizing part analysis and holistic recognition is not achieved until adolescence (Davidoff and Roberson, 2002). For faces, featural as well as configurational information may be utilized for both perceptual and recognition processes (Schwaninger, Lobmaier, and Collishaw, 2002). With respect to pattern recognition, the emergent feature or features that suffice to identify the pattern is as salient a property as any others from which it emerges (Pomerantz, 1986). Studies of the feature-Gestalt trade-off in familiar voice recognition remain to be designed and executed.

6.6.2 Summary of cortical neuroanatomical substrates for faces and voices

Despite the discrepant backgrounds in research on voices and faces, tentative generalizations about the comparative neuroanatomical substrates and cerebral processes for discrimination and recognition are possible. First, for both faces and voices, discrimination and recognition are separate abilities involving different neuroanatomical substrates. Secondly, a predominance, overall, of the right hemisphere for all these abilities has been reported, but left hemisphere involvement for both face and voice processing has also been observed. When naming is involved for faces, the left hemisphere has also been implicated in recognition; for voices, the left hemisphere has been implicated in discrimination. Names may be less strongly associated with recognition of voices. For faces, a "verbal" component has been invoked to account for the left hemisphere participation in familiar face recognition, while an "analytic" sub-strategy has been invoked to account for evidence of left hemisphere involvement in unfamiliar voice discrimination. Dissociations of familiar-intimate and familiar-famous stimulus processing have been suggested for both faces and voices, but both of these can be expected to be mediated in the right hemisphere.

So, returning to the "Fox and Hedgehog" model introduced earlier, we review again how this perspective leads to a better understanding of voice perception. We recall Isaiah Berlin's (1953, 1994) discussion of Greek poet Archilochus' original story "The Fox and the Hedgehog," in which the fox knows lots of little things and the hedgehog knows one big thing, and we utilize this dichotomy to characterize

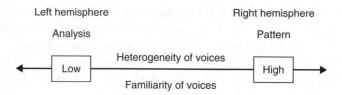

Figure 6.9 Continuum of parameters in voice sets, homogeneity–heterogeneity and unfamiliarity–familiarity, correlated with left-right hemisphere preferences

human voice perception. In voice perception, both the fox – analytic strategies – and the hedgehog – Gestalt pattern recognition – proceed more or less deftly, depending on voice status and listener experience. The fox analyzes the featural details, the hedgehog grasps the Gestalt-pattern whole. As previously mentioned, this approach draws on traditions in psychology that alternate between exemplar and rule-based descriptive approaches, and in linguistics, where various versions of analogy and structural (rule-governed) approaches have been proposed. In voice perception studies up to now, most analyses have attempted chiefly to extract features to explain listeners' performance. The Fox and Hedgehog model proposes instead that two modes are operative.

Given that voice perception utilizes both featural and configurational modes of processing; considering the large array of potential vocal parameters available for each voice; and taking into account the psychological differences inherent in familiar compared with unfamiliar voices, we propose a model of brain processing of voice patterns that accommodates all these facts. Familiar voices, each with a few unique, distinctive cues to identity (because they are known to the listener), are likely to be more perceptually heterogeneous than unfamiliar voices, which are not yet established as unique memorable patterns (see schema in Figure 5.1). The number of familiar voices typically within each person's repertory is not known, but it might be astonishingly large. "Heterogeneous" in this connection means that for the user, items within a set of familiar voices "feel" different from one another, because each is made up of a very different constellation of associations. Unfamiliar voices have not become as distinct to a listener, and do not contain a set of memorial associations. Therefore unfamiliar voices in a set of voices seem more homogeneous. The voice–listener interaction is pre-eminent in this classification scheme. In this model, similarity (homogeneity) and dissimilarity (heterogeneity) are psychological properties of the listener, correlating roughly with a (high or low) familiarity factor (see Figure 6.9). The two modes, featural and configurational, are associated with left and right hemisphere processes respectively.

Now we can place the parameters homogeneity–heterogeneity and featural–Gestalt on continua in association with familiarity with the voices and with left and right hemisphere function. The more homogeneous and unfamiliar a set of voices, the more likely featural comparison will be used to discriminate among them; the more heterogeneous and familiar the voice set, the more likely Gestalt-closure processes will be engaged. For featural analysis, matching of auditory details is used, and a few generalized templates for voices are accessed. For Gestalt-closure, distinctive cues and ad hoc combinations of cues will suffice to prompt the pattern for the familiar voice in a process called the idiosyncratic emergence of features in patterns (Pomerantz, 1986). These properties correlate with left and right hemisphere function across the continua (Figure 6.9).

6.7 Conclusions and Summary

The review of animal behavior in Chapter 5 reveals that familiar voice recognition ability is widespread, provides a clear survival advantage, and thus holds evolutionary significance. We have seen that human infants are born with the ability to recognize their mothers' voices; nonhuman animals of many types show similar abilities, the particulars of which can be explained by environmental and behavioral demands; and converging evidence from a number of paradigms suggests that a broad range of brain mechanisms, some of which are phylogenetically very old, underlie this ability. Voice recognition antedated the appearance in human development of music and language, and may have flourished long (possibly very, very long) before establishment of social groups.

For over a century, it was held that the left hemisphere was the sole arbiter of communication through the medium of speech and language (Pulvermüller, 2002). In its strictest interpretation, this fact has been borne out by continuing studies. However, much more is now known about right hemisphere involvement in communication, especially in the realm of prosodic and pragmatic function. This review of voice perception and recognition studies has shown that persons with aphasia, having intact right hemispheres, are likely well aware of the identity of the familiar-intimate and familiar-famous voices around them, along with much of the attitudinal, affective, personal, and pragmatic information provided by intonation. (We will further discuss these topics in Chapters 8 and 9.) In later discussions it will become more clear that the left hemisphere knows *what* is being said, and at the same time, the right hemisphere is considering *how*, and *by whom*, the message is expressed. Processing the voice pattern to assess who is speaking is accomplished using both featural and pattern recognition approaches, selectively and appropriately applied in various degrees and combinations to the unfamiliar or to the familiar voice, and takes much of the brain.

For several decades, the human cerebral cortex has been the focus of interest in brain function underlying important cognitive functions such as language and visual spatial processing.[23] We have reviewed evidence that these cortical regions have advanced capacity to process auditory features and auditory patterns, and to coordinate high-level interaction between these two modes of processing. These features and patterns for voice are processed independently from those for speech. With the advent of emotion psychology and advanced studies of movement, other regions of the brain, especially subcortical nuclei, have gained prominence as sophisticated mediators of human

---

[23] The PBS science documentary series called *The Mind* (1988) features the cortex, the three-millimeter layer of cells covering the brain, throughout the video presentation as the mediator of all behavior that is uniquely human.

behaviors. The work of processing auditory features and auditory patterns begins in the brainstem and has presence throughout the auditory pathway of the brain. Given the complex constitution of a voice, comprising elements of emotion, memory, and so on, many other functional entities of the brain are called upon in voice recognition. In this chapter, we have emphasized the whole brain underlay to familiar voice recognition, a cognitive process that has been greatly elaborated in the human species but is not uniquely human. While cortical areas identified in lesion and functional imaging studies constitute a final common pathway and may well be the sine qua non of successful human voice recognition, extensive neurological structures crucially participate in the process. Many of these structures are shared across biological species and reach far back into evolutionary history. These structures have enabled successful voice recognition for countless biological groupings across many millennia.

7

Identifying Unfamiliar Voices in Forensic Contexts

7.1 Introduction

We proposed in Chapters 5 and 6 that recognizing an unfamiliar voice or attempting to identify a speaker after limited exposure is not a "natural" kind of task, and that such an effort allocates perceptual and cognitive resources in a different manner than that employed when recognizing a familiar voice. However, one situation where listeners' abilities to learn an unfamiliar voice are of particular interest is when they are exposed to an unknown speaker during the commission of a crime, and as witnesses or victims are subsequently called on to recognize the voice without necessarily knowing the speaker personally or being able to identify him/her by name. Listeners may be presented with a single voice and asked to state whether it is or is not that of the perpetrator; or the witness may hear a set of speakers in a voice lineup and be asked to identify one of them as the perpetrator of the crime (e.g., Nolan, 1997). One oft-cited example of this kind of procedure occurred at the trial of Bruno Hauptmann for kidnapping the son of national hero Charles Lindbergh in 1932. Controversy continues about this case, but Lindbergh heard the voice of a man to whom ransom was paid (who may have been the perpetrator, or who may have been one of a series of con artists who plagued the case) once, uttering a short phrase (either "Hey, Doctor, over here, over here" or simply "Hey, Doctor!" – accounts of the incident varied somewhat over time) at night and from a distance of over 70 yards. Almost three years later, at Hauptmann's trial, Lindbergh testified:

Q. On the night of April the 2nd, 1932, when you were in the vicinity of St. Raymond's Cemetery and prior to delivering the money to Dr. Condon and you heard a voice hollering, "Hey Doctor," in some foreign voice, I think, as you referred to it–since that time have you heard the same voice?

Foundations of Voice Studies: An Interdisciplinary Approach to Voice Production and Perception, First Edition. Jody Kreiman and Diana Sidtis.
© 2013 Jody Kreiman and Diana Sidtis. Published 2013 by Blackwell Publishing Ltd.

A. Yes, I have.
Q. Whose voice was it, Colonel, that you heard in the vicinity of St. Raymond's Cemetery that night, saying "Hey, Doctor"?
A. That was Hauptmann's voice.
Q. You heard it again the second time where?
A. At District Attorney Foley's office in New York, in the Bronx.
       (Transcript at 109–114, *State vs. Hauptmann*, 180 A. 809 (NJ 1935) (No. 99))

Although a range of circumstantial evidence was presented at trial (for example, wood from a ladder used in the kidnapping precisely matched the grain of wood in Hauptmann's attic, and Hauptmann had a large portion of the ransom money in his possession; see e.g. Kennedy, 1985, for details of the trial), jurors afterwards reported that Lindbergh's testimony was a critical factor in their deliberations.

There are hundreds of more mundane examples: Attacks by masked robbers and rapists, crimes committed in darkness, obscene or threatening phone calls, and such events are unfortunately daily occurrences. In these situations, someone's identification of the suspect as the speaker heard during the crime is often an important piece of evidence, and is sometimes the only piece of evidence against the defendant. In cases like these, such testimony is reliable to the extent that listeners can hear a voice one time and accurately distinguish it from other, possibly similar voices at a later date.

Other criminal cases may involve recognition of a familiar voice. In one early example, in 1660 a soldier named William Hulet was tried and convicted of carrying out the decapitation of the English King Charles I in 1649. Testimony consisted largely of third-hand hearsay reports with witnesses claiming that others had told them that Hulet had told them that he was the executioner. However, one witness (Richard Gittens) testified that he had served in the army with Hulet for over 12 years, and that he recognized Hulet's voice at the time of the execution when Hulet asked the King's pardon before chopping off his head. Although Hulet denied that he had ever served in the same company with Gittens, and despite the fact that several additional witnesses testified that the ordinary hangman, one Gregory Bandon, had confessed to the killing, Hulet was convicted of regicide. The account of the trial (Howell, 1816) concludes with the report that the court, "sensible of the injury done to him" by this conviction in the face of another's confession, later reprieved Hulet, making this also an early example of misidentification by voice. Of course, there are many more mundane examples of forensic identification of a familiar voice: for example, identifying the voice of an associate from an answering machine tape or that of a suspect from a secretly recorded conversation as part of a "sting."

In the American legal system, testimony about voice recognition is usually admitted as evidence during trial, subject to cross-examination (Solan and Tiersma, 2003).[1] Considerations of admissibility often put aside issues regarding the manner in which the identification was made. Some procedures (for example, asking the victim whether or not a single suspect is the perpetrator) are inherently suggestive, and tend to bias the witness in favor of positively identifying the suspect, thus potentially violating the

---

[1] Much of the discussion in this introductory section is based on Solan and Tiersma (2003).

suspect's right to due process (*Neil vs. Biggers*, 409 US 188, 1972).[2] However, the Supreme Court ruled that such suggestive procedures are not in and of themselves fatal to eyewitness (and by extension earwitness) testimony, but that their influence should be weighed against indicators that the testimony is otherwise reliable (*Manson vs. Brathwaite*, 432 US 98, 1977). Factors the Court stated as contributing to witness reliability were the exposure the witness had to the voice at the time of the crime, the witness's attention, accuracy of the witness's description of the criminal at the time of the crime, the degree of certainty in the identification, and the delay between the crime and the identification. Even if an identification is made using biasing procedures, if it otherwise meets these criteria for admissibility (the "Biggers criteria"), it is admissible in court. This rather low threshold for admissibility leaves issues of witness reliability up to the jury to decide. Unfortunately, juries do not always have enough information about factors that affect the reliability of identifications to make informed decisions about the case at hand. This situation highlights the need for coherent research into the factors that underlie the (un)reliability of voice identification testimony.[3]

A substantial body of forensically focused research has in fact been conducted regarding speaker recognition. In contrast to the studies presented in Chapter 5 (which examine the factors and processes that facilitate speaker recognition), these studies emphasize factors that are likely to *interfere* with recognizing the voice. The earliest modern work on speaker recognition (McGehee, 1937, 1944) was motivated by issues raised during Bruno Hauptmann's trial, while more modern research has specifically addressed the Biggers reliability criteria. Additional factors affecting earwitness reliability have also been identified and evaluated, including the distinctiveness of the voice, the possibility of vocal disguise, and the method of testing recognition (Deffenbacher *et al.*, 1989). The practical, seemingly case-specific nature of studies in this research tradition benefits defendants and juries in addressing immediately relevant issues of witness reliability: Very often, a study of the reliability of voice identification under a precise set of conditions is undertaken to provide support for the defense or the prosecution in a specific legal case, with the results subsequently published. However, this approach has also led to the appearance of many superficially similar studies with discrepant results. Because individual studies are motivated by practical concerns, little effort has been invested in understanding why results differ from study to study. As a result, the forensic voice identification literature often seems spotty and confusing, with very little reference to theory. Even though the studies described in Chapter 5 have the same ostensible topic as those presented here (speaker recognition), it can be difficult to use findings and theories from one domain to make specific predictions or interpret results in the other, as we will see repeatedly in the sections that follow.

In the rest of this chapter we review threats to the accuracy of earwitness testimony. Such threats can arise at any point as information about the unfamiliar voice is transmitted

---

[2] The Biggers decision referred specifically to identifications of suspects by eyewitnesses to crime, but the criteria specified in the decision are often generalized to earwitness testimony as well. See Solan and Tiersma (2003) for more detailed discussion.

[3] Witnesses in court are sometimes asked to identify a voice from a tape recording. Courts usually require only that the tape be authenticated for such testimony to be admissible. The issues surrounding the actual voice identification itself are similar in these cases to those that arise when a "live" voice is identified, so this particular set of circumstances will not be discussed separately. See Solan and Tiersma (2003) for more information.

> Speaker → Utterance → Signal transmission → Listener → Listener response

Figure 7.1   Stages of transmitting information about an unfamiliar voice from a speaker to a listener.

from the speaker to the listener (Figure 7.1, following the speech chain introduced in Chapter 1). Proceeding through the speech chain from the speaker to the listener, we will examine the importance of the many factors (including the Biggers criteria) that hypothetically impact the relevance and accuracy of earwitness testimony.

7.2   Speaker Factors

Although the Biggers criteria describe the characteristics of a reliable witness, most forensically oriented studies of speaker identification focus on the speaker's attributes, possibly because the focus of trials is typically on the likelihood that the suspect is the perpetrator. Speakers can differ in many ways, as detailed in Chapter 4, but the factors that underlie most differences between speakers (age, sex, race, physical size, etc.) are not in general the focus of forensically oriented studies, which instead emphasize factors that are likely to interfere with recognizing the voice, as described above. We examine these factors in the following sections.

7.2.1   Speaker factor 1: Did the voice seem particularly distinctive?

Some speakers leave listeners feeling "I'll never forget that voice." This impression corresponds to the fact that some voices are apparently more recognizable than others, although both the extent and the pattern of differences vary a good deal from study to study. For example, Thompson (1985) reported large differences between speakers in the likelihood that they would be correctly identified (hit rates = 15–90% for a seven-day delay between hearing the voice and the recognition test), but smaller differences in the false alarm rate (15–50%). Unfortunately, it is not a simple matter to predict which voices will actually be recognized accurately. First, listeners are poor judges of which voices they are likely to identify correctly. For example, Van Lancker, Kreiman, and Emmorey (1985) found listeners correctly identified only 26.6% of the famous voices they predicted that they would recognize. Secondly, the association between a priori distinctiveness and recognizability is not straightforward. Orchard and Yarmey (1995) reported that voices considered "distinctive" were remembered better for two days than "undistinctive" voices (and were easier to identify when whispered), and Clifford, Rathborn, and Bull (1981) found that voices rated "high recognition" were better recognized than "low recognition" voices after delays of up to two hours, but not after longer delays. However, other studies have had opposite results. Clifford *et al.* (1981) found that unfamiliar voices rated "highly recognizable" were not recognized any better overall than those rated "hard to recognize" (for delays between learning and testing that ranged from 10 minutes to 14 days). Similarly, for delays ranging from one week to four weeks, Papcun, Kreiman, and Davis (1989) found no difference in hit rates for voices rated "hard to remember" versus "easy to remember," but the "hard to remember" voices were more likely to be *incorrectly* identified as the target voice than were the "easy to remember" voices. Thus it is not the case that voices listeners consider a priori to be distinctive are necessarily the easiest to remember.

7.2.2   Speaker factor 2: Did the voice sound familiar?

As described in Chapter 5, listeners' familiar voice recognition abilities are good, but not outstanding. Given the inherent difficulty of open-set tasks (in which the speaker could be anyone in the world, familiar or unfamiliar), error rates in recognition tasks can be high, even for the most familiar speakers. Results from forensically motivated studies have been rather mixed, but overall confirm this finding. Some studies have found that listeners can identify familiar voices with better than 90% accuracy (e.g., LaRiviere, 1972; Abberton and Fourcin, 1978; Hollien, Majewski, and Doherty, 1982). Others report worse performance; for example, Clarke and Becker (1969) found correct identification levels ranging from 58% for naive listeners to 63% for experts. Increasing familiarity provides an advantage in some test conditions, but not in others: Yarmey, Yarmey, Yarmey, and Parliament (2001) found that highly and moderately familiar voices were recognized more accurately than low-familiar or trained-to-recognize voices, but Read and Craik (1995) reported that accuracy was no better for "mildly familiar" voices than for unfamiliar voices (heard once and then identified from a voice lineup); and Ladefoged and Ladefoged (1980) reported the infamous failure of an expert listener to recognize his mother in an open set listening task.

7.2.3   Speaker factor 3: Did the speaker have an accent or speak a foreign language?

Multilingualism is a common feature of urban life, and hearing a speaker who has an accent or who is not speaking the local primary language does not even attract attention in many places. In forensic situations, it is reasonable to ask whether and to what extent differences between the victim and the perpetrator in dialect or language spoken affect the reliability of earwitness identifications. Such an effect would be consistent with the notion that articulatory information is important for recognizing voices, as discussed in Chapter 5. A listener who is unfamiliar with the phonetic inventory of a particular language may very well have a hard time distinguishing features that are idiosyncratic to the particular speaker from features that characterize the language or the accent in general, resulting in a "they all sound alike to me" perspective.

A number of studies have examined the effects of accent or language spoken on earwitness reliability. Four different situations have been examined: (1) The speaker and listener speak the same language, but have different regional or national accents (the American English of Boston vs. Los Angeles, vs. Australian English); (2) the speaker and listener speak the same language, but one is a native speaker and one has a foreign accent; (3) the speaker uses a foreign language that the listener understands; and (4) the speaker uses a foreign language that the listener does not understand. Table 7.1 summarizes typical results. Hypothetically, one might expect recognition scores to decrease as language unfamiliarity increases, so that scores should get worse

Table 7.1 Representative results of studies examining the effects of accent and/or language spoken on speaker identification performance. Values are averaged across experiments for replications within multi-experiment papers.*

Voice sample	Own dialect	Regional dialect	Foreign accent	Familiar foreign language	Unfamiliar foreign language	Reference
A brief sentence			Hit rate 0.57; false alarm rate 0.18		Hit rate 0.58; false alarm rate 0.18	Goldstein et al. (1981)
A long sentence	85% correct	82% correct	81% correct			Goldstein et al. (1981)
1 word	56% correct	55% correct	37% correct			Goldstein et al. (1981)
72–80-word passage	Hit rate = 0.65; false alarm rate ≈ 0.27[a]		Hit rate = 0.52; false alarm rate ≈ 0.27		Hit rate = 0.38; false alarm rate ≈ 0.27	Thompson (1987)
72–93-word paragraph	Average d' = 1.33		Average d' = 1.00		Average d' ≈ 0.66	Goggin et al. (1991)
72–93-word paragraph	d' = 1.34		d' = 0.95		d' = 0.72	Goggin et al. (1991)
1 min. passage				Average d' = 2.56	Average d' = 1.67	Köster and Schiller (1997)
2 sentences	Hit rate = .88		Hit rate = .13			Doty (1998)
Short phrase	62% correct	26% correct				Vanags et al. (2005)
Not specified (at least 1 sentence)	Hit rate .41; false alarm rate .44	Hit rate .34, false alarm rate .65				Kerstholt et al. (2006)
40–50 sec passage				Hit rate = .47; false alarm rate = .67	Hit rate = .47; false alarm rate = .93	Philippon et al. (2007)

Notes:

* d' is a measure of listener sensitivity used in signal detection theory (see Chapter 4). When listeners cannot discriminate at all, d' = 0. When listeners achieve 75% correct on both signal and noise trials, d' = 1.35. See Macmillan and Creelman (2005) for more information.

[a] False alarm rates did not differ across conditions and were reported as an average value.

from left to right across the table, and with the exception of two experiments by Goldstein, Knight, Bailis, and Conover (1981), results show this expected pattern, although effect sizes differ from study to study. Consistent with the notion that familiarity with a language enhances the listener's ability to make use of articulatory cues to speaker identity, bilingual speakers of English and Spanish performed equally well when asked to identify previously heard voice samples of Spanish speakers and of English speakers with and without Spanish accents (Goggin, Thompson, Strube, and Simental, 1991).

7.2.4   Speaker factor 4: Did the voice sound disguised?

Vocal disguise requires speakers to determine the primary attributes of their voice patterns – the vocal features that characterize them – and then to alter those features sufficiently to destroy the pattern's integrity. Vocal disguise can work in two different ways, both of which depend on the speaker's vocal plasticity for their success. First, a speaker can produce an utterance that differs greatly from his or her usual vocal quality, one that sounds so unusual that this particular production is unlikely to be associated with his or her "average" voice. Alternatively, the speaker can produce a quality that is close to the average for the entire population of speakers with respect to every possible vocal attribute, so that there is nothing distinctive about this particular voice sample to distinguish the speaker from many others. In practice, the first option is much easier to accomplish, and is the approach that is usually taken. Use of a computer generated voice is one possible example of the second kind of vocal disguise, more often found in crime films than in real life (Kunzel, 2000).

Table 7.2 lists some of the different ways in which voices can be disguised. As discussed in Chapter 1, it follows from the source-filter theory of speech production that speakers can vary vocal quality by making steady-state and/or dynamic changes to the voice source and/or to the vocal tract filter. Examples of these kinds of alterations are given in audio samples 7.1–7.8, all of which were produced at a single session by a single talker. (The examples of vocal plasticity in Chapter 2 can also be treated as an exercise in vocal disguise; compare audio samples 2.9–2.18.)

Although study has not been particularly systematic or theoretically motivated, experimental evidence shows that disguises do indeed disrupt the process of recognizing a voice (Table 7.3). Listeners have little difficulty detecting that vocal disguise is present – 92.6% correct detection for experts, 89.4% correct for naive listeners (Reich, 1981) – but they have significant difficulty normalizing away a disguise to recognize the underlying vocal pattern. Ability to penetrate a vocal disguise depends at least somewhat on a listener's background, as indicated by the data in Table 7.3. When presented with a disguised voice sample, expert listeners performed significantly better than did naive listeners when asked to select the correct speaker from a list of ten (although recognition rates for undisguised samples did not differ; Hollien *et al.*, 1982). Familiarity with the speaker and with the language being spoken also help recognition of the underlying vocal pattern (Reich and Duke, 1979). Familiarity with the speaker provided the largest advantage, but the effect of disguise on performance was similar for both listeners who knew the talker and listeners who were trained to recognize the target voices (about 19% decline in recognition scores in both cases). In contrast, speakers who did not

Table 7.2   Some ways to disguise a voice.

Alter the source
   Change F0
   Whisper
   Use creak, falsetto, period doubling
Alter vocal tract shape
   Change in nasality (pinching nose/lowering velum)
   Shorten vocal tract (lip retraction, larynx raising)
   Lengthen vocal tract (lip protrusion, larynx lowering)
   Alter the shape of the vocal tract (for example, through pharyngeal expansion or contraction)
Vary dynamic aspects of speech
   Use accent
   Vary intonation contour
   Vary speaking rate or rhythm
   Object in mouth, clenched teeth
Combinations of these

---

know English actually performed equally poorly in the disguised and undisguised conditions (and were worst overall at recognizing the talkers).

Of the approaches to disguise listed in Table 7.2, the effects of changes to the source (phonation) have been studied most often, possibly because source manipulations can be made without too much distortion of the information content of the spoken message (at least in languages like English that do not use tone or make only minimal use of phonation contrasts to carry word-level meaning). Even the simplest alterations appear to provide effective disguises. For example, Wagner and Köster (1999) found that hit rates decreased dramatically from 97% to 4%, when listeners were asked to identify the voices of familiar co-workers who spoke in falsetto versus normal voice. False alarm rates decreased in the falsetto condition, from 29% to 1%, indicating that listeners adopted a much more conservative response strategy when dealing with obviously disguised voices. Use of creaky voice as a disguise led to a 26% decrease in hit rates (Hirson and Duckworth, 1993), along with an increase in false alarm rates from 17% to 43%. Whisper is another commonly-used and effective disguise: Whispering a vowel resulted in a decrease of almost 50% in recognition accuracy, from 40% correct to 22% correct (LaRiviere 1975). The effectiveness of whisper as a disguise does depend somewhat on the speaker, however, at least when stimuli are longer than a single vowel: "Distinctive" voices remain recognizable at above chance levels when whispered (Orchard and Yarmey, 1995).

Sidebar: Voices of Identical Twins

The voices of monozygotic (identical) twins pose a possible challenge to forensic voice identification efforts. Because monozygotic twins are genetically identical and (usually) raised under identical circumstances, their voices should be highly confusable.

Data suggest that the voices of twins are indeed more similar than those of dizygotic twins or unrelated individuals. Identical twins are more similar in their average F0 and in the amount of variability in F0 than are either dizygotic twins or unrelated individuals (Debruyne, Decoster, Van Gijsel, and Vercammen, 2002). Similarities in vocal tract size and shape also result in rather similar acoustic spectra, especially with respect to the shape of the spectrum above the first formant (Alpert, Kurtzberg, Pilot, and Friedhoff, 1963; van Lierde, Vinck, de Ley, Clement, and Van Cauwenberge, 2005). However, detailed measurements of monosyllables produced by a single set of male twins revealed significant differences for F0 (mean, range, patterns), the frequencies of the first, second, and fourth formants (F1, F2, F4), vowel durations, and details of articulatory timing. In another study comparing monozygotic and dizygotic twins, most articulatory and vowel formant measures did not differ between the two groups. However, the dizygotic twins showed more variability in production of the stressed syllable /gi/ (Weirich, 2010). Thus, although monozygotic twins have voices that are more similar than those of dizygotic twins or unrelated individuals, their voices are still not completely identical, and both shared environment and unique physiology leave their marks on the voices.

Identification scores are consonant with these facts. When asked to name each member of a set of male identical twins from a monosyllable, six listeners who knew both speakers well succeeded approximately 72% of the time (Whiteside and Rixon, 2000). In an easier task, listeners correctly selected the twins from a set of three voices based on a sentence (about 78% correct) or a 2.5 sec sustained vowel (57.5% correct; Van Gysel, Vercammen, and Debruyne, 2001). Although these values are significantly above chance, they are far from perfect, confirming once again that both genetic and environmental factors are important determinants of how a speaker sounds. (Note in comparison that the cries of twin noctule bat pups are more similar than are the calls of unrelated pups, and remain so as the pups grow, although the cries of unrelated individuals grow more distinct with age; Knörnschild, von Helversen, and Mayer, 2007.)

Despite the fact that experimental evidence, everyday experience, and common sense support the effectiveness of vocal disguise, disguises are not particularly common in criminal cases that include voice recognition. Kunzel (1994) estimated that only about 15% of cases in German courts involved voice disguise. When disguise is present, falsetto, creaky voice, whispering, fake foreign accents, and hyponasality (produced by nose pinching) are favored, while synthetic speech is hardly ever used (Reich and Duke, 1979; Kunzel, 2000).

Finally, in addition to the intentional changes in speaking patterns introduced by disguise, speakers may also change speaking style unintentionally. Changes that occur in vocal quality due to variations in speaking style (casual vs. formal speech) or emotional state (calm vs. angry speech; manic or depressed states vs. calm or cheerful moods; see Chapter 9) may equal or exceed the effects of vocal disguise, as may changes

Table 7.3 Percentage correct voice recognition for disguised and undisguised voices, for different kinds of listeners.

	Undisguised	Old age	Hoarse	Hypernasal	Slow rate	Free disguise
Naive listeners[a]	92.3	67.6	68.4	59.4	70.3	61.3
Expert listeners[b]	92.5	79.7	81.2	72.2	79	73.8
Listeners who knew speaker[c]	98					79
Listeners trained to recognize speaker[b]	39.8					20.7
Listeners who did not speak English[b]	15.7					17.9
Listeners aged 16–50						29–30.3
Listeners aged 50–80[c]						20

Notes:
[a] Data from Reich and Duke (1979). Listeners performed a same/different task in which some voice pairs included a disguised voice and some did not.
[b] Reich and Duke (1979).
[c] Data from Hollien *et al.*, 1982. Listeners chose the correct speaker from a list of ten.
[e] Data from Hollien *et al.* (1982); Clifford, 1980. Results are averaged across experiments with four, six, and eight distracter voices.

in dialect related to the specific speaking environment or the target audience. In a study of such effects, Bahr and Pass (1996) recorded the voices of African-American males speaking casually and formally, and then asked listeners to judge whether pairs of voice samples represented the same or different speakers. When speaking styles were matched, hit rates equaled 87% (false alarm rate = 13%), but when speaking styles differed within a pair of voices, the hit rate declined sharply to 39%, while the false alarm rate increased to 21%. Shouting also serves as an effective disguise, even when disguise is not the speaker's intent (Blatchford and Foulkes, 2006). However, because shouting obscures some vocal features (loudness, obviously, but also segment durations and mean F0) but preserves others (for example, regional accent), its effect on voice recognizability should vary from talker to talker. This is in fact the case: Hit rates for a shouted two-word phrase ranged from 19 to 83% across nine familiar talkers (false alarm rate = 45%), and from 31 to 100% for a 12-syllable shouted phrase (false alarm rate = 19%). This variability is consistent with the model of voice recognition proposed in Chapters 5 and 6: The importance of a vocal attribute depends on the context in which it occurs, so no one disguise will suit every talker and circumstance equally well.

7.2.5   Might the speaker have mimicked someone else?

Mimicry and disguise are two sides of the same coin. Both require the speaker to determine the primary attributes of a voice pattern – the vocal features that characterize a speaker – and both depend for their success on the perpetrator's vocal plasticity.

While disguise requires speakers to obscure their underlying voice pattern, a mimic or impersonator reproduces or even exaggerates important vocal characteristics in sufficient detail that listeners will immediately recognize the target speaker.[4] Most speakers can easily disguise their voices, whereas convincing vocal mimicry usually requires talent, some training, and extensive practice (however much we may like to think our amateur efforts are both convincing and amusing). Finally, mimicry is usually used for entertainment, rather than with criminal intent, whereas vocal disguises, while not necessarily criminal, are seldom completely innocent. A mimic need not copy every detail of the voice pattern; in fact, it is not clear if humans can adequately mimic more than a few features at a time (Nolan, 1983). Instead, mimicry functions as a kind of verbal caricature. Just as facial caricatures are obviously not true-to-life portraits, mimicry generally involves copying and usually exaggerating a small number of the target's verbal trademarks, stereotypical utterances, or prominent idiosyncrasies, with the goal of entertaining, and not of fooling, the audience. Even though accuracy is not paramount, mimicry is not as easy as we might assume. Mimicry (at least mimicry of a specific talker) also improves with systematic practice and feedback: In one study, the rate of false identifications (successful imitations) increased significantly when a professional impersonator was allowed to listen to his efforts and provided with feedback from an automatic verification system (Blomberg, Elenius, and Zetterholm, 2004).

Although even professional mimics are not usually mistaken for the target speaker, occasionally the speaker's goal is in fact deception. It is very difficult indeed to reproduce a voice so accurately that it is actually mistaken for the target, and true impersonation usually requires a credulous audience to succeed. For example, filmgoers who saw *The Trail of the Pink Panther* (Edwards, 1982) and *The Curse of the Pink Panther* (Edwards, 1983) saw actor David Niven, and heard what they thought was his voice. Only later was it revealed that the voice onscreen was actually that of mimic Rich Little, who overdubbed Niven's dialog because Niven's serious illness made his speech unintelligible (he died of amyotrophic lateral sclerosis – Lou Gehrig's Disease – shortly before *Curse* was released).[5] Once this is known it is fairly easy to detect the difference in voices; but at the time audiences heard what they expected to hear, and suspected nothing.

Although mimicry and impersonation have not been studied extensively, research confirms that mimicked voices are caricatures rather than close approximations to their targets, and mimics overshoot and undershoot the target's characteristics as often as they match them precisely (Zetterholm, 2002, 2003). Different mimics tend to select the same features when mimicking a given voice, but the importance of a particular feature varies with the voice, consistent with the importance of the overall voice pattern in recognizing familiar voices (Chapters 5 and 6). Despite general agreement about how to mimic a particular voice, the efforts of different mimics may not sound especially similar. For example, when two professional mimics copied the voices of six well-known Swedish speakers, one listener who was unfamiliar with the target voices questioned whether the speakers were even mimicking the same targets (Zetterholm, 2002, 2003).

---

[4] Examples of the work of one famous professional mimic are available at www.richlittle.com.
[5] Internet Movie Database; http://www.imdb.com; accessed June 21, 2007.

7.3   Factors Related to Speech Samples or the Utterances Heard

Common sense dictates that some utterances provide more information about speakers than others do, and thus should enhance the reliability of earwitness testimony. For example, it seems intuitive that a witness who hears only a scream in the night is less likely to identify the voice correctly than is a witness who overhears a 20-minute telephone conversation. This intuition is enshrined in the Biggers criteria, which stipulate that the exposure the witness had to the voice at the time of the crime is an important factor contributing to earwitness reliability. The studies reviewed in this section have attempted to spell out what adequate "exposure" might mean.

7.3.1   Sample factor 1: Content and duration of the speech heard

One aspect of "exposure" is the duration and content of the speech sample heard by the witness, and many studies have examined the effect of increasing sample duration on earwitness reliability. Sample durations have ranged wildly across studies, as have performance levels. Early studies focused largely on determining the limits of performance. Performance from extremely short or static stimuli can exceed chance levels; for example, recognition of familiar speakers from a small set of colleagues was 36% correct when listeners heard only a snippet of the vowel /i/ lasting 1/40th of a second (Compton, 1963). Performance improves (not surprisingly) as sample duration increases. Some studies of unfamiliar voices suggest that in simple discrimination tasks performance exceeds chance levels for stimulus durations of 1 sec or longer, but may improve with increasing durations of up to 1 minute, after which no further improvements accrue (Pollack, Pickett and Sumby, 1954; Bricker and Pruzansky, 1966; Legge, Grosman, and Pieper, 1984). The importance of increasing duration depends on the listening task, however: Performance improves more with duration when the task is more difficult (for example, when the delay between hearing and recognizing a voice is longer than a few minutes). This finding has also been replicated more recently by Legge *et al.* (1984), who found that, given a one-minute voice sample, listeners could pick the correct speaker from two choices after 15 minutes on about 70% of trials, but performance fell below chance levels when the listeners heard only six seconds of speech. (This effect was consistent whether the listeners remembered the voices for five minutes or ten days.)

The reasons why longer stimuli produce better results have been the subject of some discussion. Classic studies and some modern replications (often using very short speech samples) argued that performance increases with duration because longer voice samples provide listeners with a better sample of the speaker's phonetic repertoire. For example, Roebuck and Wilding (1993) found no difference between short, varied voice samples and long varied voice samples, but short unvaried samples produced worse performance overall. In contrast, Cook and Wilding (1997) argued that duration was the critical factor, not the number of different sounds heard. They examined listeners' ability to identify a target voice from a six-voice lineup after a 1 week delay, based on hearing a short, unvaried voice sample (< three vowel sounds, five syllables), a short varied voice sample including five or six different vowels, or a long varied voice sample (>6 vowels, 11.33 syllables). Although correct recognition averaged only 38% across conditions, listeners who heard the longer stimuli performed better than listeners in either short-stimulus group. It is possible that longer samples produce a change in listeners' response criteria, and that this accounts for the increased percentage correct scores (i.e., hit rates) reported by Wilding and colleagues: If both hit rates and false alarm rates increase with voice sample duration, no real improvement in performance has occurred, although increased hit rates may make it appear as if subjects are more accurate (Yarmey, 1991; Yarmey and Matthys, 1992). Finally, most of these studies apparently assume that changes in duration affect only the sample of speech sounds (phonemes) available to the listener. However, making an utterance longer also increases the listener's ability to estimate the speaker-dependent prosodic characteristics of the voice, including variability in pitch and loudness, the speaker's average pitch and loudness, speaking rate, and all the other non-phonemic aspects of the voice signal whose importance for voice quality and speaker recognition have been discussed in earlier chapters. These factors probably interact with voice sample duration and phonemic inventory in ways that have not yet been adequately described.

7.3.2 Sample factor 2: Matched versus unmatched voice samples

Intuitively, it would be hard to match the memory of a cry of fear in another room to the sound of an unfamiliar person producing a normal utterance. A number of studies have addressed this issue by assessing how the extent to which the sample heard at test "matches" the sample heard originally will affect earwitness reliability. For example, speakers may yell during the commission of a crime, but not during a voice lineup; a cold may produce hoarseness at first exposure (learning), but not at test; and so on.

Committing a crime may involve significant emotion (fear, excitement, anger) for the criminal as well as for the victim. The general effects of emotion on voice and the perception of emotional state from voice have been studied extensively, and are discussed in Chapter 9. In forensic contexts, authors have mainly been concerned with the extent to which differences in emotional tone may facilitate or disrupt speaker recognition. For example, if an agitated criminal speaks with a high F0, but normally speaks with a rather low F0, how important is this difference in determining the accuracy of earwitness testimony (Boss, 1996)? When testing occurred within a few minutes of hearing the voice, a difference in emotional tone between learning and testing produced a significant decrease in recognition accuracy (Saslove and Yarmey, 1980). At a longer delay of one week, differences in emotional tone did not affect recognition accuracy, probably because performance was only slightly above chance in either the matched emotion/unmatched emotion condition ("floor effects"; Read and Craik, 1995).

In contrast to the effects of changes in emotional state or in the words uttered, delays in recording the speaker after the crime probably have little effect on voice recognition accuracy. Some changes in voice quality may occur in the short term as speakers recover from (or come down with) colds or develop (or recover from) hoarseness due to vocal abuse; but in general speakers' voices change very slowly over time (Chapter 4). The slow time-course of vocal change results in minimal impact on recognition scores (Hollien and Schwartz, 2000, 2001). When listeners heard recordings

of the same (unfamiliar) speakers that were made at sessions separated by delays ranging from four weeks up to six years, their performance in a same/different (paired
comparison) task declined from 95% for contemporary samples to 70–85% for samples
made at different times, consistent with decrements that arise from hearing two different samples recorded at the same time. This variability is thus more likely due to
normal day-to-day within-speaker variability in voice quality than to long-term changes
in the speaker's vocal apparatus. When recordings were separated by 20 years (during
which time significant physiological changes may well have occurred), ability to determine whether samples came from the same talker or not declined to 35% correct.
Although listeners were not familiar with the talkers in this study, results suggest that
naive listeners are able to adjust mentally for the kinds of within-speaker variability in
quality that they encounter in their everyday lives, consistent with common experience. However, this kind of very long delay does not arise often in legal situations; and
the negative contributions of delays in recording a voice are probably minimal relative
to other sources of error in voice recognition.

7.4   Factors Related to the Transmission System

Messages or threats delivered by telephone are often a factor in forensic situations
where earwitness testimony is at issue. The telephone filters the voice signal quite
dramatically. No information is present in a telephone signal below 300 Hz, or above
about 3,400 Hz, which means that many speech sounds (fricatives like /s/, affricates
like /tʃ/) that have most of their energy above this range may not be adequately
transmitted (Nolan, 2005).[6] In addition, telephone voices have a reduced dynamic
range; noise may be present on the line or in the background; and in some cases distortions introduced by an answering machine or voicemail system may further degrade
in the signal. All of these factors may make it harder for a listener to recognize the
person who made the bomb threat or the obscene telephone call.

Two issues surrounding the telephone (or other transmission systems) and earwitness reliability have been investigated. The first concerns the effect that filtering or
other signal degradations have on listener accuracy. Early studies (Compton, 1963)
showed that high-pass filtering had a much more dramatic effect than low-pass filtering
on speaker recognition accuracy, suggesting that the listeners might indeed perform
less well when voices were heard over the telephone than when they were heard live.
Some additional early studies found that recognition performance was consistently
worse when a telephone was involved (Rathborn, Bull, and Clifford, 1981). However,
more modern studies (Perfect, Hunt, and Harris, 2002; Kerstholt, Jansen, Van
Amelsvoort, and Broeders, 2006) have not found decrements in performance, possibly due to improvements in telephone signals in recent years. These studies suggest
that the signal filtering characteristics of the telephone are not a significant cause of
losses of accuracy that occur in these cases.

---

[6] Perception of the fundamental frequency is not affected because the auditory system can extract this
information from harmonic spacing; see Chapters 2 and 4).

A second possibility is that earwitness reliability suffers when listeners hear a voice over one transmission system (the telephone, for example, or a recording made on a specific kind of equipment, or through a pillow placed over their head) and then attempt to recognize it from playback via a different transmission system (a live person; a good-quality recording). Some combinations of sound systems have had negative effects on recognition or discrimination scores. For example, Alexander, Botti, Dessimoz, and Drygajlo (2004) reported that error rates doubled in a same/different task when voices were recorded and then played back using different instrumentation. Other studies have found no effects of mismatched transmission systems or recording conditions on recognition accuracy (McGonegal, Rabiner, and McDermott, 1978; Kerstholt, Jansen, Van Amelsvoort, and Broeders, 2004, 2006). Differences between systems probably account for these variable findings: Systems may have differed more dramatically in one study than in the others, so the listener's task was not equally difficult in all cases.

Cellular phones introduce a number of additional concerns (see Byrne and Foulkes, 2004, for extended discussion). First, a cell phone can be used virtually anywhere, leading to the possibility of increased masking of the voice signal by background noise. Speakers tend to speak much more loudly on their cells than when using a landline (possibly in response to the presence of background noise); and during cell phone use F0 may also increase by as much as 30 Hz as compared to landline use (because F0 tends to increase with loudness; see Chapter 2). Low-pass filtering characteristics of cell phones may be more dramatic than those of landlines (Kunzel, 2001). Transmission characteristics of cell phones also produce rather large increases (on the order of 29% on average, but up to 60%) in first formant values compared to direct recordings of the same voice samples (Byrne and Foulkes, 2004). Although no data appear to exist about the effects of these differences on listener accuracy, in principle the effects are large enough to influence both speaker identity judgments and perception of a speaker's personal characteristics (Chapter 4).

7.5 Listener Factors

7.5.1 Listener factor 1: Inherent ability to remember/recognize voices

Listeners differ significantly in their ability to recognize voices, but it is difficult to define listener characteristics that consistently predict who is or is not likely to produce accurate responses. Several factors predict performance in a limited way. First, Köster, Hess, Schiller, and Kunzel (1998) found a modest correlation ($r = 0.4$) between measures of speech perception acuity and speaker recognition accuracy. Additional studies reported that listeners aged 40 or older performed worse than listeners under age 40 (Clifford *et al.*, 1981; Kreiman, 1987) when asked to discriminate among or recognize the voices of young (20-ish) speakers. It is not clear if this decreased level of performance reflects declining cognitive or sensory functioning (consistent with declining speech perception scores) or a "they all sound alike" effect of the kind described in Section 7.2.3. No study has examined the ability of younger listeners to recognize the voices of older speakers.

7.5.2   Listener factor 2: Degree of attention

The Biggers criteria stipulate that a witness's attention to the voice at the time of the crime is an important determinant of earwitness reliability. The validity of the association between attention and accuracy has been investigated directly by manipulating the instructions received by a listener. Results have varied across studies, with some investigators finding large and significant effects of instructions on hit rates (but also increases in false alarm rates; Saslove and Yarmey, 1980; Armstrong and McKelvie, 1996) and others finding no differences in overall accuracy between listeners who were asked specifically to pay attention to the voice during a distracter task and those who were not so instructed (Cook and Wilding, 2001; Perfect *et al.*, 2002). This suggests that instructions may alter response criteria more than they improve accuracy, but the relevant analyses have not been reported.

A second, indirect approach to the question of listener attention is to manipulate different aspects of the listening context that are presumed to affect attention. For example, several studies have found that it is more difficult to remember several voices than it is to remember just one (e.g., McGehee, 1937; Carterette and Barnebey, 1975; Legge *et al.*, 1984). (Carterette and Barnebey suggest that differences in performance are due to increasing false alarm rates as the target voice set increases in size.) It may also be easier to recognize a voice that was learned through active conversation with the speaker than it is to recognize one that was only heard passively (Hammersley and Read, 1985). Having more than one opportunity to hear the voice may or may not facilitate subsequent recognition. In one study, listeners were significantly more accurate when they heard the same voice sample three times than when they heard it only once (Cook and Wilding, 2001). When listeners heard an additional, different voice sample from the same speaker between initial exposure and test, accuracy increased slightly; but hearing a sample from a different speaker tripled the probability that this different voice would be incorrectly identified as the target at test (Thompson, 1985). Finally, a third study found that hearing a voice twice improved performance, but hearing it three times did not (Yarmey and Matthys, 1992). It again seems likely that these manipulations affect listeners' response criteria, so that accuracy data are difficult to interpret.

One forensically important contextual effect is the ability of the listener to see the face of the perpetrator during the crime. Two hypotheses have emerged about how seeing a face and remembering a voice might interact. Seeing the face might somehow help the listener encode the voice better, consistent with the further hypothesis that associations develop at the neurological level between the voice and face during learning (Shah *et al.*, 2001; von Kriegstein, Kleinschmidt, and Giraud, 2005a; von Kriegstein, Kleinschmidt, Sterzer, and Giraud, 2005b; see Chapter 6). Alternatively, the presence of a face during learning could distract the listener from the voice, leading to worse recognition performance (the so-called "face overshadowing effect"; Cook and Wilding, 2001). As usual, evidence is ambiguous between these hypotheses. In some studies, listeners who both saw and heard the speaker at learning performed better than did those who only heard the speaker (Legge *et al.*, 1984; Armstrong and McKelvie 1996). Other investigators reported worse performance when faces were presented (McAllister, Dale, Bregman, McCabe, and Cotton, 1993; Cook and Wilding,

Table 7.4 Experimental designs for studies of blind listeners.

Study	Listeners	Speakers	Stimuli	Task	Result
Bull *et al.* (1983)	92 blind 72 sighted	1 target 5–9 foils	1 sentence	Closed-set voice parade after 5 sec delay	Blind > sighted (hit rates)
Winograd *et al.* (1984)	12 blind 24 sighted	20 male, 20 female	Short passage produced by each of 20 speakers	Label each of 40 samples as "old" or "new"	Blind > sighted (hit rates); blind > sighted (false alarm rates)
Elaad *et al.* (1998)	18 sighted; 15 blind	16 targets 2–6 foils/target	Short conversation	Open set: match target to foils	Sighted > blind

1997, 2001). Seeing a voice both at learning and at test usually benefits performance, largely due to the salience of faces (see Sheffert and Olson, 2004, for review).

One listener population – the blind – provides a natural test of the face–facilitation hypothesis, and has received special attention accordingly. Several authors (Bull, Rathborn, and Clifford, 1983; Winograd, Kerr, and Spence, 1984; Elaad, Segev, and Tobin, 1998) have speculated that blind listeners would outperform their sighted counterparts in voice recognition tasks, because dependence on hearing has either heightened auditory sensitivity or led to more efficient cognitive strategies for speaker recognition.[7] It is also possible that lack of distracting visual input could improve voice recognition performance. Methods have differed substantially from study to study, and are summarized in Table 7.4. Results have not supported the hypothesis of greater recognition or discrimination accuracy in the blind. Bull *et al.* (1983) asked listeners to pick a target voice out of a lineup after a very short delay. They reported significantly higher hit rates for blind listeners than for sighted ones, but did not report false alarm rates. Winograd *et al.* (1984) played 20 voices to listeners, and then asked them to respond "new" or "old" to each of 40 additional voices, half of which they had in fact heard before. They reported that both hit and false alarm rates were higher for blind listeners, so that no significant difference in overall accuracy occurred. Finally, Elaad *et al.* (1998) presented listeners with a target voice and a set of foils, and allowed listeners to play all the voices as often as necessary to identify or reject each sample. In this case, the sighted listeners performed slightly better than the blind, although differences were quite small.

7.5.3 Listener factor 3: Is a confident witness more likely to be accurate?

Confidence is persuasive. The witness who says, "I am absolutely positive about this" is inherently more believable than one who says, "Well, maybe …". This basic fact about human nature is reflected in the Biggers criteria, which stipulate that witness

---

[7] Note that the seemingly analogous hypothesis that deaf viewers are superior to hearing viewers at face recognition has not been tested, to our knowledge.

confidence about an identification is one of the factors that governs the admissibility of the identification as evidence. Juries also pay particular attention to witness confidence when assessing the reliability of testimony (Deffenbacher, 1980; Cutler, Penrod, and Stuve, 1988).

Unfortunately, it does not appear that earwitness confidence is related to accuracy in any straightforward way. Reviews and meta-analyses (Deffenbacher, 1980, on earwitness testimony; Bothwell, Deffenbacher, and Brigham, 1987, on eyewitness testimony) indicate that significant results are uncommon, and large correlations are almost unheard of. Across studies, the average correlation between confidence and accuracy equals about 0.25 (equivalent to about 6% variance accounted for; Bothwell *et al.*, 1987). Since these publications, numerous additional studies have produced the same result of nonsignificant correlations (Bull and Clifford 1984; Yarmey, 1986; Goggin *et al.*, 1991; Van Wallendael, Surace, Parsons, and Brown, 1994; Read and Craik, 1995; Olsson, Juslin, and Winman, 1998; Perfect *et al.*, 2002; Kerstholt *et al.*, 2004) or significant but very low correlations ($r = 0.37$, Yarmey *et al.*, 2001; $r = 0.23$, Yarmey, 1991). It is even possible to find significantly positive, nonsignificant, and significantly negative correlations between witness confidence and accuracy from a single study (Yarmey and Matthys, 1992). Thus, even in those rare cases when correlations are statistically significant, confidence provides us with very little information about the likely accuracy of the witness's testimony.

Signal detection theory (Chapter 4) provides one possible explanation for this counterintuitive state of affairs. In this framework, a listener's confidence in a response is related to decision criteria, and not to sensitivity. For a fixed level of sensitivity (perceptual ability to discriminate among stimuli), a confident listener will normally reply "I recognize the speaker" more frequently than an unconfident listener, thus generating both more hit responses (correct identifications) and more false alarms (incorrect identifications); an unconfident listener will hesitate before identifying a suspect, but will also generate fewer false identifications. Because confidence modulates both hit and false alarm rates, it has no consistent effect on accuracy in this model (the two are independent), so no consistent correlation with accuracy would be expected. This explanation is consistent with evidence from Olsson *et al.* (1998), who argue that successful recognition of familiar voices in everyday life leads some listeners to overestimate their abilities to identify unfamiliar voices, so that in forensically-relevant situations (where listening conditions are usually impoverished relative to everyday listening) they are confident out of proportion to their abilities.

An additional explanation is that the lack of correlation between confidence and recognition accuracy is due to changes over time in what is remembered about a voice. Recall that listeners apparently remember unfamiliar voices with reference to a prototype or "average voice" and a set of deviations from that average (Papcun *et al.*, 1989; Kreiman and Papcun, 1991; Chapter 5). Over time, details of how the target voice deviates from the prototype are forgotten, and listeners' memories increasingly converge on average-sounding voices. Given this, listeners may (correctly) report that the voice they hear matches their memory, but their memory is not an accurate record of what was originally heard, resulting in a lack of correspondence between confidence and accuracy.

A third possibility, proposed by Deffenbacher (1980), is that confidence predicts accuracy only when listening conditions are "optimal." This proposal captures our intuition that a witness's confidence means more under some circumstances (for example, when identifying a highly familiar voice from a very long voice sample in a quiet environment where it is unlikely that another similar-sounding person was present) than under others (an unfamiliar voice, heard through a mask for a second or two only in the presence of loud environmental noise). Deffenbacher proposes a long, ad hoc list of circumstances that might combine to define "optimal" conditions, including knowledge that a test is coming; enough stress to promote vigilance but not so much that it paralyzes the witness; a long enough voice sample; extensive personal familiarity with the speaker; a short retention interval; similar stimuli presented at learning and at test; and so on. This highlights the primary limitation of the proposal to define "optimal" conditions for voice identification: It is very difficult to specify what "optimal" means in real life forensic situations, or to determine post hoc whether conditions were or were not optimal. Further, optimal conditions do not necessarily mean that there will be a strong correlation between accuracy and confidence: Stronger associations between confidence and accuracy are *more likely* when listening conditions are optimal, but nonsignificant associations have also been observed even under optimal conditions. It thus appears that confidence is not diagnostic of witness accuracy in any meaningful way.

7.5.4   Listener factor 4: Sex of listener

Concerns about whether males or females are better at recognizing unfamiliar voices started with McGehee (1937), who found that men were better at recognition tasks than women. Differences between men and women in cognitive processes, sensitivity, or attention might be expected to affect earwitness reliability in consistent ways. For example, women's increased sensitivity to some aspects of male voices (Chapter 4) might lead to the prediction that they can recognize male voices better than men can. However, this has not proven to be the case. Researchers have found nearly every possible result in studies examining the importance of a listener's sex as a predictor of voice recognition ability, including interactions between the sex of the speaker and listener. For example, Wilding and Cook (2000) found that female listeners were more likely to recognize female voices correctly than male voices, while male listeners were equally accurate when asked to identify male and female voices. In contrast, Thompson (1985) found no significant differences between men and women in recognition accuracy. In the face of such variability in results, the only viable conclusion is that there are no consistent differences in overall recognition ability between males and females. Observed differences between studies are probably due to incidental differences between voice samples studied or the individual listeners in the two groups, which can have a particularly large effect on results when only a few individuals are studied.

7.5.5   Listener factor 5: Training

Specialized training represents yet another factor whose impact on recognition accuracy remains unknown. At first thought, it might seem that through training, practice, and experience, expert listeners would learn what features to pay attention to and develop more forgetting-resistant strategies. On the other hand, the cognitive model of unfamiliar voice recognition presented in Chapter 5 suggests that feature encoding is not necessarily a helpful strategy, and other research on the perception of voice quality (Chapter 1) has shown that listeners are not especially good at extracting features from voices in any case.

Corresponding to these rather vague predictions, phoneticians have sometimes outperformed naive listeners in voice recognition, but not always. In one study (Elaad *et al.*, 1998), phoneticians with expertise in voice recognition had both higher hit rates and lower false alarm rates than did naive listeners; in a second study (Schiller and Köster, 1998), phoneticians had higher hit rates than naive listeners, but false alarm rates did not differ; and in a third study (Shirt, 1983) no difference between expert and naive listeners was found. It is worth noting that, even if they develop superior encoding and retrieval strategies, expert listeners remain susceptible to many of the same effects that confound naive listeners. For example, Ladefoged (1978) found that half of a group of experienced phoneticians misidentified an unknown speaker as a member of the phonetics lab group, because they had just been asked to identify the voices of other lab members and thus expected that all the test voices came from the same group, despite their extensive sophistication, experience, and training.

7.5.6   Listener factor 6: Accuracy of description

One of the Biggers criteria – the accuracy with which the witness describes the perpetrator at the time of the crime – is particularly difficult to translate from the visual domain (describing a person) to the auditory domain (describing a voice). As discussed in Chapter 1, voices are very difficult to describe. They are not amenable to decomposition in the way that faces are (size and color of eyes, shape of mouth and nose, presence or absence of facial hair in males, hair length and color, and so on), and no fixed vocabulary exists for the many small details of word choice, pronunciation, speaking rate, pitch variation, accentuation, and personal voice quality (in the narrow sense) that contribute to recognition (Perfect *et al.*, 2002). In fact, producing a verbal description of the voice has the effect of fixing the witness's attention and memory on inappropriate vocal attributes, and results in significant decreases in recognition accuracy (Perfect *et al.*, 2002; Vanags, Carroll, and Perfect, 2005).

7.6   Recognizing the Voice: Testing Procedures

7.6.1   The delay between the crime and the identification

In the common sense view, time is a basic aspect of unfamiliar voice identification, and accuracy should decline in some regular fashion as a function of time. From this perspective, other factors (the number of voices heard, stress, sample duration, and so on) should affect the rate of forgetting, or the shape of the forgetting curve, but not the overall pattern of regular decline over time. The forensic concern, in this view, is straightforward: How long can the delay be between the crime and the voice lineup for the procedure to remain valid?

The data do not provide a clear answer to this reasonable question, because, as Table 7.5 indicates, it is clear that delay in and of itself is not a strong predictor of accuracy. Several explanations for this vexing situation suggest themselves. First, many, many factors affect earwitness reliability, as reviewed in this chapter, and it may simply be the case that delay does not carry as much weight in this multifactor model as our intuition tells us it should. Secondly, memory changes over time, as described in Chapter 5. Listeners forget the attributes of distinctive voices over time, so their memories converge on "hard to remember" voices, making it increasingly likely over time that these voices will be "correctly" recognized. In the present context, this means that accuracy rates may go up or down over time as a function of the voices being studied, and not as a main effect of the delay. Finally, many studies (particularly in the older literature) do not report false alarm rates. A number of more recent studies (e.g., Van Wallendael *et al.*, 1994; Kerstholt *et al.*, 2006) have suggested that the high probability of incorrectly selecting an innocent person from a lineup (the false alarm rate) is the primary threat to earwitness reliability. A seemingly reasonable overall percentage correct score may mask a false alarm rate that is unacceptably high.

7.6.2 Selecting the distracter voices and administering the lineup

In forensic situations, earwitnesses are often asked to identify the perpetrator's voice from a "voice lineup" or "voice parade," analogous to a visual lineup. The proper construction of such lineups in terms of how the distracter voices are chosen has generated discussion; in addition, the translation from a visual task to an auditory task (with the addition of a temporal dimension) introduces special demands. Authors generally agree that the distracter voices should not be chosen to match the suspect's voice, but instead should match the *description* of the suspect's voice in accent, rate, and intonational range (however difficult that may be; Nolan and Grabe, 1996; Olsson *et al.*, 1998). Listeners tend to incorrectly identify a distracter voice as the target when distracters match the suspect's voice, versus when they match the description of the suspect (Olsson *et al.*, 1998). At the same time, the distracter voices should not be so similar that the suspect stands out unduly (Yarmey, Yarmey, and Yarmey, 1994). Ideally, pre-tests will be used to ensure that the perceptual distances between the distracters and the suspect voice are approximately equal, and that the set is homogeneous, with no one voice sounding stereotypically "criminal" (Nolan and Grabe, 1996). Finally, lineups should be administered in a double blind format, so that the person presenting the samples does not know which voice is that of the suspect. These combined procedures are obviously pragmatically challenging.

Unfortunately, it is unlikely that these ideal procedures are followed in most voice lineup situations, and there is a very real possibility of bias. Listeners (at least in the laboratory) find it very difficult indeed to reject all the voices in a lineup (Philippon *et al.*, 2007), and often pick the best match available, even when the true criminal is not among the choices. In this way, poor lineup construction results in increased false alarm rates and possible wrongful convictions (Van Wallendael *et al.*, 1994). Finally, the test administrator should avoid exposing the witness to the voices before the test (which could lead to secondary learning and misidentifications), and should ensure that the witness can actually hear adequately (Hammersley and Read, 1983).

Table 7.5 Unfamiliar voice identification: Selected accuracy data for different retention intervals.

Delay	Stimuli	Results	Source
Immediate	1 sentence	Hit rate = .89; false alarm rate = .2	Kreiman and Papcun (1991)
Immediate	Telephone survey (several minutes)	Hit rate = .52; false alarm rate = .21	Yarmey (1991)
Immediate	90 sec. ad	Hit rate = .80; false alarm rate = .19	Van Wallendael *et al.* (1994)
5 min	1 min. monologue	Hit rate = .61, false alarm rate = .06	McAllister *et al.* (1993)
10 min	1 sentence	Prob.(correct) = 56%	Clifford *et al.* (1981)
15 min	1 min. passage	70% correct (old/new task)	Legge *et al.* (1984)
40 min	1 sentence	Prob.(correct) = 41%	Clifford *et al.* (1981)
100 min	1 sentence	Prob.(correct) = 41%	Clifford *et al.* (1981)
130 min	1 sentence	Prob.(correct) = 44%	Clifford *et al.* (1981)
1 day	1 sentence	Prob.(correct) = 32%	Clifford *et al.* (1981)
1 day	56-word paragraph; read live	Hit rate = .83	McGehee (1937)
2–3 days	Telephone survey (several minutes)	Hit rate = .29; false alarm rate = .31	Yarmey (1991)
3 days	56-word paragraph; read live	Hit rate = .81	McGehee (1937)
1 week	1 sentence	48% - 50% correct	Cook and Wilding 1997 (2001)
1 week	2 min. survey	Hit rate = .66; false alarm rate = .06	Papcun *et al.* (1989)
1 week	2 min. survey	Hit rate = .63; false alarm rate = .06	Kreiman and Papcun (1991)
10 days	1 min. passage	61% correct	Legge *et al.* (1984)
2 weeks	1 sentence	Prob. (correct) = 38%	Clifford *et al.* (1981)
2 weeks	2 min. survey	Hit rate = .7; false alarm rate = 0.1	Papcun *et al.* (1989)
2 weeks	A few sentences	Hit rate = .68	McGehee (1944)
2 weeks	90 sec. ad	Hit rate = 76%; false alarm rate = .22	Van Wallendael *et al.* (1994)
17 days	5 sec. utterance	20% correct	Read and Craik (1995)
4 weeks	2 min. survey	Hit rate = .57; false alarm rate = .09	Papcun *et al.* (1989)
2 months	A few sentences	Hit rate = .46	McGehee (1944)
3 months	56-word paragraph; read live	Hit rate = .35	McGehee (1937)
5 months	56-word paragraph; read live	Hit rate = .13	McGehee (1937)

7.7   Impact on Juries

However reliable (or unreliable) earwitness testimony may be, such testimony often has an influence on juries beyond what is justified. For example, as noted above, in the trial of Bruno Hauptmann the jury relied heavily on Colonel Lindbergh's voice identification testimony, despite many facts that would suggest to most reasonable people that it was not especially likely to be accurate (the foreign accent; the extremely long delay between hearing and identifying the voice; the extremely short, shouted voice sample; the large distance between the speaker and listener). Yet in general, in studies using mock trials, jurors returned a higher percentage of guilty verdicts – and mock jurors were significantly more certain of that verdict – when an earwitness was included in the scenario than when none was included (Van Wallendael *et al.*, 1994).

This heavy reliance on earwitness testimony does not appear to arise because juries hold false beliefs about voice recognition, but rather because they are not consistently well informed about research in this area. Using a questionnaire to assess knowledge of the factors that affect earwitness reliability, Philippon *et al.* (2007) found that both police and members of the general public were aware that it is more difficult to identify unfamiliar than familiar voices, and that the witness's familiarity with the language spoken may facilitate or interfere with recognition; but they were not generally knowledgeable about the lack of relationship between confidence and accuracy. Police officers were no more knowledgeable than were naive listeners. The authors suggest that expert testimony can be of great value in informing juries about the limitations of this kind of evidence.

7.8   Summary and Conclusions

Remembering and recognizing an unfamiliar voice that has forced its way into our attention is a difficult, unnatural task, involving a patchwork of pattern recognition and featural analysis processes. Because no consistent cognitive strategy apparently exists for dealing with unfamiliar voices, it is not particularly surprising that the literature provides mostly conflicting results: Variability is inherent in the enterprise. In a typical forensic voice recognition experiment, the likelihood of selecting a correct voice (and of avoiding an incorrect identification) varies across the full range of possibilities, depending on virtually every conceivable factor (e.g., the voice sample heard, the set of distracter voices, the instructions to the listener, and so on). Even in the laboratory, it has not proven possible (to date, at least) to model all the pertinent factors that determine earwitness accuracy. In real forensic situations, which lack experimental control, it is not currently possible to estimate the likelihood of accuracy with any precision. Such testimony should be regarded with the highest degree of caution and skepticism.

8

Linguistic Uses of Voice Quality: How Voice Signals Linguistic and Pragmatic Aspects of Communication

8.1 Introduction

Because human voices transmit spoken language from the speaker to listeners, the relationship of voice to language has long been of interest to linguists. Early theorists (for example, Sapir, 1921) often distinguished the linguistic[1] from the nonlinguistic aspects of a spoken message, and did not consider voice quality a part of Language. With some exceptions,[2] changes in voice quality over the course of an utterance or across speakers were considered accidental ("paralinguistic") features of utterances, individuated by the particular speaker and context, distinct from the phonology, morphology, syntax, and lexicon that constitute Language proper. For many years, speech scientists conducted studies so that such extraneous, extra-linguistic, speaker-specific material was held constant, stripped away, or perceptually normalized to reach the underlying, purely linguistic message projected by the talker.

According to recent conceptions of the role of voice quality in speech perception, however, clear separation of voice quality variations into separate linguistic and paralinguistic domains is no longer viable. It is now well understood that "paralinguistic" voice characteristics serve important linguistic functions at every level of Language. In fact, voice quality cues interact significantly with linguistic events as part of the process of recognizing words and decoding the meaning of spoken messages (for example, Mullennix, Pisoni, and Martin, 1989; Goldinger, Pisoni, and Logan, 1991), and substantial evidence indicates that familiarity with a talker's voice facilitates deciphering the spoken message itself (for example, Goldinger, Pisoni, and Logan, 1991; Nygaard and Pisoni, 1998). It follows that the traditional theoretical separation between linguistic and paralinguistic aspects of the vocal signal cannot be strictly maintained.

---

[1] In this sense, "linguistic" means "segmental" and refers to consonants and vowels. Nonsegmental or "suprasegmental" (nonlinguistic) portions are carried over longer stretches of speech.
[2] They were aware that voice quality is the carrier of phonemic contrasts in languages like Thai, which uses changes in F0 ("tones") to signal meaning changes; see Section 8.4.

Foundations of Voice Studies: An Interdisciplinary Approach to Voice Production and Perception,
First Edition. Jody Kreiman and Diana Sidtis.
© 2013 Jody Kreiman and Diana Sidtis. Published 2013 by Blackwell Publishing Ltd.

That is, the previous two-channel model of "linguistic" information comprising phonology, syntax, and semantics, and "paralinguistic" information expressing attitudes and emotions, has been superseded by the understanding that voice characteristics operate at all levels of language structure. The scope of language study has also become much broader in recent times, expanding beyond phonology, syntax, and semantics to include the pragmatics of communication, which focuses on social speech and discourse and examines principles governing actual language use. As the review below shows, it is difficult to overemphasize the role of voice quality in the pragmatics of everyday language use (see, for example, Shattuck-Hufnagel and Turk, 1996, or Cutler, Dahan, and von Donselaar, 1997, for extended review).

Given these newer perspectives on the role of voice in speech perception and the broader view of communicative structure, in this chapter we describe the uses of voice quality – or prosody (we use these terms interchangeably in this discussion) – in linguistic communication. Voice quality (broadly and narrowly considered) is the stuff of speech prosody, an area of intensive study in speech science, psycholinguistics, and neuropsychology. Prosody traditionally encompasses average pitch and pitch variability (or the mean and variability of fundamental frequency), loudness (or intensity) mean and variation, the large array of temporal factors that determine perceived speech rate and rhythm, and voice quality narrowly defined (for example, creakiness and breathiness, which function subtly – and sometimes not so subtly – in everyday speech to communicate meaning). We first consider the essential differences between language and prosody, and then review how the four primary components of prosody – pitch, loudness, timing, and voice quality – serve as indicators of linguistic structure. In the remainder of the chapter, we examine the integral role of voice in communication by reviewing its operation in signalling linguistic structure in phonology, the lexicon, grammar, semantics, and pragmatics.

8.2 Ontological Differences Between Language and Prosody

The units of language – phone, phoneme, morpheme, word, phrase, sentence, and discourse – are widely accepted among linguists as a valid and descriptively adequate framework for investigating and describing new languages, language learning, and so on. This stable, shared foundation has allowed linguistic studies to flourish cooperatively in numerous fields such as anthropology, psychology, philosophy, and sociology. Voice quality, or prosody, provides signals for all these types of linguistic structure. However, in contrast to discrete, easily transcribed linguistic units, the luxury of well-defined building blocks and stable, quantifiable objects of study has not been accorded to the study of prosody. Much of prosodic material is continuous in nature, lending itself less naturally to structural descriptions. Accordingly, terminology for prosody, proposed across several centuries, constitutes a mélange of partially overlapping, often vague descriptors. While the referent and characteristics of "phoneme" or "word" are clear to any student of language, the terms "voice quality" and "prosody" lack a stable descriptive system relating measurable features to functional significance in general use. Thus an essential ontological asymmetry lies beneath our consideration of the linguistic uses of voice quality.

Table 8.1 provides a list of modern terms that have been proposed in various linguistic treatments of voice quality, along with their definitions and functions. Terms pertain to different domains (word, phrase, sentence, conversational turn, discourse unit), and many are overlapping. Their status may be physiological and quantifiable, as in the case of fundamental frequency; it may be observable and measurable, as pausing is; or it may be relative and impressionistic, as is the case for key and register. While this mixing of quantitative and qualitative perspectives somewhat obscures the way to clarity, these terms do provide handholds for progress in understanding something about the topic, and they do reveal considerable effort and insight on the part of early researchers.

8.3   The Acoustic-Auditory Basis: The Elements of Prosody

We return to the foundations of voice, examining the four main components of prosody: pitch, loudness, timing/rate, and voice quality. Each element is reviewed in turn below with respect to what it does and how it is transcribed and measured. Transcription and measurement are challenging, in part because identifying meaningful aspects of the sounds comprising prosody is, in many cases, a most difficult undertaking.

8.3.1   Pitch changes

Most analyses of vocal quality in spoken language focus on changes in fundamental frequency (the acoustic correlate of pitch) and its patterning and variability in the utterance, also referred to popularly as "the melody of speech," intonation, or one's "tone of voice." Fundamental frequency can theoretically be measured using either analog or digital approaches, but in practice, noise bursts, subharmonic phonation and other deviations from periodicity, along with silences naturally occurring in running speech, create challenges to valid measures. However, this parameter has a very rich history of quantification and analysis in the speech signal (see, for example, Hess, 1983, for a book-length review). Although fundamental frequency is quantifiable for most spoken utterances, the appropriate formalisms for systematically representing pitch changes in speech (or the linguistic function of these changes) remains unsettled – but not for lack of trying. An array of terms in various traditions for describing intonation exists, each utilizing a different notational system, with unknown relationships to early musical notation (see Sidebar on Gregorian chant notation). Making sense of these numerous perspectives on representing linguistic prosody can be daunting. Devising methods for visually representing pitch levels and contours has proven equally challenging. There is a venerable history of treatments of speech prosody (see Danielsson, 1955; Crystal, 1969; Laver, 1981), starting, for colloquial spoken English, with the work of John Hart (1551, 1569) and Joshua Steele (1775).

In modern practice, in contrast to the universal agreement to utilize the International Phonetic Alphabet (IPA) to represent possible human speech sounds (International Phonetic Association, 1999; Ladefoged, 2006), little consensus has evolved for prosody, for which various notational systems have been proposed and remain in use. Figure 8.1 shows an example of one early representational approach from James Rush

Table 8.1 Terms used in prosodic studies of speech.

Term	A definition	Representative references
Accent	Highlighted syllable in a sentence	Bolinger (1972)
	Limited to prominences where pitch is a factor (pitch accent)	Cruttenden (1997)
Accent range	The breadth of pitch range spanning over the intonation-group	Cruttenden (1997)
Alignment	"Phonetic property of the relative timing of events in the F0 contour and events in the segmental string"	Ladd (1996)
Anacrusis	Unstressed syllables at the beginning of an utterance	Cruttenden (1997)
Boundary tone	An additional tone that lands precisely on the phrasal boundary	Pierrehumbert and Hirschberg (1990)
Broad focus	Refers to the entirety of the intonation-group being "in focus"	Cruttenden (1997)
Cadence	Variations of falling tones in "melodic sequence" that signify closure	Wichmann (2000)
Catathesis	Lowers the pitch range after any of the complex (or two-toned) accents, results in compression of the pitch range	Pierrehumbert and Hirschberg (1990)
Complex rhythm unit	The combination of two or more simple rhythm units	Pike (1945)
Contrastivity	Refers to nucleus placement when the speakers wants to keep old information in focus; "involving comparison within a limited set"	Cruttenden (1997)
Continuation rise	Rise in F0 on the last stressed syllable preceding the boundary	Cooper and Sorensen (1981)
Declination	The gradual decrease in F0 in English declarative sentences	Cooper and Sorensen (1981)
Declination unit: Loudness	Might or might not be coterminous with pitch declination unit.	Couper-Kuhlen (2000)
Declination unit: Pitch	Unit with declining pitch; may contain several intonation units	Couper-Kuhlen (1991)
Depressed pitch reset	Decreased accent	Wichmann (2000)
Direction-change point	The moment in some primary contours when the pitch movement shifts from falling to rising or rising to falling	Pike (1945)
Discourse prosody	Prosodic cues listeners use to process speech in "real time"	Wichmann (2000)
Echoes	Typically questions which excise part of the previous speaker's utterance, and convey incredulity; also, may be an exclamation	Cruttenden (1997)
Final lowering	Pitch range variation, dependent on temporal elements	Pierrehumbert and Hirschberg (1990)
Final pause	Ending after several contours	Pike (1945)

Table 8.1 (*Cont'd*).

Term	A definition	Representative references
Focus	Singular nuclear pitch accent that lands on or near the end of the intonation contour	Wennerstrom (2001); Cruttendon (1997); Ladd (1980, 1996); Selkirk (1984)
Focus: Narrow	Part of the intonation group is "out of focus," or included in a preceding group	Cruttenden (1997)
Fundamental voice frequency (F0)	Number of vocal fold vibrations per second	Cooper and Sorensen (1981)
High fall	Type of simple falling tone	Cruttenden (1997)
High-rising boundaries	Pitch boundary characterized by a rise from the last pitch accent of the phrase	Wennerstrom (2001)
Implication contour	Intonation contour characterized by a rapidly decreasing rise that concludes with the "embryo of the fall"	Delattre (1966–7)
Insists	A type of utterance in which the speaker denies something assumed in the previous speaker's utterance	Cruttenden (1997)
Intonation	The pitch or melody of the voice during speech; size of unit debated	Wennerstrom (2001)
	The result of the "interaction of features from different prosodic systems"	Crystal (1975)
	Employing suprasegmental phonetic features to express meaning on the sentence-level in a "linguistically structured" way	Ladd (1996)
Intonation: Lexical	Pitch patterns with relatively stereotyped meanings on word, phrase or sentence level	numerous authors
Intonation break	In complex rhythm units, when the first primary contour ends within the rhythm unit	Pike (1945)
Intonation contours	Standardized pitch pattern sequences that native speakers of a language employ to fit in situational models	Pike (1945)
Intonation unit	Synonymous with intonational phrase; refers to the unit where "cognition, syntax, physics, phonetics and phonology converge"	Wennerstrom (2001); Chafe (1994)
Intonational parallelism	The nuclear tone of an individual tone group repeats itself in the subsequent tone group	numerous authors

Term	Description	Reference
Intonational phrase, intermediate phrase, tone or intonation unit	Pitch contour that includes a key, some number of pitch accents and a pitch boundary	Wennerstrom (2001); Pierrehumbert (1980); Halliday (1967); Brazil (1985); Chafe (1994)
Key	Width of the pitch range that spans over an entire intonation-group	Cruttenden (1997)
Key: High	Speaker initiates an utterance high in his/her pitch range	Wennerstrom (2001)
Key: Low	Speaker begins an utterance low in his/her pitch range	Wennerstrom (2001)
Key: Mid range	Speaker does not change his pitch range upon initiation of a new utterance	Wennerstrom (2001)
Key in pitch range	Pitch at utterance onset	Wennerstrom (2001)
Length	Refers to the duration of a series of syllables relative to one another, or the duration of one syllable in different environments	Cruttenden (1997)
Low boundaries	Pitch boundary characterized by a fall, and ends at the "floor" of the speaker's range	Wennerstrom (2001)
Low fall	Type of simple falling tone	Cruttenden (1997)
Loudness	Refers to how the listener perceives the "breath-force" the speaker employs	Cruttenden (1997)
Major boundary	Viewed relative to minor boundary	Wichmann (2001)
Major continuation	In French, a rising pitch contour signifying the continuance of a sentence; higher rise relative to a minor continuation	Delattre (1966–7)
Minor boundary	Lower than major boundary	Wichmann (2000)
Minor continuation	In French, a rising pitch contour signifying the continuance of a sentence; smaller rise relative to a major continuation	Delattre (1966–7)
No pitch boundary	Occurs when the speaker hesitates or ceases speaking mid-utterance; boundary characterized by a glottal or other stop and no final lengthening	Wennerstrom (2001)
Nuclear pitch accent	Speaker's immediate focus	Couper-Kuhlen (2001); Wennerstrom (2001)
Nuclear Stress Rule (NSR)	Sentence-final position receives the primary stress	Chomsky and Halle (1968) (cited: Crystal, 1975)
Nuclear tones	Tonal movement patterns	Wichmann (2000)
Nucleus	Last pitch accent in phrase	Couper-Kuhlen (1991)
	Describes pitch accent, typically the last in the phrase; most prominent in the stereotyped intonation-groups	Cruttenden (1997)

Table 8.1 (*Cont'd*).

Term	A definition	Representative references
Onset depression	The unexpected lower topic reset at a major boundary	Wichmann (2000)
Onset level	Beginning of intonation phrases	Couper-Kuhlen (1991)
Overlay models of F0	A model of F0 which presupposes that the pitch contour is a complex function that can be broken down into smaller parts	Ladd (1996)
Paragraph intonation	How a speaker initiates the beginning of a unit of spoken text	numerous authors
Paralinguistic	Acoustic cues that reveal elements of interpersonal communication (for example, solidarity, agreement, aggression), and speaker's emotional state	numerous authors
Paratone	Prosodic organization at topic level; intonational paragraphs	Brown (1977); Yule (1980); Wennerstrom (2001)
Paratone: High	Expansion of speaker's pitch range	Wennerstrom (2001)
Paratone: Low	Compression of speaker's pitch range	Wennerstrom (2001)
Parenthesis	Plateau whose level depends upon the preceding contour type	Delattre (1966–7)
Partially falling boundaries	Pitch boundary characterized by a gradual fall that does not reach the "floor" of the interlocutor's range	Wennerstrom (2001)
Pauses	A possible demarcation of an intonation-group boundary	Cruttenden (1997)
Phrasal tones	Denotes the boundaries of a phonological phrase	Pierrehumbert and Hirschberg (1990)
Phrasing	The manner in which a complex utterance is partitioned	Pierrehumbert and Hirschberg (1990)
Phrase boundaries	Marked by some components of the tune, duration pattern and pausing	Pierrehumbert and Hirschberg (1990)
Pitch	Perceptual correlate of the acoustic measure of fundamental frequency	Cruttenden (1997); Cooper and Sorensen (1981)
Pitch accent	Tones the speaker assigns to important lexical units in the discourse; marks a prominent lexical item	Wennerstrom (2001); Pierrehumbert and Hirschberg (1990)
	Local feature of a pitch contour–usually a pitch change that signals the presence of a prominent syllable in the utterance	Ladd (1996);
Pitch boundaries	Standardized pitch patterns occurring at the ends of phrases	Wennerstrom (2001)
Pitch phonemes	Four levels of pitch relative to one another	Pike (1945)

Term	Definition	Reference
Pitch range	Distance between the highest point on the F0 contour and the lowest point, or baseline; determines how tune, or intonational patterns are realized	Pierrehumbert and Hirschberg (1990)
Plateau boundaries	Pitch boundary characterized by a leveling off from the final pitch accent of the phrase	Wennerstrom (2001)
Precontours	One or more unstressed syllables that occur immediately before the stressed syllable of the primary contour	Pike (1945)
Pre-nuclear pitch accents	Pitch accents that do not fall in the intonation-group final position	Cruttenden (1997)
Primary contours	Intonation contours that occur in sentence final position and carry significant meaning	Pike (1945)
Primary stress	Refers to the primary pitch accent (pitch prominence) in the intonation group	Cruttenden (1997)
Prominence	As a function of pitch, loudness or duration the degree to which a constituent stands out relative to others	Wennerstrom (2001)
	The interaction, to varying degrees, of length, loudness and pitch that allows one syllable to be more noticeable; sequences of prominent vs. non-prominent syllables create the outline for connected speech and "backbone for intonation"	Cruttenden (1997)
Prosodic contextualization cues	Traffic controls in interactional talk	Couper-Kuhlen (1991)
Prosody at boundaries of utterances	Various cues	Wennerstrom (2001); numerous authors
Register	Relative position of an intonation phrase within a speaker's range	Couper-Kuhlen (1991)
	The height of the pitch range spanning over an intonation-group	Cruttenden (1997)
Register shift	Relative change in pitch range during discourse	Klewitz and Couper-Kuhlen (1999)
Relative prominence	Pattern of prominence (for example, which syllables/words are emphasized) in the phrase as a whole unit	Ladd (1996)
Rhythm	Regular beat established through accented syllables	Wennerstrom (2001); Couper-Kuhlen (2001); numerous authors
Rhythm group	The range of an utterance that spans from one stressed syllable to the next (synonymous with "foot")	Cruttenden (1997)
Rhythm unit	A sentence or part of a sentence spoken in groups of syllables in the absence of pauses	Pike (1945)
Secondary stress	Refers to a subordinate prominence (pitch accent) in the intonation group	Cruttenden (1997)

Table 8.1 (*Cont'd*).

Term	A definition	Representative references
Stress	Syllable in the word that is accented; on the word level, describes the arrangement of strong and weak syllables; Configuration of rhythm or relative syllable prominence in an utterance	Bolinger (1972); Wennerstrom (2001); Pierrehumbert and Hirschberg (1990)
Stress pattern	In an utterance, how the syllables are arranged in a pattern of relative prominence	Pierrehumbert and Hirschberg (1990)
Stress-timed language	A relatively equal unit of time passes between one stressed syllable and the next	Cruttenden (1997)
Stress-timed rhythm unit	Rhythm unit whose length is determined by one strong stress, instead of the total number of syllables	Pike (1945)
Supradeclination	Trend of lowering pitch over a spoken paragraph; a succession of lower pitch onsets in the paragraph	Wichmann (2000)
Syllable-timed rhythm unit	Rhythm unit whose unstressed syllables receive one beat each, resulting in an imitative pattern of syllable prominence	Pike (1945)
Tempo	Speaking rate	Numerous authors
Tentative pause	The prolongation of the last one or two phonemes of the previous word	Pike (1945)
Tertiary stress	Refers to a prominence produced by length or loudness	Cruttenden (1997)
Timing	Many unit-types and treatments	Numerous authors
Tone	Referred to in British linguistics as "pitch movements"	Crystal (1975); Wichmann (2000); Pierrehumbert and Hirschberg (1990)
Tone group	"Chunks" of spontaneous speech that vary in length from monosyllabic to 30+ syllables	Wichmann (2000)
Topic reset	High pitch indicates shift in discourse to new topic	Wichmann (2000)
Total contour	Precontour plus primary contour; in the absence of a precontour, a primary contour constitutes the total contour	Pike (1945)
Tune	Patterns of fundamental frequency that allow for, and result in, a rich variety of intonational patterns; some have nuanced meanings	Pierrehumbert and Hirschberg (1990)
	Pitch patterns; cannot be directly related to sentence types	Ladd (1996)
Unstressed	Unaccented	Cruttenden (1997)
Upstep	Raises the boundary tone after a H (high) phrase accent	Pierrehumbert and Hirschberg (1990)
Word-stress	Syllables denoted as stressed in a dictionary or lexicon, which then endows them with the potential for "accent" in an utterance	Cruttenden (1997)

Figure 8.1 Prosody notation for speech from James Rush (1823/1859).

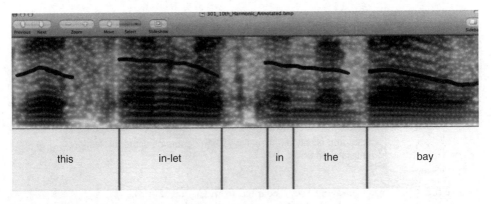

Figure 8.2 Tracing of 10th harmonic of a spoken sentence.

(1823/1859). For intonation, melodic sweeps are commonly represented by continuous curves representing pitch height and movement over time, reflecting the continuous nature of pitch changes in speech. For example, Lieberman (1968) displays pitch curves as derived from acoustic analysis, either from pitch extraction of the fundamental frequency or using a tracing of the 10th harmonic on narrow band spectrograms (Figure 8.2). Crystal (2003) has utilized curved lines placed on an iconically represented pitch range space (Figure 8.3) to show subtle nuances of intonational meanings. Crystal's more extensive work on English intonation (1975) utilizes large and small dots, capitalization, arrows, dashes, and two kinds of accent marks (grave and acute), along with curved lines placed in a vertical space to represent low fall pitch contours, high falls, low rises, and so on (Figure 8.4). Bolinger (1986) presents example sentences with individual syllables and words typewritten on curves and displacements to iconically represent their movement "up" and "down" in a given

270 *Linguistic Uses of Voice Quality*

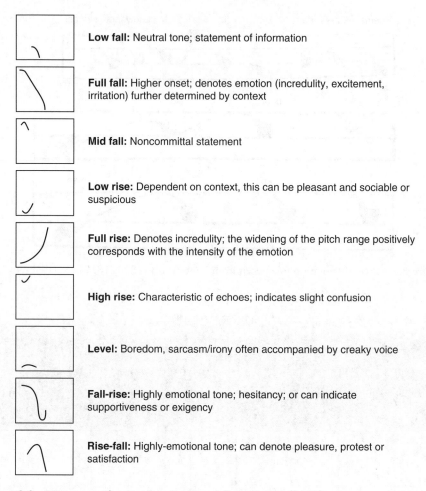

Low fall: Neutral tone; statement of information

Full fall: Higher onset; denotes emotion (incredulity, excitement, irritation) further determined by context

Mid fall: Noncommittal statement

Low rise: Dependent on context, this can be pleasant and sociable or suspicious

Full rise: Denotes incredulity; the widening of the pitch range positively corresponds with the intensity of the emotion

High rise: Characteristic of echoes; indicates slight confusion

Level: Boredom, sarcasm/irony often accompanied by creaky voice

Fall-rise: Highly emotional tone; hesitancy; or can indicate supportiveness or exigency

Rise-fall: Highly-emotional tone; can denote pleasure, protest or satisfaction

Figure 8.3 Nine ways of saying "yes," adapted from Crystal (2003).

(i) I |think _it's 'all going to be al|RIGHT|

(ii) I |think _it's ↓all going to be al|RIGHT|

Figure 8.4 Example of prosodic notation from Crystal (1969).

(but relative) pitch range (Figure 8.5). These phonetic, often impressionistic representations are sometimes supplemented with detailed measurements of F0; for example, Ladefoged (2006; Figure 8.6) combined pitch curves obtained from automatic pitch extraction algorithms with lexical items of the utterance typed along the curve (note use of voiced segments throughout to facilitate smooth pitch tracking).

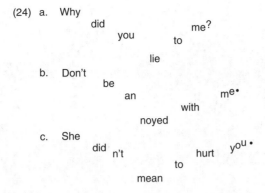

Figure 8.5   Example of prosodic notation from Bolinger (1982).

Figure 8.6   Example of prosodic notation from Ladefoged (2006).

> ### Sidebar: Gregorian Chant
>
> Plainchant, constituting the musical repertoire of the Roman Catholic Church for several centuries, consists of 3,000 melodies developed in the sixth and seventh centuries in Western Europe. Chant has been referred to as rhythmic or heightened speech, but we know of no attempts to correlate chant melodies with intonational meanings in language, or with linguistic or affective prosody (Apel, 1990). An elaborate notional system evolved for chant materials, utilizing a general format not unlike those employed by David Crystal and other modern prosodists. An example is shown in Figure 8.7.

While continuous lines visually represent the pitch movement of the utterance, in many treatments they serve mainly as idiosyncratic descriptors of a few sentences, rather than as formal systems for classifying most or all utterances according to structure, function, or meaning (but see discussion of "tunes" below). Attempts to classify intonational contours based on function or meaning have been only partially successful, because variants of any stereotyped contour can proliferate, and, in other contexts, the same or similar intonation contours (sometimes called "tunes;" Pierrehumbert and Hirschberg, 1990; Ladd, 1996) can have a different meaning. A straightforward example is an utterance-final rising pitch contour. In American English, such contours signal that the speaker is asking a question. (An international survey of prosody concluded that the majority of languages have raised pitch to indicate a question (Hirst

Figure 8.7 Gregorian note representation.

and Di Cristo, 1998), although in many dialects of British English, questions feature falling intonation and other languages use higher intonation elsewhere in the interrogative sentence (Siemund, 2001).) Rising intonation also signals an intent to continue the discourse. Further, rising intonation contours (sometimes called "uptalk") that signal neither continuation nor questioning have swept the English-speaking world. Such contours, which were stereotypical for a time of "Valley girl speech," may have had their origin in Australia and are now being heard across America from speakers of all ages. Various meanings have been given to this practice, including the expression of uncertainty, signalling subordinate status (consistent with the "size code;" Ohala, 1984), eliciting acknowledgement from the listener, and/or maintaining interlocutory control. Or perhaps it is merely a new prosodic trend. In any event, this wide range of functions for utterance-final rising pitch contours exemplifies the difficulty inherent in devising coding systems relating prosodic form, function, and meaning in a consistent manner.

One alternative to these somewhat unsatisfactory and unsystematic phonetic systems for describing or transcribing intonation is a phonologically based system of notation called "Tone and Break Indices," or ToBI (Silverman *et al.*, 1992; see Sidebar). ToBI transcriptions mark the relative pitch rises and falls that distinctively convey the underlying prosodic structure of the language. They thus reflect abstract representations of the prosodic structure of a specific language or dialect, and do not compose a "universal alphabet" for prosody. Like other phonological descriptions, separate systems must be developed for each new language or dialect, based on extensive research regarding the prosodic structure of the language. Complete systems including published standards, training materials, and interrater reliability data have been developed for English, German, Korean, and Japanese, with systems partially developed for over a dozen additional languages or dialects. A similar system, called "Gesprächsanalytisches Transkriptionssystem" or GAT (Selting *et al.*, 1998), was designed in Germany to provide a standard for transcription of conversational speech.

Sidebar: The ToBI System

ToBI (short for "Tone and Break Indices") is a widely-used system that uses discrete, universal symbols to represent meaningful, generalizable intonational properties of utterances. ToBI identifies target tones (H* for high, and L* for low) in an utterance, and places them at the appropriate syllable on the "tone tier" above the transcribed utterance (the segmental tier). A sharply rising pitch is indicated by L + H*. A scoop upwards can be represented by L* + H. A small step down in pitch is symbolized as H + !H*. These notations can be used to reflect prosodic elements occurring as prenuclear pitch accents (see Table 8.1) on stressed syllables, nuclear pitch accents, phrase accents, and boundary tones. Nuances of linguistic meaning communicated by prosody, as they are identified in specific languages, can be represented by this system.

Here are some examples, corresponding to audio samples 8.1 and 8.2:[3]

1. *We've met before.*	Tone Tier	[H*	H*	L-L%]
Simple statement.	Segmental Tier	We've	met	before
2. *We've met before?*	Tone Tier	[H*	L	H*-H%]

8.3.2   Loudness

Loudness refers to the "sensation magnitude of sound" (Gulick, Gescheider, and Frisina, 1989, p. 261), and is related to intensity, frequency and duration. Intensity, a measure of power per unit area, can be quantified using acoustic measures, but the linguistic functions of its perceptual correlate, loudness, are not as well understood as

---

[3]   **ToBI key: H*** = high stressed syllable; **L*** = low stressed syllable; **H%** = high boundary tone; **L%** = low boundary tone; **L + H*** = sharply rising pitch; **L* + H** = scoop upwards; **H + !H*** = small step down in pitch

those of fundamental frequency and pitch.[4] (Amplitude, a measure related to loudness, refers to the distance of excursion of the acoustic wave.[5]) Loudness variation usually tracks with pitch changes, such that greater loudness follows higher pitch, although it is possible to control these aspects of voice separately, as discussed in Chapter 2. In their training singers learn to uncouple pitch and loudness, and can increase pitch softly and lower pitch loudly (see Chapter 10). Ability to control these aspects of voice independently implies that loudness could in theory serve as an independent cue to linguistic contrasts, but to our knowledge no language uses intensity as an exclusive acoustic cue to systematically contrast phonemic meanings. This lacuna may arise from the vicissitudes of ambient sound transmission. Loudness is more vulnerable to conditions in communicative settings than pitch or temporal cues. Intensity varies with distance from the listener, which is not true of frequency. It has been known at least since the beginning of the twentieth century (Gamble, 1909; Mershon, Desaulniers, Kiefer, Amerson and Mills, 1981) that changes in loudness and changes in distance can produce similar auditory percepts. Perceptually, it is often difficult to determine whether a perceived contrast is due primarily to the effects of intensity, fundamental frequency, and/or duration. In particular, studies suggest that loudness judgments for short utterances are unreliable, whereas relative pitch height is more reliably perceived (McFadden, 1975).

Although loudness variations do not serve as cues to linguistically significant contrasts in classical language structure, pragmatic and emotional contrasts are so signaled under normal circumstances. For example, increased loudness on words and phrases signals thematic importance, or conveys anger on either a low or a high pitch. Softer utterances can convey sadness (Banse and Scherer, 1996; see Chapter 9). In fact, listening studies have shown that intensity is a key acoustic cue for distinguishing idiomatic from literal meanings in ditropic (ambiguous) sentences in Korean (Ahn, Yang, and Sidtis, 2010). However, in a restaurant with a great deal of background noise (everyone talking, music, dish clatter), the shouted conversational utterances of your dinner companion will be probably recognized as an attempt to be heard and understood, and not as an attempt to convey specialized linguistic or affective meaning.[6]

8.3.3 Temporal cues

Because speech exists in time, all linguistic cues are time-bound. Temporal factors in speech prosody comprise a diverse set of cues and functions, including articulatory timing, patterns of stress, rhythm, pausing, durations of segments, words, and phrases, and overall speech rate in words per minute or syllables per second. Timing details arise directly from myriad variations on laryngeal and vocal tract gestures. Their linguistic significance is indisputable in many cases. These varied aspects of the temporal organization of speech serve both linguistic and paralinguistic functions, often with

---

[4] Recall that fundamental frequency (F0) and intensity are acoustic measures, while pitch and loudness are perceptual constructs; see Chapter 2.

[5] Measurement practices for intensity, amplitude and loudness differ; see Chapter 2.

[6] In a noisy restaurant, anger might be conveyed through heightened pitch and emphatically accenting syllables and words, using a combination of temporal and F0 cues, or by visual, behavioral, or lexical cues (red face, waving arms, wild accusations …).

the same cues conveying different kinds of messages in the same manner that pitch, loudness, and voice quality changes do. For example, a prolonged phoneme may signal a drawl of boredom in one context, but a change in word meaning in a language like Finnish with geminate (duplicated) consonants.

The importance of timing as an integral part of the speech process is uncontroversial. Linguistically significant contrasts include differences in voice onset time in consonant–vowel transitions (English and Hindi), geminate consonants (Finnish and Italian), and long versus short vowels (German and Arabic). Timing contrasts also operate allophonically (that is, they are determined by phonetic context) at the word level. In English, for example, stop consonants that differ in voice onset time and degree of aspiration in initial position, for example, /d/ and /t/, are distinguished in word-final position primarily by the length of the preceding vowel, as in /bad/ and /bat/. As mentioned above, timing and pitch (with loudness) combine to signal stress and pitch-accent contrasts on words and word compounds.

Pauses are also meaningfully associated with processes at several levels of speech performance, and reflect respiratory and articulatory demands, linguistic structural planning, and stylistic effects in communication. An obvious function of pausing is to allow respiration, but the relationship between pausing in speech and breathing is not straightforward, as speakers frequently breathe sooner or later than required to replenish their air supply (Winkworth, Davis, Adams, and Ellis, 1995). Linguistic factors significantly affect breathing patterns, with deeper inspiration during reading occurring at the beginning of a paragraph or a sentence than within sentences. Subjects also pause longer and more frequently during more cognitively demanding speech tasks, and the longest pauses are often located at linguistic boundaries (Grosjean, 1980). Studies have shown that spontaneous speech, having greater cognitive demands, contained more and longer pauses than reading (Goldman-Eisler, 1972; Sabin, Clemmer, O'Connell, and Kowal, 1979), and summarizing a cartoon story induced more pauses than the less challenging task of describing the story (Goldman-Eisler, 1961, cited in Rosenfield, 1987). These findings indicate that pausing in many cases reflects speech planning. Finally, pausing is used as a stylistic device to enhance and improve communication. A judiciously placed "pregnant pause" creates special effects. It might highlight importance, build tension, foreshadow a surprise, or provide emphasis (Quirk, Greenbaum, Leech, and Svartik, 1985). In conversation, pauses may indicate surprise (Couper-Kuhlen, 2000), and they provide time for both speaker and hearer to think in the interactive process of formulating and understanding ideas (Oliveira, 2002).

Many kinds of temporal measures can reliably be undertaken, including the absolute and relative durations of phonemic segments, portions of segments, and pausing within talk, rate (in syllables per second or words per minute), and patterning of temporal elements (rhythm) per unit time. In combinations, these elements constitute rhythm and tempo in speech. Note that measures of speech rate vary in how they take pausing into account. Notational systems can easily accommodate numerous temporal measures, sometimes by representing them spatially or by assigning relative time values to note shapes. However, no universally accepted system for visually representing temporal units and their function in speech has been devised.

8.3.4 Voice quality (narrowly considered)

The last of the four prosodic constructs, voice quality, plays a subtle but pervasive role in linguistic meanings. Relatively little is known about these functions, however, due to the difficulties of defining and implementing meaningful and reliable measures of voice (see Chapters 1 and 2). Because appropriate analysis tools are generally lacking, most studies have relied on impressionistic, auditory methods, with all their attendant limitations (for example, Ní Chasaide and Gobl, 2002). For these reasons, we know much more about F0, intensity (and their auditory correlates pitch and loudness), and duration, all of which are relatively straightforward to measure, as discussed above, even though systematic correlations of these parameters with functions in speech are not usually clear.

Most linguistic investigations of the uses of voice quality in the narrow sense (for example, whispered, creaky) involve phonation types at the phonological level. These contrastive phonation types have generated considerable interest in recent phonetic studies and are reviewed below. However, voice quality changes contribute to meaning at many other linguistic levels. Creaky voice (or vocal fry) often signals prominence within a sentence, the presence of linguistic boundaries like ends of sentences, or major changes of topic (Lehiste, 1979; Kreiman, 1982; Dilley, Shattuck-Hufnagel, and Ostendoerf, 1996; Epstein, 2002). For example, listen carefully to the sentence in audio sample 8.3, and notice the "creaky" voice quality at the end of the sentence and at the boundaries of major phrases. Whisper and murmur can be recorded physiologically at the larynx and acoustically in waveforms and spectral displays. Nasality, lip rounding, and rhoticization (r-coloring) can be determined from spectrographic records, where formants appear lowered and weakened. Other dimensions, such as pharyngealization or vocal strain, lack clear acoustic or physiological correlates. While subtle nuances of meaning may be communicated by these vocal quality changes, no coherent account of these functional meanings exists.

As noted previously, voice qualities, like other prosodic phenomena, do not benefit from a systematic terminology or notational system for use in impressionistic transcription of the vocal signal. The IPA (International Phonetic Association, 1999) includes symbols for transcribing phonemically distinctive uses of "creaky" or "breathy" voice quality (and for some aspects of pathological speech), but despite the descriptive labels, such transcriptions imply only that a contrast exists within the phonology of the language, without providing a specific description of the sound produced to express the contrast. One additional phonetic notational system – the VoQS – has been proposed, derived in part from the phonetic description of voice quality developed by Laver (1980). This system uses symbols reminiscent of the IPA to separately transcribe airstream types (for example, pulmonic ingressive), phonation types (for example, whisper, falsetto) and supralaryngeal settings (for example, spread-lip voice, velarized voice) (Ball, Esling, and Dickson, 2000). These transcription systems, while potentially useful, have had little impact on voice quality research, and correspondences to communicative functions are wholly unexplored.

Attempts at quantification have also met with little success, as discussed in Chapter 2. Many different acoustic measures have been advocated over the years as "objective" measures of voice quality, including various measures of jitter (period-to-period variability in F0), shimmer (period-to-period variability in amplitude), harmonics-to-noise ratios

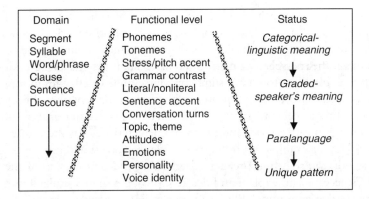

Domain	Functional level	Status
Segment	Phonemes	*Categorical-*
Syllable	Tonemes	*linguistic meaning*
Word/phrase	Stress/pitch accent	
Clause	Grammar contrast	↓
Sentence	Literal/nonliteral	*Graded-*
Discourse	Sentence accent	*speaker's meaning*
	Conversation turns	
	Topic, theme	↓
	Attitudes	*Paralanguage*
	Emotions	
	Personality	↓
	Voice identity	*Unique pattern*

Figure 8.8 The giant "Pyramid of Prosody" presents an overview of the use of prosodic cues in speech by linguistic unit, linguistic function (level), the primary property (discrete or graded) and the type of meaning (domain).

(the amount of periodic vs. aperiodic energy in a sound), and, more recently, measures of source spectral slope (Kreiman, Gerratt, and Antoñanzas-Barroso, 2007) and cepstral-based measures[7] of relative periodicity like the cepstral peak prominence (Hillenbrand, Cleveland, and Erickson, 1994). However, the usefulness of these measures is unclear because of lack of evidence concerning their perceptibility under normal speaking conditions (Kreiman and Gerratt, 2005), and their relationship to the production and perception of linguistic contrasts is even less known.

8.4 Functional Levels of Prosodic Cues in Language

As previous sections demonstrate, prosody is intrinsic to speech and serves many different communicative functions. A useful way to describe different functions of prosody in language is to consider the extent to which each is subsumed by a codified system of discrete, distinctive cues, or by a system of cues that are graded, idiosyncratic across individuals and occasions, and pattern-based. Figure 8.8 shows how different prosodic functions, considered in this fashion, form a giant "Pyramid of Prosody." At the top of this Pyramid are linguistically structured contrasts that are cued by voice quality, timing, loudness, and/or pitch. These include segmental (phonemic) contrasts based on phonation type (Section 8.4.3), tones in a tone language, the grammatical shape of a question versus statement, or the literal versus nonliteral versions of "ditropic" sentences (Van Lancker, Canter, and Terbeek, 1981). In these cases, easily described, discrete prosodic cues are sufficient to signal the discrete categories that form linguistic contrasts. This system of cues constitutes linguistic meaning to be contrasted with speaker's meaning, represented further down the Pyramid.

Proceeding down the Pyramid from sentence accent to voice identity, it is increasingly difficult to identify or describe cues to serve each subsequent prosodic function.

---

[7] A cepstrum is the spectrum of a spectrum.

The cues are graded, occur in degrees, and shade into each other. For example, cues for a happy emotion can shade into contentment or surprise, and all these categories can be conveyed in degrees of the emotion itself (extreme happiness, mild or moderate surprise). In another perspective, many interchangeable cues (pauses, creakiness, slowing speech rate, pitch contour) can signal discourse units or changes in topic, and the particular prosodic attributes associated with these functions vary idiosyncratically from speaker to speaker and utterance to utterance, reflecting aspects of speakers' meaning, communicative style, and personal characteristics. In these cases, prosodic form is variable; for example, as Bolinger (1972a, p. 633) stated long ago, "Accent is predictable – if you're a mind-reader," suggesting that knowledge of the speaker's intentions is necessary to explain and describe prosodic shapes utilized in the expression of the speaker's meaning. For these uses of linguistic prosody, the deterministic view – that linguistic structures and prosodic configurations are uniquely and regularly related – has been abandoned (Cutler *et al.*, 1997). Toward the bottom of the Pyramid, "paralinguistic" meanings like attitudes, emotions, and personality characteristics can be conveyed by an ocean of possible prosodic patterns, and it is difficult (if not impossible) to identify consistent correlations between the cues, these functions, the meanings they convey, and linguistic structure. In these realms, few prosodic details are actually obligatory, as the speaker has great freedom to use prosody to transmit fine nuances of information (Sanderman and Collier, 1995). As discussed in previous chapters, these are better described as graded rather than forming discrete units. At the very bottom lies the most idiosyncratic of prosodic signals, personal voice identity. In this case, each voice forms a unique pattern, as described in Chapters 5 and 6.

Untangling the prosodic strands of linguistic meaning, speaker's meaning, paralanguage, and personal identity in the complex tapestry of a speech signal is daunting, and many levels and layers of prosodic information occur in every utterance (although speakers and listeners possess a deep and sophisticated competence for nearly instantly deciphering these multiple levels of meaning from prosodic cues). The remainder of this chapter focuses on the relatively "easy" cases – the top half of the Pyramid – where correlations between function and structure can be observed, although with decreasing orderliness: phonology, the lexicon, grammar, semantics, and the pragmatics of discourse. Blending in with discourse elements are attitudinal perspectives expressed in speech. These form frankly paralinguistic characteristics, and are themselves related to (and often indistinguishable from) emotions (see Chapter 9).

8.4.1   The segment and syllable: Tone and voice quality contrasts

The focus of this section is linguistic tone and states of the glottis, examining production and perception of tone and phonation types. In this domain, linguists typically study (1) the cues that are utilized and the circumstances that may condition use of one cue over another; (2) the ways in which tone and voice quality interact with intonation, and the ways that F0 cues interact with voice quality cues; and (3) localization of specific cues on particular segments or parts of the syllable. Listeners have a battery of cues to chose from, including F0, phonation type, duration, and intensity (Brunelle, 2009).

The majority of the world's languages are tone languages (for example, Ladefoged, 2006) that use changes in F0 to form minimal pairs of words that contrast in meaning while holding vocalic and consonantal elements constant. For example, in Cantonese the syllable [si] means "poem" when spoken with a high tone, "history" when spoken with pitch rising from mid to high, "try" when spoken with a mid tone, "time" when tone falls from mid to low, "city" when pitch rises slightly from low-mid to mid, and "surname" when spoken with a level, low-mid tone (Khouw and Ciocca, 2007) (see also Thai contrasts in Section 3.5.2). Tones can also signal grammatical contrasts; for example, in Igbo (spoken in Nigeria) the idea of possession is expressed by a high tone (Ladefoged, 2006).

The F0 contour associated with contrasting tones can be level or can change over the course of a syllable. The simplest tone systems contrast high and low tones, as seen in many Bantu languages (Ladefoged, 2006). Other languages feature three (Yoruba), four (Mandarin Chinese), five (Thai), and even eight contrasting tones (the Wenzhou dialect of Chinese; Cao and Maddieson, 1992). The Wenzhou dialect of Chinese distinguishes high level, mid rising, high falling-rising, low rising-falling, high rising, low late-rising, high checked, and low checked tone contours (Cao and Maddieson, 1992), while the tone system in Mandarin includes a tone that dips from mid to low and then rises to high, a high tone, a rising tone, and a falling tone (Francis, Ciocca, Wong, Leung, and Chu, 2006). Some "laryngeally complex" languages (for example, Jalapa Mazatec, spoken in southern Mexico) even combine tones with creaky and breathy phonation. These interesting cases will be discussed in a subsequent section.

8.4.2 Perception of tone

In languages with tonal (but not phonation type) contrasts, the primary correlates of tone identity usually include aspects of F0, including relative F0 level, direction of change, and magnitude of change. For example, the contour and level tones of Cantonese can be described by two dimensions: direction of F0 change (rising, falling, level) and magnitude of F0 change, both measured over the last part of the vowel (Khouw and Ciocca, 2007). Perceptual data are consistent with these observations. Listeners correctly identified synthesized Thai words 93% of the time based just on F0 (Abramson, 1975). When natural amplitude variations were added to the stimuli, recognition scores increased by only 3%, and tone could not be recognized well at all from whispered speech (Abramson, 1972), again consistent with the primacy of F0 as a cue in this tonal system. Similarly, Mandarin Chinese listeners could not identify words that had been resynthesized with a flat pitch contour (see Gandour, 1978, for review); and in Yoruba, changes in amplitude and duration did not affect recognition accuracy, again indicating that F0 is the main cue to tone identity (Hombert, 1976; see Gandour, 1978, for review; and see below for discussion of other correlated cues). It is likely that allophonic changes in voice quality, such as creaky voice, also signal tonal contrasts under some circumstances (phonation types are reviewed below).

However, perception of tone varies from language to language, as might be expected given the variety of pitch patterns that occur. In a study of such differences, Gandour and Harshman (1978) played synthetic stimuli with different tonal shapes to speakers of Thai (which has level, rising, and falling tones), Yoruba (which has level tones only), and American English, which has no tones. Multidimensional scaling analyses (see Chapter 1) revealed five perceptual dimensions for tone: average pitch, contour shape (rising/level/falling), length (long/short), extreme endpoint, and slope (level/contour). Average pitch was the most important dimension for tone perception for all three language groups, but especially for the English speakers. Further, the Thai speakers paid more attention to the second dimension than did the Yoruba speakers, presumably by virtue of their experience with rising and falling tones. These results suggest the obvious: that the perceptual strategy listeners use when listening to tone languages depends in part on their native language experience. (Recall that speakers of tone languages also appear to differ from speakers of English in the manner in which pitch is processed at the level of the auditory centers of the brainstem; Krishnan *et al.*, 2005. See Chapter 3 for more discussion.)

Sentence-level prosodic variation in F0 introduces additional potential perceptual complexities for speakers of tone languages. As in nontonal languages, sentence-level prosodic variation in F0 occurs in tone languages, while tonal contrasts are localized to individual syllables or words. For example, pitch falls during statements in Cantonese and rises on questions, potentially complicating the perception of rising and falling tones. For Cantonese, Ma, Ciocca, and Whitehill (2006) found that all tones (whether nominally rising, falling, or level) were produced with rising contours in question-final position. All tones were correctly perceived in context, but many were misperceived as rising when excised, suggesting that listeners rely on context to normalize such changes. Differences in mean pitch between speakers might also pose a threat to tone perception, such that a child's low tone might be similar in F0 to a woman's high tone. However, listeners are also able to normalize interspeaker differences: Recognition of level tones improves significantly when tokens are presented one speaker at a time (80.3%) versus randomized by speaker (48.6% correct; Wong and Diehl, 2003), an effect that is enhanced when words are presented in a sentential context. The effect of context appears to depend on nonlinguistic pitch properties: In a separate study (Francis *et al.*, 2006), normalization occurred when the precursor sentence was spoken in a tone language (Cantonese) or in English, by the same talker or by different talkers. Thus, perception of tone is highly robust to F0 variations that occur for other reasons, although the manner in which listeners accomplish this remains unknown.

8.4.3 Phonation types

In addition to changes in F0, changes in the pattern of vocal fold vibration are important for conveying lexical meaning.[8] Such contrasts can occur simultaneously with tone (see below) as correlated or independent properties. Phoneticians often conceptualize such patterns as forming a continuum of glottal states from most open (voiceless) to most closed (glottal stop), with intermediate steps in between (for example, Gordon and Ladefoged, 2001). Languages divide this continuum up in different ways, and distinguish different configurations along this continuum. As many as seven modes of vocal fold vibration have been proposed for consonants (voiced and voiceless, plus breathy voice, slack voice, modal voice, stiff voice, and creaky voice), with a

---

[8] Changes in phonation commonly occur allophonically as well (e.g., breathiness occurs near /h/, creak near glottal stop), but these will not be discussed further.

slightly different set (voiceless, breathy, slack, stiff, and creaky) for vowels (Ladefoged and Maddieson, 1996), although authors differ in the number of types distinguished and the terms applied (Gerratt and Kreiman, 2001b).

Phonation contrasts on consonants can occur on sonorants like /m/ and /n/, on stops like /p/ and /b/, or on implosive consonants[9] in languages like Hausa (Gordon and Ladefoged, 2001). Most commonly observed is the presence or absence of vocal fold vibration, which in English distinguishes voiceless from voiced consonants (for example, /s/ from /z/). In other examples, the Burmese word /mǎ/ produced with a voiced bilabial nasal means "hard," but when spoken with a voiceless bilabial nasal means "notice" (Gordon and Ladefoged, 2001). Similarly, in Newar (a Tibeto-Burman language) the word /ma:/ spoken with a voiced /m/ means "garland," but means "be unwilling" when spoken with a breathy /m/. Creaky phonation contrasts with modal phonation on sonorants in Northwest American Indian languages like Hupa and Montana Salish. (See Ladefoged and Maddieson, 1996, or Gordon and Ladefoged, 2001, for many more examples and details.) Phonation contrasts on vowels also occur commonly in languages. For example, in Gujarati the word /bar/ with a modal /a/ means "twelve," but means "outside" when pronounced with a breathy /a̤/. In Jalapa Mazatec, já means "tree" with a modally phonated /a/, but with a breathy /a̤/ it means "he wears," and with a creaky /ã/ it means "he carries" (example from Gordon and Ladefoged, 2001).

Although little is known about the perception of these phonatory contrasts, many studies have examined the acoustic contrasts by which they are implemented in different languages. The contrast between murmured (breathy) and clear vowels in Gujarati is marked by significant differences in maximum and mean airflow, duration, posterior glottal opening, and amplitude of the first harmonic (Fischer-Jorgensen, 1967). Similarly, breathy vowels in Hmong differ from modal vowels in H1-H2 (the difference in relative amplitude between the first and second harmonics) and in closure duration (Huffman, 1987). In Mixtec (a language spoken in Mexico), laryngealization is marked by a drop in amplitude and/or F0, by a decrease in H1-H2, and by creak or vocal fry (Gerfen and Baker, 2005). Again, no one cue is necessary to signal the contrast between phonation types, and differences occur across speakers in addition to those that may be observed across languages (Blankenship, 2002). (See also Wayland and Jongman, 2003, who describe a similar situation with the breathy and clear vowels of Khmer.) Note, however, that native speakers of languages with phonation contrasts produce contrasts that are of greater magnitude and longer duration than do speakers of other languages, which do not have these phonemic contrasts (Blankenship, 2002), are more consistent in their perceptual strategies as a group than are listeners for whom the contrasts are allophonic (Esposito, 2010), and are more sensitive to small changes in harmonic amplitudes than are native speakers of English or Thai (Kreiman and Gerratt, 2010; Kreiman, Gerratt, and Khan, 2010).

---

[9] Implosive consonants are produced by lowering the larynx during phonation so that a negative air pressure develops in the mouth and air is sucked inward.

8.4.4   Interaction of tone and voice quality

In a final complication, tone and phonation type combine in some languages, and can interact in four different ways (Andruski and Ratliff, 2000). Phonatory mode can function as a property of a sound that is not related to tone, as in Gujarati; phonation and tone can be independent and crossed, resulting in a language with more kinds of syllables (as in the case of Mpi, a Tibeto-Burman language with six tones, all of which occur both modally and laryngealized, for a total of 12 possible contrasts; Silverman, 1997); a particular phonation type can be associated with one tone and produced inconsistently across speakers, as in Mandarin; or mode of phonation can function as a consistent correlate of a specific tones, as in Green Mong (which has seven lexically contrastive tones, one of which is always breathy and one of which is creaky; Andruski, 2006) and Northern Vietnamese (6 tones, some accompanied by creaky or breathy voice; Brunelle, 2009).

In the absence of tone, breathiness and creakiness usually last for the whole vowel (Silverman, 1997). However, when tone and phonation contrasts co-occur, creakiness and/or breathiness can interfere with the production and perception of tonal changes in F0 by introducing irregularities in F0, and by increasing levels of aperiodicity, which can mask the higher harmonics. Languages solve this seeming conflict of interest by partitioning tone and phonation contrasts to different parts of the vowel. Phonation contrasts are usually carried on the first part, and tone on second part (which is produced with modal phonation). This strategy optimizes listeners' ability to hear both contrasts on the same vowel. Similarly, when sonorant consonants are produced with phonemically creaky voice, creak often spreads onto the vowel before the sonorant or onto the following vowel (Silverman, 1997; Gordon and Ladefoged, 2001), increasing the discriminability of the formant transitions on which perception of the consonant depends (but see Bird, Caldecott, Campbell, Gick, and Shaw, 2008, for evidence of variability in timing across languages).

Finally, the question arises of how listeners deal perceptually with such complicated linguistic contrasts. Across languages and studies, breathy voice has been associated with increased levels of spectral noise (especially in the higher frequencies), lower intensity, an increase in spectral tilt and in the amplitude of the first harmonic, a decrease in F0, lower F1 (possibly due to lowering of the larynx), a longer open phase and slower closing velocity during each vibratory cycle, and an increase in segment duration. Creaky (or laryngealized) phonation is correlated with increased aperiodicity, lower intensity, decreased spectral tilt and a lower amplitude of the first harmonic, a decrease in F0, an increase in F1 (possibly due to laryngeal raising), a vibratory pattern with a shorter open phase and quicker closing, and increased duration (Huffman, 1987; Andruski and Ratliff, 2000; see Gordon and Ladefoged, 2001, for review). With so many potential cues, what do listeners actually pay attention to when they hear a phoneme as breathy, modal, or creaky?

Unfortunately, relatively little is known about the perception of phonation type across languages. It is possible to sort Green Mong vowels into the correct category 92% of the time based on H1-H2 (first and second harmonics), duration, F0, jitter and shimmer, with H1-H2 doing most of the work (Andruski and Ratliff, 2000; see also Andruski, 2006), suggesting that these features are potentially salient perceptual cues. Only one published study (Brunelle, 2009) has used speech synthesis to test specific hypotheses about perceptual salience of different cues in Northern Vietnamese, which has correlated phonation types and tones. Although listeners' responses followed the F0 contour in many cases, final glottalization (creak) overrode pitch information for one tone that was both steeply falling and glottalized, possibly because glottalization makes pitch more difficult to hear. Despite the complexity of the tonal system, only a small number of cues (pitch rise, glottalization, low offset, and a falling-rising pattern) were needed to distinguish the tones perceptually.

8.4.5 Prosodic cues in word-level rhythmic and stress contrasts

Prosodic elements operate at the level of words and phrases to produce distinctive linguistic forms, by combining pitch, loudness, and duration to signal contrasts in stress and rhythm (Fry, 1958, 1968). Most simply viewed, stress is used to indicate the importance of a word or phrase in a sentence (Bolinger, 1972b). As these accents and stress patterns occur across utterances, they combine in complex ways to determine the perception of speech rhythm, defined as regular beats brought about through the succession of accented syllables (Couper-Kuhlen, 2001; Wennerstrom, 2001; see Table 8.1). Different approaches to analysis appear for word stress, sentence accent, and phrasal intonation, all of which display differing combinations of changes in pitch, loudness, timing, and voice quality to indicate peaks or prominences, forming a rhythm group or unit (Pike, 1945; Cruttenden, 1997; Couper-Kuhlen, 2001).

Word stress is a dynamic process in English, with such paradigms as *di*plomat, di*plo*macy, diplo*ma*tic. For longer words, some practitioners have advocated a number of levels to notate stress phenomena. Ladefoged (2006) attributes variations in prominence on longer words to sentence accent processes, while at the word level itself he proposes two accent "heights." This arises from the observation that in sentences, some stresses are dropped, accommodating a rough notion of English rhythm, in which a regular, or isochronous, beat occurs. In Ladefoged's example (using an apostrophe before the accented syllable), "'Stresses in 'English 'tend to re'cur at 'regular 'intervals of 'time" (2006, p. 115). The former dichotomy between stress-timed languages (i.e., English), which features stressed and reduced syllables, and syllable-timed languages (i.e., French), for which syllable length and quality are more consistent, has been modified, because relative accent also does occur in French (see definitions on Table 8.1). In verbal interaction, rhythmic elements may become synchronized (Auer, Couper-Kuhlen, and Müller, 1999), as speakers "match" each other in intonation and rhythm (Couper-Kuhlen, 1996). Robert Port and his colleagues have argued persuasively that English and other languages adjust timing during production to conform to certain rhythmic constraints, which are hierarchically present and characterized by entrainment between these metrical levels. In this portrayal, rhythm is an organizational principle and its effects are predictable (Cummins and Port, 1998). One such effect is that information is better retained when acquired in "rhythmic chunks" (Auer *et al.*, 1999).

A comparable prosodic–phonological contrast appears in the temporal domain at the word level, where length alone distinguishes vowel or consonant contrasts, as in

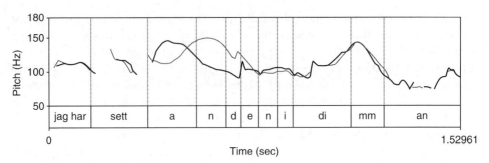

Figure 8.9   Pitch contours of two words produced by a male speaker in a carrier phrase: I have seen the duck/spirit in the fog. (Thick line = accent I, thin line = accent II). (Ambrazaitis and Bruce, 2006, p. 5).

the German contrast Stadt ("city") and Staat ("state"). A similar but limited presence of word-level prosodic contrast is seen, for example, in Swedish, English, Norwegian and Japanese. South Swedish has both stress and pitch effects on contrasting words as in the words anden (accent I, "duck") and anden (accent II, "spirit") (Ambrazaitis and Bruce, 2006; Figure 8.9). In German, verb pairs distinguish meanings by timing and pitch contrasts: for example, über*fahr*en (run over) and *über*fahren (ferry across); *um*gehen (circulate) and um*ge*hen (avoid). In English, timing and pitch elements combine to distinguish noun/verb pairs such as (English) *im*port, im*port*; *con*duct/con*duct*; *pro*duce/pro*duce*. Similar pairs occur as compound nouns contrasting with noun phrases: *green*house, green *house*; *spit*fire, spit *fire*. Native speakers of English are able to distinguish these pairs out of context, from listening, about 81% of the time. In a reversal of usual findings comparing production and comprehension abilities, a study of normal subjects revealed higher scores for accurately producing the contrasts (92%) than recognizing them (Van Lancker Sidtis, 2004).

8.4.6   Prosodic contrasts for grammatical phrases and clauses

When listening to the stream of speech, the listener must, as a first priority, perceive how portions of that stream group together into phrases and sentences, and much of prosodic study is devoted to defining phrase and sentence boundaries. Table 8.1 lists more than a dozen types of boundary notion. Prosodic cues are important for determining the ends of sentences or utterances in spoken language (for example, Slifka, 1999). For example, creaky voice serves as a marker of prosodic boundaries, either initially and/or finally, in Swedish and Finnish as well as in English (for example, Kreiman, 1982; see Gordon and Ladefoged, 2001, for review). In standard Chinese, creak occurs on 9% of syllables overall, but on almost all sentence-final syllables (Belotel-Grenié and Grenié, 2004). Pitch plays a very large role in this chunking function, as has long been recognized (Menn and Boyce, 1982). Many treatments are concerned with characterizing pitch changes (and changes in loudness, which usually track pitch changes) as reflective of important beginnings and ends of utterances. These include anacrusis (unstressed syllables at the beginning of an utterance), boundary tones (Pierrehumbert and Hirschberg, 1990), cadence (terminal material; Wichmann,

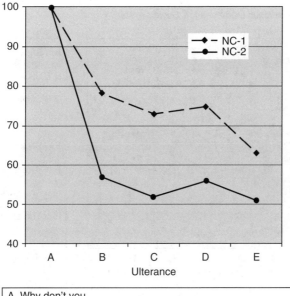

Figure 8.10 Demonstration of pre-pausal lengthening in phrases showing the duration of the utterance "A," "Why don't you," when embedded in increasingly longer utterances (B-E) for two speakers. The y axis shows length as a percentage of the original length of utterance A.

2000), declination (continual lowering of F0; Cooper and Sorensen, 1981), final lowering, key (the prominent range of F0), pitch boundaries, and register (in this context, the relative position of an intonation within the speaker's range; Couper-Kuhlen, 1999).

Also, within phrases timing cues gather constituents into informational and grammatical units. For example, in English a robust timing pattern called "prepausal lengthening" (or its converse, "initial shortening") helps signal phrasal structure in discourse. Prepausal lengthening means that syllables or words occurring toward the end of a phrase are longer than that same syllable or word occurring early in a phrase. A classic example was provided by Gaitenby (1965) in expansions of the expression "[[[[[Why don't you] get tickets] for tomorrow] night]'s performance?]" Figure 8.10 shows schematically that words and phrases become shortened when embedded in a increasing longer phrase, or, conversely, words and phrases spoken toward the end of an utterance are relatively longer. Various explanations for this fact have been offered. Probably the most convincing is that this element of temporal regularity helps to point to beginnings and ends. Other factors may include breath control – less breath is available toward the end of an utterance, leading to planned increases in rate of speaking at an earlier time in longer utterances.

The same phenomenon, called "initial shortening," is observed in single words. In word paradigms, such as "stick, sticky, stickily," the vowel /ɪ/ is longest in "stick,"

(a)
Word and Vowel Nucleus Durations for "Stick" as Stem Word

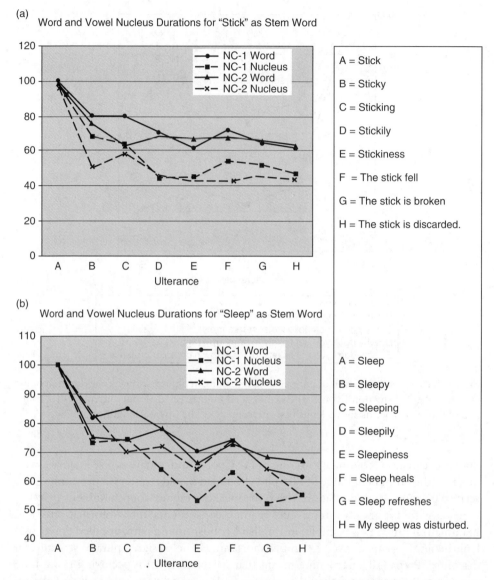

A = Stick

B = Sticky

C = Sticking

D = Stickily

E = Stickiness

F = The stick fell

G = The stick is broken

H = The stick is discarded.

(b)
Word and Vowel Nucleus Durations for "Sleep" as Stem Word

A = Sleep

B = Sleepy

C = Sleeping

D = Sleepily

E = Sleepiness

F = Sleep heals

G = Sleep refreshes

H = My sleep was disturbed.

Figure 8.11 Plots for percentage duration of the stem words "stick" and "sleep" in derived word and phrasal forms A–H spoken by two normal talkers. Plots for full word durations and word nucleus (vowel) durations are shown. The vowel sustains more shortening. The ordinate represents duration as a percentage of the A form.

somewhat shorter in "sticky," and shortest in "stickily" (Lehiste, 1972). As might be anticipated, most shortening occurs during the vowel nucleus of the word. This temporal pattern on phrases and word paradigms is quite robust, in that it is preserved in various motor speech disorders, such as the dysarthria associated with Parkinson's disease, even when other temporal disturbances of speech have arisen (Canter and Van Lancker, 1985). (Values for two normal speakers are shown in Figure 8.11.)

An important use of prosody in fluent speech, and one that has a long, distinguished history in punctuation rules and rhetoric, is the signaling of phrasal constituency. Possibilities for lexical and grammatical ambiguity abound in running speech, and because punctuation occurs only in the written mode, many such ambiguities must be unpacked by features of the voice. Prosodic cues act together to indicate how words in a string are related to each other, and all the elements – pitch, loudness, timing, and voice quality – are variously selected or comingled to indicate how speakers intend to chunk the words they say into meaningful groups. The often-cited example (rendered here punctuation-free) "Eats shoots and leaves," depending on constituency, refers either to the behavior of a panda or to the actions of a gunslinger. "Garden path sentences," in which the structure of the sentence tricks the listener into a wrong interpretation, also exemplify structural ambiguity; a classic example is "A horse raced past the barn fell." Prosody is so effective in communicating structure in these cases that such teasers work best in the written modality. Potentially ambiguous phrases and sentences are routinely – but not always – disambiguated through use of prosody. Does your spoken rendition of "the old man and woman" transmit a clear reference to two older persons or one older person and a female adult?

Grammatical contrasts of several types are signaled by the prosodic information conveyed by voice quality (Crystal, 1969; Ladd, 1996; Cutler *et al.*, 1997; Kjelgaard and Speer, 1999; Raczaszek, Tuller, Shapiro, Case, and Kelso, 1999; Schafer, Speer, Warren, and White, 2000). Grammatical use of linguistic prosody is located at the bottom of the categorical portion of the Pyramid of Prosody (Figure 8.8) as sentence types (declarative, interrogative, imperative) and clause types (dependent, conditional, restrictive) each fall into a single category that can be signaled by prosodic cues. However, while grammatical categories are stable, prosodic cues for signaling those categories are much less so. Descriptions of English prosody often state that questions are more likely to be uttered with rising intonation and declaratives with falling intonation, but exceptions occur, and many varieties of English do not systematically display falling patterns with declarative sentences (Auran, Bouzon, and Hirst, 2004), as previously discussed (see Section 8.3.1 above). In English, conditional clauses are spoken using an intonation contour different from that used in declarative clauses. For example, "If he was playing the guitar at the time ..." is intoned quite differently from "He was playing the guitar at the time" uttered as an independent clause. Prosodic structure also marks the differences between restrictive and nonrestrictive clauses. These provide convincing examples of the power of intonational contrast, because unlike the conditional/independent clause example above, these clauses are made up of the same words. A nonrestrictive clause provides identifying information about the "head" or subject of the clause in which it is embedded: "His ex-wife, who lives in Miami, is planning to visit." In a restrictive clause, the same utterance is used to narrow the referent down to a specific ex-wife from among several possibilities living in different cities. Try pronouncing the sentence with these two meanings, and note how differently they are intoned (audio samples 8.4 and 8.5). A similar function appears in the use of prosodic contrasts for reported speech in quoted and repeated utterances (Klewitz and Couper-Kuhlen, 1999).

Sidebar: List Intonation

A classic example of a stereotypic intonation pattern involving falling vocal pitch at the end of the utterance appears in the verbal production of lists. Falling intonation is nearly mandatory at the end of an orally produced list of numbers or words. (People find it difficult to produce a list without falling intonation on the last item.) When counting from one to five, for example, all words between one and four will rise slightly in pitch contour, and then the pitch of "five" will steeply fall. If the same person counts from one to six, "five" will sound like the previous numbers in the list, while "six" will have the stereotyped terminal rising-falling shape. This pattern occurs whether the lists are words, phrases, or sentences. If a long list is produced, requiring a breath before the end is attained, falling intonation is withheld until the final item in the list. This use of falling intonation clearly functions as a signal of the end of a verbal act. An interesting parallel is seen in German complex and compound sentences, which feature rising intonation on clauses in a series leading to a concluding clause, which is produced on falling intonation.

8.4.7   Meaning in prosodic shape: Intonational idioms

In "intonational idioms" or "lexical intonation," prosodic shapes themselves represent and signal discrete communicative meanings. A classic example often given in discussing prosodic "tunes" is the childhood taunt "na (na) na na na na" (Figure 8.12), where the distinctive prosodic contour, without any lexical items, communicates insolence and contempt.[10] Any sentence or phrase uttered on this contour carries an unmistakably clear meaning. For example, the sentence "Johnny's going home now" with and without the taunting prosody yields two very different meanings (audio samples 8.6 and 8.7). Interestingly, this contour exists with the same meaning in at least one other (related) language (German).

As this example shows, subtle (and not so subtle) meanings sometimes inhere in prosodic contours themselves. Writers have described numerous tunes (illustrated in audio samples 8.8 to 8.12; Pierrehumbert and Hirschberg, 1990; Ladd, 1996) that carry such independent meanings in and of themselves. Liberman and Sag (1974) speak of an intonational lexicon, exemplifying a number of these meaning-laden contours, such as surprise-redundancy (audio sample 8.8) and contradiction. Indeed, observation of one's own speech reveals a continuous flow of meaning-in-intonation contours. Echo questions – verbal repetitions of interrogative prosody – convey incredulity (audio sample 8.9) (Cruttenden, 1997; see Table 8.1). Similarly, echo questions with a final rise-fall convey emphasis or sarcasm, depend-

---

[10]   See Ladd (1980) and Bolinger (1986) for fuller treatments of this example.

Na → ····(na) → na → → na → ····na → → ····na

Figure 8.12 Childhood taunt on nonsense syllables.

ing on context (as in, "Are you ready?" "Am I ready!"; audio sample 8.10). A low fall at the end of a sentence suggests finality and definiteness (audio sample 8.11), and is generally "more uninterested, unexcited, and dispassionate" than the high fall counterpart, which is "more interested, more excited" (Cruttenden, 1997, p. 91). Delattre (1966, 1972) identified other meaningful prosodic tunes, such as the implication contour, which conveys a sense of confidence. An "insist" (audio sample 8.12; see Table 8.1) serves to deny something previously stated, and is characterized by nuclear pitch on the final verb (not noun) as in "I didn't say I'd *dance* at the party." Countless effective meaning nuances can appear on single word contrasts, as displayed by the many ways of saying "yes" illustrated in Figure 8.3 (Crystal, 2003).

Many more meaning-carrying intonation tunes appear as longer contours carried by phrases and sentences. Try saying the sentence "He didn't *think* so" with the words spoken on low, low, high, low-fall pitch values. This intonational shape with the emphasis on the word "think" implies finality and definitiveness tinged with defiance (audio samples 8.13 and 8.14). Use this intonation with "I didn't *want* to" and "She shouldn't *try* that." While the communicative import of the intonation is subtle and difficult to characterize, a consistent thread can be recognized. This communicative meaning is lost when the same utterances are intoned in other ways, as in high, high low, low-rise. Another such intonational idiom is high low high-rise fall, as in "I *want* to *see* it" (audio sample 8.15), where the high-rise syllable is higher than the initial pitch level. This communicates a demanding or rebellious (or whining) stance, and might be punctuated with an exclamation mark. When the same intonational contour is used for "*He* didn't *say* so" or "*We* couldn't *do* it," the same attitudinal meaning is conveyed. In another prosodic pattern, the notion of "also" is carried by the sentence accent (audio sample 8.16). The statement "*She* has an insane daughter," spoken on high, low, low, low rising, implies that someone else – perhaps the conversation partner – does also, while "She has an insane *daughter*" carries the notion that the other daughter is unique. The first prosodic form might be insulting to the conversational partner.

There may be thousands of these intonational meanings that interact in subtle ways with the lexical meanings of the sentences on which they are carried. Writers with a fine ear for prosodic nuance can exploit these elements in countless ways. One humorous example is reprinted in the Sidebar, in which an intonational meaning trumps the linguistic meaning in a conversation between Jeeves, the all-knowing butler, and his scatty employer, Bertie Wooster.

Sidebar: Jeeves and Wooster, *Brinkley Manor*
by P.G. Wodehouse (1934)

Bertie: "It is true, Jeeves," I said formally, "that once or twice in the past I may
have missed the bus. That, however, I attribute purely to bad luck."

Jeeves: *"Indeed, sir?"*

Bertie: "On the present occasion I shall not fail, and I'll tell you why I shall not
fail. Because my scheme is rooted in human nature."

Jeeves: *"Indeed, sir?"*

Bertie: "It is simple. Not elaborate. And, furthermore, based on the psychology
of the individual."

Jeeves: *"Indeed, sir?"*

Bertie: "Jeeves," I said, "don't keep saying 'Indeed, sir?' No doubt nothing is
further from your mind than to convey such a suggestion, but you have
a way of stressing the 'in' and then coming down with a thud on the
'deed' which makes it virtually tantamount to 'Oh, yeah?' Correct, this,
Jeeves."

Jeeves: *"Very good, sir."*

In Table 8.1, the term "key" describes relative pitch changes, extending across an entire utterance, that are used to indicate attitude changes or information status pertaining to elements in the utterance. Newscasters shift key to indicate a new unit of information (Cruttenden, 1997). Similarly, register refers to the relative pitch within a speaker's range, which can be used to delineate emotional and attitudinal stances toward the linguistic content, as well as to mark reported and parenthetic speech (Couper-Kuhlen, 1991; Cruttenden, 1997; Klewitz and Couper-Kuhlen, 1999). For example, a speaker might shift to the lower portion of her pitch range and lower her voice to introduce a highly personal topic.

8.4.8   Ditropic (idiomatic/literal) sentences and other formulaic utterances

As far as we know, all languages have idiomatic expressions. In English sentences like "It broke the ice" or "He went out on a limb," idiomatic meanings can alternate with literal ones in a special kind of ambiguity that does not depend on lexical, phrasal, or grammatical shapes. Sentence pairs like these are called "ditropic," in that they may be interpreted either literally or nonliterally. In Figure 8.8, ditropic sentences (carrying either literal or nonliteral meanings) are placed on the Pyramid at the midpoint between categorical/linguistic and graded/speaker's meaning. The categorical property arises because there is a binary choice in meaning for these types of sentences: They are either literal or idiomatic. Nonliteral language departs from linguistic meaning, because the meaning of the phrase cannot be derived from the linguistic meanings of the constituent words, and so the usage determines the meaning. This feature of ditropic sentences qualifies them for membership in the pragmatic realm of the Pyramid.

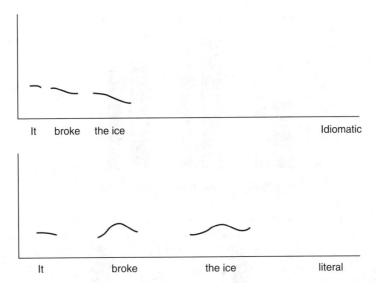

It   broke   the ice   Idiomatic

It   broke   the ice   literal

Figure 8.13 Intonation contours for idiomatic and literal meanings of ditropic sentences in American English.

In English, and undoubtedly in other languages also, idioms and other formulaic expressions are characterized by stereotyped prosodic cues and intonation contours. (For a review of the prosodic properties of formulaic expressions, see Van Lancker Sidtis, 2010). For example, the formulaic expression "I *would*n't want to be in *his* shoes" must have the prominent pitch on "his," and in "*That's* enough to drive a man to *drink*," the first and final syllable take the highest pitch. This is well known to teachers of second languages: Producing a contour different from the stereotyped form on formulaic expressions sounds non-native, even when the student learning a second language produces all the words correctly.

Because idiomatic meanings in general have stereotyped intonation contours, acoustic-auditory cues might hypothetically serve to distinguish the two kinds of meaning. In fact, listeners are able to identify the intended meaning at well above chance levels, whether the sentences are heard singly or in pairs. An analysis of the acoustic cues making up the two types of utterances revealed significant differences in prosodic variables including pitch contours, timing, and voice quality (Figure 8.13). The literal versions are longer and have a larger number of local pitch contours; the nonliteral counterparts are shorter, tend to be spoken on one contour, and often contain marked voice quality (creaky voice or murmur) (Van Lancker, Canter, and Terbeek, 1981). The nonliteral versions may also be articulated with retracted lips (and correspondingly raised formant frequencies) to indicate smiling.

Similar analyses of ditropic sentences from French also revealed acoustic differences in realization of idiomatic versus literal intended meanings, but in French, the acoustic cues were reversed. While in American English sentences, idiomatic meanings were associated with shorter durations, lower F0 and F0 range, and less F0 variability, in the French pairs, the idiomatic variants had longer durations, higher F0, and greater F0 variability and range (Abdelli-Baruh, Yang, Ahn, and Van Lancker Sidtis,

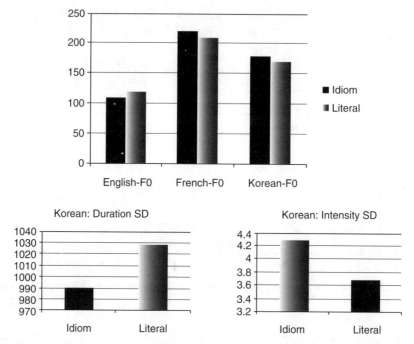

Figure 8.14   Acoustic measures for meaning contrasts in English, French and Korean ditropic sentences showing an opposite role of fundamental frequency. Korean utilizes duration and intensity as cues.

2007). For Korean ditropic sentences, pitch played a marginal role in the contrasts. Greater intensity variations were found for the idiomatic utterances (Figure 8.14), with higher durational variability for literal exemplars (Ahn, Yang, and Sidtis, 2010).

8.5   Voice Quality and the Pragmatics of Communication

Discourse functions (found toward the bottom of the Pyramid in Figure 8.8) belong to the field of pragmatics, which refers to principles of language use in social settings. In pragmatics, language scientists describe how interlocutors make assumptions or derive inferences, and how they cooperate in various ways to achieve effective verbal communication. Studies have focused on conversation (face-to-face or by telephone), storytelling, narration and picture description, and on the communication practices of auctioneers, ministers, weather forecasters, and psychotherapists (see Kuiper, 2009). For example, conversational turns and topic changes are both signaled by voice quality cues. Authenticity and sincerity, as codified in the Gricean maxims (see Sidebar), may well be inferred more from tone of voice than from the words used. Confidence, politeness, and such sociolinguistic notions as deference versus assertiveness, also manifest in the pragmatic domain, are conveyed to varying degrees by voice. Subtle variations in voice quality, pitch, intensity and duration (yielding patterns of rhythm) play a large role in the detailed regulation of communicative interactions, and "parliamentary procedure" in a group of talkers is handled by a combination of vocal signals, gesture, and eye contact (Hopper, 1992). Repetition, a practice that occurs normally in conversation (Tannen, 1989; Wolf and Sidtis, 2010), is also characterized by distinct prosodic cues under specific conditions (Wong, 2000).

Sidebar: Gricean Maxims

Paul Grice (1975) proposed four maxims describing "rules" that cooperative speakers follow in conversation, and that listeners typically assume are being followed as they interpret what they hear in discourse. These maxims – quality, quantity, relation, and manner – arose from his observations of natural language. *Quality* refers to the assumption that a speaker will not assert that for which he lacks sufficient knowledge or does not believe. *Quantity* requires that the interlocutor contribute only what is necessary to convey the message, no more or no less. *Relation* portrays the speaker's contribution as relevant to the conversation. Lastly, *Manner* presupposes that the interlocutor conveys the message in an orderly, comprehensible fashion while avoiding ambiguity. Meaning can be also found in cases where the speaker "flouts" or "violates" a maxim, but often some kind of social-interactional "trouble" ensues when this happens (for example, when the speaker takes a long detour from the main point, or when a fact is injected out of context without the flag, "Oh, before I forget …"). These elements belong to the domain of *speaker's* meaning, which is the intended meaning in a given context, to be distinguished from *linguistic* meaning, which is shared, stable, and structurally fixed in the language (Grice, 1968).

8.5.1 Prosody in discourse

Prosody has been called a "marker of information flow" in spoken discourse (Swerts and Geluykens, 1994). Topic and theme, as they are manifested in the structure of talk, are shaped in part by voice characteristics. Sentence accent indicates whether information is new or assumed ("given," as in "I *offered* Tom the book" compared to "I offered Tom the *book*" or "I offered *Tom* the book"). Such information is transmitted by graded cues, in that higher pitch on a louder and longer syllable underscores the intention to communicate that the information is new. In utterances beginning with "please," the difference between a request and a demand can easily be signaled by a shift in sentence accent. A request entails cooperativeness and mutual knowledge, as in "*Please* don't **smoke** here," which, with the pitch accent on smoke, utilizes the intonation of given information. However, placing a high pitch accent followed by falling tone on utterance-initial "please" marks it as new information (**Please** don't smoke here) and is used when the request has not been complied with. The different intonation changes the illocutionary force of the utterance (the basic purpose of a speaker in making it) from a request to something closer to a demand (Wichmann, 2005). These cues are difficult to classify and to codify, however, in part because linguistic uses of prosodic cues, such as those signaling sentence type and phrase structure, converge with conveyance of emotion and attitude. For example, the question "Are you leaving now?" is spoken with rising intonation normally signaling an interrogatory utterance, but if the pitch increase is extra high, the question includes surprise or shock. As part of pragmatic competence, listeners use such auditory cues to discern levels of importance and emphasis in the speaker's message.

In addition to providing information about phrasal and sentential units, prosody marks out larger discourse units of various kinds. Sentences combine in spoken texts to form themes or topics, which unite the talk and provide coherence. These are signaled through emphasis on syllables and words, which in turn is accomplished by changes in pitch, voice quality, duration, and rate. Units such as a "paragraph" used in discourse or in telling a story have structure which can be identified, and much of the structure is communicated through prosody (Lehiste, 1972; Kreiman, 1982). For example, speakers begin topics on high pitches and end on lower ones, with less F0 variability, and pause (often with an "um" or "uh" as a pause filler) at the end of a paragraph (see Cutler *et al.*, 1997, for extensive review). Speakers also talk more quickly and more loudly at the beginning of a topic than at the end, and these changes provide strong cues to listeners (Kreiman, 1982). Couper-Kuhlen (1986) suggests that such intonational patterns set up "frames" for comprehension of discourse. Similar to the notion of "keys" in discourse, the term "paratones" was coined to described how intonation corresponds to paragraph-like units in speech (Yule, 1980); for example, gradual changes in pitch within paragraph-size units have been reported in spontaneous speech (Swerts and Geluykens, 1994). This structure is critical to comprehension: When spoken texts were presented with altered intonation, comprehension and recognition memory for words in the text were affected. This finding suggests that linguistic prosody supplies redundant cues for determining the structure of sentences and discourses, but also aids with semantic encoding and memory retention of lexical units (Cohen, Douaire, and Elsabbagh, 2001).

Note that all of these signals can also function in the paralinguistic realm, because when a speaker utilizes intonation to identify relative importance in the information flow, attitudes toward the information are usually implied. Thus paralinguistic signaling of attitudinal stance arises from many of these linguistic-prosodic parameters, which perform multiple jobs in linguistic organization.

8.5.2   Turn-taking in conversation

Prosody performs important functions in cuing the discourse structure of a conversation as well, and in managing the flow of topics and turns. Conversational turns are organized in large part through vocal signals, although eye contact and facial expression also contribute (Auer, 1996). Prosody is used as a resource in the process of organizing conversational interactions, such as projecting next syntactic turns and setting the pitch level or tenor of the conversation at the beginning of a telephone call (Schegloff, 1998). Prosodic signals indicate when the "turn" is being yielded to another participant, or when the speaker wishes to continue talking. Prosodic cues also signal an opportunity for overlapping turn placement (Wells and Macfarlane, 1998). In Dutch conversation, a particular intonation contour is interpreted as a question as well as a signal that the speaker wants to keep the floor ("turn-keeping")

(Caspers, 1998). Changes in speech rate cue collaborative information units for conversation participants in Japanese, with presentation of new information occurring on deceleration of speech rate (Kioso, Shimojima, and Katagiri, 1998). In studies of conversation, prosodic differences in items repeated by a speaker as "understanding checks" may communicate confirmation (falling pitch and louder) or a reflective response (Couper-Kuhlen, 2000). The shimmer of prosodic meanings in conversational settings might be compared to revolving mirror balls, in that conversational partners reflect off each other and off their social and linguistic settings.

Continuation signals, usually rising intonation at a place where falling intonation would be expected, let the listener know that the speaker intends to hold the floor or continue with the same theme. However, rising pitch on filtered utterances was also shown to be judged as turn completions (Schaffer, 1983). The more usual pattern of pitch declination also serves to indicate ends (and hence beginnings) of groupings in the utterance (Cutler and Pearson, 1986), where a listener might politely assume the speaking turn. A "paralinguistic drawl" on a final syllable or on the accented syllable of a final clause can signal completion of a turn (Duncan and Fiske, 1977).

Studies reveal few differences in turn-taking structure when comparing face-to-face and telephone conversations, suggesting that prosodic and linguistic cues alone carry the day in large part (Hopper, 1992). Telephone calls are characterized by various levels of structure, starting with openings and closing, and enfolding topics, themes, and conversational turns into the form (Liberman and McLemore, 1992). On the telephone, "intonational settings" indicate length of specific turns, and signal openings and closings. High pitch in utterance onsets characterizes statements providing the reason for the call in radio call-in shows (Couper-Kuhlen, 2001). In business calls, certain intonation attributes are sustained throughout; and distinctive discourse units within this genre of telephone call can be identified (openings, business transactions, preclosures, final closures) by prosodic details. These subunits are seen mainly in two parameters: control of midpoint of the F0 contour and control of fluctuation of the F0 contour (Douglas-Cowie and Cowie, 1998). When a member of a telephonic pairing wishes to terminate the call, he or she might increase vocal pitch, lengthen phrases, and assume a different vocal quality, as in "Okay, then! It's been fun chatting! I'll talk to you soon! Bye for now!" All of these closing expressions have a signature vocal quality specialized for the purpose of ending the phone call.

8.5.3   Vocal cues in error repair

Speakers often give a quick signal to indicate that they intend to revise or abandon an expression. There are several techniques that speakers use to indicate they have uttered something prematurely or in error and wish to change their minds (Schegloff, Jefferson, and Sacks, 1977). Prosody alone can be used to mark the items to be revised or abandoned. One strategy is to use a matching prosodic signal for the correction. For example, one might say "I'm going to give the *teacher* – the *student* all those materials" using the same pitch accent on "student" as was heard for "teacher." Repetition of the intonation on the replacement word is also noticeable because it does not constitute usually-anticipated intonation for a continuing phrase (Clark and Wasow, 1998). While words such as "I mean" are often used to self-repair a verbal error, prosodic elements such as glottal stops and unusual lengthening of vowels, including schwa (mid central vowel present in reduced syllables in the repeated item), have been reported (Levinson, 1983). Prosodic cues, as in the astonished question that might initiate a repair process, can override the interactional cues functioning to move the conversation forward (Selting, 1996b).

8.5.4   Summary

Prosody in discourse has a variable relationship to the words selected by the speaker (Crystal, 1969), essentially because in this domain of communication, prosody carries a personal message and provides a vehicle for individual expression and control. Much is executed automatically and proceeds without awareness, or perhaps with partial awareness, during the speaking and listening process (Hird and Kirsner, 1998). The extent of the layering of information provided by prosodic material in pragmatic domains (Günthner, 1999) and throughout speech production is reflected in Figure 8.8. Studies such as those examining these layers in tone languages like Thai may provide insight (Luksaneeyanawin, 1998). It is also the case that prosodic structure has a certain independent status. That is, normal-sounding intonation can be produced without simultaneous comprehension of the content of the text (Koriat, Greenberg, and Kreiner, 2002). (This is commonly seen in Alzheimer's disease.) These apparent paradoxes highlight the immense complexity of the role played by prosody in signaling linguistic meaning.

8.6   Paralanguage: Attitudes and Emotions

Functionally, the least amenable to categorizing, and hence placed toward the bottom of the Pyramid of Prosody, are attitudes and emotions. For Pike (1945), all intonation was mainly attitudinal. As mentioned above, grammatical moods such as interrogative and conditional might be seen to shade imperceptibly into attitudinal categories such as complaint, doubtfulness, and irony. We address this colorful realm of human vocal expression by mentioning some specific ways that attitudes are revealed in speech. It is well known that a line between attitudes and emotions cannot convincingly be drawn. Chapter 9 describes how voice reveals emotion, personality, and psychiatric states, along with current attempts to study and measure these qualities.

8.6.1   Attitudes

We've touched upon the signaling of attitudes often in this chapter, because utterances without attitudinal stance hardly exist. The domain of attitudes takes us deeper into the realm of paralanguage, which most typically refers to emotional meanings, a topic that will be explored in Chapter 9. Attitudes reflect the speaker's viewpoint in using the utterance and so they straddle linguistic and paralinguistic domains. Most talk includes implicit evaluative commentary by the speaker carried on the spoken utterance: authenticity, sincerity; irony, sarcasm; approval, disapproval, and so on (Figure 8.3). Listeners can discern from tone of voice alone, without lexical cues, whether good or bad news is coming up in a voice mail message, but only when the negative or positive information actually follows in the message, suggesting that speakers tune their voices differently when merely announcing that they have news to impart at a later time (Swerts and Hirschberg, 2010). Even in saying that prosodic signals cue inferences, we find ourselves comingled with attitudes (Couper-Kuhlen, 2000). Our conversations in the natural state are bursting with nuances. The question "Why didn't you [any action]?" can sound like an information question, a nurturing moment of support, or a reproach, signaled by shifts in voice quality (Günthner, 1999). Similarly, the response to the question "Where is the [noun]?" ("It's in the [location]") can sound informationally responsive, defiant, or defensive, again, solely based in modifications of pitch, loudness, voice quality, and duration. While surprise is often indicated by use of formulaic expressions such as "wow," "my goodness," and so on, people also display surprise by prosodically marking questions and repeats of previous turns in the conversation (Wilkinson and Kitzinger, 2006). "Oh" as a common formulaic expression can be imbued with a huge range of attitudes and emotions, including surprise, delight, and dismay (Wilkinson and Kitzinger, 2006). As a graded attribute, surprise can be mild (as in slight puzzlement) or intense (as in loathing bewilderment), and it can have a negative or a positive valence (Bolinger, 1989). The speaker has available a vast ocean of attitudes and innuendos subtly communicated by the prosodic material. These can be directed toward self or other (the tone in "As low-man on the totem pole …," for example, can be self-deprecating or insulting) or, in that same expression, toward the content of the utterance (that is, toward the phrase, as though ridiculing the very notion expressed in the phrase "low man on the totem pole"). The value-added additudinal properties discerned from the vocal signal may be expected to reflect social norms, trends, and, of course, prejudices. In studies by Geiselman and colleagues, incidental processing of the importance of a spoken message was associated with gender of the talker's voice (Geiselman and Crawley, 1983), such that messages spoken in female voices were judged less "potent" than those spoken in a male voice. Good novelists provide the reader with hints about the psychological and social ambience by indicating how attitudinal material, even of great subtlety, is conveyed in speech. Incidental information derived from voice thus has an effect on the perceived linguistic meaning.

Sidebar: Signaling Tone of Voice in the Novel *Bonfire of the Vanities*

Using his ear for natural speech, the novelist Tom Wolfe captures the communication of attitudinal judgments vividly, when, for example, describing the tone used by Buck, a beefy bodyguard, speaking to an obtuse Englishman: "[Buck] used the sort of voice you use for someone who is blameless but dense" (1987, p. 275). Or, of a socialite during a dinner party, "Her tone said 'How on earth could you not know that?'" (p. 326). Wolfe's description of intonational nuances serves to depict the social and psychological status of his characters.

8.6.2   Irony, sarcasm, and humor

Popular attitudinal stances in conversational talk that are signaled in part by voice quality are irony and sarcasm. This phenomenon allows speakers to use a string of words to convey an intended meaning which is opposite to the usual meanings of those words. In a stereotyped prosodic contour for sarcasm, the utterance appears as high, low, low-rise. Say "*That*'s a great idea" using that intonation, and compare this form to the same sentence canonically intoned in a slowly declining pitch with a high rise on idea. Add creaky voice toward the end of the utterance. A sarcastic meaning – that is NOT a great idea – is a likely candidate for the first production.[11] Irony and sarcasm also often feature altered voice quality in the narrow sense, with pharyngealization and creaky voice, to communicate that a meaning opposite of the usual literal meaning is being expressed. Impressionistic scores for voice quality associated with irony yielded higher ratings for creaky voice and pharyngealization (Van Lancker, Canter, and Terbeek, 1981).

Languages differ in how they signal irony and sarcasm. Cheang and Pell (2009) found that the expression of sarcasm in Cantonese differs from English. Cantonese speakers express sarcasm by increasing F0, while English speakers lower F0 to express sarcasm (see also Cheang and Pell, 2008). Sarcasm in French is also marked by a higher F0, but features more monotone pitch contours than do more sincere utterances (Laval and Bert-Erboul, 2005); and Italians express sarcasm with increases in F0, F0 range, and amplitude (Anolli, Ciceri, and Infantino, 2002).

Approaches to sarcasm and irony based on acoustic analyses alone may obscure subtle dimensions of meaning or lead to wrong conclusions. For example, actor-based studies of English speakers suggested that there are consistent cues that indicate a speaker is being sarcastic or ironic (dropping or lowered pitch, louder, slower speech, reduced pitch variability; Cheang and Pell, 2008), and listeners can discern the "dripping irony" that characterizes most acted portrayals as perceptually distinct from non-ironic speech when speakers intend to communicate the contrast between ironic and literal meanings (Bryant and Fox Tree, 2005). However, studies of spontaneously occurring irony and sarcasm showed that despite some acoustic differences (Rockwell, 2007), listeners cannot reliably distinguish dryly ironic utterances from nonironic utterances without the help of contextual cues. That is, spontaneously emitted ironic utterances presented in isolation were not well recognized as ironic, while "posed" versions, or those presented as citation forms, were (Rockwell, 2000). When sarcasm was identified, acoustic cues were slower tempo, higher intensity, and lowered pitch. In real life, rhetorical devices, such as implausible exaggeration, repetition or hyperbole, serve along with tone of voice as potent cues to irony (Kreuz and Roberts, 1995). Thus, although studies that depended on acting do reveal a consistent "ironic tone of voice" (which indicates that native speakers know these prosodic cues), studies of naturally occurring irony suggest that verbal context usually provides critical information in most cases. Other factors contribute in naturalistic settings, but knowledge

---

[11]   In *Bonfire of the Vanities*, the lawyer places an early morning phone call to Peter, who is impaired by a hangover, and quickly perceiving Peter's distress, states "Jeezus, Pete, *you* sound terrific." Italics on the first word denote a sarcastic meaning using written notation (Wolfe, 1987, p. 190).

"And now a correction: Portions of last night's story on diving mules which were read with an air of ironic detachment should actually have been presented with earnest concern."

Figure 8.15   The diving mules news report: The day after.

of the prosodic cues that signal these subtle meaning differences appears to be part of the native speaker's competence. Note that in a comparison of written and verbal ironic exemplars, irony was better discerned by listeners than readers (Bryant and Fox Tree, 2002). A similar perceptual disparity has been found for idiomatic versus literal meanings of ditropic sentences (those with this special ambiguity) such as "It broke the ice." When embedded in paragraphs read aloud with contextually generated literal or idiomatic interpretations, and then excised for a listening task, utterances carrying these disparate meanings were not distinguishable (Van Lancker and Canter, 1981). In a second study, when speakers were instructed to produce ditropic utterances with one or the other meaning intended, listeners performed extremely well on the discrimination task (Van Lancker, Canter, and Terbeek, 1981).

The sensitivity of listeners to ironic tone can lead to all kinds of consequences. Figure 8.15 depicts a cartoon that was inspired by an actual incident, reported on August 9, 2007, in an article entitled "High-Diving Mule Act Concerns Animal Activists" (San Antonio, Associated Press). Newscasters had reported a story about diving mules at a carnival, using a droll, amused tone while presenting, to them, a "fluff" piece of journalism. Animal rights activists were not amused, and complained that the style of presentation made fun of animal abuse. The next evening, the news station issued an apology – for the tone in which the story was reported.

The masterpiece of prosodic management appears in humor. It's often been said that joke telling is all in the timing, and, indeed, decelerations and accelerations belong intimately to the structure of verbal humor. Articulatory rate speeds up toward the end of a punch line. (This is one of the reasons that jokes are especially difficult to grasp in a second language). Using prosody, nuances and attitudes are manipulated by the stand-up comic as if on a high wire. Subtle changes in voice quality are of paramount effect in humor, but this is a woefully understudied topic, especially given the popularity of sitcoms, movies, late night television shows, comedy clubs, and internet material, not to mention humorous moments in daily interaction, a great source of pleasure (or pain) for us all. One exception to the dearth of scientific study of prosody in humor comes from a study analyzing speech from a well-known television sitcom, *Friends* (Purandare and Litman, 2006). Speech samples were selected immediately preceding artificial laughter (designated as "humorous") and compared with other ("nonhumorous") speech in various measures of tempo, pitch, and energy. Even when gender and speaker differences were taken into account, humorous turns were faster, and had higher F0 and energy peaks, ranges, and standard deviations than nonhumorous speech. These observations were supported by listeners' abilities to identify humorous segments from the acoustic-prosodic features.

8.7   Voice Identity

We have reviewed linguistic, pragmatic, and a bit about paralinguistic uses of prosody in speech, moving down the Pyramid. Nonverbal, nonlinguistic acoustic information across all the "levels" of language converges to form the auditory pattern representing individual voice identity so that finally, referring to again Figure 8.8, we come full circle to prosody's function in personal voice production, perception and recognition, a topic amply covered elsewhere in this book.

8.8   Summary and Relation to Other Chapters

There is a long history of interest in the melody of speech, especially in the past few decades, when there has been an explosion of books and articles on the subject. Despite the ever-increasing arsenal of research on this topic, the subtlety and complexity of linguistic prosody are such that a viewpoint prevails in the language sciences that only a native speaker of a language can validly assess intonational meanings in that language (Hirst and Di Cristo, 1998). Machine signal processors have yet to adequately recreate naturalistic intonation in synthetic speech systems, as anyone who has ever winced while listening to phone trees and recorded messages can attest. While enlightening descriptions of linguistic uses of prosody are available for portions of languages and specific types of speech samples, we are still a long way from understanding how to describe and model this intricate domain of human language.

In spoken discourse, prosody is always present (Wennerstrom, 2001). Voice quality functions throughout speech to signal a large range of linguistic expression, including phonological, grammatical, and pragmatic principles of communication. Phonemic contrasts are provided by phonetic uses of voice, and tones occur on syllables in some languages to carry word meanings. Word level pitch and accent patterns appear in numerous languages, yielding different meanings on strings of identical phonological segments. Intonational contours supply a variety of grammatical modes, certain fixed conceptual meanings, and stereotyped forms for idioms and formulaic expressions. However, intonation also functions as an autonomous signaling system (Selting, 1996a) arising from the intentions of the speaker (Bolinger, 1972b). Thus prosody interweaves both natural (determined by the speaker) and linguistically structured material (Wilson and Wharton, 2006).

The great challenge faced by prosodic analysts is to separate linguistic from paralinguistic meanings in intonation (Ladd, 1996). Speakers' intentions and attitudes within the social context of the talk, woven throughout the linguistic prosodic contour, are represented and delivered using kaleidoscopic nuances of voice quality. The attitudes and intentions communicated in a verbal utterance are at least as important as the words themselves and in some instances, they carry more weight (Pike, 1945), blending with "pure" linguistic meanings of prosody. We have seen that rising question intonation is rightly categorized as linguistic meaning, but question intonation on a higher-than-usual rising pitch adds tinges of surprise, bewilderment, or amazement to the question. Can it also be said, in this case, that the utterance is more of a question, or that the underlying proposition is being more intensely questioned? Speech scientists usually consider linguistic categories to be discrete, while paralinguistic meanings are graded. In this perspective, persons do not question more or less; instead, to describe the question uttered on higher rising intonation signaling attitudinal meanings, the descriptive apparatus of paralanguage is employed. In this way, attitudes, emotions, and personality variables intertwine in the paralinguistic domain of the speech signal. These topics will be discussed in the next chapter.

9

Perception of Emotion and Personality from Voice

Emotions vary so much in a number of dimensions – transparency, intensity, behavioral expression, object-directedness, and susceptibility to rational assessment, as to cast doubt on the assumption that they have anything in common.[1]

9.1   Introduction

Some of the earliest research on voice focuses on how humans express and perceive emotion in their voices. The term προσῳδία (prosōidía) appears in Plato's *Republic* in discussions of the emotional correlates of different musical modes and how the modes are imitative of speech. The study of vocal emotion was taken up by the Romans, who were concerned with the role that emotion played in oratory, and in particular with its importance for eliciting emotions in others, enhancing persuasiveness. Other writers were concerned with the expression of emotion in and of itself, for the window it provided into the speaker's soul (see e.g. Caelen-Haumont and Pollerman, 2008, for extended review). Such views persisted into the enlightenment; for example, in 1823/1859, James Rush wrote, "The voice is the principle organ of the soul; it is that by which the mind first and immediately pours forth its thots." Voice teachers and pedagogues assisted in developing the field of emotional expression as part of elocution, with the aim of improving skills for performance and debate. These efforts included notions of how an educated person should communicate emotion. For example, Professor Robert Kidd, instructor of elocution at the Princeton Theological Seminary, described how to articulate emotions such as anger (by a strong, vehement, and elevated voice) and joy (by a quick, sweet, and clear voice) (Kidd, 1857, p. 71), echoing the same phrases used by Alden in his earlier instructional manual "The Reader" (1802, p. 13).

---

[1]   http://plato.stanford.edu/entries/emotion/; accessed November 5, 2009.

Foundations of Voice Studies: An Interdisciplinary Approach to Voice Production and Perception,
First Edition. Jody Kreiman and Diana Sidtis.
© 2013 Jody Kreiman and Diana Sidtis. Published 2013 by Blackwell Publishing Ltd.

Modern scientific studies of voice and emotion began with the publication of Darwin's book *The Expression of Emotions in Man and Animals* (1872a). Darwin claimed that voice serves as the main carrier of affective signals, and that there is a direct correspondence between particular states in the talker and the sounds produced, in part because of "direct action of the excited nervous system on the body, independently of the will, and independently, in large part, of habit" (p. 348). In this view, emotion is related largely to physiological arousal, reflected for example by the contrast between anger and depression. Because emotion is a product of a physiological state, Darwin viewed emotional displays as honest indicators of an animal's internal state that allow other animals to make quick inferences about its probable intentions and behavior.

In this chapter, we will describe what is known about how speakers express various shades of emotion, how listeners attribute emotions to speakers, and how emotion interacts with the spoken semantic message. We will argue that verbal expressions of emotion in humans may in fact share some features with those of animals, but that significant elaborations in cognitive processes differentiate humans from other animals in the manner in which emotion is expressed and perceived.

9.2   Interactions Between What is Said and How it is Said

We begin by considering the relationship between the words that are spoken and the emotional tone that carries the spoken message. In some traditions, linguists view their object of study as consisting of two disparate entities: language and speech[2] (French: *langue et parole*), where language is the abstract system of grammar, and speech is the vocal-motor performance. When considering emotional information in verbal communication, language and speech have their place under the sun in very different ways. Language has a more intimate relationship with thought than with emotion. Some people hold that language and thought are fully co-dependent or even coterminous; the extreme view is that one cannot harbor language without thought and human thought cannot exist without human language. In contrast, the relationship of language to emotion is tenuous. Emotional information is expressed very little through phonology, morphology, and syntax, and depends almost exclusively on semantics and lexical choice (Van Lancker Sidtis, 2008). Viewed from the perch that overlooks language structure, it is clear that we tell each other how we feel, sometimes directly as in "I feel horrible," sometimes indirectly as in "I had a horrible day," using the lexicon. But to account for the fullness of emotional communication, one must move to speech, where voice and prosody carry the day. Processing in the brain follows this rough dichotomy, as language and thought are more cortically than subcortically represented, while speech and emotion are alike in partaking relatively more richly of subcortical nuclei.

---

[2]   German uses one word for language and speech: "die Sprache." The term "die Redeweise" is better translated as *mode of speaking* and "die Motorik" refers to motor processes in general. One possibility for speech is "Das Sprechen," referring to the process of speaking.

Figure 9.1 From Loriot, "Scenes from a Marriage," Act 2.

Recent work has examined the manner in which verbal and emotional messages interact in spoken communication. Beyond the relatively simple messages conveyed by most animal emotional displays, the emotional tone of an utterance has a direct impact on the manner in which a listener processes spoken words. For example, Nygaard and Queen (2008) found that listeners were able to repeat happy or sad words like "comedy" or "cancer" more quickly when the words were spoken in a tone of voice that matched the word, and more slowly when the emotional tone of voice differed from the word's affective meaning. This study and others like it (e.g., Mullennix, Bihon, Bricklemyer, Gaston, and Keener, 2002) suggest that there is an emotion-specific effect of tone of voice on the cognitive processing of spoken words. Studies of electrical brain potentials leading to the same conclusion are reviewed by Schirmer and Simpson (2008).

Such studies also support the idea that listeners normally expect semantic and intonational meanings to be concordant (see Sidebar on the Gricean maxims in section 6.5). We notice when inconsistencies (which are the basis of verbal irony and sarcasm) occur, and often these incidents incite perplexity, fear, or humor (see sidebar "The Visitors"). In a scene by the German humorist, Loriot, a wife repeatedly recommends activities, such as a taking a walk or reading, to her husband, who replies each time that he wishes only to sit quietly. After (exactly) 33 quiet and patient responses from the husband, the wife says, "Why are you yelling at me?" The husband answers in a loud, screaming voice: "I'm not yelling at you!" (*Ich schreie dich nicht an!*; see Figure 9.1). This is a point of high humor in the sketch, precisely because of the incongruity embedded in the utterance: screaming to explicitly deny screaming.

Some authors (e.g., Milmoe, Rosenthal, Blane, Chafetz, and Wolf, 1967; Vargas, 1986; both cited by Graham, Hamblin, and Feldstein, 2001) have claimed that

Sidebar: "The Visitors"

Unwilling host:	Go on get out.
	All of you
	Go on.
	Get out, get out, get out!
Unwanted visitor:	I beg your pardon.
Unwilling host:	I'm turning you all out!
	I'm not having my house filled with filthy perverts!
	Now look! I'm giving you just a half a minute and then I'm going to call the police.
	So get out!
Unwanted visitor:	I don't much like the tone of your voice.

–Monty Python's Flying Circus, season 1, episode 9.

normal adults usually believe the tone of voice rather than the words (consistent with this example). Experimental studies suggest that the extent to which this is true depends on how large the discrepancy is between the emotional and the linguistic meaning and how context is guiding the listener's perceptions. For example, the contrast in "I feel just fine" spoken on a tense, tentative tone might be politely ignored, while, "I'm not angry" spoken in "hot anger" would not. Extreme discrepancies between the semantics and the emotional prosody stand out as anomalous, and may elicit a smile in experimental settings as they do in humorous skits (Vingerhoets, Berckmoes, and Stroobant, 2003). In the Vingerhoets *et al.* (2003) study, when listeners were asked to attend selectively to the emotional or the semantic channel, more errors were made on incongruent stimuli, and more errors were made on identification of emotional prosody when the semantics were neutral (86.6% correct) than on the semantics when the prosody was neutral (93.5% correct). Similarly, more prosodic errors occurred on discordant semantic information (83.7% correct) than the other way around (88.4% correct). Normative data from *The Florida Affect Battery*, which contains a subset of incongruent sentences, are also consistent with this finding (Bowers, Coslett, Bauer, Speedie, and Heilman, 1987). In half of the trials for which semantic content and prosody conflict (for example, "All the puppies are dead" said in a happy tone of voice), performance declines steeply as a function of age and brain damage in comparison to other prosodic tasks, suggesting a role of task demands or other factors (Figure 9.2). Subjects also have difficulty producing incongruent stimuli using neutral prosody and project an emotional facial expression to accomplish the task (Mehrabian, 2007).

Thus, although emotional-prosodic information is in the background of the communicative act, and the linguistic information is in the foreground, these studies show how important an understanding of the expression and perception of vocal emotion

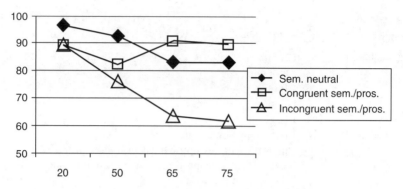

Figure 9.2   Performance by age on naming emotional intonation on semantically neutral, congruent and incongruent sentences.

is for theories of speech performance. Emotional meanings, broadly considered, are an important part of what we express when we speak, as evidenced by the painful conversational lapses that can occur when a listener misperceives the speaker's emotional state; and emotional content affects the manner in which listeners process the semantic message.

9.3   Brain Function Underlying Emotions and Emotional Nuances in Speech

We continue by reviewing brain function and structure underlying the experience and communication of emotion, mood, affect, feelings and attitude. (A more thorough overview of the neurology of vocal production and perception is offered in Chapter 3.) The limbic system (Figure 9.3; first described by Papez in 1937) plays a prominent role in emotional processing. Some people object to the term "limbic system,"[3] because the concept actually refers to a number of loosely connected structures and portions of structures with varied functions in memory, emotion, motivation, attention, and mood, and agreement about membership in the limbic system is not universal (LeDoux, 2000). This assemblage of nuclei is found beneath the neocortical mantel. The hippocampus, which is dedicated to establishing memory, is included, and it is easy to see how memory and emotion are tightly linked in mental life.[4] Other structures, such as the dentate gyrus, fornix, and mammilothalamic tract, have multiple functions, which include memory and mood. The parahippocampal gyrus (grey matter surrounding the hippocampus) establishes visual information and modulates mood, among other subtler contributions. The rhinencephalon, or olfactory system, evolutionarily among the oldest of the limbic

---

[3]   Also called the rhinencephalon (literally "smell-brain"), limbic lobe or, in French, *le grand lobe limbique*.

[4]   Emotional difficulties have been associated with deeply stored memories (Freud, 1938).

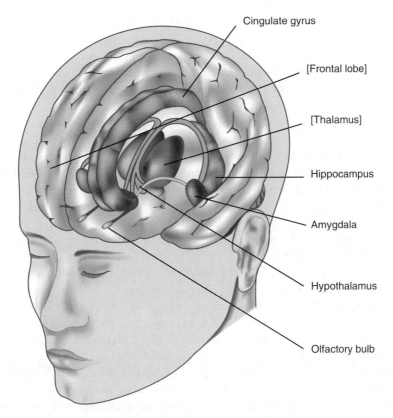

Cingulate gyrus

[Frontal lobe]

[Thalamus]

Hippocampus

Amygdala

Hypothalamus

Olfactory bulb

Figure 9.3　The limbic system, along with frontal lobe and thalamus.

structures, is included in this mix.[5] Encircling all the limbic structures are the cingulate gyri, a paleocortical ring (older cortex, in contrast to neocortex, or later evolving cortical neurons), which functions broadly in control, formation and processing of emotion, memory, and attentional responses. Some neuropsychologists include as features of the limbic system the orbito-frontal cortex and its connections to subcortical nuclei, and others highlight thalamic nuclei, which coordinate between many structures (Damasio, 1994). A key piece of the memory-mood-emotion regime is the amygdala, a structure about the size of an almond, after which it is named. The amygdala, with numerous connections to other limbic and subcortical structures, inhibits, facilitates and reflects internal and external environmental conditions related to emotion, attention and memory (Adolphs and Tranel, 1999; LeDoux, 2000), selecting from different kinds of input and functioning as a "relevance detector" (Sander, Grafman, and Zalla, 2003).

The experience and expression of emotion also depend on the subcortical motor structures or basal ganglia,[6] whose primary function is motor execution (Heilman and

[5]　The intimate relationship of the olfactory structures to the limbic system may account for the large role that disgust plays in emotion research.

[6]　Basal ganglia include the caudate nucleus (head and tail), putamen, globus pallidus, nucleus accumbens, subthalamic nucleus, and substantia nigra.

Gilmore, 1998). The limbic structures lie contiguous to and in close interconnection with the subcortical motor structures responsible for speech, rather like bedfellows, as an integrated interleaving of oddly shaped parts in an elaborate appliance. Emotions and motor speech alike emerge from the intricate interplay of these structures. It is little wonder, therefore, that nearly every verbal utterance is tinged with attitudinal and emotional nuance. As Scherer, Johnstone, and Klasmeyer (2003) state, "… we generally express emotion when we produce speech. Linguistic and expressive cues are intimately intertwined" (p. 446). Our recognition of emotional meanings is quick and independent of who is talking, according to studies using event-related potentials to track brain responses to emotional speech (Paulmann and Kotz, 2008a, b). Subjects differentiated emotional utterances from neutral ones spoken by male or female voices within 200 ms, faster than matching the vocal identity of the signal, especially when primed by the same vocal emotion (Spreckelmeyer, Kutas, Urbach, Altenmüller, and Müntee, 2009).

Primary evidence for the role of the basal ganglia in processing of mood, psychological state, and motivation comes from studies of persons with brain damage (Santamaria and Tolosa, 1992; Poncet and Habib, 1994; Masterman and Cummings, 1997; Heilman and Gilmore, 1998). Neurologists have linked the basal ganglia to establishing and selecting emotional responses in production (Ali Cherif *et al.*, 1984; Saint-Cyr, Taylor, and Nicholson, 1995), and these processes are manifest in speech patterns (Mendez, Adams, and Lewandowski, 1989). Hemispheric damage without subcortical involvement is less likely to yield prosodic deficits (Cancelliere and Kertesz, 1990; Karow, Marquardt, and Marshall, 2001). Caplan *et al.* (1990) describe motivational deficits (abulia) following damage to the caudate nucleus, with clinical signs including emotionally flat verbal responses with normal intellectual content. Production of expletives with appropriate vocal prosody is preserved in most cases of left hemisphere damage, implicating intact subcortical structures, and is hyperactivated in Tourette's syndrome, believed to be due to subcortical dysfunction (Van Lancker and Cummings, 1999). Bhatia and Marsden (1994) analyzed 240 patients with focal basal ganglia lesions of vascular etiology, and found loss of vocal emotional expression to be common following damage to the caudate nucleus, globus pallidus, or putamen (Fisher, 1983; Tranel, 1992). In spontaneous speech, prosodic features track the neurobehavioral state. Thus the limbic system, interfaced with the basal ganglia, exercises a mighty influence on the expression of emotion by means of vocal prosody.

Higher-level control of motor speech, including planning and retrieval of words, phrases, and intonation contours, is represented in cortical layers located on the cerebral hemispheres. It is from here that the cognitive component of emotion – the post-physical appraisal phase – originates. How much each hemisphere contributes to vocal emotional processing remains a vigorous controversy even in perception (Baum and Pell, 1997; Wong, 2002), for which studies are far more plentiful. For perception of affective meanings in speech prosody, dichotic listening results (see Sidebar in Chapter 3) and results from lesion studies consistently implicate right hemisphere specialization (i.e., a left ear advantage) for processing emotional meanings and left hemisphere representation for matched linguistic stimuli (Safer and Leventhal, 1977; Ley and Bryden, 1982; Voyer, Bowes, and Soraggi, 2008). However, earlier claims from lesion studies of an exclusive right hemisphere role in perception of affective meanings have failed to replicate or have given way to other explanations of the results

(Heilman, Scholes, and Watson, 1975; Van Lancker and Sidtis, 1992). Functional imaging studies of the ability to judge or discriminate emotional stimuli present ambiguous results about cerebral function, with some authors reporting right-sided activation (George *et al.*, 1996; Beaucousin *et al.*, 2007; Wiethoff *et al.*, 2008), others emphasizing bilateral activation in cortical areas (Imaizumi *et al.*, 1997; Wildgruber, Pihan, Ackermann, Erb, and Grodd, 2002; Gandour *et al.*, 2003; Kotz *et al.*, 2003; Mitchell, Elliott, Barry, Cruttenden, and Woodruff, 2003; Wildgruber *et al.*, 2004), and many reporting bilateral activation from some analyses and right-sided from others (Adolphs, Damasio, and Tranel, 2002). For example, using fMRI, Buchanan *et al.* (2000) reported bilateral and right temporal activation during the detection of angry, happy, sad, or neutral emotional tone on words. Passive listening to adjectives and nouns rated as emotionally neutral and low-arousal in the semantic channel, but produced with neutral, happy, erotic, angry, fearful, sad, or disgusted intonation, resulted in stronger responses in the superior temporal gyrus of the right hemisphere (Wiethoff *et al.*, 2008). A study utilizing components of the EEG that directly measure cortical activation (Pihan, 2006) suggested that the right hemisphere has a relatively predominant role in processing emotions expressed in the voice, combined with a clear complementary role for the left hemisphere. Laterality for emotional perception was not observed in a subsequent study when DC potentials were recorded over nine specific cortical regions (Pihan, Tabertd, Assuras, and Borod, 2007). Further analyses of activation sites by Imaizumi *et al.* (1997) pointed to different cerebral sites for speaker identification and recognition of emotional intonation.

Additional requirements for various levels of processing of these stimuli add to the confusion. For example, top-down effects for linguistically or affectively oriented attention may require involvement of the left hemisphere, as may temporal cues mediating performance. More recent functional imaging studies suggest posterior neural networks in both the left and right hemisphere which monitor task-dependent features of linguistic (or emotive) pitch effects, with major involvement of subcortical nuclei in normal discrimination and the recognition of emotional stimuli (Kotz *et al.*, 2003). Note that the contribution of subcortical systems is likely underestimated in functional imaging studies, because subcortical activation is more difficult to observe using these techniques and these areas are less often analyzed, as discussed in Chapter 6. Using fMRI scanning techniques, studies by Dietrich and her colleagues revealed bilateral temporal and subcortical activation in subjects listening passively to affective-prosodic, nonverbal interjections (Dietrich, Hertrich, Alter, Ischebeck, and Ackermann, 2008) (see Sidebar).

The most accommodating model of emotional-prosodic perception posits a bilateral temporofrontal network with subcortical involvement (Berckmoes and Vingerhoets, 2004). How much each hemisphere contributes depends a great deal on the emotional speech task (Tompkins and Flowers, 1985; Bowers *et al.*, 1987). In a study carefully controlling tasks and lesion information, no significant differences were seen between left- and right-brain-damaged groups in emotional intonation discrimination, recognition on nonsense utterances, and recognition on sentences with emotional words, although both groups performed significantly differently from normal control subjects (Pell, 2006). A later study (Pell, 2007) reported right hemisphere sensitivity to attitudinal information in speech, as represented in stimuli communicating politeness and confidence, although the results suggested that the deficits may have related to broader deficiencies in evaluating contextual information.

For emotional prosodic production, lesion studies are even more inconclusive as regards hemispheric dominance (Pell and Baum, 1997a, b). A careful study of patients with brain lesions by Cancelliere and Kertesz (1990) found that deficient production of vocal emotional meanings (in formal testing) occurred significantly more often only in association with subcortical damage, and not with damage exclusively to either cortical hemisphere. These findings agree with an early paper by Kent and Rosenbek (1982) proposing that several cerebral sites may contribute to prosodic production, including left and right cortical sites and subcortical nuclei. This perspective has been elaborated in a review article leading to a model of cerebral processing of prosody (Sidtis and Van Lancker Sidtis, 2003), outlining the conditions under which cortical and subcortical systems modulate emotional-prosodic information in speech.

In summary, the bulk of lesion and functional imaging evidence suggests that both hemispheres, as well as subcortical nuclei, contribute significantly to emotional functioning in perception and production. Vocal prosodic production in humans is mediated in large part through subcortical structures, including the limbic system and basal ganglia nuclei, following commands from left and right cortical mechanisms, allocating control of F0 to the right and control of timing to the left hemisphere. As far as can be understood, comprehension of emotional-prosodic meanings relies on this same extensive system, in the contingent ways we have outlined. In its cerebral extensiveness, the human system differs from that observed in our nonhuman animal counterparts, in which vocalizing behaviors appear to involve primarily subcortical and limbic nuclei (Jürgens, 1979, 1982; Ploog, 1979; Simonyan and Jürgens, 2003).

Sidebar: Interjections

Interjections belong to vocal communication and are defined as "an exclamation expressing emotion,"[7] "words that show emotion … not grammatically related to the rest of the sentence"[8] and "short verbal emotional utterances" (Dietrich, Ackermann, Szameitat, and Alter, 2006). An obvious matter of interest is how these verbal utterances relate to purely nonverbal cries, moans, and sighs. In part addressing this question, German emotional interjections were recorded and separated into those with high lexical content (for which both propositional and prosodic cues are important) and those with low lexical content (depending mainly on prosodic information). The latter stand closer to nonverbal expressions of emotion. Listeners' ratings of these expressions spoken with neutral and with expressive prosody indicated that the conventional lexical and the prosodic information both contribute to conveying meaning, but that the prosodic material is probably more salient. (See Section 9.8 for indications that some of these vocalizations have biological bases, as shown in cross-cultural studies).

---

[7]   Microsoft Office Word Dictionary.
[8]   www.english-grammar-revolution.com/list-of-interjections.html; (under "A," the Grammar site lists "aha, ahem, ahh, ahoy, alas, arrggg, aw" as examples).

Given the complexity of these systems in humans, it is possible to identify various sources of deficient emotional expression in speech. Defects in naturally occurring verbal expression of emotion ("dysprosody"), associated with flat speech, may arise from mood or motivational changes associated with impaired basal ganglia or limbic structures, cognitive-programming failure deriving from cortical deficits, or motor dysfunction arising from deficient modulation of F0, intensity, or timing in speech. Similarly, difficulties in recognizing emotional speech may be attributable to several factors, including dysfunctional subcortical and limbic nuclei, or damage to right or left hemisphere mechanisms, leading to faulty pitch or timing analysis in auditory receiving areas and/or to impaired comprehension of verbal-emotional content. Further, somatic and neurochemical influences, which are beyond the scope of this review, pervade these systems. Most modern authors agree that complex alliances between structures in the brain and chemistry in the body, interacting with culture and environment, account for mental phenomena, in which emotion and cognition form a blended mixture. As we will see when acoustic cues for emotional utterances are reviewed below, fundamental frequency manifesting in all its many configurations heads the list of important cues for emotional meanings, which perhaps accounts for many reports of the effects of right hemisphere damage on production and perception of emotional prosody as determined in formal testing using actor generated stimuli.[9] Yet a large array of other acoustic parameters – intensity, timing elements, voice quality – collaborate in various weightings and combinations to convey emotional meaning in speech.

9.4 The Nature and Function of Emotions

Another issue in the study of vocal emotion is the difficulty inherent in defining emotion in general, in specifying what emotions exist, and in distinguishing different emotions. These are important issues because they affect the manner in which investigators approach the study of emotion – what they choose to study, how they determine what their subjects feel or hear, what they measure, how they relate their findings to behavior or physiology, and so on.

Difficulties emerge at the onset of such inquiries due to differences among investigators in distinctions among such concepts as emotion, affect, mood, and feeling, independent of questions about what emotions (or feelings, or moods) there are. One perspective is that emotion and feeling refer to a physiological quality, affect is subjective and conscious, and mood is the longer-lasting subjective state (Ketai, 1975). Many other definitions have also been proposed. In typical voice research usage, emotions are "brief and intense reactions to goal-relevant changes in the environment" (Laukka, 2008). Benson (1994) defines "mood" as a basic aspect of emotion, calling it a "relatively pervasive but often impersistent internal disposition" (p. 101). Affect, in Benson's system, "represents the observable physical manifestations of emotion" (p. 101). Behavioral neurologists classify emotions into two major

---

[9] Convergent observations indicate a superiority of the right hemisphere in processing pitch patterns; see Chapter 3.

divisions: experience and behavior (Heilman and Gilmore, 1998). Affect has been defined as direct knowledge-by-acquaintance of feelings and desires derived from neurochemical systems (LeDoux, 1994; Buck, 2000). In another perspective, Rolls (1995) defines emotions as states that are produced by positive or negative reinforcing stimuli. For Rolls, subcortical structures, crucial to emotions, process reinforcement and select competing responses. As Izard (1977) stated, "a complete definition of emotion must take into account … the experience or conscious feeling of emotion … the processes that occur in the brain and nervous system and the observable expressive patterns of emotion" (p. 4).

In this chapter, as we attempt to discuss the manifestation of emotional meanings in voice, the cover term "emotion" is meant to encompass all of these subcategories, and we employ the term "emotion" to refer broadly to any awake, internalized state that is not strictly identified as "thinking" or "cognition." It is important to remember that both mood and affect are routinely revealed in speech prosody in natural speech. The fact that these may be discordant at any given time reflects the complexity of vocal signaling. In this presentation, we go even further in exploring the untamed vagaries of attitudinal stance as well, mainly because, as we shall see below, attitude is more prevalent in speech than emotion and there is no clear line between attitudes and emotions.

9.4.1   Why express emotions?

Authors have also speculated widely about the reasons for the existence of emotions, and why animals (including humans) would express them in the first place. Many functions for emotions have been suggested: Emotions may direct attention to significant events, reflect the relevance and significance of the event to an individual, signal whether or not the event is a good thing or a bad thing, prepare the individual to act physically and/or psychologically, and/or inform both the individual and other individuals about its internal state and readiness to act (Scherer, 1981; Tatham and Morton, 2004). These complex functions involve cognitive appraisal, subjective feeling, physiological arousal, action tendency, and regulation (Laukka, 2008).

There is also much speculation regarding the reasons why animals communicate vocally about emotion. Such speculation is complicated by the difficulty of determining the meaning of animal vocalizations in the first place: Semantic, social, and emotional information are convolved in the calls of many species (Rendall, Owren, and Ryan, 2009), which may also be playful and pleasurable, and/or usefully release tension. When vocalization occurs as adjunctive behavior to breathing, its cost (measurable as the rate of oxygen consumption) is negligible. For example, there is low physiological cost to humans in normal speaking, as the source of energy for speech belongs to resting metabolism (Fitch, 2004b). For canaries, singing rather than sitting quietly on the perch raises the metabolic rate only slightly (Ward, Speakman, and Slater, 2003). In other cases (for example, when animals make "advertisement calls"), vocalizations are expensive in terms of physical energy. Intense calling by the Gray Treefrog, for example, can draw seven times as much oxygen as that utilized at rest during the daytime (Bucher, Ryan, and Bartholomew, 1982). Vocalization also bears the additional cost of drawing the attention of predators. Such costs suggest that benefits to callers must also be potentially significant, or emotional displays would not have evolved so universally.

Snowdon (2003) has suggested three general benefits of emotional vocalizations in animals. First, communicating feelings (particularly negative feelings) may allow other animals to anticipate behaviors (particularly attacks) so that they can avoid the caller; or benefits to the caller may be more direct (for example, angry vocal displays may make the animal sound larger than it is, so that others will avoid it); or animals may use emotional vocalizations to manage others, but also monitor others' calls to gather information about their intentions. Bachorowski and Owren (2003) have also proposed an "affect induction" account of vocalized emotion, in part because none of these explanations is consistent with all of the data on production and perception of emotion (as we will describe below; see also Snowdon, 2003, for review). They argue that the function of emotion in speech is not to inform listeners that the speaker is feeling something specific, because this kind of information is useful only if the information modulates listeners' behavior in ways that benefit the speaker. From this perspective, emotional signals exploit listener sensitivities to influence the emotional systems of the listeners, thus influencing listeners to behave in beneficial ways toward the speakers.[10]

9.4.2 Where do emotions come from?

Given the complexity of emotional experience, it should not be surprising that different views of the origins of emotion have emerged. An early controversy arose from the James–Lange theory, which described experienced emotion as a response to bodily sensations. According to William James (1884), we do not cry because we feel sorry, but we feel sorry because we cry. This was largely replaced by a modified version called the Cannon–Bard theory (Cannon, 1927), whereby limbic and subcortical nuclei send information simultaneously to the cerebral cortex and the autonomic system evoking two parallel reactions, the physiological excitement and the awareness of the emotion. These views have reappeared over the years in various guises. In psychology, a long debate about whether emotion and cognition are independent or commingled, and which of the two is the more "fundamental" in human consciousness, has taken many turns. Two prominent positions were exemplified by Zajonc (1984), who maintained that affect occurs before and independently of cognition, while Lazarus (1984) stated that emotion can't happen without "cognitive appraisal." Part of the disagreement hinged on the particular definition of "cognition," which for Zajonc signified something like "mental work," while for Lazarus cognition entailed primarily "primitive evaluative perception" (Buck, 2000). Both viewpoints may be right, depending on the time frame being considered in the emotional responses (LeDoux, 1994). These debates were more recently

---

[10] Note that extensive studies of vervet monkeys in the field do not conclusively indicate that that monkeys have self-awareness or that they attribute mental states to others (Cheney and Seyfarth, 1990), suggesting that these effects cannot occur consciously.

synthesized by Damasio (1994), who presents an argument from clinical observations in patients with brain damage that emotion plays a central role in human rationality (see also LeDoux, 1996, who provides the foundation to describe human minds as both cognitive and emotional.)

In speech research, Tatham and Morton (2004) review three different possible sources of emotion: physiological effects, cognitive responses to stimuli, and "bio-psychological" factors, which meld the two types of source. These views have been upgraded to accommodate current interests in the role of evolution in development of such competences. Descriptions based on physiological factors state that emotions derive from systems that evolved to deal with biologically significant events, emphasizing the James–Lang view. Such reactions include basic states like fear, rage, panic, distress, isolation/loneliness, and so on. In this view, emotionally conditioned changes in voice happen when the talker's affect causes changes in the voice production process, so that every unique emotion should have a specific pattern of acoustic cues (Cowie and Cornelius, 2003; Scherer, 2003). For example, arousal emotions (often associated with "fight or flight" reactions) are associated with dry mouth, changes in respiration, tension, and/or tremors, all of which are part of voice production. Because of their biological basis, in this view emotion should be expressed and perceived in similar ways by all humans (and possibly non-human animals as well).

Cognitive approaches to emotion state that, while emotions may start out as simple biologically based reactions to stimuli, what an animal feels is ultimately more dependent on additional factors like experience, memory of previous stimuli, and cognitive processing than it is on physiological response; this is the modernized version of the Cannon–Bard theory. In this elaborated view, emotions are cultural products that owe much of their meaning and expression to social rules, so no fixed set of emotions exists, and the expression and perception of emotion should vary from culture to culture.

9.4.3   How many emotions are there?

The first step in designing a study of the expression or perception of vocal emotion is usually to decide what emotions there are, when they can be expected to occur, and/or which ones you want to study. Because of the amorphous nature of this topic and the different approaches to its study, labeling and classification systems for emotions are not neatly in place, and an entirely satisfactory general-purpose classification may be unobtainable, in part because of the uneasy boundary that exists between emotions and other loosely defined categories, such as attitude (defiance, indifference), feelings (nervousness, fear) and mood (depression, elation) (See Sidebar on Emotions and Attitudes). Investigators have used a range of emotive words (happy, angry, sad) to describe the emotional content of speech. In some cases, terms are chosen based on a theory of emotion (e.g., Scherer, 1986); in others, an empirical approach like factor analysis (Huttar, 1968) or multidimensional scaling (Green and Cliff, 1975) is applied to sort out the emotional structure of the stimuli, and to relate this structure to voice samples. In other cases, however, no particular basis is apparent for the investigator's choices.

Sidebar: Emotions and Attitudes

Both lay and scientific opinion acknowledge a distinction between two kinds of signaling in speech, emotional and attitudinal expression. When someone says "I don't like your attitude," they are referring in large part to vocal tones that give color to the expression and have an impact on the communication. Typical examples are impudence, defiance, sarcasm, and the like. It is possible to say "I like your attitude," referring to a signal in the voice of pleasantness, cooperativeness, or optimism. In contrast, take the classic emotions, sadness, fear and anger: It is inappropriate to say, "I don't like your emotion," perhaps because we consider that attitudes are chosen in the moment and can be adjusted, but emotions are involuntary and cannot. Further, attitudes are toward something: toward oneself, one's conversation partner, or toward the topic at hand. Emotions are about something. Most can agree on this simplistic level of distinction between attitudes and emotions. Yet these phenomena are not, and probably cannot be, reliably or obviously differentiated.

How do we classify human expressions of surprise, contempt, bewilderment, doubt, disgust, indifference, defiance, and so on? The fullest study of attitudes was performed by Osgood and colleagues, who used bipolar ratings of adjectives to develop the "semantic differential," which consisted of three dimensions: evaluation, potency, and activity (Osgood, Suci, and Tannenbaum, 1957). Positions on these three dimensions permitted depiction of attitudinal positioning in response to any topic, person, subject or word. Studies of vocal "emotional" expression in humans typically include a mix of emotions and attitudes. In contrast, studies of vocal expression in nonhuman animals focus exclusively on a few classic emotions (fear, rage). This discrepancy might suggest that we exercise caution in drawing comparisons between vocal behaviors in nonhuman animals and humans. Of course, pet owners anecdotally discern a broad range of "attitudes" in their animal companions, including hope, defiance, regret, embarrassment, and compliance. Science is a very long way from studying these behavioral stances in animals. As for human speech, it is difficult to conceive of an utterance that does not convey at least a bit of attitude and nuances of feeling, while fewer in everyday discourse communicate the classic "Big 6" emotions (Cowie *et al.*, 1999; see below). We note that most laboratory studies have used posed, actor-generated stimulus representing a small set of emotional meanings, and therefore are probing stereotypes of emotional prosody.

In part, the difficulty of selecting emotional material to study derives from the size of the available vocabulary. There are hundreds of English words for emotional and attitudinal states. A compilation of "feeling, attitude, emotion and heart words" accumulated at an internet site has grown to 1,200 words.[11] Although word lists vary from author to author, more conservative estimates range from 107 to 558 words with

---

[11] http://www.selfcraft.net/writeyourself/Thewords.htm; accessed November 5, 2009.

"emotional connotations," at least 60 of which are distinct enough to merit study (Cowie and Cornelius, 2003). As daunting as the study of 60 distinct emotions might be, even this large a sample may be too small to include the distinctions that humans make and think are important. For example, many people distinguish multiple kinds of anger (hot anger or fury, cold anger, suppressed anger, frustration anger, self-righteousness, pouting, hostility, passive-aggression...) and many kinds of love (passionate, motherly, worshipful, platonic, obsessive, and so on), and these may be characterized by rather different acoustic cues (Frick, 1986). To stir the pot of emotional words even further, researchers warmly disagree on whether to include "neutral" in the set of emotional stimuli; some even claim that "neutral" is an emotion. It is unclear how researchers could gather data on so many different states, how to chose the stimuli to apply, or how the small number of cues that are usually studied can represent so many seemingly distinct phenomena, leaving emotion researchers in a bit of a quandary.

One common tactic adopted in response to the overwhelming diversity of emotional states is to limit the selection to a set of "basic emotions." This set varies somewhat from study to study, but usually includes some subset of the so-called "Big 6" emotions (fear, anger, happiness, sadness, surprise, and disgust), sometimes supplemented with hot versus cold anger, contempt, love, and/or desire. It is easy to see how phenomenologically different these six are: fear and anger have possible animal counterparts; happiness features a subtler hue; surprise may be said to arise from psychological set (*Einstellung*) and attentional mechanisms rather than emotion, and disgust ranges from a primative response to one relying on cognitive judgment. However, despite these limitations, the "basic" emotions are usually viewed as biologically-based in some way.[12] For example, Juslin and Laukka (2003) describe them as "fast and frugal algorithms" (p. 771) that let organisms quickly evaluate and respond to a situation when they have limited information or limited time to act (see e.g. Laukka, 2003, for review). This view is consistent with evidence (reviewed in Section 9.6.1 below, and by Juslin and Laukka, 2003) linking some emotional states to physiological changes (for example, those associated with fear).

In an alternative approach, investigators do not try to specify or distinguish the emotions under study. Instead, investigators study the level of undifferentiated emotional response, sometimes calling this "arousal" (or "activation," or "stress;" e.g., Williams and Stevens, 1972; Scherer, 1986). In this approach, arousal is assumed to produce involuntary physiological responses, by virtue of which it should produce predictable and detectable changes in speech production (so, for example, F0 tends to increase with muscle tension as activation/arousal increases). These studies then relate continuously changing levels of arousal to changes in some acoustic variable or variables. Patterns of change in F0 appear in some studies to be better explained by activity or degree across emotions than by the particular emotion under study, consistent with this view (Banse and Scherer, 1996; Bänziger and Scherer, 2005). This approach is particularly apparent in studies of vocal stress and lying, which we review in Section 9.9.

---

[12] Although some authors consider them to be semantically basic or prototypical instead, so that they represent the best or most typical example of a relatively large clusters of loosely related terms (Mervis and Rosch, 1981).

This basic approach can be generalized to create dimensional models of emotion, in contrast to the categorical models described above. Dimensional approaches allow investigators to avoid the use of specific vocabulary for emotions, while retaining the option of placing specific emotions within the space formed by these dimensions if desired. They are also consistent with the graded and noncategorical nature of emotional information in speech (in contrast to categorical grammatical information; see Chapter 8). Evidence exists (reviewed by Laukka, Juslin, and Bresin, 2005) for four or more dimensions: arousal, valence (from positive to negative), potency (ability to cope), and intensity (e.g., slightly angry, extremely angry).

A few studies have used voice synthesis to examine the categorical versus dimensional nature of perceived emotion directly. These have had variable results. Laukka (2003, 2005) recorded an actress producing "prototypical" utterances for fear, anger, sadness, and happiness, and then manipulated F0, intensity, amounts of spectral energy above and below 500 Hz, F1, and pause duration to create six continua in which emotion gradually morphed from the values appropriate for one emotion into those for another (anger–fear, anger–sadness, fear–happiness, fear–sadness, happiness–anger, and happiness–sadness). Listeners were asked to discriminate among stimuli on the continuum. Results showed a clear crossover point for each continuum, such that stimuli that fell on one side of that point on the continuum were nearly always perceived as expressing one emotion, and stimuli on the other side as expressing the other, and discrimination was better across category boundaries than within categories (although discrimination within categories was above chance levels). Consistent with usual practice in the perceptual literature, these results were interpreted as supporting categorical rather than dimensional models of emotion. In contrast, Kakehi, Sogabe, and Kawahara (2009) used a different synthesis approach[13] to morph stimuli from one emotion to another (happy/sad/angry–neutral, sad/angry–happy, sad-angry), and then asked listeners to discriminate among stimuli across degrees of morphing. Like Laukka, they found that identification judgments were consistent with categorical perception models; but discrimination was equally accurate both within and across categories, contrary to categorical perception models. Differences in synthesis techniques and experimental tasks may account for these inconsistencies. It is also possible that the methods employed measure features of cognition about emotion rather than the emotions themselves. In either event, the matter remains an open question.

Finally, feelings are more subtle and multilayered than verbal expression is, so that even if distinct emotions exist, their expression in voice is continuous and dimensional (Laukka *et al.*, 2005). This in part may explain why much of vocal signaling is apprehended as attitudinal, which is a subtle mixture of a range of emotions and cognitive stance, rather than purely emotional in nature. Bio-evolutionary explanations and some data appear more consistent with dimensional accounts; but neither model is entirely satisfactory. Nor are they necessarily mutually exclusive, although they are often treated as such. For example, it is possible that expressions associated with arousal are universal, while culturally-specific display rules tune these dimensions into quasi-independent categories. It is also likely that the design of the formal experiment, and how listeners are expected to respond, has an influence on the outcome.

---

[13] The vocoder Straight; for example, Kawahara (2001).

9.5 Experimental Approaches to the Study of Vocal Emotion

Not surprisingly, the study of vocal emotion (and of emotion in general) has proven a very, very complicated topic. As discussed above, by their very definition emotions are ephemeral: They arise quickly in response to environmental or cognitive stimuli, and they typically dissipate quickly as the animal responds and the situation changes. They also depend on the (unobservable) internal state of an individual, about which the individual him- or herself may have limited insight. Studying such varying, transitory, inaccessible states of being has proven challenging, beyond the difficulties discussed above of distinguishing, defining, and identifying emotional states.

Vocalized emotion has been studied using four experimental approaches: use of naturally occurring emotions, inducing emotional states in the laboratory, portrayals of specific emotions by actors, and synthesizing stimuli to depict specific emotions.[14] Each of these has advantages and disadvantages. In particular, a trade-off exists between realism and control. For example, it is impossible to control anything prospectively in field recordings of real emotions: The stimuli generating the emotional state can be anything, and can vary over time; speakers may experience complex or simple emotional states, which may also change as the event unfolds; there may be little actual emotion in the talk; speakers may say whatever they wish (or nothing), or may scream, laugh, or cry instead of speaking; recording conditions may be good or terrible; and so on. It can also be rather difficult to determine what emotion or emotions are felt in naturally occurring emotional situations (particularly because different people may respond differently to the same circumstances), to separate the effects of multiple simultaneous emotion-like responses (relief and guilt; simultaneous happiness and sadness; Tatham and Morton, 2004), or to separate emotion in voice from the emotional content of the words uttered in natural contexts (Greasley, Sherrard, and Waterman, 2000). Attempts to gather emotional speech from group discussions and other spontaneous discourse have been disappointing (Cowie *et al.*, 1999), because intense, strong emotional expression seldom occurred. This explains in part why naturalistic studies tend to focus on strong, negative emotions and on rather dramatic and/or gross events, including plane crashes (Ruiz, Absil, Harmegnies, Legros, and Poch, 1996; Protopapas and Lieberman, 1997), the fiery crash of the zeppelin Hindenburg (audio sample 9.1; Williams and Stevens, 1972), and the New York City blackout (Streeter, MacDonald, Apple, Krauss, and Galotti, 1983). Data on naturally occurring positive emotions are generally lacking (although public displays of great joy at major sporting events could potentially provide such data).

Other authors have attempted to balance realism with control by inducing emotional responses from subjects under laboratory conditions. For example, subjects can be asked to perform difficult tasks with severe time restrictions (mental arithmetic (Hecker, Stevens, von Bismarck, and Williams, 1968); an impossible lexical decision task (Bachorowski and Owren, 1995)); they can be shown disgusting or otherwise affecting videos (Tolkmitt and Scherer, 1986); they can be asked to chat

---

[14] Use of naturalistic versus actor-elicited emotions corresponds to studies of spontaneous versus posed facial expressions, for which important neuropsychological differences are seen (Borod, 1993).

about the recent deaths of close friends or family members (Erickson *et al.*, 2006); they can play difficult or frustrating computer games (Johnstone, van Reekum, Hird, Kirsner, and Scherer, 2005); and so on. Such tasks can provide good recording conditions and control of content – subjects can be asked to utter standard phrases at any time during the experiment – but not all emotions are equally easy to elicit, and ethical considerations and restrictions inherent in working with human subjects limit an experimenter's ability to elicit very strong emotions, so that the stimuli may not adequately model natural emotions. Some evidence suggests that concerns about representativeness are exaggerated. For example, Ruiz *et al.* (1996) compared speech produced under stressful conditions in the laboratory (a Stroop task[15]) and outside of the laboratory (cockpit recordings from a plane that was about to crash). They reported very similar effects in each case, with stressed speech showing higher F0 and an increase in energy in the higher frequencies. Based on these data, they argue that laboratory induction paradigms are valid models of naturally-occurring stress.

Studies using actors to portray specific emotions provide another partial remedy for these concerns. Actors can produce a wide range of emotions at different levels of intensity, without the experimenter having to sacrifice control of text or recording conditions. Actors can also be asked to portray specific emotions, reducing concerns about the complexity of the feelings that may arise during real emotional situations and the difficulty of sorting out precisely what is being expressed under such circumstances. As a result, studies using actors are very common, particularly when authors seek the acoustic correlates associated with specific emotions (e.g., Williams and Stevens, 1972; Banse and Scherer, 1996; Laukka *et al.*, 2005, and many others). Such portrayals (although posed) may provide reasonable approximations to naturally occurring emotions, depending on the circumstances and the experimental question under investigation. For example, Williams and Stevens (1972) compared naturally occurring emotion (a radio announcer's eyewitness description of the Hindenburg crash; audio sample 9.1) with a version of the same text produced by a professional actor (unfamiliar with the recording) who performed the text based on a transcript. They noted a number of differences between the original and acted versions of the text, but concluded that the comparison served overall to validate the use of acted emotional portrayals. Even minimal differences between acted and natural emotions may have importance, however, and some evidence indicates that significant differences exist between acted and genuine, spontaneous emotions, at least for sadness (Erickson *et al.*, 2006) and happiness (Aubergé and Cathiard, 2003). As in other such effects (sarcasm, irony), actors likely draw on stereotypes to express the emotional content. Other limitations to acting-based studies are apparent as well. Actors vary in their skill (Scherer, Banse, Wallbott, and Goldbeck, 1991), and even the most able may overemphasize obvious cues to an emotional state, and omit more subtle cues, so that their portrayals resemble cultural stereotypes more than they do genuine emotions (Scherer, 2003). Portrayals may also emphasize socially-learned characteristics of emotional expression at the expense of those that derive from genuine physiological

---

[15] In a Stroop task (Stroop, 1935), subjects see the name of a color printed in a different color (the word 'red' in green type, for example) and are asked to identify either the word or the color as quickly as possible.

arousal (although all emotional expression is modulated by social rules; Scherer *et al.*, 1991).These kinds of discrepancies may obscure subtle dimensions of meaning or lead to wrong conclusions.

The fourth approach, utilizing computer-synthesized emotions to examine questions about how listeners and speakers process emotional meaning in voices, has the obvious advantage of allowing complete control over the stimuli. Of course, theories about the essential characteristics of the stimuli must be up to par in the design of such stimuli. Until now these approaches have had the strongest presence in engineering working papers (many are found without attribution or date on the internet). As has been mentioned, the ever-growing field of computer speech synthesis is constantly striving to achieve ways to produce appropriate paralinguistic material in automatic telephone voice trees, announcements, and text to speech translations. A few scientific studies using the methods of speech synthesis to study human responses to vocal emotion are reviewed below (Section 9.7). Such studies typically begin with naturally produced utterances and manipulate them using speech and voice synthesis techniques.

In conclusion, there is no one optimal method for obtaining examples of emotional speech. Considerations of realism versus control, emotional intensity versus ethics, and the underlying complexity of emotional reactions, suggest that the best strategy is to look for convergences between experimental approaches, so that laboratory- and field-based studies can validate each other (Scherer, 2003). This is the strategy we will pursue in the following sections, wherein we review data concerning the production and perception of emotions in (mostly English language) speech. After examining the manner in which speakers encode emotion and listeners decode it, we will consider the extent to which these data are consistent with biologically- or culturally-driven models of emotion. For humans, studies of prosodic performance during brain imaging in normal subjects and in performance by persons with brain damage may further elucidate how listeners hear and produce emotional meanings in speech. Our caveat through this exploration is that the broad range of emotions studied and the dimension of cognitive appraisal, both so prominent in human studies, pertain little or not at all to models of emotional vocal behaviors in animals. This discrepancy underlies the intrinsic difficulty before us in referencing human emotion insights to evolutionary theory.

9.6   How Does Emotion Affect the Voice?

With these considerations in mind, we proceed to the question of how speakers express emotions in their voices. Many studies have examined the extent to which speakers "leak" subtle signs of emotion into their voices and the manner in which different emotions are expressed (or not expressed). Results have been fairly consistent across studies, at least for arousal or active emotions (Table 9.1; for extensive reviews of this large literature, see e.g. Frick, 1985; Scherer, 1986, 2003; Murray and Arnott, 1993; Juslin and Laukka, 2001, 2003; or Bachorowski and Owren, 2003, 2008). For example, Williams and Stevens (1972) evaluated actors' utterances produced in angry, fearful, or sorrowful tones of voice. Compared to neutral utterances,

Table 9.1 Commonly-reported associations between acoustic features of posed emotions and the speaker's affect. Values indicated are relative to normal or emotionally neutral speech. Adapted from reviews by Scherer (1986, 2003), Murray and Arnott (1993), and Juslin and Laukka (2001).

	Sadness	*Fear*	*Anger*	*Joy/Happiness*	*Boredom*
Mean F0	Slightly lower	Very much higher	Very much higher	Much higher	Lower or normal
F0 range	(Slightly) more monotone	Wider or narrower	Much wider	Much wider	More monotone or normal
F0 variability/ contour	Downward inflections	Normal, or abrupt changes/ upward inflections	Abrupt changes/ upward inflections	Smooth, upward contours	Less variability
Intensity	Quieter	Normal	Louder	Louder	Quieter
Speaking rate	Slightly slower	Much faster	Slightly faster	Faster or slower	Slower
Spectral slope	Less high- frequency energy	More or less	More	More	Less

anger was associated with increased F0, with a wider range of F0 values, and also with extra emphasis on some syllables, more extreme articulation, and in some cases with longer durations. Like anger, fear was expressed via precise articulation and increased durations, but F0 was lower than for anger, and F0 increased and decreased more quickly, so that contours were "peakier." Finally, sorrow was characterized by low F0, a monotone voice, and by increases in the duration of speech sounds and pauses (cf. Scherer *et al.*, 1991, who reported similar results). More elaborately, Hammerschmidt and Jürgens (2007) asked actors to portray rage, despair, contempt/disgust, joy, joyful surprise, voluptuous enjoyment, and affection, and examined the extent to which the correct emotion could be determined based on 90 different acoustic measurements. They found that measures of the energy distribution in the spectrum (relating to the stiffness of the vocal folds) were good indices of negative emotions. Van Lancker and Sidtis (1992) asked a single actor to produce four utterances with emotional intonation contrasts (sad, angry, happy, surprised) but with neutral linguistic content, and then used discriminant function analysis to determine the degree to which six acoustic cues (F0 mean and variation, intensity mean and variation, and duration mean and variation) could differentiate the emotional meanings based on four exemplars each. Figure 9.4 provides examples of the syllable-by-syllable values for each of the acoustic measures. Listening studies yielded a 96% accuracy rate in identifying the intended emotional meanings (Van Lancker and Sidtis, 1992). The discriminant function analysis result produced two functions that accounted for 98.7% of the variance in the acoustic data. The first function was most highly correlated with F0 variability, while function two was most highly correlated with mean F0.

Other changes in vocal quality carry subtler nuances of emotional meaning, but these are more difficult to quantify and are seldom examined. Intensity is not always measured in these studies, but its impact is considerable when assessed (see Laukka *et al.*, 2005). Breathy voice has been associated with intimacy and sadness and tense voice with anger (Gobl and Ní Chasaide, 2003), and creak has also been associated with "victim voice" that communicates desperation and neediness (Sidtis and Van Lancker Sidtis, 2003). Studies of naturally occurring emotion also point to similar cues. For example, examination of three recordings made when death was imminent revealed increased F0, increased F0 variability, and vocal tremors as the situation worsened (Williams and Stevens, 1969).

When considering these results, it is important to remember that speakers differ quite a bit from one another in the manner and extent to which they express emotions naturally in their speech. A brief mental survey of our family and friends' varying styles of expression will verify this general point. In one published demonstration, Streeter, MacDonald, Apple, Krauss, and Galotti (1983) examined recordings of telephone conversations between Con Edison's system operator and his supervisor before and

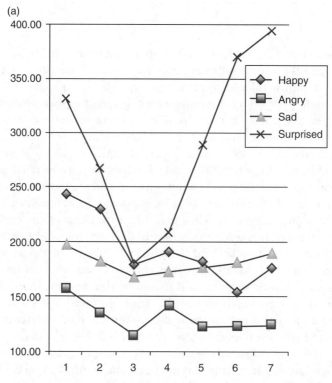

Figure 9.4   (a) Mean fundamental frequency by syllable for happy, angry, sad, and surprised utterances spoken by an actress. (b) Mean syllable durations for happy, angry, sad, and surprised utterances. (c) Mean amplitude by syllable for happy, angry, sad, and surprised utterances. Data from Van Lancker and Sidtis (1992).

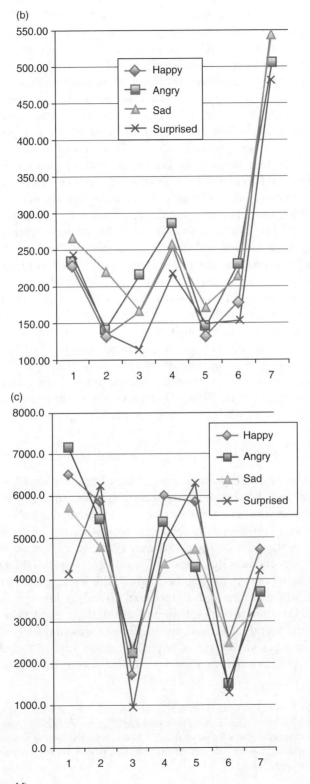

Figure 9.4 (*cont'd*).

after the 1977 New York City blackout.[16] They measured a variety of F0, intensity, and rate cues for voice samples from recorded telephone conversations between the system officer (who was directly responsible for maintaining the power grid) and his supervisor as the event unfolded. Interestingly, they found opposite patterns of changes over time for each speaker. As the blackout became more and more inevitable (and stress presumably increased), F0 and intensity decreased for the system officer, but increased for his supervisor. The system officer's F0 contours and speaking rate remained constant throughout the event, but the supervisor's F0 variability and speaking rate both increased. Perceptual evaluation confirmed that the system officer actually sounded less emotional over time, in contrast to the supervisor, who sounded increasingly upset.

Large intersubject differences in the manner and extent to which emotion is expressed have also been found in studies of laboratory-induced stress. For example, Bachorowski and Owren (1995) induced positive and negative feelings by giving listeners an impossible task (determining if a string of letters was a real word or not after only 100 msec of exposure) and providing random feedback ("good job" vs. "try harder") with the proportion of positive feedback as the independent variable in the study. They found that female speakers who reported that they usually experienced positive emotions strongly and who received large amounts of positive feedback showed significantly higher levels of vocal emotion (measured by F0, jitter, and shimmer) than did subjects who reported less habitual reactivity. In males, the highest levels of vocal emotion were associated with subjects who experienced negative emotions strongly and received negative feedback. Thus, vocal characteristics in this task depended on the talker's sex, their underlying habitual emotional traits, and the emotional context in which the speech was produced (see also Tolkmitt and Scherer, 1986). This gives a hint of the numerous variables that talkers and listeners juggle while expressing and perceiving vocal emotion.

9.6.1 Emotional expression, arousal, and the size code

Many studies of emotional expression in voice have been motivated by the hypothesis (reviewed above) that the physiological effects of emotion (modulated to a greater or lesser extent by cognitive/evaluative factors) are necessarily leaked into the voice, so that there is a direct correspondence between particular states in the signaler and the communicative display produced (e.g., Scherer, 1986; we will discuss some alternative hypotheses in later sections of this chapter.) For example, respiration rate increases with arousal, as an animal prepares for "fight or flight." This increase leads to increased subglottal pressure, which in turn leads to increased F0 and/or intensity (see Chapter 2). Thus, mean F0, F0 contour shapes, temporal relationships, and loudness should (and often do) vary with emotion, because of the effects of arousal on respiration. Similarly, arousal-related changes in patterns of respiration might lead to shorter durations of speech between breaths, altering a speaker's typical speech rhythm or producing an

---

[16] On July 13, 1977, a series of lightning strikes, compounded by human error, lead to complete failure of the electrical distribution system in New York City and Westchester County, New York. Power was completely lost over the entire area for more than 24 hours. Fires and looting ensued, and over 9,000 travelers had to be rescued from the subways. At the time, Con Edison was the sole provider of electricity in the New York City area.

increased rate of speech; and decreased motor control with increasing emotion (related to trembling, for example) could lead to increased jitter and shimmer, changes in F0 contour, or decreased articulatory precision (Williams and Stevens, 1972). Increased muscular tension related to anger or arousal might also lead to increased loudness or a strangled voice quality (Fonagy, 1981); and arousal emotions might lead to increased high-frequency energy in the voice, compared to "relaxed" emotions like quiet happiness, which should be characterized by less high-frequency energy (Scherer, 1986).

At least some of these physiologically-based emotional signals may also derive in part from an innate "frequency code" shared by many animals. Because smaller animals typically have voices with higher F0 and higher frequency resonances than do larger animals (e.g., Fitch, 1994; Smith, Patterson, Turner, Kawahara, and Irino, 2005; see Chapter 4 for review), utterances with higher F0 through their association with small size may have acquired secondary meanings of submission, lack of threat, fear, reticence, passivity, and so on; and utterances with low F0 through their association with large size carry connotations of assertiveness, dominance, aggression, and threat (Ohala, 1983, 1984). Facial expressions associated with submission or lack of threat (retracting lip corners, as dogs do, or the human smile) shorten the vocal tract and result in increased formant frequencies, also like those typical of a smaller animal (e.g., Ohala, 1980; Tartter and Braun, 1980; Bachorowski, 1999). Some experimental evidence (Chuenwattanapranithi, Xu, Thipakorn, and Maneewongvatan, 2008) adds detail to this view linking emotional expression to a size code. Listeners heard synthetic speech generated with statically or dynamically lengthened or shortened vocal tracts, and with static or varying F0. They rated these vocalizations as emanating from a larger or smaller body size, or as expressions of anger or happiness. In general, constant resonances and F0 were associated with larger or smaller body sizes as hypothesized; but dynamically changing resonances and F0 led to perception of happiness or anger. (Note that in these studies – and in many others – the contribution of voice quality is not taken into account.)

These results suggest to many researchers that much of what speakers express in their voices and listeners perceive is the level of arousal, expressed on an active–passive dimension. For example, activation emotions like fear, anger, and joyful happiness all share similar acoustic correlates like higher F0, more F0 variability, faster speech rates, increased intensity, and increases in high-frequency energy; and the cues listed in Table 9.1 do not obviously distinguish related emotions from one another as required by categorical views. Further, the data in Table 9.1 do not provide very much evidence for other emotional dimensions like valence, intensity, or potency (but see Goudbeek and Scherer, 2010), although it is difficult to evaluate differences due to the small number of positive emotions generally studied. In a study explicitly seeking evidence for different dimensions of emotion in voice, Laukka *et al.* (2005) found that the cues to activation and emotional intensity largely overlapped (both were associated with mean and maximum F0, F0 standard deviation, mean and standard deviation of intensity, F1, F2, and spectral balance[17]), while very few reliable cues to valence (positive or negative) were identified, suggesting that valence is not well represented in the voice. In the context of physiologically-motivated models of emotional expression, this is not unreasonable: An emotion's positive or negative nature is a priori less strongly related to autonomic

[17] Spectral levels in contiguous frequency bands.

physiological changes than are activation or intensity, whose shared relationship to physiological arousal also makes sense of their shared acoustic correlates. However, whether an emotion is negative or positive in the current state of affairs is obviously of immense importance to both the sender and the receiver of the signal, and listeners often can tell, so that we are again confronted by a great deal of successful emotional-prosodic communication that is not accounted for.

If the expression of emotion is integral to emotional experience, as these biological views imply, then talking in an emotional tone of voice might actually influence the speaker's mood. Some evidence suggests that this is in fact the case (Siegman, Anderson, and Berger, 1990; Siegman and Boyle, 1993). Speakers who discussed fear- and anxiety-producing events (for example, living through a missile attack) using a fast and loud voice had higher blood pressure and heart rate than they did when speaking slowly and softly about similar topics. Similarly, subjects who discussed sad or depressing events using a slow and soft voice also had higher blood pressure than they did when speaking about these events in a loud and fast or neutral voice. Note that using an emotional tone of voice is not enough to elicit emotions on its own: Effects were not consistently observed when speakers discussed neutral topics.

9.7   How do Listeners Perceive Emotion from Voices?

The data discussed in the previous section suggest that listeners should be rather good at distinguishing an aroused speaker – whether happy or angry, triumphant or terrified – from a calm one, but should be rather less able to determine the specific emotion being experienced. These data also suggest that listeners should rely on similar cues no matter what their linguistic or cultural background, because most emotional expression appears to derive from physiological processes that are common to all humans, and indeed to most mammals.

In fact, listeners' accuracy at discriminating among individual emotions in formal testing (summarized in Table 9.2) appears to exceed levels that might be expected from the cues available to them. Meta-analyses of many studies using different sets of emotional stimuli indicate that listeners correctly identify a specific target emotion about 60% of the time, a rate about five times greater than what would be expected by chance (e.g., Scherer, 2003).[18] It is difficult to account for this level of accuracy, particularly given the extent of overlap between the apparent cues for individual emotions (Scherer, 1986). Note that extrapolation of these success rates to emotional information transmitted in natural speech is not established.

Although overall accuracy is reasonably consistent across studies of adult listeners, depending on the categories and numbers of emotions used, posed emotions are not equally well recognized, as Table 9.2 shows. When listeners agree about the emotion

---

[18]   Experimenters have argued about the appropriateness of adjusting this value to correct for guessing, pointing out that most studies give listeners a list of responses to choose from so that a certain number of responses will be correct just by chance. In addition, most studies include only one or two positive emotions, which could make it easier for listeners to identify those tokens. This could also inflate overall percentage correct scores. However, even when corrected for these factors, accuracy rates still average about 50% correct across emotions, still well above chance levels (which depend on the number of emotions studied, but are usually about 12% correct).

Table 9.2 Listeners' accuracy in discriminating among different posed emotions. Values are not corrected for guessing.

	Fear	Disgust	Happiness/ Joy	Sadness	Anger	Surprise
van Bezooijen (1984)	58%	49%	72%	67%	74%	–
Scherer *et al.* (1991)	52%	28%	59%	72%	68%	–
Van Lancker and Sidtis (1992)	–	–	100%	100%	100%	96%
Scherer *et al.* (2001)	74%	–	48%	80%	79%	–
Juslin and Laukka (2001)[a]	50%/69%	37%/43%	50%/52%	65%/62%	41%/75%	–
Elfenbein and Ambady (2002) (crosscultural meta-analysis)	50.8%	–	28.9%	62.8%	63.7%	–
Thompson and Balkwill (2006) (across 5 languages)	59%	–	62%	82%	74.5%	–
Graham *et al.* (2001)	55%	–	70%	39%	76%	–

[a] Weak/strong intensity

they perceive, that emotion is usually related to arousal or activation, and the acoustic cues implicated in their judgments are fairly similar (and related to F0, amplitude, and duration) whatever the arousal emotion. Listeners generally agree poorly and inconsistently about non-arousal emotions and about emotional valence. In most studies, listeners are most accurate at identifying sadness and anger, followed by fear and joy; but they cannot recognize disgust at above chance levels. (Sadness, of course, exists in both aroused and depressed versions, adding some confusion to this picture.) Errors in discrimination are not random – listeners tend to confuse emotions with others that are "near," rather than with unrelated feelings (e.g., Graham *et al.*, 2001).

In general, accuracy studies suffer from significant limitations. First, they typically measure discrimination, rather than recognition, because listeners select the best label for what they hear from a short list of choices (Frick, 1985). The listeners' task may also have an effect – for example, words heard in isolation may sound angry, but the same words presented in a sentence context may not (Frick, 1986). Finally, results are typically presented as correlations between perceptual and acoustic measures, so that they cannot demonstrate causation between the signals and the perceptual judgments. Thus, the emotion perceived, the reported accuracy levels, and conclusions about the perceptual processes underlying these scores may be confounded to an unknown extent with effects of the testing method used.

One solution to at least some of these problems is the application of voice synthesis to confirm relationships between acoustic parameters and the qualities perceived. If changes in an acoustic parameter produce corresponding changes in the emotion heard, then we can safely conclude that listeners in fact attend to that parameter when judging that emotion. An early application (Protopapas and Lieberman, 1997) examined a gradient of "stress" from none to extreme using synthetic /a/ vowels whose F0 contour mimicked the voice of a helicopter pilot during conversations with the control tower prior to a fatal crash. The results of tests showed that perception of the degree of stress depended primarily on the maximum or mean F0, but not on the precise shape of the F0 contour or on the direction (rising/falling) of the melodic pattern. Speech rate also provides a cue to emotional meaning. Breitenstein, Van Lancker, and Daum (2001) asked listeners to label actor-generated utterances (in German) as happy, sad, angry, frightened, or neutral after F0 variability and speaking rate had been manipulated. Subjects' responses were less affected by changes in F0 variation than they were by changes in speech rate. Slower speaking rates were reliably associated with the "sad" label; faster rates were classified as angry, frightened, or neutral. In general, sad and neutral responses were more frequent when F0 variation decreased (so voices were more monotone) whereas frightened, angry, and happy responses increased with greater F0 variation. In addition, stimuli were rated significantly more "active" as they increased in rate and F0 variability, regardless of the emotion. These results are again consistent with the existence of an activation/arousal dimension in the production and perception of vocal emotion.

Finally, it is important to remember that in natural circumstances listeners attend to the words spoken and to many nonverbal cues – body language, facial expressions, context, blushing, tears, and so on. Although these ordinarily occur in combination, a meta-analysis of studies focusing on distinctive behavioral channels showed comparable abilities to assess expressive behavior considered separately (Ambady and Rosenthal, 1992). Nonetheless, in daily interaction, we rely on a striking number and variety of cues when assessing the emotional state of someone we know well (an average of six or seven cues, up to more than a dozen; Planalp, DeFrancisco, and Rutherford, 1996). Vocal cues may well play the largest role. Complex vocal cues ("His voice became louder, his speech more like a bark;" "He began in a raised voice, higher pitch, was talking faster than normal and incessantly;" p. 146) were cited most often as the single most important way subjects could tell that their partners were experiencing an emotion (24% of "most important" cues, and 19% of cues overall, used by over two-thirds of subjects). The discrepancy between the importance and

---

Sidebar: Emotion Recognition in Children

The ability to recognize vocal emotion in formal testing develops slowly over time. Children aged four to five have difficulty discriminating among vocal emotions presented in an experimental setting, but accuracy increases steadily over time until it peaks rather late, at about age 25 (McCluskey and Albas, 1981; Matsumoto and Kishimoto, 1983). It is assumed, however, that young infants and children discern emotional meaning naturalistically in the voices around them. The failure of children younger than age 7 to recognize emotional prosody is most likely attributable to the meta-cognitive nature of the task, and the relative backgrounding of affective-prosodic information compared to the verbal information in the stimuli (Van Lancker, Cornelius, and Kreiman, 1989).

usefulness of vocal cues to emotion and our inability to account for this behavior scientifically is one of the more unsatisfying aspects of the study of voice.

9.8   Biological, Social, and Cross-Cultural Perspectives on Vocal Emotion

The data reviewed in the previous sections are largely consistent with theories of emotion that describe biological processes shaped by cognitive and social contingencies. Recognition accuracy and acoustic explanations are both best for arousal-related emotions and for dimensional models of emotion, with the strongest evidence for only one arousal/activation related dimension. However, acoustic analyses to date have failed to account for the lion's share of the variance in listeners' judgments. For example, Sobin and Alpert (1999) used teams of raters to identify voice samples that scored highest on perceived joy, fear, anger, and sadness, while simultaneously scoring low on the other three emotions. They then attempted to predict the emotion each quasi-prototypical voice expressed via correlations with amplitude mean and variance, mean and variance of F0, mean and variance of duration of stressed syllables, speaking and pausing time, and a variety of other measures. Prediction was far from perfect. Joy was best at 72% rating variance accounted for (the prototypical joyous utterances were characterized by high F0 variability but low variability in loudness, many emphasized syllables, and long utterance durations); but for fear, only 24% of rating variance was explicable by the acoustic measures. Analyses accounted for 45% of the variance in anger ratings, and 51% for sadness. Thus, as much as three-quarters of the variance in perceptual judgments of emotion cannot be explained by even a relatively large set of acoustic measures. Accuracy is even lower when cultural factors are entered into the equation: British-English and Dutch speakers differed considerably in evaluating prosodic cues for self-confidence, surprise, and emphaticness (Chen, Gussenhoven, and Rietveld, 2004).

Failure to identify the acoustic cues underlying perceptual judgments can be explained in many ways. Emotional information in conversational speech is layered, fluid and vague; listeners' perceptions provide many kinds of psychological and experiential filters; acoustic cues are normally embedded in other physical, linguistic, and social-contextual cues. Individual differences in vocal expression occur, although their impact on accuracy of identification may be quite limited (Spackman, Brown, and Otto, 2009). Exemplars obtained in the laboratory may exaggerate or underrepresent emotional cues. And, of course, cultural factors are likely to play a significant role in the establishment of processes that allow for production and perception of emotion, as they do in all human affairs. Even if emotions ultimately have biological bases, the process of learning to control emotions and emotional displays, and algorithms for decoding vocal and facial expressions, have much that is culture-specific. A large literature (with a predominant focus on facially expressed emotion) has addressed this possibility. In such studies, experimenters typically employ one group of speakers, and two or more groups of listeners from different national, cultural, or linguistic communities, along with posed emotional expressions. Accuracy at discriminating emotions is then compared for listeners whose background matches that of the speakers (the "in-group") versus those from a different background (the "out-group"), with the typical result of an in-group advantage. Insofar as the native language relates to cultural identity, verbal emotional expression heard in the first language is generally stronger and more meaningful than the same material heard in the second or third language, and there is an influence of the "dominant language" on these findings. Autobiographical memories are influenced by the language spoken at the time the events occurred (Marian and Neisser, 2000; Matsumoto and Stanny, 2006). Dewaele (2008) surveyed nearly 1,500 multilingual adults using an online questionnaire asking them to evaluate the emotional weight of the phrase "I love you" in their first, second and other languages. Most speakers felt the phrase most strongly in their native language, and some endorsed strength of meaning in the dominant language (which might not be the first language) was found.

Across studies, meta-analysis indicates that this advantage varies by emotion, ranging from about 7% for anger and sadness to about 18% for happiness (Elfenbein and Ambady, 2002; see Table 9.1). For example, Albas, McCluskey, and Albas (1976) asked speakers of Cree and of Canadian English to discriminate among happy, sad, angry, and loving utterances spoken in Cree and in English, but filtered to obscure the semantic content of the utterances. The listener groups did not differ in overall accuracy, but each was more accurate when judging tokens produced in their native language (an interaction effect; cf. Breitenstein *et al.*, 2001). Similarly, van Bezooijen, Otto, Heenan, and Francais (1983) asked Dutch, Taiwanese, and Japanese listeners to identify (from ten choices) the emotions expressed in three word phrases spoken in Dutch. All listeners performed above chance levels; however, scores were higher for Dutch listeners than for Taiwanese or Japanese, who did not differ. When patterns of errors were examined, confusions could best be explained by the similarity of the two emotions in activation level. This indicates that the same primary dimension underlies evaluation of vocal emotions across cultures, despite finding of an in-group advantage. The authors attribute the consistency underlying apparent differences between cultural groups to the biological basis of cues to activity/arousal, and suggest that cues to other dimensions like valence may be both learned and more subtle than those for arousal. Similarly, Graham *et al.* (2001) found that both Japanese and Spanish speakers had more difficulty recognizing emotions from English speech than did English speakers, but patterns of errors for the Spanish speakers were more similar to those of the English speakers than were errors made by Japanese speakers, presumably due to closer cultural correspondences. (See also Thompson and Balkwill, 2006, who examined English-speaking listeners' discrimination of emotions produced in English, German, Chinese, Tagalog, and Japanese.) Finally, a cross-cultural study of nonverbal emotional vocalizations was conducted with the Himba, a seminomadic group in Namibia (Sauter, Eisner, Ekman, and Scott, 2010) using stimuli generated by Himba and British English speakers. Nine nonverbal emotional vocalizations (e.g., cheers, laughs, growls representing the emotions of achievement, amusement, and anger) from their own and from the other culture were successfully identified by British English and Himba listeners (by matching the stimuli to the appropriate story). The only exception was the sigh representing relief, which was not successfully matched to the relief story by the Himba listeners in either the English or the Himba-generated version (although English listeners successfully identified both cultures' renditions of relief). In general, while within-culture recognition was somewhat higher than across-culture recognition, these results suggest a biological reality to these vocalizations, in line with the universality of many facial emotional expressions, such as smiling. In-group versus out-group differences can also be demonstrated electrophysiologically. In bilingual speakers, greater autonomic reactivity as measured by galvanic skin responses was recorded for emotional words in the native language than in the second language (Ayçiçegi and Harris, 2004). Taboo words and reprimands also elicited greater physiological reactivity in the first than in the second language (Harris, Ayçiçegi, and Gleason, 2003; for review, see Harris, Gleason, and Ayçiçegi, 2006).

The moderate in-group advantage in recognizing emotional meanings in speech stands in contrast to the difficulties foreign-language learners face when learning the phonology of a second language. This contrast was revealed in a study of brain auditory evoked responses to a phonological versus an emotional stimulus. Evoked response data using the p300 response (a relatively late brain wave believed to reflect cognitive processes of discrimination) showed that Japanese listeners (who have difficulty distinguishing /r/ and /l/; e.g., Strange and Dittman, 1984; Logan, Lively, and Pisoni, 1991) could not distinguish between the syllables "rip" and "lip," but the waveforms for both American and Japanese listeners were strong and clear for angry and happy productions of the same words, indicating robust discriminatory ability in both groups for emotional contrasts on these short stimuli (Figure 9.5a; Buchwald, Erwin, Guthrie, Schwafel, and Van Lancker, 1994). Identification performance for "rip" and "lip" from audio recordings was at chance, but accuracies were high for the pair "angry/happy" (Figure 9.5b), confirming this finding.

A few studies have also examined cross-cultural differences in the expression of attitudes. Using semantic scales to rate such parameters as "confident" and "friendly" on utterances that varied systematically on F0, British English and Dutch listeners were found to differ considerably in the perception of these attitudes in their native languages (Chen, Gussenhoven, and Rietveld, 2004). According to these authors, while these paralinguistic meanings may be based in universal biological codes, the specific signals are language specific. Features related to F0 are important for expressing sarcasm and other emotions across cultures, but the particular details vary substantially from language to language (Pell, Paulmann, Dara, Alasseri, and Kotz, 2009). Despite such variability, speakers of Arabic, English, German, and Hindi were all able to recognize emotions expressed in each others' languages at above chance levels (Pell *et al.*, 2009).

Data from studies of nonhuman animals can also contribute to our understanding of the innate versus social nature of emotion. Because the neural control structures and voice production mechanisms used to express vocal emotion are fairly comparable across many mammal species (Hauser, 1996; Scherer, 2003), similarities between animal and human expressions of emotion tend to support bio-evolutionary models, at least when the emotional categories compared are severely limited. (For review of the neurology of vocal production, see Chapter 3). At the same time, a discontinuity exists between models of vocalized emotion in nonhuman animals, where arousal seemingly refers to aversive and hedonistic domains, and models of vocalized emotion in humans, where the mantle of cognitive appraisal covers the entire scene. Among nonhuman animals, it seems likely that few if any vocalizations are free from affect. Predator alerts, separation calls, and cries used to signal finding food all contain emotional aspects (Snowdon, 2003), so separating out those aspects of the call that are uniquely emotional, and not caused by other factors, is not straightforward.

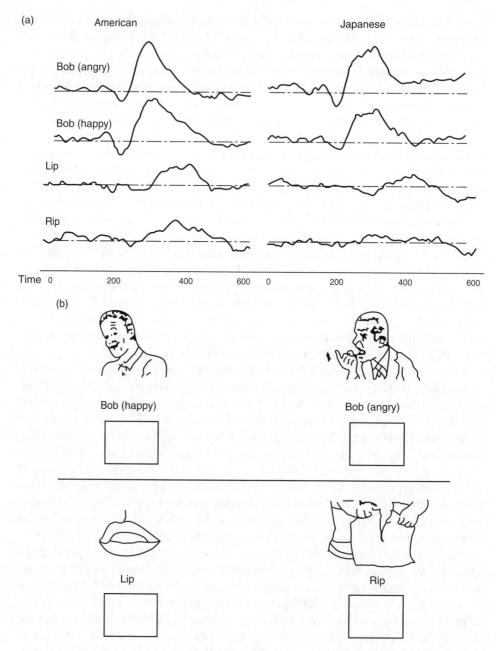

Figure 9.5 (a) Auditory evoked responses (P300) wave for American and Japanese subjects listening to repetitions of Bob (angry) and Bob (happy) or *lip* and *rip*. (b) An answer sheet for the listening task. Japanese speakers could not discriminate between spoken samples of *rip* and *lip* but discriminated as well as American English speakers between Bob (angry) and Bob (happy).

The usefulness of examining animal vocalizations in the study of emotion is limited not only by the problem of separating emotional from social/cognitive aspects of vocalization, but also by the problem of determining what an animal is feeling. Several clever studies have addressed this limitation by carefully determining the circumstances under which the calls were emitted. For example, Fichtel, Hammerschmidt, and Jürgens (2001) analyzed calls produced by squirrel monkeys in an experiment where vocalizations were produced by brain stimulation, but the animals controlled the stimulation they received by moving from one room (which turned stimulation on) to another (which turned stimulation off). The amount of time spent in each room was considered an index of the aversiveness of the stimulation (which the animals would seek or avoid, as appropriate), so that calls associated with stimulation could be graded according to emotional valence. Increased aversion resulted in increases in high-frequency spectral energy, increased F0, and/or in increases in the amount of spectral noise (aperiodicity) in the call (see also Jürgens, 1979, 1982).

In a different approach, Bastian and Schmidt (2008) used behavioral observations to classify bat vocalizations (produced as the bats approached roosting places, or in response to these approach calls) into high- and low-intensity calls, and then examined the acoustic attributes of each call type. They assumed that more pronounced displays would be produced in situations that were more important to the bats, so that it was possible to infer the animal's internal state from the intensity of its display. They found that call duration, the number and frequency of calls produced, and F0 all increased with intensity, for both the approach and response calls, and they argued that bats encode emotion in two ways: by using a call that is context-specific (it only occurs when the bat is approaching the roost), and then modulating that call to reflect the intensity of the situation. Emotional intensity is coded in a similar fashion (by some subset of increased call frequency, intensity, and F0) in many mammals, including tree shrews and baboons; and such cues separate cold from hot anger and anxiety from fear in humans. Some evidence also confirms our intuitive impressions that we can accurately judge a nonhuman animal's emotional state from its cries (Leinonen, Laakso, Carlson, and Linnankoski, 2003; Nicastro and Owren, 2003; Pongracz, Molnar, Miklosi, and Csanyi, 2005).

These studies reveal the value as well as inherent limitation in comparing nonhuman animal and human studies of vocalized emotion. The scope of human studies lying under the umbrella term "emotion" is quite vast and undifferentiated, including, as we have said, elements of mood, attitude, affect, motivation, and so on, all interwoven with cognitive material. Frank expressions of classic emotions are infrequently encountered under most speaking circumstances (Pittam and Scherer, 1993). Animal studies, on the other hand, deal at most with a limited set of emotions like fear and anger whose presence must be inferred, or (more convincingly) with such constrained and more general categories as aversion and attraction, or hedonic versus aversive states. In combination, such studies suggest that vocal repetition rate and F0 express emotional arousal across animal species separated evolutionarily by tens of millions of years (for example, bats separated from other mammalian lines about 95,000,000 years ago; Bastian and Schmidt, 2008). These commonalities across such different species suggest that these parameters function as widespread affect cues. We conclude that there are universal (i.e., biologically based), species-specific, and culture-specific aspects to the production and perception of vocal emotion, and that at least some aspects of human vocal emotion reach back historically into the earliest appearance of vocalized sound.

9.8.1   Laughter and the affect induction account of emotion

The studies discussed in the previous sections treat emotional vocalizations largely as a means of communicating information about one animal's internal state to another. As a result, these studies focus on the manner in which emotions are encoded and decoded, with the results that we have just reviewed. However, as noted previously, a different way of thinking about emotion – the affect induction account (Bachorowski and Owren, 2008) – focuses instead on the possible importance of emotional communications for influencing the listener's feelings and behavior. In this view, information about what an animal is feeling is useful to the extent that it influences the listener in some way (whether or not this effect is intentional), and it is these effects on subsequent listener behavior that could have shaped signaling behavior over evolutionary time. Because one role of emotional vocalization in this view is to induce emotion in a listener, and not only to communicate the speaker's internal state, the relationship between signals and speakers is probabilistic, and not absolute: It may benefit speakers to produce similar responses in listeners to (their own) different emotional states (Bachorowski and Owren, 2008). Conclusions that listeners draw about the speaker's internal state may thus be based on inferences that listeners draw from their own affective responses to the sounds, their experience, and the context in which the sounds occur. These conclusions may or may not reflect the speaker's internal state.

This view of vocal emotion is in tune with relatively consistent correlations between acoustic attributes and perceived emotions, but its intuitive appeal goes somewhat further. We all have emotional responses to sounds all the time – feelings of fear or excitement in response to sirens, smiles when we hear laughter, a sense of urgency (or irritation) when babies cry – and cardiac and electrodermal data show that many environmental and human sounds produce responses on the arousal (active-passive) and valence (positive-negative) dimensions. Further, this kind of view allows for sounds to have different affective impacts depending on context. For example, a high-pitched shriek has one meaning at a party, but an entirely different one in a dark alley late at night. In both cases, the sound causes listener arousal. As always in our rendition of vocal matters, the role of the listener must crucially be included in the mix, and affect induction accounts accomplish this goal.

Most of the formal evidence for this affect induction view of emotion comes from studies of laughter. Laughter is apparently "hard wired" in mammals: It occurs in many mammal species (e.g., Panksepp and Burgdorf, 2003; Meyer, Baumann, Wildgruber, and Alter, 2007; see Provine, 2000, for review), occurs in similar circumstances, at similar places in the pauses of conversation, with similar acoustic characteristics, across unrelated cultures and in congenitally deaf speakers who have never heard laughter (Provine and Emmorey, 2006; Makagon, Funayama, and Owren, 2008). This strongly suggests its basis is biological, although some social learning also takes place (consider how awkward inappropriate laughter can be in a social setting). In addition to this consistency in occurrence, laughter has traditionally been described as a highly stereotyped behavior, in which speakers produce homogeneous, vowel-like, song-like sounds of the "hohoho hehehe hahaha" variety (see Sidebar for a review of this literature). However, more recent evidence underscores the variability inherent in

laughter. Studies comparing laughter produced in contexts consistent with joy, taunting, *Schadenfreude*,[19] and during tickling are acoustically and perceptually distinct
(Szameitat *et al.*, 2009). Even within a single context, laughs are surprisingly heterogeneous. Detailed analyses of a large corpus of naturally-occurring laughs (1,024
examples from 97 different speakers who watched a funny video; Bachorowski,
Smoski, and Owren, 2001) showed that laughs fell into three categories: song-like
and voiced, snort-like (mostly unvoiced, with nasal turbulence), and unvoiced grunts
(breathy pants, harsh cackles, not nasal, but noisy).[20] Only 30% were voiced; 47.6%
were fully unvoiced. A whopping 62.8% of laughs included a snort, and 37.2% included
grunts (21.8% of laughs include more than one kind of vocalization). Laughs are variable in form within speakers as well as across speakers: over 40% of speakers produced
all three kinds of laugh, and 43% produced two of the three. Some consistent differences between males and females were observed. Notably, females produced more
song-like laughs than males did, and males produced more unvoiced grunts than
females did.

The question that arises from these data is the functional significance of all this
variability, which is likely to serve some purpose. Evidence (reviewed in Bachorowski
and Owren, 2003; Owren and Bachorowski, 2003) suggests that both males and
females use laughter unconsciously, but strategically, as follows. First, highly variable
pitch contours like those that characterize voiced laughter (see Sidebar) have been
associated with inducing and maintaining arousal in listeners (laughter attracts attention, and it is contagious). However, more than half of laughs are unvoiced, with
unvoiced laughs much more common among males than females. Finally, voiced,
songlike laughs are significantly more likely to elicit positive responses than unvoiced
grunts, pants, or snortlike sounds (Bachorowski and Owren, 2001). Listeners actually actively dislike these unvoiced sounds, especially when produced by females; for
example, the personality of the beautiful title character in the film *Miss Congeniality*
(Petrie and Bullock, 2000) is indexed primarily by her snorting laughter, which marks
her as undesirable. These facts suggest that females should produce the most voiced
laughs when talking to male strangers (whom they seek to attract), but males talking
with strangers (potential competitors) should especially avoid voiced laughter. This
appears to be the case: Speakers produce the kind of laugh that affects listeners when
it serves their purpose, but avoid that kind of laughter at other times (e.g., Bachorowski
and Owren, 2008). In this way, laughter can help form and maintain relationships,
and can improve cooperation among unrelated individuals. Note that laughter has
both direct and indirect effects on listeners in this view: Laughs can affect behavior
by directly inducing affect (in the same way that a loud noise induces a startle reflex),
because laughter, like yawning, is contagious, or through learned associations between
the sound produced and the animal's subsequent behavior (so that, for example,
dogs respond with enthusiasm to the sounds that they have learned signal an imminent walk).

---

[19] Amusement at the discomfort or suffering of others, as in much slapstick humor.
[20] Examples of these different laughs can be heard at http://www.psy.vanderbilt.edu/faculty/
bachorowski/laugh.htm; accessed November 5, 2009.

9.9   Stress and Lie Detection from Voice

The lady doth protest too much, methinks.

William Shakespeare, *Hamlet*, III.2.239

Within the study of vocal emotion, the detection of stress and lying from voice has received substantial attention. Because lying is such a common and distasteful behavior, detecting lies has always held interest – for parents concerned about where their children *really* were last night, for employers who wish to screen potential employees for honesty, for police departments interrogating suspects, and for government agencies worried about spying and terrorism. Ability to accurately recognize stress in pilots, astronauts, or law enforcement personnel noninvasively could help mission officers determine whether a mission or task should continue (Williams and Stevens, 1969; Johannes, Salnitski, Gunga, and Kirsch, 2000). More mundanely, systems to assess stress from voice could also allow automatic telephone call routing systems to determine when a customer is growing irritated or angry so that transfer to a human operator could be expedited (Maffiolo and Chateau, 2003).

Two research areas along these lines have developed: the study of listeners' abilities to detect lies by listening in everyday circumstances, and studies focusing on the development and evaluation of electronic systems for detecting stress and deception in voice. (Automatic lie detection systems are discussed in detail in Chapter 10.) Both kinds of investigation are based on the assumption that lying is stressful, and that stress leaves marks on the voice that can be detected. The basic logic underlying studies of lie detection from voice goes as follows. In most non-psychopathic people, producing a convincing lie requires significant cognitive effort and control, which is stressful (e.g., Anolli and Ciceri, 1997). In one version of this view, lie-related stress derives from the tension, anxiety, or heightened arousal that inhere in the situation that led to the lie, producing a kind of "fight or flight" response in the liar. This heightened arousal is incompatible with ongoing, precise control of F0, loudness, and voice quality (e.g., Tanner and Tanner, 2004), resulting in increased vocal variability during a lie. Alternatively, stress may be related to the substantial mental effort needed to control one's voice during the lie so as to minimize cues and mistakes. Efforts to prevent leakage of emotion into the voice signal may result in an overcontrolled voice with *less* variability than the speaker evinces when telling the truth (Anolli and Ciceri, 1997). Thus, the view that lying requires cognitive effort and control actually predicts that two kinds of liars may exist: those who show increased variability in their utterances when lying due to "fight or flight" responses, and those who show less variability because of vocal over-control. Anolli and Ciceri (1997) also point out that a substantial proportion of liars (about 32% of subjects in their study) are good at lying, and manage to keep F0 and other cues constant. The variety of liars that exists presents a challenge to those who seek a single set of cues that will consistently separate truthful from deceitful utterances.

Given the assumption that lying is stressful, most investigations seeking cues to lying have focused on F0 (Hansen, Zhou, and Pellom, 1999), because of the general relationship between stress and F0 (e.g., Hecker *et al.*, 1968), and because F0 is sensitive to many of the physiological changes associated with arousal and/or fight or flight responses, as noted above (Tanner and Tanner, 2004). Cognitive loads (planning the lie; anticipating challenges) may also lead to slower speech rates, or to more speech errors when the talker is deceptive (Mehrabian, 1971).

In fact, many cues related to F0 or speech tempo/rhythm have emerged from studies of dishonest speech (most of which used conditions simulated in the field or laboratory, with varying fidelity to naturally-occurring situations). F0 often increases in deceptive utterances, by about 6–7 Hz on average (Ekman, Friesen, and Scherer, 1976; Streeter, Krauss, Geller, and Olson, 1977; Anolli and Ciceri, 1997), although Anolli and Ciceri reported that F0 *decreased* for five out of 31 liars and did not change for eight out of 31 liars. Response latencies may increase when the speaker is lying (Kraut, 1978; Vrij, Edward, and Bull, 2001), but differences may be very small (on the order of 0.2 sec; Harrison *et al.*, 1978). Liars are typically more dysfluent (DePaulo, Rosenthal, Rosenkrantz, and Green, 1982) and/or more verbose than non-liars, and produce more pauses, as predicted (DePaulo and Pfeifer, 1986; Anolli and Ciceri, 1997; Vrij *et al.*, 2001), although answers to questions may also be shorter (Kraut, 1978). Which cues are active, and to what extent, depends on the speaker and the situation, and combined with the fact that lying comes easily to some people, detection of lying from the voice is a precarious business. Perhaps the only safe conclusion is that no typical deceptive behavior exists (Vrij *et al.*, 2001).

Listeners typically believe that they are reasonably adept at lie detection, and many also believe that they are not particularly good at lying themselves (Elaad, 2003). In fact, people in general are much better at concealing lies than at detecting lies. Many laboratory studies have shown that lie detection accuracy hovers near chance levels, rarely exceeding 60% correct when 50% correct is expected just by guessing (Harrison, Hwalek, Raney and Fritz, 1978; Zuckerman, DeFrank, Hall, Larrance, and Rosenthal, 1979; DePaulo and DePaulo, 1989; see Kraut, 1980, or Bond and DePaulo, 2006, for review). Listeners did not differ in honesty and deception ratings for filtered or full speech, when hearing randomized samples of deceptive and honest utterances (Ekman, Friesen, and Scherer, 1976). Although there is some evidence that people can improve at detecting the lies of a specific individual if they are given feedback (Zuckerman, Koestner, and Colella, 1985), improvements are very small (on the order of 2–6%). Extensive experience with liars and lie detection in general does not appear to increase listeners' accuracy under laboratory conditions. Professionals like customs inspectors, police officers, polygraph examiners, and intelligence officers, who detect deception as part of their jobs, do not perform any better at this task than do generic American undergraduate students (DePaulo and Pfeifer, 1986; Ekman, O'Sullivan, Friesen, and Scherer, 1991; Elaad, 2003). Despite the consistent finding that practice does not make perfect, professionals are significantly more confident of their lie detection responses than are ordinary citizens, although all listeners typically believe that they are more accurate than they are (DePaulo and Pfeifer, 1986).

Why are listeners so bad at detecting lies? In part, poor performance is related to the extent to which speakers are able to conceal lies (it is hard to perceive something when no cues are present; DePaulo *et al.*, 1982) and to the high levels of speaker variability (different speakers have different "tells" that indicate lying, as noted above, and no one cue or set of cues is consistently associated with deceptive speech, so there is no typical "sound" of lying, and no single perceptual strategy is sufficient; see Vrij *et al.*, 2001, for review). In addition, due to the operation of stereotypes, discrepancies exist between the cues that mark deceptive speech and cues that occur with speech that is honest but is nonetheless perceived as deceptive (Zuckerman, Spiegel, DePaulo, and Rosenthal, 1982). Increased numbers of "ums" and "ers," slower speaking rates, and a high rate of dysfluencies may lead listeners to conclude that an honest speaker is lying (DePaulo *et al.*, 1982). Finally, most of the cues to lying can also be associated with the stress of being under scrutiny by a figure of authority (your mother; a customs official). For example, nervousness due to being scrutinized can result in increases in F0; stopping to think before answering a question in order to avoid inaccuracy can result in a long response latency that ironically makes the answer seem more dishonest; and so on. These effects increase false alarm rates and decrease the overall accuracy of lie detection.

As a group, studies of lie detection by listening suffer from a number of technical limitations. In general, only a few speakers produce only a few utterances. In real life lying situations there is often a significant emotional or legal penalty associated with lying, and getting caught is terrible; in the laboratory, experiments cannot ethically incorporate realistic kinds or levels of jeopardy, and getting caught is no big deal, making it unlikely that speakers perform in ways that accurately model real lying. At the same time, studies using acting may result in exaggerated or caricatured emotions rather than realistic expressions of stress. Experimental subjects may also experience emotions other than lie-related stress that introduce experimental confounds, adding to the problem of experimental control. Nevertheless, it also appears that lying is not difficult, and that many speakers are proficient liars, even when they think they're not. For these reasons, it is not particularly surprising that studies of lie detection by listening have produced such consistently weak or negative results. Alas, lying is just not easy to detect.

Sidebar: The Case of the Lying Presidents

American history offers an unfortunately large number of good examples of recorded lies by public figures that have subsequently been detected. Such lies, whatever their political or social repercussions, provide excellent data for the study of lying from voice, because they represent real lies about important matters, and because the cost associated with detection is extremely high. For the sake of fairness, we will consider one such incident from each major political party: Republican Richard Nixon's lies about the Watergate break-in, and Democrat William Jefferson Clinton's about his relationship with Monica Lewinsky (Cozen-Harel, 2007).

Examples of President Nixon's truthful and lying speech are included as audio samples 9.2 and 9.3. Most notably, the utterances differ in pitch: the lying statement has a much higher F0 than does the truthful statement. Pitch in the Watergate statement is also more variable than in the truthful statement, and pauses are more in evidence, as are word repetitions.

Audio sample 9.4 is a selection from President Clinton's State of the Union address, while tracks 9.5 and 9.6 contain a lie and a truthful statement about the Lewinsky matter, respectively. In his untrue statement, President Clinton's utterances are particularly uneven and choppy, in sharp contrast to the more usual fluent speech evident in the truthful samples. Pauses in the lying speech are extremely homogeneous in duration; in his truthful speech, pauses are less frequent and vary in duration. The sharp rhythm of the lying speech gives it a somewhat unnatural, mechanical quality, again in contrast to his usual warm style. Word repetitions are also in evidence during the lie. This pattern suggests that Mr. Clinton's attempts to control his speech have resulted in an overcontrolled voice (at least with respect to rhythm), despite the tension and anger evident in his intonation.

9.10 Summary and Conclusions

To summarize, we can account for something under half (and maybe as little as a quarter) of listeners' perceptions of a limited number of "primary" vocal emotions based on acoustic cues like F0, intensity, duration, and details of voice quality, which seem to reflect primarily the speaker's state of arousal beyond a certain threshold. Still less is known about the processing of vocal emotional information in naturalistic human speech. A considerable array of emotions cannot be characterized adequately using these measures. The search for nonhuman antecedents yields only limited insight, but there is some convincing correspondence between animal and human in the foundations of emotional expression as revealed in their comparable subcortical/limbic substrates for emotional vocalization. This is the view of emotion as a phylogenetically continuous mechanism with functional adaptability, as elaborated by Scherer (1984, 1985).

In humans, there has been a copious cognitive flowering of appraisal processes, which have given rise to more complex dimensions of emotion identified by researchers. Details remain to be worked out about when emotions can be classified as arousal or active, how this dimension interacts with other putative dimensions such as potency and intensity, and how (and why) this theoretical apparatus maps onto measurable acoustic cues. Human cultures differ in terms of how emotional meanings in prosody are expressed and perceived, but these differences are minimal compared to linguistic differences. If we extend Grice's conversational maxims of quality ("Do not say what you believe to be false") and manner ("Avoid ambiguity") to the expression of emotional intonation in the verbal message, then it is apparent that we expect these two channels to be concordant (Grice, 1975, 1978). When they are not, perplexity ensues, sociolinguistic trouble is unleashed, or pathology is revealed. How often such events occur, how they are handled and resolved, and what they mean in communicative interactions have yet to be examined. These perspectives cast doubt on the value of incongruent expressions – those with conflicting semantic and affective-prosodic information – as key in experimental tasks.

Given that emotions, mood, attitude, and affect are produced and perceived as layered, graded, and fleeting presences, it is not surprising that, on the whole, we have a rather limited understanding of how listeners naturally reach the conclusions they do about emotions in voice. Little consistent evidence links any auditory/acoustic cues either to discrete emotional states or to emotional valence: Cues to a speaker's precise emotional state are ambiguous, even for laughter (which can be associated with embarrassment, nervousness, appeasement, etc., as well as with amusement or happiness; see Owren and Bachorowski, 2003, or Szameitat *et al.*, 2009, for review); but many effects of vocal emotion on listeners are clear and easy to demonstrate (try not to smile when you hear someone else laughing). These observations are inconsistent with either dimensional or categorical models of emotion, which predict the existence of consistent cues to speaker affect and good listener ability to agree and/or to accurately decode the emotions in voice, neither of which has been consistently reported. Instead, many studies have revealed relatively undifferentiated cues to emotions and context-dependent responses from listeners, which are more consistent with affect induction accounts of emotion. Many limitations are apparent in these studies – heterogeneous speaker and listener groups limit our ability to examine consistent individual differences; small numbers of speakers typically studied (usually less than 10); use of actors; limited statistical and acoustic analysis techniques – but these pale beside the complexity of the problem to be studied. There is no satisfactory answer for all of this at this time.

Finally, it is important to remember that in real life listeners have access to many channels of information (face, voice, posture, context ...) when perceiving and identifying emotions. For example, cues to disgust probably involve facial grimacing more than verbal expressions. Similarly, joy is better recognized from the face – especially the eyes – than from voice; conversely, anger can be hard to judge from the face, but is relatively easy to hear in the voice (Scherer *et al.*, 2001). Satisfactory explanations for such discrepancies have not emerged to date. Nonetheless, as separated lovers know from spending weeks or months communicating exclusively by telephone, a universe of feeling can be conveyed by voice alone.

Sidebar: Laughter: Details, Details.

As described above, laughter is highly variable. Voiced laughs are characterized by high F0 (mean for females = 405 Hz; mean for males = 272 Hz, with maxima of 2,083 Hz and 1,245 Hz, respectively). F0 is also quite variable for both males and females: the average F0 excursion about the mean is 59 Hz for males, and 86 Hz for females. Only 38% of laughs are monotone; 29% have falling F0 contours, in 19% F0 varies sinusoidally, and 14% have rising/falling or plain rising F0 contours. Laughs do not, however, vary very much in formant frequencies. Measures indicate that they occur almost entirely on a single central "schwa" type vowel. Alas, the mythical "ho ho ho" of Santa Claus does not occur in real laughing (Bachorowski *et al.*, 2001). Patterns of variability are fairly constant across age groups: 3-year-olds squeal more than adults do (Nwokah, Davies, Islam, Hsu, and Fogel, 1993), and 70-year-old males laugh slightly longer and with a somewhat compressed F0 range as compared to 20-year-old males (LaPointe, Mowrer, and Case, 1990), but similarities far outweigh differences across age and sex groups.

Neurologically, laughter is highly complex, and depends on precise coordination of many different brain areas (many in the right cerebral hemisphere) that work together in a functional network (Meyer, Zysset, von Cramon, and Alter, 2005; Meyer *et al.*, 2007). Perception of laughter also involves many different brain regions, especially the right cerebral hemisphere, and hearing laughter may activate some of the same brain regions that are involved in producing it. This pattern of coactivation may explain in part the contagious nature of laughter.

Sidebar: Smiling and Frowning

Smiling and frowning are universal expressions among humans. Spontaneous smiling emerges within 24 hours of birth (Kawakami *et al.*, 2006). These expressions may have correlates in other animals as well (for example, lip gestures used by many animals to exaggerate their size or signal submission during agonistic encounters; see Chapter 4 for review). Because these articulatory adjustments are easy to hear in other contexts, it seems likely that listeners can hear a speaker's smile as well, without reference to the accompanying facial display. Early studies (Tartter and Braun, 1980) confirmed that naive listeners could hear smiles in short utterances, and that these utterances generally sounded happy; further, formant frequencies (but also F0) increased for the smiled utterances compared to utterances produced without smiles. Later studies using smiled and frowned whispered syllables (Tartter and Braun, 1994) showed that smiles and frowns are perceived with equal accuracy in whisper and in regular phonation, so that F0 cannot be the primary cue to these expressions. Results confirmed the importance of resonances in the perception of these expressions: Perceived frowning was correlated with lower F2 values and increased syllable durations in whisper, while smiling was marked by higher F2 values. Other vocal tract effects related to pharyngeal and nasal resonances may also be in play. Interestingly, frowns were less well-recognized in syllables with rounded vowels, because of the ambiguity introduced by the phonemic lip rounding. Overall, these data underscore yet again the importance of considering formant frequencies in models of emotion and of voice quality in general (e.g., Bachorowski, 1999).

More recent studies suggest that there is more to the perception of smiling happiness than the acoustic changes associated with mechanical lip gestures. Listeners are easily able to hear the difference between speech produced with open smiles, suppressed smiles, or no smile, and accuracy increases the more "smiley" the smile is (again relying on resonance cues, which were sometimes misleading due to inter-speaker differences; Drahota, Costall, and Reddy, 2008). Similarly, French listeners found it easy to distinguish spontaneous amused speech from speech produced with a mechanical smile (Aubergé and Cathiard, 2003): Spontaneous amusement (in French speakers, at least) was typically louder than mechanically smiled speech. Interestingly, resonance cues do not distinguish different kinds of laughter, which vary in laryngeal but not articulatory features (Szameitat *et al.*, 2009).

9.11   Personality and Voice

The study of how personality is expressed and/or perceived from voice signals provides an interesting contrast to emotion. In many views, emotion and personality are related concepts, with emotion by definition a transient state and personality encompassing the more enduring (but by no means stable or permanent) aspects of the manner in which individuals respond to stimuli. Links between personality and voice have been apparent from early times. According to Kramer (1964), the word "personality" originally derived from the Latin *personare*, "to sound through," apparently referring to the mouth opening in an actor's mask. The meaning shifted over time to refer to actor himself, and then to mean any particular individual. Hence, the etymology of "personality" traces back to the voice of the speaker.

Like the study of emotion, work on personality dates at least to the Greeks and Romans, who had rather elaborate views about the relationship between voice and personality. According to the Greeks, a deep and tense voice indicates bravery, while a high and slack voice indicates cowardice. A voice rising from low to high signals disgruntlement; a nasal voice signals spitefulness and moral laxity; high, clangy, birdlike voices indicate greed and vanity, and a cracked or broken voice signals gluttony and violence. Stupid people bleat like sheep or goats; but a dry quality indicates a wily person (Stanford, 1967; see also Laver, 1981, for an interesting historical review). Formal studies of personality and voice began in the 1930s, especially in England and in Germany. Voice screening was an important part of the process of selecting officers in the German army prior to World War II: Warm melody, softness of quality and accentuation were associated with a person capable of strong sympathetic and emotional participation, while a monotone, hard or harsh vocal quality and staccato accentuation were treated as evidence of calm, determined will power (Diehl, 1960). Similar views were held elsewhere at the time. For example, Diehl also quotes from an American personnel manual of the era: "If the voice is loud and harsh, its owner is inclined to be domineering and likes his own way too much. If the voice is breathy, soft, weak and lacks force, it belongs to the person who will spend his time in wishful thinking, rather than in actually doing; a daydreamer" (p. 193).

It is not hard to understand why the study of personality and voice has drawn (and continues to draw) so much attention. Most listeners have had the common experience of hearing a voice that gives the strong impression of a particular personality type. For example, the voice in audio sample 9.7 almost rings with apparent good nature and a sunny disposition, while that in audio sample 9.8 gives many listeners the impression of a certain restraint and/or snobbery. Because such impressions are so strong and so common, it seems obvious that we must be able to infer personality from voice; as Sanford (1942) wrote, "With respect to voice and personality, we can start with the evidence that they are related. The analytical approach, if judiciously employed, may clarify the relationship. If such an approach reveals no relationship, we would be forced to conclude that it may be the fault of the approach" (p. 838).

Despite such assertions, the study of the expression and perception of personality from voice has not evolved in a smooth or particularly satisfactory manner, as we shall see in what follows. Difficulties begin with the issue of defining personality. As with the study of emotional expression in voice, ability to define and measure the speaker's personality (like their emotional state) is a prerequisite for examining the accuracy of listeners' judgments or the acoustic cues to a given personality, but such definitions are so broad that it is difficult to operationalize them into a measurement approach (possibly because personality itself is a broad concept). For example, researchers have suggested that personality comprises enduring individual differences in the nature of the cognitive processes, the relative dominance of specific motivational states, the degree of emotional reactivity and the preference for certain behavior patterns (Revelle and Scherer, 2009). Although this definition distinguishes personality from emotional state (largely on the basis of duration), it does not readily suggest a method for quantification, despite the fact that ability to quantify personality is a critical component of many studies of personality and voice.

The solution to this dilemma adopted by many researchers has been to assess personality by means of semantic differential scaling. In this approach, subjects rate a large set of individuals on a large number of bipolar scales for different personality (or vocal) "traits." Factor analysis is then applied to reduce this large set of scales to a smaller number of relatively complex orthogonal "factors." Summary labels are assigned to these factors to describe the clusters of behavior patterns. The precise factors that emerge from this approach depend on the scales used as input, and on the individuals being rated. The scales need not be obviously related to personality or to voice; for example, many studies apply the fairly generic scales derived by Osgood *et al.* (1957), who reduced a set of 40 original scales like sweet–sour, fast–slow, and thick–thin to a set of three superordinate factors: evaluation, potency, and activity. Authors in early studies of voice and personality typically assessed personality with respect to some subset of the 40 original Osgood *et al.* scales and also frequently augmented the subset with additional scales to tune it to their specific application; or they used some other, similar set, derived in the same manner from another study (e.g., Table 9.3; Addington, 1968). More modern approaches often refer to the "big five" personality factors: Neuroticism versus Emotional Stability, Agreeableness versus Antagonism, Extraversion versus Introversion, Open versus Closed to Experience, and Conscientiousness versus Impulsiveness (e.g., John, 1990). Some studies assess personality from voice using a variety of formal personality tests; but most authors use self-reports via this kind of ad hoc personality inventory and rating forms.

The literature on vocal expressions of personality includes three primary approaches, each reviewed briefly in what follows. The oldest studies seek to determine if listeners agree in their perceptions of personality from voice, and if those impressions are accurate. Much of this literature is impressionistic, rather than strictly scientific. Such studies are most often based on observation and lack experimental controls, making interpretation and generalization difficult. More recent studies have focused on "externalization" (how speakers' "true" personalities are expressed in their voices) or "attribution" (how listeners gather impressions – correctly or incorrectly – from voice), but seldom both in the same paper.

Table 9.3 Factors and rating scales for personality assessment from voice (Addington, 1968).

Factor	Representative underlying scales
Hearty/Glum	Talkative–Quiet
	Extroverted–Introverted
Potent/Impotent	Self-respecting–Servile
	Well adjusted–Neurotic
Soft-Hearted/	Kind–Cruel
Hard-Hearted	Sensitive–Insensitive
Gregarious/Antisocial	Jovial–Morose
	Extroverted–Introverted
Aggressive/Unresisting	Energetic–Lazy
	Active–Passive
Urbane/Coarse	Rich–Poor
	Educated–Uneducated
Hardy/Fragile	Tall–Short
	Unemotional–Emotional
Appealing/	Polite–Boorish
Disagreeable	Convincing–Unconvincing

9.11.1   Studies of accuracy in personality perception from voice

Studies focused on listeners' accuracy typically begin with measurement of the speakers' personalities, sometimes using a standardized personality inventory, but more often via the speakers' self-reports on ad hoc sets of rating scales like those described above. Investigators then gather assessments of voice, and compare these two sets of subjective measures. In one of the earliest examples of this kind of study, Pear (1931) played nine voices (a police detective, a secretary, a minister, a fashion buyer, an army officer, an 11-year-old child, a judge, an electrical engineer, and an actor) over the radio, which was itself a relative novelty at the time. Each speaker read the same passage from Dickens (the study was conducted in England). Nearly 5000 listeners participated in the study by submitting an answer form published in the newspaper, and over 600 also provided detailed comments about the speakers (see Sidebar). (Identification of the speakers' vocations was part of the process.)

Pear's primary finding was the existence and importance of vocal stereotyping, the notion of which frames his entire book. For example, listeners correctly guessed the professions of some speakers (notably the actor and the judge), but for other speakers agreement greatly exceeded accuracy: Over 50% of listeners thought that speaker 1 (a police detective) was a farmer or a rancher, and most believed that speaker 8 (an electrical engineer) worked in a manual trade of some sort. Similarly, the highest leadership ratings were given to speakers whose voices were professionally important to them (the actor, the judge, and the clergyman). The informal nature of this pioneering study makes it difficult to draw specific conclusions from the data, but Pear makes it clear that he considers stereotyping to be an important aspect of the perception of personality from voice.

Findings of stereotyping have been repeatedly and consistently replicated over the years. More formal evidence emerged from a series of similar experiments (some performed in the laboratory, some over the radio) undertaken in Boston by Allport and Cantril (1934; Cantril and Allport, 1935). Three male speakers participated in each of eight laboratory experiments, in which listeners judged "outer" characteristics like age, height, and appearance, and "inner" characteristics like vocation, political preference, extroversion, dominant values, and ascendance. Listeners also matched voice samples to summary sketches of personality. Participation in the radio experiments was limited: only 285 responses were submitted, in contrast to the nearly 5000 received by Pear (the authors explained that the experiments were broadcast opposite the popular show *Amos 'n' Andy*, pointing out that science has a hard time competing with comedy), but results were consistent with those from the laboratory studies. Loud, boisterous voices were judged to be extroverted; gentle, restrained voices were judged to be introverted, sometimes mistakenly. Forceful, aggressive voices were rated as ascendant; passive, meek voices were heard as submissive, but often incorrectly. Summary descriptions of personality were easier to match to voices than were individual traits; but accuracy seemed a matter of coincidence rather than insight. That is, listeners were accurate when trait bundles happened coincidentally to correspond to speaker's measured personality, but the two dimensions did not often correspond. Allport and Cantril concluded that these data are evidence for stereotypes in action, saying, "The uniformity of opinion regarding the personality of radio speakers is somewhat in excess of the accuracy of such opinion" (p. 50).

Sidebar: Some Comments from the Listeners
in Pear (1931)

Regarding the child (the author's daughter): "A girl scholar, but with full intention to excel, and unless baulked would be a leader or director of others, as a schoolteacher, or over a body of women in a room or factory or business; neat and careful in her dress; fair complexion" (p. 215).

Regarding the army officer: "Can do more than he thinks he can. Has not been sufficiently encouraged with praise. Nervous. Not a vast amount of education. Is inclined to be disgusted with the world and the people. Does not make allowances. Has not sufficient patience. Needs praise and encouragement and some sympathy" (p. 213).

Regarding the minister: "This poor fellow must have had a lot of reverses in life, if his voice is not assumed. I should say he has suffered considerably and is very sympathetic ... He has been anything but successful, and has great difficulty in making ends meet. I would imagine him as being tall and cadaverous, round-shouldered, with a long neck and protruding chin, but oh, so sad; very nervous and lacking confidence" (p. 197).

More formal experimental studies have reached similar conclusions with respect to issues of listener accuracy and agreement, with results again replicated robustly across studies and decades. For example, Taylor (1934) recorded 20 male speakers on a "Speakophone" aluminum disk, and asked 20 listeners to tick off the characteristics they associated with each voice from a list of 136 questions, statements, and words describing personality traits (including all the items from standard tests of neurosis and introversion). Listeners agreed consistently with one another, but their judgments were not in agreement with the speakers' self-ratings on the same scales. More recently, Hunt and Lin (1967) used essentially the same methodology to compare personality self-ratings of two male speakers to 78 listeners' ratings based on voice samples. They found some agreement between listeners' and speakers' assessments; error rates ranged from 13% ("forceful/gentle") to 74% (agile/slow), but results are difficult to interpret given the very small number of speakers. In fact, despite the common intuition that judgments about personality *must* be accurate sometimes (and hence the corresponding effort to define those circumstances), the many weaknesses of these studies have had the result that the question of accuracy must be considered as still unresolved. The totally subjective nature of the protocols (which involve comparing two sets of ratings), variations in the number and nature of the voices studied and the speech samples used, differences in the definitions of personality and the rating instruments applied, the fact that "personality" comprises complex and often contradictory factors, and the general absence of theory make it virtually impossible to compare studies or to draw solid conclusions, apart from the existence and importance of stereotypes in perception of personality from voice.

9.11.2   What are the cues to apparent personality?

In general, description of vocal parameters underlying stereotyped personality perceptions has been a challenging enterprise for the reasons stated above. Four different approaches to this question have appeared in the literature: (1) purely descriptive, rating-based studies; (2) studies in which experimenters examine correlations between acoustic measures of voices and ratings of the speakers' personalities; (3) studies in which speakers vary their delivery in some manner, and experimenters examine the impact of these variations; and (4) applications of speech synthesis to examine the effects of specific acoustic parameters on perceived personality. Of these approaches, only the first (which is also the most subjective and least scientifically rigorous) offers the opportunity to examine (albeit informally) how differences in actual personality are expressed by (or "cause") differences in the vocal signal. Such approaches cannot apply truly experimental methodology, because it is not possible to manipulate the personality of a single speaker and observe how his/her voice changes. For example, Stagner (1936) asked students to rate five male and five female voices on aggressiveness, nervousness, "general impression," intensity, poise, flow of speech, and clearness. He reported good social agreement on all scales except aggressiveness. In women, vocal intensity was moderately associated with aggressiveness, and flow of speech and clearness were correlated with nervousness; but no significant correlations were observed between rated vocal and personality characteristics in men. Other studies have found associations between introversion and lower dominance and a breathy quality (Moore, 1939), between dominance and loudness, resonance, and low pitch (Mallory and Miller, 1958), between rated vocal effort and extroversion, sociability, and emotional stability (Scherer, 1974), and between the lack of pauses and/or speaking rate and extroversion, competence, and likeability (Scherer, 1974).

A more modern rating-based take on vocal stereotyping is the so-called "vocal attractiveness stereotype" (e.g., Zuckerman and Driver, 1989; Zuckerman, Hodgins, and Miyake, 1990; see Section 4.3.5). It has long been known that physically attractive people benefit from "halo effects" and are judged to be more competent, smarter, nicer, more successful, and so on, than are less attractive individuals (the so-called "what is beautiful is good" stereotype; Dion, Berscheid, and Walster, 1972). An analogous process based on vocal quality has also been observed: People with more attractive voices (measured by ratings) are perceived as more powerful, more competent (Berry, 1992), more dominant, higher achieving, and more likeable than those with voices rated as less attractive (Zuckerman and Driver, 1989). Vocal attractiveness has a large effect on perceived neuroticism, a moderate effect on extraversion, openness, and conscientiousness, but no significant impact on perceived agreeableness (Zuckerman *et al.*, 1990), suggesting that an attractive voice is stereotypically associated with a relaxed, confident person who may or may not be pleasant. Interestingly, the vocal attractiveness stereotype is most prominent when listeners are unfamiliar with the talkers, but disappears at high levels of familiarity (Zuckerman *et al.*, 1990). The negative impressions created by an unattractive voice are exacerbated when such a voice is paired with an attractive face, an effect that has often been exploited to comic effect in film (for example, in the shrill, high-pitched voice used by Leslie Ann Warren in her performance as scheming gangster's moll Norma Cassady in *Victor, Victoria* (Edwards, 1982), or Jean Hagen's portrayal of the beautiful but discordantly-voiced silent film star Lina Lamont in *Singin' in the Rain* (Freed, Donen, and Kelly, 1952)). Similarly, politicians with attractive faces but unattractive voices are perceived as significantly less attractive, competent, trustworthy, and as lacking in leadership ability compared to those whose faces and voices are both attractive (Surawski and Ossoff, 2006).

The effects of vocal attractiveness may also be modulated by other stereotypes related to the relative maturity or babyishness of the voice in question. Childlike or babyish adult voices (those perceived as higher pitched and "tighter") are stereotypically associated with less power and more warmth and approachability than more mature-sounding voices (Montepare and Zebrowitz-McArthur, 1987); they lead to impressions that the speaker is weaker, less assertive or dominant, less competent, and more vulnerable, but also more kind and honest than a more mature speaker (Berry, 1990, 1992). Voices that are both babyish and unattractive received particularly negative ratings on a variety of personality attributes related to power (Berry, 1992). Stereotypes associated with the speaker's sex further modulate these findings. Attractive female voices (but not male voices) are associated with warm and likeable personalities, while attractive male voices (but not female voices) are associated with dominant personalities (Berry, 1990). Babyishness in female speakers is particularly strongly associated with perceived weakness, whether or not the speaker's voice is attractive; and perceived maturity affects perceived competence only for females with attractive voices, and not for other speakers. These interactions suggest that positive

personality attributions associated with vocal maturity may arise because the characteristics associated with mature voices overlap with those that signal masculinity
(Zuckerman, Miyake, and Elkin, 1995), as discussed in Chapter 4.

Sidebar: What is an Attractive Voice, Anyway?

Surprisingly little is known about what it is that makes a voice attractive, despite
the apparent importance of vocal attractiveness in interpersonal relations. Some
research (reviewed in Chapter 10) has described the characteristics of a good
operatic singing voice, but information about good quality in normal speaking
voices is generally lacking (although most of us feel we know a good voice when
we hear one, and listeners agree reasonably well about whether or not a given
voice is attractive). This limitation extends to the study of pathological voice
quality: No generally agreed-upon standards exist for attributes that distinguish
a normal voice from a disordered one.

One correlational study (Zuckerman and Miyake, 1993) has explored the
attributes that characterize attractive voices. In this study, one group of listeners
rated the attractiveness of 110 voice samples from males and females, and a
second group rated the voices on subjective scales for pitch, pitch range,
shrillness, loudness and loudness range, resonance, monotonousness, nasality,
deepness, squeakiness, articulation, and throatiness. Vocal attractiveness was
significantly associated with good articulation, low shrillness, low nasality,
moderate pitch and pitch range, and good resonance ($R^2 = 0.74$). Attempts to
explain these associations via additional correlations with acoustic measures of
the voice samples were not successful, however. Thus, it is not currently possible to estimate a priori how attractive or appealing a voice will be from its
acoustic attributes, or to determine objectively which attributes should be
addressed in attempts at vocal improvement or rehabilitation. More recent
evidence (Bruckert *et al.*, 2010) indicates that synthetic voices created by averaging together many individual voices are more attractive the more voices are
included in the average. This effect may occur because averaging decreases the
aperiodicities in each voice, or because the averaged voices better approximate
prototypes for voices in a given culture. In any event, for the time being vocal
beauty remains in the ear of the listener.

One reasonable question about the importance of stereotyped vocal cues in personality perception concerns the importance of such cues in contexts where other, factual
information about a person's competence and/or warmth are available – for example,
in a job interview where a résumé documents the speaker's background and achievements. Evidence suggests that such influence is substantial (Ko, Judd, and Stapel,
2009). When male and female speakers with voices rated high or low on masculinity
or femininity (independent of their biological sex) read aloud résumés containing
stereotypically masculine or feminine data (e.g., documenting past employment as a
security guard or as an aerobics instructor), speakers with voices rated low in femininity

Table 9.4   Associations between measured vocal characteristics and ratings of personality for males vs. females (adapted from Aronovitch, 1976).

Female speakers:

Mean intensity	Self-doubting/self-confident
	Extraversion/introversion
	Boldness/caution
	Laziness/energy
Speaking rate	Self-doubting/self-confident
	Boldness/caution
Mean F0	Kindness/cruelty
	Maturity/immaturity
	Emotionality/unemotionally
Pausing	Self-doubting/self-confidence
	Extraversion/introversion

Male speakers:

Intensity variance	Self-doubting/self-confident
	Extraversion/introversion
	Boldness/caution
	Submissiveness/dominance
F0 variance	Submissiveness/dominance

were perceived as more competent than speakers with highly feminine voices, independent of sex, and regardless of résumé type. Speakers with highly feminine voices were also perceived as warmer. In these studies, femininity was significantly correlated with babyishness (as in the studies reviewed above), consistent with the suggestion above that a chain of associations links perceived femininity (independent of biological sex) with babyishness and both to weakness and incompetence (because babies are less competent than adults; Ko *et al.*, 2009).

In summary, rating-based studies have consistently reported that listeners' agreement exceeds their accuracy in perceiving personality characteristics from voice. Some evidence has emerged regarding the nature of some of these stereotypes, but because these studies depend entirely on listeners' subjective ratings and on correlational analyses (which cannot demonstrate causation), it is difficult to draw firm conclusions, either about the nature of the stereotypes or about the relationships among the different variables studied.

In the second class of studies examining the basis for listeners' stereotypical judgments of personality from voice, experimenters gather ratings of perceived personality (as above) but then evaluate the correlations between those ratings and acoustic measures of the voices. For example, Aronovitch (1976) asked listeners to rate the personalities of 57 speakers on 10 bipolar scales (self-doubting/self-confident, extraverted/introverted, kind/cruel, bold/cautious, lazy/energetic, sociable/unsociable, humorous/serious, mature/immature, submissive/dominant, and emotional/unemotional), based on recorded readings of a standard passage. He found high interrater reliability in assignment of particular traits to particular voices, but different patterns of correspondences for male and female speakers (Table 9.4). For female speakers,

Table 9.5   Effects of varied speaking styles on personality attributions (Addington, 1968).

Increased breathiness:
   Younger, more artistic (males)
   More feminine, prettier, more petite, more effervescent, more highly strung, shallower
   (females)

Increased flatness:
   More masculine, more sluggish, colder, more withdrawn (males and females)

Increased throatiness:
   Older, more realistic, more mature, more sophisticated (males)
   Less intelligent, more masculine, lazier, more boorish, uglier, more careless, more neurotic,
   more apathetic (females)

Faster rate:
   More animated, more extroverted (males and females)

More pitch variability:
   More dynamic, feminine, aesthetic (males)
   More dynamic, extroverted (females)

Increased vocal tenseness:
   Older, more unyielding (males)
   Younger, more emotional, more feminine, more high strung, less intelligent (females)

Increased vocal orotundity:
   More energetic, healthier, more artistic, more sophisticated, prouder, more interesting,
   more enthusiastic (males)
   Livelier, more gregarious, more sensitive, prouder, more humorless (females)

personality judgments were related to static aspects of speech (average intensity, F0, pausing, and speaking rate); for males, personality judgments varied with dynamic aspects of speech (variability in intensity and F0). Like studies based solely on listeners' ratings, such studies cannot demonstrate that listeners' judgments depend on the particular acoustic attribute. They can only demonstrate that an association exists between the rated personality and measured vocal characteristics.

Other kinds of studies are more amenable to experimental approaches from which causal relations can be inferred. For example, speakers can vary their delivery, while holding everything else as constant as possible. Addington (1968) asked two male and two female speakers to read a standard passage with seven different voice qualities (breathy, tense, thin, flat, throaty, nasal, and "orotund"), at three speaking rates, with three levels of F0 variability. He then gathered personality ratings on 40 scales for all 144 voice samples. Listeners agreed very well in their ratings, with reliability ranging from 0.94 for the scale masculine/feminine to 0.64 for ratings of extroversion/introversion. The effects of the different voice quality manipulations are listed in Table 9.5. As this table shows, changes to speaking rate, F0 variability, flatness, and "orotundity" had similar effects on perceived personality for male and female speakers, but the effects of changes in breathiness, throatiness, and vocal tenseness were sex-dependent, reminiscent of the varying effects of babyishness described above.

Acoustic manipulations or speech synthesis can also be used to vary single acoustic parameters while holding others constant, to examine the effects on perceived personality. To date, such studies are few in number and have focused on a small number of acoustic parameters and a short, varying list of personality dimensions. For example, Page and Balloun (1978) examined the relationship between loudness and perceived personality by adjusting playback volume for the voice of a female talker in conversation with a male (whose voice was not manipulated). Rated assertiveness for the female increased with volume, but ratings of self-assurance (maturity, relaxation, independence) and desirability (sincerity, good work partner) decreased with increased volume. In a more ambitious design, Brown, Strong, and Rencher (1974) used speech synthesis to modify the speaking rate (normal, one half normal, 1.5 times normal), mean F0 (normal, 70% of normal, 1.8 times normal), and F0 variance (normal, 20% of normal, 1.8 times normal) of two male voices saying the sentence "We were away a year ago," thereby creating 54 voices from two original tokens. Thirty-seven listeners rated these stimuli on 15 scales related to the personality factors "competence" and "benevolence." Rate manipulations had the largest effects on perceived personality. Decreasing the speaking rate resulted in large decreases in perceived competence and smaller decreases in rated benevolence, while increasing the speaking rate decreased perceived benevolence, and increased perceived competence. Effects of F0 manipulations were also reliable, but smaller. Increasing F0 variability resulted in increased benevolence ratings, while decreasing F0 variability decreased both perceived competence and perceived benevolence; and increasing mean F0 caused decreases in ratings of both competence and benevolence. A subsequent study (Smith, Parker, and Noble, 1975) focused exclusively on the effects of rate, and applied less extreme manipulations, along with more, smaller steps (+/– 12.5%, 25%, 37.5%, 50%), and a larger set of speakers (six rather than two). This study confirmed that a strong, linear relationship exists between speaking rate and perceived competence, such that fast talkers are perceived as significantly more competent than slow talkers. The relationship between rate and benevolence proved curvilinear, however: Either very fast or very slow speaking rates were associated with less benevolent personalities. Increased speaking rates have also led to perceptions of a more active personality, while normal speaking rates were judged most fluent, persuasive, and emphatic, and least nervous. Decreasing the speaking rate had a large negative impact on these variables, and may also decrease perceived potency (Apple, Streeter, and Krauss, 1979). Finally, increasing F0 produced significant decreases in perceived potency; but neither changes in rate nor changes in F0 had any effect on perceived goodness (the "evaluation" factor derived by Osgood *et al.*, 1957).

In conclusion, evidence from synthesis experiments demonstrates that listeners' perceptions of a speaker's personality do depend in part on vocal characteristics. Impressions of high-pitched voices or slower-talking speakers are particularly negative (Apple *et al.*, 1979). The effects of speaking rate on personality attribution are large and consistent: Fast speaking rates are associated with more activity, dynamism, potency, extroversion, and competence, while slow talking is associated with less truthfulness, less fluency, less emphaticness, lack of seriousness and persuasiveness, and increased passivity (but also with more potency). The effects of F0 are more variable; higher F0 is associated with greater extroversion, assertiveness, confidence, and competence, but also with immaturity, emotionality and emotional instability, nervousness, and less truthfulness.

Increased pitch variability results in perception of a more dynamic, extroverted, outgoing, benevolent, and submissive personality; and increased vocal effort creates the impression of a person who is more extroverted, less self-doubting, and less lazy.

   Because of the many limitations inherent in these studies, the data do not allow us to fairly conclude whether the impressions listeners form reflect actual differences in personality, or whether they are the product of vocal stereotypes only tenuously tied to fact (Kramer, 1964; Scherer, 1972; Giles and Powesland, 1975). As noted above, studies have applied different definitions of personality or have focused on different aspects of personality, and have used widely differing measurement instruments to estimate personality traits. Because such tests (particularly the ad hoc tests typically applied in the studies reviewed above) do not measure personality in a consistent or comprehensive manner, it is not surprising that consistent associations between personality ratings from voice and measures from formal personality tests have not emerged. Because neither approach to personality measurement can account for all the details of personality, it is inevitable that they sample different parts of the variance in personality. In this case, both measurement approaches would be valid, but they would be uncorrelated because they simply measure different things (Kramer, 1964). Finally, most studies use voice samples that are recorded from monologue. This approach may limit the extent to which listeners can accurately judge attributes like dominance and submission, which are related to interactions with others (Mallory and Miller, 1958). For these reasons, despite the significant evidence that exists for stereotyping with respect to personality, the question of accuracy must be considered still an open one.

Sidebar: Speaking Rate and Personality

Speaking rate has significant, but complex, effects on listeners' personality judgments. In general, faster rates are associated with increases in perceived competence, while both fast and slow rates convey the impression of lower benevolence (Smith *et al.*, 1975; a moderate rate is best for this dimension; see Stewart and Ryan, 1982, for review). Speakers who increase their rate by avoiding hesitation pauses are also perceived as more extroverted, competent, and likeable than are speakers who pause frequently (Scherer, 1974). Faster speaking rates (up to about 130% of normal) may also increase the listener's interest in what is being said, and may lead to increased recall (LaBarbera and MacLachlan, 1979).

   However, additional factors complicate this simple picture. Primary among these is the fact that listeners may perceive speaking rates with reference to their own habitual rate, rather than in absolute terms (Feldstein, Dohm, and Crown, 2001), so that judgments of competence and benevolence vary depending on both the talker's and the listener's voices. Judgments of social attractiveness may also depend on the speaker's relative, rather than absolute, speaking rate (Streeter *et al.*, 1983). The context in which speech is produced also affects the relationship between rate and perceived personality: Slower rates are generally more acceptable when produced in the context of a formal interview than they are in informal conversational settings (Streeter *et al.*, 1983).

9.11.3 Cross-cultural differences in personality perception

Although speculation abounds, the origins of stereotypes remain mysterious. Pear (1931) suggested that they are based in theatrical portrayals that have become conventionalized through the development of modern mass media, but this seems unlikely given the clear views held by the Greeks and Romans about the relationship between voice and personality (unless they emerged from the classical theater itself). Modern arguments about the origins of vocal stereotypes hinge on the extent to which such stereotypes are shared across cultures. If stereotypes linking certain vocal characteristics to specific personality attributes have a basis in biology, then such stereotypes should occur commonly in unrelated cultures; but if they are culture-specific and learned, then we would expect differences to occur across cultures.

Following this line of reasoning, Montepare and Zebrowitz-McArthur (1987) argued that voice stereotypes have their basis in "ecologically derived behavioral factors," and thus persist because they have a foundation in truth. For example, perceptual cues associated with babyish voices might be shared across cultures, because the underlying biological process – aging – is universal. If this is the case, listeners might reasonably overgeneralize vocal cues associated with such factors, leading to vocal stereotyping. To test this hypothesis, they examined the perception of babyish voices in Korea and in the United States. Listeners in both countries heard 32 American speakers recite the alphabet, and rated their voices on nine scales representing the dimensions social/physical weakness, competence, and interpersonal warmth. Listeners also rated the speakers' vocal characteristics (e.g., their pitch, loudness, articulation, speech rate; mature/childlike voice, feminine/masculine voice). Results for Korean and American listeners were very similar. After controlling for the relationship between babyishness and femininity, both groups associated childlike voices with weak, incompetent, and warm personalities, and perceived speakers with feminine voices as weak, but not incompetent. American listeners, but not Korean listeners, also associated feminine voices with warmth, the only difference between groups. Listeners' judgments were not significantly correlated with the speakers' self-assessments, indicating that these shared perceptions represent stereotypes common to the two cultures.

Additional studies have revealed differences between cultures in vocal stereotypes associated with different personalities, consistent with social learning hypotheses. For example, Peng, Zebrowitz, and Lee (1993) hypothesized that differences in the social status accorded to the aged in Korea and in the United States might lead to different associations between vocal characteristics associated with aging (rated speaking rate, vocal tension, vocal loudness) and perceived personality, predicting that Americans (who value youth above age) should hear faster or louder male voices as more dominant and competent, consistent with the impression of youth, while Koreans should hear louder or slower male talkers as more dominant and competent, consistent with the impression of age. Consistent with these predictions, loud voices conveyed power for all listeners, but the effects of rate differed by culture. American listeners heard louder and faster-talking speakers (both Koreans and Americans) and more powerful and competent, while Korean listeners heard only the louder talkers as more powerful and competent (regardless of the talker's nationality). No effect of speaking rate on perceived personality was observed for Korean listeners. Because a slow speaking rate is often associated with an elderly speaker, these differential effects of speaking rate on personality attributions are consistent with differences in the value placed on the elderly in Korean versus American culture, and thus are consistent with social learning views of personality perception from speech.

Similarly, F0 differs for females according to nationality, with significantly higher values for Japanese women (about 232 Hz on average) than for Americans (mean = about 214 Hz) or Swedish women (mean = about 196 Hz; van Bezooijen, 1995). These differences could be due to sociocultural factors; Japanese women's higher F0 may correspond to the perception of greater politeness or of stereotypically female roles within Japanese culture. To test this hypothesis, male and female Dutch and Japanese listeners rated Japanese and Dutch female speakers on a variety of personality scales related to powerfulness and attractiveness. Voice samples were pitch-altered to create three conditions (lower than normal, normal, and higher than normal). Both listener groups heard the higher-than-normal-pitch samples as expressing less power, but groups differed in the voices they found attractive: Dutch listeners preferred medium- or low-pitched voices, while Japanese listeners preferred medium- or high-pitched voices, consistent with the hypothesis that Japanese women increase their speaking F0 to meet cultural standards for femininity.

Cultural effects on the perception of personality from voice are also apparent in studies examining how speakers' accents affect the way in which they are perceived. In general, speakers with General American or big-city accents are perceived as more intelligent, industrious, and confident than are those with regional accents, but regional accents are associated with greater integrity, sincerity, generosity, friendliness, and warmth (see Tsalikis, DeShields, and LaTour, 1991, for review). For example, speakers with an accent from Buffalo, New York, are perceived as nicer, less potent, and less active than those with a New York City accent (Markel, Eisler, and Reese, 1967); and English speakers with a Jewish accent received higher ratings for humor, entertainingness, and kindness, but lower ratings for leadership, than did the same speakers when talking with a General American accent (Anisfeld, Bogo, and Lambert, 1962). General American appears to enhance a speaker's credibility, while social attractiveness is enhanced somewhat by an accent, foreign or regional (Tsalikis *et al.*, 1991). Recent research (Lev-Ari and Keysar, 2010) confirms these accent-related decreases in credibility; however, these data suggest such effects are due to the fact that non-native speech is more difficult to understand than native speech, rather than to social prejudices.

Thus, evidence from studies of adult speakers is consistent with both biological and cultural influences on the manner in which personality is perceived from voice, and each explanation may be true for some aspects of personality perception. Some additional evidence from studies of vocal attractiveness in children's voices suggests an additional possible influence on such judgments: the "self-fulfilling prophecy" view as proposed by Scherer and Scherer (1981). In this view, others treat speakers in ways that are consistent with the personality stereotypically associated with their voice quality; and because of the manner in which they are treated, speakers eventually learn to behave in ways that are consistent with how they sound. In other words, it is not who we are that makes us sound as we do; it is how we sound that, over time, makes us who we are. This view contrasts to the more common view implicit in most of literature on voice and personality, which assumes that voice reflects personality (the "externalization" approach).

Although this view appears incompatible with modern evidence concerning the genetic basis of personality (Eysenck, 1990; Gjone and Stevenson, 1997), some empirical evidence consistent with an influence of voice on personality does exist (Berry, Hansen, Landry-Pester, and Meier, 1994). In this study, male and female five-year-old children counted to 10, and adult listeners rated their voice samples on scales related to competence, leadership, dominance, honesty, warmth, attractiveness, and babyishness. Results were very similar to the vocal attractiveness and babyishness stereotypes that have been reported for adult speakers. Attractive boys' voices suggested the personality of a competent, warm leader; attractive girls' voices suggested someone who was warm and competent, but not a leader. Independent of attractiveness, babyish voices of both sexes were associated with less perceived competence, leadership, and dominance, but more honesty and (for boys only) more warmth. The strong similarities between stereotyped associations between voice and perceived personality for adults and very young children suggests (but of course cannot prove) a basis for the persistent belief that there is a "kernel of truth" in personality stereotypes, via the treatment individuals receive as they grow, based on how they sound.

9.12   Voice in Psychiatric Disease

If emotions are thought to leak into the speech signal, it follows naturally that voice quality is a topic of interest in psychiatry and that psychiatric status may be assessed systematically, and occasionally with success, by the listener. However, in the same way that the changeful and contradictory forces in every human psyche wreak havoc with speech scientists' attempts to correlate stable vocal parameters with individual personality types, the effort to read character in the voice encounters even more daunting circumstances in psychiatric disease. The public has become resigned to reading in the newspaper that a recently discovered perpetrator of heinous, murderous acts was a nice guy and good neighbor. We can assume that seldom, if ever, without other information, does something in the voice of the criminally insane stand out as suspicious. As an example, consider Ted Bundy:

> Serial Killer, Rapist, Necrophiliac. He was attractive, smart, and had a future in politics. He was also one of the most prolific serial killers in U.S. history.[21]

Public officials in Washington, DC, among whom Bundy lived and worked, described him as normal-seeming and sincere. Video footage[22] verifies that his voice sounds masculine, competent, and intelligent; listeners might well rate the voice high on attractiveness.

[21]   http://crime.about.com/od/serial/p/tedbundy.htm; accessed November 9, 2009.
[22]   Available at http://www.youtube.com/watch?v=jAHgJFPcOvY; accessed November 9, 2009.

   While the more perplexing and egregious examples of mental illness remain intrac-
table to voice analysis, we often believe we can discern aberrant mental and emotional
states in a person's voice, and a few insights about vocal characteristics associated with
certain classic psychiatric conditions have been gained. In a study of social phobics in
naturalistic conditions (public speaking), acoustic parameters accompanying state
anxiety before therapeutic treatment (mean and maximum F0, high-frequency components in the spectrum, and pauses) decreased with treatment (Laukka *et al.*, 2008),
and listeners' ratings of the voice quality tracked the acoustic changes. In another
study, psychopaths, described as "con artists," were found to speak more quietly and
to use word emphasis differently than did nonpsychopathic male offenders; when
using prosodic emphasis, they did not distinguish between emotional and nonemo-
tional words, unlike the control group (Louth, Williamson, Alpert, Pouget, and Hare,
1998). However, it is not known whether these speech patterns are discernable to
listeners in social settings.
   Scientific inquiry has also examined abilities of psychiatric patients to produce emotional prosody in speech and to perceive emotional information in others to gain
clearer understanding of major depression, mania, and schizophrenia, to aid in diagnosis, and to track recovery using quantitative methods (Alpert, 1983; Alpert, Rosen,
Welkowitz, Sobin, and Borod, 1989; Alpert, Pouget, and Silva, 2001). As listeners,
schizophrenic subjects are poor at recognizing emotional information in speech
(Leentjens, Wielaert, van Harskamp, and Wilmink, 1998; Shaw *et al.*, 1999;
Pijnenborg, Withaar, Bosch, and van den Brouwer, 2007). Similar deficits in subjects
diagnosed with bipolar disorder were also reported (Bozikas *et al.*, 2007). Unusual
prosody in the speech of psychosis has long been noted. Emile Kraepelin, who first
described schizophrenia, established "flat" and impoverished speech (alogia) as diagnostic criteria (Kraepelin, 1921), and acoustic analyses of speech have borne this out,
showing low F0 and amplitude mean and variability and more pausing in negative
symptom schizophrenia (Andreasen, Alpert, and Martz, 1981; Alpert, Shaw, Pouget,
and Lim, 2002). Voice quality ratings by five judges significantly distinguished schizophrenics from non-schizophrenics (Todt and Howell, 1980). In another approach,
schizophrenic subjects had lower F0 than bipolar subjects (Bozikas *et al.*, 2007).
Measures of pausing and rate in speech may be useful in differentiating early stage
Parkinson's disease from major depression (Flint, Black, Campbell-Taylor, Gailey, and
Levinton, 1992). However, a study examining the relationship of acoustic measures
to measures of psychopathology did not yield correlations between speech parameters
and test results (Stassen, Bomben, and Gunther, 1991). Effects of pharmacological
treatment on acoustic measures are variable, with little change in prosody observed
following a course of antidepressant medication in subjects who improved clinically
(Garcia-Toro, Talavera, Saiz-Ruiz, and Gonzalez, 2000), while other authors reported
close tracking of improved behavior and voice in two-thirds of the subjects (Helfrich,
Standke, and Scherer, 1984; Stassen, Kuny, and Hell, 1998). Mood, especially depression, has been tracked with some reliability, if not specificity, by vocal indicators
(Ellgring and Scherer, 1996), in that an increase in speech rate and decrease of pausing were associated with improved mood. Both depressed and schizophrenic subjects
showed a decrease in F0 following therapy, interpreted as a reduction of arousal
(Tolkmitt, Helfrich, Standke, and Scherer, 1982). Pausing was reduced following

pharmacological treatment in another study (Greden, Albala, Smokler, Gardner, and Carroll, 1981). Factors such as subjective diagnostic criteria, a broad range of individual differences, and inconsistent longitudinal changes confound efforts to successfully establish vocal characteristics in psychiatric disease. Few such quantitative aids to subjective clinical diagnostic procedures have been reliably established.

9.13   Detection of Intoxication from Voice

Most of us have spent time in the company of someone who is under the influence of alcohol, but even those who have been spared the experience are familiar with the stereotypical sounds (and images) of drunken revelers and tearful inebriates, thanks to portrayals in films like *The Lost Weekend* (Wilder, 1945), *Leaving Las Vegas* (Regen and Figgis, 1995), *Who's Afraid of Virginia Woolf?* (Lehman and Nichols, 1966), *Animal House* (Landis, 1978), *Days of Wine and Roses* (Edwards, 1962), and many others. The complex effects of alcohol on human cognitive, motor, and sensory processes are well known (see e.g. Chin and Pisoni, 1997, for extensive review). At low doses, alcohol affects mood but may also contribute to increased nerve cell activity, which may actually improve motor functioning somewhat by relieving anxiety. Motor functioning decreases with increasing doses of alcohol. When blood alcohol concentrations (BACs) reach levels between 0.05% and 0.08%, muscle control is affected, so that there are increases in both reaction times and lack of coordination. These disabilities become more and more prominent as blood alcohol concentrations approach 0.1% (a concentration of 0.08% defines legal drunkenness in the United States), so that fine movements and skilled operations (including speaking clearly) become difficult to perform without clumsiness, and it may be difficult to walk without staggering or stumbling. With continued consumption, gait, speech, and other functions are further compromised, until coma develops at a blood alcohol concentration of about 0.3%. Death from respiratory failure may occur at blood alcohol concentrations above 0.4%.

9.13.1   The effects of alcohol on voice and speech

Because alcohol affects human cognition, sensation, and motor function, alcohol consumption produces many different kinds of changes to speech and voice, and affects both phonation and articulation (see Chin and Pisoni, 1997, for extensive review). At the level of the larynx, alcohol irritates the mucosa lining the larynx and alters the sensitivity of the tissue to mechanical stimulation. It also causes decreases in the amplitude of vocal fold vibration and in mucosal waves, corresponding to the slightly hoarse quality (dysphonia) that sometimes occurs with drinking. Consistent with these physical effects (and with the impression of mild dysphonia), alcohol consumption produces significant changes in the harmonics to noise ratio and in F0 when compared to a speaker's sober voice (Klingholz, Penning, and Liebhardt, 1988).

    Effects on articulation are sundry, and include *segmental*, *suprasegmental*, and *gross effects* (Johnson, Pisoni, and Bernacki, 1990). Segmental effects occur when alcohol impairs the speaker's ability to coordinate movements of the different articulators, resulting in changes to the ways in which sounds and words are pronounced. Errors in this category include substituting one sound for another (e.g., *r* for *l*, *s* for *sh*), devoicing the last sound of a word (so that *iz* becomes *is*), or deleting consonants altogether. More subtle changes may also occur, including inappropriate lengthening of vowels and consonants, incomplete stop closure in affricates, deaffrication, and so on, leading to an overall impression of sloppy or imprecise pronunciation. The speaker may also have trouble maintaining the relative timing of different gestures needed to produce sounds, resulting in misordered speech sounds or production of the incorrect sound; for example, mistiming the stop consonant release relative to the onset of vocal fold vibration can cause perception of different consonant (so that /d/ will become /t/ if the onset of voicing is delayed by as little as 20 ms; Lisker and Abramson, 1964; Johnson *et al.*, 1990). These errors typically occur with heavy drinking (blood alcohol levels over 0.1%). Suprasegmental effects are easier for most listeners to hear than segmental effects, but not all talkers produce them (Hollien, DeJong, Martin, Schwartz, and Liljegren, 2001b). They include changes to intonation, rhythm, speaking rate, and loudness. For example, speakers may produce words more quietly than usual (Sobell, Sobell, and Coleman, 1982), or may speak with increased F0 and amplitude; they may use an unusually breathy voice, or increase pitch variability. Severely intoxicated speakers often speak significantly more slowly than they do when sober (Sobell and Sobell, 1972; Sobell *et al.*, 1982; Hollien, Liljegren, Martin, and DeJong, 2001a); and the number and duration of pauses during speech may also increase with increasing alcohol consumption. Gross effects include mangling words, omitting words, interjecting unnecessary words, using the wrong word, misordering words, and so on. They occur most often with heavy drinking (for example, 1 liter of wine; 5–10 oz 86 proof alcohol; Sobell and Sobell, 1972).

9.13.2　Can listeners tell if someone is drunk?

Despite the large number of potential vocal cues to drunkenness, listeners are not always able to tell whether or not a speaker is sober, particularly at mild to moderate levels of intoxication. Listener accuracy ranged from 62 to 74% correct for judgments of speakers who produced a single sentence when their blood alcohol concentrations equaled at least 0.1% (Pisoni and Martin, 1989). Students and police officers achieved similar results as listeners: Students averaged 61.5% correct, officers 64.7% correct. Performance was slightly better in a simpler discrimination task in which listeners heard pairs of sentences produced by four talkers when sober or drunk, and were asked to say which was which. Phoneticians labeled the stimuli correctly about 82% of the time on average, while naive listeners were correct 74% of the time (Pisoni, Yuchtman, and Hathaway, 1986). In both cases, performance exceeded chance levels, but listeners were far from perfect.

　　Given the plethora of changes in voice that follow from alcohol consumption, why should listeners be less than perfect in hearing drunkenness? One possible explanation is that there are other factors that produce similar effects on articulation and phonation. For example, stress and fatigue may result in slowed speech or misarticulation, and shouting in a noisy pub or restaurant may cause inflammation or swelling of the vocal folds, altering their mass and stiffness and thus leading to changes in their pattern of vibration similar to those that occur with exposure to alcohol (see e.g. Colton, Casper, and Leonard, 2005, for extended discussion). Some neurological disorders, notably ataxic speech due to cerebellar disease, are also characterized by vocal quality and/or speech patterns resembling those associated with mild to moderate intoxication. A second possibility is that listeners are more attuned to stereotypes of drunkenness than to the actual sequelae, and thus overlook or misinterpret the relevant speech cues. Evidence for this view comes from a study by Hollien, DeJong, and Martin (1998), who asked 12 actors to portray drunkenness when sober and sobriety when drunk. The actors simulated mild, legal, and severe drunkenness, and then consumed alcohol until they were in fact mildly, legally, and severely drunk, at which points they tried to sound sober. Listeners perceived the actors as being more drunk when they were acting drunk than when they were actually drunk; and when the actors were drunk but trying to sound sober listeners rated them as less drunk than they were (so the actors succeeded in fooling people). Comparisons of feigned versus actual intoxication indicated that the actors exaggerated the vocal attributes associated with different levels of drunkenness. For example, F0 increased with increasing intoxication, but it increased more when the speakers simulated intoxication than when they were truly drunk (Hollien *et al.*, 2001a). Similarly, nonfluencies and speech errors doubled for actual intoxication, but quadrupled for simulated intoxication. It is less clear how the actors managed to sound sober. Comparisons of simulated versus actual sobriety showed no changes in F0 or intensity, and differences in speaking rate and nonfluencies did not change significantly.

9.13.3   Is a "verbal breathalyzer" possible?

If listeners cannot be fully relied on to identify the drunk, can instrumental measures of voice do a better job? Probably not, for two major reasons. First, as noted above, the effects of alcohol on voice are similar to those that arise from vocal abuse or strain. Because these changes can arise from causes other than alcohol consumption, and because even a non-drinker may need to shout in a bar or at a party, these cues cannot unambiguously signal mild-to-moderate intoxication (e.g., Klingholz *et al.*, 1988). Secondly, speakers differ substantially in the extent to which alcohol affects their voices, and up to 20% of speakers will not show the typical effects described above. With this caveat, it appears that segmental and gross effects (word additions, repetitions, substitutions, wrong voicing/devoicing, omissions, distortions, lengthenings) may be the best signs that someone is severely intoxicated. In one study, the rate of such dysfluencies nearly tripled for speakers with blood alcohol levels of 0.12%, compared to 0.04 and 0.08% conditions (Hollien *et al.*, 2001b). Increases in rates of interrupting and overlapping speech during conversation are also good cues to severe drunkenness (Smith, Parker, and Noble, 1975), although of course these can sometimes be explained by personality or emotional factors.

In summary, alcohol produces some predictable changes in voice and speech production, but there are often other explanations for the same phenomena (emotion, stress, vocal fatigue, neurological impairment, and so on), particularly at low to moderate doses. Most attentive listeners probably can tell when someone familiar is seriously drunk, but it is probably not possible to detect low to moderate levels of intoxication with any degree of certainty or consistency.

Sidebar: The *Exxon Valdez* Accident

On March 24, 1989, the oil tanker *Exxon Valdez* ran aground and spilled 11,000,000 gallons of crude oil into Alaska's Prince William Sound, causing massive environmental damage and the deaths of hundreds of thousands of sea birds and thousands of marine mammals. Cleanup costs to repair the appalling environmental damage exceeded $2 billion.

One issue raised by the National Transportation Safety Board during its investigation of this accident was the possibility that the boat's captain, Joseph Hazelwood, was drunk at the time of the incident. To investigate that possibility, Johnson, Pisoni, and Bernacki (1990; see also Tanford, Pisoni, and Johnson, 1992) reviewed six taped samples of Captain Hazelwood's voice, recorded 33 hours before the accident, one hour before, immediately after, one hour after, and nine hours after, plus an additional sample from a televised interview. When they compared the samples recorded just before and after the accident to the samples recorded 33 hours before and during the television interview, they found an increase in segmental errors, along with a reduced speaking rate, changes in F0 range, and increased vocal jitter. They also found some gross speech errors, but could not evaluate the specific pattern without knowledge of how common these were in Captain Hazelwood's usual manner of speaking.

These data are consistent with drunkenness, but do they *prove* drunkenness? To fairly conclude that the captain must have been drunk, vocal changes must exist that always occur when someone is drunk, and never occur at any other time. In other words, investigators must be able to separate the effects of alcohol on voice from the individual and combined effects of emotion, fatigue, stress, and talking in a noisy environment. In the case of Captain Hazelwood, Johnson *et al.* determined that the overall vocal pattern was more consistent with the effects of alcohol than with those of stress, sorrow, or fatigue on voice, but were unable to state conclusively that *only* alcohol intoxication could have caused the observed changes in voice. Because other explanations were possible, they could not fairly conclude Captain Hazelwood was drunk from the recorded voice data, and he was in fact acquitted by a jury.

10

Miscellany: Voice in Law Enforcement, Media and Singing

10.1   Introduction and Overview

As previous chapters imply, voice plays a compelling role in many aspects of everyday life. We review some of these applications here: legal cases and forensic investigations, advertising, dubbing and voiceover work, public and informational announcements, and news- and sportscasting. We close with an overview of the singing voice. The background in the previous chapters helps us to evaluate these applications of voice in the real world.

10.2   Legal Issues

The importance of voice in communicating personal identity has many ramifications, some of which entail legal actions. The special intensity of personal familiarity in the voice has inspired ad producers to chose famous actors to promote their products. It is cheaper, of course, to find someone to imitate the famous voice. However, laws have been passed that prevent ad producers from simulating or imitating a famous voice without permission or compensation. For example, California Civil Code section 3344 prohibits using "another's name, voice, signature, photograph, or likeness, in any manner, on or in products, merchandise, or goods, or for purposes of advertising or selling, or soliciting purchases of, products, merchandise, goods or services, without such person's prior consent." In this law, the voice pattern attains the personal status of the person's name, signature, or photograph. Several suits mounted by movie stars and other public figures whose voices have been used in commercials or other media have been successfully argued.

Other legal issues arise from the application of systems to recognize speakers or to detect lying from the voice. The limitations of speaker identification or lie detection by

Foundations of Voice Studies: An Interdisciplinary Approach to Voice Production and Perception,
First Edition. Jody Kreiman and Diana Sidtis.
© 2013 Jody Kreiman and Diana Sidtis. Published 2013 by Blackwell Publishing Ltd.

listening, discussed in Chapters 7 and 9 respectively, have long frustrated forensic phoneticians and law enforcement officials. Large bodies of research have been devoted to the search for "objective" methods to augment or replace flawed human listeners in the detection of miscreants. These are described in the following sections.

10.2.1   "Voiceprints" in speaker recognition

One early alternative to auditory voice recognition in criminal cases was the sound spectrogram, popularly known as a "voiceprint." As described in Chapter 2, spectrograms combine intensity, time, and frequency information in a single three-dimensional display, allowing the user to easily visualize changes in formant frequencies over time, intonation patterns, timing of articulatory events, areas of relative high and low spectral energy, and other aspects of the voice signal, in a single relatively detailed and accessible display.

Although the term "voiceprint" implies that spectrograms directly link a voice sample to the speaker in the same manner that fingerprints are physically linked to the body that produced them, this is not in fact the case. A fingerprint is a direct physical impression of the surface of a finger. In contrast, a spectrogram is a visual image of a sound, created by a series of acoustic transformations, whose precise appearance depends on the kind of transformation, the method of recording, the printer used, and other factors that have nothing to do with either the speaker or the voice. Secondly, fingerprints remain essentially constant during all uses throughout life. However, no speaker ever says the same thing in precisely the same way twice, so that intraspeaker differences as well as between-speaker differences must be taken into account when deciding if two "voiceprints" represent the same or different speakers (Bolt *et al.*, 1979; Kent and Chial, 2002). For these reasons, the catchy term "voiceprint" is more misleading than illuminating, and the impression of direct, physical evidence that the term creates is incorrect. Nevertheless, voiceprints have played an important role in speaker recognition research, and the interesting history of their use and fall from favor will be discussed in some detail.

Development of a sound spectrograph[1] began in 1941, motivated in part by military needs for a way to identify individual German radio operators[2] in order to track troop movements, and for a way to represent other sounds visually. (See Tosi, 1979, or Potter *et al.*, 1947/1966, for more history of the spectrograph.) The original analog sound spectrographs operated as follows. A sample of speech (or any other sound) up to 2.4 sec in duration was recorded magnetically. This sample was played back repeatedly while a variable electronic filter passed only certain frequencies on each repetition. Two filter bandwidths were available: 300 Hz or 45 Hz. An electronic stylus produced a dark line on special recording paper as the filter scanned through the

---

[1]   By analogy to "telegram" and "telegraph," spectrograms are images and spectrographs are the machines that produce them.

[2]   This remains an issue today. For example, the Civil Aviation Authority has issued a safety alert because of reported occurrences of unauthorised transmissions being made on British air traffic frequencies giving pilots bogus instructions at the time of landing their aircraft. In some cases, these malicious messages were identified only by a sudden change in the voice characteristics purporting (falsely) to be the flight controller.

frequency range of the device (usually 0–4 kHz). The darkness of the printed line corresponded to the intensity of acoustic energy at that frequency. The pass band of the filter increased in frequency with each sound repetition, and the stylus moved up the paper. The final result was a visual representation of the sound, with time on the x axis, frequency on the y axis, and amplitude represented by the darkness of the marks on the paper. The ability to generate images of dynamic speech events quickly and easily was a critical development in speech research, and it would be hard to over-state its historical importance. Modern digital spectrographic displays are available in most acoustic analysis software. In current approaches spectral analyses (usually fast Fourier transforms, or FFTs) are produced over very short segments of speech, and then plotted as traditional time vs. frequency vs. intensity displays (although modern implementations may represent intensity in color, rather than grayscale). Modern implementations allow better control of the filter bandwidth and sample duration, so displays provide much clearer images of voices with high F0. Thus, spectrographic analysis remains a popular, convenient way of visualizing dynamic changes in con-nected speech.

The notion of voiceprints as analogous to fingerprints in their usefulness had its ori-gin shortly after the exciting development of acoustic recording technologies and was nurtured by phonetic theories of the time. Forensic applications of sound spectrogra-phy began in the early 1960s (Kersta, 1962; see, for example, Hennessy and Romig, 1971a, for review). These applications were based on the "theory of invariant speech," which stated "that a greater and recognizable difference exists among speakers and that the differences within a speaker are not significant. In addition, there is no overlap between the intraspeaker variability and the interspeaker variability. Each individual's voice pattern is unique to that person" (Hennessy and Romig, 1971b, p. 447). In this theory, the greatest challenge to accurate voice identification comes from physical changes in the speech apparatus with age and disease; differences in voice signals due to vocal plasticity are considered negligible. Application of spectrograms to voice identifi-cation required the additional assumption that spectrograms accurately and sufficiently display the unique attributes of each individual voice – that "the spectrogram shows acoustic reality, not subjective perception" (Hennessy and Romig, 1971b, p. 450).

In a typical examination, the examiner produced spectrograms of voice samples recorded during a crime and a sample or samples from a suspect. The examiner then compared the spectrograms, examining features like formant frequencies, patterns of transitions between sounds, fricative spectra, fundamental frequency, and so on. Many (but not all) examiners listened to the voice as well. Depending on the extent to which the two voice samples matched, the examiner could declare that samples came from the same person, different people, or that no determination was possible. (See, for example, Tosi, 1975, for a more detailed discussion.) Thus, spectrographic voice identification was a subjective decision by the examiner based on evidence, rather than an objective result produced algorithmically by a machine. Different examiners could and did weigh evidence differently, and could reach different conclu-sions based on the same evidence, because interpreting spectrograms was "an art rather than a science" (Hecker, 1971, p. 69).

The appeal of this technique is easy to understand, and, interestingly, it has today regained a foothold in the popular press and in action films following the advent of digital technology. First, spectrographic analyses turn auditory pattern matching tasks into visual pattern matching tasks. When matching two visual patterns, all the information is present at once, overcoming the temporal offset inherent in listening. The examiner can scan both images, isolating and comparing different aspects at leisure. In contrast, auditory patterns are by their nature distributed across time, making it difficult to isolate comparable features in two signals and creating memory demands that may add variability to results. Spectrograms also have advantages over other acoustic analysis techniques, in that they provide a dynamic display of many aspects of the speech signal. Waveform displays show frequency, but resonance information is hard to extract visually; spectral displays show summary frequency and resonance information, but have limited ability to resolve and highlight dynamic changes in the speech signal over time. In contrast, a spectrogram provides both spectral and frequency information in one display. Producing a spectrogram requires very little equipment and only limited sophistication in acoustic analysis. The technique is very simple, with few parameters to manipulate, and provides a handy "one-size-fits-all" kind of analysis. Thanks to dedicated analog hardware, spectrograms were also easy and fast to produce compared to other analysis techniques that were available in the 1960s. Finally, spectrograms gave the impression of a scientific, technologically advanced tool, objectively applied by trained and credentialed examiners, in contrast to the opinions offered by witnesses who might or might not remember the voice of a perpetrator accurately.

All spectrographic analyses have significant practical and theoretical limitations, however. Technically, resolution on the time or frequency dimension can only be increased at the expense of resolution on the other dimension, as described above. Because resolution is limited, it is possible for two spectrograms to look nearly identical, but represent different utterances, especially when the recorded signals are noisy or limited in frequency range (Hecker, 1971). Analyses were difficult to calibrate, and the technique was not robust to variations in recording conditions or procedures. Differences in the equipment used in recording the test and comparison utterances could affect the outcome of analyses, and noise in the voice recordings could obscure important details, resulting in artefactually increased or decreased resemblances among spectrograms. Finally, when the speaker's fundamental frequency was high, the 300 Hz filter bandwidth used by the original analog spectrographs could not resolve vowel formants adequately. This meant that spectrograms of women's and children's voices were very difficult to evaluate. Forensic applications of spectrography entailed further limitations. First, examiners were often police officers who were not necessarily sophisticated in phonetics or speech science. They took a two-week course on voice identification via spectrography, and then apprenticed with a mentor for up to two years; but hardly anyone completed the training (Tosi, 1975). Finally, at the time speech research had focused almost entirely on the acoustics of speech, and relatively little on the aspects of sound that characterize individual talkers. Thus, little information was available to examiners about the features that distinguish different talkers, as compared to those that represent intraspeaker variability. As a result, examiners appear to have confused aspects related to differences in what was said with speaker-related differences, and intra- with interspeaker variations in voice quality.

Theoretical limitations are also apparent. The "theory of invariant speech" now seems very naive, given an appreciation of the extent to which individuals can voluntarily vary their vocal quality (Chapter 1). Evidence from studies of vocal disguise further undermined this theory. Endress, Bambach, and Flosser (1971) reported that original analog spectrograms were useless when a common falsetto disguise was applied, because spectrograms cannot adequately resolve formants and other features when F0 is high. In a more detailed study, Reich, Moll, and Curtis (1976) asked 30 speakers to disguise their voices in various ways. They then presented spectrograms of 15 undisguised and 15 disguised test voice samples, along with 15 undisguised reference spectrograms, to four experienced voiceprint examiners who were asked to match the test to the reference samples. This was an open set task: In reality, a correct match existed for only 11/15 test samples. Undisguised samples were correctly identified 56.7% of the time, but disguised samples were correctly identified only 21.7% of the time. Thus, vocal disguise does significantly interfere with spectrographic identification (although recognition from undisguised samples was not impressive to start with), contrary to the central assumption of the method.

Experimental evidence regarding the reliability of spectrographic voice identification varies widely from study to study, with error rates across studies ranging from 0% to 85% (Kent and Chial, 2002). Proponents of the method often argued that most errors represented misses (failing to correctly identify the true perpetrator) rather than false alarms (identifying an innocent person as the perpetrator); but high overall error rates reduced the evidentiary value of the method. Variations in accuracy and reliability were usually attributed to differences in experimental protocols (as they are in studies of voice recognition by listening). However, researchers were never able to define the effects of different experimental manipulations on accuracy and reliability, so no consensus was reached on which procedures were optimal. Further, no consistent criteria were specified for what constituted a match between voiceprints. Neither the absolute nor the relative importance of different voice features was ever established, so it was never clear how much weight should be given to testimony regarding matches or nonmatches between spectrograms. Given these difficulties, legal testimony based on spectrograms was controversial almost from the start, and voice identifications based solely on spectrograms have fallen into legal disfavor. (See Faigman, Kaye, Saks, and Sanders, 2002, for review of the past and present legal status of spectrograms in courtroom proceedings.)

Modern approaches to forensic voice recognition may include reference to spectrograms, but typically experts make use of both auditory and acoustic analysis in preparing testimony about the likelihood that two voice samples represent the same speaker (Rose, 2002). Listening to the voice samples allows the expert to screen for recording quality or for unusual auditory characteristics, but on its own listening is not efficient because voices can sound very similar but be acoustically rather different. Similarly, acoustic analysis (including reference to spectrographic displays) remains a useful manner of visualizing dynamic changes in speech; but no acoustic analysis is adequate on its own because it is never clear without listening which dimensions should be analyzed.

10.2.2 Voice recognition by computers

Voice recognition by computer is quite different from the traditional forensic case, where a listener hears a voice sample and recognizes or even names the speaker. Computer systems capable of positively identifying any subject from a recorded voice sample do not exist at present. Instead, in the usual procedure a cooperative speaker produces a specific test phrase, which is analyzed acoustically and compared to a stored template that has been created for the person the speaker claims to be. A statistical index of the match is created, and if the match exceeds some threshold, the person's identity is verified. The precise details of the algorithm vary from product to product, but such "speaker verification" can be very accurate indeed, with false alarm and miss rates of less than 1% (Kunzel, 1994). To ensure that the template for each speaker adequately represents the range of voice qualities that the speaker uses (to keep the incorrect rejection rate below the threshold of irritation), such systems generally require substantial training, and voice templates are normally constructed from multiple recordings of a single speaker gathered over a period of time (Hammersley and Read, 1996).

Because comparisons utilized in automatic speaker recognition usually depend on the overall voice spectrum, and not on any particular feature or phonetic details of the voice, such algorithms provide little insight into human voice recognition processes or performance. The specific parameters analyzed do not necessarily relate in any straightforward way to traditional linguistic articulatory features or acoustic parameters; they are typically more robust under controlled conditions, and under those conditions, they are more powerful than traditional parameters (Rose, 2002). Of course, they are not human-free, in that humans write the programs, select the parameters for the analysis, and provide the samples of speech. Verification procedures also differ substantially from traditional forensic speaker recognition scenarios (Kunzel, 1994). First, in most computer voice verification applications, speakers wish to be recognized and accordingly comply with the verification protocol. They make no attempt at vocal disguise, and produce the correct phrase clearly (and repeatedly, if necessary). Criminals do not usually wish to be recognized, and may make vigorous efforts to confound identification attempts. The test phrase used in computer recognition is carefully designed to incorporate words that discriminate well among speakers. In contrast, no control at all is possible over what is said during a crime; and under most Western legal systems a suspect cannot be compelled to repeat the phrases used during a crime, or even to provide any comparison voice sample at all.

In a computer verification task, the voice sample is acquired under ideal recording conditions. The environment is quiet, good-quality equipment is available, and the line to the computer is noise-free. (In fact, such systems tend to be very sensitive to transmission channel characteristics and environmental noise; Rose, 2002). In contrast, during the commission of a crime the voice sample (if one exists) is often a recording of a telephone call or the low-fidelity soundtrack from a video recorder. The environment is usually noisy, and may include a background of other voices or traffic sounds, and the transmission system and/or recording device may filter the signal rather drastically. For example, telephone systems are subject to filtering, hissing, static, and dropouts to varying extents. Improving system performance almost always means improving control of recording conditions, but because almost no control is possible in forensic situations, almost nothing can be done to improve recognition rates.

In the case of computer verification of speaker identity, there are only a small number of target speakers, and the task for the verification algorithm is to match a test sample to one single target from the test set, or to declare that no satisfactory match exists. Thus, only one (reiteratively applied) paired comparison need take place between the target and test voice samples. In contrast, the target in the case of a crime could be anyone at all. There may be multiple suspects, and there is no guarantee that the target is in fact one of the suspects. This unlimited open set task is far more difficult than the constrained verification case.

Finally, the recognition threshold in a computer verification scheme can be adjusted based on the particular application to balance false alarm and miss rates. Recall that the likelihood of a false alarm (an incorrect recognition) depends in part on a listener's response criterion – the listener's willingness to declare that he or she has recognized the speaker. A very strict criterion will minimize false alarms, at the cost of a decrease in the rate of correct recognitions; a loose criterion will minimize misses but will also produce a high false alarm rate. In automatic speaker verification systems, system designers can choose a strict verification threshold in high security situations where false alarms (incorrectly admitting someone who is not a target speaker) constitute security catastrophes. Such a threshold will lead to the occasional exclusion of someone who has right to entry (a higher miss rate), but rarely if ever will someone be admitted by mistake. However, an incorrectly rejected speaker has the opportunity to appeal the rejection, for example by presenting identification to a security guard. By adjusting the threshold for verification, users can balance the likelihood of a false alarm and a miss to fine-tune system performance as desired.

This kind of fine-tuning is not possible in the case of forensic speaker recognition, because there is not a comparable appeal level in this type of procedure. A miss in a criminal case means a guilty person is set free, but a false alarm means an innocent person is convicted. Under these circumstances, a very strict threshold for recognition is appropriate, even if this results in the probability of a miss approaching 100% (Kunzel, 1994).

In conclusion, recognition systems that are commonly assumed to be "automatic" and "objective" are not human-free: Humans write the programs, select the analysis parameters, determine the criteria for acceptance or rejection of a speaker, and provide the speech samples (Rose, 2002). Commercial voice verification algorithms have very good results because we make the task easy for them. Humans asked to recognize voices do not perform statistically as well as computers do, but humans undertake a much harder task. They separate the voice from a background of noise, possibly including other voices; they map an uncontrolled, degraded voice signal, which is a member of an open-ended set, onto some decayed memory trace; and, somehow, they sometimes recognize the talker. Although human performance in this task is not well understood, it remains an amazing ability.

10.2.3 Computerized voice stress evaluators and lie detectors

Like automated systems to identify individuals by their voices and voiceprint machines to convict criminals, computerized voice stress analysis systems promise huge benefits to society with very little trouble to anyone. Such systems assume that a link exists between stress (which is further assumed to be associated with lying) and physiological changes, which in turn are unambiguously and uncontrollably expressed in the voice. This supposed link between a precise emotional state and precise acoustic signal characteristics allows very specific conclusions to be drawn from analysis of voice signals. As one manufacturer states:

> The technology detects minute, involuntary changes in the voice reflective of various types of brain activity. By utilizing a wide range spectrum analysis to detect minute changes in the speech waveform, LVA [layer voice analysis] detects anomalies in brain activity and classifies them in terms of stress, excitement, deception, and varying emotional states, accordingly. In this way, LVA detects what we call "brain activity traces," using the voice as a medium. The information that is gathered is then processed and analyzed to reveal the speaker's current state of mind. (www.nemesysco.com; accessed 2/1/2007)

The same manufacturer goes on to claim that the system can:

> ...distinguish between stress resulting from excitement and any other emotional stress. Distinctions are also made between confusion and other cognitive or global stress resulting from the circumstances surrounding the issue being discussed. It also distinguishes between "acceptable levels" of stress and between stresses emanating from attempts at deception. ... LVA detects levels of tension, rejection, fear, embarrassment and attempts to outsmart or answer cynically. It also measures the subject's level of thinking. ... Using Deception Patterns, LVA can achieve the greatest accuracy rate in detecting deceptions. (www.nemesysco.com; accessed 8/27/2007)

The first system for detecting stress in voice appeared in 1971, and usage of such systems as lie detectors has become increasingly common in a number of applications. (Table 10.1 includes a partial list of systems and their acronyms.) In the United States, over 1700 police departments use such systems when interviewing suspects[3] (Damphousse, Pointon, Upchurch, and Moore, 2007); and stress detectors are increasingly used to screen insurance claims as a deterrent to fraud. One company stated that the proportion of insurance claims turned down doubled from 5% to 10% after it began to use a stress detection system,[4] and another insurer reported that 25% of automotive insurance claims were withdrawn after use of voice stress analysis over the telephone.[5] The 2001 Aviation and Transportation Security Act even cites voice stress analysis as a possible screening tool for airline security, and the *New York Times* reported that systems are under development that would help airport screeners determine whether passengers should be further screened or allowed to proceed to their flights.[6]

These are high-stakes issues; but beyond the important goals of deterring fraud and making transportation safe, systems for detecting lies and stress from voice have great

[3] *New York Times*, "Could your voice betray you?" by Douglas Heingartner; published July 1, 2004; accessed 2/27/2006.

[4] "Truth testing for insurance claims," BBC News, August 14, 2003; news.bbc.co.uk/go/pr/fr-/1/hi/business/3150675.stm; accessed 2/27/2006.

[5] "Lie detectors 'cut car claims'"; news.bbc.co.uk/go/pr/fr/-/hi/uk/3227849.stm; published 10/30/2003; accessed 2/27/2006.

[6] *New York Times*, "Could your voice betray you?" by Douglas Heingartner; published July 1, 2004; accessed 2/27/2006.

Table 10.1 Voice stress analysis systems and their acronyms.

Acronym	System	Manufacturer
CVSA	Computerized Voice Stress Analyzer	National Institute for Truth Verification
	Lantern	Diogenes Co.
LVA	Layer Voice Analysis	Nemesysco
PSE	Psychological Stress Evaluator	Diogenes Co.
	Truster Pro	Nemesysco
	Vericator	Nemesysco
	Deceptech	Diogenes Co.

practical appeal. Polygraph screening (the primary current alternative to such systems) is time-consuming and expensive; it requires a trained operator and the physical presence of the person to be questioned; and it can only be used with yes/no questions. In contrast, voice stress analysis systems are advertised as cheaper, easier to use, less invasive, and less constrained than polygraph devices. Manufacturers claim that these devices can be applied to any speech sample, even one that is surreptitiously recorded or transmitted over the telephone; that they are not affected by drugs or caffeine or by the speaker's medical condition or age; and that they can detect lies from any utterance. They thus offer the promise of detecting any kind of lie – from a teenager's excuse for coming home late to an employee's misstatement on an expense report to a car salesperson's insistence that a price is the best he can do – with the same rigor and accuracy applied to matters of national security.

10.2.4   How do the systems "work"?

Systems to detect lies from voice signals require a large number of assumptions. For lies to be detectable, there must first exist a "lie response" – a measurable physiological or psychological event (stress-related or not) that always occurs when a person lies (Lykken, 1981; Hollien, Geison, and Hicks, 1987). Systems that detect lies by measuring "stress" require the further assumption that lying is stressful, and that this kind of stress produces physiological changes that affect the voice production system (Haddad, Walter, Ratley, and Smith, 2001). In most cases, this physiological response is assumed to be the so-called "microtremor," a tiny, low-amplitude oscillation of the reflex mechanism that controls the length and tension of stretched muscles (Gamer, Rill, Vossel, and Godert, 2006; Meyerhoff, Saviolakis, Koenig, and Yourick, 2001). These oscillations have a frequency of about 8–14 Hz, and are believed to be a function of signal delays in the reflex loops that regulate the amount of stretch in the muscle. Because microtremors exist in other muscles, it is further assumed that they exist in laryngeal muscles as well (Meyerhoff *et al.*, 2001). Stress is believed to decrease the blood supply to a muscle, causing microtremors to decrease in amplitude or disappear altogether – in other words, microtremors are assumed to be *inversely* related to stress.[7] Voice stress analyzers claim to measure microtremors in speech and convert them to a graphical representation that depicts the level and kind of stress felt by the subject. The final assumptions are that the presence of vocal indices of stress indicates that the person is lying, and that stress related to lying can be distinguished from other kinds of stress that may arise at the same time (Brown, Senter, and Ryan, 2003; Gamer *et al.*, 2006).

Although the proprietary nature of voice stress analysis technology makes it impossible to determine exactly what any system does, not all systems claim to evaluate microtremors. For example, Nemesysco (Natania, Israel) claims that its Layer Voice Analysis system (LVA) "does not use any previously known method for detecting voice stress, such as measuring 'micro-tremors' in the voice," but instead uses "unique signal-processing algorithms" that extract a large number of "emotional parameters" from each voice segment. Nemesysco cites 8,000 mathematical algorithms applied to 129 voice frequencies; up to eight "final analysis formulas" are also applied to generate measures of truthfulness, attention, arousal, and other attributes. No details are provided concerning the algorithms employed, so it is again not possible to determine what these systems actually do.

A number of logical, technical, and empirical problems are apparent with this chain of argumentation. The first difficulty is the assumption that lying is always stressful. It is easy to imagine a situation in which telling a lie might be less stressful than conveying an unpleasant truth; and for some people, lying in general appears not at all stressful, but natural or even exhilarating. Participants may also experience more than one emotion at the same time, which might also introduce ambiguity into results (Hansen, Zhou, and Pellom, 1999); and emotional states similar to those associated with lying may arise for other reasons (National Research Council, 2003). For example, Sommers (2006) found that a Computerized Voice Stress Analyzer (CVSA; National Institute for Truth Verification, West Palm Beach, FL) detected similar rates of "lying" (i.e., stress) from students playing a stressful video game (where lying was not an issue) as it did from subjects participating in a mock theft paradigm (20% versus 24% correct detection). In any event, a theoretical basis for associating particular measures with emotional states has not been elaborated by system manufacturers so there is no scientific basis offered for associating a given system output with a particular state in the subject. Secondly, muscular function in the larynx is highly complex. The laryngeal muscles are the smallest and fastest in the body (Chapter 2), and contractions shift very rapidly as muscles act synergistically and in opposition to one another to meet the demands of linguistic voicing, linguistically meaningful phonation contrasts, and vocal prosody (Chapter 8). It is difficult to understand how relatively slow, low-amplitude microtremors could be detected in the face of such a complex and rapid sequence of physiological events (Hollien *et al.*, 1987). It is also unclear how microtremors could be separated from the other many kinds of F0 variability that exist in voice, including jitter, shimmer, normal vibrato-like modulations, and pathological vocal tremors due to neurological disorders like benign familial tremor or Parkinson disease. Further,

---

[7] Although some manufacturers state that preparing for "fight or flight" increases readiness in all muscles and thus increases muscle vibration, implying that stress/fear *enhance* tremor (e.g., http://www.lie-detection.com/).

microtremors have never been found in the muscles of the larynx, even when those muscles were studied with electromyography (which measures electrical potentials directly from the muscles as they contract; Shipp and Izdebski, 1981; see Hollien *et al.*, 1987, for review). An additional difficulty is apparent with the claim that systems can evaluate virtually any voice sample, including recorded voices or voices heard over the telephone. Telephones filter out information in the 8–14 Hz range of interest, and many recording devices add wow (a slow frequency distortion in reproduced sound, due to speed fluctuations in a system component) or flutter (rapid variations in F0 fidelity) to the recorded signal, potentially contaminating results (for example, Titze, 1995; Jiang, Lin, and Hanson, 1998). Finally, like spectrographic analysis, many voice stress analysis systems ultimately depend on the subjective judgments of a trained operator. Subjective scoring, variability resulting from the particular utterances chosen for analysis, variations in recording quality, and other factors potentially limit the ability of the systems to perform as described (Brenner, Branscomb, and Schwartz, 1979; Brenner and Branscomb, 1979).

10.2.5   Attempts to validate voice stress detectors by comparison to other measures of stress

Several studies have attempted to validate the claims that voice stress analysis systems actually detect stress by comparing the output of such systems to more traditional physiological measures of stress. For example, Horvath (1978, 1979) compared the Psychological Stress Evaluator (PSE; Diogenes Company, Kissimmee, FL) to a traditional polygraph device in a study in which subjects lied about the identity of a concealed card. The polygraph was able to distinguish lies from honest statements at better than chance levels (hit rate = 0.65; false alarm rate = 0.15), but performance for the PSE did not exceed chance levels (hit rate = 0.28, false alarm rate = 0.28), even when subjects were highly motivated. Cestaro (1996) compared performance of the CVSA to a traditional polygraph examination. Neither system performed especially well in this paradigm, possibly because subjects were not at risk if the lie was detected. However, the CVSA underperformed the polygraph by a significant margin (38.7% accuracy, versus 62.5% for the polygraph). Meyerhoff *et al.* (2001) compared the CVSA's ability to detect stress to validated stress indices like salivary cortisol, blood pressure, and heart rate, in a stressful interview paradigm. All the physiological indices of stress increased during the interview, but no effect was observed for the CVSA data. These results are not consistent with claims that microtremor-based voice stress analysis systems do in fact detect stress. To our knowledge, data attempting to validate the LVA system against other measures of stress or emotion have not been published.

The validity of voice stress evaluation systems is also threatened by problems with interoperator reliability. Several studies have reported that results for different system operators were not significantly correlated (CVSA: Meyerhoff *et al.*, 2001; PSE: Horvath, 1978; Waln and Downey, 1987). More recently, Damphousse *et al.* (2007) compared the performance of expert and newly-trained users of the LVA and CVSA systems. They found between-group correlations averaging 0.34 for the CVSA (representing only 12% shared variance), and 0.19 for the LVA, indicating poor reliability when comparing expert and neophyte interpretations of the same data. (Interestingly (or alarmingly?), the newly-trained users were more accurate than the experts in this study.) Horvath (1979) reported that interrater agreement (but not accuracy) increased when subjects were highly motivated to avoid detection. Cestaro (1996) also reported that investigators using the CVSA agreed highly, despite the fact that their performance at separating truth-tellers from liars did not exceed chance levels (in other words, they agreed largely because as a group they were consistently wrong).

10.2.6   How accurate are voice stress detection systems?

Table 10.2 provides the results of an array of studies evaluating the accuracy of voice stress analyzers at detecting stress and/or lies. As this table shows, evidence does not support the belief that lies can be detected from voice using systems like those described here.

System manufacturers and proponents of voice stress analysis systems often argue that these consistently unimpressive results do not reflect actual system performance in the field, because laboratory conditions do not mimic the levels of jeopardy and stress that apply in real lie-producing situations. It is somewhat novel to hear claims that a commercial product only works in the real world but not in the laboratory; laboratory studies more typically overestimate accuracy, because they provide better control of extraneous factors (National Research Council, 2003). However, these arguments are inconsistent with validation studies described above, which demon-strated that subjects in laboratory tests did in fact experience stress that was detectable by other, more traditional means (Meyerhoff et al., 2001). Further, lack of realistic stress in laboratory experiments does not account for the very high false alarm rates reported in studies of voice stress analyzers. If the lack of jeopardy and relatively low stress created in experimental situations are responsible for the consistent reports of poor performance by such systems, then these studies should produce a large number of false negative responses (misses), rather than false alarms (Meyerhoff et al., 2001), but this does not occur.

Two pertinent studies (Damphousse et al., 2007; Hollien, Harnsberger, Martin, and Hollien, 2008) did examine the accuracy of the LVA and CVSA systems in a real-world setting. In the first (Damphousse et al., 2007), a total of 319 male arrestees awaiting processing at county jails in Oklahoma were asked about recent drug use, after which a drug test (urinalysis) was administered to assess truthfulness. The experi-menters were trained by system manufacturers, and experimental procedures were verified with system manufacturers prior to the beginning of the study. Neither system performed any better in this setting than it did in laboratory tests (see Table 10.2). The second study (Hollien et al., 2008; see also Hollien and Harnsberger, 2006) evaluated the performance of the CVSA under both laboratory and field conditions, and compared the performance of five phoneticians, two experimenters trained and certified by the manufacturer, and three experienced system operators provided by the manufacturer (who approved all of the procedures). Hit rates for the laboratory data ranged from 50 to 65% correct, but false alarm rates were very high (62–70%). For field data, hit rates were lower (19–38%); false alarm rates were also lower, but remained higher than hit rates (41–49%). In neither condition did performance exceed chance levels; and trained operators did not perform better than did phoneticians.

Table 10.2 Representative studies examining the accuracy of voice stress analysis systems. (FA = false alarm)

Device	Task	Results	Reference
PSE	Identity of hidden card	Hit rates below chance	Horvath (1978, 1979)
PSE	Public speaking; electrical shocks	Hit rates at chance; FA rate 42%	Hollien *et al.* (1987)
CVSA	Mock theft	Accuracy below chance (39–50%)	Janniro and Cestaro (1996); Cestaro (1996)
Vericator,[a] Diogenes Lantern	Mock theft	Accuracy below chance	Haddad *et al.* (2001)
Vericator	Smuggling	Hit rate 15%; FA rate 21%	Brown *et al.* (2003)
TrusterPro[b]	Theft	Hit rate 30%	Gamer *et al.* (2006)
Vericator	Mock theft	Hit rate 24%; FA rate 18%	Sommers (2006)
LVA, CVSA	Drug screening in prison setting	Hit rates: LVA = 21% CVSA = 8% FA rates: LVA = 5 FAs for every hit CVSA = 14.1 FAs for every hit	Damphousse *et al.* (2007)
CVSA	Lying under shock-induced stress	Hit rates = 64–65% FA rates = 62–70%	Hollien *et al.* (2008)
CVSA	Lying during hostile interrogation as part of military survival training	Hit rates = 19–38% FA rates = 41–49%	Hollien *et al.* (2008)

[a] An earlier version of the LVA system. Vericator was used as a trade name for this product in the United States.
[b] Another early version of the LVA system.

10.2.7 Screening applications

The above evidence suggests that use of voice stress analysis systems to determine whether a specific individual is lying at a given time is problematic. Use of the same software to screen large numbers of individuals for truthfulness (for example, in airport security applications) is limited by the same issues of reliability and validity, but additional problems arise when we try to detect an occasional liar from amongst a mass of honest individuals (National Research Council, 2003). As discussed above, the likelihood of correctly apprehending the liar (a hit) is a function of both the sensitivity of the detection system and of the user's tolerance for false alarms (accusing or detaining the innocent). This means that, for fixed sensitivity, detecting all liars also means accusing or detaining a large number of innocent, honest citizens (a high false alarm rate); and lowering the false alarm rate means failing to detect all the liars. This is a particular problem if we assume that most people are honest. Imagine an airport security queue on a bad day: 10,000 people are waiting to be screened, ten of whom are up to no good. Imagine further that a voice stress screening system with the improbably high accuracy level of 90% is installed at the airport. If this system is set to produce a high hit rate, then it must also have a high false alarm rate, so that detecting eight out of ten malefactors among the 10,000 people screened would entail detaining 1,606 individuals, only eight of whom are actually lying, for a false alarm rate of 1,598 people (National Research Council, 2003). (Of course, the screeners would still have to separate those eight miscreants from the other innocent individuals by some other means; and two liars are not detected at all.) If the system operators adjust their criteria to reduce the number of innocent people who are detained, the hit rate will go down as well; for example, reducing the false alarm rate to a more reasonable 39/10,000 people also reduces the hit rate to two of ten real liars detected. The inevitable trade-offs between hit and false alarm rates in detection paradigms mean that screening applications for voice stress analyzers are simply impractical when the actual proportion of liars is small.

Empirical studies of screening applications confirm this rather depressing state of affairs. When subjects attempted to smuggle federal trial evidence past a security checkpoint, screening with the "Vericator" (predecessor to the Nemesysco LVA products; Nemesysco, Ltd.) detected only nine out of 59 smugglers, while falsely implicating 23 out of 111 innocent individuals. This level of performance did not exceed chance, and did not differ significantly from the human inspector's ability to detect evidence smugglers (Brown *et al.*, 2003). Similarly, Gamer *et al.*, (2006) asked subjects to steal the contents of a wallet. A battery of physiological measures of stress significantly detected the guilty individuals in this paradigm (hit rate = .9; false alarm rate = .13); but the "TrusterPro" (another Nemesysco product) produced a hit rate of only .3 (false alarm rate .13).

10.2.8   Why do people believe in lie detectors?

"Voiceprinting," the promising but flawed technique described above, was debunked by the scientific community, and appropriate changes to legal procedures were implemented as a result. In contrast, voice stress analysis technology has never been shown to be reliable or valid, and has been thoroughly debunked several times since its first appearance (Disner, 2004; Damphousse *et al.*, 2007). Despite this fact, systems sell in increasing numbers every year, and legislation calling for new applications of what seemingly amounts to a useless technology is passed by a gullible Congress. What can explain society's insistence on clinging to a technology that does not appear to work?

A number of possible explanations suggest themselves. First, voice stress analysis systems may be useful even in the absence of accuracy, because (misguided) belief in their accuracy produces a deterrent effect (National Research Council, 2003). For example, Damphousse *et al.* (2007) found that arrestees were much less likely to lie about recent drug abuse when they thought interviewers were using "lie detectors" than when no detectors were used. Similarly, Disner (2004) relates an anecdote about a police department that uses an empty leatherette case with flashing red and green lights when interrogating subjects, to much the same effect. One manufacturer (National Institute for Truth Verification (NITV)) cites the results of a survey of users to validate its approach, stating, "It is clear that the majority of the survey respondents believe the CVSA is a useful tool. Key factors in this usefulness appear to be its ease of use, timeliness, affordability, and ability to help convince guilty subjects to confess. It appears to be very helpful in clearing cases."[8]

The current political and social climate also encourages buyers who want to believe. The voice stress analysis industry has been in operation for over 30 years, and systems are widely applied by law enforcement agencies who find them useful whether or not they are accurate. Advocates of such systems often point out their non-invasive nature, and sometimes cite in-house, unpublished studies supporting the validity and reliability of the systems. The respectability provided by the age of the industry, combined with the belief of users in the system, may create a culture that encourages continued (or even expanded) use of such systems despite the fact that no independent study has ever shown them to perform with better than chance accuracy. The seriousness of the problems that voice stress analysis systems purport to address further contributes to their appeal. Who could say "no" to a non-invasive, automatic terrorist detector? Even a flawed system may have appeal as a quick, stopgap solution to a serious long-term problem (Brown *et al.*, 2003).

Finally, a mystical aura pervades much discussion of voice stress analysis. For example, the Nemesysco website states that its LVA technology:

> … can detect various cognitive states, such as whether your subject is excited, confused, stressed, concentrating, anticipating your responses, or unwillingly sharing information. The technology also can provide an in-depth view of the subject's range of emotions, including those relating to "love."[9]

Voice stress analysis systems promise to give their users access to a speaker's deepest, most intimate thoughts and feelings – in essence, it offers the ability to read minds. These promises of access to hidden information and concealed feelings enhance the impression of secret, mystical rituals administered by figures of authority who by virtue of the power of the ritual are able to divine the truth (National Research Council, 2003). Limited access further enhances the aura of secrecy and power that pervades discussion of voice stress analysis technology. For example, NITV claims that it withdrew its CVSA product from the commercial market to prevent criminals from applying the technology to identify undercover law enforcement agents;[10] and the Nemesysco website refers to "secret" algorithms withheld even from patent applications. Whatever the explanation, it is unfortunate that limited law enforcement budgets are being invested in a product whose efficacy remains so much in question.

[8]   http://www.cvsa1.com/DOD%20Survey.htm; viewed 8/27/2007.
[9]   http://www.nemesysco.com/technology-sense.html; accessed 8/30/2007.
[10]   http://www.cvsa1.com/; accessed 8/30/2007.

10.3   Advertising, Marketing, Persuasion, and Other Related Applications

Television and radio advertising take up an increasing amount of broadcast time in the United States, and interest in how voices can affect sales has increased accordingly. Advertising is an interesting application of vocal expressions of emotion and personality, and of other topics discussed in this volume as well. The ad man faces a number of difficult decisions. Should a foreign accent be used to promote a product? A foreign accent might attract attention by being exotic and interesting, but it may be less intelligible than a native speaker, and may even provoke mildly xenophobic responses. Some voices in advertising have an importuning tone, which attracts attention, but may also be annoying or off putting. Voice quality in advertisements may do many things: It may be chosen primarily to seize the viewer's attention (by any means), or to represent positive attributes of the product, and/or to be entertaining. A deft combination of these attributes appears in a recent Superbowl advertisement created by Cars.com.[11] A salesman in a car dealership and a customer have a conversation closing the car purchase deal, using voices that communicate assurance, competence, and bonding. They begin to agree on Plan A. The customer mentions that Plan B would have involved bringing in a witchdoctor to shrink the salesman's head. The salesman's voice communicates nuances of uncertainty and fear. A second salesman looks into the office and asks for leave to go home, because, he says, of his tiny head, which we see perched on his ample frame. His speaking voice uses helium speech to increase vocal resonant frequencies to correspond to his now reduced head size. This advertisement uses voice quality first to simulate a successful transaction and then to entertain the viewer, who has intuitions about how vocal resonances correlate with head size.

10.3.1   What kind of voice should be used in an advertisement?

A well-chosen voice should help attract consumers' attention to the advertisement, increasing the likelihood that they will actually listen to it and remember its content; and an attractive voice may generate favorable responses and create positive attitudes towards the product. Further, the speaker's sex and age, his or her apparent personality, socioeconomic status, and race, and the style of delivery (upper-class; adolescent; accented) can reinforce the brand's image and focus the ad to the correct audience (Chattopadhyay, Dahl, Ritchie, and Shahin, 2003). Thus, an ideal ad should include a voice that is credible, attractive, and projects an image consistent with the product and tuned to the target audience, so that appropriate consumers identify with the voice and with the product.

Some research has examined how the voices used in radio or television ads affect a consumer's attitude toward the product or service on offer or their intent to buy, but these efforts have been fragmentary. The effects of music on advertising efficacy are fairly well understood (see, for example, Alpert, Alpert, and Maltz, 2003; Zander,

---

[11]   This ad can be viewed at www.blogs.cars.com/kickingtires/2008/02/super_bowl_ads.html.

2006), but at present ad directors usually rely largely on intuition to select a voice whose gender, age, ethnicity, and delivery style will attract the correct audience and produce the correct product image (for example, Chattopadhyay *et al.*, 2003). Most studies have focused on a simple evaluation of listeners' preferences for certain types of voices; for example, most listeners like younger voices better than older voices, and formal speaking styles produce the impression of someone who is bright and competent, while an informal style gives the impression of someone likeable (for example, Cantril and Allport, 1937; see Levi and Pisoni, 2007, for a recent review). Selecting an announcer based on fit between voice and product can enhance ad effectiveness. For example, North, MacKenzie, Law, and Hargreaves (2004) asked listeners to evaluate mock radio ads for five brands (for example, Rhapsody chocolate bar; image – indulgent, extravagant, pleasant, luxurious), delivered either in a voice that matched the brand or in one that did not fit the brand's image, as judged by a separate panel of raters. They found that the extent of voice fit to the product image served to highlight specific brand attributes, influencing listeners' perceptions of the advertisement so that they corresponded more closely with the desired product image (for example, made a car seem more "American"). Listeners also remembered the specific information in the advertisement better when the voice fit the product, but there was no effect on memory for brand name or class of product. These results suggest that it is important to select the voices for an advertisement very, very carefully, but highlight our lack of knowledge about how voice quality may project certain images, how different vocal attributes or combinations of attributes contribute to image formation, and about how subtle changes in image-related vocal attributes can influence advertisement effectiveness.

Two formal theories have been proposed to explain how voice quality influences consumers in advertising contexts. The first focuses on the manner in which voice affects the listener's attitude toward the advertisement and the vocal factors that increase the consumer's positive feelings about the brand. In this view, a pleasant voice is effective because it conditions the listener's preference for the brand or product associated with it. The second theory – the elaboration likelihood model (or ELM; Petty and Cacioppo, 1979; see Gelinas-Chebat and Chebat, 1992, for review) – argues that ads persuade consumers via two different mechanisms: central and peripheral. Attitudes formed via the central route are generated by actively thinking about the informative content of the advertisement and making a choice. Consumers who are persuaded via the central route are assumed to be highly involved with the ad, which is of significant interest to them, and as a result they should pay little attention to cues like voice quality. In the peripheral route, attitudes are formed by associating the product with positive or negative cues that condition the response, but without active, direct thinking. Consumers persuaded via this mechanism are not significantly involved in the ad, and may pay it little direct attention. This model proposes that indirect or peripheral cues like voice should be most important when listeners are not particularly interested in the product and either do not or will not pay attention to a message whose value to them does not merit an investment of direct cognitive effort.

Formal tests of the elaboration likelihood model have assessed the hypothesis that voice will interact with the consumer's view of the ad's importance, and have had somewhat mixed results. Gelinas-Chebat and Chebat (1992) asked one speaker to produce high-involvement and low-involvement ads directed at students (for student loans and an ATM card, respectively) while varying intensity and F0 variability (both at low and high levels, yielding four versions of each ad). Undergraduate students listened to each advertisement and responded to a 16-item questionnaire that measured the comprehensibility, clarity, interest, usefulness, and informativeness of the ads. Vocal characteristics affected attitude towards the advertisement only in the low-involvement condition, as hypothesized. When interest in the advertisement was high, changes in voice quality had no effect on ratings of the ad's effectiveness. In the low-involvement condition, the effect of F0 variability on advertisement acceptance was significant only when the intensity was low. Overall, low intensity and low F0 variability lead to better advertisement acceptance, possibly because less exaggerated vocal styles are more consistent with a low-involvement message and with indirect influences. A subsequent study using the same methods extended the inquiry to examine the relative effects of message content and voice quality on the credibility of the advertisement and on the listener's intent to buy (Gelinas-Chebat, Chebat, and Vaninsky, 1996). In the low-involvement condition, vocal intensity affected credibility; credibility affected listeners' attitudes toward the message, and attitude toward the service affected intent to buy, so a chain of association linked voice to intent to buy despite limited evidence for a direct connection. In the high-involvement condition, F0 variability had a significant effect on source credibility, contrary to predictions, with increased variability corresponding to a less credible speaker.

A final test of the elaboration likelihood model examined the influence of speaking rate on the speaker's credibility when the listener agrees with the message being advocated (a "pro-attitudinal" message) compared to an advertisement with which the listener disagrees (a "counter-attitudinal" message). Hypothetically, rapid speech should increase the credibility of counter-attitudinal messages, because increased speech rates are associated with extroversion, competence, likeability, and other positive personality traits (see Chapter 9), and because the faster rate of speech limits the extent to which the listener can process the details or implications of the spoken message. In contrast, faster speech rates might decrease the credibility of pro-attitudinal messages, because the quick delivery (hypothetically) undermines the listener's ability to process and elaborate on an argument with which they agree (and evokes the stereotype of the fast-talking unscrupulous salesman). To test these hypotheses, listeners heard pro- or counter-attitudinal messages at a normal speaking rate or at a rate that was increased or decreased with speech synthesis. In each case, they rated the speaker's credibility and knowledgeableness. For the counter-attitudinal message, credibility increased with speaking rate; and for the pro-attitudinal message, credibility decreased with rate, both consistent with predictions of this model (Smith and Shaffer, 1991).

10.3.2   Tailoring an advertisement to an audience: Differences between listeners

Because subtle cues like speaking rate, vocal intensity, and F0 variability appear to have different effects depending on the listener's a priori interest in the product or agreement with the position being advocated, these results highlight the importance of knowing whom the advertisement is directed at, and then tailoring the vocal message to the specific target audience. For example, campaign advertising aimed at "swing voters" who have not yet committed to one candidate or the other may rely heavily on such cues to fine-tune the advertisement to one specific target group (Kinser, 2009). In one example, a radio advertisement aired in support of 2008 US presidential candidate Barack Obama[12] begins with a negative message about rival candidate John McCain. This negative message is delivered at the relatively slow speaking rate of 128 words per minute. The contrasting second half of the advertisement is a positive message about Obama, delivered at 164 words per minute. This pattern of speech rate change suggests the advertisement is targeted to voters who think badly of McCain but have not yet reconciled themselves to voting for Obama. It gives listeners who agree that McCain is not a good candidate the chance to absorb the negative message, and impresses the same voters with the speaker's expertise with regard to Obama.

In addition to pre-existing attitudes, listeners' underlying cognitive and emotional profiles may also influence the likelihood that a given sales approach will succeed. For example, Hall (1980) examined differences between listeners who were good or bad at perceiving and decoding nonverbal cues in their responses to telephone solicitors who attempted to persuade them to volunteer for a research project. Two types of callers participated: "good senders," who were adept at expressing emotional meanings via nonverbal cues, and "bad senders," who were less adept. Both caller types made calls in which they attempted to be highly persuasive (the so-called "hard-sell" approaches) and calls that used a less aggressive approach. All callers also used the same fixed script in their calls, and thus had to persuade listeners to volunteer based solely on voice quality cues. Good and bad senders succeeded equally well overall in convincing listeners to volunteer, but the persuasive approach applied interacted significantly with the listeners' decoding skills. Good decoders responded better (i.e., volunteered more hours to the project) to "hard-sell" approaches than did poor decoders, while poor decoders volunteered more hours when the caller used a stiffer, colder voice. The authors speculated that poor decoders, hearing hard-sell approaches, may not understand the caller's intentions and become defensive. Such listeners respond better to a more businesslike, less aggressive appeal.

10.3.3 Speech rates, advertising, and sales

Results reviewed above indicate that effects of speaking rate are important aspects of person perception, and can have a significant impact on the effectiveness of an advertisement (see Sidebar on speech rates in Chapter 4). In advertising contexts, as in other contexts, listeners prefer faster speaking rates (up to about 130% of normal; LaBarbera and MacLachlan, 1979; MacLachlan, 1982), and faster speakers are generally judged more credible, persuasive, intelligent, and knowledgeable than slower speakers (for example, Miller *et al.*, 1976). Because airtime is expensive, speech compression is commonly used in advertisement production to maximize the information transmitted (think of the disclaimers at the ends of ads for

---

[12] This ad can be heard at www.livingroomcandidate.org/commercials/2008/low-road.

medications or financial products, which are often spoken so quickly that they are almost unintelligible). Because advertisement directors actively manipulate speaking rates, it is important to understand the effects of such manipulations on advertisement effectiveness.

Depending on the ad, a significant amount of time (up to 15% of advertisement duration, in one estimate; Megehee, Dobie, and Grant, 2003) is taken up by pauses. This suggests that ads can be speeded up (or slowed down) in two different ways: by compressing or expanding pauses, or by compressing or expanding both speech and pauses together. Several studies have compared the effects of these different kinds of shortening on advertisement effectiveness. Megehee *et al.* (2003) expanded and compressed a single original radio-style advertisement by +/– 15%, and asked listeners to assess the advertisement on scales related to their attitudes toward the product, the message, and the speaker, and their intent to purchase the product (a combination identification/debit card). Faster speaking rates generated more emotional responses from the listeners than did slower rates, and slower rates reflected more cognitive responses (more thoughts about the product). However, the rate manipulations did not produce any significant effects on intention to buy. Megehee *et al.* interpreted these results as consistent with the elaboration likelihood model (the proposal that ads persuade consumers either through central – via content – or peripheral – via nuances – mechanisms): Faster speech produced more responses related to the message, but not to the product per se. They concluded that a slow rate is appropriate if the ad's purpose is to persuade college-aged listeners with detailed product information, but if the goal is to evoke feelings about the product, a faster rate is better. Method of speech compression is irrelevant in either case.

In contrast, Chattopadhyay *et al.* (2003) reported that increasing syllable speed by compressing speech (by about 10%) interfered with advertisement processing. Listeners who heard ads at the original rate paid more attention and had better recall of advertisement content than did those who heard the compressed speech version. However, shortening only pauses (from an average duration of 0.6 sec to 0.1 sec) had no negative effect on attention or recall. Ads that combined a high syllable speed with low pitch were better liked, and enhanced attitudes toward the product, but no effect of pitch was observed in the normal speed condition. These results are consistent overall with the elaboration likelihood model. Note, however, that although results met conventional standards for statistical reliability, they accounted for very little variance in the data (about 2%), limiting the conclusions that can be drawn from the study.

Pause compression does seem to have a more substantial positive effect on sales success in the field, however. Peterson, Cannito, and Brown (1995) measured total speaking time, pause duration, F0 mean, variability, and contour shape, and loudness variability for 21 experienced male salesmen as they delivered their standard sales script to a research assistant. Sales performance (obtained from company records) was significantly correlated with speaking rate, mostly because pause durations were shorter for good sellers (possibly because short pauses make it more difficult for the listener to interrupt the speaker; see section 7.5.3). Salesmen who used falling F0 contours also had better sales results, but there was no relationship between sales performance and mean F0, F0 variance, or variance in intensity. Similarly, telephone interviewers who have short pauses, falling intonation contours (especially early in the conversation), variable F0, and higher mean F0 were more successful at convincing listeners to cooperate than were interviewers who lacked these characteristics (Sharf and Lehman, 1984).

10.3.4   Male versus female voices: Which works better?

Debate about the suitability and desirability of male versus female voices in broadcasting has raged since the early days of radio. According to Cantril and Allport (1937), 95% of listeners reported that they preferred male to female radio announcers (although they felt women's voices were more attractive than men's). Men were particularly preferred as announcers when the material being broadcast was factual (for example, news reports). However, women's voices were preferred over men's when the text was reflective (for example, poetry or abstract passages). Based on the discrepancy between the reported overwhelming preference for male announcers and simultaneous evidence that female voices are in fact preferred in some contexts, Cantril and Allport concluded that the differences in preference rates were due solely to prejudice. Despite the increasing number of women in broadcasting today, evidence indicates that prejudice against women broadcasters remains a significant factor in voice casting, in both advertising and commercial programming. Men continue to serve much more frequently as announcers in radio ads than do women (Whipple and McManamon, 2002). For example, 70% of advertisements on British television that included a voiceover announcer used a male in that role, compared to 81% of ads on Saudi television (Nasif and Gunter, 2008).

Some evidence suggests that this preponderant reliance on male announcers may be counterproductive, at least under some circumstances. Whipple and McManamon (2002) asked listeners to assess the effectiveness of ads with male and female announcers and spokespeople (product endorsers) for sex-specific products (a male cologne, a female perfume) and sex-neutral ads (shampoo, a shower head). Sex of announcer and spokesperson had no effect (either positive or negative) on the ad's effectiveness for gender neutral products, or for male-targeted products. For female-targeted products and female listeners, results were best when both the announcer and the spokesperson were female. Male listeners responded better to a male spokesperson when hearing an advertisement for a female-targeted product (for example, a male endorsing a female perfume), but sex of the announcer had no effect. Peirce (2001) found that matching the sex of animated spokes-characters to that of the product image significantly enhanced listeners' likings of the characters and the products, although subtle effects of mismatches on product images were also observed. These results again highlight the importance of carefully considering target audience when selecting the voices to be used in an ad.

10.3.5   Summary

It is apparent that using vocal quality to tune an advertisement to an audience is an important task that requires attention to many subtle aspects of voice and a detailed consideration of the specific goals of the ad. Ad managers must determine which product attributes they wish to highlight, and what vocal attributes might correspond to those aspects of the product's image. (For example, what makes a voice project freedom and innovation?) They must decide what kind of speaker will best catch the attention of the target audience and help them to identify with the brand. They must estimate the importance of the product to the target audience and determine what kind of quality and delivery will persuade that audience in the most effective manner; and they must find a pleasant-sounding, credible speaker who can accomplish these diverse goals in a short utterance. Finally, they must balance considerations of a voice's memorability with those of how appropriate the voice is to represent the product. Unfortunately, the literature documents the difficulty of the voice casting process, but provides only limited general-purpose advice for the ad manager. If time is constrained, it may be better to shorten pauses than to increase speaking speed. However, if you are persuading via peripheral cues, increasing syllable speed can make these cues more important to listeners. When the announcer is male, low pitch can't hurt, and it can help. Beyond these limited dicta, intuition and tradition remain the primary tools of voice casting.

10.4   Dubbing and Voiceovers

10.4.1   Dubbing

When a film is dubbed into another language, it is challenging to determine how to represent the original actors' voices, especially when the whole range of voice characteristics is considered to include accent, dialect, emotional nuances, and all the intangibles we have discussed. Some have said that the dubbing profession is undervalued, considering the complexity of the process and its broad impact. Most foreign movies shown in Germany, Spain and France are dubbed in the native language by active dubbing studios in Berlin, Barcelona and Paris (Whitman-Linsen, 1992). Dubbing, or *Synchronization*, as it is called, constitutes a venerated tradition in Germany, with a large industry devoted to this art. There is a large group of German voice actors (*Synchronsprecher*) who are known only as the voices of stars in American and other films. Similarly active industries are found in France and Spain, where more that 1,200 film and television dubbers form two unions.

In addition to visually synchronizing spoken words to movements of the lips, many other aspects of the speech act require attention during dubbing. Syllable and phrase length, as well as pausing and emphasis, must be plausibly rendered in the dubbed version (Götz and Herbst, 1987). However, in general the most important goal of a dub is to match "vocal type" by correctly modeling the paralinguistic and prosodic elements of the target speech, as well as accents and dialects that might be in play in the original film. Interestingly, lip synchrony can be overlooked if the more "top-down" characteristics in overall vocal expression are convincing (Whitman-Linsen, 1992). It is also not important that the voice of the dubber precisely matches that of the original actor. In a poll of professionals in the dubbing business, the top ranked criterion for selection of the appropriate voices for a film to be dubbed indicated that the voice of the dubbing actor must correspond to the original character's type, rather than to the precise sound of the original actor's voice. Only ten percent of the

225 respondents indicated that the voices of the dubbing and target actors should be similar (Hesse-Quack, 1969). As an example of this view, only one of the five German practitioners vocally representing Columbo, the character played by Peter Falk, can be said to actually sound like Falk.[13]

This complex domain leads to a range of quirky problems. The audience may start to notice when the same dubbing voice appears for a variety of different characters in different films. On the other hand, using a different voice in different movies for a well-known actor can also raise eyebrows. To minimize this source of distress for moviegoers, some dubbing studios use the same domestic voice for a well-known, frequently appearing actor.

Vocal characteristics other than those signaling character and personality present strong challenges in the dubbing process. In the original film, dialect and accent may be used to convey cultural details, humor, traditional values, and so on. As Whitman-Linsen (1992) asked, should American cowboys speak German using proper High German (the standard, educated dialect) or should they speak German with American accents? How are regional accents to be handled in the dubbed version? Some expression of emotion and attitude conveyed in the voice is reliant on cultural differences. How can the dubbing professional ensure that these meanings have been recognized and transmitted in the dubbed language? The related matter of register and style, formality and other sociolinguistic properties of talk might be the most difficult to capture. Caution and care are required to handle these crucial aspects of vocal communication in the dubbing process, and often exact correspondences are not possible, in which case changes to the script may be required to capture the desired meaning.

Many of these challenges were faced head-on in the German-dubbed version of the American television situation comedy *Hogan's Heroes*, which originally ran from 1965 to 1971. The sitcom took place in a German prisoner of war camp called Stalag 13, using as plotline the premise that the Allied prisoners of war were actually engaged in sabotaging the German war effort. The show was dubbed into German and released for the second time in Germany in 1994 as *Ein Käfig voller Helden* (A Cage of Heroes). In the original version, the German officers spoke in German-accented English, which has intrinsic comic value to American English listeners. By contrast, in the German-language version, the German officers in the camp speak in different dialectal accents, some of which are humorous to a German audience. The camp commander portrays a Prussian stereotype (who would ordinarily speak Standard German or *Hochdeutsch*) but has a Saxony accent, a dialect coming from a very different kind of German culture. His underling, who portrays a Bavarian stereotype, speaks Bayerish, a dialect which is generally regarded with disdain. One of the prisoners, who has a strong lower-class British accent in the American series, speaks with an exaggerated stutter in the German version. Here we see that a variety of adjustments to vocal patterns were selected to adapt humorous aspects in the voices of the original actors for the dubbed version.

Other dubbing is done not to translate to another language, but to manipulate the voice patterns toward certain ends. Italian films are mostly dubbed by other

---

[13] Woody Allen stated humorously that his dubber's voice (in German films) fits him better than his own (Whitman-Linsen, 1992, p. 42).

actors – speaking Italian. One reason is that because most Italian films are made on location rather than on soundstages, live sound would be too chaotic and noisy. An important goal of the director is to represent both the right appearance and the right accent, considering the broad array of Italian dialects, each with its nuances and connotations. The Italian director finds an actor who has the appropriate appearance for the film, and uses the voiceovers of an actor with the right voice pattern at a later time.

Casting for animation presents similar cross-cultural challenges. In the United States, current practice dictates "name brand" casting for feature-length animated films, but soundtracks prepared for foreign releases of these films must match the voice to the character in a culturally specific manner, as described above. Cultures differ in the stereotypes associated with different vocal qualities (see Chapter 9), so that a vocal "good guy" in one country may not sound sufficiently heroic in another. For example, "good guy" voices in the United States typically speak with deep, relaxed, and clear voices and avoid monotone, while bad guys sound soft, not clear, monotonous, and stiff (Yarmey, 1993). Villains and heroes in Japanese anime films are not distinguishable by F0. Instead, villains use voices produced with pharyngeal expansion or constriction, while heroes use neutral pharyngeal configurations and may sound breathy (Teshigawara, 2003). Other such examples certainly exist, but have not been systematically studied.

Sidebar: Disney Princesses

A mainstay of feature-length animation is the Disney Princess. Starting with Snow White in 1937 and continuing to the present day, these charming characters are noted for their youthful, feminine voices. The first princess, Snow White, speaks with a voice that sounds almost comical to modern ears: Due to her very high falsetto, extreme breathiness, quick speaking rate, and short utterances, Snow White sounds more like a small overexcited animal than like a princess. Subsequent princesses (such as Cinderella (1950) and Sleeping Beauty (1959)) lowered their F0 into more human ranges, but retained the extreme breathiness, pitch variability, low volume, and smiling vocal tones appropriate for young, very feminine, and helpless characters. More modern princesses like Ariel (*The Little Mermaid*, 1989), Belle (*Beauty and the Beast*, 1991), and Jasmine (*Aladdin*, 1992) were heralded as departures from the "helpless heroine" stereotype, but such departures are not especially apparent vocally. All speak with high and variable F0, moderate to rapid speaking rates, and a smiling, soft quality stereotypically appropriate for a lively, lovely, but very youthful female (although they may occasionally raise their voices, and Belle and Jasmine are not consistently breathy).

10.4.2   Voiceovers

Voiceover roles provide interesting and challenging work for a wide range of talented actors. Numerous courses, workshops, and books provide instruction in manipulating the voice to produce character voices of all kinds. Lewis (2003) illustrates (on the CD accompanying her book) five basic vocal states that are foundational to a cornucopia of sounds useful to the voiceover artist: head voice, nasal voice, adenoidal voice, throat voice, and chest voice. Similarly, Blu, Mullin, and Songé (2006) distinguish ten placements: head, eyes, nasal, adenoidal, near the ears ("munchkin" voice), lower mouth, throat, back of the throat, chest, and diaphragm. Each of these voice "placements" can give rise to variations to convey distinctive sounds signaling age, energy, social class, and personality. To achieve the desired effects, the voiceover actor is instructed to work with vocal stereotypes. This is a pragmatic approach, given the cultural reality of vocal stereotypes and findings that listeners agree on ratings of personality stereotypes conveyed in the voice, although personality measures obtained from the individuals producing the voice often do not match these stereotypes (see Chapter 9 for more discussion). As stated by Lewis (2003, CD), "There's nothing wrong with stereotypes: They are the foundation on which we build our unique, personal characterization." In a similar vein, vocal coaches advocate learning foreign dialects from pop culture, using Hollywood Slavic and Hollywood French accents (as purveyed by Maurice Chevalier, who reportedly cultivated an exaggerated accent for use in public appearance and film).

10.4.3 How does voiceover voice differ from "normal" voice?

Despite the importance of vocal characteristics in advertising, surprisingly little is known about what makes a voice attractive, or about what differentiates a "professional" voice from everyday speaking. Professional voiceover artists have in common a voice that captures attention, the ability to vary voice quality while maintaining relatively low pitch, normal articulation, and varied intonation. Their delivery in voiceover mode features some modifications in speaking rhythm and rate, including "strategic pausing" and prolongation of key words in the advertisement copy (Medrado, Ferreira, and Behlau, 2005). These attributes may be discernable in normal speech as well as in performance modes: Listeners in one study correctly distinguished voiceover artists from naive talkers about 79% of the time, even when speech was produced in a neutral setting (Medrado *et al.*, 2005).

To achieve these somewhat vague goals, professional voice coaches often advocate creating an entire character as preparation for even a small voiceover role. For example, Alburger (2007) describes a process that involves specifying the audience being addressed, the character's back story that led to the utterances to come, the desires, lifestyle, physical appearance, clothing, habits, emotional makeup and current emotional state, attitudes, underlying personality, and physical movements of the character, along with more specific aspects of the desired voice, including speaking rate, rhythm, volume, accent or idiosyncrasies of pronunciation, pitch characteristics, and the way the character laughs. Like singing teachers, instructions for achieving these ambitious goals are more commonly based on intuition and experience than on research. However, we do note the emphasis in this tradition on the relationship between a whole person – a physical being with a history and an emotional profile – and the voice produced, reminiscent of the view that emerged from the neuroanatomical overview in Chapter 3 and the neuropsychological studies described in Chapter 6.

10.5   Announcing, Newscasting, and Sportscasting

In public places, we are surrounded by announcements: over loud speakers, on airplanes, answering machines and phone systems, in line at a theme park, while boarding a subway or train, and while driving thanks to navigational GPS systems. (Many of these announcements are recorded by real talkers producing whole utterances or words which are concatenated to produce new utterances, although some are generated with text-to-speech synthesis.) In the early days of broadcasting, announcing drew considerable scientific interest (Pear, 1931; Cantril and Allport, 1935), and a number of studies examined the ability of listeners to draw conclusions about speakers' intelligence, truthfulness, occupation, personality, level of fatigue, body type, and so on (Fay and Middleton, 1939a,b; 1940a,b,c; 1941) from voices transmitted over public address systems. Like similar studies reviewed in Chapter 9, results generally showed low to moderate agreement among listeners, with listeners showing much more agreement about some voices than about others, consistent with stereotyping. However, little modern research has focused specifically on the manner in which announcers' voices should be matched to the announcement and the context. Possibly as a result, informal listening reveals a wide variety of approaches to the question of what public address announcers (and GPS systems) should sound like, as system designers balance considerations of attracting attention, intelligibility, authority, friendliness, and an appropriate level of alarm. For example, automated tornado alert systems need to transmit information concisely and accurately, but must also convey a sense of urgency appropriate to the level of threat, which varies over time from location to location.[14] Some choices can seem mysterious to listeners. For example, in New York Verizon Telephone abruptly changed its voice mail announcements, without warning or explanation, from a light, cheerful voice to one that is serious, businesslike, and cold, possibly confusing and upsetting millions of customers who no longer felt as welcome to leave a message as they had before. In the New York City subway, the frequently repeated announcement ("Stand clear of the closing doors, please") transmits a tinge of irony in the vocal quality to some listeners, whether intentionally or unintentionally, leaving one to wonder what the disembodied male really thinks about the passengers. Broader questions also arise – Should New York dialects be employed in New York airports, Chicago dialects at O'Hare Airport? Should a public address announcer's voice emphasize a quality that is alert, friendly, calm, authoritative, or something else? These questions have serious communicative implications, but answers are not available at present.

As a special case of announcers, newscasters have a daunting responsibility to convey messages with a well-managed vocal quality. They should sound friendly but also serious; their tone should be professional but not haughty; and the voice should subtly change with the content of the story. Again, formal study is lacking, but informal observation indicates that most newscasters lower pitch and slow their speaking rate somewhat for reports of tragic or serious events, but increase rate and pitch (and smile, raising resonant frequencies) when reporting cheery public interest stories. Errors can occur: A minor

[14]   An example of such a system can be heard at http://www.npr.org/templates/story/story.php?storyId=1046719.

outcry occurred when a story about diving mules was reported in the evening news with a tone that reflected amusement rather than concern or outrage (Figure 8.15).

Sportscasters are faced with the need to generate (or reflect) fan enthusiasm, sometimes in the face of a less than thrilling sporting spectacle, and must also somehow communicate the atmosphere at the game to a home audience. In one notable example, golf announcers on television whisper their commentary as a shot is being prepared, despite the fact that they are typically sitting in a trailer nowhere near the events they are describing. In a thrilling example of the art of sportscasting, consider Vin Scully's call of Sandy Koufax's first no-hitter.[15] As the ninth inning begins, Scully maintains a slow speaking rate and calm delivery, especially between pitches. This is appropriate – after all, in baseball a no-hitter can evaporate at any time – and also gives the call a kind of calmness and an air of excited waiting, so that the drama builds naturally, and the listener is not worn out by constant vocal hyperbole or hysteria. When a pitch is thrown, Scully's rate, F0, and F0 variability all increase as the ball is put into play. This pattern lasts until just before the last pitch, when there are two out and two strikes on the final batter. At this time Scully uses a consistently faster speaking rate and high and variable F0, expressing the excitement of the moment. His voice erupts with happiness when the batter is thrown out and the no-hitter is recorded. The rhythm of increases and decreases in the dynamic aspects of speech perfectly captures the starts and stops of baseball, and the growing drama of the events that are unfolding on the field.

In contrast to live announcers, synthesized announcements are universally disdained, mostly because of their emotional and attitudinal vapidity. The lack of normal sounding paralinguistic material in speech synthesized by rule is a major cause of listeners' dissatisfaction and perceptions of unpleasantness. For example, alert messages that convey the proper sense of urgency can be more effective than those that sound either hysterical or robotic and uninvolved (Park and Jang, 1999). Similarly, better ability to modulate vocal emotion in voice synthesis could allow businesses to tailor the spoken messages listeners hear from voice response systems, so that the speaker conveyed sympathy, happiness, encouragement when a wrong key has been pressed, or other contextually appropriate feelings. Such emotionally tailored messages could greatly enhance users' satisfaction with telephone response systems, and also ensure that the auditory image conveyed is consistent with the desired corporate image (Maffiolo and Chateau, 2003).

10.6 Singing

The study of the singing voice highlights several themes that were developed in previous chapters, among them interactions between the source and filter in determining voice quality, the power of the voice to convey emotional messages, and the extent to which individuals can control the sound of their voices. Vocalists can produce an amazing range of different voice qualities. Even casual listening to country, rock and roll, and classical artists reveals many differences in vocal quality beyond those related to personal quality and musical style. Describing such rich, complex signals is difficult, and the issue

---

[15] The call of the ninth inning of this game can be heard at http://www.npr.org/templates/story/story.php?storyId=9752592.

Table 10.3 F0 ranges for different kinds of singing voices (data adapted from Titze, 1994).

Voice type	Approximate singing range
Bass	80–330 Hz
Baritone	100–400 Hz
Tenor	130–530 Hz
Contralto	150–600 Hz
Mezzosoprano	220–880 Hz
Soprano	200–1,200 Hz

of how to classify singing voices is confused by conflicting intellectual traditions. Much of the writing about singing has been done by vocal pedagogues whose assumptions and terminology often vary widely from those current in the scientific community.

This introduction describes several of the main issues in the scientific study of singing. For more complete discussion, see, for example, Vennard (1967), Sundberg (1987), Titze (1994), or Bunch (1997).

10.6.1   Kinds of singers and singing

Singing voices are most often classified on the basis of F0, from basses to sopranos (Table 10.3). However, harmonic amplitudes and formant frequencies are also important in voice classification, because the frequency at which source energy is best transmitted varies with voice classification. Across singers, spectral peaks (averaged over long stretches of phonation) occur at higher frequencies for voices with higher fundamental frequencies (and shorter vocal tracts), and decrease in frequency as the vocal tract lengthens (Sundberg, 2001; Cleveland, 1977). Lower pitched voices naturally tend to coincide with longer vocal tracts, and the longer the vocal tract, the lower its resonant frequencies. Interesting vocal effects may occur when vocal fold size and vocal tract length do not covary as expected (Erickson, 2004). For example, a singer who has a long neck but short vocal folds may produce a voice that is pitched high but sounds "dark" (Titze, 1994). Titze suggests that some subclassifications of voices in opera (for example, lyric baritone) may be based on this kind of hybrid case, but relevant data are lacking.

Significant differences in voice quality may also occur within a single singer across styles of singing. Many singers and teachers of singing distinguish styles like belt, mix, blues, and legit, but singing in these styles is learned mostly by listening and by trial and error. Although singers seem to know what such terms mean and may produce these different qualities at will, clear definitions have not been agreed upon, and singing teachers themselves may not understand precisely how these qualities are produced (but see Lovetri, Lesh, and Woo, 1999). Despite the fact that authors (and the public at large) distinguish many kinds of singing, few data are available about what differentiates the different types, other than the style of the music (for example, popular versus operatic). Some consistent differences in voice source characteristics may occur across styles. Thalen and Sundberg (2000) reported data from a single professional singer who could produce many different styles of voice. They found that blues singing required more vocal compression[16] and higher subglottal pressures, resulting in a decrease in the energy in the fundamental frequency and an increase in the energy in the higher harmonics (sometimes called "pressed" phonation). Pop-style singing used a more neutral glottal configuration; jazz singing was characterized by lower subglottal pressures and less glottal compression, adding energy to the fundamental. More recently, Lebowitz and Baken (2010) compared acoustic and physiological characteristics for professional singers engaged in belt and legit vocal styles. No differences were found in the duration of the closed portion of the glottal cycle, but belt revealed a significantly higher speed quotient.[17] In addition, the third and fourth formants were higher in frequency in legit than belt mode. The authors conclude that belting may be an extension of the chest register to a higher frequency.

Breathing during singing has been studied from several points of view. Opera singers were observed to use more breath during "emotional" than "technical" singing of the same material (Foulds-Elliott, Thorpe, Cala, and Davis, 2000). Respiratory function for opera and other professional singing differs considerably from respiration in speaking, in that greater lung volumes are used in a consistent manner and subglottal pressure is carefully calibrated by continuous adaptation of the respiratory muscles (Leanderson and Sundberg, 1988; Thomasson and Sundberg, 1999). Such breath pattern differences were not observed in country singers, whose respiratory behaviors were similar for singing and speaking (Hoit, Jenks, Watson, and Cleveland, 1996).

10.6.2   Register

Descriptions of the singing voice often (but not always) distinguish a number of vocal registers (for example, chest, middle (or mixed), and head register; heavy and light voice; or vocal fry, modal, falsetto, flageolet, and whistle, although many other terms are common; Titze, 1994; see Henrich, 2006, for an interesting historical review). Although authors generally agree that registers exist, the number that should be distinguished and how to define individual registers remain contentious, making this a confusing area of study. Register in singing is commonly defined as the phonation frequency range in which all tones are perceived and felt kinesthetically as being produced in a similar way and possess similar vocal timbre (Sundberg, 1987). The notion is that "areas" of the voice each have a different quality, as sets of pipes in an organ do; the name "register" is also used to refer to clusters of organ pipes (Alderson, 1979). Vocal registers occur in many species other than humans. Dogs bark in modal voice, and howl or whine in a falsetto-like register. Cats, with their smaller larynges, meow in a higher register, but growl in a lower register (Appelman, 1973); and male Diana monkeys use "pulse" register when producing alarm calls signaling the presence of predators (Riede and Zuberbühler, 2003).

The perception of a register change probably reflects a change in the way the vocal folds vibrate, although singing teachers sometimes describe register with respect to

---

[16]   Vocal or glottal compression refers to a technique utilized in professional singing. Air pressure is built up below the glottis via increased respiratory effort for a time during which the glottis is closed more tightly than during regular phonation. Once the vocal folds are allowed to vibrate, airflow resumes resulting in enhanced vocal quality, or the air flow may be controlled to allow for a longer vocal line on a single breath.

[17]   A measure of temporal symmetry of vocal fold openings and closings.

"where the voice resonates in the body." Chest register as usually described is more or less the same as modal phonation, and is often defined as a typical quality in speaking and low-pitched singing (for which vibrations are supposedly felt in the chest and trachea). Head register is sometimes described as a mixture of chest and falsetto, or as a typical male quality in high-pitched singing that approximates female quality, or as the upper half of a singer's range. Whistle register refers to the very highest part of the range of a few sopranos. The vocal folds are (hypothetically) stretched very tight, the amplitude of oscillations is reduced, and only the front part of the folds may vibrate (Miller and Schutte, 1993). Early studies associated register changes with actions of the vocalis (thyroarytenoid) muscle. Further, laryngeal regulatory mechanisms for F0 are thought to differ depending on register of phonation, associated with "heavy" (chest, mid, head voice) and "light" (falsetto and light head voice) vocal qualities (Hirano, Vennard, and Ohala, 1970). Some articulatory and resonance changes have been implicated in the production and perception of register as well; for example, changes in the shape of the supralaryngeal cavities (including those associated with vowel production), velum and uvula action, laryngeal lowering and forward tilt (Appelman, 1973), and epiglottal lowering and elevation have all been observed in register changes. Untrained singers may experience a "break" in vocal production when moving from one register to another. Singers use the term "lift" to speak of the action of the breath at register changes; transition into an upper register is referred to as the "passagio."

Sidebar: "Feeling" the Voice During Singing

Singing teachers and singers often describe register in terms of "where the voice vibrates" in the body. Thus, for example, chest register voice is felt to vibrate in the chest, and head register is felt in the face or head. Although these vibrations may be important cues for learning and recreating particular kinds of phonation, they do not correspond to where vocal resonance actually occurs. There is no evidence that vibration of facial bones is associated with areas of registration, and the term "head resonance" is a misnomer (Vennard, 1967). The tissues of the face are poor resonators in the normal sense of the word "resonance." They do not filter the sound and boost spectral energy at selected frequencies, they do not radiate energy efficiently into the air, and energy dissipates quickly within the soft tissues of the head so that the net effect may actually be a loss of energy. The sensation of vibration in the face is probably the result of an acoustic interaction between the vibrating vocal folds and the vocal tract. This interaction occurs when the impedances of the vocal tract and the glottis match, so that energy feeds back to the sound source, strengthening its harmonic content. In this explanation, the feeling of vibration in the head or face signals an ideal acoustic match between the source and filter to the singer, but is not the result of actual resonation in the sinuses or the nasal airways. See Titze (2001, 2004) for more discussion.

Register boundaries do not correspond precisely to particular F0 ranges. Depending on talent and training, professional singers may be able to sing most of their vocal range in a single register without a break. Transitions between registers can cause problems or "breaks" in singing, especially when this happens involuntarily. (See Titze, 1994, for discussion about how and why such register transitions occur.) Like the supraglottal vocal tract, the trachea also has resonances, and the manner in which the voice source interacts with the trachea and the vocal tract is important in singing. Research suggests that the break between modal and falsetto (which is accompanied by a jump in frequency in untrained voices) is triggered when interactions between the source and trachea change the way in which vocal folds vibrate (for example, Austin and Titze, 1997; Zhang, Neubauer, and Berry, 2006a, b). Such register breaks are cultivated in yodel (Echternach and Richter, 2010) and in Hawaiian music, while operatic singers are trained to avoid abrupt register transitions.

Sidebar: Are Music and Speech Related?

The question of how (or if) music (and singing) and speech are related in cognition and evolution has been the subject of several recent investigations (Juslin and Laukka, 2003; Jackendoff and Lerdahl, 2006; Patel, 2008). In one study, persons identified as having deficits in detecting pitch changes were found to normally discriminate the intonation contours of speech (Patel, Foxton, and Griffiths, 2005). Others claim that musical ability, like language ability, is innate, noting that among biological species, only humans have both. Children aged between five and nine years of age showed good responses to emotional information in music (Doherty, Fitzsimons, Asenbauer, and Staunton, 1999). In another study of "occasional" singers asked to produce a well-known song at a slow tempo, all but two sang with accurate F0 and timing, consistent with universal ability (Dalla Bella, Giguere, and Peretz, 2007). If both music and speech are innate to humans, then certain universals should be appear in all languages and cultures; yet questions about universality remain controversial in both domains (Sachs and Kunst, 1962).

10.6.3   How does singing voice differ from speaking voice?

Given these distinctions, how does singing differ from speech? The answer to this question depends on the kind of singing. Differences in vocal function between speaking and singing are quite small for singers without classical training (for example, Mendes, Brown, Rothman, and Sapienza, 2004), although data are restricted to descriptions of only a few singers and singing styles (Hoit *et al.*, 1996; Cleveland, Stone, Sundberg, and Iwarsson, 1997; Sundberg, Cleveland, Stone, and Iwarsson, 1999; Cleveland, Sundberg, and Stone, 2001). This is not at all the case for classically trained singers, for whom large differences occur between singing and speech. These are partly due to the special demands of operatic and other classical singing. In contrast to popular singing, a good operatic singing voice should have a large overall intensity range, stable vibrato, a prominent low-frequency resonance (i.e., an efficient voice source, so that the amplitude of the second harmonic is larger than that of the first harmonic), and a prominent high frequency resonance, or singer's formant (see below; Bartholomew, 1934). Operatic singers also need the ability to keep quality constant while varying pitch and loudness (Titze, 1994), and to keep pitch constant while varying loudness. Several gender-specific accommodations are required to accomplish these goals.

First, classically trained male voices are often characterized by a so-called "singer's formant," a resonance that appears at approximately 3 kHz regardless of the vowel being sung. A singer's formant is an essential component of a well-trained male voice, because it allows the singer to increase loudness so much that he can be heard over a symphony orchestra without amplification, and without damaging his vocal folds. The loudest harmonics in an orchestral performance tend to be at about the same frequency as the loudest harmonics in the normal human voice (about 450 Hz), so one would normally expect an orchestra to drown out a voice. Increasing loudness enough to be heard by increasing subglottal pressure and glottal resistance can result in damage to the vocal folds, and is not a viable long-term strategy for a professional voice user. However, a singer's formant adds an acoustic boost to the harmonics in the 3 kHz region of the spectrum, which is the weakest part of the orchestral spectrum. This boost is achieved by lowering the larynx, and by widening the pharynx, laryngeal ventricle, and piriform sinuses just above the vocal folds. Changing the dimensions of the vocal tract in this way changes the frequencies of the third, fourth, and fifth formants so that they cluster, boosting the spectrum in the 3 kHz region (Sundberg, 1974). (Some singers may not have to make articulatory adjustments, having been gifted with appropriate anatomy to begin with.) Besides increasing loudness in this critical area of acoustic orchestral weakness, the higher harmonics of the voice radiate forward, rather than backward or sideways, so that more of the voice goes toward the audience when a singer's formant is present (Sundberg, 1987, 2001). Thanks to these two effects, a singer's formant allows the singer to be heard over the sound of an orchestra; and because these effects are achieved by simple articulatory changes, rather than by "singing louder," the increase in loudness is achieved without any increased vocal effort or risk of damage to the vocal folds.

Female operatic singers typically use other mechanisms to achieve sufficient vocal loudness. F0 for a soprano may climb to over 1,400 Hz, producing harmonics at 2,800 Hz, 4,200 Hz, and so on. Typical values for the first and second formants for the vowel /a/ spoken by a female are about 936 Hz and 1,551 Hz, respectively (Hillenbrand, Getty, Clark, and Wheeler, 1995), so that when F0 is high the first formant may not be excited at all, and the second formant may be excited only by the fundamental or the second harmonic. Further, harmonics are widely spaced when F0 is high, so individual harmonics may not line up well with the center frequencies of the vocal tract resonances, even in the cases when F0 is lower than F1. Thus, the part of the sound spectrum that is most efficiently radiated does not appear in the output spectrum at all, because no harmonics are produced in that frequency range. Despite this apparently built-in inefficiency, singing is much louder than speech for trained female singers, as it is for males. The mechanism used to accomplish this boost in loudness is different for females than for males, however. While males typically lower the larynx to adjust the frequencies of the higher formants, female singers open their jaws more as F0 increases, regardless of the vowel being sung. Female singers may also shorten the vocal tract somewhat by retracting the corners of the mouth, which also increases the frequencies of the formants, moving them toward the high F0. Opening the jaw in this way "tunes" F1 to a value near F0 (Joliveau, Smith, and Wolfe, 2004a, b), increasing the sound energy to a level like that present in a singer's formant (a nearly 1000-fold increase in energy, according to Sundberg (1987); see also Barnes, Davis, Oates, and Chapman, 2004). As with the singer's formant, this adjustment increases loudness as a passive effect of the facts of vocal resonance. It does not require much muscular energy or any change to the voice source, thus decreasing the likelihood of injury or vocal strain.

These increases in loudness often come at the cost of substantial decreases in intelligibility (Hollien, Mendes-Schwartz, and Nielsen, 2000). The frequencies of the first two or three formants are strong cues to the identity of the vowel being spoken. The articulatory manipulations needed to generate vocal loudness necessarily restrict the ability of a singer to produce a target vowel accurately. Further, formant resolution is poor when F0 is high and harmonics are widely spaced, as mentioned above. Fortunately, other cues to vowel identity are available from continuous song, including information from the transitions between consonantal and vowel sounds and the semantic context of the lyrics, so listeners need not be completely baffled when trying to decipher operatic plots.

Vibrato also distinguishes singing from speaking, and in general seems to be an essential part of a warm, human vocal tone. It is usually described as nearly periodic modulations of the fundamental frequency about its mean value; in other words, the pitch of the voice varies slowly but regularly around the singer's target pitch when vibrato is present. Examples of voices with and without vibrato are given in audio samples 10.1 to 10.4, and changes in F0 over time for these voice samples are shown in Figure 10.1.

Vibrato develops quasi-automatically during singing training, and occurs in popular singing as well as in classically trained voices. It is more conspicuously present in trained women's voices than in men's voices (Kwalwasser, 1926). Vibrato occurs naturally but is much less frequent – by about 65% – in untrained voices, and for most trained singers, inhibiting vibrato is difficult. However, not all styles of singing require vibrato. Classical Indian singing is produced without vibrato (Deva, 1959); and singers of European early music (medieval and renaissance sacred and secular compositions) often use straight tone almost exclusively as a feature of performance practice. The "straight tone" voice quality was probably the standard in the historical period, due to the frequent use of young males as singers, in whom this sort of intonation is more natural. (As a group, children use vibrato infrequently when singing, and straight tone is desirable in ensemble singing to better achieve blend.) As examples, a study of nine German Lieder performed by Dietrich Fischer-Dieskau revealed a range of 21% to 70% straight tone usage, with an overall average of 40% non-vibrato tone (Large and Iwata, 1971), and medieval songs performed by four females contain little or no vibrato (Anonymous 4, 2002). An additional variant of vibrato technique may be heard in Wagnerian and popular singing, in which a tone is first sustained without vibrato, giving way to small and then larger amounts of vibrato.

In vibrato, F0 modulates about the mean value in a sine-wave-like pattern, as described above. Thus, vibrato can be quantified in terms of the rate of frequency modulation, its extent above and below the center frequency, and the regularity and

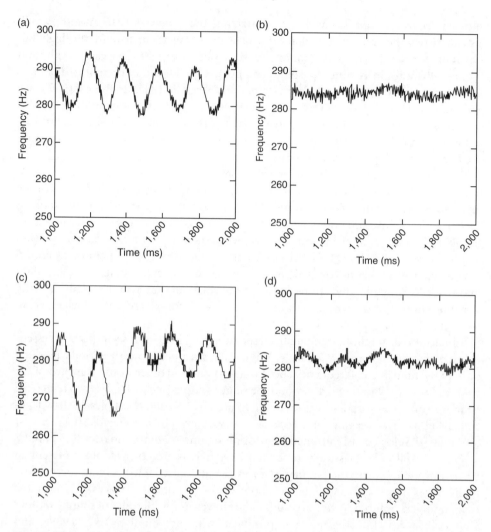

Figure 10.1 F0 tracks for voices with (a, c) and without (b, d) vibrato, for two amateur female singers.

pattern of modulation (Sundberg, 1995). Vibrato rates are usually about 4–7 Hz; in professional voices, the range is smaller (about 5–6 Hz), and frequency tends to increase toward the end of the sustained note (Prame, 1994). Studies of artistic vibrato indicate an extent ranging from a half step (in the diatonic scale[18]) to more than a whole step from tone to tone (Metfessel, 1928). With aging, vibrato rates tend to slow down, producing a less-than-pleasant "wobble." Exaggerated or intentional vibrato sounds like "tremolo," a generally unpreferred vocal sound in which F0 fluctuations are almost twice as fast as those of the normal vibrato (Kwalwasser, 1926). Although F0 varies constantly during vibrato, the presence of vibrato does not imply

[18] The seven-note musical scale made up of five whole tone steps and two half tone steps, forming the foundation of the European musical tradition.

that the singer can be less precise in hitting the target note. This is because the perceived pitch of tones with vibrato corresponds almost perfectly to the tone's average fundamental frequency, and the physical F0 changes "fuse" during perception into one salient pitch (Tiffin and Seashore, 1936; Shonle and Horan, 1980).

The range of normal vibrato rates is very similar to that found in pathological vocal tremors, suggesting that the rate derives from a natural central nervous system process, although it is not understood why vibrato (or vocal tremor) occurs. One hypothesis is that vibrato is related to a reflex loop that controls the tension of the vocal folds by modulating activity in the cricothyroid and thyroarytenoid muscles, which function as an agonist/anagonist pair (Titze, Story, Smith, and Long, 2002). The relatively long latency of this loop (more than 40 msec) corresponds to frequency modulation rates of about 5–7 Hz. Electromyographic recordings from the thyroarytenoid and cricothyroid muscles of one singer who had a vocal tremor with a rate different than her vibrato showed that modulation rates in the cricothyroid activity were similar to vibrato rates, but activity modulation rates in the thyroarytenoid matched tremor rates during speech (Dromey and Smith, 2008). This finding is consistent with the reflex resonance account of vibrato suggested by Titze *et al.* (2002), and casts some doubt on traditional accounts that associate vibrato with tremors.

Many reports argue that vibrato occurs in the amplitude domain as well as in the frequency domain (for example, Horii and Hata, 1988). Certainly the amplitude of the acoustic signal often modulates along with the frequency in vibrato, but in normal singing this primarily represents the interaction of frequency modulations with the vocal tract resonances (Sundberg, 1995; Schutte and Miller, 1991; but see also Dromey, Reese, and Hopkin, 2009), rather than an independent aspect of vibrato. As described by the acoustic theory of speech production (Fant, 1960), harmonics that are closer to the formant frequencies are passed with relatively greater energy than harmonics farther from the vocal tract resonances. Thus, as F0 varies in vibrato, the harmonics of the voice move toward and away from the center frequencies of the vocal tract resonances (assuming vowel quality remains fairly constant), producing amplitude modulations as a by-product of the frequency modulation. However, other kinds of vibrato may occur in nonwestern singing (or pathological tremors) that depend on respiratory action, and which might be better described as amplitude modulations. Some voice scientists also speak of vibrato as including periodic variations in vocal timbre (Tiffin and Seashore, 1936). These effects have not been well studied and are not understood.

Because singers vary greatly in their use of vibrato, and because its purpose is not fully understood, there are still many unanswered questions. For example, vibrato is not more efficient than straight tone: Across registers, it requires 10% higher airflow than phonation without vibrato (Large and Iwata, 1971). What, then, is the function of vibrato? One suggestion is that the vibratory movements prevent laryngeal fatigue, since in pendulum-like movements, the musculature alternately works and rests (Large and Iwata, 1971). Other studies suggest vibrato may enhance vowel intelligibility, by providing more information about where the vowel formants are. Because the source and vocal tract filter can be manipulated independently, the harmonics in a voice may not be very close to the formant frequencies, especially when F0 is very high. Including vibrato in voice makes the harmonics move around a bit, so that there is more of a chance of getting a good acoustic response from a formant. Still others suggest that vibrato allows the singing voice to achieve a pattern distinct from accompanying instruments, such as piano, violin, or orchestra (although most string players also use vibrato on sustained notes). Vibrato may also function to make the singing tone more effective as a medium for conveying emotion, based in the notion that trembling is associated with human emotional experiences. Many listeners find vibrato more exciting, while straight tone might signal coldness and monotony, or sometimes mystery and foreboding. Although these explanations are all plausible, why voices vibrate remains mysterious (Bunch, 1997).

10.6.4   Non-classical singing

Most studies of singing have focused on approaches needed for Western classical music. However, many interesting vocal phenomena occur in non-classical and non-Western singing as well. One example is overtone singing (also called [Tuvan] throat singing, double-voice singing, biphonic singing, and Xöömij), which is used in music from Tibet, China, and Mongolia, and also appears in performances by Flamenco singers and in the traditional music of the Andes (Dmitriev, Chernov, and Maslov, 1983; Bloothooft, Bringmann, van Cappellen, van Luipen, and Thomassen, 1992; Klingholz, 1993; Adachi and Yamada, 1999). A celebrated example may be heard in the "chordal chanting" practiced by the Gyoto monks of Tibet. In this complex kind of vocalization, a high melody pitch is combined with a low drone pitch, both produced simultaneously by the same person and always in a harmonic relationship, usually at the interval of a fifth above the fundamental. Two explanations have been suggested for how singers accomplish this sustained effect. One is that a second sound source (possibly vibrations of the ventricular folds) provides one of the tones. However, evidence is much more consistent with the alternative explanation that overtone singing is produced by exploiting resonance in a manner similar to that used to increase loudness in operatic singing. Singers producing overtone phonation use modal phonation or vocal fry, but add articulatory adjustments to tune the formants to one of the higher harmonics of the voice. At the same time, they narrow the bandwidth of the tuned resonance, so that the higher harmonic is increased in prominence, and they lower the amplitude of the first harmonic by increasing the amount of time the vocal folds remain closed during each glottal cycle (which increases the high frequency energy in the source relative to the fundamental; Fant and Lin, 1988). Articulatory data (including fMRI images; Adachi and Yamada, 1999) indicate that formant and bandwidth tuning are accomplished by narrowing the pharynx, adding a very narrow tongue constriction, keeping the mouth opening very small (to reduce radiation effects on the spectrum), and by increasing the tension of the walls of the mouth cavity to reduce damping losses. Singers may also add nasalization to create a spectral zero[19] that acoustically isolates the overtone resonance from the other harmonics of the voice. Perceptual data confirm that overtone singing as performed by the Gyoto monks is perceived as more nasal, stressed, and pressed than normal

---

[19]   A spectral zero is an antiresonance, or a frequency for which no source energy passes through the vocal tract; in essence, the opposite of a vocal tract resonance.

phonation, consistent with resonance and articulatory explanations for how it is produced (Bloothooft *et al.*, 1992), and indicating that the chordal effect arises from enhancement of a harmonic at a fifth interval above the fundamental pitch.

Within Western music, heavy metal vocalists and contemporary vocal improvisers use a variety of interesting vocal effects that differ markedly from those heard in classical music (even when it is contemporary). In rock singing, "dist" tones or "death grunts" containing subharmonics and/or broadband noise are employed as ornaments for high or loud tones (Borch, Sundberg, Lindestad, and Thalen, 2004). These tones may also be characterized by regular patterns of variation in pulse amplitudes, for example in an A-A-B-A-A-B pattern. Dist tones seem to be produced by using very high subglottal pressures and flow levels to set the mucosa above the vocal folds into vibration. These vibrations may be periodic and/or aperiodic; when they are periodic, they need not be harmonically related to F0 (unlike the high tones in throat singing). As the mucosa vibrates during production of dist tones, it may partially obstruct the airway, blocking the transmission of sound from the vocal folds through the vocal tract and intermittently reducing the amplitudes of glottal pulses to produce the patterns of amplitude modulation described above. Similar phenomena have been described in the production of vocal improvisers, who intentionally use nonlinear phenomena like period doubling (generation of subharmonic frequencies), biphonation (disparate frequencies in each vocal fold; see case study below), and broadband noise in a reproducible manner during their performances (Neubauer, Edgerton, and Herzel, 2004; see Chapter 2 and also Edgerton, 2004, who provides tutorials on how to produce some of these kinds of vocalization).

Finally, Ward, Sanders, Goldman, and Moore (1969) reported the case of a woman who produced "double voice" when singing. High-speed imaging confirmed that the singer was able to control the vibratory frequency of each vocal fold separately, so that she could sing in harmony with herself (unlike throat singers, who produce a varying overtone and a fairly constant background droning tone). Although this kind of phonation (sometimes called "diplophonia" or "biphonation"; see Gerratt and Kreiman, 2001b, for review) occurs sometimes in vocal pathology (when it cannot be controlled), reports in normal speakers are uncommon, and the degree of control this speaker had is particularly noteworthy.

To summarize, phonation can assume a rich array of forms, yielding many styles in singing and as well as in speaking. In general, many aspects of the singing voice can be understood in terms of standard theories of voice production. However, the scientific study of singing is in its infancy. Much remains to be learned about how singers control different aspects of the voice. Many styles of singing also remain to be described (for example, Boersma and Kovacic, 2006). Collaboration between artists and scientists has great potential to illuminate such issues, as interdisciplinary approaches in general can illuminate the essential role of vocal function in human existence.

References

Abberton, E. and Fourcin, A.J. (**1978**). "Intonation and speaker identification," *Language and Speech* **21**, 305–318.

Abdelli-Baruh, N., Yang, S.-Y., Ahn, J.S., and Van Lancker Sidtis, D. (**2007**). "Acoustic cues differentiating idiomatic from literal expressions across languages," Paper presented at the American Speech-Language Hearing Association, Boston, MA.

Abercrombie, D. (**1967**). *Elements of General Phonetics* (Chicago: Aldine).

Abitbol, J., Abitbol, P., and Abitbol, B. (**1999**). "Sex hormones and the female voice," *Journal of Voice* **13**, 424–446.

Abramson, A.S. (**1972**). "Tonal experiments with whispered Thai," in *Papers in Linguistics and Phonetics to the Memory of Pierre Delattre*, edited by A. Valdman (Mouton, The Hague), pp. 31–44.

Abramson, A.S. (**1975**). "The tones of Central Thai: Some perceptual experiments," in *Studies in Tai Linguistics*, edited by J.G. Harris and J. Chamberlain (Bangkok: Central Institute of English Language), pp. 1–16.

Abramson, A.S. (**1977**). "Laryngeal timing in consonant distinctions," *Phonetica* **34**, 295–303.

Ackermann, H. and Riecker, A. (**2004**). "The contribution of the insula to motor aspects of speech production: A review and a hypothesis," *Brain and Language* **89**, 320–328.

Adachi, S. and Yamada, M. (**1999**). "An acoustical study of sound production in biphonic singing, Xöömij," *Journal of the Acoustical Society of America* **105**, 2920–2932.

Addington, D.W. (**1968**). "The relationship of selected vocal characteristics to personality perception," *Speech Monographs* **35**, 492–503.

Adolphs, R., Cahill, L., Schul, R., and Babinski, R. (**1997**). "Impaired memory for emotional stimuli following bilateral damage to the human amygdala," *Learning and Memory* **4**, 291–300.

Adolphs, R., Damasio, H., and Tranel, D. (**2002**). "Neural systems for recognition of emotional prosody: A 3-D lesion study," *Emotion* **2**, 23–51.

Adolphs, R. and Tranel, D. (**1999**). "Preferences for visual stimuli following amygdala damage," *Journal of Cognitive Neuroscience* **11**, 610–616.

Ahn, J.S., Yang, S.Y., and Sidtis, D. (**2010**). "The perception and acoustic features of Korean ditropic sentences," *Acoustical Society of America* **27**, 1955.

Ajmani, M.L. (**1990**). "A metrical study of the laryngeal skeleton in adult Nigerians," *Journal of Anatomy* **171**, 187–191.

Albas, D.C., McCluskey, K.W., and Albas, C.A. (**1976**). "Perception of the emotional content of speech: A comparison of two Canadian groups," *Journal of Cross-Cultural Psychology* **7**, 481–490.

Alburger, J.R. (**2007**). *The Art of Voice Acting*, 3rd edition (Focal Press, Amsterdam).

Alcock, K.J., Wade, D., Anslow, P., and Passingham, R.E. (**2000**). "Pitch and timing abilities in adult left-hemisphere-dysphasic and right hemisphere damaged subjects," *Brain and Language* **75**, 47–65.

Alden, A. (**1802**). *The Reader [microform] : being the third part of a Columbian exercise: The whole comprising an easy and systematical method of teaching and of learning the English language / [selected] by Abner Alden* (Boston: I. Thomas and E.T. Andrews).

Alderson, R. (**1979**). *Complete Handbook of Voice Training* (Upper Saddle River, NJ: Prentice-Hall).

Alexander, A., Botti, F., Dessimoz, D., and Drygajlo, A. (**2004**). "The effect of mismatched recording conditions on human and automatic speaker recognition in forensic applications," *Forensic Science International* **146** (Suppl. S), S95–S99.

Ali Cherif, A., Royere, M.L., Gosset, A., Poncet, M., Salamon, G., and Khalil, R. (**1984**). "Troubles du comportement et de l'activité mentale après intoxication oxycarbonée: Lesions pallidales bilaterales," *Review Neurologique* **140**, 32–40.

Allport, G.W. and Cantril, H. (**1934**). "Judging personality from the voice," *Journal of Social Psychology* **5**, 37–55.

Alpert, M. (**1983**). "Encoding of feelings in voice," in *Treatment of Depression: Old Controversies and New Approaches,* edited by P.J. Clayton and J.E. Barrett (New York: Raven Press), pp. 217–228.

Alpert, M., Alpert, J., and Maltz, E. (**2005**). "Purchase occasion influence on the role of music in advertising," *Journal of Business Research* **58**, 369–376

Alpert, M., Kurtzberg, R.L., Pilot, M., and Friedhoff, A.J. (**1963**). "Spectral characteristics of the voices of twins," *Acta Genetica Med.Gemellol.* **12**, 335–341.

Alpert, M., Pouget, E.R., and Silva, R.R. (**2001**). "Reflections of depression in acoustic measures of the patient's speech," *Journal of Affective Disorders* **66**, 59–69.

Alpert, M., Rosen, A., Welkowitz, J., Sobin, C., and Borod, J.C. (**1989**). "Vocal acoustic correlates of flat affect in schizophrenia. Similarity to Parkinson's disease and right hemisphere disease and contrast with depression," *British Journal of Psychiatry* Suppl. **4**, 51–56.

Alpert, M., Shaw, R.J., Pouget, E.R., and Lim, K.O. (**2002**). "A comparison of clinical ratings with vocal acoustic measures of flat affect and alogia," *Journal of Psychiatric Research* **36**, 347–353.

Altmann, J. (**1980**). *Baboon Mothers and Infants* (Chicago: University of Chicago Press).

Ambady, N. and Rosenthal, R. (**1992**). "Thin slices of expressive behavior as predictors of interpersonal consequences: A meta-analysis," *Psychological Bulletin* **111**, 256–274.

Ambrazaitis, G. and Bruce, G. (**2006**). "Perception of south Swedish word accents," Lund University, Centre for Languages & Literature, Dept. of Linguistics & Phonetics Working Papers **52**, 5–8.

Amir, O. and Biron-Shental, T. (**2004**). "The impact of hormonal fluctuations on female vocal folds," *Current Opinions in Otolaryngology Head and Neck Surgery* **12**, 180–184.

Amir, O., Biron-Shental, T., and Shabtai, E. (**2006**). "Birth control pills and nonprofessional voice: Acoustic analyses," *Journal of Speech, Language, and Hearing Research* **49**, 1114–1126.

Amir, O., Biron-Shental, T., Tzenker, O., and Barer, T. (**2005**). "Different oral contraceptives and voice quality – An observational study," *Contraception* **71**, 348–352.

Amir, O. and Kishon-Rabin, L. (**2004**). "Association between birth control pills and voice quality," *Laryngoscope* **114**, 1021–1026.

Andersen, R.A. (**1997**). "Multimodal integration for the representation of space in the posterior parietal cortex," *Phil. Trans. R. Soc. Lond. B* **352**, 1421–1428.

Anderson, B., and Annakin, K. (Director) (**1960**). *Swiss Family Robinson* (Walt Disney, United States).

Andreasen, N.C., Alpert, M., and Martz, M.J. (**1981**). "Acoustic analysis: An objective measure of affective flattening," *Archives of General Psychiatry* **38**, 281–285.

Andrew, R.J. (**1976**). "Use of formants in the grunts of baboons and other nonhuman primates," *Annals of the New York Academy of Sciences* **280**, 673–693.

Andrianopoulos, M.V., Darrow, K., and Chen, J. (**2001**). "Multimodal standardization of voice among four multicultural populations: formant structures," *Journal of Voice* **15**, 61–77.

Andruski, J. (**2006**). "Tone clarity in mixed pitch/phonation-type tones," *Journal of Phonetics* **34**, 388–404.

Andruski, J. and Ratliff, M. (**2000**). "Phonation types in production of phonological tone: The case of Green Mong," *Journal of the International Phonetic Association* **30**, 37–61.

Anisfeld, M., Bogo, N., and Lambert, W.E. (**1962**). "Evaluational reactions to accented English speech," *Journal of Abnormal and Social Psychology* **65**, 223–231.

Anolli, L. and Ciceri, R. (**1997**). "The voice of deception: Vocal strategies of naive and able liars," *Journal of Nonverbal Behavior* **21**, 259–284.

Anolli, L. and Ciceri, R. (**2002**). "Analysis of the vocal profiles of male seduction: From exhibition to self-disclosure," *Journal of General Psychology* **129**, 149–169.

Anolli, L., Ciceri, R., and Infantino, M.G. (**2002**). "From 'blame by praise' to 'praise by blame': Analysis of vocal patterns in ironic communication," *International Journal of Psychology* **37**, 266–276.

Anonymous 4 (**2002**) *La BeLe Marie* (Compact Disc). Harmonia Mundi, USA.

ANSI (**1960**). ANSI S1.1-1960, "Acoustical terminology" (New York: American National Standards Institute).

Apel, W. (**1990**). *Gregorian Chant* (Bloomington, IN: Indiana University Press).

Appelman, R. (**1973**). "Radiological findings in the study of vocal registers," in *Vocal Registers in Singing: Proceedings of a Symposium*, edited by J.W. Large (Paris: Mouton), pp. 59–62.

Apple, W., Streeter, L.A., and Krauss, R.M. (**1979**). "The effects of pitch and speech rate on personal attributions," *Journal of Personality and Social Psychology* **37**, 715–727.

Arends, N., Povel, D.J., Van Os, E., and Speth, L. (**1990**). "Predicting voice quality of deaf speakers on the basis of glottal characteristics," *Journal of Speech and Hearing Research* **33**, 116–122.

Armstrong, H.A. and McKelvie, S. (**1996**). "Effect of face context on recognition memory for voices," *Journal of General Psychology* **123**, 259–270.

Aronovitch, C.D. (**1976**). "The voice of personality: Stereotyped judgments and their relation to voice quality and sex of speaker," *Journal of Social Psychology* **99**, 207–220.

Ashmore, J. (**2000**). "Hearing," in *Sound*, edited by P. Kruth and H. Stobart (Cambridge: Cambridge University Press), pp. 65–88.

Asquith, A. and Altig, R. (**1990**). "Male call frequency as a criterion for female choice in Hyla cinerea," *Journal of Herpetology* **24**, 198–201.

Assal, G., Aubert, C., and Buttet, J. (**1981**). "Asymétrie cérébrale et reconnaissance de la voix," *Revue Neurologique* (Paris) **137**, 255–268.

Assal, G., Zander, E., Kremin, H., and Buttet, J. (**1976**). "Discrimination des voix lors des lésions du cortex cérébrals," *Archives Suisses de Neurologie, Neurochirurgie, et de Psychiatrie* **119**, 307–315.

Au, W.W.L. (**1993**). *The Sonar of Dolphins* (New York: Springer-Verlag).

Aubergé, V. and Cathiard, M. (**2003**). "Can we hear the prosody of smile?," *Speech Communication* **40**, 87–97.

Aubin, T. and Jouventin, P. (**1998**). "Cocktail-party effect in king penguin colonies," *Proceedings of the Royal Society of London B: Biological Sciences* **265**, 1665–1673.

Aubin, T., Jouventin, P., and Hildebrand, C. (**2000**). "Penguins use the two-voice system to recognize each other," *Proceedings of the Royal Society of London B: Biological Sciences* **267**, 1081–1087.

Auer, P. (**1996**). "On the prosody and syntax of turn-continuations," in *Prosody in Conversation: Interactional Studies*, edited by E. Couper-Kuhlen and M. Selting (Cambridge: Cambridge University Press), pp. 57–100.

Auer, P., Couper-Kuhlen, E., and Müller, F. (**1999**). *Language in Time: The Rhythm and Tempo of Spoken Interaction* (New York: Oxford University Press).

Auran, C., Bouzon, C., and Hirst, D.J. (**2004**). "The Aix-MARSEC database: Towards an evolutive database for spoken British English," in *Proceedings of the Second International Conference on Speech Prosody*, Nara, pp. 561–564.

Austin, G. (**1806**). *Chironomia* (London: Cadell and Davies). Reprinted by Southern Illinois University Press, Carbondale, IL, 1996.

Austin, S.F. and Titze, I.R. (**1997**). "The effect of subglottal resonance on vocal fold vibration," *Journal of Voice* **11**, 391–402.

Avery, J.D. and Liss, J. (**1996**). "Acoustic characteristics of less-masculine-sounding male speech," *Journal of the Acoustical Society of America* **99**, 3738–3748.

Ayçiçegi, A. and Harris, C. L. (**2004**). "Bilinguals' recall and recognition of emotion words," *Cognition and Emotion* **18**, 977–987.

Bachorowski, J.-A. (**1999**). "Vocal expression and perception of emotion," *Current Directions in Psychological Science* **8**, 53–57.

Bachorowski, J.-A. and Owren, M.J. (**1995**). "Vocal expression of emotion: Acoustic properties of speech are associated with emotional intensity and context," *Psychological Science* **6**, 219–224.

Bachorowski, J.-A. and Owren, M.J. (**1999**). "Acoustic correlates of talker sex and individual talker identity are present in a short vowel segment produced in running speech," *Journal of the Acoustical Society of America* **106**, 1054–1063.

Bachorowski, J.-A. and Owren, M.J. (**2001**). "Not all laughs are alike: Voiced but not unvoiced laughter readily elicits positive affect," *Psychological Science* **12**, 252–257.

Bachorowski, J.-A. and Owren, M.J. (**2003**). "Sounds of emotion: Production and perception of affect-related vocal acoustics," *Annals of the New York Academy of Science* **1000**, 244–265.

Bachorowski, J.-A. and Owren, M.J. (**2008**). "Emotion-related vocal acoustics: Cue-configuration, dimensional, and affect-induction perspectives," in *Emotions in the Human Voice*, volume 1, edited by K. Izdebski (San Diego, CA: Plural), pp. 87–100.

Bachorowski, J.-A., Smoski, M.J., and Owren, M. (**2001**). "The acoustic features of human laughter," *Journal of the Acoustical Society of America* **110**, 1581–1597.

Baeckman, L. (**1991**). "Recognition memory across the adult lift span: The role of prior knowledge," *Memory and Cognition* **19**, 63–71.

Bahr, R.H. and Pass, K.J. (**1996**). "The influence of style-shifting on voice identification," *Forensic Linguistics* **3**, 24–38.

Bahrick, H., Bahrick, P., and Wittlinger, R. (**1975**). "Fifty years of memory for names and faces: A cross-sectional approach," *Journal of Experimental Psychology: General* **104**, 54–75.

Baken, R.J. (**1987**). *Clinical Measurement of Speech and Voice* (Boston: College Hill).

Baken, R.J. and Orlikoff, R.F. (**1999**). *Clinical Measurement of Speech and Voice,* second edition (San Diego, CA: Singular).

Baker, J. (**1999**). "A report on alterations to the speaking and singing voices of four women following hormonal therapy with virilizing agents," *Journal of Voice* **13**, 496–507.

Balcombe, J.P. and McCracken, G.F. (**1992**). "Vocal recognition in Mexican free-tailed bats: Do pups recognize mothers?," *Animal Behaviour* **43**, 79–87.

Ball, M.J., Esling, J., and Dickson, C. (**2000**). "The transcription of voice quality," in *Voice Quality Measurement,* edited by R.D. Kent and M.J. Ball (San Diego, CA: Singular), pp. 49–58.

Bandler, R. and Shipley, M.T. (**1994**). "Columnar organization in the midbrain periaqueductal gray: Modules for emotional expression?," *Trends in Neuroscience* **17**, 379–389.

Banse, R. and Scherer, K.R. (**1996**). "Acoustic profiles in vocal emotion expression," *Journal of Personality and Social Psychology* **70**, 614–636.

Bänziger, T. and Scherer, K.R. (**2005**). "The role of intonation in emotional expressions," *Speech Communication* **46**, 252–267.

Barker, B.A. and Newman, R.S. (**2004**). "Listen to your mother! The role of talker familiarity in infant streaming," *Cognition* **94**, B45–B53.

Barnes, J.J., Davis, P., Oates, J., and Chapman, J. (**2004**). "The relationship between professional operatic soprano voice and high range spectral energy," *Journal of the Acoustical Society of America* **116**, 530–538.

Bartholomeus, B.N. (**1973**). "Voice identification by nursery school children," *Canadian Journal of Psychology* **27**, 464–472.

Bartholomew, W.T. (**1934**). "A physical definition of 'good voice-quality' in the male voice," *Journal of the Acoustical Society of America* **6**, 25–33.

Bastian, A. and Schmidt, S. (**2008**). "Affect cues in vocalizations of the bat, Megaderma lyra, during agonistic interactions," *Journal of the Acoustical Society of America* **124**, 598–608.

Baudouin, J.Y., Gilibert, D., Sansone, S., and Tiberghien, G. (**2000**). "When the smile is a cue to familiarity," *Memory* **8**, 285–292.

Bauer, R. and Rubens, A.B. (**1985**). "Agnosia," in *Clinical Neuropsychology,* 2nd edition, edited by K. M. Heilman and E. Valenstein (New York: Academic Press), pp. 187–284.

Baum, S.R. and Pell, M. (**1997**). "Production of affective and linguistic prosody by brain-damaged patients," *Aphasiology* **11**, 177–198.

Baum, S.R. and Pell, M.D. (**1999**). "The neural bases of prosody: Insights from lesion studies and neuroimaging," *Aphasiology* **13**, 581–608.

Bazúa-Durán, C. and Au, W.W.L. (**2002**). "The whistles of Hawaiian spinner dolphins," *Journal of the Acoustical Society of America* **112**, 3064–3072.

Bazúa-Durán, C. and Au, W.W.L. (**2004**). "Geographic variations in the whistles of spinner dolphins (Stenella longirostris) of the Main Hawaiian Islands," *Journal of the Acoustical Society of America* **116**, 3757–3769.

Beauchemin, M., De Beaumont, L., Vannasing, P., Turcotte, A., Arcand, C., Belin, P., and Lassonde, M. (**2006**). "Electrophysiological markers of voice familiarity," *European Journal of Neuroscience* **23**, 3081–3086.

Beaucousin, V., Lacheret, A., Turbelin, M.R., Morel, M., Mazoyer, B., and Tzourio-Mazoyer, N. (**2007**). "fMRI study of emotional speech comprehension," *Cerebral Cortex* **17**, 339–352.

Bee, M.A. (**2004**). "Within-individual variation in bullfrog vocalizations: Implications for a vocally mediated social recognition system," *Journal of Acoustical Society of America* 116, 3770–3782.

Bee, M.A. and Gerhardt, H.C. (**2002**). "Individual voice recognition in a territorial frog (*Rana catesbeiana*)," *Proceedings of the Royal Society of London B: Biological Sciences* 269, 1443–1448.

Bee, M.A., Kozich, C.E., Blackwell, K.J., and Gerhardt, H.C. (**2001**). "Individual variation in advertisement calls of territorial male green frogs, *Rana Clamitans*: Implications for individual discrimination," *Ethology* 107, 65–84.

Beer, C.G. (**1969**). "Laughing gull chicks: Recognition of their parents' voices," *Science* 166, 1030–1032.

Belin, P., Fecteau, S., and Bedard, C. (**2004**). "Thinking the voice: Neural correlates of voice perception," *Trends in Cognitive Science* 8, 129–135.

Belin, P. and Zatorre, R.J. (**2003**). "Adaptation to speaker's voice in right anterior temporal lobe," *NeuroReport* 14, 2105–2109.

Belin, P., Zatorre, R.J., and Ahad, P. (**2002**). "Human temporal-lobe response to vocal sounds," *Cognitive Brain Research* 13, 17–26.

Belin, P., Zatorre, R.J., Lafaille, P., Ahad, P., and Pike, B. (**2000**). "Voice-selective areas in human auditory cortex," *Nature* 403, 309–312.

Belotel-Grenié, A. and Grenié, M. (**2004**). "The creaky voice phonation and the organization of Chinese discourse," in *Proceedings of the International Symposium on Tonal Aspects of Languages: With Emphasis on Tone Languages*.

Bendor, D. and Wang, X. (**2005**). "The neuronal representation of pitch in primate auditory cortex," *Nature* 436, 1161–1165.

Bendor, D. and Wang, X. (**2006**). "Cortical representations of pitch in monkeys and humans," *Current Opinion in Neurobiology* 16, 391–399.

Bennett, S. and Montero-Diaz, L. (**1982**). "Children's perception of speaker sex," *Journal of Phonetics* 10, 113–121.

Bennett, S. and Weinberg, B. (**1979**)."Acoustic correlates of perceived sexual identity in pre-adolescent children's voices," *Journal of the Acoustical Society of America* 66, 989–1000.

Benowitz, L.I., Finkelstein, S., Levine, D.N., and Moya, K. (**1990**). "The role of the right cerebral hemisphere in evaluating configurations," in *Brain Circuits and Functions of the Mind*, edited by C.B. Trevarthern (Cambridge: Cambridge University Press), pp. 320–333.

Benson, D.F. (**1994**). *The Neurology of Thinking* (Oxford: Oxford University Press).

Benton, A.L. (**1980**). "The neuropsychology of facial recognition," *American Psychologist* 35, 176–186.

Benton, A.L. and Van Allen, M.W. (**1972**). "Prosopagnosia and facial discrimination," *Journal of Neurological Science* 15, 167–172.

Berckmoes, C. and Vingerhoets, G. (**2004**). "Neural foundations of emotional speech processing," *Current Directions in Psychological Science* 13, 182–185.

Berlin, I. (**1953; 1994**). *The Hedgehog and the Fox: An Essay on Tolstoy's View of History* (London: Weidenfeld & Nicolson). Reprinted in *Russian Thinkers* (Oxford: Penguin).

Berlin, I. (**1978**). *Russian Thinkers* (New York: Viking).

Berry, D.A. (**2001**). "Mechanisms of modal and nonmodal phonation," *Journal of Phonetics* 29, 431–450.

Berry, D.A., Montequin, D.W., and Tayama, N. (**2001**). "High-speed digital imaging of the medial surface of the vocal folds," *Journal of the Acoustical Society of America* 110, 2539–2547.

Berry, D.S. (**1990**). "Vocal attractiveness and vocal babyishness: Effects on stranger, self, and friend impressions," *Journal of Nonverbal Behavior* 14, 141–153.

Berry, D.S. (**1992**). "Vocal types and stereotypes: Joint effects of vocal attractiveness and vocal maturity on person perception," *Journal of Nonverbal Behavior* **16**, 41–54.

Berry, D.S., Hansen, J.S., Landry-Pester, J.C., and Meier, J.A. (**1994**). "Vocal determinants of first impressions of young children," *Journal of Nonverbal Behavior* **18**, 187–197.

Bertau, M.-C. (**2008**). "Voice: A pathway to consciousness as 'social contact to oneself'," *Integrative Psychological & Behavioral Science* **42**, 92–113.

Best, C.T. and Avery, R.A. (**1999**). "Left-hemisphere advantage for click consonants is determined by linguistic significance and experience," *Psychological Science* **10**, 65–70.

Bever, T.G. (**1975**). "Cerebral asymmetries in humans are due to the differentiation of two incompatible processes: Holistic and analytic," *Annals of the New York Academy of Science* **263**, 251–262.

Bhatia, K.P. and Marsden, C.D. (**1994**). "The behavioural and motor consequences of focal lesions of the basal ganglia in man," *Brain* **117**, 859–876.

Bielamowicz, S., McGowan, R.S., Berke, G.S., Kreiman, J., Gerratt, B.R., and Green, D.C. (**1995**). "The effect of gas density on glottal vibration and exit jet particle velocity," *Journal of the Acoustical Society of America* **97**, 2504–2510.

Bird, S., Caldecott, M., Campbell, F., Gick, B., and Shaw, P.A. (**2008**). "Oral-laryngeal timing in glottalised resonants," *Journal of Phonetics* **36**, 492–507.

Blank, S.C., Scott, S., Murphy, K., Warburton, E., and Wise, R. (**2002**). "Speech production: Wernicke, Broca and beyond," *Brain* **125**, 1829–1838.

Blankenship, B. (**2002**). "The timing of nonmodal phonation in vowels," *Journal of Phonetics* **30**, 163–191.

Blatchford, H. and Foulkes, P. (**2006**). "Identification of voices in shouting," *International Journal of Speech, Language and the Law* **13**, 241–254.

Blomberg, M., Elenius, D., and Zetterholm, E. (**2004**). "Speaker verification scores and acoustic analysis of a professional impersonator," *Proceedings of FONETIK 2004* (Dept. of Linguistics, Stockholm University).

Bloothooft, G., Bringmann, E., van Cappellen, M., van Luipen, J., and Thomassen, K. (**1992**). "Acoustics and perception of overtone singing," *Journal of the Acoustical Society of America* **92**, 1827–1836.

Blu, S., Mullin, M.A., and Songé, C. (**2006**). *Word of Mouth* (Los Angeles: Silman-James).

Blumstein, S. and Cooper, W.E. (**1974**). "Hemispheric processing of intonation contours," *Cortex* **10**, 146–158.

Blumstein, S. and Goodglass, H. (**1972**). "The perception of stress as a semantic cue in aphasia," *Journal of Speech and Hearing Research* **15**, 800–806.

Bodamer, J. (**1947**). "Die prosopagnosie," *Arch. Psychiatrie Z. Neurol.* **179**, 6–54.

Bodden, M. (**1997**). "Instrumentation for sound quality evaluation," *Acustica* **83**, 775–783.

Boersma, P.D. and Kovacic, G. (**2006**). "Spectral characteristics of three styles of Croatian folk singing," *Journal of the Acoustical Society of America* **119**, 1805–1816.

Boersma, P. and Weenink, D. (2009). Praat: Doing phonetics by computer (Version 5.1.11) [Computer program]. Retrieved July 19, 2009, from http://www.praat.org/.

Bogen, J.D. and Gordon, H.W. (**1971**). "Musical tests for functional lateralization with intracarotid amobarbitol," *Nature* **230**, 524–525.

Bolhuis, J.J. and Van Kampen, H.S. (**1992**). "An evaluation of auditory learning in filial imprinting," *Behaviour* **122**, 195–230.

Boliek, C., Hixon, T.J., Watson, P., and Morgan, W. (**1996**). "Vocalization and breathing during the first year of life," *Journal of Voice* **10**, 1–22.

Bolinger, D. (**1964**). "Around the edge of language: Intonation," *Harvard Educational Review* **34**, 282–296. Reprinted in D. Bolinger, *Intonation: Selected Readings* (Harmondsworth: Penguin Books).

Bolinger, D. (**1972a**). "Accent is predictable (if you're a mind-reader)," *Language* **48**, 633–644.

Bolinger, D. (**1972b**). *Intonation: Selected Readings* (Harmondsworth: Penguin Books).

Bolinger, D. (**1982**). "Intonation and its parts," *Language* **58**, 505–533.

Bolinger, D. (**1986**). *Intonation and Its Parts* (Stanford, CA: Stanford University Press).

Bolinger, D. (**1989**). *Intonation and Its Uses: Melody in Grammar and Discourse* (Stanford, CA: Stanford University Press).

Bolt, R., Cooper, F., Green, D.M., Hamlet, S.L., McKnight, J.G., Pickett, J., Tosi, O., Underwood, B.D., and Hogan, D.L. (**1979**). *On the Theory and Practice of Voice Identification* (Washington, DC: National Academy of Sciences).

Bond, C.F. Jr. and DePaulo, B.M. (**2006**). "Accuracy of deception judgments," *Personality and Social Psychology Review* **10**, 214–234.

Boone, D. (**1991**). *Is Your Voice Telling on You?* (San Diego, CA: Singular).

Borch, D.Z., Sundberg, J., Lindestad, P.-A., and Thalen, M. (**2004**). "Vocal fold vibration and voice source aperiodicity in 'dist' tones: A study of a timbral ornament in rock singing," *Logopedics Phoniatrics Vocology* **29**, 147–153.

Borod, J.C. (**1993**). "Cerebral mechanisms underlying facial, prosodic, and lexical emotional expression: A review of neuropsychological studies and methodological issues," *Neuropsychology* **7**, 445–463.

Boshoff, P.H. (**1945**). "The anatomy of the South African Negro larynges," *South African Journal of Medical Sciences* **10**, 35–50.

Boss, D. (**1996**). "The problem of F0 and real–life speaker identification: A case study," *Forensic Linguistics* **3**, 155–159.

Bothwell, R.R., Deffenbacher, K.A., and Brigham, J. (**1987**). "Correlation of eyewitness accuracy and confidence: Optimality hypothesis revisited," *Journal of Applied Psychology* **72**, 691–695.

Bourget, D. and Whitehurst, L. (**2004**). "Capgras syndrome: A review of the neurophysiological correlates and presenting clinical features in cases involving physical violence," *Canadian Journal of Psychiatry* **49**, 719–725.

Bowers, D., Bauer, R.M., and Heilman, K.M. (**1993**). "The nonverbal affect lexicon: Theoretical perspectives from neurological studies of affect perception," *Neuropsychology* **7**, 433–444.

Bowers, D., Coslett, H.B., Bauer, R.M., Speedie, L.J., and Heilman, K.M. (**1987**). "Comprehension of emotional prosody following unilateral hemispheric lesions: Processing defect versus distraction defect," *Neuropsychologia* **25**, 317–328.

Bozikas, V.P., Kosmidis, M.H., Tonia, T., Andreou, C., Focas, K., and Karavatos, A. (**2007**). "Impaired perception of affective prosody in remitted patients with bipolar disorder," *Journal of Neuropsychiatry and Clinical Neuroscience* **19**, 436–440.

Brackett, C. (Producer) and Wilder, B. (Director) (**1945**). *The Lost Weekend* (Paramount, United States).

Brackett, I.P. (**1971**). "Parameters of voice quality," in *Handbook of Speech Pathology and Audiology*, edited by L.E. Travis (Englewood Cliffs, NJ: Prentice-Hall), pp. 441–463.

Bradlow, A.R., Torretta, G.M., and Pisoni, D.B. (**1996**). "Intelligibility of normal speech I: Global and fine-grained acoustic-phonetic talker characteristics," *Speech Communication* **20**, 255–272.

Bradshaw, J.L. and Mattingly, J.B. (**1995**). *Clinical Neuropsychology: Behavioral and Brain Science* (New York: Academic Press).

Bradshaw, J.L. and Nettleton, N.C. (**1983**). *Human Cerebral Asymmetry* (Englewood Cliffs, NJ: Prentice-Hall).

Brainard, M. and Doupe, A. (**2002**). "What songbirds teach us about learning," *Nature* **417**, 351–358.

Braun, A. (**1996**). "Age estimation by different listener groups," *Forensic Linguistics* **3**, 65–73.

Brazil, D. (**1985**). *The Communicative Value of Intonation in English* (Birmingham: Cambridge University Press).

Bregman, A.S. (**1994**). *Auditory Scene Analysis* (Cambridge, MA: MIT Press).

Bregman, A.S. (**2001**). "Auditory scene analysis: Hearing in complex environments," in *Thinking in Sound: The Cognitive Psychology of Human Audition*, edited by S. McAdams and E. Bigand (Oxford, UK: Clarendon Press), pp. 10–36.

Breitenstein, C., Van Lancker, D., and Daum, I. (**2001**). "The contribution of speech rate and pitch variation to the perception of vocal emotions in a German and an American sample," *Cognition and Emotion* **15**, 57–79.

Brenner, M. and Branscomb, H. (**1979**). "The psychological stress evaluator: Technical limitations affecting lie detection," *Polygraph* **8**, 127–132.

Brenner, M., Branscomb, H., and Schwartz, G. (**1979**). "Psychological stress evaluator – Two tests of a vocal measure," *Psychophysiology* **16**, 351–357.

Bricker, P.D. and Pruzansky, S. (**1966**). "Effects of stimulus content and duration on talker identification," *Journal of the Acoustical Society of America* **40**, 1441–1449.

Broniatowski, M., Grundfest–Broniatowski, S., Nelson, D.R., Dessoffy, R., Shields, R.W., and Strome, M. (**2002**). "Electronic analysis of intrinsic laryngeal muscles in canine sound production," *Annals of Otology, Rhinology & Laryngology* **111**, 542–552.

Brown, B.L., Strong, W.J., and Rencher, A.E. (**1974**). "54 voices from 2: The effects of simultaneous manipulations of rate, mean fundamental frequency, and variance of fundamental frequency on ratings of personality from speech," *Journal of the Acoustical Society of America* **55**, 313–318.

Brown, C.J. (**1979**). "Reactions of infants to their parents' voices," *Infant Behavior and Development* **2**, 295–300.

Brown, G. (**1977**). *Listening to Spoken English* (London: Longman).

Brown, J.W. (**1972**). *Aphasia, Apraxia and Agnosia: Clinical and Theoretical Aspects* (Springfield: Charles C. Thomas).

Brown, J.W. (**1988**). *The Life of the Mind: Selected Papers* (Hillsdale, NJ: Lawrence Erlbaum).

Brown, J.W. (**1998a**). "Morphogenesis and mental process," in *Learning as Self Organization*, edited by C. Pribram and J. King (Mahwah, NJ: Lawrence Erlbaum), pp. 295–310.

Brown, J.W. (**1998b**). "Foundations of cognitive metaphysics," *Process Studies* **21**, 79–92.

Brown, J.W. (**2002**). *The Self Embodying Mind* (Barrytown: Station Hill Press).

Brown, R. and Kulik, J. (**1977**). "Flashbulb memories," *Cognition* **5**, 73–93.

Brown, T.E., Senter, S.M., and Ryan, A.H. Jr. (**2003**). "Ability of the Vericator to detect smugglers at a mock security checkpoint," Report DoDPI03–R–0002, Fort Jackson, SC, Department of Defense Polygraph Institute.

Brownell, H.H., Gardner, H., Prather, P., and Martino, G. (**1995**). "Language, communication, and the right hemisphere," in *Handbook of Neurological Speech and Language Disorders*, vol. 33, edited by H.S. Kirshner (New York: Marcel Dekker), pp. 325–349.

Bruce, V. (**1990**). "Perceiving and recognising faces," *Mind and Language* **5**, 342–364.

Bruce, V. and Young, A.W. (**1986**). "Understanding face recognition," *Br J Psychol.* **77**, 305–327.

Bruck, M., Cavanagh, P., and Ceci, S.J. (**1991**). "Fortysomething: recognizing faces at one's 25th reunion," *Memory and Cognition* **19**, 221–228.

Bruckert, L., Bestelmeyer, P., Latinus, M., Rouger, J., Charest, I., Rousselet, G., Kawahara, H., and Belin, P. (**2010**). "Vocal attractiveness increases by averaging," *Current Biology* **20**, 116–120.

Bruckert, L., Lienard, J.–S., Lacroix, A., Kreutzer, M., and Leboucher, G. (**2006**). "Women use voice parameters to assess men's characteristics," *Proceedings of the Royal Society of London Series B – Biological Sciences* **273**, 83–89.

Brunelle, M. (**2009**). "Tone perception in Northern and Southern Vietnamese," *Journal of Phonetics* **37**, 79–96.

Bruyer, R. (**1981**). "Asymmetry of facial expression in brain damaged subjects," *Neuropsychologia* **19**, 615–624.

Bryant, G.A. and Fox Tree, J.E. (**2002**). "Recognizing verbal irony in spontaneous speech," *Metaphor and Symbol* **17**, 99–117.

Bryant, G.A. and Fox Tree, J.E. (**2005**). "Is there an ironic tone of voice?," *Language and Speech* **48**, 257–277.

Bryant, G.A. and Haselton, M.G. (**2009**). "Vocal cues of ovulation in human females," *Biological Letters* **5**, 12–15.

Buchanan, T.W., Lutz, K., Mirzazade, S., Specht, K., Shah, N.J., Zilles, K., and Jancke, L. (**2000**). "Recognition of emotional prosody and verbal components of spoken language: An fMRI study," *Cognitive Brain Research* **9**, 227–238.

Bucher, T.L., Ryan, M.J., and Bartholomew, G.A. (**1982**). "Oxygen consumption during resting, calling and nest building in the frog *Physalaemus pustulosus*," *Physiological Zoology* **55**, 10–22.

Buchwald, J.S., Erwin, R.J., Guthrie, D., Schwafel, J., and Van Lancker, D. (**1994**). "Influence of language structure on brain–behavior development," *Brain and Language* **46**, 607–619.

Buck, R.W. (**2000**). "The epistemology of reason and affect," in *The Neuropsychology of Emotion*, edited by J.C. Borod (New York: Oxford University Press), pp. 31–55.

Buder, E.H. (**2000**). "Acoustic analysis of voice quality: A tabulation of algorithms 1902–1990," in *Voice Quality Measurement*, edited by R.D. Kent and M.J. Ball (San Diego, CA: Singular), pp. 119–244.

Bull, R. and Clifford, B.R. (**1984**). "Earwitness voice recognition accuracy," in *Eyewitness Testimony: Psychological Perspectives*, edited by G.L. Wells & E.F. Loftus (New York: Cambridge University Press), pp. 92–123.

Bull, R., Rathborn, H., and Clifford, B.R. (**1983**). "The voice-recognition accuracy of blind listeners," *Perception* **12**, 223–226.

Bunch, M. (**1997**). *Dynamics of the Singing Voice* (Vienna: Springer).

Burke, E.J. and Murphy, C.G. (**2007**). "How female barking tree frogs, *Hyla gratiosa*, use multiple call characteristics to select a mate," *Animal Behaviour* **74**, 1463–1472.

Burklund, C.W. and Smith, A. (**1977**). "Language and the cerebral hemispheres," *Neurology* **27**, 627–633.

Burling, R. (**1993**). "Primate calls, human language, and nonverbal communication," *Current Anthropology* **34**, 25–53.

Burton, T. (Producer/director) and Di Novi, D. (Producer) (**1990**). *Edward Scissorhands* (Twentieth–Century Fox, United States).

Busby, P. and Plant, G. (**1995**). "Formant frequency values of vowels produced by preadolescent boys and girls," *Journal of the Acoustical Society of America* **97**, 2603–2606.

Butler, R., Diamond, E., and Neff, W. (**1957**). "Role of auditory cortex in discrimination of changes in frequency," *Journal of Neurophysiology* **20**, 108–120.

Byrne, C. and Foulkes, P. (**2004**). "The 'mobile phone effect' on vowel formants," *Forensic Linguistics* **11**, 83–102.

Cabeza, R. and Nyberg, L. (**2000**). "Neural basis of learning and memory: Functional neuroimaging evidence," *Current Opinion in Neurology* **13**, 415–421.

Caelen–Haumont, G. and Pollerman, B.Z. (**2008**). "Voice and affect in speech communication," in *Emotions in the Human Voice*, volume 1, edited by K. Izdebski (San Diego, CA: Plural), pp. 215–232.

Callan, D.E., Tsytsarev, V., Hanakawa, T., Callan, A., Katsuhara, M., Fukuyama, H., and Turner, R. (**2006**). "Song and speech: Brain regions involved with perception and covert production," *NeuroImage* **31**, 1327–1342.

Campisi, P., Low, A.J., Papsin, B.C., Mount, R.J., and Harrison, R.V. (**2006**). "Multidimensional voice program analysis in profoundly deaf children: Quantifying frequency and amplitude control," *Perceptual and Motor Skills* **103**, 40–50.

Cancelliere, A. and Kertesz, A. (**1990**). "Lesion localization in acquired deficits of emotional expression and comprehension," *Brain and Cognition* **13**, 133–147.

Cannon, W.B. (**1927**). "The James–Lange theory of emotion: A critical examination and an alternative theory," *American Journal of Psychology* **39**, 10–124.

Canter, G.J. and Van Lancker, D. (**1985**). "Disturbances of the temporal organization of speech following bilateral thalamic surgery in a patient with Parkinson's disease," *Journal of Communication Disorders* **18**, 329–349.

Cantril, H. and Allport, G.W. (**1935**). *The Psychology of Radio* (New York: Harper).

Cao, J. and Maddieson, I. (**1992**). "An exploration of phonation types in Wu dialects of Chinese," *Journal of Phonetics* **20**, 77–92.

Capgras, J. and Reboul-Lachaux, J. (**1923**) "L'illusion de 'Sosies' dans un délire systématisé chronique," *Bulletin de la Société de Médecine Mentale* **2**, 6–16.

Caplan, L.R., Schmahmann, J.D., Kase, C.S., Feldman, E., Baquis, G., Greenberg, J.P., Gorelick, P.B., Helgason, C., and Hier, D.B. (**1990**). "Caudate infarcts," *Archives of Neurology* **47**, 133–143.

Carbary, T.J., Patterson, J.T., and Snyder, P.J. (**2000**). "Foreign accent syndrome following a second catastrophic injury: MRI correlates, linguistic and voice pattern analysis," *Brain and Cognition* **43**, 78–85.

Carlesimo, G.A. and Caltagirone, C. (**1995**). "Components in the visual processing of known and unknown faces," *Journal of Clinical and Experimental Neurpsychology* **17**, 691–705.

Carterette, E.C. and Barnebey, A. (**1975**). "Recognition memory for voices," in *Structure and Process in Speech Perception*, edited by A. Cohen and S.G. Nooteboom (New York: Springer), pp. 246–265.

Caspers, J. (**1998**). "Who's next? The melodic marking of question vs. continuation in Dutch," *Language and Speech* **41**, 375–398.

Catania, A.C. (**1998**). *Learning* (Englewood Cliffs, NJ: Prentice Hall).

Cavagna, G. and Margaria, R. (**1965**). "An analysis of the mechanics of phonation," *Journal of Applied Physiology* **20**, 301–307.

Cerrato, L., Falcone, M., and Paoloni, A. (**2000**). "Subjective age estimation of telephonic voices," *Speech Communication* **31**, 107–112.

Cestaro, V.L. (**1996**). "A comparison between decision accuracy rates obtained using the polygraph instrument and the computer voice stress analyzer (CVSA) in the absence of jeopardy," Report DoDPI95-R-0002 (Fort McClellan, AL, Department of Defense Polygraph Institute).

Chae, S.W., Choi, G., Kang, H.J., Choi, J.O., and Jin, S.M. (**2001**). "Clinical analysis of voice change as a parameter of premenstrual syndrome," *Journal of Voice* **15**, 278–283.

Chafe, W.L. (**1994**). *Discourse, Consciousness, and Time* (Chicago: The University of Chicago Press).

Charlton, B.D., Reby, D., and McComb, K. (**2007**). "Female perception of size–related formant shifts in red deer, *Cervus elaphus*," *Animal Behaviour* **74**, 707–714.

Charlton, B.D., Reby, D., and McComb, K. (**2008**). "Effect of combined source (F0) and filter (formant) variation on red deer hind responses to male roars," *Journal of the Acoustical Society of America* **123**, 2936–2943.

Charrier, I., Mathevon, N., and Jouventin, P. (**2001b**). "Mother's voice recognition by seal pups," *Nature* **412**, 873.

Charrier, I., Mathevon, N., and Jouventin, P. (**2002**). "How does a fur seal mother recognize the voice of her pup? An experimental study of Arctocephalus tropicalis," *Journal of Experimental Biology* **205**, 603–612.

Charrier, I., Mathevon, N., and Jouventin, P. (**2003**). "Individuality in the voice of fur seal females: An analysis study of the pup attraction call in Arctocephalus tropicalis," *Marine Mammal Science* **19**, 161–172.

Charrier, I., Mathevon, N., Jouventin, P., and Aubin, T. (**2001a**). "Acoustic communication in a Black–headed Gull colony: How chicks identify their parents?," *Ethology* **107**, 961–974.

Chattopadhyay, A., Dahl, D.W., Ritchie, R.J.B., and Shahin, K.N. (**2003**). "Hearing voices: The impact of announcer speech characteristics on consumer response to broadcast advertising," *Journal of Consumer Psychology* **13**, 198–204.

Cheang, H.S. and Pell, M.D. (**2008**). "The sound of sarcasm," *Speech Communication* **50**, 366–381.

Cheang, H.S. and Pell, M.D. (**2009**). "Acoustic markers of sarcasm in Cantonese and English," *Journal of the Acoustical Society of America* **126**, 1394–1405.

Chen, A., Gussenhoven, C., and Rietveld, T. (**2004**). "Language-specificity in the perception of paralinguistic intonational meaning," *Language and Speech* **47**, 311–349.

Cheney, D.L. and Seyfarth, R.M. (**1980**). "Vocal recognition in free-ranging vervet monkeys," *Animal Behaviour* **28**, 362–367.

Cheney, D.L. and Seyfarth, R.M. (**1990**). *How Monkeys See the World* (Chicago: University of Chicago Press).

Cheney, D.L. and Seyfarth, R.M. (**1999**). "Recognition of other individuals' social relationships by female baboons," *Animal Behaviour* **58**, 67–75.

Chernobelsky, S.I. (**2002**). "A study of menses-related changes to the larynx in singers with voice abuse," *Folia Phoniatrica et Logopaedica* **54**, 2–7.

Childers, D., Hicks, D.M., Eskanazi, L., Moore, G.P., and Lalwani, A.L. (**1990**). "Electroglottography and vocal fold physiology," *Journal of Speech and Hearing Research* **33**, 245–254.

Chin, S.B. and Pisoni, D.B. (**1997**). *Alcohol and Speech* (New York: Academic Press).

Chomsky, N. and Halle, M. (**1968**). *The Sound Pattern of English* (New York: Harper and Row).

Christianson, S.-Å. (**1992**). "Do flashbulb memories differ from other types of emotional memories?," in *Affect and Accuracy in Recall: Studies of "Flashbulb Memories*, edited by E. Winograd and U. Neisser (Cambridge: Cambridge University Press), pp. 191–211.

Chuenwattanapranithi, S., Xu, Y., Thipakorn, B. and Maneewongvatan, S. (**2008**). "Encoding emotions in speech with the size code," *Phonetica* **65**, 210–230.

Ciaramelli, E., Grady, C.L., and Moscovitch, M. (**2008**). "Top-down and bottom-up attention to memory: A hypothesis (AtoM) on the role of the posterior parietal cortex in memory retrieval," *Neuropsychologia* **46**, 1828–1851.

Cimino, C.R., Verfaellie, M., Bowers, D. and Heilman, K.M. (**1991**). "Autobiographical memory: Influence of right hemisphere damage on emotionality and specificity," *Brain and Cognition* **15**, 106–118.

Clark, H.H. and Wasow, T. (**1998**). "Repeating words in spontaneous speech," *Cognitive Psychology* **37**, 201–242.

Clarke, F.R. and Becker, R.W. (**1969**). "Comparison of techniques for discriminating among talkers," *Journal of Speech and Hearing Research* **12**, 747–761.

Cleveland, T.F. (**1977**). "Acoustic properties of voice timbre types and their influence on voice classification," *Journal of the Acoustical Society of America* **61**, 1622–1629.

Cleveland, T.F., Stone, R.E., Sundberg, J., and Iwarsson, J. (**1997**). "Estimated subglottal pressure in six male country singers," *Journal of Voice* **11**, 403–409.

Cleveland, T.F., Sundberg, J., and Stone, R.E. (**2001**). "Long-term-average spectrum characteristics of country singers during speaking and singing," *Journal of Voice* **15**, 54–60.

Clifford, B.R. (**1980**). "Voice identification by human listeners: On earwitness reliability," *Law and Human Behavior* **4**, 373–394.

Clifford, B.R., Rathborn, H., and Bull, R. (**1981**). "The effects of delay on voice recognition accuracy," *Law and Human Behavior* **5**, 201–208.

Code, C. (**1987**). *Language, Aphasia, and the Right Hemisphere* (London: John Wiley & Sons).

Code, C. (**1994**). "Speech automatism production in aphasia," *Journal of Neurolinguistics* **8**, 135–148.

Code, C. (**2005**). "First in, last out? The evolution of aphasic lexical speech automatisms to agrammatism and the evolution of human communication," *Interaction Studies* **6**, 311–334.

Cohen, H., Douaire, J., and Elsabbagh, M. (**2001**). "The role of prosody in discourse processing," *Brain & Cognition* **46**, 73–82.

Cohen, J.R., Crystal, T.H., House, A.S., and Neuberg, E.P. (**1980**). "Weighty voices and shaky evidence: A critique," *Journal of the Acoustical Society of America* **68**, 1884–1886.

Coleman, R.O. (**1971**). "Male and female voice quality and its relationship to vowel formant frequencies," *Journal of Speech and Hearing Research* **14**, 565–577.

Coleman, R.O. (**1976**). "A comparison of the contributions of two voice quality characteristics to the perception of maleness and femaleness in the voice," *Journal of Speech and Hearing Research* **19**, 168–180.

Collins, S.A. (**2000**). "Men's voices and women's choices," *Animal Behaviour* **60**, 773–780.

Collins, S.A. and Missing, C. (**2003**). "Vocal and visual attractiveness are related in women," *Animal Behaviour* **65**, 997–1004.

Colton, R.H., Casper, J.K., and Leonard, R. (**2005**). *Understanding Voice Disorders*, 2nd edition (Baltimore: Lippincott Williams & Wilkins).

Compton, A.J. (**1963**). "Effects of filtering and vocal duration upon the identification of speakers, aurally," *Journal of the Acoustical Society of America* **35**, 1748–1752.

Conway, M.A. (**1995**). *Flashbulb Memories* (Hove, Sussex: Lawrence Erlbaum Associates).

Cook, S. and Wilding, J. (**1997**). "Earwitness testimony: Never mind the variety, hear the length," *Applied Cognitive Psychology* **11**, 95–111.

Cook, S. and Wilding, J. (**2001**). "Earwitness testimony: Effects of exposure and attention on the face overshadowing effect," *British Journal of Psychology* **92**, 617–629.

Cooper, W.E. and Sorensen, J.M. (**1981**). *Fundamental Frequency in Sentence Production* (New York: Springer-Verlag).

Corcoran, D.W.J. (**1971**). *Pattern Recognition* (Harmondsworth: Penguin Books).

Couper-Kuhlen, E. (**1986**). *An Introduction to English Prosody* (London: Edward Arnold).

Couper-Kuhlen, E. (**1991**). "English Speech Rhythm: Form and Function in Everyday Verbal Interaction." PhD Thesis, the University of Zurich.

Couper-Kuhlen, E. (**1996**). "The prosody of repetition: On quoting and mimicry," in *Prosody in Conversation: Interactional Studies*, edited by E. Couper-Kuhlen and M. Selting (Cambridge: Cambridge University Press), pp. 366–405.

Couper-Kuhlen, E. (**1999**). "Coherent voicing: On prosody in conversational reported speech," in *Coherence in Spoken and Written Discourse: How to Create It and How to Describe It*, edited by W. Bublitz and U. Lenk (Amsterdam: Benjamins), pp. 11–32.

Couper-Kuhlen, E. (**2000**). "Prosody," in *Handbook of Pragmatics Online*, edited by J. Verschueren, J.-O. Östman, J. Blommeart, and C. Bulcaen (Amsterdam: Benjamins).

Couper-Kuhlen, E. (**2001**). "Interactional prosody: High onsets in reason-for-the-call turns," *Language in Society* **30**, 29–53.

Cowie, R. and Cornelius, R.R. (**2003**). "Describing emotional states that are expressed in speech," *Speech Communication* **40**, 5–32.

Cowie, R., Douglas-Cowie, E., Apolloni, B., Taylor, J., Romano, A., and Fellenz, W. (**1999**). "What a neural net needs to know about emotion words," in *Computational Intelligence and Applications*, edited by N. Mastorakis (Dallas, TX: World Scientific and Engineering Society Press), pp. 109–114.

Cozen-Harel, J. (**2007**). "Vocal cues of American presidents during times of deception," unpublished manuscript, UCLA Department of Communication Studies.

Critchley, M. (**1953**). *The Parietal Lobes* (London: Edward Arnold & Co.).

Cruttenden, A. (**1997**). *Intonation*, 2nd edition (New York: Cambridge University Press).

Crystal, D. (**1969**) *Prosodic Systems and Intonation in English* (Cambridge: Cambridge University Press).

Crystal, D. (**1975**). *The English Tone of Voice* (New York: St. Martin's Press).

Crystal, D. (**2003**). *The Cambridge Encyclopedia of the English Language*, 2nd edition (Cambridge: Cambridge University Press).

Cumming, J. (**1856**). *Cumming's Minor Works: The Finger of God; Christ Our Passover; The Comforter* (Philiadelphia: Lindsay and Blakiston).

Cummins, F. and Port, R.F. (**1998**). "Rhythmic constraints on stress timing in English," *Journal of Phonetics* **26**, 145–171.

Curio, G., Neuloh, G., Numminen, J., Jousmäki, V., and Hari, R. (**2000**). "Speaking modifies voice-evoked activity in the human auditory cortex," *Human Brain Mapping* **9**, 1983–191.

Cutler, A. and Pearson, M. (**1986**). "On the analysis of turn-taking cues," in *Intonation in Discourse*, edited by C. Johns-Lewis (London: Croom Helm), pp. 139–155.

Cutler, A., Dahan, D., and van Donselaar, W. (**1997**). "Prosody in the comprehension of spoken language: A literature review," *Language and Speech* **40**, 141–201.

Cutler, B.L., Penrod, S.D., and Stuve, T.E. (**1988**). "Juror decision making in eyewitness identification cases," *Law and Human Behavior* **12**, 41–55.

Cutting, J. (**1990**). *The Right Cerebral Hemisphere and Psychiatric Disorders* (Oxford: Oxford University Press).

Dabbs, J.M. Jr. and Malinger, A. (**1999**). "High testosterone levels predict low voice pitch among men," *Personality and Individual Differences* **27**, 801–804.

Dahmen, J.C. and King, A. (**2007**). "Learning to hear: Plasticity of auditory cortical processing," *Current Opinion in Neurobiology* **17**, 456–464.

Dalla Bella, S., Giguère, J–F., and Peretz, I. (**2007**). "Singing proficiency in the general population," *Journal of the Acoustical Society of America* **121**, 1182–1189.

Daly, N. and Warren, P. (**2001**). "Pitching it differently in New Zealand English: Speaker sex and intonation patterns," *Journal of Sociolinguistics* **5**, 85–96.

Damasio, A.R. (**1994**). *Descartes' Error* (New York: Avon Books).

Damasio, A.R., Damasio, H., and Van Hoesen, G.W. (**1982**). "Prosopagnosia: Anatomic basis and behavioral mechanisms," *Neurology* **32**, 331–341.

Damjanovic, L. and Hanley, J.R. (**2007**). "Recalling episodic and semantic information about famous faces and voices," *Memory & Cognition* **35**, 1205–1210.

Damphousse, K.R., Pointon, L., Upchurch, D., and Moore, R.K. (**2007**). "Assessing the validity of voice stress analysis tools in a jail setting," Report 219031, Project 2005–IJ–CX–0047, US Department of Justice.

Danielsson, B. (ed.) (**1955**). *Works on English Orthography and Pronunciation: 1551, 1569, 1570* (Stockholm: Almqvist & Wiksell).

Danly, M. and Shapiro, B. (**1982**). "Speech prosody in Broca's aphasia," *Brain and Language* **16**, 171–190.

Darwin, C. (**1872a**). *The Expression of the Emotions in Man and Animals* (New York: Oxford University Press).

Darwin, C. (**1872b**). *The Origin of Species* (sixth edition) (London: John Murray).

Davidoff, J. and Roberson, D. (**2002**). "Development of animal recognition: A difference between parts and wholes," *Journal of Experimental Child Psychology* **81**, 217–234.

Davis, P.J., Zhang, S.P., Winkworth, A., and Bandler, R. (**1996**). "Neural control of respiration: Respiratory and emotional influences," *Journal of Voice* **10**, 23–38.

de Boer, J. and Thornton, R.D. (**2008**). "Neural correlates of perceptual learning in the auditory brainstem: Efferent activity predicts and reflects improvement at a speech–in–noise discrimination task," *Journal of Neuroscience* **28**, 4929–4937.

de Bruin, M.D., Coerts, M.J., and Greven, A.J. (**2000**). "Speech therapy in the management of male–to–female transsexuals," *Folia Phoniatrica et Logopaedica* **52**, 220–227.

DePaulo, P.J. and DePaulo, B.M. (**1989**). "Can deception by salespersons and customers be detected through nonverbal behavioral cues?," *Journal of Applied Social Psychology* **19**, 1552–1577.

De Renzi, E. (**1986**). "Prosopagnosia in two patients with CT scan evidence of damage confined to the right hemisphere," *Neuropsychologia* **24**, 385–389.

Deacon, T. (**1997**). *The Symbolic Species: The Co-evolution of Language and the Brain* (New York: W.W. Norton).

Debruyne, F., Decoster, W., Van Gijsel, A., and Vercammen, J. (**2002**). "Speaking fundamental frequency in monozygotic and dizygotic twins," *Journal of Voice* **16**, 466–471.

DeCasper, A.J. and Fifer, W.P. (**1980**). "Of human bonding: Newborns prefer their mothers' voice," *Science* **208**, 1174–1176.

DeCasper, A.J., Lecanuet, J.P. Maugais, R., Granier-Deferre, C., and Busnel, M. C. (**1994**). "Fetal reactions to recurrent maternal speech," *Infant Behavioral and Development* **17**, 159–164.

DeCasper, A.J. and Prescott, P.A. (**1984**). "Human newborns' perception of male voices: Preference, discrimination, and reinforcing value," *Developmental Psychobiology* **17**, 481–491.

Decoster, W. and Debruyne, F. (**2000**). "Longitudinal voice changes: Facts and interpretation," *Journal of Voice* **14**, 184–193.

Deffenbacher, K.A. (**1980**). "Eyewitness accuracy and confidence: Can we infer anything about their relationship?," *Law and Human Behavior* **4**, 243–260.

Deffenbacher, K.A., Cross, J.F., Handkins, R.E., Chance, J.E., Goldstein, A.G., Hammersley, R., and Read, J.D. (**1989**). "Relevance of voice identification research to criteria for evaluating reliability of an identification," *Journal of Psychology* **123**, 109–119.

Delattre, P. (**1966**). "Les dix intonations de base du français," *French Review* **40**, 1–14.

Delattre, P. (**1972**). "The distinctive function of intonation," in *Intonation*, edited by D. Bolinger (Harmondsworth: Penguin Books), pp. 159–174.

Deliyski, D.D., Petrushev, P.P., Bonilha, H.S., Gerlach, T.T., Martin-Harris, B., and Hillman, R.E. (**2008**). "Clinical implementation of laryngeal high-speed videoendoscopy: Challenges and evolution," *Folia Phoniatrica et Logopaedica* **60**, 33–44.

Denenberg, V.H. (**1967**). "Stimulation in infancy, emotional reactivity, and exploratory behavior," in *Neurophysiology and Emotion*, edited by D.C. Glass (New York: Rockefeller University Press and Russell Sage Foundation), pp. 161–190.

Denes, P.B. and Pinson, E.N. (**1993**). *The Speech Chain: The Physics and Biology of Spoken Language*, second edition (New York: W.H. Freeman).

Dennis, M. and Whitaker, H. (**1976**). "Language acquisition following hemidecortication: Linguistic superiority of the left over the right hemisphere," *Brain and Language* **3**, 404–433.

DePaulo, B.M. and Pfeifer, R.L. (**1986**). "On-the-job experience and skill at detecting deception," *Journal of Applied Social Psychology* **16**, 249–267.

DePaulo, B.M., Rosenthal, R., Rosenkrantz, J., and Green, C.R. (**1982**). "Actual and perceived cues to deception: A closer look at speech," *Basic and Applied Social Psychology* 3, 291–312.

Deva, B.C. (**1959**). "The vibrato in Indian music," *Acustica* 9, 175–180.

Dewaele, J.-M. (**2008**). "The emotional weight of I love you in multilinguals' languages," *Journal of Pragmatics* 40, 1753–1780.

Dewson, J. (**1964**). "Speech sound discrimination by cats," *Science* 144, 555–556.

Dickens, M. and Sawyer, G. (**1962**). "An experimental comparison of vocal quality among mixed groups of Whites and Negroes," *Southern Speech Journal* 18, 178–185.

Dickson, D.R. and Maue-Dickson, W.M. (**1982**). *Anatomical and Physiological Bases of Speech* (Boston: Little, Brown).

Diehl, C.F. (**1960**). "Voice and personality: An evaluation," in *Psychological and Psychiatric Aspects of Speech and Hearing*, edited by D.A. Barbara (Springfiled: Chas. C. Thomas), pp. 171–203.

Dietrich, S., Ackermann, H., Szameitat, D.P., and Alter, K. (**2006**). "Psychoacoustic studies on the processing of vocal interjections: How to disentangle lexical and prosodic information?," *Progress in Brain Research* 156, 295–302.

Dietrich, S., Hertrich, I., Alter, K., Ischebeck, A., and Ackermann, H. (**2008**). "Understanding the emotional expression of verbal interjections: A functional MRI study," *NeuroReport* 19, 1751–1755.

Dilley, L., Shattuck–Hufnagel, S., and Ostendorf, M. (**1996**). "Glottalization of word-initial vowels as a function of prosodic structure," *Journal of Phonetics* 24, 423–444.

Dion, K.K., Berscheid, E., and Walster, E. (**1972**). "What is beautiful is good," *Journal of Personality and Social Psychology* 24, 285–290.

Disner, S. (**2004**). "Voice lie detectors." Presented at SpeechTEK, September 14, 2004.

Dmitriev, L.B., Chernov, B.P., and Maslov, V.T. (**1983**). "Functioning of the voice mechanism in double–voice Touvinian singing," *Folia Phoniatrica* 35, 193–197.

Dobson, F.S. and Jouventin, P. (**2003**). "How mothers find their pups in a colony of Antarctic fur seals," *Behavioural Processes* 61, 77–85.

Doty, N.D. (**1998**). "The influence of nationality on the accuracy of face and voice recognition," *American Journal of Psychology* 111, 191–214.

Douglas-Cowie, E. and Cowie, R. (**1998**). "Intonational settings as markers of discourse units in telephone conversations," *Language and Speech* 41, 351–374.

Drahota, A., Costall, A., and Reddy, V. (**2008**). "The vocal communication of different kinds of smile," *Speech Communication* 50, 278–287.

Drake, C. and Iadecola, C. (**2007**). "The role of neuronal signaling in controlling cerebral blood flow," *Brain and Language* 102, 141–152.

Draper, M.H., Ladefoged, P., and Whitteridge, D. (**1960**). "Expiratory pressure and air flow during speech," *British Medical Journal* 1, 1837–1843.

Dromey, C., Kumar, R., Lang, A.E., and Lozano, A.M. (**2000**). "An investigation of the effects of subthalamic nucleus stimulus on acoustic measures of voice," *Movement Disorders* 15, 1132–1138.

Dromey, C., Reese, L., and Hopkin, J.A. (**2009**). "Laryngeal-level amplitude modulation in vibrato," *Journal of Voice* 23, 156–163.

Dromey, C. and Smith, M.E. (**2008**). "Vocal tremor and vibrato in the same person: Acoustic and electromyographic differences," *Journal of Voice* 22, 541–545.

Dubner, R., Sessle, B.J., and Storey, A.T. (**1978**). *The Neural Basis of Oral and Facial Function* (New York: Plenum Press).

Duchaine, B.C. (**2006**). "Selective deficits in developmental cognitive neuropsychology: An introduction," *Cognitive Neuropsychology* 23, 675–679.

Duncan, S. Jr. and Fiske, D.W. (**1977**). *Face-to-Face Interaction: Research, Methods, and Theory* (New York: John Wiley & Sons).

Echternach, M. and Richter, B. (**2010**). "Vocal perfection in yodeling – pitch stabilities and transition times," *Logopedics Phoniatrics Vocology* **35**, 6–12.

Eckel, H.E., Koebke, J., Sittel, C., Sprinzl, G.M., Pototschnig, C., and Stennert, E. (**1999**). "Morphology of the human larynx during the first five years of life studied on whole organ serial sections," *Annals of Otology, Rhinology & Laryngology* **108**, 232–238.

Edgerton, M.E. (**2004**). *The 21st Century Voice: Contemporary and Traditional Extra-Normal Voice* (Lanham, MD: Scarecrow Press).

Edwards, B. (Director) & Manulis, M. (Producer) (**1962**). *The Days of Wine and Roses* (Warner Brothers, United States).

Edwards, B. (Producer/Director) (**1982**). *The Trail of the Pink Panther* (United Artists, United States).

Edwards, B. (Producer/Director) (**1982**). *Victor/Victoria* (Metro-Goldwyn-Mayer, United States).

Edwards, B. (Producer/Director) (**1983**), *The Curse of the Pink Panther* (United Artists, United States).

Eggermont, J.J. (**2001**). "Between sound and perception: Reviewing the search for a neural code," *Hearing Research* **157**, 1–42.

Ehret, G. (**1997**). "The auditory cortex," *Journal of Comparative Physiology A* **181**, 547–557.

Ekman, P., Friesen, W.V., and Scherer, K.R. (**1976**). "Body movement and voice pitch in deceptive interaction," *Semiotica* **16**, 23–27.

Ekman, P., O'Sullivan, M., Friesen, W.V., and Scherer, K.R. (**1991**). "Face, voice, and body in detecting deceit," *Journal of Nonverbal Behavior* **15**, 125–135.

Elaad, E. (**2003**). "Effects of feedback on the overestimated capacity to detect lies and the underestimated ability to tell lies," *Applied Cognitive Psychology* **17**, 349–363.

Elaad, E., Segev, S., and Tobin, Y. (**1998**). "Long-term working memory in voice identification," *Psychology, Crime, and Law* **4**, 73–88.

Elfenbein, H.A. and Ambady, N. (**2002**). "On the universality and cultural specificity of emotion recognition: A meta-analysis," *Psychological Bulletin* **128**, 203–235.

Eliades, S.J. and Wang, X. (**2005**). "Dynamics of auditory-vocal interaction in monkey auditory cortex," *Cerebral Cortex* **15**, 1510–1523.

Ellgring, H. and Scherer, K.R. (**1996**). "Vocal indicators of mood change in depression," *Journal of Nonverbal Behavior* **20**, 83–110.

Endress, W., Bambach, W., and Flosser, G. (**1971**). "Voice spectrograms as a function of age, voice disguise, and voice imitation," *Journal of the Acoustical Society of America* **49**, 1842–1848.

Epstein, M. (**2002**). "Voice Quality and Prosody in English." Unpublished Ph.D. Dissertation, UCLA.

Erickson, D., Yoshida, K., Menezes, C., Fujino, A., Mochida, T., and Shibuya, Y. (**2006**). "Exploratory study of some acoustic and articulatory characteristics of sad speech," *Phonetica* **63**, 1–25.

Erickson, M.L. (**2004**). "The interaction of formant frequency and pitch in the perception of voice category and jaw opening in female singers," *Journal of Voice* **18**, 24–37.

Esposito, A., Demeurisse, G., Alberti, B., and Fabbro, F. (**1999**). "Complete mutism after midbrain periaqueductal gray lesion," *NeuroReport* **10**, 681–685.

Esposito, C. (**2010**). "The effects of linguistic experience on the perception of phonation," *Journal of Phonetics.* **38**, 306–316.

Estenne, M., Zocchi, L., Ward, M., and Macklem, P.T. (**1990**). "Chest wall motion and expiratory muscle use during phonation in normal humans," *Journal of Applied Physiology* **68**, 2075–2082.

Evans, S., Neave, N., and Wakelin, D. (**2006**). "Relationships between vocal characteristics and body size and shape in human males: An evolutionary explanation for a deep male voice," *Biological Psychology* **72**, 160–163.

Evans, S., Neave, N., Wakelin, D., and Hamilton, C. (**2008**). "The relationship between testosterone and vocal frequencies in human males," *Physiology & Behavior* **93**, 783–788.

Ey, E., Pfefferle, D., and Fischer, J. (**2007**). "Do age- and sex-related variations reliably reflect body size in non–human primate vocalizations? A review," *Primates* **48**, 253–267.

Eysenck, H. (**1990**). "Genetic and environmental contributions to individual differences: The three major dimensions of personality," *Journal of Personality* **58**, 245–261.

Fagel, W.P.F., van Herpt, L.W.A., and Boves, L. (**1983**). "Analysis of the perceptual qualities of Dutch speakers' voice and pronunciation," *Speech Communication* **2**, 315–326.

Faigman, D.L., Kaye, D.H., Saks, M.J., and Sanders, J. (**2002**). *Modern Scientific Evidence: The Law and Science of Expert Testimony*, vol. 3, sec. 31–1 ("Talker identification"), (Fagan, MN: West Group Publishing). pp. 588–598.

Fair, C.M. (**1988**). *Memory and Central Nervous System Organization* (New York: Paragon House).

Fair, C.M. (**1992**). *Cortical Memory Functions* (Boston: Birkhäuser).

Fant, G. (**1960**). *Acoustic Theory of Speech Production* ('s-Gravenhage: Mouton).

Fant, G. and Lin, Q. (**1988**). "Frequency domain interpretation and derivation of glottal flow parameters," *Speech Transmission Laboratory Quarterly Progress and Status Report* **2–3**, 1–21.

Farah, M.J., Hammond, K.M., and Mehta, Z. (**1989**). "Category-specificity and modality-specificity in semantic memory," *Neuropsychologia* **27**, 193–200.

Farah, M.J., Levinson, K.L., and Klein, K.L. (**1995**). "Face perception and within-category discrimination in prosopagnosia," *Neuropsychologia* **33**, 661–674.

Fay, P. and Middleton, W.C. (**1939a**). "Judgment of occupation from the voice as transmitted over a public address system and over a radio," *Journal of Applied Psychology* **23**, 586–601.

Fay, P. and Middleton, W.C. (**1939b**). "Judgment of Spranger personality types from the voice as transmitted over a public address system," *Character and Personality* **8**, 144–155.

Fay, P. and Middleton, W.C. (**1940a**). "Judgment of Kretschmerian body types from the voice as transmitted over a public address system," *Journal of Social Psychology* **12**, 151–162.

Fay, P. and Middleton, W.C. (**1940b**). "Judgment of intelligence from the voice as transmitted over a public address system," *Sociometry* **3**, 186–191.

Fay, P. and Middleton, W.C. (**1940c**). "The ability to judge the rested or tired condition of a speaker from his voice as transmitted over a public address system," *Journal of Applied Psychology* **24**, 645–650.

Fay, P. and Middleton, W.C. (**1941**). "The ability to judge truth-telling, or lying, from the voice as transmitted over a public address system," *Journal of General Psychology* **24**, 211–215.

Fecteau, S., Armony, J.L., Joanette, Y., and Belin, P. (**2005**). "Sensitivity to voice in human prefrontal cortex," *Journal of Neurophysiology* **94**, 2251–2254.

Feinberg, D.R., DeBruine, L.M., Jones, B.C., and Perrett, D.I. (**2008**). "The role of femininity and averageness of voice pitch in aesthetic judgments of women's voices," *Perception* **37**, 615–623.

Feinberg, D.R., Jones, B.C., Law Smith, M.J., Moore, F.R., DeBruine, L.M., Cornwell, R.E., Hillier, S.G., and Perrett, D.I. (**2006**). "Menstrual cycle, trait estrogen level, and masculinity preferences in the human voice," *Hormones and Behavior* **49**, 215–222.

Feinberg, D.R., Jones, B.C., Little, A.C., Burt, D.M., and Perrett, D.I. (**2005**). "Manipulations of fundamental and formant frequencies influence the attractiveness of human male voices," *Animal Behaviour* **69**, 561–568.

Feldstein, S., Dohm, F.-A., and Crown, C.L. (**2001**). "Gender and speech rate in the perception of competence and social attractiveness," *Journal of Social Psychology* **141**, 785–806.

Fellowes, J.M., Remez, R.E., and Rubin, P.E. (**1997**). "Perceiving the sex and identity of a talker without natural vocal timbre," *Perception and Psychophysics* **59**, 839–849.

Fellows, L., Heberlein, A.S., Morales, D.A., Shivde, G., Waller, S., and Wu, D. (**2005**). "Method matters: An empirical study of impact in cognitive neuroscience," *Journal of Cognitive Neuroscience* **17**, 850–858.

Ferguson, S.H. (**2004**). "Talker differences in clear and conversational speech: Vowel intelligibility for normal–hearing listeners," *Journal of the Acoustical Society of America* **116**, 2365–2373.

Fichtel, C., Hammerschmidt, K., and Jürgens, U. (**2001**). "On the vocal expression of emotion. A multi–parametric analysis of different states of aversion in the squirrel monkey," *Behaviour* **138**, 97–116.

Fischer, J. (**2004**). "Emergence of individual recognition in young macaques," *Animal Behaviour* **67**, 655–661.

Fischer, J., Kitchen, D.M., Seyfarth, R.M., and Cheney, D.L. (**2004**). "Baboon loud calls advertise male quality: Acoustic features and their relation to rank, age, and exhaustion," *Behavioral Ecology and Sociobiology* **56**, 140–148.

Fischer-Jorgensen, E. (**1967**). "Phonetic analysis of breathy (murmured) vowels in Gujarati," *Indian Linguistics* **28**, 71–139.

Fisher, C.M. (**1983**). "Abulia minor versus agitated behavior," *Clinical Neurosurgery* **31**, 9–31.

Fitch, J. and Holbrook, A. (**1970**). "Modal vocal fundamental frequency of young adults," *Archives of Otolaryngology Head and Neck Surgery* **92**, 379–382.

Fitch, W.T. (**1994**). Vocal Tract Length Perception and the Evolution of Language. Unpublished Brown University doctoral dissertation.

Fitch, W.T. (**1997**). "Vocal tract length and formant frequency dispersion correlate with body size in rhesus macaques," *Journal of the Acoustical Society of America* **102**, 1213–1222.

Fitch, W.T. (**2000a**). "The evolution of speech: A comparative review," *Trends in Cognitive Sciences* **4**, 258–266.

Fitch, W.T. (**2000b**). "Skull dimensions in relation to body size in nonhuman mammals: The causal bases for acoustic allometry," *Zoology–Analysis of Complex Systems* **103**, 40–58.

Fitch, W.T. (**2002**). "Comparative vocal production and the evolution of speech: Reinterpreting the descent of the larynx," in *The Transition to Language*, edited by A. Wray (Oxford University Press, Oxford), pp. 21–45.

Fitch, W.T. (**2004a**). "The evolution of language," in *The Cognitive Neurosciences*, 3rd edition, edited by M. Gazzaniga (Cambridge, MA: MIT Press).

Fitch, W.T. (**2004b**). "Kin selection and 'mother tongues': A neglected component in language evolution," in *Evolution of Communication Systems: A Comparative Approach*, edited by D.K. Oller and U. Griebel (Boston, MA: MIT Press), pp. 275–296.

Fitch, W.T. (**2006**). "The biology and evolution of music: A comparative perspective," *Cognition* **100**, 173–215.

Fitch, W.T. (**2010**). *The Evolution of Language* (New York: Cambridge University Press).

Fitch, W.T. and Giedd, J. (**1999**). "Morphology and development of the human vocal tract: A study using magnetic resonance imaging," *Journal of the Acoustical Society of America* **106**, 1511–1522.

Fitch, W.T. and Hauser, M.D. (**1995**). "Vocal production in nunhuman primates: Acoustics, physiology, and functional constraints on 'honest' advertisement," *American Journal of Primatology* **37**, 191–219.

Fitch, W.T. and Hauser, M.D. (**2003**). "Unpacking 'honesty': Vertebrate vocal production and the evolution of acoustic signals," in *Acoustic Communication*, edited by A.M. Simmons, A.N. Popper, and R.R. Fay (New York: Springer), pp. 65–137.

Fletcher, H. and Munson, W.A. (**1933**). "Loudness: its definition, measurement, and calculation," *Journal of the Acoustical Society of America* **5**, 82–108.

Flint, A.J., Black, S.E., Campbell-Taylor, I., Gailey, G.F., and Levinton, C. (**1992**). "Acoustic analysis in the differentiation of Parkinson's disease and major depression," *Journal of Psycholinguistic Research* **21**, 383–399.

Fonagy, I. (**1981**). "Emotions, voice and music," in *Research Aspects on Singing*, edited by J. Sundberg (Stockholm: Royal Swedish Academy of Music), pp. 51–79.

Formby, D. (**1967**). "Maternal recognition of infant's cry," *Developmental Medicine and Child Neurology* **9**, 293–298.

Formby, C., Thomas, R.G., and Halsey, J.H. Jr. (**1989**). "Regional cerebral blood flow for singers and nonsingers while speaking, singing, and humming a rote passage," *Brain and Language* **36**, 690–698.

Foulds-Elliott, S.D., Thorpe, C.W., Cala, S.J, and Davis, P.J. (**2000**). "Respiratory function in operatic singing: Effects of emotional connection," *Logopedics Phoniatrics Vocology* **25**, 151–168.

Francis, A.L., Ciocca, V., Wong, N.K., Leung, W.H., and Chu, P.C. (**2006**). "Extrinsic context affects perceptual normalization of lexical tone," *Journal of the Acoustical Society of America* **119**, 1712–1726.

Francis, A.L. and Driscoll, C. (**2006**). "Training to use voice onset time as a cue to talker identification induces a left-ear/right hemisphere processing advantage," *Brain and Language* **98**, 310–318.

Freed, A. (Producer), Donen, S. (Director), and Kelly, G. (Director) (**1952**). *Singin' in the Rain* (Metro Goldwyn Mayer, United States).

Freud, S. (**1938**). *The Basic Writings of Sigmund Freud* (edited by A.A. Brill) (Oxford, UK: Modern Library).

Frey, R., Volodin, I., and Volodina, E. (**2007**). "A nose that roars: Anatomical specializations and behavioral features of rutting male saiga," *Journal of Anatomy* **211**, 717–736.

Frick, R.W. (**1985**). "Communicating emotion: The role of prosodic features," *Psychological Bulletin* **97**, 412–429.

Frick, R.W. (**1986**). "The prosodic expression of anger: Differentiating threat and frustration," *Aggressive Behavior* **12**, 121–128.

Frohlich, M., Michaelis, D., Strube, H.W., and Kruse, E. (**2000**). "Acoustic voice analysis by means of the hoarseness diagram," *Journal of Speech, Language, and Hearing Research* **43**, 706–720.

Fry, D.B. (**1958**). "Experiments in the perception of stress," *Language and Speech* **1**, 126–152.

Fry, D.B. (**1968**). "Prosodic phenomena," in *Manual of Phonetics*, edited by B. Malmberg (Amsterdam: North-Holland), pp. 365–410.

Fry, D.B. (**1979**). *The Physics of Speech* (Cambridge: Cambridge University Press).

Gaitenby, J. (**1965**). "The elastic word," *Haskins Laboratories Status Report on Speech Research* **SR-2**, 3.1–3.12.

Gamble, E. (**1909**). "Minor studies from the psychological laboratory of Wellesley College, I. Intensity as a criterion in estimating the distance of sounds," *Psychological Review* **16**, 416–426.

Gamer, M., Rill, H.G., Vossel, G., and Godert, H.W. (**2006**). "Psychophysiological and vocal measures in the detection of guilty knowledge," *International Journal of Psychophysiology* **60**, 76–87.

Gandour, J.T. (**1978**). "The perception of tone," in *Tone: A Linguistic Survey*, edited by V. Fromkin (New York: Academic Press), pp. 41–76.

Gandour, J.T. and Dardarananda, R. (**1983**). "Identification of tonal contrasts in Thai aphasic patients," *Brain and Language* **18**, 98–114.

Gandour, J.T. and Harshman, R. (**1978**). "Crosslanguage differences in tone perception: A multidimensional scaling investigation," *Language and Speech* **21**, 1–33.

Gandour, J.T., Wong, D., Dzemidzic, M., Lowe, M., Tong, Y., and Li, X. (**2003**). "Cross-linguistic fMRI study of perception of intonation and emotion in Chinese," *Human Brain Mapping* **18**, 149–157.

Gandour, J.T., Wong, D., Hsieh, L., Weinzapfel, B., Van Lancker, D., and Hutchens, G.A. (**2000**). "A crosslinguistic PET study of tone perception," *Journal of Cognitive Neuroscience* **12**, 207–222.

Garcia, J. and Riley, A.L. (**1998**). "Conditioned taste aversions," in *Comparative Psychology: A Handbook*, edited by G. Greenberg & M.M. Haraway (New York: Garland Publishing), pp. 549–561.

Garcia-Toro, M., Talavera, J.A., Saiz-Ruiz, J., and Gonzalez, A. (**2000**). "Prosody impairment in depression measured through acoustic analysis," *Journal of Nervous Medical Disorders* **188**, 824–829.

Garvin, P.L. and Ladefoged, P. (**1963**). "Speaker identification and message identification in speech recognition," *Phonetica* **9**, 193–199.

Gasser, H., Amézquita, A., and Hödl, W. (**2009**). "Who is calling? Intraspecific call variation in the aromobatid frog *Allobates femoralis*," *Ethology* **115**, 596–607.

Gaudio, R. (**1994**). "Sounding gay: Pitch properties in the speech of gay and straight men," *American Speech* **69**, 30–57.

Gay, T., Strome, M., Hirose, H., and Sawashima, M. (**1972**). "Electromyography of the intrinsic laryngeal muscles during phonation," *Annals of Otology, Rhinology & Laryngology* **81**, 401–408.

Gazzaniga, M.S., Irvy, R.B., and Mangun, G.R. (**2002**). *Cognitive Neuroscience: Biology of the Mind* (New York: Norton & Company).

Gazzaniga, M.S. and Smylie, C.S. (**1983**). "Facial recognition and brain asymmetries: Clues to underlying mechanisms," *Annals of Neurology* **13**, 536–540.

Geiselman, R.E. and Bellezza, F.S. (**1977**). "Incidental retention of speaker's voice," *Memory & Cognition* **5**, 658–665.

Geiselman, R.E. and Crawley, J.M. (**1983**). "Incidental processing of speaker characteristics: Voice as connotative information," *Journal of Verbal Learning and Verbal Behavior* **22**, 15–23.

Geissmann, T. (**2002**). "Gibbons songs and human music from an evolutionary perspective," in *The Origins of Music*, edited by N.L. Wallin, B. Merker, and S. Brown (Cambridge, MA: MIT Press).

Gelfer, M.P. (**1988**). "Perceptual attributes of voice: Development and use of rating scales," *Journal of Voice* **2**, 320–326.

Gelfer, M.P. (**1993**). "A multidimensional scaling study of voice quality in females," *Phonetica* **50**, 15–27.

Gelfer, M.P. and Schofield, K.J. (**2000**). "Comparison of acoustic and perceptual measures of voice in male-to-female transsexuals perceived as female versus those perceived as male," *Journal of Voice* **14**, 22–33.

Gelinas-Chebat, C. and Chebat, J.-C. (**1992**). "Effects of two voice characteristics on the attitudes toward advertising messages," *Journal of Social Psychology* **132**, 447–459.

Gelinas-Chebat, C., Chebat, J., and Vaninsky, A. (**1996**). "Voice and advertising – Effects of intonation and intensity of voice on source credibility, attitudes toward the advertised service and the intent to buy," *Perceptual and Motor Skills* **83**, 243–262.

George, M.S., Parekh, P.I., Rosinsky, N., Ketter, T.A., Kimbrell, T.A., Heilman, K.M., Herscovitch, P., and Post, R.M. (**1996**). "Understanding emotional prosody activates right hemisphere regions," *Archives of Neurology* **53**, 665–670.

Gerard, H.B., Green, D., Hoyt, M., and Conolley, E.S. (**1973**). "Influence of affect on exposure frequency estimates," *Journal of Personality and Social Psychology* **28**, 151–154.

Gerfen, C. and Baker, K. (**2005**). "The production and perception of laryngealized vowels in Coatzospan Mixtec," *Journal of Phonetics* **33**, 311–334.

Gerhardt, K.J. and Abrams, R.M. (**2000**). "Fetal exposures to sound and vibroacoustic stimulation," *Journal of Perinatology* **20**, S21–S30.

Gerratt, B.R. and Kreiman, J. (**2001a**). "Measuring vocal quality with speech synthesis," *Journal of the Acoustical Society of America* **110**, 2560–2566.

Gerratt, B.R. and Kreiman, J. (**2001b**). "Toward a taxonomy of nonmodal phonation," *Journal of Phonetics* **29**, 365–382.

Gerratt, B.R., Kreiman, J., Antoñanzas-Barroso, N., and Berke, G.S. (**1993**). "Comparing internal and external standards in voice quality judgments," *Journal of Speech and Hearing Research* **36**, 14–20.

Gerratt, B.R., Till, J., Rosenbek, J.C., Wertz, R.T., and Boysen, A.E. (**1991**). "Use and perceived value of perceptual and instrumental measures in dysarthria management," in *Dysarthria and Apraxia of Speech*, edited by C.A. Moore, K.M. Yorkston, and D.R. Beukelman (Baltimore: Brookes), pp. 77–93.

Gescheider, G.A. (**1997**). *Psychophysics: The Fundamentals* (Mahwah, NJ, Lawrence Erlbaum).

Geschwind, N. (**1970**). "The organization of language and the brain: Language disorders after brain damage help in elucidating the neural basis of verbal behavior," *Science* **170**, 940–944.

Geschwind, N. and Galaburda, A.M. (**1987**). "Cerebral lateralization: Biological mechanisms, associations and pathology: I. A hypothesis and program for research," *Archives of Neurology* **42**, 428–459.

Ghazanfar, A.A., Turesson, H.K., Maier, J.X., Van Dinther, R., Patterson, R.D., and Logothetis, N.K. (**2007**). "Vocal-tract resonances as indexical cues in rhesus monkeys," *Current Biology* **17**, 425–430.

Gilbert, C.D. and Sigman, M. (**2007**). "Brain states: top-down influences in sensory processing," *Neuron* **54**, 677–696.

Giles, H. and Powesland, P.F. (**1975**). *Speech Style and Social Evaluation* (London: Academic Press).

Gjone, H. and Stevenson, J. (**1997**). "A longitudinal twin study of temperament and behavior problems: Common genetic or environmental influences?," *Journal of the American Academy of Child and Adolescent Psychiatry* **36**, 1448–1456.

Glass, C., Bradshaw, J.L., Day, R.H., and Umiltà, C. (**1985**). "Familiarity, special frequency and task determinants in processing laterally presented representations of faces," *Cortex* **21**, 513–31.

Glover, H., Kalinowski, J., Rastatter, M., and Stuart, A. (**1996**). "Effect of instruction to sing on stuttering frequency at normal and fast rates," *Perceptual and Motor Skills* **83**, 511–522.

Gobl, C. and Ní Chasaide, A. (**2003**). "The role of voice quality in communicating emotion, mood and attitude," *Speech Communication* **40**, 189–212.

Goehl, H. and Kaufman, D.K. (**1983**). "Do the effects of adventitious deafness include disordered speech?," *Journal of Speech and Hearing Disorders* **49**, 53–58.

Goggin, J.P., Thompson, C.P., Strube, G., and Simental, L.R. (**1991**). "The role of language familiarity in voice identification," *Memory & Cognition* **19**, 448–458.

Gold, P.E. (**1985**). "A proposed neurobiological basis for regulating memory storage for significant events," in *Affect and Accuracy in Recall: Studies of "Flashbulb" Memories*, edited by E. Winograd and U. Neisser (Cambridge: Cambridge University Press), pp. 141–161.

Goldberg, G. (**1987**). "Supplementary motor area structure and function: Review and hypotheses," *Journal of Neurological Rehabilitation* **1**, 19–24.

Goldberg, S. (**2007**). *Clinical Neuroanatomy Made Ridiculously Simple*, 3rd edition (Miami, FL: Medmaster).

Goldinger, S.D. and Azuma, T. (**2003**). "Puzzle-solving science: The quixotic quest for units in speech perception," *Journal of Phonetics* **31**, 305–320.

Goldinger, S.D., Pisoni, D.B., and Logan, J.S. (**1991**). "On the nature of talker variability effects on recall of spoken word lists," *Journal of Experimental Psychology: Learning, Memory and Cognition* **17**, 152–162.

Goldman, J.A., Phillips, D.P., and Fentress, J.C. (**1995**). "An acoustic basis for maternal recognition in timber wolves (Canis lupus)?," *Journal of the Acoustical Society of America* **97**, 1970–1973.

Goldman, J.L. and Roffman, J.D. (**1975**). "Indirect laryngoscopy," *Laryngoscope* **85**, 530–533.

Goldman-Eisler, F. (**1961**). "The significance of changes in the rate of articulation," *Language and Speech* **4**, 171–188.

Goldman-Eisler, F. (**1972**). "Pauses, clauses, sentences," *Language and Speech* **15**, 103–113.

Goldstein, A.G., Knight, P., Bailis, K., and Conover, J. (**1981**). "Recognition memory for accented and unaccented voices," *Bulletin of the Psychonomic Society* **17**, 217–220.

Gombrich, E.H. (**1995**). *The Story of Art* (London: Phaidon Press).

Gonzalez, J. (**2003**). "Estimation of speakers' weight and height from speech: A re–analysis of data from multiple studies by Lass and colleagues," *Perceptual and Motor Skills* **96**, 297–304.

Gonzalez, J. (**2004**). "Formant frequencies and body size of speaker: A weak relationship in adult humans," *Journal of Phonetics* **32**, 277–287.

Goodglass, H. and Kaplan, E. (**1972**). *Assessment of Aphasia and Related Disorders* (Philadelphia, PA: Lea and Febiger).

Goozee, J.V., Murdoch, B.E., Theodoros, D.G., and Thompson, E.C. (**1998**). "The effects of age and gender on laryngeal aerodynamics," *International Journal of Language & Communication Disorders* **33**, 221–238.

Gordon, H.W. (**1970**). "Hemispheric asymmetries for the perception of musical chords," *Cortex* **6**, 387–398.

Gordon, M. and Ladefoged, P. (**2001**). "Phonation types: A cross-linguistic overview," *Journal of Phonetics* **29**, 383–406.

Götz, D. and Herbst, T. (**1987**). "Der frühe Vogel fängt den Wurm: Erste Überlegungen zu einer Theorie der Synchronisation (Englisch–Deutsch)," in *Arbeiten aus Anglistic und Amerikanistik* **12**.

Goudbeek, M. and Scherer, K. (**2010**). "Beyond arousal: Valence and potency/control cues in the vocal expression of emotion," *Journal of the Acoustical Society of America* **128**, 1322–1336.

Graddol, D. and Swann, J. (**1983**). "Speaking fundamental frequency: Some physical and social correlates," *Language and Speech* **26**, 351–366.

Grafman, J., Salazar, A.M., Weingartner, H., and Amin, D. (**1986**). "Face memory and discrimination: An analysis of the persistent effects of penetrating brain wounds," *International Journal of Neuroscience* **29**, 125–139.

Graham, C.R., Hamblin, A.W., and Feldstein, W. (**2001**). "Recognition of emotion in English voices by speakers of Japanese, Spanish and English," *IRAL* **39**, 19–37.

Gray, G.W. (**1943**). "The 'voice qualities' in the history of elocution," *Quarterly Journal of Speech* **29**, 475–480.

Greasley, P., Sherrard, C., and Waterman, M. (**2000**). "Emotion in language and speech: Methodological issues in naturalistic approaches," *Language and Speech* **43**, 355–375.

Greden, J.F., Albala, A.A., Smokler, I.A., Gardner, R., and Carroll, B.J. (**1981**). "Speech pause time: A marker of psychomotor retardation among endogenous depressives," *Biological Psychiatry* **16**, 851–859.

Green, D.M. and Swets, J.A. (**1966**). *The Theory of Signal Detection* (New York: John Wiley & Sons).

Green, J.A. and Gustafson, G.E. (**1983**). "Individual recognition of human infants on the basis of cries alone," *Developmental Psychobiology* **16**, 485–493.

Green, R.S. and Cliff, N. (**1975**). "Multidimensional comparisons of structures of vocally and facially expressed emotion," *Perception and Psychophysics* **17**, 429–438.

Grice, H.P. (**1968**). "Utterer's meaning, sentence-meaning, and word-meaning," *Foundations of Language* **4**, 225–42.

Grice, H.P. (**1975**). "Logic and conversation," in *Syntax and Semantics, Vol. 3: Speech Acts*, edited by P. Cole and J.L Morgan (New York: Academic Press), pp. 41–58.

Grice, H.P. (**1978**). "Further notes on logic and conversation," in *Syntax and Semantics vol. 9: Pragmatics*, edited by P. Cole (New York: Academic Press), pp. 113–127.

Grosjean, F. (**1980**). "Linguistic structures and performance structures: Studies in pause distribution," in *Temporal Variables in Speech*, edited by W. Dechert and M. Raupach (The Hague: Mouton), pp. 271–285.

Gross, M. (**1999**). "Pitch–raising surgery in male-to-female transsexuals," *Journal of Voice* **13**, 246–250.

Grossmann, T., Oberecker, R., Koch, S.P., and Friederici, A.D. (**2010**). "The developmental origins of voice processing in the human brain," *Neuron* **25**, 852–858.

Gulick, W. (**1971**). *Hearing: Physiology and Psychophysics* (New York: Oxford University Press).

Gulick, W., Gescheider, G.A., and Frisina, R.D. (**1989**). *Hearing: Physiological Acoustics, Neural Coding, and Psychoacoustics* (Oxford: Oxford University Press).

Gunter, C.D. and Manning, W.H. (**1982**). "Listener estimations of speaker height and weight in unfiltered and filtered conditions," *Journal of Phonetics* **10**, 251–257.

Günthner, S. (**1999**). "Polyphony and the 'layering of voices' in reported dialogues : An analysis of the use of prosodic devices in everyday reported speech," *Journal of Pragmatics* **31**, 685–708.

Gunzburger, D. (**1993**). "An acoustic analysis and some perceptual data concerning voice change in male–female transsexuals," *European Journal of Disorders of Communication* **28**, 13–21.

Gunzburger, D., Bresser, A., and ter Keurs, M. (**1987**). "Voice identification of prepubertal boys and girls by normally sighted and visually handicapped subjects," *Language and Speech* **30**, 47–58.

Gurd, J.M., Bessel, N.J., Bladon, R.A.W., and Bamford, J.M. (**1988**). "An unlearned foreign accent in a patient with aphasia," *Brain and Language* **28**, 86–94.

Habermann, G. (**1969**). "Zur Geschichte des Kehlkopfspiegels," *HNO (Hals-Hasen-Ohren)* **9**, 257–261.

Haddad, D., Walter, S., Ratley, R., and Smith, M. (**2001**). "Investigation and evaluation of voice stress analysis technology," Report AFRL-IF-RS-TM-2001-7, Rome, NY, Air Force Research Laboratory Information Directorate.

Hagen, P., Lyons, G.D., and Nuss, D.W. (**1996**). "Dysphonia in the elderly: Diagnosis and management of age–related voice changes," *Southern Medical Journal* **89**, 204–207.

Haggard, M., & Gaston, J.B. (**1978**). "Changes in auditory perception in the menstrual cycle," *British Journal of Audiology* **12**, 105–118.

Hahn, J. (**1988**). *Die Gießenklösterle-Höhle im Achtal bei Blaubeuren* (Stuttgart: Karl Thiess Verlagt).

Hain, T.C., Burnett, T.A., Larson, C.R., and Kiran, S. (**2000**). "Effects of pitch–shift velocity on voice F0 responses," *Journal of the Acoustical Society of America* **107**, 559–564.

Haines, D. (**2007**). *Neuroanatomy: An Atlas of Structures, Sections, and Systems* (Philadelphia, PA: Lippincott Williams & Wilkins).

Hall, J.A. (**1980**). "Voice tone and persuasion," *Journal of Personality and Social Psychology* **38**, 924–934.

Halliday, M.A.K. (**1967**). "Notes on transitivity and theme in English," Part 2, *Journal of Linguistics* **3**, 199–244.

Hamdan, A.L., Mahfoud, L., Sibai, A., and Seoud, M. (**2009**). "Effect of pregnancy on the speaking voice," *Journal of Voice* **23**, 490–493.

Hammarberg, B., Fritzell, B., Gauffin, J., Sundberg, J., and Wedin, L. (**1980**). "Perceptual and acoustic correlates of abnormal voice qualities," *Acta Otolaryngologica* (Stockholm) **90**, 441–451.

Hammerschmidt, K. and Jürgens, U. (**2007**). "Acoustical correlates of affective prosody," *Journal of Voice* **21**, 531–540.

Hammersley, R. and Read, J.D. (**1983**). "Testing witnesses' voice recognition: Some practical recommendations," *Journal of the Forensic Science Society* **23**, 203–208.

Hammersley, R. and Read, J.D. (**1985**). "The effect of participation in conversation on recognition and identification of the speakers' voices," *Law and Human Behavior* **9**, 71–81.

Hammersley, R. and Read, J.D. (**1996**). "Voice identification by humans and computers," in *Psychological Issues in Eyewitness Identification*, edited by S.L. Sporer, R.S. Malpass, and G. Koehnken (Hillsdale, NJ: Lawrence Erlbaum), pp. 117–152.

Hamsher, K., Levin, H.S., and Benton, A.L. (**1979**). "Facial recognition in patients with focal brain lesions," *Archives of Neurology* **36**, 837–839.

Hanley, J.R. and Turner, J.M. (**2000**). "Why are familiar-only experiences more frequent for voices than for faces?," *The Quarterly Journal of Experimental Psychology Section A* **53**, 1105–1116.

Hansen, E.W. (**1976**). "Selective responding by recently separated juvenile rhesus monkeys to the calls of their mothers," *Developmental Psychobiology* **9**, 83–88.

Hansen, J.H.L., Zhou, G., and Pellom, B.L. (**1999**). "Methods for voice stress analysis and classification," Report RSPL-99-August, Boulder, CO, Robust Speech Processing Laboratory, Center for Spoken Language Understanding, University of Colorado.

Hanson, H.M. (**1997**). "Glottal characteristics of female speakers: Acoustic correlates," *Journal of the Acoustical Society of America* **101**, 466–481.

Hanson, H.M. and Chuang, E.S. (**1999**). "Glottal characteristics of male speakers: Acoustic correlates and comparison with female data," *Journal of the Acoustical Society of America* **106**, 1064–1077.

Haramati, S., Soroker, N., Dudai, Y., and Levy, D.A. (**2008**). "The posterior parietal cortex in recognition memory: A neuropsychological study," *Neuropsychologia* **46**, 1756–1766.

Hardouin, L.C., Reby, D., Bavoux, C., Burneleau, G., and Bretagnolle, V. (**2007**). "Communication of male quality in owl hoots," *The American Naturalist* **169**, 552–562.

Harnsberger, J.D., Shrivastav, R., Brown, W.S. Jr., Rothman, H., and Hollien, H. (**2008**). "Speaking rate and fundamental frequency as speech cues to perceived age," *Journal of Voice* **22**, 58–69.

Harries, M.L., Hawkins, S., Hacking, J., and Hughes, I.A. (**1998**). "Changes in the male voice at puberty: Vocal fold length and its relationship to the fundamental frequency of the voice," *Journal of Laryngology and Otology* **112**, 451–454.

Harries, M.L., Walker, J.M., Williams, D.M., Hawkins, S., and Hughes, I.A. (**1997**). "Changes in the male voice at puberty," *Archives of Disease in Childhood* **77**, 445–447.

Harris, C.L., Ayçiçegi, A. and Gleason, J.B. (**2003**). "Taboo words and reprimands elicit greater autonomic reactivity in a first than in a second language," *Applied Psycholinguistics* **4**, 561–578.

Harris, C.L., Gleason, J.B., and Ayçiçegi, A. (**2006**). "When is a first language more emotional? Psychophysiological evidence from bilingual speakers," in *Bilingual Minds: Emotional Experience, Expression, and Representation*, edited by A. Pavlenko (Clevedon, UK: Multilingual Matters), pp. 257–283.

Harris, T.R., Fitch, W.T., Goldstein, L.M., and Fashing, P.I. (**2006**). "Black and white colobus monkey (Colobus guereza) roars as a source of both honest and exaggerated information about body mass," *Ethology* **112**, 911–920.

Harrison, A.A., Hwalek, M., Raney, D.F., and Fritz, J.G. (**1978**). "Cues to deception in an interview situation," *Social Psychology* **41**, 156–161.

Hart, J. (**1551**). *The Opening of the Unreasonable Writing of Our Inglish Toung*. Available as B. Danielsson (1955), *John Hart's Works on English Orthography and Pronunciation* (Stockholm: Almqvist & Wiksell).

Hart, J. (**1569**). *An Orthographie, Conveying the Due Order and Reason, How to Write or Paint Thimage of Mannes Voice, Most Like to the Life of Nature* (London: Serres).

Hartman, D.E. (**1979**). "The perceptual identity and characteristics of aging in normal male adult speakers," *Journal of Communication Disorders* **12**, 53–61.

Hartman, D.E. and Danhauer, J.L. (**1976**). "Perceptual features of speech for males in four perceived age decades," *Journal of the Acoustical Society of America* **59**, 713–715.

Hasek, C.S., Singh, S., and Murry, T. (**1980**). "Acoustic attributes of preadolescent voices," *Journal of the Acoustical Society of America* **68**, 1262–1265.

Hauser, M. (**1996**). *The Evolution of Communication* (Cambridge, MA: MIT Press).

Hazan, V. and Markham, D. (**2005**). "Acoustic-phonetic correlates of talker intelligibility for adults and children," *Journal of the Acoustical Society of America* **116**, 3108–3118.

Hébert, S., Racette, A., Gagnon, L., and Peretz, I. (**2003**). "Revisiting the dissociation between singing and speaking in expressive aphasia," *Brain* **126**, 1838–1850.

Hecker, M.H.L. (**1971**). *Speaker Recognition: An Interpretive Survey of the Literature*. ASHA Monographs **16**.

Hecker, M.H.L., Stevens, K.N., von Bismarck, G., and Williams, C.E. (**1968**). "Manifestations of task–induced stress in the acoustic speech signal," *Journal of the Acoustical Society of America* **44**, 993–1001.

Heckmann, J.G., Lang, C.J.G., and Neundörfer, B. (**2001**). "Brief communications: Recognition of familiar handwriting in stroke and dementia," *American Academy of Neurology* **57**, 2128–2131.

Heilman, K.M. and Gilmore, R.L. (**1998**). "Cortical influences in emotion," *Journal of Clinical Neurophysiology* **15**, 409–423.

Heilman, K.M., Scholes, R., and Watson, R. (**1975**). "Auditory affective agnosia: Disturbed comprehension of affective speech," *Journal of Neurology, Neurosurgery and Psychiatry* **38**, 69–72.

Helfrich, H. (**1979**). "Age markers in speech," in *Social Markers in Speech*, edited by K.R Scherer and H. Giles (Cambridge: Cambridge University Press), pp. 63–108.

Helfrich, H., Standke, R., and Scherer, K.R. (**1984**). "Vocal indicators of psychoactive drug effects," *Speech Communication* **3**, 245–252.

Helmholtz, H. (**1885**). *On the Sensations of Tone* (New York: Dover; reprinted 1954).

Hennessy, J. and Romig, C. (**1971a**). "A review of experiments involving voiceprint identification," *Journal of Forensic Sciences* **16**, 183–198.

Hennessy, J. and Romig, C. (**1971b**). "Sound, speech, phonetics, and voiceprint identification," *Journal of Forensic Sciences* **16**, 438–454.

Henrich, N. (**2006**). "Mirroring the voice from Garcia to the present day: Some insights into singing voice registers," *Logopedics Phoniatrics Vocology* **31**, 3–14.

Henton, C.G. (**1989**). "Fact and fiction in the description of female and male pitch," *Language & Communication* **9**, 299–311.

Henton, C.G. and Bladon, R.A.W. (**1985**). "Breathiness in normal female speech: Inefficiency versus desirability," *Language & Communication* **5**, 221–227.

Hepper, P.G., Scott, D., and Shahidullah, S. (**1993**). "Newborn and fetal response to maternal voice," *Journal of Reproductive and Infant Psychology* **11**, 147–153.

Hertegard, S. and Gauffin, J. (**1995**). "Glottal area and vibratory patterns studied with simultaneous stroboscopy, flow, glottography, and electroglottography," *Journal of Speech and Hearing Research* **38**, 85–100.

Hess, E.H. (**1973**). *Imprinting: Early Experience and the Developmental Psychobiology of Attachment* (New York: Van Nostrand).

Hess, W. (**1983**). *Pitch Determination of Speech Signals* (Berlin: Springer).

Hesse-Quack, O. (**1969**). *Der Übertragungsprozess bei der Synchronization von Filmen. Eine interkulturelle Untersuchung*. Neue Beiträge zur Film- und Fernsehforschung, Vol. **12** (Munich/Basel: Ernst Reinhardt).

Higgins, M.B. and Saxman, J.H. (**1989**). "Variations in vocal frequency perturbation across the menstrual cycle," *Journal of Voice* **3**, 233–243.

Hihara, S., Yamada, H., Iriki, A., and Okanoya, K. (**2003**). "Spontaneous vocal differentiation of coo–calls for tools and food in Japanese monkeys," *Neuroscience Research* **45**, 383–389.

Hillenbrand, J. and Clark, M.J. (**2009**). "The role of f(0) and formant frequencies in distinguishing the voices of men and women," *Attention Perception and Psychophysics* **71**, 1150–66.

Hillenbrand, J., Cleveland, R.A., and Erickson, R. L. (**1994**). "Acoustic correlates of breathy vocal quality," *Journal of Speech and Hearing Research* **37**, 769–778.

Hillenbrand, J., Getty, L.A., Clark, M.J., and Wheeler, K. (**1995**). "Acoustic characteristics of American English vowels," *Journal of the Acoustical Society of America* **97**, 3099–3111.

Hirano, M. (**1974**). "Morphological structure of the vocal cord as a vibrator and its variations," *Folia Phoniatrica* **26**, 89–94.

Hirano, M. (**1981**). *Clinical Examination of Voice* (New York: Springer).

Hirano, M., Kurita, S., and Nakashima, T. (**1983**). "Growth, development and aging of human vocal folds," in *Vocal Fold Physiology: Contemporary Research and Clinical Issues*, edited by D.M. Bless and J.H. Abbs (San Diego, CA: College Hill Press), pp. 22–43.

Hirano, M., Kurita, S., Yukizane, K., and Hibi, S. (**1989**). "Asymmetry of the laryngeal framework: A morphologic study of cadaver larynges," *Annals of Otology, Rhinology & Laryngology* **98**, 135–140.

Hirano, M., Ohala, J., and Vennard, W. (**1969**). "The function of laryngeal muscles in regulating fundamental frequency and intensity of phonation," *Journal of Speech and Hearing Research* **12**, 616–628.

Hirano, M., Vennard, W., and Ohala, J. (**1970**). "Regulation of register, pitch and intensity of voice," *Folia Phoniatrica* **22**, 1–20.

Hird, K. and Kirsner, K. (**1998**). "Control processes in prosody," in *Implicit and Explicit Mental Processes*, edited by K. Kirsner, C. Speelman, M. Maybery, A. O'Brien-Malone, M. Anderson, and C. MacLeod (Mahwah, NJ: Lawrence Erlbaum), pp. 201–218.

Hirson, A. and Duckworth, M. (**1993**). "Glottal fry and voice disguise: A case study in forensic phonetics," *Journal of Biomedical Engineering* **15**, 193–200.

Hirst, D. and Di Cristo, A. (**1998**). "A survey of intonation systems," in *Intonation Systems: A Survey of Twenty Languages*, edited by D. Hirst and A. Di Cristo (Cambridge: Cambridge University Press), pp. 1–44.

Hixon, T.J. (**1987**). "Respiratory function in speech," in *Respiratory Function in Speech and Song*, edited by T.J. Hixon (Boston College-Hill), pp. 1–54.

Hixon, T.J., Goldman, M., and Mead, J. (**1973**). "Kinematics of the chest wall during speech production: Volume displacements of the rib cage, abdomen, and lung," *Journal of Speech and Hearing Research* **16**, 78–115.

Hixon, T.J., Mead, J., and Goldman, M. (**1976**). "Dynamics of the chest wall during speech production: Function of the thorax, rib cage, diaphragm and abdomen," *Journal of Speech and Hearing Research* **19**, 297–356.

Hixon, T.J. and Weismer, G. (**1995**). "Perspectives on the Edinburgh study of speech breathing," *Journal of Speech and Hearing Research* **38**, 42–60.

Hochberg, J. (**1971**). "Perception," In *Woodworth & Schlosberg's Experimental Psychology*, edited by J.W. Kling and L.A. Riggs (New York: Holt, Rinehart and Winston), pp. 396–474.

Hoit, J.D. and Hixon, T.J. (**1987**). "Age and speech breathing," *Journal of Speech and Hearing Research* **30**, 351–366.

Hoit, J.D., Hixon, T.J., Altman, M., and Morgan, W. (**1989**). "Speech breathing in women," *Journal of Speech and Hearing Research* **32**, 353–365.

Hoit, J.D., Hixon, T.J., Watson, P., and Morgan, W. (**1990**). "Speech breathing in children and adolescents," *Journal of Speech and Hearing Research* **33**, 51–69.

Hoit, J.D., Jenks, C.L., Watson, P.J., and Cleveland, T.F. (**1996**). "Respiratory function during speaking and singing in professional country singers," *Journal of Voice* **10**, 39–49.

Holeckova, I., Fischer, C., Giard, M.–H., Delpeuch, C., and Morlet, D. (**2006**). "Brain responses to a subject's own name uttered by a familiar voice," *Brain Research* **1082**, 142–152.

Hollien, H. (**1990**). *The Acoustics of Crime: The New Science of Forensic Phonetics.* (New York: Plenum).

Hollien, H. (**1995**). "The normal aging voice," in *Communication in Later Life*, edited by R.A. Huntley and K.S. Helfer (Boston, MA: Butterworth-Heinemann), pp. 23–40.

Hollien, H., DeJong, G. and Martin, C.A. (**1998**). "Production of intoxication states by actors: Perception by lay listeners," *Journal of Forensic Sciences* **43**, 1153–1162.

Hollien, H., DeJong, G., Martin, C.A., Schwartz, R., and Liljegren, K. (**2001b**). "Effects of ethanol intoxication on speech suprasegmentals," *Journal of the Acoustical Society of America* **110**, 3198–3206.

Hollien, H., Geison, L., and Hicks, J.W. Jr. (**1987**). "Voice stress evaluators and lie detection," *Journal of Forensic Sciences* **32**, 405–418.

Hollien, H., Green, R., and Massey, K. (**1994**). "Longitudinal research on adolescent voice change in males," *Journal of the Acoustical Society of America* **96**, 2646–2654.

Hollien, H. and Harnsberger, J.D. (**2006**). *Voice Stress Analyzer Instrumentation Evaluation.* Final report, CIFA Contract FA 4814-04-0011.

Hollien, H., Harnsberger, J.D., Martin, C.A., and Hollien, K.A. (**2008**). "Evaluation of the NITV CVSA," *Journal of Forensic Sciences* **53**, 183–193.

Hollien, H., Hollien, P.A., and DeJong, G. (**1997**). "Effects of three parameters on speaking fundamental frequency," *Journal of the Acoustical Society of America* **102**, 2984–2992.

Hollien, H., Liljegren, K., Martin, C.A., and DeJong, G. (**2001a**). "Production of intoxication states by actors – acoustic and temporal characteristics," *Journal of Forensic Sciences* **46**, 68–73.

Hollien, H. and Malcik, E. (**1967**). "Evaluation of cross-sectional studies of adolescent voice change in males," *Speech Monographs* **34**, 80–84.

Hollien, H., Mendes-Schwartz, A.P., and Nielsen, K. (**2000**). "Perceptual confusions of high–pitched sung vowels," *Journal of Voice* **14**, 287–298.

Hollien, H., Moore, P., Wendahl, R.W., and Michel, J. (**1966**). "On the nature of vocal fry," *Journal of Speech and Hearing Research* **9**, 245–247.

Hollien, H. and Paul, P. (**1969**). "A second evaluation of the speaking fundamental frequency characteristics of post–adolescent girls," *Language and Speech* **12**, 119–124.

Hollien, H. and Schwartz, R. (**2000**). "Aural–perceptual speaker identification: Problems with noncontemporary samples," *Forensic Linguistics* **7**, 199–211.

Hollien, H. and Schwartz, R. (**2001**). "Speaker identification utilizing noncontemporary speech," *Journal of Forensic Sciences* **46**, 63–67.

Hollien, H. and Shipp, T. (**1972**). "Speaking fundamental frequency and chronologic age in males," *Journal of Speech and Hearing Research* **15**, 155–159.

Hollien, H., Majewski, W., and Doherty, E.T. (**1982**). "Perceptual identification of voices under normal, stress, and disguise speaking conditions," *Journal of Phonetics* **10**, 139–148.

Holmberg, E.B., Hillman, R.E., and Perkell, J.S. (**1988**). "Glottal airflow and transglottal air pressure measurements for male and female speakers in soft, normal and loud voice," *Journal of the Acoustical Society of America* **84**, 511–529.

Holmgren, G.L. (**1967**). "Physical and psychological correlates of speaker recognition," *Journal of Speech and Hearing Research* **10**, 57–66.

Holywell, K. and Harvey, G. (**1964**). "Helium speech," *Journal of the Acoustical Society of America* **36**, 210–211.

Hombert, J.M. (**1976**). "Perception of tones of bisyllabic nouns in Yoruba," *Studies in African Linguistics* **Suppl. 6**, 109–121.

Honjo, I. and Isshiki, N. (**1980**). "Laryngoscopic and voice characteristics of aged persons," *Archives of Otolaryngology* **106**, 149–150.

Hopper, R. (**1992**). *Telephone Conversation* (Bloomington, IN: Indiana University Press).

Horii, Y. (**1975**). "Some statistical characteristics of voice fundamental frequency," *Journal of Speech and Hearing Research* **18**, 192–201.

Horii, Y. and Hata, K. (**1988**). "A note on phase relationships between frequency and amplitude modulations in vocal vibrato," *Folia Phoniatrica* **40**, 303–311.

Horn, G. (**1985**). *Memory, Imprinting and the Brain*, Oxford Psychology Series No. 10 (Oxford, Clarendon Press).

Hornstein, S., Brown, A., and Mulligan, N. (**2003**). "Long-term flashbulb memory for learning of Princess Diana's death," *Memory* **11**, 292–306.

Horvath, F.S. (**1978**). "An experimental comparison of the psychological stress evaluator and the galvanic skin response in detection of deception," *Journal of Applied Psychology* **63**, 338–344.

Horvath, F.S. (**1979**). "Effect of different motivational instructions on detection of deception with the psychological stress evaluator and the galvanic skin response," *Journal of Applied Psychology* **64**, 323–330.

Houde, J.F., Nagarajan, S.S., Sekihara, K., and Merzenich, M.M. (**2002**). "Modulation of the auditory cortex during speech: An MEG study," *Journal of Cognitive Neuroscience* **14**, 1125–1138.

Howell, T.B. (**1816**). *A Complete Collection of State Trials and Proceedings for High Treason and Other Crimes and Misdemeanors from the Earliest Period to the Year 1783. Volume V: Charles II, 1650–1661* (London: Longman), pp. 1185–1195.

Hudson, A. and Holbrook, A. (**1981**). "A study of the reading fundamental vocal frequency of young black adults," *Journal of Speech and Hearing Research* **24**, 197–201.

Hudson, A. and Holbrook, A. (**1982**). "Fundamental frequency characteristics of young black adults: Spontaneous speaking and oral reading," *Journal of Speech and Hearing Research* **25**, 25–28.

Huffman, M.K. (**1987**). "Measures of phonation type in Hmong," *Journal of the Acoustical Society of America* **81**, 495–504.

Hugdahl, K. (Editor) (**1988**). *Handbook of Dichotic Listening: Theory, Methods and Research* (Oxford, UK: John Wiley & Sons).

Hughes, S., Dispenza, F., and Gallup, G. (**2004**). "Ratings of voice attractiveness predict sexual behavior and body configuration," *Evolution and Human Behavior* **25**, 295–304.

Hughes, S., Harrison, M., and Gallup, G. (**2002**). "The sound of symmetry: Voice as a marker of developmental instability," *Evolution and Human Behavior* **23**, 173–180.

Hughlings Jackson, J. (**1874**). "On the nature of the duality of the brain," in *Selected Writings of John Hughlings Jackson*, vol. 2, edited by J. Taylor (London: Hodder & Stoughton), pp. 129–145.

Hunt, R.G. and Lin, T.K. (**1967**). "Accuracy of judgments of personal attributes from speech," *Journal of Personality and Social Psychology* **6**, 450–453.

Hunter, M.D., Phang, S.Y., Lee, K.H., and Woodruff, P.W. (**2005**). "Gender-specific sensitivity to low frequencies in male speech," *Neuroscience Letters* **375**, 148–150.

Hurford, J.R., Studdert-Kennedy, M., and Knight, C. (Editors) (**1998**). *Approaches to the Evolution of Language: Social and Cognitive Bases* (Cambridge, Cambridge University Press).

Huttar, G.L. (**1968**). "Relations between prosodic variables and emotions in normal American English utterances," *Journal of Speech and Hearing Research* **11**, 481–487.

Hyvärinen, J. (**1982a**). "Posterior parietal lobe of the primate brain," *Physiological Reviews* **62**, 1060–1129.

Hyvärinen, J. (**1982b**). *The Parietal Cortex of Monkey and Man* (Berlin: Springer–Verlag).

Imaizumi, S., Mori, K., Kiritani, S., Kawashima, R., Sugiura, M., Fukuda, H., Itoh, K., Kato, T., Nakamura, A., Hatano, K., Kojima, S., and Nakamura, K. (**1997**). "Vocal identification of speaker and emotion activates different brain regions," *Neuroreport* **8**, 2809–2812.

Ingemann, F. (**1968**). "Identification of the speaker's sex from voiceless fricatives," *Journal of the Acoustical Society of America* **44**, 1142–1144.

Insley, S.J. (**2001**). "Mother–offspring vocal recognition in northern fur seals is mutual but asymmetrical," *Animal Behaviour* **61**, 129–137.

International Phonetic Association (**1999**). *Handbook of the International Phonetic Association* (Cambridge: Cambridge University Press).

Iseli, M. and Alwan, A. (**2004**). "An improved correction formula for the estimation of harmonic magnitudes and its application to open quotient estimation," *Proceedings of ICASSP*, pp. 669–672.

Ishii, K., Yamashita, K., Akita, M., and Hirose, H. (**2000**). "Age–related development of the arrangement of connective tissue fibers in the lamina propria of the human vocal fold," *Annals of Otology, Rhinology & Laryngology* **109**, 1055–1064.

Isshiki, N. (**1964**). "Regulatory mechanism of voice intensity variation," *Journal of Speech and Hearing Research* **7**, 17–29.

Isshiki, N., Okamura, H., Tanabe, M., and Morimoto, M. (**1969**). "Differential diagnosis of hoarseness," *Folia Phoniatrica* **21**, 9–19.

Ives, D.T., Smith, D.R.R., and Patterson, R.D. (**2005**). "Discrimination of speaker size from syllable phrases," *Journal of the Acoustical Society of America* **118**, 3816–3822.

Izard, C. (**1977**). *Human Emotions* (New York: Plenum).

Jacewicz, E., Fox, R.A., and O'Neill, C. (**2009**). "Articulation rate across dialect, age, and gender," *Language Variation and Change* **21**, 233–256.

Jackendoff, R. and Lerdahl, F. (**2006**). "The human music capacity: What is it and what's special about it?," *Cognition* **100**, 33–72.

James, W. (**1884**). "What is an emotion?," *Mind* **9**, 188–205.

Jamison, H.L., Watkins, K.E., Bishop, D.V.M., and Matthews, P.M. (**2006**). "Hemispheric specialization for processing auditory nonspeech stimuli," *Cerebral Cortex* **16**, 1266–1275.

Janniro, M.J. and Cestaro, V.L. (**1996**). "Effectiveness of detection of deception examinations using the computer voice stress analyzer," Report DoDPI96-R-0005, Fort McClellan, AL, Department of Defense Polygraph Institute.

Jaynes, J. (**1977**). *The Origin of Consciousness in the Breakdown of the Bicameral Mind* (Wilmington, MA: Houghton Mifflin Company).

Jespersen, O. (**1950**). *Language. Its Nature, Development and Origin* (London: Allen & Unwin).

Joanette, Y. and Brownell, H.H. (**1990**). *Discourse Ability and Brain Damage: Theoretical and Empirical Perspectives* (New York: Springer-Verlag).

Johannes, B., Salnitski, P., Gunga, H.-C., and Kirsch, K. (**2000**). "Voice stress monitoing in space – possibilities and limits," *Aviation, Space and Environmental Medicine* **71**, A58–A65.

John, O.P. (**1990**). "The 'Big Five' factor taxonomy: Dimensions of personality in the natural language and in questionnaires," in *Handbook of Personality: Theory and Research*, edited by L.A. Pervin (New York: Guilford Press), pp. 66–100.

Johnson, K., Pisoni, D.B., and Bernacki, R.H. (**1990**). "Do voice recordings reveal whether a person is intoxicated? A case study," *Phonetica* **47**, 215–237.

Johnson, M.H., Dziurawiec, S., Ellis, H., and Morton, J. (**1991**). "Newborns' preferential tracking of face-like stimuli and its subsequent decline," *Cognition* **40**, 1–19.

Johnstone, T., Van Reekum, C.M., Hird, K., Kirsner, K., and Scherer, K.R. (**2005**). "Affective speech elicited with a computer game," *Emotion* **5**, 513–518.

Joliveau, E., Smith, J., and Wolfe, J. (**2004a**). "Vocal tract resonances in singing: The soprano voice," *Journal of the Acoustical Society of America* **116**, 2434–2439.

Joliveau, E., Smith, J., and Wolfe, J. (**2004b**). "Acoustics: Tuning of vocal tract resonance by sopranos," *Nature* **427**, 116.

Jonas, S. (**1987**). "The supplementary motor region and speech," in *The Frontal Lobes Revisited*, edited by E. Perecman (Hillsdale, NJ: Lawrence Erlbaum Associates), pp. 225–240.

Jouventin, P. (**1982**). "Visual and vocal signals in penguins, their evolution and adaptive characters," *Advances in Ethology* **24**, 1–149.

Jouventin, P. and Aubin, T. (**2002**). "Acoustic systems are adapted to breeding ecologies: Individual recognition in nesting penguins," *Animal Behaviour* **64**, 747–757.

Jürgens, U. (**1979**). "Vocalization as an emotional indicator: A neuroethological study in the squirrel monkey," *Behaviour* **69**, 88–117.

Jürgens, U. (**1982**). "Afferents to the cortical larynx area in the monkey," *Brain Research* **239**, 377–389.

Jürgens, U. (**2002**). "Neural pathways underlying vocal control," *Neuroscience and Biobehavioral Reviews* **26**, 235–258.

Jürgens, U. and Ploog, D. (**1970**). "Cerebral representation of vocalization in the squirrel monkey," *Experimental Brain Research* **10**, 532–554.

Juslin, P. N. and Olsson, H. (**2004**). "Note on the rationality of rule–based versus exemplar-based processing in human judgment," *Scandinavian Journal of Psychology* **45**, 37–47.

Juslin, P.N. and Laukka, P. (**2001**). "Impact of intended emotion intensity on cue utilization and decoding accuracy in vocal expression of emotion," *Emotion* **1**, 381–412.

Juslin, P.N. and Laukka, P. (**2003**). "Communication of emotions in vocal expression and music performance: Different channels, same code?," *Psychological Bulletin* **129**, 770–814.

Kaganovich, N., Francis, A., and Melara, R.D. (**2006**). "Electrophysiological evidence for early interaction between talker and linguistic information during speech perception," *Brain Research* **1114**, 161–172.

Kahane, J.C. (**1978**). "A morphological study of the human prepubertal and pubertal larynx," *American Journal of Anatomy* **151**, 11–20.

Kahane, J.C. (**1982**). "Growth of the human prepubertal and pubertal larynx," *Journal of Speech and Hearing Research* **25**, 446–455.

Kakehi, K., Sogabe, Y., and Kawahara, H. (**2009**). "Research on emotional perception of voices based on a morphing method," in *Emotions in the Human Voice*, volume III, edited by K. Izdebski (San Diego, CA: Plural), pp. 1–14.

Kamachi, M., Hill, H., Lander, K., and Vatikiotis-Bateson, E. (**2003**). "Putting the face to the voice: Matching identity across modality," *Current Biology* **13**, 1709–1714.

Karow, C.M., Marquardt, T.P., and Marshall, R.C. (**2001**). "Affective processing in left and right hemisphere brain-damaged subjects with and without subcortical involvement," *Aphasiology* **15**, 715–729.

Kawahara, H. (**2001**). "Straight: An extremely high quality vocoder for auditory and speech perception research," in *Computational Models of Auditory Function*, edited by S. Greenberg & M. Slaney (Amsterdam: IOS Press), pp. 343–354.

Kawakami, K., Takai-Kawakami, K., Tomonaga, M., Suzuki, J., Kusaka, T., and Okai, T. (**2006**). "Origins of smile and laughter: A preliminary study," *Early Human Development* **82**, 61–66.

Kayser, C. and Logothetis, N.K. (**2007**). "Do early sensory cortices integrate cross-modal information?," *Brain Structure and Function* **212**, 121–132.

Kazial, K.A., Masters, W.M., and Mitchell, W. (**2004**). "Female big brown bats, Eptesicus fuscus, recognize sex from a caller's echolation signals," *Animal Behaviour* **67**, 855–863.

Keidel, W.D., Kallert, S., and Korth K. (**1983**). *The Physiological Basis of Hearing: A Review* (New York: Thieme-Stratton, Inc.).

Kelly, A.H., Beaton, L.E., and Magoun, H.W. (**1946**). "A midbrain mechanisms for facio-vocal activity," *Journal of Neurophysiology* **9**, 185–189.

Kempler, D. and Van Lancker, D. (**2002**). "The effect of speech task on intelligibility in dysarthria: Case study of Parkinson's disease," *Brain and Language* **80**, 449–464.

Kennedy, L. (**1985**). *The Airman and the Carpenter: The Lindbergh Kidnapping and the Framing of Richard Hauptmann* (New York: Harper Collins).

Kent, R.D. (**1994**). *Reference Manual for Communicative Sciences and Disorders* (Austin, TX: Pro–ed).

Kent, R.D. (**1997**). *Speech Sciences* (San Diego, CA: Singular Publishing Co.).

Kent, R.D. (**2000**). "Research on speech motor control and its disorders: A review and prospective," *Journal of Communication Disorders* **33**, 391–428.

Kent, R.D. and Chial, M.R. (**2002**). "The scientific basis of expert testimony on talker identification," in *Modern Scientific Evidence*, edited by D.L. Faigman, D. Kaye, M.J. Saks, and J. Sanders (St Paul, MN: West Publishing Co.), pp. 598–632.

Kent, R.D. and Rosenbek, J. (**1982**). "Prosodic disturbance and neurological lesion," *Brain and Language* **15**, 259–291.

Kent, R.D. and Vorperian, H.K. (**1995**). "Development of the craniofacial–oral–laryngeal anatomy: A review," *Journal of Medical Speech-Language Pathology* **3**, 145–190.

Kersta, L. (**1962**). "Voiceprint identification," *Nature* **196**, 1253–1257.

Kerstholt, J.H., Jansen, N.J.M., Van Amelsvoort, A.G., and Broeders, A.P.A. (**2004**). "Earwitnesses: Effects of speech duration, retention interval and acoustic environment," *Applied Cognitive Psychology* **18**, 327–336.

Kerstholt, J.H., Jansen, N.J.M., Van Amelsvoort, A.G., and Broeders, A.P.A. (**2006**). "Earwitnesses: Effects of accent, retention and telephone," *Applied Cognitive Psychology* **20**, 187–197.

Kertesz, A. (Editor) (**1994**). *Localization and Neuroimaging in Neuropsychology* (San Diego, CA: Academic Press).

Ketai, R. (**1975**). "Affect, mood, emotion, and feeling: Semantic considerations," *American Journal of Psychiatry* **132**, 1215–1217.

Khosla, S., Muruguppan, S., Paniello, R., Ying, J., and Gutmark, E. (**2009**). "Role of vortices in voice production: Normal versus asymmetric tension," *Laryngoscope* **119**, 216–221.

Khosla, S., Muruguppan, S., Gutmark, E., and Scherer, R.C. (**2007**). "Vortical flow field during phonation in an excised canine larynx model," *Annals of Otology, Rhinology, and Laryngology* **116**, 217–228.

Khouw, E. and Ciocca, V. (**2007**). "Perceptual correlates of Cantonese tones," *Journal of Phonetics* **35**, 104–117.

Kidd, R. (**1857**). *Vocal Culture and Elocution* (Cincinnati: Van Antwerp, Bragg & Co,).

Kimura, D. (**1967**). "Functional asymmetry of the brain in dichotic listening," *Cortex* **3**, 163–178.

King, D.B. and Wertheimer, M. (**2007**). *Max Wertheimer and Gestalt Theory* (Piscataway, NJ: Transaction Publishers).

Kinsbourne, M. (**1970**). "The cerebral basis of lateral asymmetries in attention," *Acta Psychologica* **33**, 193–201.

Kinsbourne, M. (**1974**). "Lateral interactions in the brain," in *Hemispheric Disconnection and Cerebral Function*, edited by M. Kinsbourne and W.L. Smith (Springfield, IL: C.C. Thomas), pp. 239–259.

Kinser, S. (**2009**). "Political persuasions: Vocal characteristics of campaign advertisements," unpublished manuscript, Department of Communication Studies, UCLA.

Kioso, H., Shimojima, A., and Katagiri, Y. (**1998**). "Collaborative signaling of informational structures by dynamic speech rate," *Language and Speech* **41**, 323–350.

Kisilevsky, B.S., Hains, S.M.J., Lee, K., Xie, X., Huang, H., Ye, H.H., Zhang, K., and Wang, Z. (**2003**). "Effects of experience on fetal voice recognition," *Psychological Science* **14**, 220–224.

Kitchen, D.M., Fischer, J., Cheney, D.L., and Seyfarth, R.M. (**2003**). "Loud calls as indicators of dominance in the male baboon (Papio cynocephalus ursinus)," *Behavioral Ecology and Sociobiology* **53**, 374–384.

Kitzing, P. (**1982**). "Photo- and electroglottographical recording of the laryngeal vibratory pattern during different registers," *Folia Phoniatrica* **34**, 234–241.

Kjelgaard, M.M. and Speer, S. (**1999**). "Prosodic facilitation and interference in the resolution of temporary syntactic closure ambiguity," *Journal of Memory and Language* **40**, 153–194.

Kjelgaard, M.M., Titone, D.A., and Wingfield, A. (**1999**). "The influence of prosodic structure on the interpretation of temporary syntactic ambiguity by young and elderly listeners," *Experimental Aging Research* **25**, 187–207.

Klatt, D.H. and Stefanski, R.A. (**1974**). "How does a mynah bird imitate human speech?," *Journal of the Acoustical Society of America* **55**, 822–832.

Klein, D., Zatorre, R.J., Milner, B., and Zhao, V. (**2001**). "A cross-linguistic PET study of tone perception in Mandarin Chinese and English speakers," *NeuroImage* **13**, 646–653.

Klewitz, G. and Couper-Kuhlen, E. (**1999**). "Quote–unquote: The role of prosody in the contextualization of reported speech sequences," *Pragmatics* **9**, 459–485.

Klingholz, F. (**1993**). "Overtone singing: Productive mechanisms and acoustic data," *Journal of Voice* **7**, 118–122.

Klingholz, F., Penning, R., and Liebhardt, E. (**1988**). "Recognition of low-level alcohol intoxication from speech signal," *Journal of the Acoustical Society of America* **84**, 929–935.

Knörnschild, M., Von Helversen, O., and Mayer, F. (**2007**). "Twin siblings sound alike: Isolation call variation in the noctule bat, Nyctalus noctula," *Animal Behaviour* **74**, 1055–1063.

Knösche, T.R., Lattner, S., Maess, B., Schauer, M., and Friederici, A.D. (**2002**). "Early parallel processing of auditory word and voice information," *NeuroImage* **17**, 1493–1503.

Knudsen, E.I. (**1987**). "Early experience shapes auditory localization behavior and the spatial tuning of auditory units in the barn owl," in *Imprinting and Cortical Plasticity*, edited by J.P. Rauschecker and P. Marler (New York: John Wiley & Sons), pp. 3–7.

Ko, S.J., Judd, C.M., and Stapel, D.A. (**2009**). "Stereotyping based on voice in the presence of individuating information: Vocal femininity affects perceived competence but not warmth," *Personality and Social Psychology Bulletin* **35**,198–211.

Koelsch, S., Gunter, T., Schröger, E., and Friederici, A.D. (**2003**). "Processing tonal modulations: An ERP study," *Journal of Cognitive Neuroscience* **15**, 1149–1159.

Koike, Y. and Hirano, M. (**1973**). "Glottal–area time function and subglottal pressure variation," *Journal of the Acoustical Society of America* **54**, 1618–1627.

Koriat, A., Greenberg, S.N., and Kreiner, H. (**2002**). "The extraction of structure during reading: Evidence from reading prosody," *Memory & Cognition* **30**, 270–80.

Köster, O., Hess, M.M., Schiller, N.O., and Kunzel, H.J. (**1998**). "The correlation between auditory speech sensitivity and speaker recognition ability," *Forensic Linguistics* **5**, 22–32.

Köster, O. and Schiller, N.O. (**1997**). "Different influences of the native language of a listener on speaker recognition," *Forensic Linguistics* **4**, 18–28.

Kotz, S.A., Meyer, M., Alter, K., Besson, M., von Cramon, D., and Friederici, A.D. (**2003**). "On the lateralization of emotional prosody: An event related functional MR investigation," *Brain and Language* **86**, 366–376.

Kovacic, G. and Hedever, M. (**2000**). "Interpopulation differences in acoustic characteristics of phonation," *Collegium Antropologicum* **24**, 509–519.

Kraepelin, E. (**1921**). *Manic-Depressive Insanity and Paranoia*, edited by G.M. Robertson (Edinburgh: E. & S. Livingstone).

Kramer, C. (**1977**). "Perceptions of male and female speech," *Language and Speech* **20**, 151–161.

Kramer, E. (**1964**). "Personality stereotypes in voice: A reconsideration of the data," *Journal of Social Psychology* **62**, 247–251.

Krane, M.H. (**2005**). "Aeroacoustic production of low–frequency unvoiced speech sounds," *Journal of the Acoustical Society of America* **118**, 410–427.

Kraus, N. and Nicol, T. (**2005**). "Brainstem origins for cortical 'what' and 'where' pathways in the auditory system," *Trends in Neurosciences* **28**, 176–181.

Krauss, R.M., Freyberg, R., and Morsella, E. (**2002**). "Inferring speakers' physical attributes from their voices," *Journal of Experimental Social Psychology* **38**, 618–625.

Kraut, R. (**1978**). "Verbal and nonverbal dues in the perception of lying," *Journal of Personality and Social Psychology* **36**, 380–391.

Kraut, R. (**1980**). "Humans as lie detectors: Some second thoughts," *Journal of Communication* **30**, 209–216.

Kreiman, J. (**1982**). "Perception of sentence and paragraph boundaries in natural conversation," *Journal of Phonetics* **10**, 163–175.

Kreiman, J. (**1987**). *Human Memory for Unfamiliar Voices*, University of Chicago doctoral dissertation.

Kreiman, J. (**1997**). "Listening to voices: Theory and practice in voice perception research," in *Talker Variability in Speech Processing*, edited by K. Johnson and J.W. Mullennix (New York: Academic), pp. 85–108.

Kreiman, J. and Gerratt, B.R. (**1996**). "The perceptual structure of pathologic voice quality," *Journal of the Acoustical Society of America* **100**, 1787–1795.

Kreiman, J. and Gerratt, B.R. (**1998**). "Validity of rating scale measures of voice quality," *Journal of the Acoustical Society of America* **104**, 1598–1608.

Kreiman, J. and Gerratt, B.R. (**2000a**). "Sources of listener disagreement in voice quality assessment," *Journal of the Acoustical Society of America* **108**, 1867–1879.

Kreiman, J. and Gerratt, B.R. (**2000b**). "Measuring vocal quality," in *Voice Quality Measurement*, edited by R.D. Kent and M.J. Ball (San Diego, CA: Singular), pp. 73–102.

Kreiman, J. and Gerratt, B.R. (**2005**). "Perception of aperiodicity in pathological voice," *Journal of the Acoustical Society of America* **117**, 2201–2211.

Kreiman, J. and Gerratt, B.R. (**2010**). "Perceptual sensitivity to first harmonic amplitude in the voice source," *Journal of the Acoustical Society of America* **128**, 2085–2089.

Kreiman, J., Gerratt, B.R., and Antoñanzas-Barroso, N. (**2007**). "Measures of the glottal source spectrum," *Journal of Speech, Language and Hearing Research* **50**, 595–610.

Kreiman, J., Gerratt, B.R., and Berke, G.S. (**1994**). "The multidimensional nature of pathologic vocal quality," *Journal of the Acoustical Society of America* **96**, 1291–1302.

Kreiman, J., Gerratt, B.R., and Ito, M. (**2007**). "When and why listeners disagree in voice quality assessment tasks," *Journal of the Acoustical Society of America* **122**, 2354–2364.

Kreiman, J., Gerratt, B.R., Kempster, G.B., Erman, A., and Berke, G.S. (**1993**). "Perceptual evaluation of voice quality: Review, tutorial, and a framework for future research," *Journal of Speech and Hearing Research* **36**, 21–40.

Kreiman, J., Gerratt, B.R., and Khan, S. (**2010**). "Effects of native language on perception of voice quality," *Journal of Phonetics*, **38**, 588–593.

Kreiman, J., Gerratt, B.R., and Precoda, K. (**1990**). "Listener experience and perception of voice quality," *Journal of Speech and Hearing Research* **33**, 103–115.

Kreiman, J., Gerratt, B.R., Precoda, K., and Berke, G.S. (**1992**). "Individual differences in voice quality perception," *Journal of Speech and Hearing Research* **35**, 512–520.

Kreiman, J. and Papcun, G. (**1991**). "Comparing discrimination and recognition of unfamiliar voices," *Speech Communication* **10**, 265–275.

Kreiman, J. and Van Lancker, D. (**1988**). "Hemispheric specialization for voice recognition: Evidence from dichotic listening," *Brain and Language* **34**, 246–252.

Kreuz, R.J. and Roberts, R.M. (**1995**). "Two cues for verbal irony: Hyperbole and the ironic tone of voice," *Metaphor and Symbolic Activity* **10**, 21–31.

Krishnan, A., Gandour, J.T., and Bidelman, G.M. (**2010**). "The effects of tone language experience on pitch processing in the brain," *Journal of Neurolinguistics* **23**, 81–95.

Krishnan, A., Xu, Y., Gandour, J.T., and Cariani, P. (**2005**). "Encoding of pitch in the human brainstem is sensitive to language experience," *Brain Research Cognitive Brain Research* **25**, 61–168.

Krumhansl, C.L. and Iverson, P. (**1992**). "Perceptual interactions between musical pitch and timbre," *Journal of Experimental Psychology: Human Perception and Performance* **18**, 739–751.

Kubovy, M. and Wagemans, J. (**1995**). "Grouping by proximity and multistability in dot lattices: A quantitative Gestalt theory," *Psychological Science* **6**, 225–234.

Kuhl, P.K. and Miller, J.D. (**1978**). "Speech perception by the chinchilla: Identification functions for synthetic VOT stimuli," *Journal of the Acoustical Society of America* **63**, 905–917.

Kuhnert, K. (**2005**). *Jeden Tag ein kleines Wunder: Das Geschenk der Delphine* (Each day brings a small miracle: The gift of the dolphins) (Munich: Ariston Auflage 1).

Kuiper, K. (**2009**). *Formulaic Genres* (Basingstoke, UK: Palgrave Macmillan).

Kunachak, S., Prakunhungsit, S., and Sujjalak, K. (**2000**). "Thyroid cartilage and vocal fold reduction: A new phonosurgical method for male-to-female transsexuals," *Annals of Otology, Rhinology & Laryngology* **109**, 1082–1086.

Kunzel, H.J. (**1989**). "How well does average fundamental frequency correlate with speaker height and weight?," *Phonetica* **46**, 117–125.

Kunzel, H.J. (**1994**). "Current approaches to forensic speaker recognition," *Proceedings of the ESCA Workshop on Automatic Speaker Recognition, Identification and Verification*, 135–142.

Kunzel, H.J. (**2000**). "Effects of voice disguise on speaking fundamental frequency," *Forensic Linguistics* 7, 149–179.

Kunzel, H.J. (**2001**). "Beware of the 'telephone effect': The influence of telephone transmission on the measurement of formant frequencies," *Forensic Linguistics* 8, 80–99.

Kuwabara, H. and Sagisak, Y. (**1995**). "Acoustic characteristics of speaker individuality: Control and conversion," *Speech Communication* 16, 165–173.

Kuwabara, H. and Takagi, T. (**1991**). "Acoustic parameters of voice individuality and voice–quality control by analysis–synthesis method," *Speech Communication* 10, 491–495.

Kwalwasser, J. (**1926**). "The vibrato," *Psychological Monographs* 36, 84–108.

LaBarbera, P. and MacLachlan, J. (**1979**). "Time compressed speech in radio advertising," *Journal of Marketing* 43, 30–36.

Lachs, L. and Pisoni, D.B. (**2004**). "Cross-modal source information and spoken word recognition," *Journal of Experimental Psychology: Human Perception and Performance* 30, 378–396.

Ladd, D.R. (**1980**). *The Structure of Intonational Meaning* (Bloomington, IN: Indiana University Press).

Ladd, D.R. (**1996**). *Intonational Phonology* (Cambridge: Cambridge University Press).

Ladefoged, P. (**1978**). "Expectation affects identification by listening," *Language and Speech* 21, 373–374.

Ladefoged, P. (**1996**). *Elements of Acoustic Phonetics* (Chicago: University of Chicago Press).

Ladefoged, P. (**2006**). *A Course in Phonetics* (Boston, MA: Thomson Wadsworth).

Ladefoged, P. and Ladefoged, J. (**1980**). "The ability of listeners to identify voices," *UCLA Working Papers in Phonetics* 49, 43–51.

Ladefoged, P. and Loeb, G. (**2002**). "Preliminary studies on respiratory activity in speech," *UCLA Working Papers in Phonetics* 101, 50–60.

Ladefoged, P. and Maddieson, I. (**1996**). *The Sounds of the World's Languages* (London: Blackwell).

Lammers, M.O., Au, W.W.L., and Herzing, D.L. (**2003**). "The broadband social acoustic signaling behavior of spinner and spotted dolphins," *Journal of the Acoustical Society of America* 114, 1629–1639.

Lander, K., Hill, H., Kamachi, M., and Vatikiotis-Bateson, E. (**2007**). "It's not what you say but the way you say it: Matching faces and voices," *Journal of Experimental Psychology: Human Perception and Performance* 33, 905–14.

Landis, J. (**1978**) (Director). *Animal House* (Universal, United States).

Landis, T., Cummings, J.L., Benson, D.F. and Palmer, E.P. (**1986**). "Loss of topographic familiarity," *Archives of Neurology* 43, 132–136.

LaPointe, L.L., Mowrer, D.M., and Case, J.L. (**1990**). "A comparative acoustic analysis of the laugh responses of 20- and 70- year-old males," *International Journal of Aging and Human Development* 31, 1–9.

Large, J. and Iwata, J. (**1971**). "Aerodynamic study of vibrato and voluntary 'straight tone' pairs in singing," *Folia Phoniatrica* 23, 50–65.

LaRiviere, C. (**1972**). "Some acoustic and perceptual correlates of speaker identification," in *Proceedings of the 7th International Congress of Phonetic Sciences*, pp. 558–564.

LaRiviere, C. (**1975**). "Contributions of fundamental frequency and formant frequencies to speaker identification," *Phonetica* 31, 185–197.

Lass, N.J. (**1981**). "A reply to Cohen et al.'s, Weighty voices and shaky evidence: A critique'," *Journal of the Acoustical Society of America* 69, 1204–1206.

Lass, N.J., Almerino, C.A., Jordan, L.F., and Walsh, J.M. (**1980**). "The effect of filtered speech on speaker race and sex identifications," *Journal of Phonetics* **8**, 101–112.

Lass, N.J. and Brown, W.S. (**1978**). "Correlational study of speakers' heights, weights, body surface areas, and speaking fundamental frequencies," *Journal of the Acoustical Society of America* **63**, 1218–1220.

Lass, N.J. and Davis, M. (**1976**). "An investigation of speaker height and weight identification," *Journal of the Acoustical Society of America* **60**, 700–703.

Lass, N.J. and Harvey, L.A. (**1976**). "An investigation of speaker photograph identification," *Journal of the Acoustical Society of America* **59**, 1232–1236.

Lass, N.J., Hughes, K.R., Bowyer, M.D., Waters, L.T., and Bourne, V.T. (**1976**). "Speaker sex identification from voiced, whispered and filtered isolated vowels," *Journal of the Acoustical Society of America* **59**, 675–678.

Lass, N.J., Mertz, P.J., and Kimmel, K.L. (**1978**). "The effect of temporal speech alterations on speaker race and sex identifications," *Language and Speech* **21**, 279–290.

Lass, N.J., Scherbick, K.A., Davies, S.L., and Czarnecki, T.D. (**1982**). "Effect of vocal disguise on estimations of speakers' heights and weights," *Perceptual and Motor Skills* **54**, 643–649.

Lass, N.J., Tecca, J.E., Mancuso, R.A., and Black, W.I. (**1979**). "The effect of phonetic complexity on speaker race and sex identifications," *Journal of Phonetics* **7**, 105–118.

Lattal, K.A. (**1995**). "Contingency and behavior analysis," *The Behavior Analyst* **18**, 204–224.

Lattner, S., Meyer, M.E., and Friederici, A.D. (**2005**). "Voice perception: Sex, pitch, and the right hemisphere," *Human Brain Mapping* **24**, 11–20.

Laukka, P. (**2003**). "Categorical perception of emotion in vocal expression," *Annals of the New York Academy of Science* **1000**, 283–287.

Laukka, P. (**2005**). "Categorical perception of vocal emotion expressions," *Emotion* **5**, 277–295.

Laukka, P. (**2008**). "Research on vocal expression of emotion: State of the art and future directions," in *Emotions in the Human Voice*, volume 1, edited by K. Izdebski (San Diego, CA: Plural), pp. 153–170.

Laukka, P., Juslin, P.N., and Bresin, R. (**2005**). "A dimensional approach to vocal expression of emotion," *Cognition and Emotion* **19**, 633–654.

Laukka, P., Linnman, C., Åhs, F., Pissiota, A., Frans, Ö., Faria, V., Michelgård, Å., Appel, L., Fredrikson, M., and Furmark, T. (**2008**). "In a nervous voice: Acoustic analysis and perception of anxiety in social phobics' speech," *Journal of Nonverbal Behavior* **32**, 195–214.

Laval, V. and Bert-Erboul, A. (**2005**). "French-speaking children's understanding of sarcasm: The role of intonation and context," *Journal of Speech, Language, and Hearing Research* **48**, 610–620.

Laver, J. (**1968**). "Voice quality and indexical information," *British Journal of Disorders of Communication* **3**, 43–54.

Laver, J. (**1980**). *The Phonetic Description of Voice Quality* (Cambridge: Cambridge University Press).

Laver, J. (**1981**). "The analysis of vocal quality: From the classical period to the 20th century," in *Toward a History of Phonetics*, edited by R. Asher and E. Henderson (Edinburgh: Edinburgh University Press), pp. 79–99.

Laver, J. (**2000**). "Phonetic evaluation of voice quality," in *Voice Quality Measurement*, edited by R.D. Kent and M.J. Ball (San Diego, CA: Singular), pp. 37–48.

Laver, J., Wirz, S., Mackenzie, J., and Hiller, S.M. (**1981**). "A perceptual protocol for the analysis of vocal profiles," *Edinburgh University Department of Linguistics Work in Progress* **14**, 139–155.

Lavner, Y., Gath, I. and Rosenhouse, J. (**2000**). "The effects of acoustic modifications on the identification of familiar voices speaking isolated vowels," *Speech Communication* **30**, 9–26.

Lazarus, R.S. (**1984**). "On the primacy of cognition," *American Psychologist* **30**, 124–129.

Leanderson, R. and Sundberg, J. (**1998**). "Breathing for singing," *Journal of Voice* **2**, 2–12.

Lebowitz, A. and Baken, R.J. (**in press**). "Correlates of the belt voice: A broader examination," to appear in *Journal of Voice*.

LeDoux, J.E. (**1994**). "Emotional experience as an ouput of, not a cause of, emotional processing," in *The Nature of Emotion: Fundamental Questions*, edited by P. Ekman and R.J. Davidson (New York: Oxford University Press), pp. 394–395.

LeDoux, J.E. (**1996**). *The Emotional Brain* (New York: Simon and Schuster).

LeDoux, J.E. (**2000**). "Emotional circuits in the brain," *Annual Review of Neuroscience* **23**, 155–184.

Lee, S., Potamianos, A., and Narayanan, S. (**1999**). "Acoustics of children's speech: Developmental changes of temporal and spectral parameters," *Journal of the Acoustical Society of America* **105**, 1455–1468.

Leehey, S.C. and Cahn, A. (**1979**). "Lateral asymmetries in the recognition of words, familiar faces and unfamiliar faces," *Neuropsychologia* **17**, 619–628.

Leentjens, A.F., Wielaert, S.M., van Harskamp, F., and Wilmink, F.W. (**1998**). "Disturbances of affective prosody in patients with schizophrenia; a cross sectional study," *Journal of Neurology, Neurosurgery and Psychiatry* **64**, 375–378.

Legge, G.E., Grosman, C., and Pieper, C.M. (**1984**). "Learning unfamiliar voices," *Journal of Experimental Psychology: Learning, Memory and Cognition* **10**, 298–303.

Lehiste, I. (**1972**). "The timing of utterances and linguistic boundaries," *Journal of the Acoustical Society of America* **51**, 2018–2024.

Lehiste, I. (**1979**). "Perception of sentence and paragraph boundaries," in *Frontiers of Speech Communication Research*, edited by B. Lindblom and S. Ohman (New York: Academic), pp. 191–291.

Lehman, E. (Producer) and Nichols, M. (Director) (**1966**). *Who's Afraid of Virginia Woolf?* (Warner Brothers, United States).

Leinonen, L., Laakso, M.-L., Carlson, S., and Linnankoski, I. (**2003**). "Shared means and meanings in vocal expression of man and macaque," *Logopedics Phoniatrics Vocology* **28**, 53–61.

Lengagne, T., Lauga, J., and Aubin, T. (**2001**). "Intra-syllabic acoustic signatures used by the king penguin in parent–chick recognition: An experimental approach," *Journal of Experimental Biology* **204**, 663–672.

Lerman, J.W. and Damste, P.H. (**1969**). "Voice pitch of homosexuals," *Folia Phoniatrica* **21**, 340–346.

Lev-Ari, S. and Keysar, B. (**2010**). "Why don't we believe non-native speakers? The influence of accent on credibility," *Journal of Experimental Social Psychology* **46**, 1093–1096.

Levelt, W.J.M. (**1989**). *Speaking: From Intention to Articulation* (Cambridge, MA: MIT Press).

Levi, S.V. and Pisoni, D.B. (**2007**). "Indexical and linguistic channels in speech perception: Some effects of voiceovers on advertising outcomes," in *Psycholinguistic Phenomena in Marketing Communications*, edited by T.M. Lowrey (Mahwah, NJ: Lawrence Erlbaum Associates), pp. 203–219.

Levinson, S. (**1983**). *Pragmatics* (Cambridge: Cambridge University Press).

Levy, D.A., Granot, R., and Bentin, S. (**2001**). "Processing specificity for human voice stimuli: electrophysiological evidence," *Neuroreport* **28**, 2653–2657.

Levy, D.A., Granot, R., and Bentin, S. (**2003**). "Neural sensitivity to human voices: ERP evidence of task and attentional influences," *Psychophysiology* **40**, 291–305.

Lewis, M.B., Sherwood, S., Moselhy, H., and Ellis, H.D. (**2001**). "Autonomic responses to familiar faces without autonomic responses to familiar voices: Evidence for voice-specific Capgras delusion," *Cognitive Neuropsychiatry* **6**, 217–228.

Lewis, P. (**2003**). *Talking Funny for Money* (New York: Applause Theatre and Cinema Books).

Ley, R. and Bryden, M.P. (**1982**). "A dissociation of right and left hemispheric effects for recognizing emotional tone and verbal content," *Brain and Language* **1**, 3–9.

Liang, J. (**2006**). "Experiments on the modular nature of word and sentence phonology in Chinese Broca's patients," *Trans 10* (Utrecht, The Netherlands: Netherlands Graduate School of Linguistics/Landelijke – LOT).

Liang, J. and van Heuven, V.J. (**2004**). "Evidence for separate tonal and segmental tiers in the lexical specifications of words: A case study of a brain–damaged Chinese speaker," *Brain and Language* **91**, 282–293.

Liberman, M. and McLemore, C. (**1992**). "Structure and intonation of business telephone openings," *Penn Review of Linguistics* **16**, 68–83.

Liberman, M. and Sag, I.A. (**1974**). "Prosodic form and discourse function," *Chicago Linguistics Society* **10**, pp. 416–427.

Lieberman, P. (**1968**). *Intonation, Perception, and Language* (Cambridge, MA: MIT Press).

Lieberman, P. (**1975**). "The evolution of speech and language," in *The Role of Speech in Language*, edited by J.F. Kavanaugh & J.E. Cutting (Cambridge, MA: MIT Press).

Lieberman, P. (**2002a**). *Human Language and Our Reptilian Brain: The Subcortical Bases of Speech, Syntax, and Thought* (Cambridge, MA: Harvard University Press).

Lieberman, P. (**2002b**). "The evolution of speech in relation to language and thought," in *New Perspectives in Primate Evolution and Behaviour*, edited by C.S. Harcourt and B.R. Sherwood (Otley, UK: Westbury), pp. 105–126.

Lieberman, P., Crelin, E.S., and Klatt, D.H. (**1972**). "Phonetic ability and related anatomy of the newborn and adult human, Neanderthal man, and the chimpanzee," *American Anthropologist*, **NS 74**, 287–307.

Liederman, J. (**1988**). "Misconceptions and new conceptions about early brain damage, functional asymmetry, and behavioral outcome," in *Brain Lateralization in Children*, edited by D. Molfese and S. Segalowitz (New York: Guilford Press), pp. 375–399.

Liégeois-Chauvel, C., de Graaf, J.B., Laguitton, V., and Chauvel, P. (**1999**). "Specialization of left auditory cortex for speech perception in man depends on temporal coding," *Cerebral Cortex* **9**, 484–496.

Linville, S.E. (**1996**). "The sound of senescence," *Journal of Voice* **10**, 190–200.

Linville, S.E. (**1998**). "Acoustic correlates of perceived versus actual sexual orientation in men's speech," *Folia Phoniatrica et Logopaedica* **50**, 35–48.

Linville, S.E. (**2001**). *Vocal Aging* (San Diego, CA: Singular).

Linville, S.E. and Fisher, H.B. (**1985**). "Acoustic characteristics of perceived versus actual vocal age in controlled phonation by adult females," *Journal of the Acoustical Society of America* **78**, 40–48.

Linville, S.E. and Fisher, H.B. (**1992**). "Glottal gap configurations in two age groups of women," *Journal of Speech and Hearing Research* **35**, 1209–1215.

Linville, S.E. and Rens, J. (**2001**). "Vocal tract resonance analysis of aging voice using long-term average spectra," *Journal of Voice* **15**, 323–330.

Lisker, L. and Abramson, A.S. (**1964**). "A cross-language study of voicing in initial stops: Acoustical measurements," *Word* **20**, 384–422.

Lisker, L. and Abramson, A.S. (**1971**). "Distinctive features and laryngeal control," *Language* **47**, 767–785.

Livingston, R.B. (**1967**). "Reinforcement," in *The Neurosciences: A Study Program*, edited by G. Quarton, T. Melnechuk, and F. Schmitt (New York: Rockefeller Press), pp. 514–76.

Locke, J.L. (**2008**). "Cost and complexity: Selection for speech and language," *Journal of Theoretical Biology* **251**, 640–652.

Locke, J.L. (**2009**). "Evolutionary developmental linguistics: Naturalization of the faculty of language," *Language Sciences* **31**, 33–59.

Locke, J.L. and Bogin, B. (**2006**). "Language and life history: A new perspective on the development and evolution of human language," *Behavioral and Brain Sciences* **29**, 259–325.

Logan, J.S., Lively, S.E., and Pisoni, D.B. (**1991**). "Training Japanese listeners to identify English /r/ and /l/: A first report," *Journal of the Acoustical Society of America* **89**, 874–86.

Longfellow, H. (**1866**). In *The Prose Works of Henry Wadsworth Longfellow*, Volume 2, edited by S. Longfellow (New York: Houghton, Mifflin & Co.), p. 217.

Lorenz, K. (**1935**). "Der Kumpan in der Umwelt des Vogels," *Journal of Ornithology* **83**, 137–413.

Loriot (Vicco von Bülow) (**2005**). *Scenes from a Marriage* (Zürich, Switzerland: Diogenes Verlag).

Louth, S.M., Williamson, S., Alpert, M., Pouget, E.R., and Hare, R.D. (**1998**). "Acoustic distinctions in the speech of male psychopaths," *Journal of Psycholinguistic Research* **27**, 375–384.

Lovetri, J., Lesh, S., and Woo, P. (**1999**). "Preliminary study on the ability of trained singers to control the intrinsic and extrinsic laryngeal musculature," *Journal of Voice* **13**, 219–226.

Luchsinger, R. and Arnold, G.E. (**1965**). *Voice-Speech-Language Clinical Communicology: Its Physiology and Pathology* (Belmont: Wadworth Publishing Co.).

Ludlow, C.L. (**2005**). "Central nervous system control of the laryngeal muscles in humans," *Respiratory Physiology and Neurobiology* **147**, 205–222.

Ludlow, C.L. and Loucks, T. (**2003**). "Stuttering: A dynamic motor control disorder," *Journal of Fluency Disorders* **28**, 273–295.

Luksaneeyanawin, S. (**1998**). "Intonation in Thai," in *Prosody: Models and Measurements*, edited by A. Cutler & D. Ladd (New York: Springer-Verlag), pp. 376–394.

Luo, H., Ni, J.-T., Li, Z.-O., Zhang, D. R., Zeng, F.G., and Chen, L. (**2006**). "Opposite patterns of hemispheric dominance for early auditory processing of lexical tones and consonants," *Proceedings of the National Academy of Sciences* **103**, 19558–19563.

Luria, A.R. (**1980**). *Higher Cortical Functions in Man*, 2nd edition (New York: Basic Books).

Lykken, D. (**1981**). *A Tremor in the Blood* (New York: McGraw-Hill).

Ma, J.K.-Y., Ciocca, V., and Whitehill, T.L. (**2006**). "Effect of intonation on Cantonese lexical tones," *Journal of the Acoustical Society of America* **120**, 3978–3987.

MacLachlan, J. (**1982**). "Listener perception of time compressed spokespersons," *Journal of Advertising Research* **2**, 47–51.

MacLarnon, A. and Hewitt, G. (**1999**). "The evolution of human speech: The role of enhanced breathing control," *American Journal of Physical Anthropology* **109**, 341–363.

MacLean, P.D. (**1987**). "The midline frontolimbic cortex and the evolution of crying and laughter," in *The Frontal Lobes Revisited*, edited by E. Perecman (Hillsdale, NJ: Lawrence Erlbaum Associates), pp. 121–140.

MacLean, P.D. (**1990**). *The Triune Brain in Evolution* (New York: Plenum).

Macmillan, N.A. and Creelman, C.D. (**2005**). *Detection Theory: A User's Guide*, 2nd edition (Mahwah, NJ: Lawrence Erlbaum Associates).

Maffiolo, V. and Chateau, N. (**2003**). "The emotional quality of speech in voice services," *Ergonomics* **46**, 1375–1385.

Majer, E.J. (**1980**). "Zur Geschichte der HNO-Heilkunde in Österreich [On the history of ear–nose–throat medicine in Austria]," *Laryng. Rhinol.* **59**, 406–411.

Makagon, M.M., Funayama, E.S., and Owren, M.J. (**2008**). "An acoustic analysis of laughter produced by congenitally deaf and normally hearing college students," *Journal of the Acoustical Society of America* **124**, 472–483.

Mallory, E.B. and Miller, V.R. (**1958**). "A possible basis for the association of voice character-istics and personality traits," *Speech Monographs* **25**, 255–260.

Malone, D.R., Morris, H.H., Kay, M.C., and Levin, H.S. (**1982**). "Prosopagnosia: A double dissociation between recognition of familiar and unfamiliar faces," *Journal of Neurology Neurosurgery, and Psychiatry* **45**, 820–822.

Mann, V.A., Diamond, R., and Carey, S. (**1979**). "Development of voice recognition: Parallels with face recognition," *Journal of Experimental Child Psychology* **27**, 153–165.

Marian, V. and Neisser, U. (**2000**). "Language-dependent recall of autobiographical memo-ries," *Journal of Experimental Psychology: General* **129**, 361–368.

Marin, O.S.M. and Perry, D.W. (**1999**). "Neurological aspects of music perception and per-formance, in *The Psychology of Music*, 2nd edition, edited by D. Deutsch (Academic Press, New York), pp. 653–724.

Markel, N.N., Eisler, R.M., and Reese, H.W. (**1967**). "Judging personality from dialect," *Journal of Verbal Learning and Verbal Behavior* **6**, 33–35.

Marler, P. (**1998**). "Animal communication and human language," in *The Origin and Diversification of Language*, edited by G. Jablonski and L. C. Aiello. Wattis Symposium Series in Anthropology, Memoirs of the California Academy of Sciences No. 24 (San Francisco: California Academy of Sciences), pp. 1–19.

Marler, P. and Hobbett, L. (**1975**). "Individuality in a long-range vocalization of wild chim-panzees," *Zeitschrift für Tierpsychologie* **38**, 97–109.

Marsden, C.D. (**1982**). "The mysterious motor function of the basal ganglia: The Robert Wartenberg Lecture," *Neurology* **32**, 514–539.

Marshall, J., Robson, J., Pring, T., and Chiat, S. (**1998**). "Why does monitoring fail in jargon aphasia? Comprehension, judgment, and therapy evidence," *Brain and Language* **63**, 79–107.

Maryn, Y., Roy, N., de Bodt, M., van Cauwenberge, P., and Corthals, P. (**2009**). "Acoustic measurement of overall voice quality: A meta-analysis," *Journal of the Acoustical Society of America* **126**, 2619–2634.

Marzi, C.A. and Berlucchi, G. (**1977**). "Right visual field superiority for accuracy of recogni-tion of famous faces in normals," *Neuropsychologia* **15**, 751–756.

Masataka, N. (**1985**). "Development of vocal recognition of mothers in infant Japanese macaques," *Developmental Psychobiology* **18**, 107–114.

Masataka, N. (**1994**). "Lack of correlation between body size and frequency of vocalizations in young female Japanese macaques (Macaca fuscata)," *Folia Primatologica (Basel)* **63**, 115–118.

Mason, M.J. and Narins, P.M. (**2002**). "Seismic sensitivity in the desert golden mole (Eremitalpa granti): A review," *Journal of Comparative Psychology* **116**, 158–163.

Masterman, D.L. and Cummings, J.L. (**1997**). "Frontal-subcortical circuits: The anatomic basis of executive, social, and motivated behaviors," *Journal of Psychopharmacology* **11**, 107–114.

Mathevon, N., Charrier, I., and Aubin, T. (**2004**). "A memory like a female Fur Seal: Long lasting recognition of pup's voice by mothers," *Anais da Academia Brasileira de Ciências* **76**, 237–241.

Matsumoto, A. and Stanny, C.J. (**2006**). "Language–dependent access to autobiographi-cal memory in Japanese–English bilinguals and US monolinguals," *Memory* **14**, 378–390.

Matsumoto, D., and Kishimoto, H. (**1983**). "Developmental characteristics in judgments of emotion from nonverbal vocal cues," *International Journal of Intercultural Relations* **7**, 415–424.

Matsumoto, H., Hiki, S., Sone, T., and Nimura, T. (**1973**). "Multidimensional representation of personal quality of vowels and its acoustical correlates," *IEEE Transactions on Audio and Electroacoustics* **AU-21**, 428–436.

McAdams, S. (**2001**). "Recognition of sound sources and events," in *Thinking in Sound: The Cognitive Psychology of Human Audition*, edited by S. McAdams and E. Bigand (Oxford, UK: Clarendon Press), pp. 146–198.

McAdams, S. and Bigand, E. (Editors) (**2001**). *Thinking in Sound: The Cognitive Psychology of Human Audition* (Oxford: Clarendon Press).

McAllister, H.A., Dale, R.H., Bregman, N.J., McCabe, A., and Cotton, C.R. (**1993**). "When eyewitnesses are also earwitnesses: Effects on visual and voice identifications," *Basic & Applied Social Psychology* **14**, 161–170.

McCluskey, K.W. and Albas, D.C. (**1981**). "Perception of the emotional content of speech by Canadian and Mexican children, adolescents and adults," *International Journal of Psychology* **16**, 119–132.

McComb, K., Moss, C., Sayialel, S., and Baker, L. (**2002**). "Unusually extensive networks of vocal recognition in African elephants," *Animal Behaviour* **59**, 1103–1109.

McComb, K., Reby, D. Baker, L. Moss, C., and Sayialel, S. (**2003**). "Long-distance communication of cues to social identity in African elephants," *Animal Behaviour* **65**, 317–329.

McFadden, D. (**1975**). "Duration-intensity reciprocity for equal loudness," *Journal of the Acoustical Society of America* **57**, 702–704.

McFarland, D.H. (**2001**). "Respiratory markers of conversational interaction," *Journal of Speech, Language, and Hearing Research* **44**, 128–143.

McGehee, F. (**1937**). "The reliability of the identification of the human voice," *Journal of General Psychology* **17**, 249–271.

McGehee, F. (**1944**). "An experimental study of voice recognition," *Journal of General Psychology* **31**, 53–65.

McGlone, R. and Hicks, J. (**1979**). "Speaker identification from photographs," *Journal of the Acoustical Society of America* **65 supp. 1**, 116.

McGonegal, C., Rabiner, L., and McDermott, B. (**1978**). "Speaker verification by human listeners over several speech transmission systems," *Bell System Technical Journal* **57**, 2887–2900.

McGowan, R.S. (**1988**). "An aeroacoustic approach to phonation," *Journal of the Acoustical Society of America* **83**, 696–704.

McNeill, E.J. (**2006**). "Management of the transgender voice," *Journal of Laryngology and Otology* **120**, 521–523.

McNeill, E.J., Wilson, J.A., Clark, S., and Deakin, J. (**2008**). "Perception of voice in the transgender client," *Journal of Voice* **22**, 727–733.

Mead, J., Bouhuys, A., and Proctor, D.F. (**1968**). "Mechanisms generating subglottic pressure," *Annals of the New York Academy of Sciences* **155**, 177–182.

Meadows, J.C. (**1974**). "The anatomical basis of prosopagnosia," *Journal of Neurology, Neurosurgery and Psychiatry* **37**, 489–501.

Meditch, A. (**1975**). "The development of sex-specific speech patterns in young children," *Anthropological Linguistics* **17**, 421–433.

Medrado, R., Ferreira, L.P., and Behlau, M. (**2005**). "Voice–over: Perceptual and acoustic analysis of vocal features," *Journal of Voice* **19**, 340–349.

Megehee, C.M., Dobie, K., and Grant, J. (**2003**). "Time versus pause manipulation in communications directed to the young adult population: Does it matter?," *Journal of Advertising Research* **43**, 281–292.

Mehl, M.R., Vazire, S., Ramirez-Esparza, N., Slatcher, R.B., and Pennebaker, J.W. (**2007**). "Are women really more talkative than men?," *Science* **317**, 82.

Mehler, J., Bertoncini, J., Barriere, M., and Jassik-Gerschenfeld, D. (**1978**). "Infant recognition of mother's voice," *Perception* **7**, 491–497.

Mehrabian, A. (**1971**). "Nonverbal betrayal of feeling," *Journal of Experimental Research in Personality* **5**, 64–73.

Mehrabian, A. (**2007**). *Nonverbal Communication* (Piscataway, NJ: Transaction Publishers).

Melara, R.D. and Marks, L.E. (**1990**). "Interaction among auditory dimensions: Timbre, pitch, and loudness," *Perception and Psychophysics* **48**, 169–178.

Mendes, A.P., Brown, W.S. Jr., Rothman, H.B., and Sapienza, C. (**2004**). "Effects of singing training on the speaking voice of voice majors," *Journal of Voice* **18**, 83–89.

Mendez, M.F., Adams, N.L., and Lewandowski, K.S. (**1989**). "Neurobehavioral changes associated with caudate lesions," *Neurology* **39**, 349–354.

Menn, L. and Boyce, S. (**1982**). "Fundamental frequency and discourse structure," *Language and Speech* **25**, 341–383.

Mershon, D.H., Desaulniers, D.H., Kiefer, S.A., Amerson, T.L., and Mills, J.T. (**1981**). "Perceived loudness and visually-determined auditory distance," *Perception* **10**, 531–543.

Mervis, C.B. and Rosch, E. (**1981**). "Categorization of natural objects," *Annual Review of Psychology* **32**, 89–115.

Metfessel, M. (**1928**). "What is the voice vibrato?," *Psychological Monographs* **31**, 126–134.

Meudell, P.R., Northen, B., Snowden, J.S., and Neary, D. (**1980**). "Long term memory for famous voices in amnesic and normal subjects," *Neuropsychologia* **18**, 133–139.

Meyer, M., Baumann, S., Wildgruber, D., and Alter, K. (**2007**). "How the brain laughs: Comparative evidence from behavioral, electrophysiological and neuroimaging studies in human and monkey," *Behavioural Brain Research* **182**, 245–260.

Meyer, M., Zysset, S., Von Cramon, D.Y., and Alter, K. (**2005**). "Distinct fMRI responses to laughter, speech, and sounds along the human peri-sylvian cortex," *Brain Research and Cognitive Brain Research* **24**, 291–306.

Meyerhoff, J.L., Saviolakis, G.A., Koenig, M.L., and Yourick, D.L. (**2001**). "Physiological and biochemical measures of stress compared to voice stress analysis using the computer voice stress analyzer (CVSA)," Report DoDPI98-R-0004, Fort Jackson, SC, Department of Defense Polygraph Institute.

Miller, C.L., Younger, B.A. and Morse, P.A. (**1982**). "The categorization of male and female voices in infancy," *Infant Behavior and Development* **5**, 143–159.

Miller, D.G. and Schutte, H.K. (**1993**). "Physical definition of the 'flageolet register'," *Journal of Voice* **7**, 206–212.

Miller, N., Lowit, A., and O'Sullivan, H. (**2006**). "What makes foreign accent syndrome foreign?," *Journal of Neurolinguistics* **19**, 385–409.

Miller, N., Maruyama, G., Beaber, R.J., and Valone, K. (**1976**). "Speed of speech and persuasion," *Journal of Personality and Social Psychology* **34**, 615–624.

Milmoe, S. Rosenthal, R., Blane, H.T., Chafetz, M.E., and Wolf, I. (**1967**). "The doctor's voice: Postdictor of successful referral of alcoholic patients," *Journal of Abnormal Psychology* **72**, 78–84.

Milner, B. (**1962**). "Laterality effects in audition," in *Interhemispheric Relations and Cerebral Dominance,* edited by V. Mountcastle (Baltimore: The Johns Hopkins University Press).

Mitchell, R.L., Elliott, R., Barry, M., Cruttenden, A., and Woodruff, P.W. (**2003**). "The neural response to emotional prosody, as revealed by functional magnetic resonance imaging," *Neuropsychologia* **41**, 1410–1421.

Mobbs, D. (**2003**). "Humor modulates the mesolimbic reward centers," *Neuron* **40**, 1041–1048.

Moen, I. (**1991**). "Functional lateralization of pitch accents and intonation in Norwegian: Monrad Krohn's study of an aphasic patient with altered 'melody of speech'," *Brain and Language* **41**, 538–554.

Monrad-Krohn, G. (**1947**). "Dysprosody or altered 'melody of language'," *Brain* **70**, 405–415.

Monsen, R.B. (**1979**). "Acoustic qualities of phonation in young hearing-impaired children," *Journal of Speech and Hearing Research* **22**, 270–288.

Montepare, J.M. and Zebrowitz-McArthur, L. (**1987**). "Perceptions of adults with childlike voices in two cultures," *Journal of Experimental Social Psychology* **23**, 331–349.

Moore, B.C.J. (**1982**). *An Introduction to the Psychology of Hearing*, 2nd edition (London: Academic Press).

Moore, D.M. and Berke, G.S. (**1988**). "The effect of laryngeal nerve stimulation on phonation: A glottographic study using an in vivo canine model," *Journal of the Acoustical Society of America* **83**, 705–715.

Moore, P. (**1964**). *Organic Voice Disorders* (Englewood Cliffs, NJ: Prentice-Hall).

Moore, W.E. (**1939**). "Personality traits and voice quality deficiencies," *Journal of Speech and Hearing Disorders* **4**, 33–36.

Morris, R.J. (**1997**). "Speaking fundamental frequency characteristics of 8- through 10-year-old white and African-American boys," *Journal of Communication Disorders* **30**, 101–116.

Morris, R.J. and Brown, W.S. Jr. (**1994a**). "Age-related differences in speech variability in women," *Journal of Communication Disorders* **27**, 49–64.

Morris, R.J. and Brown, W.S. Jr. (**1994b**). "Age-related differences in speech intensity among adult females," *Folia Phoniatrica et Logopedica* **46**, 64–69.

Morrison, H.M. (**2008**). "The locus equation as an index of coarticulation in syllables produced by speakers with profound hearing loss," *Clinical Linguistics and Phonetics* **22**, 726–240.

Morsbach, G. and Bunting, C. (**1979**). "Maternal recognition of their neonates' cries," *Developmental Medicine and Child Neurology* **21**, 178–185.

Morse, P.A. and Snowdon, C.T. (**1975**). "An investigation of. categorical speech discrimination by rhesus monkey," *Perception and Psychophysics* **17**, 9–16.

Mount, K.H., and Salmon, S. (**1988**). "Changing the vocal characteristics of a post–operative transsexual patient: A longitudinal study," *Journal of Communication Disorders* **21**, 229–238.

Mufwene, S.S., Rickford, J.R., Bailey, G., and Baugh, J. (Editors) (**1998**). *African-American English: Structure, History and Use* (New York: Routledge).

Mullennix, J.W., Bihon, T., Bricklemyer, J., Gaston, J., and Keener, J.M. (**2002**). "Effects of variation in emotional tone of voice on speech perception," *Language and Speech* **45**, 255–283.

Mullennix, J.W., Pisoni, D.B., and Martin, C.S. (**1989**). "Some effects of talker variability on spoken word recognition," *Journal of Acoustical Society of America* **85**, 365–378.

Munson, B. (**2007**). "The acoustic correlates of perceived masculinity, perceived femininity, and perceived sexual orientation," *Language and Speech* **50**, 125–142.

Munson, B. and Babel, M. (**2007**). "Loose lips and silver tongues, or, projecting sexual orientation through speech," *Language and Linguistics Compass* **1/5**, 416–449.

Munson, B., McDonald, E.C., DeBoe, N.L., and White, A.R. (**2006**). "The acoustic and perceptual bases of judgments of women and men's sexual orientation from read speech," *Journal of Phonetics* **34**, 139–294.

Murayama, J., Kashiwagi, T., Kashiwagi, A., and Mimura, M. (**2004**). "Impaired pitch production and preserved rhythm production in a right brain–damaged patient with amusia," *Brain and Cognition* **561**, 36–42.

Murphy, K. Corfield, D. R. Guz, A. Fink, G. R. Wise, R. J. S. Harrison, J., and Adams, L. (**1997**). "Cerebral areas associated with motor control of speech in humans." *Journal of Applied Physiology* **83**, 1438–1446.

Murphy, P.J. (**2000**). "Spectral characterization of jitter, shimmer, and additive noise in synthetically generated voice signals," *Journal of the Acoustical Society of America* **107**, 978–988.

Murray, I.R. and Arnott, J.L. (**1993**). "Toward the simulation of emotion in synthetic speech: A review of the literature on human vocal emotion," *Journal of the Acoustical Society of America* **93**, 1097–1108.

Murry, T., Hollien, H., and Muller, E. (**1975**). "Perceptual responses to infant crying: Maternal recognition and sex judgments," *Journal of Child Language* **2**, 199–204.

Murry, T. and Singh, S. (**1980**). "Multidimensional analysis of male and female voices," *Journal of the Acoustical Society of America* **68**, 1294–1300.

Murry, T., Singh, S., and Sargent, M. (**1977**). "Multidimensional classification of abnormal voice qualities," *Journal of the Acoustical Society of America* **61**, 1630–1635.

Myers, C.S. (**1915**). "A contribution to the study of shell shock: Being an account of three cases of loss of memory, vision, smell, and taste, admitted into the Duchess of Westminster's War Hospital, Le Touquet," *The Lancet*, 316–320.

Myers, P. (**1998**). *Right Hemisphere Damage* (San Diego, CA: Singular Publishing).

Myers, R.E. (**1976**). "Comparative neurology of vocalization and speech: Proof of a dichotomy," *Annals of the New York Academy of Science* **280**, 745–757.

Mysak, E.D. and Hanley, T.D. (**1958**). "Aging processes in speech: Pitch and duration characteristics," *Journal of Gerontology* **13**, 309–313.

Naeser, M.A. and Chan, W.-C.S. (**1980**). "Case study of a Chinese aphasic with the Boston Diagnostic Aphasia Exam," *Neuropsychologia* **18**, 389–410.

Nakamura, K., *et al.* (**2001**). "Neural substrates for recognition of familiar voices: A PET study," *Neuropsychologia* **39**, 1047–1054.

Nasif, A. and Gunter, B. (**2008**). "Gender representation in television advertisements in Britain and Saudi Arabia," *Sex Roles* **52**, 752–760.

National Research Council (**2003**). *The Polygraph and Lie Detection* (Washington, DC: National Academies Press).

Neiman, G.S. and Applegate, J.A. (**1990**). "Accuracy of listener judgments of perceived age relative to chronological age in adults," *Folia Phoniatrica* **42**, 327–330.

Neisser, U. (**1967**). *Cognitive Psychology* (New York: Appleton-Century-Crofts).

Neisser, U. (**1976**). *Cognition and Reality* (San Francisco: Freeman and Company).

Neisser, U. and Harsch, N. (**1992**). "Phantom flashbulbs: False recollections of hearing the news about the Challenger," in *Affect and Accuracy in Recall: Studies of "Flashbulb" Memories*, vol. 4, edited by E. Winograd and U. Neisser (New York: Cambridge University Press), pp. 9–31.

Nelken, I. (**2004**). "Processing of complex stimuli and natural scenes in the auditory cortex," *Current Opinion in Neurobiology* **14**, 474–480.

Neubauer, J., Edgerton, M., and Herzel, H. (**2004**). "Nonlinear phenomena in contemporary vocal music," *Journal of Voice* **18**, 1–12.

Neuner, F. and Schweinberger, S.R. (**2000**). "Neuropsychological impairments in the recognition of faces, voices, and personal names," *Brain and Cognition* **44**, 342–366.

Newman, J.D. (**2003**). "Vocal communication and the triune brain," *Physiology and Behavior* **79**, 495–502.

Ní Chasaide, A. and Gobl, C. (**2002**). "Voice quality and the synthesis of affect," in *Improvements in Speech Synthesis*, edited by E. Keller, G. Bailly, A. Monaghan, J. Terken, and M. Huckvale (New York: John Wiley & Sons), pp. 252–263.

Nicastro, N. and Owren, M.J. (**2003**). "Classification of domestic cat (Felis catus) vocalizations by naive and experienced human listeners," *Journal of Comparative Psychology* 117, 44–52.

Noback, C.R., Ruggiero, D.A., Demarest, R.J., and Strominger, N.L. (Editors) (**2005**). *The Human Nervous System: Structure and Function*, 6th edition (Totowa, NJ; Humana Press).

Nolan, F. (**1983**). *The Phonetic Bases of Speaker Recognition* (Cambridge: Cambridge University Press).

Nolan, F. (**1997**). "Speaker recognition and forensic phonetics," in *The Handbook of Phonetic Sciences*, edited by W.J. Hardcastle & J. Laver (Oxford: Blackwell), pp. 744–767.

Nolan, F. and Grabe, E. (**1996**). "Preparing a voice lineup," *Forensic Linguistics* 3, 74–94, 1996.

North, A.C., MacKenzie, L.C., Law, R.M., and Hargreaves, D.J. (**2004**). "The effects of musical and voice 'fit' on responses to advertisements," *Journal of Applied Social Psychology* 34, 1675–1708.

Nudo, R.J. (**2003**). "Adaptive plasticity in motor cortex: Implications for rehabilitation after brain injury," *Journal of Rehabilitative Medicine* **Suppl. 41**, 7–10.

Nwokah, E., Davies, P., Islam, A., Hsu, H., and Fogel, A. (**1993**). "Vocal affect in three-year-olds: A quantitative acoustic analysis of child laughter," *Journal of the Acoustical Society of America* 94, 3067–3090.

Nygaard, L.C. and Pisoni, D.B. (**1998**). "Talker-specific learning in speech perception," *Perception and Psychophysics* 60, 335–376.

Nygaard, L.C. and Queen, J.S. (**2008**). "Communicating emotion: Linking affective prosody and word meaning," *Journal of Experimental Psychology: Human Perception and Performance* 34, 1017–1030.

Nygaard, L.C., Sommers, M.S., and Pisoni, D.B. (**1994**). "Speech perception as a talker-contingent process," *Psychological Science* 5, 42–46.

O'Connell-Rodwell, C. (2005). "Keeping an 'ear' to the ground: Seismic communication in elephants," *Physiology* 22, 287–294.

O'Connell-Rodwell, C., Wood, J., Kinzley, C., Rodwell, T., Poole, J., and Puria, S. (**2007**). "Wild African elephants (Loxodonta africana) discriminate between familiar and unfamiliar conspecific seismic alarm calls," *Journal of the Acoustical Society of America* 122, 823–830.

Ohala, J.J. (**1980**). "The acoustic origin of the smile," *Journal of the Acoustical Society of America* 68, S33.

Ohala, J.J. (**1983**). "Cross-language use of pitch: An ethological view," *Phonetica* 40, 1–18.

Ohala, J.J. (**1984**). "An ethological perspective on common cross-language utilization of F0 of voice," *Phonetica* 41, 1–16.

Ojemann, G.A. (**1983**). "Brain organization for language from the perspective of electrical stimulation mapping," *Brain and Behavioral Sciences* 6, 189–230.

Ojemann, G.A. and Mateer, C. (**1979**). "Cortical and subcortical organization of human communication: Evidence from stimulation studies," in *Neurobiology of Social Communication in Primates*, edited by H.D. Steklis and M.J. Raleigh (New York: Academic Press), pp. 111–132.

Oliveira, M. (**2002**). "The role of pause occurrence and pause duration in the signaling of narrative structure," *Advances in Natural Language Processing* 2389, 43–51.

Olsson, N., Juslin, P., and Winman, A. (**1998**). "Realism of confidence in earwitness versus eyewitness identification," *Journal of Experimental Psychology: Applied* 4, 101–118.

Orchard, T.L. and Yarmey, A.D. (**1995**). "The effects of whispers, voice-sample duration, and voice distinctiveness on criminal speaker identification," *Applied Cognitive Psychology* 9, 249–260.

Orlikoff, R.F. (**1999**). "The perceived role of voice perception in clinical practice," *Phonoscope* 2, 87–106.

Orlikoff, R.F. and Baken, R.J. (**1989**). "The effect of the heartbeat on vocal fundamental fre-quency perturbation," *Journal of Speech and Hearing Research* **32**, 576–582.

Orlikoff, R.F., Baken, R.J., and Kraus, D.H. (**1997**). "Acoustic and physiologic characteristics of inspiratory phonation," *Journal of the Acoustical Society of America* **102**, 1838–1845.

Osgood, C.E., Suci, G.J., and Tannenbaum, P.H. (**1957**). *The Measurement of Meaning* (Urbana, IL: University of Illinois Press).

Owren, M.J. and Bachorowski, J.-A. (**2003**). "Reconsidering the evolution of nonlinguistic communication: The case of laughter," *Journal of Nonverbal Behavior* **27**, 183–200.

Owren, M.J., Berkowitz, M., and Bachorowski, J.-A. (**2007**). "Listeners judge talker sex more efficiently from male than from female vowels," *Perception and Psychophysics* **69**, 930–941.

Oyer, H. and Deal, L.V. (**1985**). "Temporal aspects of speech and the aging process," *Folia Phoniatrica (Basel)* **37**, 109–112.

Packman, A., Onslow, M., and Menzies, R. (**2000**). "Novel speech patterns and the treatment of stuttering," *Disability and Rehabilitation* **22**, 65–79.

Page, R.A. and Balloun, J.L. (**1978**). "The effect of voice volume on the perception of person-ality," *Journal of Social Psychology* **105**, 65–72.

Palmer, J.M. (**1973**). "Dynamic palatography. General implications of locus and sequencing patterns," *Phonetica* **28**, 76–85.

Palmeri, T.J., Goldinger, S.D., and Pisoni, D.B. (**1993**). "Episodic encoding of voice attributes and recognition memory for spoken words," *Journal of Experimental Psychology: Learning, Memory, and Cognition* **19**, 309–328.

Palmerino, C.C., Rusiniak, K.W., and Garcia, J. (**1980**). "Flavor–illness aversions: The peculiar roles of odor and taste in memory for poison," *Science* **208**, 753–755.

Panksepp, J. (**1998**). *Affective Neuroscience: The Foundations of Human and Animal Emotions* (New York: Oxford University Press).

Panksepp, J. (**2003**). "At the interface of affective, behavioral and cognitive neurosciences: Decoding the emotional feelings of the brain," *Brain and Cognition* **52**, 4–14.

Panksepp, J. (**2005**). "Affective consciousness: Core emotional feelings in animals and humans," *Consciousness & Cognition* **14**, 30–80.

Panksepp, J. (**2008**). "The power of the word may reside in the power of affect," *Integrative Psychological and Behavioral Science* **43**, 47–55.

Panksepp, J. and Burgdorf, J. (**2003**). "'Laughing' rats and the evolutionary antecedents of human joy?," *Physiology & Behavior* **79**, 533–547.

Pannbacker, M. (**1984**). "Classification systems of voice disorders: A review of the literature," *Language, Speech, and Hearing Services in Schools* **15**, 169–174.

Papanicolaou, A.C., Raz, H., Loring, D.W., and Eisenberg, H.M. (**1986**). "Brain stem evoked response suppression during speech production," *Brain and Language* **27**, 50–55.

Papcun, G., Kreiman, J., and Davis, A. (**1989**). "Long-term memory for unfamiliar voices," *Journal of the Acoustical Society of America* **85**, 913–925.

Papez, J.W. (**1937**). "A proposed mechanism of emotion," *Archives of Neurology and Psychiatry* **38**, 725–743.

Pardo, J.S. (**2006**). "On phonetic convergence during conversational interaction," *Journal of the Acoustical Society of America* **119**, 2382–2393.

Park, K.S. and Jang, P.S. (**1999**). "Effects of synthesized voice warning parameters on per-ceived urgency," *International Journal of Occupational Safety and Ergonomics* **5**, 73–95.

Pasricha, N., Dacakis, G., and Oates, J. (**2008**). "Communication satisfaction of male-to-female transsexuals," *Logopedics Phoniatrics Vocology* **33**, 25–34.

Patel, A.D. (**2008**). *Music, Language, and the Brain* (New York: Oxford University Press).

Patel, A.D., Foxton, J.M., and Griffiths, T.D. (**2005**). "Musically tone-deaf individuals have difficulty discriminating intonation contours extracted from speech," *Brain and Cognition* **59**, 310–313.

Paulmann, S. and Kotz, S.A. (**2008a**). "An ERP investigation on the temporal dynamics of emotional prosody and emotional semantics in pseudo- and lexical-sentence context," *Brain and Language* **105**, 59–69.

Paulmann, S. and Kotz, S.A. (**2008b**). "Early emotional prosody perception based on different speaker voices," *Neuroreport* **19**, 209–213.

Payne, K. (**1998**). *Silent Thunder* (New York: Penguin Putnam Inc.).

Payri, B. (**2000**). "Perception de la Voix Parlée: La Cohérence du Timbre du Locuteur," Doctoral thesis, University of Paris XI, Orsay. Published as Notes et Documents LIMSI number 2000-01, LIMSI, Orsay, France.

PBS television series. (**1988**). "The Mind." Nine–part series. WNET.

Pear, T.H. (**1931**). *Voice and Personality* (London: Chapman and Hall).

Peirce, K. (Director) (**1999**). *Boys Don't Cry* (Fox Searchlight Pictures, United States).

Peirce, K. (**2001**). "What if the Energizer bunny were female? Importance of gender in perceptions of advertising spokes–character effectiveness," *Sex Roles* **45**, 845–858.

Pell, M.D. (**2006**). "Cerebral mechanisms for understanding emotional prosody in speech," *Brain and Language* **97**, 221–234.

Pell, M.D. (**2007**). "Reduced sensitivity to prosodic attitudes in adults with focal right hemisphere brain damage," *Brain and Language* **101**, 64–79.

Pell, M.D. and Baum, S.R. (**1997a**). "Unilateral brain damage, prosodic comprehension deficits, and the acoustic cues to prosody," *Brain and Language* **57**, 195–214.

Pell, M.D. and Baum, S.R. (**1997b**). "The ability to perceive and comprehend intonation in linguistic and affective contexts by brain–damaged adults," *Brain and Language* **57**, 80–99.

Pell, M.D., Paulmann, S., Dara. C., Alasseri, A., and Kotz, S. (**2009**). "Factors in the recognition of vocally expressed emotions: A comparison of four languages," *Journal of Phonetics* **37**, 417–435.

Pemberton, C., McCormack, P., and Russell, A. (**1998**). "Have women's voices lowered across time? A cross sectional study of Australian women's voices," *Journal of Voice* **12**, 208–213.

Penfield, W. and Roberts, L. (**1959**). *Speech and Brain Mechanisms* (Princeton, NJ: Princeton University Press).

Peng, Y., Zebrowitz, L.A., and Lee, H.K. (**1993**). "The impact of cultural background and cross-cultural experience on impressions of American and Korean male speakers," *Journal of Cross-Cultural Psychology* **24**, 203–220.

Penrose, R. (**1994**). *Shadows of the Mind* (Oxford: Oxford University Press).

Peretz, I. (**2001**). "Auditory agnosia: A functional analysis," in *Thinking in Sound: The Cognitive Psychology of Human Audition*, edited by S. McAdams and E. Bigand (Oxford, UK: Clarendon Press), pp. 199–230.

Peretz, I. (**2001**). "Brain specialization for music: New evidence from congenital amusia," *Annals of the New York Academy of Sciences* **930**, 153–165.

Peretz, I. and Zatorre, R.J. (**2005**). "Brain organization for music processing," *Annual Review of Psychology* **56**, 89–114.

Perfect, T.J., Hunt, L.J., and Harris, C.M. (**2002**). "Verbal overshadowing in voice recognition," *Applied Cognitive Psychology* **16**, 973–980.

Perkins, W. and Kent, R.D. (**1991**). *Functional Anatomy of Speech, Language and Hearing: A Primer* (Boston, MA: Allyn & Bacon).

Perrachione, T.K., Chiao, J.Y., and Wong, P.C.M. (**2010**). "Asymmetric cultural effects on perceptual expertise underlie an own–race bias for voices," *Cognition* **114**, 42–55.

Perry, D.W., Zatorre, R.J., Petrides, M., Alivisatos, B., Meyer, E., and Evans, A.C. (**1999**). "Localization of cerebral activity during simple singing," *Neuroreport* **10**, 3453–3458.

Perry, T.L., Ohde, R.N., and Ashmead, D.H. (**2001**). "The acoustic bases for gender identification from children's voices," *Journal of the Acoustical Society of America* **109**, 2988–2998.

Peters, K.S., Applebury, M.L., and Rentzepis, P.M. (**1977**). "Primary photochemical event in vision: Proton translocation," *Proceedings of the National Academy of Science* **74**, 3119–3123.

Peterson, G.E. and Barney, H.L. (**1952**). "Control methods used in study of the vowels," *Journal of the Acoustical Society of America* **24**, 175–184.

Peterson, R.A., Cannito, M.P., and Brown, S.P. (**1995**). "An exploratory investigation of voice characteristics and selling effectiveness," *Journal of Personal Selling and Sales Management* **15**, 1–15.

Petkov, C.I., Kayser, C., Augath, M., and Logothetis N.K. (**2006**). "Functional imaging reveals numerous fields in the monkey auditory cortex," *PloS Biol* **4**, e215.

Petrie, D. (Director), & Bullock, S. (Producer) (**2000**). *Miss Congeniality* (Castle Rock Entertainment, United States).

Petrovici, J.-N. (**1980**). "Speech disturbances following stereotaxic surgery in ventrolateral thalamus," *Neurosurgical Review* **3**, 189–195.

Petty, R.E. and Cacioppo, J.T. (**1979**). "Issue involvement can increase or decrease persuasion by enhancing message-relevant cognitive responses," *Journal of Personality and Social Psychology* **37**, 1915–1926.

Pfefferle, D. and Fischer, J. (**2006**). "Sounds and size: Identification of acoustic variables that reflect body size in hamadryas baboons, Papio hamadryas," *Animal Behaviour* **72**, 43–51.

Pfefferle, D., West, P.M., Grinnell, J., Packer, C., and Fischer, J. (**2007**). "Do acoustic features of lion, Panthera leo, roars reflect sex and male condition?," *Journal of the Acoustical Society of America* **121**, 3947–3953.

Philippon, A.C., Cherryman, J., Bull, R., and Vrij, A. (**2007**). "Earwitness identification performance: The effect of language, target, deliberate strategies and indirect measures," *Applied Cognitive Psychology* **21**, 539–559.

Pierrehumbert, J., Bent, T., Munson, B., Bradlow, A.R., and Bailey, J.M. (**2004**). "The influence of sexual oreintation on vowel production," *Journal of the Acoustical Society of America* **116**, 1905–1908.

Pierrehumbert, J. and Hirschberg, J. (**1990**). "The meaning of intonational contours in the interpretation of discourse," in *Intentions in Communication*, edited by P.R. Cohen, J. Morgan, and M.E. Pollack (Cambridge, MA: MIT Press), pp. 271–311.

Pihan, H. (**2006**). "Affective and linguistic processing of speech prosody: DC potential studies," in *Progress in Brain Research*, vol. 156, edited by S. Anders, G. Ende, M. Junghöfer, J. Kissler, and D. Wildgruber. (Mahwah, NJ: Elsevier), pp. 269–284.

Pihan, H., Tabertd, M., Assuras, S., and Borod, J. (**2007**). "Unattended emotional intonations modulate linguistic prosody processing," *Brain and Language* **105**, 141–147.

Pijnenborg, G.H.M., Withaar, F.K., Bosch, R.J., and van den Brouwer, W.H. (**2007**). "Impaired perception of negative emotional prosody in schizophrenia," *Clinical Neuropsychologist* **21**, 762–75.

Pike, K. (**1945**). *The Intonation of American English* (Ann Arbor, MI: University of Michigan Press).

Pineda, J.A., Sebestyen, G., and Nava, C. (**1994**). "Face recognition as a function of social attention in non-human primates: an ERP study," *Brain Research Cognitive Brain Research* **2**, 1–12.

Pinker, S. (**1994**). *The Language Instinct* (New York: William Morrow & Co.).

Piske, T., MacKay, I.R.A., and Flege, J.E. (**2001**). "Factors affecting degree of foreign accent in an L2: A review," *Journal of Phonetics* **29**, 191–215.

Pisoni, D.B. (**1993**). "Long–term memory in speech perception: Some new findings on talker variability, speaking rate, and perceptual learning," *Speech Communication* 13, 109–125.

Pisoni, D.B. and Martin, C.S. (**1989**). "Effects of alcohol on the acoustic–phonetic properties of speech: Perceptual and acoustic analyses," *Alcoholism: Clinical and Experimental Research* 13, 577–587.

Pisoni, D.B., Yuchtman, M., and Hathaway, N. (**1986**). "Effects of alcohol on the acoustic–phonetic properties of speech," in *Alcohol, Accidents and Injuries* (Pittsburgh, PA: Society of Automotive Engineers), pp. 131–150.

Pittam, J. and Scherer, K.R. (**1993**). "Vocal expression and communication of emotion," in *The Handbook of Emotions,* edited by M. Lewis, and J.M. Haviland (New York: The Guilford Press), pp. 185–197.

Planalp, S., DeFrancisco, V.L., and Rutherford, D. (**1996**). "Varieties of cues to emotion in naturally occuring situations," *Cognition & Emotion* 10, 137–153.

Plant, R.L., Freed, G.L., and Plant, R.E. (**2004**). "Direct measurement of onset and offset phonation threshold pressure in normal subjects," *Journal of the Acoustical Society of America* 116, 3640–3646.

Pliny the Younger (**1963**). *The Letters of the Younger Pliny,* translated by Betty Radice (New York: Penguin Classics).

Plomp, R. (**1976**). *Aspects of Tone Sensation* (London: Academic Press).

Ploog, D. (**1975**). "Vocal behavior and its 'localization' as prerequisite for speech," in *Cerebral Localization,* edited by K. J. Zülch, O. Creutzfeldt, and G. C. Galbraith (Berlin: Springer-Verlag).

Ploog, D. (**1979**). "Phonation, emotion, cognition, with reference to the brain mechanisms involved," *Ciba Foundation Symposium* 69, 79–98.

Poeppel, D. (**2003**). "The analysis of speech in different temporal integration windows: Cerebral lateralization as 'asymmetric sampling in time'," *Speech Communication* 41, 245–255.

Pollack, I., Pickett, J., and Sumby, W.H. (**1954**). "On the identification of speakers by voice," *Journal of the Acoustical Society of America* 26, 403–406.

Pollack, S. (Producer/Director) and Richards, D. (Producer). (**1982**). *Tootsie* (Columbia, United States).

Pomerantz, J.R. (**1986**). "Visual form perception: An overview," In *Pattern Recognition by Humans and Machines,* edited by E. C. Schwab and H. C. Nusbaum (San Diego, CA: Academic Press).

Poncet, M. and Habib, M. (**1994**). "Atteinte isolée des comportements motives et lesions des noyaux gris centraux," *Revue Neurologique (Paris)* 150, 588–593.

Pongracz, P., Molnar, C., Miklosi, A., and Csanyi, V. (**2005**). "Human listeners are able to classify dog (canis familiaris) barks in different situations," *Journal of Comparative Psychology* 119, 136–144.

Poremba, A., Malloy, M., Saunders, R.C., Carson, R.E., Herscovitch, P., and Mishkin, M. (**2004**). "Species–specific calls evoke asymmetric activity in the monkey's temporal lobes," *Nature* 427, 448–51.

Port, R.F. (**2007**). "The graphical basis of phones and phonemes," in *Second–Language Speech Learning: The Role of Language Experienced in Speech Perception and Production,* edited by M. Monro and O.-S. Bohn (Amsterdam: Benjamins), pp. 349–365.

Port, R.F. and Leary, A. (**2005**). "Against formal phonology," *Language* 81, 927–964.

Potter, R.K., Kopp, G.A., and Kopp, H.G. (**1947/1966**). *Visible Speech* (New York: Dover).

Prame, E. (**1994**). "Measurements of the vibrato rate of ten singers," *Journal of the Acoustical Society of America* 96, 1979–1984.

Protopapas, A. and Lieberman, P. (**1997**). "Fundamental frequency of phonation and perceived emotional stress," *Journal of the Acoustical Society of America* 101, 2267–2277.

Provine, R.R. (**2000**). *Laughter: A Scientific Investigation* (New York: Viking).

Provine, R.R. and Emmorey, K. (**2006**). "Laughter among deaf signers," *Journal of Deaf Students and Deaf Education* 11, 403–409.

Ptacek, P.H. and Sander, E.K. (**1966**). "Age recognition from voice," *Journal of Speech and Hearing Research* 9, 273–277.

Ptacek, P.H., Sander, E.K., Maloney, W.H., and Jackson, C.C.R. (**1966**). "Phonatory and related changes with advanced age," *Journal of Speech and Hearing Research* 9, 353–360.

Pulvermüller, F. (**2002**). *The Neuroscience of Language: On Brain Circuits of Words and Serial Order* (Cambridge: Cambridge University Press).

Purandare, A. and Litman, D. (**2006**). "Humor: Prosody analysis and automatic recognition for F.R.I.E.N.D.S.," presented at EMNLP 2006, Sydney, Australia.

Purhonen, M., Kilpelainen-Lees, R., Valkonen-Korhonen, M., Karhu, J., and Lehtonen, J. (**2004**). "Cerebral processing of mother's voice compared to unfamiliar voice in 4-month-old infants," *International Journal of Psychophysiology* 52, 257–266.

Purhonen, M., Kilpelainen-Lees, R., Valkonen-Korhonen, M., Karhu, J., and Lehtonen, J. (**2005**). "Four-month-old infants process own mother's voice faster than unfamiliar voices–Electrical signs of sensitization in infant brain," *Cognitive Brain Research* 24, 627–633.

Puts, D.A. (**2005**). "Mating context and menstrual phase affect women's preferences for male voice pitch," *Evolution and Human Behavior* 26, 388–397.

Puts, D.A., Gaulin, S.J.C., and Verdolini, K. (**2006**). "Dominance and the evolution of sexual dimorphism in human voice pitch," *Evolution and Human Behavior* 27, 283–296.

Puts, D.A., Hodges, C.R., Cardenas, R.A., and Gaulin, S.J.C. (**2007**). "Men's voices as dominance signals: Vocal fundamental and formant frequencies influence dominance attributions among men," *Evolution and Human Behavior* 28, 340–344.

Quené, H. (**2008**). "Multilevel modeling of between–speaker and within–speaker variation in spontaneous speech tempo," *Journal of the Acoustical Society of America* 123, 1104–1113.

Querleu, D., Lefebvre, C., Titran, M., Renard, X., Morillion, M., and Crepin, G. (**1984**). "Reactivité du nouveau-né de moins de deux heures de vie à la voix maternelle," *Journal de Gynecologie, Obstetrique et Biologie de la Reproduction* 13, 125–134.

Quirk, R., Greenbaum, S., Leech, G., and Svartik, J. (**1985**). *A Comprehensive Grammar of the English Language* (London: Longman).

Racette, A., Bard, C., and Peretz, I. (**2006**). "Making non-fluent aphasics speak: Sing along!," *Brain* 129, 2571–2584.

Raczaszek, J., Tuller, B., Shapiro, L.P., Case, P., and Kelso, S. (**1999**). "Categorization of ambiguous sentences as a function of a changing prosodic parameter: A dynamical approach," *Journal of Psycholinguistic Research* 28, 367–393.

Radcliffe, M., Williams, M.G., and Williams, R. (Producers) and Columbus, C. (Director) (**1993**). *Mrs. Doubtfire* (Twentieth Century-Fox, USA).

Rämä, P., et al. (**2004**). "Dissociable functional cortical topographies for working memory maintenance of voice identity and location," *Cerebral Cortex* 14(7), 768–780.

Ramig, L. (**1986**). "Aging speech: Physiological and sociological aspects," *Language & Communication* 6, 25–34.

Ramig, L., Gray, S., Baker, K., Corbin-Lewis, K., Buder, E., Luschei, E., Coon, H., and Smith, M. (**2001**). "The aging voice: A review, treatment data and familial and genetic perspectives," *Folia Phoniatrica et Logopaedica* 53, 252–265.

Ramig, L. and Ringel, R. (**1983**). "Effects of physiological aging on selected acoustic characteristics of voice," *Journal of Speech and Hearing Research* 26, 22–30.

Randestad, A., Lindholm, C.E., and Fabian, P. (**2000**). "Dimensions of the cricoid cartilage and the trachea," *Laryngoscope* 110, 1957–1961.

Rapcsak, S.Z., Polster, M.R., Comer, J.F., and Rubens, A.B. (**1994**). "False recognition and misidentification of faces following right hemisphere damage," *Cortex* **30**, 565–83.

Rastatter, M.P., McGuire, R.A., Kalinowski, J., and Stuart, A. (**1997**). "Formant frequency characteristics of elderly speakers in contextual speech," *Folia Phoniatrica et Logopaedica* **49**, 1–8.

Rathborn, H., Bull, R., and Clifford, B.R. (**1981**). "Voice recognition over the telephone," *Journal of Police Science and Administration* **9**, 280–284.

Rauschecker, J.P. and Marler, P. (Editors) (**1987**). *Imprinting and Cortical Plasticity* (New York: John Wiley & Sons).

Read, D. and Craik, F.I.M. (**1995**). "Earwitness identification: Some influences on voice recognition," *Journal of Experimental Psychology: Applied* **1**, 6–18.

Reby, D. and McComb, K. (**2003**). "Anatomical constraints generate honesty: Acoustic cues to age and weight in the roars of red deer," *Animal Behaviour* **65**, 519–530.

Reby, D., McComb, K., Cargnelutti, B., Darwin, C., Fitch, W.T., and Clutton-Brock, T. (**2005**). "Red deer stags use formants as assessment cues during intrasexual agonistic interactions," *Proceedings. Biological Sciences* **272**, 941–947.

Recanzone, G.H., Schreiner, C.E., and Merzenich, M.M. (**1993**). "Plasticity in the frequency representation of primary auditory cortex following discrimination training in adult owl monkeys," *Journal of Neuroscience* **13**, 87–103.

Reed, S. (**1972**). "Pattern recognition and categorization," *Cognitive Psychology* **3**, 382–407.

Regen, S. (Producer) and Figgis, M. (Director) (**1995**). *Leaving Las Vegas* (Initial Productions, United States).

Reich, A.R. (**1981**). "Detecting the presence of vocal disguise in the male voice," *Journal of the Acoustical Society of America* **69**, 1458–1461.

Reich, A.R. and Duke, J.E. (**1979**). "Effects of selected vocal disguise upon speaker identification by listening," *Journal of the Acoustical Society of America* **66**, 1023–1028.

Reich, A.R., Moll, K.L., and Curtis, J.F. (**1976**). "Effects of selected vocal disguises upon spectrographic speaker identification," *Journal of the Acoustical Society of America* **60**, 919–925.

Reid, I., Young, A.W., and Hellawell, D.J. (**1993**). "Voice recognition impairment in a blind Capgras patient," *Behavioural Neurology* **6**, 225–228.

Remez, R.E. (2005). The perceptual organization of speech, in *The Handbook of Speech Perception*, edited by D. B. Pisoni and R. E. Remez, (Oxford: Blackwell), pp. 28–50.

Remez, R.E., Fellowes, J.M., and Rubin, P.E. (**1997**). "Talker identification based on phonetic information," *Journal of Experimental Psychology: Human Perception and Performance* **23**, 651–666.

Remez, R.E., Rubin, P.E., Berns, S.M., Pardo, J.S., and Lang, J.M. (**1994**). "On the perceptual organization of speech." *Psychological Review* **101**, 129–156.

Rendall, D. (**2003**). "Acoustic correlates of caller identity and affect intensity in the vowel-like grunt vocalizations of baboons," *Journal of the Acoustical Society of America* **113**, 3390–3402.

Rendall, D., Kollias, S., Ney, C., and Lloyd, P. (**2005**). "Pitch (F0) and formant profiles of human vowels and vowel-like baboon grunts: The role of vocalizer body size and voice-acoustic allometry," *Journal of the Acoustical Society of America* **117**, 944–955.

Rendall, D., Owren, M.J., and Rodman, P.S. (**1998**). "The role of vocal tract filtering in identity cueing in rhesus monkey (Macaca mulatta) vocalizations," *Journal of the Acoustical Society of America* **103**, 602–614.

Rendall, D., Owren, M.J., and Ryan, M. J. (**2009**). "What do animal signals mean?," *Animal Behaviour* **78**, 233–240.

Rendall, D., Owren, M.J., Weerts, E., and Hienz, R.J. (**2004**). "Sex differences in the acoustic structure of vowel-like grunt vocalizations in baboons and their perceptual discrimination by baboon listeners," *Journal of the Acoustical Society of America* **115**, 411–421.

Rendall, D., Rodman, P.S., and Edmond, R.E. (**1996**). "Vocal recognition of individuals and kin in free-ranging rhesus monkeys," *Animal Behaviour* **51**, 1007–1015.

Rendall, D., Vasey, P.L., and McKenzie, J. (**2008**). "The queen's English: An alternative, bio-social hypothesis for the distinctive features of 'gay speech'," *Archives of Sexual Behavior* **37**, 188–204.

Rendall, D., Vokey, J.R., and Nemeth, C. (**2007**). "Lifting the curtain on the Wizard of Oz: Biased voice-based impressions of speaker size," *Journal of Experimental Psychology: Human Perception and Performance* **33**, 1208–1219.

Rendall, D., Vokey, J.R., Nemeth, C., and Ney, C. (**2005**). "Reliable but weak voice-formant cues to body size in men but not women," *Journal of the Acoustical Society of America* **117**, 2372.

Revelle, W. and Scherer, K.R. (**2009**). "Personality and emotion," In *Oxford Companion to the Affective Sciences*, edited by D. Sander and K.R. Scherer (Oxford: Oxford University Press).

Reynolds, D.A. (**1995**). "Large population speaker identification using clean and telephone speech," *IEEE Signal Processing Letters* **2**, 46–48.

Richards, D.S., Frentzen, B., Gerhardt, K.J., McCann, M.E., and Abrams, R.M. (**1992**). "Sound levels in the human uterus," *Obstetrics and Gynecology* **80**, 186–190.

Richter, D., Waiblinger, J., Rink, W. J., and Wagner, G.A. (**2000**). "Thermoluminescence, electron spin resonance and C-14-dating of the late middle and early upper palaeolithin site of Geißenklösterle Cave in southern Germany," *Journal of Archaeological Science* **27**, 71–89.

Riding, D., Lonsdale, D., and Brown, B. (**2006**). "The effects of average fundamental frequency and variance of fundamental frequency on male vocal attractiveness to women," *Journal of Nonverbal Behavior* **30**, 55–61.

Riecker, A., Kassubek, J., Gröschel, K., Grodd, W., and Ackermann, H. (**2006**). "The cerebral control of speech tempo: Opposite relationship between speaking rate and bold signal changes at striatal and cerebellar structures," *NeuroImage* **29**, 46–53.

Riecker, A., Wildgruber, D. Dogil, G., Grodd, W., and Ackermann, H. (**2002**). "Hemispheric lateralization effects of rhythm implementation during syllable repetitions: An fMRI study," *NeuroImage* **16**, 169–176.

Riede, T. and Fitch, W.T. (**1999**). "Vocal tract length and acoustics of vocalization in the domestic dog (Canis familiaris)," *Journal of Experimental Biology* **202**, 2859–2867.

Riede, T. and Titze, I. (**2008**). "Vocal fold elasticity of the Rocky Mountain elk (Cervus elaphus nelsoni) – Producing high fundamental frequency vocalization with a very long vocal fold," *Journal of Experimental Biology* **211**, 2144–2154.

Riede, T. and Zuberbühler, K. (**2003**). "Pulse register phonation in Diana monkey alarm calls," *Journal of the Acoustical Society of America* **113**, 2919–2926.

Robinson, B.W. (**1972**). "Anatomical and physiological contrasts between human and other primate vocalizations," in *Perspectives on Human Evolution 2*, edited by S.L. Washburn and P. Dolhinow (Holt, Rinehart & Winston, New York), pp. 438–443.

Robinson, B.W. (**1976**). "Limbic influences on human speech," *Annals of the New York Academy of Sciences* **280**, 761–771.

Rockwell, P. (**2000**). "Lower, slower, louder: Vocal cues of sarcasm," *Journal of Psycholinguistic Research* **29**, 483–495.

Rockwell, P. (**2007**). "Vocal features of conversational sarcasm: A comparison of methods," *Journal of Psycholinguistic Research* **36**, 361–369.

Roebuck, R. and Wilding, J. (**1993**). "Effects of vowel variety and sample length on identification of a speaker in a line-up," *Applied Cognitive Psychology* **7**, 475–481.

Roederer, J.G. (**1995**). *The Physics and Psychophysics of Music* (New York: Springer).

Rolls, E.T. (**1995**). "A theory of emotion and consciousness, and its application to understanding the neural basis of emotion," in *The Cognitive Neurosciences*, edited by M. Gazzaniga (Cambridge, MA: MIT Press), pp. 1091–1106.

Rose, P. (**2002**). *Forensic Speaker Identification* (London: Taylor & Francis).

Rose, P. and Duncan, S. (**1995**). "Naive auditory identification and discrimination of similar voices by familiar listeners," *Forensic Linguistics* **2**, 1–17.

Rosenblum, L.D., Smith, N.M., Nichols, S.M., Hale, S., and Lee, J. (**2006**). "Hearing a face: Cross-modal speaker matching using isolated visible speech," *Perception and Psychophysics* **68**, 84–93.

Rosenfield, B. (**1987**). *Pauses in Oral and Written Narratives* (Boston, MA: Boston University).

Rosenthal, V. (**2004**). "Microgenesis, immediate experience and visual processes in reading," in *Seeing, Thinking and Knowing*, edited by A. Carsetti (Dordrecht: Kluwer Academic Publishers), pp. 221–244.

Rosenzweig, M.R. (**1951**). "Representations of the two ears at the auditory cortex," *American Journal of Psychology* **67**, 147–158.

Rosenzweig, M.R. (**1954**). "Cortical correlates of auditory localization and of related perceptual phenomena," *Journal of Comparative and Physiological Psychology* **47**, 269–276.

Rosenzweig, M.R. (**1961**). "Auditory localization," *Scientific American* **205**, 132–142.

Rouder, J. N. and Ratcliff, R. (**2006**). "Comparing exemplar- and rule-based theories of categorization," *Current Directions in Psychological Science* **15**, 9–13.

Roy, N., Gouse, M., Mauszycki, S.C., Merrill, R.M., and Smith, M.E. (**2005**). "Task specificity in adductor spasmodic dysphonia versus muscle tension dysphonia," *Laryngoscope* **115**, 311–316.

Ruiz, R., Absil, E., Harmegnies, B., Legros, C., and Poch, D. (**1996**). "Time- and spectrum-related variabilities in stressed speech under laboratory and real conditions," *Speech Communication* **20**, 111–129.

Rush, J. (**1823/1859**). *The Philosophy of the Human Voice: Embracing its physiological history: together with a system of principles, by which criticism in the art of elocution may be rendered intelligible and instruction, definite and comprehension to which is added a brief analysis of song and recitative*, 5th edition (Philadelphia: J. B. Lippencott & Co,).

Russell, A., Penny, L., and Pemberton, C. (**1995**). "Speaking fundamental frequency changes over time in women: A longitudinal study," *Journal of Speech and Hearing Research* **38**, 101–109.

Ryalls, J. and Reinvang, I., (**1986**). "Functional lateralization of linguistic tones: Acoustic evidence from Norwegian," *Language and Speech* **29**, 389–398.

Ryan, M. and Kenny, D.T. (**2009**). "Perceived effects of the menstrual cycle on young female singers in the western classical tradition," *Journal of Voice* **23**, 99–108.

Ryan, W.J. (**1972**). "Acoustic aspects of the aging voice," *Journal of Gerontology* **27**, 265–268.

Ryan, W.J. and Capadano, H. (**1978**). "Age perceptions and evaluative reactions toward adult speakers," *Journal of Gerontology* **33**, 98–102.

Sabin, E.J., Clemmer, E.J., O'Connell, D.C., and Kowal, S. (**1979**). "A pausological approach to speech development," in *Of Speech and Time*, edited by A.W. Siegman and S. Felstein (Hillsdale, NJ: Lawrence Erlbaum Associates), pp. 35–55.

Sachs, C. and Kunst, J. (**1962**). *The Wellsprings of Music* (The Hague: Martinus Nijhoff).

Sachs, J., Lieberman, P., and Erickson, D. (**1973**). "Anatomical and cultural determinants of male and female speech," in *Language Attitudes: Current Trends and Prospects*, edited by R.W. Shuy and R. Fasold (Washington, DC: Georgetown University Press), pp. 152–171.

Safer, M.A. and Leventhal, H. (**1977**). "Ear differences in evaluating emotional tones of voice and verbal content," *Journal of Experimental Psychology: Human Perception and Performance* **3**, 75–82.

Saint-Cyr, J.A., Taylor, A.E., and Nicholson, K. (**1995**). "Behavior and the basal ganglia," in *Behavioral Neurology of Movement Disorders. Advances in Neurology,* volume 65, edited by W.J. Weiner and A.E. Lang (New York: Raven Press), pp. 1–28.

Samson, S. and Zatorre, R.J. (**1994**). "Contribution of the right temporal lobe to musical timbre discrimination," *Neuropsychologia* **32**, 231–240.

Sander, D., Grafman, J., and Zalla, T. (**2003**). "The human amygdala: An evolved system for relevance detection," *Reviews in the Neurosciences* **14**, 303–316.

Sanderman, A. and Collier, R. (**1995**). "Prosodic phrasing at the sentence level," in *Producing Speech: Contemporary Issues (for Katherine Safford Harris),* edited by F. Bell–Berti and L.J. Raphael (New York: AIP Press), pp. 321–332.

Sanders, I., Rai, S., Han, Y.S., and Biller, H. F. (**1998**). "Human vocalis contains distinct superior and inferior subcompartments: Possible candidates for the two masses of vocal fold," *Annals of Otology, Rhinology and Laryngology* **107**, 826–833.

Sanford, F.H. (**1942**). "Speech and personality," *Psychological Bulletin* **39**, 811–845.

Sankoff, G. and Cedegren, H. (**1971**). "Some results of a sociolinguistic study of Montreal French," in *Linguistic Diversity in Canadian Society,* edited by R. Darnell (Edmonton and Champaign: Linguistic Research) pp. 61–87. Cited by Smith (1979).

Santamaria, J. and Tolosa, E. (**1992**). "Clinical subtypes of Parkinson's disease and depression," in *Parkinson's Disease: Neurobehavioral Aspects,* edited by S.J. Huber and J.L. Cummings (New York: Oxford University Press), pp. 217–228.

Sanvito, S., Galimberti, F., and Miller, E.H. (**2007**). "Having a big nose: Structure, ontogeny and function of the elephant seal proboscis," *Canadian Journal of Zoology* **85**, 207–220.

Sapienza, C.M. (**1997**). "Aerodynamic and acoustic characteristics of the adult African American voice," *Journal of Voice* **11**, 410–416.

Sapienza, C.M. and Dutka, J. (**1996**). "Glottal airflow characteristics of women's voice production along an aging continuum," *Journal of Speech and Hearing Research* **39**, 322–328.

Sapir, E. (**1921**). *Language* (New York: Harcourt, Brace, & World).

Sapir, E. (**1927**). "Speech as a personality trait," *American Journal of Sociology* **32**, 892–905.

Saslove, H. and Yarmey, A.D. (**1980**). "Long-term auditory memory: Speaker identification," *Journal of Applied Psychology* **65**, 111–116.

Sauter, D., Eisner, F., Ekman, P., and Scott, S. (**2010**). "Cross-cultural recognition of basic emotions through nonverbal emotional vocalizations," *Proceedings of the National Academy of Sciences* **107**, 2408–2412.

Sawusch, J.R. (**1986**). "Auditory and phonetic coding of speech," in *Pattern Recognition by Humans and Machines: Speech perception* (Volume 1), edited by E.C. Schwab and H.C. Nusbaum (New York: Academic Press), pp. 51–88.

Saxman, J.H. and Burk, K. (**1967**). "Speaking fundamental frequency characteristics of middle-aged females," *Folia Phoniatrica* **19**, 167–172.

Saxton, T.K., Caryl, P.G., and Roberts, S.C. (**2006**). "Vocal and facial attractiveness judgments of children, adolescents and adults: The ontogeny of mate choice," *Ethology* **112**, 1179–1185.

Schafer, A.J., Speer, S.R., Warren, P., and White, S.D. (**2000**). "Intonational disambiguation in sentence production and comprehension," *Journal of Psycholinguistic Research* **29**, 169–182.

Schaffer, D. (**1983**). "The role of intonation as a cue to turn taking in conversation," *Journal of Phonetics* **11**, 243–257.

Schaltenbrand, G. (**1965**). "The effects of stereotactic electrical stimulation in the depth of the brain," *Brain* **88**, 835–840.

Schegloff, E.A. (**1979**). "Identification and recognition in telephone conversation openings," in *Everyday Language: Studies in Ethnomethodology*, edited by G. Psathas (New York: Irvington Publishers, Inc.), pp. 23–78.

Schegloff, E.A. (**1998**). "Reflections on studying prosody in talk-in-interaction," *Language and Speech* **41**, 235–263.

Schegloff, E.A., Jefferson, G., and Sacks, H. (**1977**). "The preference for self-correction in the organisation of repair in conversation," *Language* **53**, 361–82.

Scherer, K.R. (**1972**). "Judging personality from voice: A cross-cultural approach to an old issue in inter-personal perception," *Journal of Personality* **40**, 191–210.

Scherer, K.R. (**1974**). "Voice quality analysis of American and German speakers," *Journal of Psycholinguistic Research* **3**, 281–298.

Scherer, K.R. (**1979**). "Personality markers in speech," in *Social Markers in Speech*, edited by K.R. Scherer & H. Giles (Cambridge: Cambridge University Press), pp. 147–210.

Scherer, K.R. (**1981**). "Speech and emotional states," in *Speech Evaluation in Psychiatry*, edited by J.K. Darby (New York: Grune and Stratton), pp. 189–220.

Scherer, K.R. (**1984**). *On the Nature and Function of Emotion: A Component Process Approach* (Hillsdale, NJ: Lawrence Erlbaum).

Scherer, K.R. (**1985**). *Vocal Affect Signalling: A Comparative Approach* (New York: Academic Press).

Scherer, K.R. (**1986**). "Vocal affect expression: A review and a model for future research," *Psychological Bulletin* **99**, 143–165.

Scherer, K.R. (**2003**). "Vocal communication of emotion: A review of research paradigms," *Speech Communication* **40**, 227–256.

Scherer, K.R., Banse, R., and Wallbott, H.G. (**2001**). "Emotion inferences from vocal expression correlate across languages and cultures," *Journal of Cross-Cultural Psychology* **32**, 76–92.

Scherer, K.R., Banse, R., Wallbott, H.G., and Goldbeck, T. (**1991**). "Vocal cues in emotion encoding and decoding," *Motivation and Emotion* **15**, 123–148.

Scherer, K.R., Johnstone, T., and Klasmeyer, G. (**2003**). "Vocal expression of emotion," in *Handbook of Affective Sciences*, edited by R.J. Davidson, K.R. Scherer, and H.H. Goldsmith (Oxford: Oxford University Press), pp. 433–456.

Scherer, K.R. and Scherer, U. (**1981**). "Speech behavior and personality," in *Speech Evaluation in Psychiatry*, edited by J. Darby (New York: Grune & Stratton), pp. 115–135.

Scherrer, J.A. and Wilkinson, G.S. (**1993**). "Evening bat isolation calls provide evidence for heritable signatures," *Animal Behaviour* **46**, 847–860.

Schiffman, H.R. (**1976**). *Sensation and Perception: An Integrated Approach* (New York: John Wiley & Sons).

Schiller, N.O. and Köster, O. (**1998**). "The ability of expert witnesses to identify voices: A comparison between trained and untrained listeners," *Forensic Linguistics* **5**, 1–9.

Schirmer, A. (**2004**). "Timing in speech: A review of lesions and neuroimaging findings," *Brain Research and Cognitive Brain Research* **21**, 269–287.

Schirmer, A., Alter, K., Kotz, S., and Friederici, A.D. (**2001**). "A lateralization of prosody during language production: A lesion study," *Brain and Language* **76**, 1–17.

Schirmer, A. and Simpson, E. (**2008**). "Brain correlates of vocal emotional processing in men and women," in *Emotions in the Human Voice*, volume 1, edited by K. Izdebski (San Diego, CA: Plural), pp. 75–86.

Schlanger, G., Schlanger, P., and Gerstman, L. (**1976**). "The perception of emotionally toned sentences by right hemisphere-damaged and aphasic subjects," *Brain and Language* **4**, 396–403.

Schmidt-Nielsen, A. and Stern, K.R. (**1985**). "Identification of known voices as a function of familiarity and narrow-band coding," *Journal of the Acoustical Society of America* 77, 658–663.

Schon Ybarra, M. (**1995**). "A comparative approach to the nonhuman primate vocal tract: Implications for sound production," in *Current Topics in Primate Vocal Communication*, edited by E. Zimmermann, J.D. Newman, and U. Jürgens (New York: Plenum), pp. 185–198.

Schroeder, C.E., Smiley, J., Fu, K.G. O'Connell, M.N., McGinnis, T., and Hackett, T.A. (**2003**). "Anatomical mechanisms and functional implications of multisensory convergence in early cortical processing," *International Journal of Psychophysiology* 50, 5–17.

Schulz, G.M., Varga, M., Jeffires, K., Ludlow, C.L., and Braun, A.R. (**2005**). "Functional neuro-anatomy of human vocalization: An H2150 PET study," *Cerebral Cortex* 15, 1835–1847.

Schuster, M., Lohscheller, J., Kummer, P., Eysholdt, U., and Hoppe, U. (**2005**). "Laser projection in high-speed glottography for high-precision measurements of laryngeal dimensions and dynamics," *European Archives of Oto-Rhino-Laryngology* 262, 477–481.

Schutte, H.K. and Miller, D.G. (**1991**). "Acoustic details of vibrato cycle in tenor high notes," *Journal of Voice* 5, 217–223.

Schwaninger, A., Lobmaier, J.S., and Collishaw, S.M. (**2002**). "Role of featural and configural information in familiar and unfamiliar face recognition," *Lecture Notes in Computer Science* 2525, 643–650.

Schwartz, M.F. (**1968**). "Identification of speaker sex from isolated, voiceless fricatives," *Journal of the Acoustical Society of America* 43, 1178–1179.

Schwartz, M.F. and Rine, H.E. (**1968**). "Identification of speaker sex from isolated whispered vowels," *Journal of the Acoustical Society of America* 44, 1736–1737.

Schweinberger, S.R. (**2001**). "Human brain potential correlates of voice priming and voice recognition," *Neuroposychologia* 39, 921–936.

Schweinberger, S.R., Herholz, A., and Sommer, W. (**1997a**). "Recognizing famous voices: Influence of stimulus duration and different types of retrieval cues," *Journal of Speech, Language, and Hearing Research* 40, 453–463.

Schweinberger, S.R., Herholz, A., and Stief, V. (**1997b**). "Auditory long–term memory: Repetition priming of voice recognition," *Quarterly Journal of Experimental Psychology Section A–Human Experimental Psychology* 50, 498–517.

Searby, A. and Jouventin, P. (**2003**). "Mother–lamb acoustic recognition in sheep: A frequency coding," *Proceedings of the Royal Society of London B: Biological Sciences* 270, 1765–1771.

Searby, A., Jouventin, P., and Aubin, T. (**2004**). "Acoustic recognition in macaroni penguins: An original signature system," *Animal Behaviour* 67, 615–625.

Seddoh, S.A.K. (**2004**). "Prosodic disturbance in aphasia: speech timing versus intonation production," *Clinical Linguistics and Phonetics* 18, 17–38.

Seddon, N. (**2005**). "Ecological adaptation and species recognition drives vocal evolution in Neotropical suboscine birds," *Evolution* 59, 200–215.

Seeck, M., Mainwaring, N., Ives, J., Blume, H., Dubuisson, D., Cosgrove, R., Mesulam, M.M., and Schomer, D.L. (**1993**). "Differential neural activity in the human temporal lobe evoked by faces of family members and friends," *Annals of Neurology* 34, 369–372.

Seikel, J.A., King, D.W., and Drumright, D.G. (**2000**). *Anatomy and Physiology for Speech, Language, and Hearing* (San Diego, CA: Singular).

Selkirk, E. (**1984**). *Phonology and Syntax. The Relation between Sound and Structure.* (Cambridge, MA: MIT Press).

Selting, M. (**1996a**). "On the interplay of syntax and prosody in the constitution of turn-constructional units and turns in conversation," *Pragmatics* 6, 371–388.

Selting, M. (**1996b**). "Prosody as an activity-type distinctive due in conversation: The case of so-called 'astonished' questions in repair initiation," in *Prosody in Conversation: Interactional Studies*, edited by E. Couper-Kuhlen and M. Selting (Cambridge: Cambridge University Press), pp. 231–270.

Selting, M., Auer, P., Barden, B., Bergmann, J., Couper-Kuhlen, E., Günthner, S., Meier, C., Quasthoff, U., Schlobinski, P., and Uhmann, S. (**1998**) "Gesprächsanalytisches Transkriptionssystem (GAT)," *Linguistische Berichte* **173**, 91–122.

Semenza, C. and Zettin, M. (**1988**). "Generating proper names: A case of selective ability," *Cognitive Neuropsychology* **5**, 711–721.

Semple, S. and McComb, K. (**2000**). "Perception of female reproductive state from vocal cues in a mammal species," *Proceedings of the Royal Society of London Series B: Biological Sciences* **267**, 707–712.

Shah, N.J., Marshall, J.C., Zafiris, O., Schwab, A., Zilles, K., Markowitsch, H.J., and Fink, G.R. (**2001**). "The neural correlates of person familiarity. A functional magnetic resonance imaging study with clinical implications," *Brain* **124**, 804–815.

Shahidullah, S. and Hepper, P.G. (**1994**). "Frequency discrimination by the fetus," *Early Human Development* **36**, 13–26.

Shanahan, J. (**2007**). *Language, Feeling, and the Brain: The Evocative Sector* (New Brunswick, NJ: Transaction Publishers).

Sharf, D.J. and Lehman, M.E. (**1984**). "Relationship between the speech characteristics and effectiveness of telephone interviewers," *Journal of Phonetics* **12**, 219–228.

Sharp, S.P., McGowan, A., Wood, M.J., and Hatchwell, B.J. (**2005**). "Learned kin recognition cues in a social bird," *Nature* **434**, 1127–1130.

Shattuck–Hufnagel, S. and Turk, A.E. (**1996**). "A prosody tutorial for investigators of auditory sentence processing," *Journal of Psycholinguistic Research* **25**, 193–247.

Shaw, G.B. (**1916**). *Pygmalion: A Romance in Five Acts* (London: Constable).

Shaw, R.J., Dong, M., Lim, K.O., Faustman, W.O., Pouget, E.R., and Alpert, M. (**1999**). "The relationship between affect expression and affect recognition in schizophrenia," *Schizophrenia Research* **37**, 245–50.

Sheffert, S.M. and Olson, E. (**2004**). "Audiovisual speech facilitates voice learning," *Perception and Psychophysics* **66**, 352–362.

Shipp, T. and Hollien, H. (**1969**). "Perception of the aging male voice," *Journal of Speech and Hearing Research* **12**, 703–710.

Shipp, T. and Izdebski, K. (**1981**). "Current evidence for the existence of laryngeal macro-tremor and microtremor," *Journal of Forensic Sciences* **26**, 501–505.

Shipp, T., Qi, Y., Huntley, R., and Hollien, H. (**1992**). "Acoustic and temporal correlates of perceived age," *Journal of Voice* **6**, 211–216.

Shirt, M. (**1983**). "An auditory speaker–recognition experiment comparing the performance of trained phoneticians and phonetically naive listeners," *University of Leeds Papers in Linguistics and Phonetics* **1**, 115–117.

Shonle, J.K. and Horan, K.E. (**1980**). "The pitch of vibrato tones," *Journal of the Acoustical Society of America* **67**, 246–252.

Sidtis, D., Cameron, K., Bonura, L., and Sidtis, J.J. (**2011**). "Dramatic effects of speech task on motor and linguistic planning in severely dysfluent parkinsonian speech," in review.

Sidtis, D., Canterucci, G., and Katsnelson, D. (**2009**). "Effects of neurological damage on production of formulaic language," *Clinical Linguistics and Phonetics* **23**, 270–284.

Sidtis, D., Rogers, T., Godier, V., Tagliati, M., and Sidtis, J.J. (**2010**). "Voice and fluency changes as a function of speech task and deep brain stimulation," *Journal of Speech Language and Hearing Research* **53**, 1167–1177.

Sidtis, J.J. (**1980**). "On the nature of the cortical function underlying right hemisphere auditory perception," *Neuropsychologia* **18**, 321–330.

Sidtis, J.J. (**1982**). "Predicting brain organization from dichotic listening performance: cortical and subcortical functional asymmetries contribute to perceptual asymmetries," *Brain and Language* **17**, 287–300.

Sidtis, J.J. (**2007**). "Some problems for representations of brain organization based on activation in functional imaging," *Brain and Language* **102**, 130–140.

Sidtis, J.J., Ahn, J.S., Gomez, C., and Sidtis, D. (**2010**). "Speech characteristics associated with three genotypes of ataxia" (submitted).

Sidtis, J.J., Gomez, C., Naoum, A., Strother, S.C., and Rottenberg, D.A. (**2006**). "Mapping cerebral blood flow during speech production in hereditary ataxia," *NeuroImage* **31**, 246–254.

Sidtis, J.J., Strother, S.C., and Rottenberg, D.A. (**2003**). "Predicting performance from functional imaging data: Methods matter," *NeuroImage* **20**, 615–624.

Sidtis, J.J., Strother, S.C., and Rottenberg, D.A. (**2004**). "The effect of set on the resting state in functional imaging: A role for the striatum?," *NeuroImage* **22**, 1407–1413.

Sidtis, J.J., Strother, S.C., Anderson, J.R., and Rottenberg, D.A. (**1999**). "Are brain functions really additive?," *NeuroImage* **9**, 490–496.

Sidtis, J.J. and Van Lancker Sidtis, D. (**2003**). "A neurobehavioral approach to dysprosody," *Seminars in Speech and Language* **24**, 93–105.

Siegman, A.W., Anderson, R.A., and Berger, T. (**1990**). "The angry voice: Its effects on the experience of anger and cardiovascular reactivity," *Psychosomatic Medicine* **52**, 631–643.

Siegman, A.W. and Boyle, S. (**1993**). "Voices of fear and anxiety and sadness and depression: The effects of speech rate and loudness on fear and anxiety and sadness and depression," *Journal of Abnormal Psychology* **102**, 430–437.

Siemund, P. (**2001**). "Interrogative constructions," in *Language Typology and Language Universals*, edited by M. Haspelmath, E. König, W. Oesterreicher, and W. Raible (Berlin: de Gruyter), pp. 1010–1028.

Silva, J.A., Leong, G.B., and Wine, D.B. (**1993**). "Misidentification delusions, facial misrecognition, and right brain injury," *Canadian Journal of Psychiatry* **38**, 239–241.

Silverman, D. (**1997**). "Laryngeal complexity in Otomanguean vowels," *Phonology* **14**, 235–261.

Silverman, E. and Zimmer, C.H. (**1978**). "Effect of the menstrual cycle on voice quality," *Archives of Otolaryngology Head and Neck Surgery* **104**, 7–10.

Silverman, K., Beckman, M., Pitrelli, J., Ostendorf, M., Wightman, C., Price, P., Pierrehumbert, J., and Hirschberg, J. (**1992**). "ToBI: A standard for labeling English prosody," *Proceedings of International Congress on Speech and Language Processing–1992*, 866–870.

Simonet, P., Versteeg, D., and Storie, D. (**2005**). "Dog-laughter: Recorded playback reduces stress related behavior in shelter dogs," *Proceedings of the 7th International Conference on Environmental Enrichment*.

Simons, J.S. and Mayes, A.R. (**2008**). "What is the parietal lobe contribution to human memory?," *Neuropsychologia* **46**, 1739–1742.

Simons, J.S., Peers, P.V., Hwang, D.Y., Ally, B.A., Fletcher, P.C., and Budson, A.E. (**2008**). "Is the parietal lobe necessary for recollection in humans?," *Neuropsychologia* **46**, 1185–1191.

Simonyan, K. and Jürgens, U. (**2003**). "Subcortical projections of the laryngeal motorcortex in the rhesus monkey," *Brain Research* **974**, 43–59.

Singh, S. & Murry, T. (**1978**). "Multidimensional classification of normal voice qualities," *Journal of the Acoustical Society of America* **64**, 81–87.

Skousen, R. (**1989**). *Analogical Modeling of Language* (Dortrecht: Kluwer).

Skousen, R., Lonsdale, D., and Parkinson, D. B. (Editors) (**2002**). *Analogical Modeling – An Exemplar-Based Approach to Language* (Amsterdam: Benjamins).

Slifka, J. (**1999**). "Respiratory system changes in relation to prosodic cues at the beginning of speech," *Journal of the Acoustical Society of America* **106**, 2241–2242.

Smith, A. (**1966**). "Speech and other functions after left dominant hemispherectomy," *Journal of Neurology, Neurosurgery and Psychiatry* **29**, 467–471.

Smith, B.L., Brown, B.L., Strong, W.J., and Rencher, A.E. (**1975**). "Effects of speech rate on personality perception," *Language and Speech* **18**, 145–152.

Smith, D.R., Patterson, R.D., Turner, R., Kawahara, H., and Irino, T. (**2005**). "The processing and perception of size information in speech sounds," *Journal of the Acoustical Society of America* **117**, 305–318.

Smith, D.R., Walters, T.C., and Patterson, R.D. (**2007**). "Discrimination of speaker sex and size when glottal-pulse rate and vocal-tract length are controlled," *Journal of the Acoustic Society of America* **122**, 3628–3639.

Smith, P.M. (**1979**). "Sex markers in speech," in *Social Markers in Speech*, edited by K.R. Scherer and H. Giles (Cambridge: Cambridge University Press), pp. 109–146.

Smith, R.C., Parker, E.S., and Noble, E.P. (**1975**). "Alcohol's effect on some formal aspects of verbal social communication," *Archives of General Psychiatry* **32**, 1394–1398.

Smith, S.M. and Shaffer, D.R. (**1991**). "Celebrity and cajolery: Rapid speech may promote or inhibit persuasion through its impact on message elaboration," *Personality and Social Psychology Bulletin* **17**, 663–669.

Smyth, R., Jacobs, G., and Rogers, H. (**2003**). "Male voices and perceived sexual orientation: An experimental and theoretical approach," *Language in Society* **32**, 329–350.

Snowdon, C.T. (**2003**). "Expression of emotion in nonhuman animals," in *Handbook of Affective Sciences*, edited by R.J. Davidson, K.R. Scherer, and H.H. Goldsmith (Oxford: Oxford University Press), pp. 457–480.

Sobell, L.C. and Sobell, M.B. (**1972**). "Effects of alcohol on the speech of alcoholics," *Journal of Speech and Hearing Research* **15**, 861–868.

Sobell, L.C., Sobell, M.B., and Coleman, R.F. (**1982**). "Alcohol induced dysfluency in nonalcoholics," *Folia Phoniatrica* **34**, 316–323.

Sobin, C. and Alpert, M. (**1999**). "Emotion in speech: The acoustic attributes of fear, anger, sadness, and joy," *Journal of Psycholinguistic Research*, **28**, 347–365.

Sokolov, E.N. (**1960**). "Neuronal models and the orienting influence," in *The Central Nervous System and Behavior: Transactions of the Third Conference*, edited by M.A.B. Brazier (New York: Josiah Macy Foundation), pp. 187–276.

Solan, L.M. and Tiersma, P.M. (**2003**). "Hearing voices: Speaker identification in court," *Hastings Law Journal* **54**, 373.

Soltis, J. (**2004**). "The signal functions of early infant crying," *Behavioral and Brain Sciences* **27**, 443–458.

Sommers, M.S. (**2006**). "Evaluating voice-based measures for detecting deception," *Journal of Credibility Assessment and Witness Psychology* **7**, 99–107.

Song, J.H., Skoe, E., Wong, P.C., and Kraus, N. (**2008**). "Plasticity in the adult human auditory brainstem following short-term linguistic training," *Journal of Cognitive Neuroscience* **20**, 1892–1902.

Spackman, M. P., Brown, B.L., and Otto, S. (**2009**). "Do emotions have distinct vocal profiles? A study of idiographic patterns of expression," *Cognition and Emotion* **23**, 1565–1588.

Speedie, L.J., Wertman, E., Ta'ir, J., and Heilman, K.M. (**1993**). "Disruption of automatic speech following a right basal ganglia lesion," *Neurology* **43**, 1768–1774.

Spence, M.J. and DeCasper, A.J. (**1987**). "Prenatal experience with low–frequency maternal-voice sounds influence neonatal perception of maternal voice samples," *Infant Behavior and Development* **10**, 133–142.

Spence, M.J. and Freeman, M.S. (**1996**). "Newborn infants prefer the maternal low-pass filtered voice, but not the maternal whispered voice," *Infant Behavior and Development* **19**, 199–212.

Spence, M.J., Rollins, P.R., and Jerger, S. (**2002**). "Children's recognition of cartoon voices," *Journal of Speech, Language, and Hearing Research* **45**, 214–222.

Sperry, R.W., Zaidel, E., and Zaidel, D. (**1979**). "Self-recognition and social awareness in the disconnected minor hemisphere," *Neuropsychologia* **17**, 153–166.

Spreckelmeyer, K. N., Kutas, M., Urbach, T., Altenmüller, E., and Müntee, T. F. (**2009**). "Neural processing of vocal emotion and identity," *Brain and Cognition* **69**, 121–126.

Sroufe, L.A. and Wunsch, J.P. (**1972**). "The development of laughter in the first year of life," *Child Development* **43**, 1326–1344.

Stagner, R. (**1936**). "Judgments of voice and personality," *Journal of Educational Psychology* **27**, 272–277.

Stanford, W.B. (**1967**). *The Sound of Greek* (Berkeley, CA: University of California Press).

Stassen, H.H., Bomben, G., and Gunther, E. (**1991**). "Speech characteristics in depression," *Psychopathology* **24**, 88–105.

Stassen, H.H., Kuny, S., and Hell, D. (**1998**). "The speech analysis approach to determining onset of improvement under antidepressants," *European Neuropsychopharmacology* **8**, 303–310.

Stathopoulos, E. and Sapienza, C.M. (**1993a**). "Respiratory and laryngeal measures of children during vocal intensity variation," *Journal of the Acoustical Society of America* **94**, 2531–2543.

Stathopoulos, E. and Sapienza, C.M. (**1993b**). "Respiratory and laryngeal function of women and men during vocal intensity variation," *Journal of Speech and Hearing Research* **36**, 64–75.

Steele, J. (**1775**). *An Essay Towards Establishing the Melody and Measure of Speech, to be Expressed and Perpetuated by Certain Symbols* (London: Bowyer and Nichols).

Stephens, L.L. (**1988**). "The role of memory in the relationship between affect and familiarity," *Cognition and Emotion* **2**, 333–349.

Stevens, A.A. (**2004**). "Dissociating the cortical basis of memory for voices, words and tones," *Cognitive Brain Research* **18**(**2**), 162–171.

Stevens, K.N. (**1972**). "Sources of inter– and intra–speaker variability in the acoustic properties of speech sounds," in *Proceedings of the 7th International Congress of Phonetic Sciences*, edited by A. Rigault and R. Charbonneau (The Hague: Mouton), pp. 206–232.

Stevens, K.N. (**1998**). *Acoustic Phonetics* (Cambridge, MA: MIT Press).

Stevens, S.S. (**1968**). "Measurement, statistics, and the schemapiric view," *Science* **161**, 849–856.

Stewart, M. and Ryan, E.B. (**1982**). "Attitudes toward younger and older adult speakers: Effects of varying speech rates," *Journal of Language and Social Psychology* **1**, 91–109.

Stoicheff, M.L. (**1981**). "Speaking fundamental frequency of middle–aged females," *Folia Phoniatrica* **19**, 167–172.

Strange, W. and Dittman, S. (**1984**). "Effects of discrimination training on the perception of /r-l/ by Japanese adults learning English," *Perception & Psychophysics* **36**, 131–145.

Streeter, L.A., Krauss, R.M., Geller, V., and Olson, C. (**1977**). "Pitch changes during attempted deception," *Journal of Personality and Social Psychology* **35**, 345–350.

Streeter, L.A., MacDonald, N.H., Apple, W., Krauss, R.M., and Galotti, K.M. (**1983**). "Acoustic and perceptual indicators of emotional stress," *Journal of the Acoustical Society of America* **73**, 1354–1360.

Stroop, J.R. (**1935**). "Studies of interference in serial verbal reactions," *Journal of Experimental Psychology* **18**, 643–662.

Studdert-Kennedy, M. and Shankweiler, D. (**1970**). "Hemispheric specialization for speech perception," *Journal of the Acoustical Society of America* **48**, 579–594.

Suga, N. (**2008**). "Role of corticofugal feedback in hearing, " *Journal of Comparative Physiology A* **194**, 169–183.

Suga, N., Ma, X., Gao, E., Sakai, M., and Chowdhury, S.A. (**2003**). "Descending system and plasticity for auditory signal processing: Neuroethological data for speech scientists," *Speech Communication* **41**, 189–200.

Sundberg, J. (**1974**). "Articulatory interpretation of the 'singing formant'," *Journal of the Acoustical Society of America* **55**, 838–844.

Sundberg, J. (**1987**). *The Science of the Singing Voice* (DeKalb, IL: Northern Illinois University Press).

Sundberg, J. (**1995**). "Acoustic and psychoacoustic aspects of vocal vibrato," in *Vibrato*, edited by P.H. Dejonckere, M. Hirano, and J. Sundberg (San Diego, CA: Singular), pp. 35–62.

Sundberg, J. (**2001**). "Level and center frequency of the singer's formant," *Journal of Voice* **15**, 176–186.

Sundberg, J., Cleveland, T.F., Stone, R.E. Jr., and Iwarsson, J. (**1999**). "Voice source characteristics in six premier country singers," *Journal of Voice* **13**, 168–183.

Surawski, M.K. and Ossoff, E.P. (**2006**). "The effects of physical and vocal attractiveness on impression formation of politicians," *Current Psychology: Developmental, Learning, Personality, Social* **25**, 15–27.

Swaminathan, J., Krishnan, A., and Gandour, J.T. (**2008**). "Pitch encoding in speech and non-speech contexts in the human auditory brainstem," *NeuroReport* **19**, 1163–1167.

Swerts, M. and Geluykens, R. (**1994**). "Prosody as a marker of information flow in spoken discourse," *Language and Speech* **37**, 21–43.

Swerts, M. and Hirschberg, J. (**2010**). "Prosodic predictors of upcoming positive or negative content in spoken messages," *Journal of the Acoustical Society of America* **128**, 1337–1345.

Swets, J.A. and Pickett, R.M. (**1982**). *Evaluation of Diagnostic Systems: Methods From Signal Detection Theory* (New York: Academic).

Syka, J. (**2002**). "Plastic changes in the central auditory system after hearing loss, restoration of function, and during learning," *Physiology Review* **82**, 601–636.

Szameitat, D.P., Alter, K., Szameitat, A.J., Wildgruber, D., Sterr, A., and Darwin, C.J. (**2009**). "Acoustic profiles of distinct emotional expressions in laughter," *Journal of the Acoustical Society of America* **126**, 354–366.

Tanaka, S. and Tanabe, M. (**1986**). "Glottal adjustment for regulating vocal intensity," *Acta Otolaryngologica (Stockholm)* **102**, 315–324.

Tanford, J.A., Pisoni, D.B., and Johnson, K. (**1992**). "Novel scientific evidence of intoxication: Acoustic analysis of voice recordings from the Exxon Valdez," *Journal of Criminal Law and Criminology* **82**, 579–609.

Tannen, D. (**1989**). *Talking Voices. Repetition, Dialogue and Imagery in Conversational Discourse*, Studies in Interactional Sociolinguistics No. 6 (Washington, DC: Georgetown University).

Tanner, D.C. and Tanner, M.E. (**2004**). *Forensic Aspects of Speech Patterns: Voice Prints, Speaker Profiling, Lie and Intoxication Detection* (Tucson, AZ: Lawyers and Judges Publishing Company).

Tartter, V.C. and Braun, D. (**1980**). "Perceptual and acoustic effects of smiling on speech," *Perception and Psychophysics* **27**, 24–27.

Tartter, V.C. and Braun, D. (**1994**). "Hearing smiles and frowns in normal and whisper registers," *Journal of the Acoustical Society of America* **96**, 2101–2107.

Tatham, M. and Morton, K. (**2004**). *Expression in Speech: Analysis and Synthesis* (Oxford: Oxford University Press).

Taylor, A.M. and Reby, D. (**2010**). "The contribution of source–filter theory to mammal vocal communication research," *Journal of Zoology* **280**, 221–236.

Taylor, A.M., Reby, D., and McComb, K. (**2008**). "Human listeners attend to size information in domestic dog growls," *Journal of the Acoustical Society of America* **123**, 2903–2909.

Taylor, H.C. (**1934**). "Social agreement on personality traits as judged from speech," *Journal of Social Psychology* **5**, 244–248.

Terango, L. (**1966**). "Pitch and duration characteristics of the oral reading of males on a masculinity dimension," *Journal of Speech and Hearing Research* **9**, 590–595.

Terrazas, A., Serafin, N., Hernandez, H., Nowak, R., and Poindron, P. (**2003**). "Early recognition of newborn goat kids by their mother: II. Auditory recognition and evidence of an individual acoustic signature in the neonate," *Developmental Psychobiology* **43**, 311–320.

Teshigawara, M. (**2003**). *Voices in Japanese Animation: A Phonetic Study of Vocal Stereotypes of Heroes and Villains in Japanese Culture.* Unpublished Doctoral dissertation, University of Victoria.

Thalen, M. and Sundberg, J. (**2000**). "A method for describing different styles of singing. A comparison of a female singer's voice source in 'classical', 'pop', 'jazz', and 'blues'," *Royal Institute of Technology Quarterly Progress and Status Reports* **1**, 45–54.

Thomas, E.R. and Reaser, J. (**2004**). "Delimiting perceptual cues used for the ethnic labeling of African American and European American voices," *Journal of Sociolinguistics* **8**, 54–87.

Thomas, I.B. (**1969**). "The perceived pitch of whispered vowels," *Journal of the Acoustical Society of America* **46**, 468–470.

Thomas, L.B., Harrison, A.L., and Stemple, J.C. (**2008**). "Aging thyroarytenoid and limb skeletal muscle: Lessons in contrast," *Journal of Voice* **22**, 430–450.

Thomasson, M. and Sundberg, J. (**2001**). "Consistency of inhalatory breathing patterns in professional operatic singers," *Journal of Voice* **15**, 373–383.

Thompson, C.P. (**1985**). "Voice identification: Speaker identifiability and a correction of the record regarding sex effects," *Human Learning* **4**, 19–27.

Thompson, C.P. (**1987**). "A language effect in voice identification," *Applied Cognitive Psychology* **1**, 121–131.

Thompson, R. (**1967**). *Foundations of Physiological Psychology* (New York: Harper & Row).

Thompson, W.F. and Balkwill, L.L. (**2006**). "Decoding speech prosody in five languages," *Semiotica* **158**, 407–424.

Tiago, R., Pontes, P., and do Brasil, O.C. (**2007**). "Age-related changes in human laryngeal nerves," *Otolaryngology Head and Neck Surgery* **136**, 747–751.

Tian, B., Reser, D., Durham, A., Kustov, A., and Rauschecker, J.P. (**2001**). "Functional specialization in rhesus monkey auditory cortex," *Science* **292**, 290–293.

Tiffin, J. and Seashore, H. (**1936**). "Summary of the established facts in experimental studies on the vibrato up to 1932," in *The Vibrato*, edited by C.E. Seashore (Iowa City: University of Iowa), pp. 344–376.

Titova, N. and Näätänen, R. (**2001**) "Preattentive voice discrimination by the human brain as indexed by the mismatch negativity," *Neuroscience Letters* **308**, 63–65.

Titze, I.R. (**1989**). "Physiologic and acoustic differences between male and female voices," *Journal of the Acoustical Society of America* **85**, 1699–1707.

Titze, I.R. (**1992**). "Phonation threshold pressure: A missing link in glottal aerodynamics," *Journal of the Acoustical Society of America* **91**, 2926–2935.

Titze, I.R. (**1994**). *Principles of Voice Production* (Englewood Cliffs, NJ: Prentice-Hall).

Titze, I.R. (**1995**). *Workshop on Acoustic Voice Analysis. Summary Statement* (Denver: National Center for Voice and Speech).

Titze, I.R. (**2001**). "Acoustic interpretation of resonant voice," *Journal of Voice* **15**, 519–528.

Titze, I.R. (**2004**). "A theoretical study of F0-F1 interaction with application to resonant speaking and singing voice," *Journal of Voice* **18**, 292–298.

Titze, I.R., Luschei, E.S., and Hirano, M. (**1989**). "The role of the thyroarytenoid muscle in regulation of fundamental frequency," *Journal of Voice* **3**, 213–224.

Titze, I.R., Story, B., Smith, M., and Long, R. (**2002**). "A reflex resonance model of vocal vibrato," *Journal of the Acoustical Society of America* **111**, 2272–2282.

Todd, N.P. (**2007**). "Estimated source intensity and active space of the American alligator (Alligator Mississippiensis) vocal display," *Journal of the Acoustical Society of America* **122**, 2906–2915.

Todt, E.H. and Howell, R.J. (**1980**). "Vocal cues as indices of schizophrenia," *Journal of Speech and Hearing Research* **23**, 517–526.

Tolkmitt, F., Helfrich, H., Standke, R., and Scherer, K,R (**1982**). "Vocal indicators of psychiatric treatment effects in depressives and schizophrenics," *Journal of Communication Disorders* **15**, 209–22.

Tolkmitt, F. and Scherer, K.R. (**1986**). "Effect of experimentally induced stress on vocal parameters," *Journal of Experimental Psychology: Human Perception and Performance* **12**, 302–313.

Tompkins, C.A. and Flowers, C.R. (**1985**). "Perception of emotional intonation by brain–damaged adults," *Journal of Speech and Hearing Research* **28**, 527–538.

Torriani, M.V.G., Vannoni, E., and McElligott, A.G. (**2006**). "Mother–young recognition in an ungulate hider species: A unidirectional process," *American Naturalist* **168**, 412–420.

Tosi, O. (**1975**). "The problem of speaker identification and elimination," in *Measurement Procedures in Speech, Hearing, and Language*, edited by S. Singh, (Baltimore: University Park Press), pp. 399–431.

Tosi, O. (**1979**). *Voice Identification: Theory and Legal Applications* (Baltimore: University Park Press).

Tranel, D. (**1992**). "Neuropsychological correlates of cortical and subcortical damage," in *Textbook of Neuropsychiatry, volume II*, edited by S.C. Yudofsky and R.E. Hales (Washington, DC: American Psychiatric Press), pp. 57–88.

Tropea, C. (**1995**). "Laser Doppler anemometry: Recent developments and future challenges," *Measurement Science & Technology* **6**, 605–619.

Tsalikis, J., DeShields, O.W. Jr., and LaTour, M.S. (**1991**). "The role of accent on the credibility and effectiveness of the salesman," *Journal of Personal Selling & Sales Management* **11**, 31–41.

Tucker, J.A. and Tucker, G.F. (**1979**). "A clinical perspective on the development and anatomical aspects of the infant larynx and trachea," in *Laryngo-tracheal Problems in the Pediatric Patient*, edited by G.B. Healy and T.J.I. McGill (Springfield, IL: Charles C. Thomas), pp. 3–8.

Tunturi, A.R. (**1946**). "A study on the pathway from the medial geniculate body to the acoustic cortex in the dog, " *American Journal of Physiology* **147**, 311–319.

Tuomi, S.K. and Fisher, J.F. (**1979**). "Characteristics of simulated sexy voice," *Folia Phoniatrica* **31**, 242–249.

Umiltà, C., Brizzolara, D., Tabossi, P., and Fairweather, H. (**1978**). "Factors affecting face recognition in the cerebral hemispheres – familiarity and naming," in *Attention and Performance*, vol. 7, edited by J. Requin (Hillsdale, New Jersey: Erlbaum), pp. 363–374.

Uttal, W.R. (**2001**). *The New Phrenology: The Limits of Localizing Cognitive Processes in the Brain* (Cambridge, MA: MIT Press).

van Bezooijen, R. (**1984**). *Characteristics and Recognizability of Vocal Expressions of Emotion* (Dordrecht: Foris Publications).

van Bezooijen, R. (**1995**). "Sociocultural aspects of pitch differences between Japanese and Dutch women," *Language and Speech* **38**, 253–265.

van Bezooijen, R., Otto, S., Heenan, T., and Francais, A. (**1983**). "Recognition of vocal expressions of emotion," *Journal of Cross-Cultural Psychology* **14**, 387–406.

Van Borsel, J., De Cuypere, G., Rubens, R., and Destaerke, B. (**2000**). "Voice problems in female-to-male transsexuals," *International Journal of Language and Communication Disorders* **35**, 427–442.

Van Borsel, J., De Cuypere, G., and Van den Berghe, H. (**2001**). "Physical appearance and voice in male-to-female transsexuals," *Journal of Voice* **15**, 570–575.

Van Borsel, J., Van Eynde, E., De Cuypere, G., and Bonte, K. (**2008**). "Feminine after crico-thyroid approximation?," *Journal of Voice* **22**, 379–384.

van den Berg, J. W. (**1958**). "Myoelastic-aerodynamic theory of voice production," *Journal of Speech and Hearing Research* **1**, 227–244.

van den Berg, J.W. (**1968**). "Sound production in isolated human larynges," *Annals of New York Academy of Sciences* **155**, 18–27.

van Dommelen, W.A. (**1990**). "Acoustic parameters in human speaker recognition," *Language and Speech* **33**, 259–272.

van Dommelen, W.A. (**1993**). "Speaker height and weight identification: A re-evaluation of some old data," *Journal of Phonetics* **21**, 337–341.

van Dommelen, W.A. and Moxness, B.H. (**1995**). "Acoustic parameters in speaker height and weight identification: Sex-specific behavior," *Language and Speech* **38**, 267–287.

Van Gysel, W.D., Vercammen, J., and Debruyne, F. (**2001**). "Voice similarity in identical twins," *Acta Otorhinolaryngolica Belgique* **55**, 49–55.

Van Lancker, D. (**1991**). "Personal relevance and the human right hemisphere," *Brain and Cognition* **17**, 64–92.

Van Lancker, D. (**1997**). "Rags to riches: Our increasing appreciation of cognitive and communicative abilities of the human right cerebral hemisphere," *Brain and Language* **57**, 1–11.

Van Lancker, D. and Canter, G.J. (**1981**). "Idiomatic versus literal interpretations of ditropically ambiguous sentences," *Journal of Speech and Hearing Research* **24**, 64–69.

Van Lancker, D. and Canter, G.J. (**1982**). "Impairment of voice and face recognition in patients with hemispheric damage," *Brain and Cognition* **1**, 185–195.

Van Lancker, D., Canter, G.J., and Terbeek, D. (**1981**). "Disambiguation of ditropic sentences: Acoustic and phonetic cues," *Journal of Speech and Hearing Research* **24**, 330–335.

Van Lancker, D., Cornelius, C., and Kreiman, J. (**1989**). "Recognition of emotional–prosodic meanings in speech by autistic, schizophrenic, and normal children," *Developmental Neuropsychology* **5**, 207–226.

Van Lancker, D. and Cummings, J.L. (**1999**). "Expletives: neurolinguistic and neurobehavioral perspectives on swearing," *Brain Research Reviews* **31**, 83–104.

Van Lancker, D. Cummings, J.L., Kreiman, J., and Dobkin, B.H. (**1988**). "Phonagnosia: A dissociation between familiar and unfamiliar voices," *Cortex* **24**, 195–209.

Van Lancker, D., and Fromkin, V.A. (**1973**). "Hemispheric specialization for pitch and 'tone': Evidence from Thai," *Journal of Phonetics* **1**, 101–109.

Van Lancker, D. and Fromkin, V.A. (**1978**). "Cerebral dominance for pitch contrasts in tone language speakers and in musically untrained and trained English speakers," *Journal of Phonetics* **6**, 19–23.

Van Lancker, D. and Kreiman, J. (**1984**). *The Voice Recognition Test.* Copyright, 1984.

Van Lancker, D. and Kreiman, J. (**1986**). "Preservation of familiar speaker recognition but not unfamiliar speaker discrimination in aphasic patients," *Clinical Aphasiology* **16**, 234–240.

Van Lancker, D. and Kreiman, J. (**1987**). "Unfamiliar voice discrimination and familiar voice recognition are independent and unordered abilities," *Neuropsychologia* **25**, 829–834.

Van Lancker, D., Kreiman, J., and Cummings, J.L. (**1989**). "Voice perception deficits: Neuroanatomic correlates of phonagnosia," *Journal of Clinical and Experimental Neuropsychology* **11**, 665–674.

Van Lancker, D., Kreiman, J., and Emmorey, K. (**1985**). "Familiar voice recognition, Patterns and parameters. Part I: Recognition of backward voices," *Journal of Phonetics* **13**, 19–38.

Van Lancker, D., Kreiman, J., and Wickens, T.D. (**1985**). "Familiar voice recognition: Patterns and parameters. Part II: Recognition of rate–altered voices," *Journal of Phonetics* **13**, 39–52.

Van Lancker, D. and Ohnesorge, C. (**2002**). "Personally familiar proper names are relatively successfully processed in the human right hemisphere, or, the missing link," *Brain and Language* **80**, 121–129.

Van Lancker, D. and Pachana, N. (**1998**). "The influence of emotion on language and communication disorders," in *The Handbook of Neurolinguistics*, edited by B. Stemmer & H.A. Whitaker (San Diego, CA: Academic), pp. 302–313.

Van Lancker, D. and Rallon, G. (2004). "Tracking the incidence of formulaic expressions in everyday speech: Methods for classification and verification," *Language and Communication* **24**, 207–240.

Van Lancker, D. and Sidtis, J.J. (**1992**). "The identification of affective-prosodic stimuli by left- and right-brain damaged subjects: All errors are not created equal," *Journal of Speech and Hearing Research* **35**, 963–970.

Van Lancker Sidtis, D. (**2004**). "When only the right hemisphere is left: Language and communication studies," *Brain and Language* **91**, 199–211.

Van Lancker Sidtis, D. (**2007**). "Does functional neuroimaging solve the questions of neurolinguistics?," *Brain and Language* **102**, 200–214.

Van Lancker Sidtis, D. (**2008**). "Formulaic and novel language in a 'dual process' model of language competence: Evidence from surveys, speech samples, and schemata," in *Formulaic Language: Volume 2. Acquisition, Loss, Psychological Reality, Functional Applications*, edited by R.L. Corrigan, E.A. Moravcsik, H. Ouali, and K.M. Wheatley (Amsterdam: Benjamins), pp. 151–176.

Van Lancker Sidtis, D. (**2010**). "Two–track mind: Formulaic and novel language support a dual–process model," in *Advances in the Neural Substrates of Language: Toward a Synthesis of Basic Science and Clinical Research*, edited by M. Faust (New York: Blackwell), to appear.

Van Lancker Sidtis, D., Kempler, D., Jackson, C., and Metter, E.J. (**2010**). "Prosodic changes in aphasic speech: Timing," *Journal of Clinical Linguistics and Phonetics* **24**, 155–167.

Van Lancker Sidtis, D., Pachana, N., Cummings, J., and Sidtis, J.L. (**2006**). "Dysprosodic speech following basal ganglia insult: Toward a conceptual framework for the study of the cerebral representation of prosody," *Brain and Language* **97**, 135–153.

Van Lancker Sidtis, D. and Postman, W.A. (**2006**). "Formulaic expressions in spontaneous speech of left- and right-hemisphere damaged subjects," *Aphasiology* **20**, 411–426.

Van Lierde, K.M., Claeys, S., De Bodt, M., and Van Cauwenberge, P. (**2006**). "Response of the female vocal quality and resonance in professional voice users taking oral contraceptive pills: A multiparameter approach," *Laryngoscope* **116**, 1894–1898.

Van Lierde, K.M., Vinck, B., de Ley, S., Clement, G., and Van Cauwenberge, P. (**2005**). "Genetics of vocal quality characteristics in monozygotic twins: A multiparameter approach," *Journal of Voice* **19**, 511–518.

Van Opzeeland, I.C. and Van Parijs, S.M. (**2004**). "Individuality in harp seal, Phoca groenlandica, pup vocalizations," *Animal Behaviour* **68**, 1115–1123.

Van Wallendael, L.R., Surace, A., Parsons, D.H., and Brown, M. (**1994**). "'Earwitness' voice recognition: Factors affecting accuracy and impact on jurors," *Applied Cognitive Psychology* **8**, 661–677.

Vanags, T., Carroll, M., and Perfect, T.J. (**2005**). "Verbal overshadowing: A sound theory in voice recognition?," *Applied Cognitive Psychology* **19**, 1127–1144.

Vargas, M.F. (**1986**). *Louder Than Words: An Introduction to Nonverbal Communication* (Ames, IA: Iowa State University Press).

Vennard, W. (**1967**). *Singing: The Mechanism and the Technic* (New York: Carl Fischer).

Verhulst, J. (**1987**). "Development of the larynx from birth to puberty," *Revue de Laryngologie Otologie Rhinologie* **108**, 269–270. Cited by Kent and Vorperian (1995).

Vilkki, J. and Laitinen, L.V. (**1974**). "Differential effects of left and right ventrolateral thalamotomy on receptive and expressive verbal performances and face-matching," *Neuropsychologia* **12**, 11–19.

Vingerhoets, G., Berckmoes, C., and Stroobant, N. (**2003**). "Cerebral hemodynamics during discrimination of prosodic and semantic emotion in speech," *Neuropsychology* **17**, 93–99.

Voiers, W.D. (**1964**). "Perceptual bases of speaker identity," *Journal of the Acoustical Society of America* **36**, 1065–1073.

von Kempelen, W. (**1791**). *Mechanismus der menschlichen Sprache nebst der Beschreibung seiner sprechenden Machine* (Vienna, Austria: J.B. Degen).

von Kriegstein, K., Eger, E., Kleinschmidt, A., and Giraud, A.L. (**2003**). "Modulation of neural responses to speech by directing attention to voices or verbal content," *Brain Research Cognitive Brain Research* **17**, 48–55.

von Kriegstein, K. and Giraud, A.L. (**2004**). "Distinct functional substrates along the right superior temporal sulcus for the processing of voices," *NeuroImage* **22**, 948–955.

von Kriegstein, K., Kleinschmidt, A., and Giraud, A.L. (**2005**). "Voice recognition and cross-modal responses to familiar speakers' voices in prosopagnosia," *Cerebral Cortex* **16**, 1314–1322.

von Kriegstein, K., Kleinschmidt, A., Sterzer, P., and Giraud, A.L. (**2005**). "Interaction of face and voice areas during speaker recognition," *Journal of Cognitive Neuroscience* **17**, 367–376.

Vorperian, H.K. and Kent, R.D. (**2007**). "Vowel acoustic space development in children: A synthesis of acoustic and anatomic data," *Journal of Speech, Language and Hearing Research* **50**, 1510–1545.

Vorperian, H.K., Kent, R.D., Lindstrom, M.J., Kalina, C.M., Gentry, L.R., and Yandell, B.S. (**2005**). "Development of vocal tract length during early childhood: A magnetic resonance imaging study," *Journal of the Acoustical Society of America* **117**, 338–350.

Vorperian, H.K., Wang, S., Chung, M.K.,, Schimek, E.M., Durtschi, R.B., Kent, R.D., Ziegert, A.J., and Gentry, L.R. (**2009**). "Anatomic development of the oral and pharyngeal portions of the vocal tract: an imaging study," *Journal of the Acoustical Society of America* **125**, 1666–1678.

Voyer, D., Bowes, A., and Soraggi, M. (**2008**). "Response procedure and laterality effects in emotion recognition: Implications for models of dichotic listening," *Neuropsychologia* **47**, 23–29.

Vrij, A., Edward, K., and Bull, R. (**2001**). "People's insights into their own behavior and speech content while lying," *British Journal of Psychology* **92**, 373–389.

Vukovic, J., Jones, B.C., Feinberg, D.R., DeBruine, L.M., Smith, F.G., Welling, L.M., and Little, A.C. (**2010**). "Variation in perceptions of physical dominance and trustworthiness predicts individual differences in the effect of relationship context on women's preferences for masculine pitch in men's voices," *British Journal of Psychology*, in press.

Wagner, A.D., Shannon, B.J., Kahn, I., and Buckner, R.L. (**2005**). "Parietal lobe contributions to episodic memory retrieval," *Trends in Cognitive Sciences* **9**, 445–453.

Wagner, I. and Köster, O. (**1999**). "Perceptual recognition of familiar voices using falsetto as a type of voice disguise," in *Proceedings of the XIVth International Congress of Phonetic Sciences, San Francisco*, pp. 1381–1385.

Wahlin, A., Backman, L., Mantylea, T., Herlitz, A., Viitanen, M., and Winblad, B. (**1993**). "Prior knowledge and face recognition in a community based sample of healthy, very old adults," *Journal of Gerontology* **48**, 54–61.

Waksler, S. (**2001**). "Pitch range and women's sexual orientation," *Word* **52**, 69–77.

Walden, B.E., Montgomery, A.A., Gibeily, G.J., Prosek, R.A., and Schwartz, D.M. (**1978**). "Correlates of psychological dimensions in talker similarity," *Journal of Speech and Hearing Research* **21**, 265–275.

Walker, V.G. (**1988**). "Durational characteristics of young adults during speaking and reading tasks," *Folia Phoniatrica* **40**, 12–20.

Waln, R.F. and Downey, R.G. (**1987**). "Voice stress analysis: Use of telephone recordings," *Journal of Business and Psychology* **1**, 379–389.

Walton, J.H. and Orlikoff, R.F. (**1994**). "Speaker race identification from acoustic cues in the vocal signal," *Journal of Speech and Hearing Research* **37**, 738–745.

Wang, X. (**2007**). "Neural coding strategies in auditory cortex," *Hearing Research* **229**, 81–93.

Wang, X. and Kadia, S.C. (**2001**). "Differential representation of species–specific primate vocalizations in the auditory cortices of marmoset and cat," *Journal of Neurophysiology* **86**, 2616–2620.

Wang, Y., Liu, D., and Wang, Y. (**2003**). "Discovering the capacity of human memory," *Brain and Mind*, **4**, 189–198.

Ward, C.D. and Cooper, R.P. (**1999**). "A lack of evidence in 4-month-old human infants for paternal voice preference," *Developmental Psychobiology* **35**, 49–59.

Ward, P.H., Sanders, J.W., Goldman, R., and Moore, G.P. (**1969**). "Diplophonia," *Annals of Otology, Rhinology & Laryngology* **78**, 771–777.

Ward, S., Speakman, J.R., and Slater, P.J.B. (**2003**). "The energy cost of song in the canary, *Serinus canaria*," *Animal Behaviour* **66**, 893–902.

Warren, D. (**1996**). "Regulation of speech aerodynamics," in *Principles of Experimental Phonetics*, edited by N.J. Lass (St. Louis: Mosby), pp. 46–92.

Warren, J.D., Scott, S.K., Price, C.J., and Griffiths, T.D. (**2006**). "Human brain mechanisms for the early analysis of voices," *NeuroImage* **31**, 1389–1397.

Warrington, E.K. and James, M. (**1967**). "An experimental investigation of facial recognition in patients with unilateral cerebral lesions," *Cortex* **3**, 317–326.

Watanabe, T. and Katsuki, Y. (**1974**). "Response patterns of single auditory neurons of the cat to species-specific vocalization," *Japanese Journal of Physiology* **24**, 135–155.

Wayland, R. and Jongman, A. (**2003**). "Acoustic correlates of breathy and clear vowels: The case of Khmer," *Journal of Phonetics* **31**, 181–201.

Weinberg, B. and Bennett, S. (**1971**). "Speaker sex recognition of 5- and 6- year old children's voices," *Journal of the Acoustical Society of America* **50**, 1210–1213.

Weirich, M. (**2010**). "Articulatory and acoustic inter-speaker variability in the production of German vowels," *ZAS Papers in Linguistics* **52**, 19–42.

Weismer, G. (**1997**). "Motor speech disorders," in *The Handbook of Phonetic Sciences*, edited by W. Hardcastle and J. Laver (Oxford: Blackwell), pp. 191–219.

Weismer, G. and Liss, J. (**1991**). "Reductionism is a dead–end in speech research: Perspectives on a new direction," in *Dysarthria and Apraxia of Speech: Perspectives on Management*, edited by K. Yorkston, C. Moore, & D. Beukelman (Baltimore, MD: Brookes), pp. 15–27.

Welch, A.M., Semlitsch, R.D., and Gerhardt, H.C. (**1998**). "Call duration as an indicator of genetic quality in male gray tree frogs," *Science* **280**, 1928–1930.

Welles, O. (Producer/Director) (**1941**). *Citizen Kane* (Mercury Productions, United States).

Wells, B. and Macfarlane, S. (**1998**). "Prosody as an interactional resource: Turn–projection and overlap," *Language and Speech* **41**, 265–294.

Wennerstrom, A. (**2001**). *The Music of Everyday Speech* (Oxford, UK: Oxford University Press).

Werner, H. (**1956**). "Microgenesis and aphasia," *Journal of Abnormal Social Psychology* **52**, 347–353.

Werner, H. and Kaplan, B. (**1963**). *Symbol Formation: An Organismic Developmental Approach to Language and the Expression of Thought* (New York: John Wiley & Sons).

Wertheimer, M. (**1944**). *Gestalt Theory* (West Orange, NJ: Barton Press).

Whalen, D.H. and Kinsella-Shaw, J. M. (**1997**). "Exploring the relationship of inspiration duration to utterance duration," *Phonetica* **54**, 138–152.

Whipple, T.W. and McManamon, M.K. (**2002**). "Implications of using male and female voices in commercials: An exploratory study," *Journal of Advertising* **31**, 79–91.

Whiteley, A.M. and Warrington, E.K. (**1977**). "Prosopagnosia: A clinical psychological, and anatomical study of three patients," *Journal of Neurology, Neurosurgery, and Psychiatry* **40**, 395–403.

Whiteside, S.P. (**1998**). "The identification of a speaker's sex from synthesized vowels," *Perceptual and Motor Skills* **87**, 595–600.

Whiteside, S.P. (**1999**). "A comment on women's speech and its synthesis," *Perceptual and Motor Skills* **88**, 110–112.

Whiteside, S.P. and Rixon, E. (**2000**). "Identification of twins from pure (single speaker) and hybrid (fused) syllables: An acoustic and perceptual case study," *Perceptual and Motor Skills* **91**, 933–947.

Whitman-Linsen, C. (**1992**). *Through the Dubbing Glass* (Frankfurt am Main: Peter Lang).

Wichmann, A. (**2000**). *Intonation in Text and Discourse: Beginnings, Middles and Ends* (Harlow, Essex: Pearson Education).

Wichmann, A. (**2005**). "Please – from courtesy to appeal: the role of intonation in the expression of attitudinal meaning," *English Language and Linguistics* **9**, 229–253.

Wicklund, K., Seikel, A., Dillman, R., Glynn, S., Bond, V., Murphy, S., Neal, H., Newton, T., Hipp, E., Archambault, N., Jones, C., and Zarko, K. (**1998**). "Fundamental frequency changes in singers and non-singers related to menstruation," *Medical Problems of Performing Artists* **13**, 100–108.

Wiethoff, S., Wildgruber, D., Kreifelts, B., Becker, H., Herbert, C., Grodd, W., and Ethofer, T. (**2008**). "Cerebral processing of emotional prosody–influence of acoustic parameters and arousal," *NeuroImage* **39**, 885–893.

Wilder, B. (Director) and Brackett, C. (Producer) (**1945**). *The Lost Weekend* (Paramount, United States).

Wilder, B. (Producer/Director) (**1959**). *Some Like It Hot* (Metro-Goldwyn-Mayer, United States).

Wildgruber, D., Hertrich, I., Riecker, A., Erb, M., Anders, S., Grodd, W., and Ackermann, H. (**2004**). "Distinct frontal regions subserve evaluation of linguistic and emotional aspects of speech intonation," *Cerebral Cortex* **14**, 1384–1389.

Wildgruber, D., Pihan, H., Ackermann, H., Erb, M., and Grodd, W. (**2002**). "Dynamic brain activation during processing of emotional intonation: Influence of acoustic parameters, emotional valence, and sex," *NeuroImage* **15**, 856–869.

Wilding, J. and Cook, S. (**2000**). "Sex differences and individual consistency in voice identification," *Perceptual and Motor Skills* **91**, 535–538.

Wilkinson, S. and Kitzinger, C. (**2006**). "Surprise as an interactional achievement: Reaction tokens in conversation," *Social Psychology Quarterly* **69**, 150–182.

Williams, C.E. and Stevens, K.N. (**1969**). "On determining the emotional state of pilots during flight: An exploratory study," *Aerospace Medicine* **40**, 1369–1372.

Williams, C.E. and Stevens, K.N. (**1972**). "Emotion and speech: Some acoustical correlates," *Journal of the Acoustical Society of America* **52**, 1238–1250.

Williams, J.R. (**1998**). "Guidelines for the use of multimedia in instruction," *Proceedings of the Human Factors and Ergonomics Society 42nd Annual Meeting*, 1447–1451.

Williams, M.D. and Hollan, J.D. (**1981**). "Processes of retrieval from very long-term memory," *Cognitive Science* **5**, 87–119.

Willis, E.C. and Kenny, D.T. (**2008**). "Relationship between weight, speaking fundamental frequency, and the appearance of phonational gaps in the adolescent male changing voice," *Journal of Voice* **22**, 451–471.

Wilson, D. and Wharton, T. (**2006**). "Relevance and prosody," *Journal of Phonetics* **38**, 1559–1579.

Winer, J.A. and Lee, C.C. (**2007**). "The distributed auditory cortex," *Hearing Research* **229**, 3–13.

Winkworth, A.L., Davis, P.J., Adams, R.D., and Ellis, E. (**1995**). "Breathing patterns during spontaneous speech," *Journal of Speech and Hearing Research* **38**, 124–144.

Winkworth, A. L., Davis, P. J., Ellis, E., and Adams, R. D. (**1994**). "Variability and consistency in speech breathing during reading: lung volumes, speech intensity, and linguistic factors," *Journal of Speech and Hearing Research* **37**, 535–556.

Winograd, E., Kerr, N.H., and Spence, M.J. (**1984**). "Voice recognition: Effects of orientating task, and a test of blind versus sighted listeners," *American Journal of Psychology* **97**, 57–70.

Winters, S.J., Levi, S.V., and Pisoni, D.B. (**2008**). "Identification and discrimination of bilingual talkers across languages," *Journal of the Acoustical Society of America* **123**, 4524–4538.

Wirz, S. and Mackenzie Beck, J. (**1995**). "Assessment of voice quality: The vocal profiles analysis scheme," in *Perceptual Approaches to Communication Disorders*, edited by S. Wirz (London: Whurr), pp. 39–55.

Wodehouse, P.G. (**1934**). *Brinkley Manor* (New York: Triangle Books).

Wolf, R. and Sidtis, D. (**2010**). "Pragmatic repetition in conversational discourse: Method for quantification and functional analysis," submitted.

Wolfe, T. (**1987**). *Bonfire of the Vanities* (New York: Farrar Straus Giroux).

Wolfe, V., Ratusnik, D., Smith, F., and Northrop, G. (**1990**). "Intonation and fundamental frequency in male-to-female transsexuals," *Journal of Speech and Hearing Disorders* **55**, 43–50.

Wong, J. (**2000**). "Repetition in conversation: A look at 'first and second sayings,'" *Research on Language and Social Interaction* **33**, 401–424.

Wong, P.C.M. (**2002**). "Hemispheric specialization of linguistic pitch patterns," *Brain Research Bulletin* **59**, 83–95.

Wong, P.C.M. and Diehl, R.L. (**2003**). "Perceptual normalization for inter- and intratalker variation in Cantonese level tones," *Journal of Speech, Language, and Hearing Research* **46**, 413–421.

Woo, P., Casper, J., Colton, R.H., and Brewer, D. (**1992**). "Dysphonia in the aging: Physiology versus disease," *Laryngoscope* **102**, 139–144.

Woodson, G.W. (**1999**). "The autonomic nervous system and laryngology," *Handbook of Clinical Neurology, 74: The Autonomic Nervous System, Part I. Normal Function*, edited by O. Appenzeller (Mahwah, NJ: Elsevier), pp. 387–398.

Wray, A. (**2000**). "Holistic utterances in protolanguage: The link from primates to humans, " in *The Evolutional Emergence of Language*, edited by C. Knight, M. Studdert-Kennedy, and J.A. Hurford (Cambridge: Cambridge University Press), pp. 285–302.

Wray, A. (**2002a**). *Formulaic Language and the Lexicon* (Cambridge: Cambridge University Press).

Wray, A. (**2002b**). "Dual processing in protolanguage: Performance without competence," in *The Transition to Language*, edited by A. Wray (Oxford: Oxford University Press), pp. 113–160.

Wray, A. and Perkins, M. (**2000**). "The functions of formulaic language: an integrated model," *Language and Communication* **20**, 1–28.

Wuyts, F.L., De Bodt, M.S., Molenberghs, G., Remacle, M., Heylen, L., Millet, B., Van Lierde, K., Raes, J., and Van de Heyning, P.H. (**2000**). "The dysphonia severity index: An objective measure of vocal quality based on a mutliparameter approach," *Journal of Speech, Language, and Hearing Research* **43**, 796–809.

Xue, S.A. and Fucci, D. (**2000**). "Effects of race and sex on acoustic features of voice analysis," *Perceptual and Motor Skills* **91**, 951–958.

Xue, S.A. and Hao, J.G. (**2006**). "Normative standards for vocal tract dimensions by race as measured by acoustic pharyngometry," *Journal of Voice* **20**, 391–400.

Xue, S.A., Hao, G.J., and Mayo, R. (**2006**). "Volumetric measurements of vocal tracts for male speakers from different races," *Clinical Linguistics and Phonetics* **20**, 691–702.

Yarmey, A.D. (**1986**). "Verbal, visual, and voice identification of a rape suspect under different levels of illumination," *Journal of Applied Psychology* **71**, 363–370.

Yarmey, A.D. (**1991**). "Voice identification over the telephone," *Journal of Applied Social Psychology* **21**, 1868–1876.

Yarmey, A.D. (**1993**). "Stereotypes and recognition memory for faces and voices of good guys and bad guys," *Applied Cognitive Psychology* **7**, 419–431.

Yarmey, A.D. and Matthys, E. (**1992**). "Voice identification of an abductor," *Applied Cognitive Psychology* **6**, 367–377.

Yarmey, A.D., Yarmey, A.L., and Yarmey, M.J. (**1994**). "Face and voice identifications in showups and lineups," *Applied Cognitive Psychology* **8**, 453–464.

Yarmey, A.D., Yarmey, A.L., Yarmey, M.J., and L. Parliament. (**2001**). "Common sense beliefs and the identification of familiar voices," *Applied Cognitive Psychology* **15**, 283–299.

Yin, R.K. (**1970**). "Face recognition by brain–injured patients: A dissociable ability?," *Neuropsychologia* **8**, 395–402.

Yoshida, Y., Tanaka, Y., Saito, T., Shimazaki, T., and Hirano, M. (**1992**). "Peripheral nervous system in the larynx," *Folia Phoniatrica (Basel)* **44**, 194–219.

Yost, W.A., Braida, L., Hartmann, W.W., Kidd, G.D. Jr., Kruskal, J., Pastore, R., Sachs, M.B., Sorkin, R.D., and Warren, R.M. (**1989**). *Classification of Complex Nonspeech Sounds* (Washington, DC: National Academy Press).

Young, A.W. (Editor). (**1983**). *Functions of the Right Cerebral Hemisphere* (London: Academic Press).

Young, A.W., Flude, B.M., Hay, D.C., and Ellis, A.W. (**1993**). "Impaired discrimination of familiar from unfamiliar faces," *Cortex* **29**, 65–75.

Young, A.W., Newcombe, F., de Haan, E.H., Small, M., and Hay, D.C. (**1993**). "Face perception after brain injury. Selective impairments affecting identity and expression," *Brain*, 941–959.

Young, A.W. and Ratcliff, G. (**1983**). *Functions of the Right Cerebral Hemisphere* (Burlington, MA: Academic Press).

Young, A.W., Reid, I., Wright, S., and Hellawell, D.J. (**1993**). "Face-processing impairments and the Capgras delusion," *British Journal of Psychiatry* **162**, 695–698.

Young, P.A., Young, P.H., and Tolbert D.L. (**2007**). *Basic Clinical Neuroscience* (Philadelphia, PA: Lippincott, Williams & Wilkins).

Yule, G. (**1980**). "Speaker's topics and major paratones," *Lingua* **52**, 33–47.

Zajonc, R. (**1968**). "Attitudinal effects of mere exposure," *Journal of Personality and Social Psychology Monograph* **9**, 1–28.

Zajonc, R. (**1980**). "Feeling and thinking: Preferences need no inferences," *American Psychologist* **35**, 151–175.

Zajonc, R. (**1984**). "On the primacy of emotion," *American Psychologist* **39**, 117–123.

Zander, M.R. (**2006**). "Musical influences in advertising: How music modifies first impressions of product endorsers and brands," *Psychology of Music* **34**, 465–480.

Zatorre, R.J. (**1988**). "Pitch perception of complex tones and human temporal-lobe function," *Journal of the Acoustical Society of America* **84**, 566–572.

Zatorre, R.J. and Belin, P. (**2001**). "Spectral and temporal processing in human auditory cortex," *Cerebral Cortex* **11**, 946–953.

Zemlin, W.R. (**1998**). *Speech and Hearing Science: Anatomy and Physiology*, fourth edition (Needham Heights, MA: Allyn & Bacon).

Zetterholm, E. (**2002**). "A comparative survey of phonetic features of two impersonators," *Royal Institute of Technology Quarterly Status and Progress Reports* **44**, 129–132.

Zetterholm, E. (**2003**). *Voice Imitation: A Phonetic Study of Perceptual Illusions and Acoustic Success*, Travaux de l'Institute de Linguistique de Lund, Lund University, Sweden.

Zhang, Z. (**2008**). "Influence of flow seperation location on phonation onset," *Journal of the Acoustical Society of America* **124**, 1689–1694.

Zhang, Z., Neubauer, J., and Berry, D.A. (**2006a**). "The influence of subglottal acoustics on laboratory models of phonation," *Journal of the Acoustical Society of America* **120**, 1158–1569.

Zhang, Z., Neubauer, J., and Berry, D.A. (**2006b**). "Aerodynamically and acoustically driven modes of vibration in a physical model of the vocal folds," *Journal of the Acoustical Society of America* **120**, 2841–2849.

Zhao, W., Zhang, C., Frankel, S.H., and Mongeau, L.G. (**2002**). "Computational aeroacoustics of phonation, Part I: Computational methods and sound generation mechanisms," *Journal of the Acoustical Society of America* **112**, 2134–2146.

Zuckerman, M., DeFrank, R.S., Hall, J.A., Larrance, D.T., and Rosenthal, R. (**1979**). "Facial and vocal cues of deception and honesty," *Journal of Experimental Social Psychology* **15**, 378–396.

Zuckerman, M. and Driver, R. (**1989**). "What sounds beautiful is good: The vocal attractiveness stereotype," *Journal of Nonverbal Behavior* **13**, 67–82.

Zuckerman, M., Hodgins, H., and Miyake, K. (**1990**). "The vocal attractiveness stereotype: Replication and elaboration," *Journal of Nonverbal Behavior* **14**, 97–112.

Zuckerman, M., Koestner, R., and Colella, M.J. (**1985**). "Learning to detect deception from three communication channels," *Journal of Nonverbal Behavior* **9**, 188–194.

Zuckerman, M. and Miyake, K. (**1993**). "The attractive voice: What makes it so?," *Journal of Nonverbal Behavior* **17**, 119–135.

Zuckerman, M., Miyake, K., and Elkin, C.S. (**1995**). "Effects of attractiveness and maturity of face and voice on interpersonal impressions," *Journal of Research in Personality* **29**, 253–272.

Zuckerman, M., Spiegel, N.H., DePaulo, B.M., and Rosenthal, R. (**1982**). "Nonverbal strategies for decoding deception," *Journal of Nonverbal Behavior* **6**, 171–187.

Author Index

Abberton, E., 6, 178, 241
Abdelli-Baruh, N., 291
Abercrombie, D., 8, 19
Abitbol, B., 126
Abitbol, J., 126
Abitbol, P., 126
Abrams, R.M., 160, 162
Abramson, A.S., 105, 279, 358
Absil, E., 318
Ackermann, H., 81–2, 198, 309–10
Adachi, S., 396
Adams, N.L., 308
Adams, R.D., 31, 275
Addington, D.W., 343–4, 350
Adolphs, R., 227, 230, 307, 309
Ahad, P., 216–17
Ahn, J.-S., 79, 274, 291–2
Ajmani, M.L., 148
Akita, M., 112
Alasseri, A., 331
Albala, A.A., 357
Albas, C.A., 330
Albas, D.C., 328, 330
Alberti, B., 85
Alburger, J.R., 385
Alcock, K.J., 102, 193–4
Alden, A., 302
Alderson, R., 389
Alexander, A., 251

Ali Cherif, A., 308
Allport, G.W., 345, 377, 381, 386
Almerino, C.A., 149
Alpert, J., 377
Alpert, M., 245, 329, 356, 377
Alter, K., 102, 193, 309–10, 334, 341
Altenmüller, E., 308
Altig, R., 151
Altman, M., 120
Altmann, J., 170
Alwan, A., 55
Ambady, N., 327–8, 330
Ambrazaitis, G., 284
Amerson, T.L., 274
Amézquita, A., 185
Amin, D., 205
Amir, O., 126
Andersen, R.A., 228
Anderson, B., 147
Anderson, J.R., 81
Anderson, R.A., 326
Andreasen, N.C., 356
Andrew, R.J., 88
Andrianopoulos, M.V., 148
Andruski, J., 282
Anisfeld, M., 354
Annakin, K., 147
Anolli, L., 142, 298, 336–7
Anonymous 4, 393

Foundations of Voice Studies: An Interdisciplinary Approach to Voice Production and Perception, First Edition. Jody Kreiman and Diana Sidtis.
© 2013 Jody Kreiman and Diana Sidtis. Published 2013 by Blackwell Publishing Ltd.

Author Index

Subject Index

Foundations of Voice Studies: An Interdisciplinary Approach to Voice Production and Perception,
First Edition. Jody Kreiman and Diana Sidtis.
© 2013 Jody Kreiman and Diana Sidtis. Published 2013 by Blackwell Publishing Ltd.